D0075888

Hispanic American Religious Cultures

VOLUME 1: A–M

Miguel A. De La Torre, Editor

A B C ⬤ C L I O

Santa Barbara, California • Denver, Colorado • Oxford, England

can

Library of Congress Cataloging-in-Publication Data

Hispanic American Religious Cultures /
    Miguel A. De La Torre, editor.
        p. cm. – (American religious cultures)
    Includes bibliographical references and index.
    ISBN 978–1–59884–139–8 (hardcopy : alk. paper) – ISBN 978–1–59884–140–4 (ebook)
1. Hispanic Americans–Religion–Encyclopedias. I. De La Torre, Miguel A.
BL2525.H57   2009
200.89'68073—dc22   2009012661

13 12 11 10 9   1 2 3 4 5

This book is also available on the World Wide Web as an eBook.
Visit www.abc-clio.com for details.

ABC-CLIO, LLC
130 Cremona Drive, P.O. Box 1911
Santa Barbara, California 93116-1911

This book is printed on acid-free paper ∞

Manufactured in the United States of America

To the millions of Hispanic congregations throughout the United States, accept this encyclopedia as our way of worshipping the Creator with all of our minds.

Contents

VOLUME 2

PART 2 ESSAYS

Acknowledgments

Most Hispanic religious academicians insist that they conduct their scholarship through a process known as *teología en conjunto*, a collaborative methodology rooted in the social and historical contexts of the Latina/o community. Scholarship ceases to be an individual task as it becomes a shared endeavor that relies on the richness of our multiple views and voices to articulate the diversity of divergent religious perspectives within our community. *Teología en conjunto* corrects the misconception that Hispanics are some type of monolithic group by revealing the complexity of our religious lives. To that end, this book is not, nor could it ever be, the product of one person. In a very real sense, it is the collective effort of the Latina/o scholarly and religious community. To the hundreds of colleagues who had a hand in bringing this work to completion, I say, "¡Gracias!" Egos were set aside as we worked together toward the common goal of creating this unique and timely contribution to the overall religious discourse.

I also wish to express my deepest gratitude to Debbie McLaren who worked tirelessly beside me, helping with the proof-texting so that we could meet all of the publisher's deadlines. Also, I express my thanks to the publishing editors, Steven Danver, who conceived the project with me, and Lynn Jurgensen, who brought the project to its conclusion. And finally, I am grateful to my wife, Deb, and children, Vincent and Victoria, for their unending belief in the work to which I am called.

Introduction

For many, the religious history of the United States began at Plymouth Rock with the first Thanksgiving dinner, and then moved westward. Obviously, this view of religious history ignores the centuries of Native American spirituality. Even if we were to limit the movement of religion to faiths imported from Europe—specifically Christianity and, to a lesser extent, Judaism—Plymouth Rock would not be our starting point. The start of the European-based religious history of the United States was both Spanish and Roman Catholic. It began in May 1493 when Pope Alexander VI, at the insistence of the king and queen of Spain—Ferdinand and Isabella—issued two bulls, the *Inter Caetera I* and *II*. Through these documents, all lands within the so-called "New World" that were not under a Christian ruler were granted to Spain (although a line of demarcation was drawn to carve out a space for Portugal). What was to eventually become the United States was first and foremost a Spanish colony under Spanish political and religious rule, even though the native inhabitants of the continent had no knowledge of Spaniards or of popes.

In 1526, Lucas Vásquez de Ayllón set out with about 600 individuals from Hispaniola and founded the colony of San Miguel de Gualdape, the first European colony on North American soil. San Miguel was located in what would become the Carolinas near the vicinity of what would eventually be Jamestown, the English colony founded nearly a century later. A chapel was eventually built on the site, and for the first time on the North American continent, the Christian God was worshipped. The first prayers to the Christian God offered on the land that was to become the United States were offered in Spanish. And though the colony eventually failed, another more permanent colony further to the south was established. By 1565 San Augustine was established by Pedro Menéndez de Avilés off the coast of what would become Florida, making this site the oldest continuous city within the United States.

When we think of the expansion of Christianity within the United States, we have been taught to see it as an east-to-west movement. In reality, it has been a south-to-north movement—from the Spanish Caribbean northward along the eastern U.S. coast and from what would become Mexico northward along the western U.S. coast. Before English pilgrims celebrated their first Thanksgiving dinner in 1621, San Augustine already existed, and Santa Fe was the permanent center of Spanish dominion in the lands that eventually would become the southwestern United States. This historical presence of Hispanics is evident when we survey any map of the United States, where we will find states named Florida, not Flowered; Nevada, not Snow; and Colorado, not Red-Colored. Likewise, we have cities called Santa Fe, not Holy Faith; Los Angeles, not The Angels; and El Paso, not The Pass. Our map bears witness to the early presence of speakers of Spanish.

The descendants of Hispanics were the earliest immigrants to arrive in what would become the United States. Their presence precedes the creation of this nation. Ironically, not only were they the first immigrants, they are also the latest immigrants. Nevertheless, their presence has mostly been ignored and marginalized throughout U.S. history, even though they are deemed to be the group most likely to change the face of America, which one can even call the "browning" of America. While their presence impacts many aspects of American life, the concern of this encyclopedia is focused on the religious influences of Latina/os. Before we can understand these influences, it is important that we understand who these Hispanics are. What are their demographics? Why are they here? And what characteristics seem to define Latina/o religiosity?

WHO ARE LATINA/OS?

In 1992, ketchup ceased being America's favorite condiment. According to sales figures, most Americans preferred salsa. But taste buds are not the only thing the Hispanic presence in this country is affecting. Many Americans cheer for sports personalities like baseball figure Jose Canseco or boxing legend Oscar de la Hoya. They read the literary works of Oscar Hijuelos, Christina Garcia, and Sandra Cisneros. They dance to the Latin beat of Celia Cruz, Ricky Martin, and Gloria Estefan. And their lives have been improved by the contributions made by Nobel Prize winners like Luis Walter Alvarez, Mario Molina, and Severo Ochoa. Every aspect of American life has been influenced by the Hispanic presence, including religion—specifically, how Americans conduct rituals, understand doctrinal "truths," or do "church." To ignore the Hispanic contribution to the discourse of U.S. religiosity is to ignore a major segment of the American population's spirituality.

The sheer numbers of Latina/os living in the United States will, whether we wish to admit it or not, impact U.S. discourse on American religiosity. Having recently become the largest minority group in the nation, they are impacting and restructuring the social, political, and economic ethos of the areas in which they settle. This makes the use of the word "minority" problematic. Hispanics constitute either the majority of the population or the largest portion of residents in several of the largest cities within the United States. For example, the 2006 U.S. census information showed that Latina/os represent 61 percent of Miami, Florida; 60 percent of San Antonio, Texas; and 49 percent of Los Angeles, California. Basically, in some of our largest urban areas, the major religious influence is Hispanic. Latina/os are mainly located in four states: California (31 percent of the Hispanic population), Texas (19 percent), New York (8 percent), and Florida (8 percent). This means that over 66 percent of the Hispanic population is located in these four states. Yet the states with the largest percentage of the state's Hispanic population are New Mexico (42.1 percent), California (32.4 percent), Texas (32 percent), and Arizona (25.3 percent).

According to the 2007 population estimates produced by the U.S. Census Bureau, the Latina/o population is at 45.5 million or about 15 percent of the U.S. population, with a projection of reaching 102 million by 2050 or about 25 percent of the population. Some experts believe the 25 percent mark could be reached much earlier—in 2030. It is safe to say that by 2050 at the latest, one in four Americans will be a Latino/a! When we consider that in 1950 Hispanics represented 4 million residents, comprising 2.6 percent of the population, their growth has been unparalleled, making them the fastest growing ethnic or racial group in this county. In the year 2000, Hispanics contributed to 37 percent of the nation's growth. The Census Bureau estimates that between the years 2000 and 2014, their contribution to growth will be 43 percent. This growth rate is expected to increase to 57 percent between the years 2030 and 2050.

Nevertheless, the numbers reported by the Census Bureau are deceiving. Excluded from the count are about 3.9 million residents of Puerto Rico and about 12 million undocumented "immigrants" who are treated as nonentities. These tallies are further complicated by the Census Bureau's own admission of underrepresenting Latina/os (and other minority groups) by as much as 3 percent. Misrepresented in the national consciousness, Hispanics become misrepresented also in demographic statistics. If we were to adjust these figures to count every Latina/o living under the domain of the United States, there would appear to be more than 62.75 million Hispanics or about 20.6 percent of the population. In other words, one out of every five Americans is presently a Latina/o!

A danger exists that this group of people we call Hispanics or Latina/os are seen as some type of monolithic group. For many Euro-Americans, there exists little difference between a Chicana/o, a Mexican American, a Central American, or a Spanish Caribbean native. In reality, Hispanics represent a very diverse population—some of whom are White, some indigenous, others Black, and most somewhere in between. They are a *mestizaje* (mixture) of cultures, races, and ethnicities. Some are heir to different indigenous cultures (such as Taíno, Mayan, Aztec, and Zapotec); others trace their roots to medieval Catholic Spain (influenced by Muslims and Jews), or Africa (specifically those who come from the Caribbean and Brazil), or even Asia. This mixture is further complicated by their continuous presence in the United States, which adds new dimensions to their ethnic backgrounds due to interethnic marriages. In a very real sense, Hispanics represent all the colors of the human rainbow of skin pigmentation, coming from a multitude of cultural and ethnic backgrounds.

It would be an error to assume that all Hispanics speak Spanish. Some only speak Spanish, but others only speak English, some are bilingual, and others prefer to speak *Spanglish* (a mixture of English and Spanish). Some barely know Spanish and instead speak one or several Mayan languages. It is also an error to assume all Hispanics crossed the borders into the United States. For some, the borders crossed them. Their forbearers have been on the land that would become the United States before there was a United States. Others are born U.S. citizens, while others are naturalized citizens. Some are resident aliens, while others are undocumented. Some groups were well received and quickly integrated into the U.S. fabric, while others have faced significant discrimination. It would also be misleading to assume that all Latina/os belong to the same economic stratum. Yes, many are poor, but several are multimillionaires. They live in the despair of the *barrio*, the comfort of middle-class suburbia, the open spaces of rural America, and the luxury of gated communities. Some pick grapes for a living, while others pick stocks and bonds. Consequently, there is no such thing as a "pure" or "typical" Hispanic.

Likewise, there is no such thing as one Hispanic religious expression. According to research done by the Hispanic Churches in American Public Life (HCAPL), 93 percent of all Latina/os identify with Christianity. Many may be Catholics—70 percent of those claiming to be Christian—but surely this does not represent the totality of the Latina/o religious experience. About 22 percent are scattered among the other non-Catholic Christian expressions, specifically Protestants, Pentecostals, and Evangelicals, with the highest concentration among Pentecostal groups—specifically the Assembly of Christian Churches, the Pentecostal Church of God, and the Apostolic Assembly of Faith in Christ Jesus.

The breakdown in faith affiliation reported by HCAPL was confirmed by a study conducted by the Pew Hispanic Center, which found that 68 percent of Latina/os claim to be Catholic, of which Mexicans (74 percent) and South Americans (71 percent) were disproportionately higher. Of the 15 percent of Hispanics who claimed to be Evangelicals, Puerto Ricans (27 percent) and Central Americans (22 percent) had larger representation than the average. And of those Hispanics who self-identified as secular, 8 percent, Cubans represented the largest share (14 percent).

The Pew Hispanic Center estimated that one-third of U.S. Catholics and 6 percent of Evangelical Protestants are Hispanics. These numbers are expected to grow along with the overall demographic growth of Hispanics within the United States, thus impacting the nation's religious expression. For example, if the conversion rate over the past quarter century remains constant, the overall Catholic population will decline from 68 percent in 2006 to 61 percent in 2030. Yet, over that same period, the proportion of Catholics who are Latina/o will increase from 33 percent to 41 percent.

While many are loyal to one Christian tradition, others participate in more than just one belief system. Although they may be Christians by day, by night, or in cases of emergencies, they might consult the *orishas*—African quasi-deities of the religion Santería—or visit a *curandera/o* (healer) to access ancestral Amerindian religious traditions. For some Latina/os, spiritual succor is found in U.S.-based faiths like the Jehovah Witnesses representing (according to HCAPL) the largest Hispanic membership to a non-Catholic Christian tradition, and Mormonism, which ranks eighth among Hispanic's largest religious traditions. For others (about 1 percent), spiritual solace is found within other world religious traditions like Islam, Judaism, or Buddhism. And, of course, there are those Hispanics who chose no particular religious preference (about 6 percent) or are atheist (about 0.37 percent).

HISPANIC DEMOGRAPHICS

According to 2002 Census information, the largest ethnic group among Hispanics is from Mexican origin, representing 59.3 percent of the Latina/o population and 7.4 percent of the overall U.S. population. The second largest Hispanic group is the Puerto Ricans who comprise 9.6 percent of the Latina/o population and 1.2 percent of the total U.S. population. The third largest group is the Cubans who consist of 3.5 percent of the Latina/o population and 0.4 percent of the U.S. population. For the past half-century, these three groups have been considered the big three Hispanic groups. However, the spot for third place is being challenged, and if current demographic shifts continue, Dominicans (2.3 percent of Hispanics) or Salvadorians (2 percent of Latina/os) could very well become the third largest U.S. Latina/o ethnic group.

If we consider the median age of Hispanics at 26, as noted by *The Hispanic Databook*, we notice that they are younger than the overall U.S. population age of 35.4. Cubans at 40.3, Spaniards at 35.8, and Uruguayans at 37.3 years of age are the only three Latina/o groups older than the U.S. median age. The youngest group, which is also the most populist group, is the Mexicans at age 24.4. Puerto Ricans are also among the younger Hispanic groups at 27.7 years.

The Hispanic Databook goes on to show that Hispanic families of 3.59 persons in a household tend to be larger than overall U.S. households of 2.59. The largest household sizes are among Salvadorians at 4.14 persons, followed by Guatemalans at 4.08 persons. There are no Latina/o ethnic groups that have household sizes smaller than the average U.S. household. Only one group, Spaniards, have an equal household size of 2.59 persons. The other two groups that come closest to the U.S. household size are Argentineans at 2.75 persons and Cubans at 2.76 persons. When it comes to those five years of age and older who speak English only in Hispanic households, Spaniards top the list at 40 percent of their population. The next closest groups are Paraguayans at 28.1 percent of its population and Panamanians at 26.1 percent. Salvadorians at 6 percent, Guatemalans at 6.9 percent, and Dominicans at 7.1 percent are the ethnic groups with the fewest household members speaking English only at home. Mexicans (21.2 percent) and Puerto Ricans (24.6 percent) are closer to the average at 21.4 percent. Cubans are below that average at 13.7 percent.

Of the entire Latina/o population, 40.2 percent, according to *The Hispanic Databook*, are foreign born. With the exception of Puerto Ricans at 1.4 percent and Mexicans at 41.5 percent, all other Latina/o groups have a vast majority of foreign born. Cubans at 68.5 percent and Dominicans at 68.2 percent have the least foreign born among those groups with a majority, with Venezuelans at 80.1 percent having the most. All other groups have about three-quarters of their population born outside the United States. Of the entire U.S. Hispanic population, only 11.2 percent of those who are foreign born are naturalized citizens. Cubans have the largest group of naturalized citizens at 41.4 percent of its foreign-born population. If we ignore Puerto Ricans at 0.6 percent of its foreign-born population because they are born with U.S. citizenship, the group with the lowest percentage of its foreign-born population who have obtained naturalized citizenship are Mexicans at 9.2 percent of its population.

Almost half of the Hispanic population (47.6 percent) that is 25 years and older do not have a high school diploma, compared to 80.4 percent of the U.S. population that has a diploma. Argentineans (80.44 percent), Bolivians (84.6 percent), Chileans (83.1 percent), Panamanians (84.9 percent), Peruvians (82.5 percent), and Venezuelans (88 percent) all exceed the U.S. population average. Among the "big three," Cubans (63 percent) and Puerto Ricans (63.3 percent) are above the Hispanic average while Mexicans (45.8 percent) fall below. The groups least likely to graduate from high school are Salvadorians with only 36.1 percent obtaining a diploma and Guatemalans at 38.9 percent. When it comes to a four-year college degree for those who are 25 years and over, only 10.4 percent of the Hispanic population has a degree, compared to 24.4 percent of the overall U.S. population. Those least likely to have a college degree are Salvadorians at 5.5 percent of its population, Guatemalans at 6.9 percent, and Mexicans at 7.5 percent. Puerto Ricans (12.5 percent) and Cubans (21.1 percent) are above the Hispanic average. Venezuelans are the most likely to have a college degree at 44.1 percent.

In 2004, *The Hispanic Databook* reported that the Hispanic median household income at $33,676 is below the overall U.S. population median income. Mexicans are very close to the Hispanic median at $33,621. Puerto Ricans fall below the Hispanic median at $30,644, while Cubans are placed above the median at $36,671. The lowest household income is among Dominicans at $29,099, while the highest is among Bolivians at $47,245. But these numbers can be deceiving. When we examine the per capita income, we note the extent of poverty among Hispanics whose per capita income at $12,111 is almost half of the overall nation at $21,587. Mexicans have the lowest per capita income at $10,918. Puerto Ricans per capita income stands at $13,518, slightly above the Hispanic average, with Cubans at $20,451, slightly below the national average. Only three groups have a per capita income greater than the national average: Argentineans at $26,121, Spaniards at $23,046, and Uruguayans at $22,870. While 12.4 percent of the overall U.S. population falls below the poverty level, 22.6 percent of Hispanics lives below the poverty line. Dominicans (27.5 percent of its population), Puerto Ricans (25.8 percent), Hondurans (24.3 percent), and Mexicans (23.51 percent) are the ethnic groups with the largest portion of people living below the poverty line. Only Paraguayans (11.5 percent), Peruvians (12.2 percent), and Uruguayans (11.2 percent) have a lower percentage of their population living in poverty than the overall U.S. population. Not surprisingly Latina/os who own their own homes (45.7 percent of the Hispanic population) are less than the U.S. overall average (66.2 percent).

WHY ARE THEY HERE?

As previously mentioned, Hispanics have been present on lands that would become part of the United States before the United States existed. Before the English colonial venture began, the ancestors of Latina/os occupied these lands as either the original inhabitants (through their Native American roots) or as the first colonizers (through their Medieval Spaniard roots). For most Latina/os, especially those who trace their roots to Mexico and Central America, they are the product of the violent clash of these two cultures, making them children of the conquistador oppressors and their Indian victims. For others, especially those from the Caribbean, they are the children of slave-holding Spanish plantation owners and their slaves. Most Latina/os find themselves within the boundaries of the United States because their lands were conquered through military superiority (Mexico). Others find themselves here because their lands were annexed (Puerto Rico) or economically exploited (most of Central America, South America, and the Caribbean).

The first major "influx" of Latina/os to the United States occurred with the territorial conquest of Northern Mexico, recognized by the 1848 signing of the Treaty of Guadalupe-Hidalgo. The treaty brought a cessation to the Mexican-American War and created a border between the two nations by drawing a surveyor line across the sand, literally through an area that, according to the archeological evidence, has historically experienced fluid migration. This border created through military conquest resulted in Mexico's loss of 40 percent of its northern territory to the United States. The immediate consequence of creating this artificial 1,833-mile border is that the United States acquired gold deposits in California, silver deposits in Nevada, oil in Texas, and all of the natural harbors (except Veracruz) necessary for commerce. The acquisition of these natural resources contributed to the wealth building of the United States at the expense of Mexico. Also lost with the signing of the treaty were some 50,000 of their citizens who were residing on those lands. Overnight, these Mexican citizens who were the majority in their nation became a minority Mexican American population within a foreign land.

The second major "influx" of Hispanics to the United States occurred with the annexation of Puerto Rico at the close of the Spanish-American War in 1898. The war, to a great extent, was a fight for control of colonial territories between the declining empire of Spain and the emerging empire of the United States. With U.S. victory came the territorial acquisition of almost all of Spain's colonial possessions, including the Philippines, Guam, Cuba, and Puerto Rico. The Philippines fought for independence against the United States in the Philippine-American War. Millions died before they became a commonwealth in 1935 and an independent nation after World War II. Cuba was declared independent from the start, but in reality remained under U.S. economic control until the 1959 Castro Revolution. Guam and Puerto Rico, to this day, have remained colonies of the United States. The annexation of Puerto Rico and the granting of citizenship during World War I to acquire needed soldiers have facilitated easy migration to the U.S. mainland.

The U.S. history of conquest and annexation explains why the two largest Hispanic groups within the United States are from Mexico and Puerto Rico. For many representing the remaining Latina/o population, their presence is a result of economic exploitation. According to the Census Bureau, the component most responsible for the increase of the Hispanic population between 2000 and 2006 was "Net International Migration" at 52.4 percent.

A century of "gunboat diplomacy" where Latin American governments were overthrown to install "banana republics" responsible for protecting U.S. business interests created poverty and death in many Latin American countries, specifically in Central

America and the Caribbean. For many Latin Americans, specifically the poor exploited due to foreign business interests, resistance was manifested as either fight or flight. Many chose the former, resulting in hundreds of thousands being killed or "disappearing." Others chose the latter and fled north. They mainly settled in urban areas including New York City, Los Angeles, and Washington, D.C. For example, Salvadorians and Nicaraguans immigrated because the United States conducted wars in their countries by either supporting an oppressive regime (as in the case of El Salvador) or funding the rebel forces (as in the case of Nicaragua). When the century-long policy of "gunboat diplomacy" provided U.S.-based multinational corporations (i.e., the United Fruit Company) the ability to build roads into these developing countries to extract, by brute force if necessary, their natural resources, or when U.S. factories known as *maquiladoras* were built along the border to extract cheap labor, some of the inhabitants of Latin America, deprived of a livelihood, took these same roads following the resources taken.

CHARACTERISTICS OF HISPANIC RELIGIOSITY

A comprehensive 2007 study done by the Pew Hispanic Center on how Hispanics are transforming American religion showed that as a whole, Latina/os express greater commitment to religion (68 percent) than the overall U.S. population (60 percent). Nine out of ten Hispanics identify with a specific religion. The sheer increase in numbers of Hispanics is not the only variable impacting U.S. religiosity. Latina/os are bringing change to religious communities, and these religious communities are bringing change to Hispanics. These changes are rooted in the prevailing characteristics of the Latina/o religious experience.

One of the prevailing characteristics defining Hispanic religiosity is its emphasis on ethnic-oriented worship. The Pew study showed that two-thirds of all Latina/o worshippers attend churches that have Hispanic clergy, conduct services in Spanish, and have a large Latina/o portion of worshippers in the congregation. While one can expect this phenomenon to be predominant among immigrants and/or Spanish speakers, it is just as prevalent among U.S.-born and English-speaking Hispanics. This indicates that Latina/os mainly worship with Hispanic congregations due to reasoning rooted in ethnic identity more so than simply being a product of immigration or language. As the growth of the Hispanic population continues, so too will the continuous emergence of Hispanic-oriented congregations within all U.S. religious traditions.

A second characteristic of Latina/o religiosity, according to the same Pew study, is the prevalence of "spirit-filled" religious experiences. This renewalist movement emphasizes the Holy Spirit and its daily intervention in the lives of believers. The Spirit is present within the faith community through metaphysical manifestations, which include speaking in tongues (glossolalia), performing miracles (including healing), and prophesying. The renewalist movement encompasses both Pentecostal and charismatic groups—both Catholic and Protestants. While about a fifth of non-Hispanic Protestants identify with a spirit-filled religion, more than half of Latina/o

Protestants do (57 percent). Likewise, more than half of Latina/o Catholics (54 percent) self-identify as charismatics compared to only an eighth of non-Hispanic Catholics.

This renewalist movement may explain some of the major beliefs held by Hispanic Christians. According to the Pew study, a majority of these Latina/os view God as an active force in the world and in their daily lives; thus three out of four Hispanics believe that miracles still occur today as they did in biblical times. Half of all Latina/os (76 percent of Evangelical Latina/os) believe the Bible is the literal word of God compared to 35 percent of non-Hispanics (62 percent of Evangelical Non-Hispanics). They are more likely than non-Hispanics to claim religion as an important component of their lives, many subscribing to a "prosperity gospel," believing that God rewards the faithful with financial prosperity and good health. Also, when compared to the rest of the population, Latina/os are more likely (52 percent) than non-Hispanics (33 percent) to hold the belief of Jesus' second coming within their lifetime. Finally, about two-thirds of Latina/os say that their political thinking is influenced by their religious beliefs and commitments, and thus more than half of them say that the pulpit is an appropriate place to address political and social issues. Not surprisingly, a correlation exists between political party affiliation and religious conviction.

CONCLUSION

Over the past few decades, Americans have started to take notice of the Hispanics among them. Most automated phone services begin by asking the caller to press two if they want to continue in Spanish. Daily newspapers carry stories on undocumented Latina/o immigrants. And most are finding, with increasing frequency, Hispanics living in the same neighborhoods, shopping in the same malls, eating in the same restaurants, and attending the same schools as Euro-Americans. Hispanics are here, they are here to stay, and with each passing year their numbers are growing. Their presence is changing many aspects of American life—including the religious landscape. This is the first encyclopedia ever written to provide an academic resource to Hispanic religiosity within the United States. Many scholars have contributed to this project from their areas of expertise in the hope that a resource can exist that provides an intellectual understanding of the Hispanic religious experience.

—Miguel A. De La Torre

REFERENCES AND FURTHER READING

Aponte, Edwin David, and Miguel A. De La Torre. *Handbook of Latina/o Theologies* (St. Louis, MO: Charlice Press, 2006).

De La Torre, Miguel A., and Edwin David Aponte. *Introducing Latino/a Theologies* (Maryknoll, NY: Orbis Books, 2001).

Espinosa, Gastón. "Methodological Reflections on Latino Social Science Research." *Rethinking Latino(a) Religion and Identity*, ed. Miguel A. De La Torre and Gastón Espinosa (Cleveland, OH: Pilgrim Press, 2006).

The Hispanic Databook (Millerton, NY: Grey House Publishing, 2004).

Pew Hispanic Center. *Changing Faiths: Latinos and the Transformation of American Religion* (Washington, DC: Pew Forum on Religion and Public Life, 2007).

Rodríguez, Havidán, Rogelio Sáenz, and Cecilia Menjívar, eds. *Latinas/os in the United States: Changing the Face of América* (New York: Springer, 2008).

U.S. Census Bureau. http://www.census.gov/.

Part I
ENTRIES

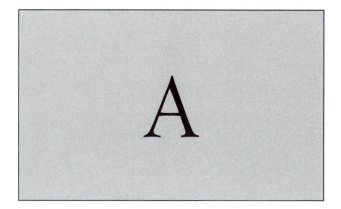

ACOMPAÑAMIENTO

The notion of acompañamiento, or "accompaniment," emerges within U.S. Latino/a theologies and Latin American liberation theologies as a development of the preferential option for the poor that grounds these theological movements. In his groundbreaking work *A Theology of Liberation* (1971), Peruvian theologian Gustavo Gutiérrez argues that theology must be "critical reflection on Christian praxis in the light of the Word" (Gutiérrez 1988, 11). Christian theology must be rooted in Christian action in the world as a critical reflection on that lived commitment that will nurture and embolden the struggle for social change. Conversely, when theological reflection is undertaken in isolation from such social engagement, it will, by its silence, implicitly support the unjust status quo. A politically neutral theology is thus not possible; either theology reflects on and contributes to the struggle for justice or, by its silence on political questions, theology—and the theologian—will be complicit in existing injustices. The work of Gutiérrez and other Latin American theologians was very influential throughout Latin American Christianity and beyond. Indeed, in their general conferences at Medellín, Colombia (1968), and Puebla, Mexico (1979), the Catholic bishops of Latin America committed themselves to a preferential option for the poor; they called for the Church to become a "Church of the poor."

Gutiérrez insisted that the option for the poor and all Christians as both individuals and Church is rooted in the Bible itself, suggesting that there are two principal overarching themes in Scripture: (1) the universality and gratuity of God's love and (2) God's preferential love for the poor. Though, at first glance, these themes appear to be incommensurable, they are in fact mutually implicit. If we live in a world divided between the powerful and the powerless, and if God loves everyone equally, then God's love for the powerful must manifest itself differently than God's love for the powerless. For purposes of illustration, one

At sunrise on Good Friday, members of Tucson's Los Dorados organization walk up a mountain near the city, carrying a cross. (Stephanie Maze/Corbis)

might take an example from family life. If a father comes upon his teenage son fighting with his younger, smaller daughter, the daughter would not appreciate the father's refusal to take any action on the ground that he loves his children equally and, therefore, must not take sides. Were the father to step in and restrain the son, such an act would not diminish the father's love for the son, nor would it mean that the father loves the daughter more than he loves the son. It would simply mean that, in that context, the father's equal love for the two must manifest itself in different forms. Equal or universal love does not imply neutrality; indeed, the former precludes the latter.

In the years since its earliest articulations, the notion of the preferential option for the poor has been critiqued, developed, and deepened. Further

analyses have focused, for instance, on clarifying terms such as "the poor." Other analyses have focused on the nature of a "preferential option." In what, precisely, does a preferential option consist? If a commitment to justice is central to such an option, what would constitute such a commitment? It is in the context of these latter questions that the term "acompañamiento" emerges, as an attempt to specify an essential dimension of the preferential option for the poor and the commitment to social justice.

The notion of accompaniment as central to the struggle for justice was already present among Latin American pastoral workers who, informed by liberation theology, "accompanied" the poor in their struggles during the 1970s and 1980s. Acompañamiento meant the act of being present alongside the poor in their everyday lives and struggles. Gutiérrez averred that any genuine commitment to the liberation of the poor must be grounded in concrete, particular friendships with poor persons. In other words, one might infer, the simple (yet dangerous!) act of being present with poor persons, of befriending them, in such a way that their humanity and worth is affirmed and valued is the most fundamental form of liberation, which grounds and gives rise to the more explicitly political forms of liberation.

Such inferences have been further developed and systematized in the work of U.S. Latino/a theologians influenced by the insights of Latin American liberation theology, especially the preferential option for the poor. Where the poor are treated as— in Gutiérrez's words— "non-persons," the act of accompaniment, of being present with, of walking alongside the poor is the most fundamental way in which we affirm the personhood of poor persons, not as an abstraction ("the poor"), but as particular human beings worthy of respect. Such an affirmation of another's dignity, through the simple act of everyday presence with them, contributes to that struggle for survival which itself is the most basic form of resistance in a society that seeks the destruction or, at least, disappearance of the poor.

U.S. Latino/a theologians have drawn attention to the liberating dimensions of U.S. Latino/a popular religion as a key context of acompañamiento. Though not overtly political, the religious practices of the poor are important instances in which the poor accompany each other, are present to each other, and give expression to the bonds that unite them so that, even in the midst of much suffering, they are empowered to continue

hoping and struggling. More importantly, such religious practices give expression to their experience of a God who accompanies them in their suffering and struggle. Thus, for example, the Good Friday *Via Crucis*, in which the community comes together to walk with Jesus on his way to Calvary, is an important way in which the community reaffirms its bonds with a God who suffers and struggles with them. Those bonds become sources of hope, which can form the basis not only of the everyday struggle for survival, but of more public and political struggles for change. The connection between the experience of empowerment in everyday relationships and empowerment for political and structural change is one that has been especially developed by Latin American feminist, U.S. Latina feminist, and *mujerista* theologians in their concept of *lo cotidiano* (the everyday).

By contributing to our understanding of Christian praxis, or Christian action in the world, such reflections have contributed to the further development of a "critical reflection on Christian praxis in the light of the Word." Thus, the act of acompañamiento becomes an essential source and context for the theological task, particularly as that task seeks to promote the liberation of the poor and a more just society.

Roberto S. Goizueta

References and Further Reading

Aquino, María Pilar. *Our Cry for Life* (Eugene, OR: Wipf and Stock, 2002).

Berryman, Phillip. *Stubborn Hope: Religion, Politics, and Revolution in Central America* (Maryknoll, NY: Orbis Books, 1994).

Espín, Orlando. *The Faith of the People: Theological Reflections on Popular Catholicism* (Maryknoll, NY: Orbis Books, 1997).

Goizueta, Roberto S. *Caminemos con Jesús: Toward a Hispanic/Latino Theology of Accompaniment* (Maryknoll, NY: Orbis Books, 1995).

Gutiérrez, Gustavo. *A Theology of Liberation: History, Politics, and Salvation* (Maryknoll, NY: Orbis Books, 1988).

Isasi-Díaz, Ada María. *Mujerista Theology: A Theology for the Twenty-First Century* (Maryknoll, NY: Orbis Books, 1996).

AESTHETICS

The noun "aesthetics" usually refers to a branch of philosophical inquiry dealing with the nature, meaning, and interpretation of art; the creative processes used to create it; and the kinds of experience that art offers. The adjective "aesthetic" commonly refers to the perceptual, the beautiful, and the artistic. This entry provides a brief sketch of how the term has been used in philosophical and religious discourse, with the aim of showing the contributions that U.S. Latino/a theologians and scholars of religion are making today.

Historical Development

Western theories of art and beauty may be traced back to Plato, but the concept of aesthetics is a distinctly modern one. Drawing on the Greek word "aesthesis" (perception), Alexander Gottlieb Baumgarten coined the term in 1735 to mean the science of sensory knowledge. Whereas initially aesthetics was broadly conceived of as an inquiry into the sensory knowledge of any (or, indeed, all) experience, many theorists soon limited this inquiry to the sensory knowledge of exceptional pieces of fine art. One sees this shift clearly, for example, when comparing Immanuel Kant's wide-ranging discussion of the transcendental aesthetic in his *Critique of Pure Reason* (1781) and G. W. F. Hegel's more limited thoughts on the fine arts in *Introductory Lectures on Aesthetics* (1835). This shift was not a completely decisive one. Subsequent thinkers, like the Romantics, would highlight the broad reach of aesthetics, as witnessed by their fascination with the beautiful and sublime features of nature and the human body.

In spite of the Romantics' gains, aesthetic theory since the late eighteenth century has been premised largely on the more limited idea that aesthetics is a matter of art proper, and perhaps more importantly, that art is to be contemplated by a perceiver in a disinterested and detached way. This contemplative view of art, which is often described as "art for art's sake" or "art-as-such," emerged largely in the writings of Joseph Addison, the third Earl of Shaftesbury, and, most notably, in Kant's later writings, particularly the *Critique of Aesthetic Judgment* (1790). For the later Kant, aesthetic experience refers to a pure judgment of taste. The perceiver contemplates the object in an immediate way, irrespective of its use or external end. This view was fueled by the rise of a new leisure class in Europe who, at the time, sought to enjoy the fine arts for their intrinsic value.

This eighteenth- and nineteenth-century contemplative model of "art-as-such" differed significantly from the more long-standing constructive approach to art. Since Aristotle's *Poetics*, theorists of art had approached the topic largely through the viewpoint of the maker, rather than the perceiver, of art. An art object was seen as a true work or craft, and it was designed specifically to affect certain external ends. This construction model made function and context integral to the meaning of art. The contemplative model of art, on the other hand, stripped art from its multifaceted environment and derived meaning instead from its inherent worth.

Today, scholars still draw upon both contemplative and constructive approaches to art, sometimes highlighting the tension between the two. Critical theorists and post-structuralists, for instance, have taught us to be suspicious of intrinsic or culturally independent conceptions of art. Yet, at the same time, thinkers in these traditions often affirm that, in certain respects, aesthetic experiences and objects do enjoy a relative autonomy from their material, historical, and cultural preconditions. Much of the ensuing debate has to do with how best, exactly, to understand the relation of the relative and the autonomous qualities of the aesthetic.

Religious Discourse and Aesthetics

There is a natural fit between religious and aesthetic discourse. Insofar as an aesthetic object or experience transcends ordinary experience, it may approach, if not approximate, a sense of the sacred. According to Paul Tillich, "All the arts penetrate into the depths of things which are beyond the reach of cognition" (Tillich 1989, 15). Theologians and religious scholars often invoke the discussion of aesthetics to highlight a dimension of human experience that in some way exceeds the normal "reach of cognition."

Many of the classic themes in the philosophy of art discussed above—detached contemplation, active construction, and relative autonomy—may be reinterpreted in more religious terms. The eighteenth-century idea of "art-as-such" had already functioned previously in the realms of metaphysics and theology, primarily in the writings of Plato and Plotinus, and, later, Augustine. In one of the strangest turns in intellectual history, early Christian theology began to identify the God of the Old Testament —a personal, relational, and historical God—with the Greeks' pagan notion of an autonomous and self-sufficient Absolute Beauty. According to M. H. Abrams, Augustine was mainly responsible for this fusion of the Hebrew God and the classical Absolute. Augustine's understanding of *caritas* pitted *uti*, which suggests, in a constructive fashion, loving things for their utility as a means to something else—against *frui*, which connotes, in a more contemplative way, loving God as an end in God's-self and for pure enjoyment. Within Christianity, the seed for the idea of "art-as-such" had been planted as early as the fifth century.

Today, religious studies scholars and theologians continue to debate many of the classic issues in aesthetics. Among other things, they continue to differ as how best to *approach* creative objects and practices ("art" in the largest sense). Some opt for an Augustinian model of contemplation, whereas others prefer a more Aristotelian (and often, by extension, Marxian) approach.

Furthermore, while most theologians and religionists would not want to restrict aesthetics to the realm of art proper, many continue to debate *where* aesthetic objects and experiences can best be found. Those interested in theological

RETABLOS

Even though retablo means literally "behind the table," the first retablos were made to be placed on a table that would serve as an altar for Christian worship in the ninth century. These retablos were made of sheets of wood or metal and depicted scenes from the life of Christ or a particular saint. Oftentimes, it would also have the portrait of Jesus or the saint being venerated. In the twelfth century retablos were installed in the apses behind the altars in many churches throughout Europe. It was not until after the Tridentine reform, however, that retablos became an important part of the altar. In Spain and other parts of Europe, as retablos became a permanent part of the main altar, they became larger and more ornate. These ornamental retablos with statuary, reliquaries, and tabernacles made their way into many large towns in Latin America. At the same time, missionaries recovered the use of small portable retablos to be placed upon tables and altars for the purpose of worship and teaching Christian doctrine. In many parts of Latin America and Southwestern United States it is these small, movable works of folk art that come to mind when the word "retablo" is used.

—GCG

aesthetics, for example, tend to focus on the texts, doctrines, worship practices, and ethical norms of a single religious tradition, such as Christianity. They tend to highlight beauty as an important attribute of God, revelation, and moral character. Others interested in religious aesthetics tend to foreground the aesthetic-religious dimensions of human experience at large. These scholars are more prone to look at aesthetics across cultures and religious traditions as well as to utilize nonsectarian language and categories.

The Contribution of U.S. Hispanics to the Discourse of Aesthetics

As important and instructive as the European discourse on aesthetics is, one cannot overlook the fact that it has not significantly addressed the aesthetic works and experiences of much of the world's population. In light of this void, scholars of U.S. Latino/a religion have made significant contributions to our understanding of the aesthetic dimensions of religion. These scholars borrow from inherited classical and European frameworks, but they also bring a distinctly American approach to the subject, drawing on a rich and varied religious history.

One of the greatest contributions made by scholars of U.S. Latino/a religion has been to take account of the indigenous roots of Hispanic religiosity. Scholars have identified at least three distinct premodern aesthetic sensibilities that continue to inform the religious practices of many Latino/as today: the Amerindian, the Iberian, and the African. Within each, there is no sharp distinction between the realm of the sacred and the realm of the profane. Instead, everyday experience may qualify as religiously significant. The divine is sacramentally mediated, through a variety of aesthetic forms, as an intensification of everyday experience. As Allan Deck and Chris Tirres have noted, Africans, Amerindians, and the newly arrived Iberian Christians imbued their rituals, symbols, and polyrhythmic music with sensuality, power, and a sense of freedom, in effect, making their world holy. Today, such aesthetic expressions continue to play a major part in Latino/a culture, serving often as sites where the sacred is experienced. Furthermore, the ongoing cultural exchange between Latin America and the United States, fostered by the ongoing movement of immigrants, continues to infuse U.S. Latino/a religious practices with a vital and integral sense of the sacred.

In addition to drawing attention to indigenous and premodern cosmologies, scholars of Latino/a religion have also broached aesthetic themes by demonstrating how, in the colonial encounter, human creativity and imagination helped subjugated peoples forge a sense of identity and agency. In his study of Mesoamerican religion, historian of religion Davíd Carrasco notes that the story of religion in the New World is, in many ways, the story of colonial conquest and the overcoming of this hardship through human striving and artistic ingenuity. Through the creative, transcultural processes of what Carrasco calls "worldmaking," "worldcentering," and "worldrenewing," colonized people not only made their world bearable, but also meaningful. Carrasco shows how this is so through such diverse examples as the Virgin of Guadalupe, the peyote hunt of the Huichol Indians, the celebration of *Día de los Muertos*, the Fiesta of Santiago among the Tzutujil Maya, and the Chicano Movement in the United States. Numerous other scholars also highlight various types of human creativity and imagination utilized by Latino/as in the face of oppression, including visual art, murals, women's literature, film, music, and popular ritual. Though these aesthetic media may differ greatly, at their best they all may reflect what theologian Harold Recinos refers to as a "poetics of power."

Far from taking a detached view of aesthetics or religion, scholars of Latino/a religiosity tend to root their discourse in particular histories, stories, artistic forms, or ways of life in the Latino/a context. Such is seen in the works of Alejandro García-Rivera and Roberto S. Goizueta. García-Rivera laments the fact that Western thought, beginning with Plato and continuing through Kant, has tended to divorce aesthetic experience from religious experience. Noting the impressive efforts of Latin Americans to reconstruct their own history and philosophy, García-Rivera calls for theology to expand beyond the confines of "textual" theology and to explore the richness of "living" theological and artistic texts—such as symbols, images, music, poems, drama, and dance. When this happens, García-Rivera believes that we may witness the beautiful as a means for the soul to ascend to a blissful union with God. As he puts it, theological aesthetics "attempts to make clear once again the connection between Beauty and the beautiful, between Beauty's divine origins and its appropriation by the human heart" (García-Rivera 1999, 11).

Goizueta is similarly interested in validating Latino/a "lived" religion, with a focus on how popular Catholicism may be an authentic and liberating form of human action. Goizueta draws, in part, on José Vasconcelos's notion of "empathic fusion" in order to underscore the communal character of human action (praxis). Over and against modern (constructive) notions of praxis that reduce human action to a mere "making," Goizueta argues for a (more contemplative) version of praxis—what he calls "aesthetic praxis"—as an intrinsic end in itself. Aesthetic praxis is interpersonal relationship at its best, and its value is intrinsically, rather than extrinsically, derived. As Goizueta suggests, such human action serves as the seedbed of all ethical-political action (Goizueta 1995, 77–131).

In turning to everyday experience, many Latino/a theologians and scholars of religion have utilized the category of *lo cotidiano* (daily life) and have thereby widened the definition of what counts as aesthetic. This category of analysis, first developed by feminist critical theorists in the 1960s and 1970s, has exposed problematic social hierarchies, such as patriarchy, that pervade people's daily living. As theologian María Pilar Aquino has noted, *lo cotidiano* highlights aspects of daily life that have been passed over by androcentric theories, including questions of sexuality, culture, and aesthetics. In privileging the category of *lo cotidiano,* Latino/a theologians and scholars of religion have rooted aesthetics—and, by extension, claims about sacred power or God's revelation—to the experience of the lifeworld.

Michelle Gonzalez broaches the intersecting themes of theological aesthetics and *lo cotidiano* in her study of Sor Juana Inés de la Cruz, the first female theologian of the Americas. Gonzalez explores how Sor Juana's plays and poetry pushed the borders of the dominant male academic theology of her time, and she argues that Sor Juana's literary creations continue to challenge the

patriarchal and scholarly norms by which we do theology today. In terms of her literary form, Sor Juana drew on Baroque excess in order to affirm the dramatic as a powerful vehicle for probing theological questions. As for theological content, Sor Juana probed the sacrality of everyday life (*lo cotidiano*) and affirmed a relational and egalitarian anthropology that is compatible with contemporary approaches by many Latino/a theologians.

Finally, Miguel De La Torre, who also relies on *lo cotidiano*, develops a Cuban Christology constructed from the margins of society. Influenced by sociologist Pierre Bourdieu, De La Torre uses visual art to tackle serious ethical issues of the ruptured Cuban community separated between those on the island and those in exile. Art, as a sign, contains within it the meaning given to it by the culture from which it arises. For De La Torre, the work of art, as "text," can raise human consciousness by unmasking the false utopias of the Cuban culture when the marginalized of that culture resignifies the sign, thus destabilizing the normative power structures.

Scholars of Latino/a religion and theology have made significant contributions to our understanding of the aesthetic dimensions of religion. Aesthetic practices and products continue to offer useful entry points for understanding the complex reality of Latino/a religiosity. One area that scholars of Latino/a religion seem especially well suited to pursue further is the ethico-political dimension of aesthetics. Historians, anthropologists, and sociologists have underscored the fact that Latino/a religiosity carries the postcolonial scar of asymmetrical power relations, while, at the same time, showing that aesthetic practices and products may serve a life-giving and liberative function. In his groundbreaking work, Virgilio Elizondo has begun to explore the theological implications of this theme, inspiring others to probe the dialectic even further.

Although the relationship between aesthetics and ethics may often prove indirect and elusive, Latino/a scholars of religion and theology are in a unique position to explore how cultural identity may help to bridge aesthetics and ethics. Their starting claim is a promising one: when religious aesthetics is rooted in the cultural memory of a people, it remains true not only to a reality of suffering but also to the eschatological promise that the horizon of history is still open.

Christopher Tirres

References and Further Reading

Carrasco, David. *Religions of Mesoamerica: Cosmovision and Ceremonial Centers* (San Francisco: Harper & Row, 1990).

Casarella, Peter. "Art and the U.S. Latina and Latino Religious Experience." *Introduction to the U.S. Latina and Latino Religious Experience*, ed. Hector Avalos (Boston: Brill Academic Publishers, 2004).

Deck, Allan, and Christopher Tirres. "Latino Popular Religion and the Struggle for Justice." *Religion, Race, and Justice in a Changing America*, ed. Gary Orfield and Holly Lebowitz Rossi (New York: The Century Foundation Press, 2000).

De La Torre, Miguel A. *The Quest for the Cuban Christ: A Historical Search* (Gainesville: University Press of Florida, 2002).

Elizondo, Virgilio. *Galilean Journey: The Mexican-American Promise* (Maryknoll, NY: Orbis Books, 1983).

García-Rivera, Alejandro. *The Community of the Beautiful: A Theological Aesthetics* (Collegeville, MN: The Liturgical Press, 1999).

Goizueta, Roberto. *Caminemos con Jesús: Toward a Hispanic/Latino Theology of Accompaniment* (Maryknoll, NY: Orbis Books, 1995).

Gonzalez, Michelle A. *Sor Juana: Beauty and Justice in the Americas* (Maryknoll, NY: Orbis Books, 2003).

Tillich, Paul. *On Art and Architecture*, ed. John Dillenberger and Jane Dillenberger (New York: Crossroad, 1989).

AFRICANS

This entry is an examination of the story of African culture encountering the Iberian modern west within the social confines of slavery. It will map a path from the experiences of Africans in the construction of the modern west to the emergence of Afro-Hispanic religiosity. However, to properly do so, this entry explores the story of "the things themselves," that is, the story of African slaves encountering the so-called New World. Without this story of the trials that African culture survived, the history of the socioreligious encounter between African and Hispanic worlds is fatally truncated. The examination begins with the sociohistorical development of African slavery in the Iberian west, and then moves to a look at the Africans' Middle Passage into the New World. Next it observes how African cosmology, even in the chains of slavery, functioned to inform the religious nature of Iberian colonial territories. Lastly, a brief examination of the *mulatez* controversy highlights ways that the mixing of African/Latino/a identity has functioned to problematize modern racial and ethnic reasoning.

As it is, this entry speaks more broadly of African religious traditions and cosmologies, giving preference to those traits that are evidenced in Afro-Hispanic religiosity. A continent as large and diverse as Africa contains more religious traditions than can be abundantly examined in this entry. Nonetheless, it is the persistence of an African perspective or worldview that is most important for the topic at hand. At the conclusion of this entry, the reader should have an understanding of how and why African slaves became the staple product in building the modern west; why Iberian Catholicism was more tenable than the Protestantism of other European nations in providing religious space for the survival of African gods; how African religiosity was able to mask and manifest itself within the Catholicism of slave masters; and how the confluence of African culture and Latina/o religiosity contributes to racial and ethnic (i.e., identity) complexities in modern Hispanic communities.

The Emergence of African Slavery in the Iberian West

Nearly a century before a Dutch ship carrying 20 Africans docked in British North America in 1619, the enslavement of Africans in the Iberian colonies of Central and South America was already common. By 1510, the Spanish were receiving African slaves in the Caribbean via Portuguese ships. The slaves from these ships were put to work in the mines at Hispaniola. In 1518, Spain shipped 4,000 slaves to its colonized islands in the so-called "New World." Furthermore, by 1540, the Spanish were

transporting about 10,000 slaves per year to the newly colonized west. Meanwhile, the Portuguese, by the mid-1500s, were combining indigenous and African bodies to work on northeastern Brazilian sugar plantations. Though northern European countries—especially England, France, Denmark, and Holland—would eventually challenge the Iberian strongholds of the Caribbean, the earliest activity in the trade of African slaves took place in Caribbean areas where Spanish and Portuguese colonizers controlled the land.

Slavery was not a novelty of fifteenth-century European society. It had been a part of every major civilization in recorded history and had been a regular practice dating back to the Hellenistic Empire of the sixth century BCE. Forced labor was also a part of Islamic nations in the Mediterranean from the eighth century CE forward, and the use of slaves was likewise vital to the functionality of many African nations. Yet in most of these cases, slavery was limited to domestic servitude. While the social status and treatment afforded to slaves were never things to be envied, they were a far cry from the dehumanized status of those forced to work themselves to death on the sunup to sundown plantations that developed in the west. Rarely before the sixteenth century was a slave system central to market and industrial production; yet this, combined with western European politics of identity, ideology, and power, was precisely the role that slavery played for Spain and Portugal.

In the early part of the fifteenth century, Portuguese ships were already making trips to sub-Saharan Africa. However, these pre-1492 traders did not have the same interests that would develop into the desire for large quantities of bodies forced to perform free labor in the New World. Instead, they sought to undermine the dominance of North African trade routes by discovering new pathways to trade with sub-Saharan Africa. These early Portuguese vessels were more interested in spices, fabric, and especially gold than they were in slaves. When these ships did begin to attain Africans through trade in the 1440s, the slaves were typically shipped to the Iberian ports at Lisbon and Seville where they were usually put to work in domestic roles.

After Columbus's encounter with what are now known as the Americas, Spain and Portugal raced to capitalize on the new lands. The initial victims of these Iberian colonizers were the Natives, but these indigenous peoples were quickly decimated by a combination of disease, murder, and slave labor. Spain and Portugal needed to replace the nearly exterminated Natives with other bodies that could be forced to build their "New World." Along with the exigency for new free labor, the Iberian nations had to contend with Northern European nations that were now following Spain and Portugal across the Atlantic and into the Americas. Out of this race for free labor emerged the transatlantic slave trade, through which Africans became the new fodder for Spain and Portugal's westward colonial machine.

The desire for African slave labor increased as sugar plantations became the new money-maker for the Iberian nations. Around 1517—the same year that Bishop Bartolomé de Las Casas successfully advocated for the transportation of African slaves to the New World, an event which officially legitimized an already existing practice—slaves began to be disbursed to the islands of Cuba, Puerto Rico, and Jamaica (all colonies of Spain at the time) as well as to mainland Brazil (land claimed by Portugal), which was Europe's biggest supplier of sugar by 1580. By the mid-seventeenth century, sugar had surpassed tobacco as the most desired commodity in the New World colonies, and the rapid establishment of sugar plantations helped mold the makeup of Caribbean populations. The sugar plantations replaced smaller farms, and an enormous influx of African slaves forced to work on the plantations displaced farmers and indentured servants. The production of sugar was a major reason that areas south of the United States are estimated to have received approximately 95 percent of the Africans brought as slaves to the New World. Sugar, however, was not the only reason that the Caribbean received so many slaves. Slaving patterns, which will be examined later, were another contributing factor to the large African-born slave population.

The Middle Passage and African Existence in the Iberian New World

The Middle Passage was the second leg of the tripartite journey that displaced Africans from their native lands to the New World by European nations. The Middle Passage was preceded by a journey from Europe to the west coast of Africa where a combination of trading and kidnapping was used to attain African slaves. Once in the New World slaves were exchanged for goods (e.g., minerals, gold, spices, and cotton), which they would eventually farm, harvest, and mine for their masters. These goods would

TIPO TIB'S FRESH CAPTIVES BEING SENT INTO BONDAGE—WITNESSED BY STANLEY.

Africans captured by Tippu Tip, the Arab slave trader from Zanzibar, are sent into bondage, as purportedly witnessed by British explorer Henry Morton Stanley, about 1850. (Library of Congress)

then be returned to European countries through a final excursion; the return voyage was the third and final leg of the triangular trade. Most scholars agree that, at the least, somewhere between 10 and 15 million Africans survived the torturous journey across the Atlantic. However, there is no precise method to calculate how much higher the actual number of slaves might have been. Because of the death of slaves on the scandalous westward voyage, and the illegal transportation of Africans after various pieces of legislature limited or banned the slave trade, the exact number of slaves brought to the Americas will perhaps remain a mystery.

The journey across the Atlantic was hell for the slaves. The ships were inhumanely packed and food, water, and air were scarce for the African captives. Chained below deck, enveloped in their own urine, vomit, feces, and blood, it is no wonder that the slave ship has been described as a floating deathtrap. Historians have differed as to whether the deaths of slaves were more a result of sickness or the overall time spent at sea in cramped space. Nonetheless, whether one, the other, or a combination of both were the cause of death, the regularity of slave casualty was a fact accepted as normative by European governments, slave traders, ship captains, and their crews. In the early stages of the mass transportation of African slaves, it is estimated that 15 to 20 percent of the human cargo died before reaching the land that their captors had destined for them. This number, in some cases, saw a significant

LIMPIEZA DE SANGRE

Limpieza de sangre, known in English as "washing the blood," is a concept that originated in Medieval Spain. It was an attempt to prevent the lost of a family's reputation due to an interreligious marriage. The idea was to "wash the blood," specifically Christian blood from contamination due to marrying a Jew or a Muslim. With Spain's conquest of the New World, the danger existed of Spaniards marrying or cohabitating with Indians, Blacks, or any mixture thereof. What was once considered a religious concept now became racialized. A self-imposed prerequisite developed to always marry a lighter person so as to perform la limpieza de sangre. This phraseology indicated a metaphysical notion of blood being a vehicle toward lineage equality. For most of the first half of the nineteenth century, parents' concern with the socioeconomic consequences of their "white" child marrying a person of darker complexion was argued in terms of "washing the blood." Pursuing racial endogamy, parents felt a marriage across racial barriers degraded the family's reputation and contaminated the metaphysical purity of blood.

—MAD

drop to 5 to 10 percent mortality rate in the seventeenth century when the Portuguese passed formal legislation limiting the tonnage of cargo on slave ships. It should be clear, however, that Portugal's legislature regarding the capacity of slave ships was far from a sanguine expression of concern for the well-being of the slaves who had been relegated to the bowels of the ship. Instead, these precautionary measures sought a mode of transportation that might be more economically efficient. After all, the death of a slave often meant the loss of revenue for colonial powers.

Slavery in the New World marked a significant period not only in the development of Europe's economic power, but also in the history of European thought. The westward push reinforced Western Europe's imperial status, and also reified Europe's xenophobic worldview. These nations traveled, not in order to learn more about the world, and hence about themselves, but to prosper—even and especially at the expense of non-

European peoples. Hence, while slavery itself was not unique to Europeans, the type of slavery practiced by European colonists beginning in the late fifteenth and early sixteenth centuries is what made these European nations unique. Theirs was an especially peculiar type of inhumane bondage through which the existence of African slaves was relegated to a space *outside* of the western societies that emerged in the aftermath of Christopher Columbus's 1492 journey. No longer were slaves the unenviable beings that existed beneath even the peasants (as was the case in many slavery-practicing nations prior to the advent of western colonization). African slaves were actually chained to a mode of *nonexistence* in what would become known as the Americas. Beyond the economic prosperity that slave labor produced, the lives of slaves were worthless in the eyes of the slaveholding Europeans.

Slaves in the Caribbean who survived the Middle Passage found no mercy on dry land. Constantly vulnerable to the most whimsical forms of torture from their masters, slaves could, at any moment, be subjected to whipping, branding, rape, and even murder. To compound this agonizing existence, the high volume of slaves transported directly from Africa made it more cost-effective to work a slave to death, rather than provide her/him with the food, shelter, and medical care necessary for a prolonged life. In parts of the Caribbean, seven years was considered an average life span for an African slave. This technique of replacing slaves was radically different from the method employed in the United States, where slaves were bred domestically more often than they were shipped directly from Africa. As a result of these different slaving patterns, Iberian territories maintained a much larger population of African-born slaves than did the United States. The disparity in the number of African-born slaves in Iberian territories vis-à-vis the United States contributed to the forging of a radically different social and cultural existence for slaves under Spanish and Portuguese ownership. These differences would be especially evident in the religiosity of slaves in the Caribbean.

Two Worlds Collide: The Formation of Afro-Hispanic Religiosity

As recently as the 1930s, African-born former slaves could be found in the Caribbean; this fact has a melancholy affect on how the existence of Africans in the new world is understood. On one hand, the presence of African-born former slaves in the Caribbean is a reminder of the recent nature of slavery, the institution in which White masters rendered

Black life disposable. On the other hand, the perseverance of African life, culture, and especially religion in the lives of these former slaves and their descendants makes the memory of slavery a dangerous, potentially liberating one. The existence and cultural persistence of people of African descent testifies to a mode of history that challenges White supremacist renderings. In the margins of White history, in the blind spots of White supremacy, African life survived and thrived brilliantly and defiantly vis-à-vis a White society that treated them as something less than human. Central to the slaves' defiance against being finally conquered by White supremacy and slavery was an African religiosity that, in the Caribbean, was masked in the culture and religion of White oppressors.

The religious infrastructure of the White supremacist culture to which African slaves were subjected was totally foreign to the worldview of the Africans themselves. According to philosopher Cornel West, the "secretion" of the idea of White supremacy was a result of the scientific revolution, the adoption of neo-classical ideals, and the shift to subjectivism in philosophy. These three traits, within the context of imperial Western Europe, were vital to the development of what West names the "normative gaze" of White supremacy. This normative gaze created a racist vacuum that engulfed the lives of African slaves as they arrived in the New World. Within this vacuum, religion functioned to "divinely" sanction the most horrendous system of slavery. The White Christian God, in the lives of the slaves, was the God who had "saved" the savage Africans from eternal damnation, and the temporal hardships of slavery were nothing compared to the eternal reward of

---

LUCUMÍ

"Lucumí" is a term from the Yoruba people of Africa that means friendship. The Yoruba were brought to the Caribbean, specifically Cuba, as slaves. The term is believed to be derived from the Yoruba greeting "oluki mi," which literally means "my friend." Some scholars believe it refers to the ancient Yoruba kingdom called Ulkumi. The word has come to be used in reference to any characteristic of the Yoruba culture, including their language. For some contemporary believers and scholars of the religion Santería, there is an attempt to use the term Lucumí, or "Regal de Ocha" (Rule of Ocha), to describe their faith. "Santería," a term that became popular during the 1940s in Cuba, was originally a pejorative term employed by Catholic clerics on the island to signify what they considered to be a syncretism of African traditional spirituality and the veneration of Catholic saints.

—MAD

---

salvation. Yet the very structure of the normative gaze, with its religious and philosophical limits set in the humanistic boundaries of the Enlightenment, could not finally contain the immemorial nature of African divinity.

The culture of Africa has been described as extremely religious, and, in a sense, this is certainly true. Based on the modern White understanding of religiosity, African culture could be described as immensely religious. Religion certainly pervades African life. Yet, in another sense, there was no "religious realm" in African life. Stated differently, the Eurocentric separation between church and state, and between sacred and secular, which molds and delimits religious life in the modern West, did not exist in the cosmology of the traditional African religiosity that crossed the Atlantic Ocean in the bodies, hearts, and minds of enslaved Africans. It is not the case that African culture had no conception of the sacred; however, the English language, restricted as it is by a Eurocentric worldview, struggles to express the conception of "sacred" that

was and is vital to African existence. As Africans were brought to the Caribbean as slaves, they brought with them conceptions of the divine that could not be comprehended by the racist God of their masters. The religious worlds, though altered, of the Yoruba, the Ibo, the Bakongo, and the Mandike—to name a few—sustained the slaves in their most dire situations. In these African religions, everything has value and meaning. From one's family members, to a rock lying on the side of the road, all things have been created to contribute to the experience of human life. Hence, harmony—not control, domination, or the ability to conquer—is the aim of life within African religiosity.

While imperial European cosmology sought to give colonial countries mastery over nature, African cosmology recognized humanity's dependence on nature and sought harmony with, not dominance over, the world. Where imperial European theology set out to interpret God in light of its colonial aspirations, Africans knew the divine as the source of all things and sought harmony with God's

NEGRITUDE AND NEGRISMO

Negritude emerged from a literary and ideological movement of the 1930s–1950s led by three French-speaking Black intellectuals: Aimé Césaire from Martinique, educated in Paris; the poet Leopoldo Sédar Senghor, the first president of Senegal; and Léon-Gontran Damas, a French Guyanese poet and member of the National Assembly. The literary contributions of women such as the Nardal sisters (Martinique) also require mention. Césaire coined the term in his 1939 poem "Notebook of a Return to my Native Land," *Return to my Native Land* (1969). For him, "negritude" meant recognition of one's blackness and the acceptance of the common destiny of Black people. Negritude called for the revalorization of Black African culture and heritage and the rejection of Western social, political, and cultural domination. The movement was also influenced by Afro-centric movements such as the Harlem Renaissance in New York City. In the Spanish-speaking Caribbean, a similar movement emerged as "Negrismo," as represented in the work of Afro-Cuban poet Nicolas Guillen's *Songoro Cosongo* (1931) and from Puerto Rican Luis Palés Matos's *Tun tun de pasa y griferia* (1937). In the Dominican Republic, Manuel del Cabral was noted for his *Tropico Negro* (1942) and *Compadre Mon* (1943). The Cuban Caribbean contributions predated the French-speaking movement.

—AMF

wonderful creation. When these two worlds collided in slavery, African religiosity was not simply destroyed. In spite of the agony that African bodies and minds were subjected to at the hands of Iberian colonists, African culture and religiosity endured. It would be incredibly idealistic to say that enslaved African existence in the New World was identical to African life on the continent. It is true, however, that the gods of Africa created a space, even in the depths of slavery, where Africans could worship in forms that testified to the malleability of African religiosity. This remarkable persistence is especially evident in Santería in Cuba and Candomblé in Brazil. The *why* of African religiosity in the New World is clear: the gods traveled in the minds and bodies of African slaves and were far too vital to life itself to be killed off even amidst the evils of slavery. However, in order to fully understand the *how*

of African religious perseverance, it is essential to understand the structure of Catholicism as practiced by the Iberian colonizers. It is not the case that colonial religion helped Africans survive. Colonial religion, as already discussed, sought dominance for Whites and only cared about Black bodies as sources of economic advancement. Thus, the importance of understanding Iberian Catholicism has nothing to do with giving credit to White religion. Instead, the aim is to understand the space that African gods (re)claimed in order to show faithfulness to African slaves.

Unlike the colonial United States, the early stages of Iberian-controlled territories were lorded over by mostly Catholic colonists. While the racist culture of these regions mirrored that of the colonial United States, the religious and cultural differences contributed to a radically different religious life for slaves in these regions. Catholic-Iberian nations also had a radically different notion of what evidenced salvation. Where Protestant conversion was to be accompanied by a "sanctified" (read: immersed in White culture) lifestyle, conversion to the Catholic faith was a much less dogmatic process. This is not to imply that Africans experienced total religious freedom in the Caribbean—far from it. The very fact that Africans were enslaved was a constant challenge to any semblance of complete freedom. However, the less socially stringent expectations around conversion in the Iberian Catholicism of Latin America was much more conducive to a more ocular survival of African faith than was White U.S. Protestantism.

The Catholicism of Iberian colonizers gave primacy not to holy sacraments, but to religiously significant persons, especially the Virgin Mary, Jesus, and, most importantly for African religiosity, saints. Where traditional Catholicism aimed to maintain a clear distinction between veneration of the saints and worship of the triune God, the distinguishing lines were often blurred and even crossed in the religious lives of Iberian colonists. Saints were worshipped for their ability to provide immediate aid in the face of existential urgencies; thus Iberian colonists lit candles to saints, knelt before their images, and also observed days set aside for saint celebration with remarkable discipline. In the practice of saint veneration or worship, many Africans saw striking parallels with divine conceptions of Africa. Many African religions held that there was one High God responsible for creation. This God was largely transcendent in nature and was thus only marginally concerned with the affairs of the earth. There were,

however, lesser gods that were constantly involved in the workings of the world. Africans would appeal to these gods when the vicissitudes of life caused physical and spiritual anguish. When slaves saw their masters kneeling before these lesser but immediately important figures, they discovered a medium through which the gods of Africa might commune with them even in the New World. Africans began to "mask" their gods in the form of Catholic saints and, in doing so, brilliantly resisted spiritual colonization. This masking process was aided by the fact that the roles and iconographic appearances of many Catholic saints were strikingly similar to those of African gods. For example, Shango, the god of thunder and lightning, wore the mask of St. Barbara the saint trusted with protecting Catholics from thunder and lightning, while Oshossi, god of hunting, was often masked by St. George or St. Michael, saints who were traditionally depicted holding swords.

The masking of African gods is far more significant than the word "syncretism" denotes. This was not simply a case of a defeated people mixing their belief system with that of their conquerors as a last, desperate attempt to claim some semblance of Africa. Instead, the masking of African gods reminds one that the strength of African religiosity is its ability to transform itself when confronted by other religious traditions without dehumanizing those that practice other faiths. In the deepest sense, the persistence of African religiosity in the face of Iberian colonization functioned to challenge the European attempt to name everyone and everything in the world. Because the ability to name one's self and one's world is central to being a free human being, the masking of African gods was a way to resist complete bondage. As long as African slaves remembered African culture and religiosity, they could never be finally conquered.

The Mulatez Controversy: A Part of Contemporary Afro-Hispanic Existence

The persistence of African religiosity provided space for slaves to control a part of their lives that was otherwise widely dominated by the evil wills of their masters. Along with control over one's life comes control over one's identity. Yet in the same way that African slaves had only marginal control of their worlds, they had only partial control over naming themselves. This crisis of identity still pervades contemporary Afro-Hispanic societies as Spanish descendants of African slaves wrestle with the frustrating complexities of White, modern racial, and ethnic reasoning. White supremacist notions of the self force many Afro-Hispanics to feel that one must choose a racial or ethnic side. This side-choosing ethic combined with the stigma of being Black in a White supremacist society reveals the extent to which African existence is still rejected —even by those who have African ancestors. The controversy surrounding the term *mulatez* is a prime example of the difficulty that comes with attempting to name one's self after having been named by others for so long.

Mulatez is a term used to denote the interracial "mixing" of African and Hispanic peoples, but its use has been interpreted many different ways. For some, *mulatez* is potentially liberating because it (along with *mestizaje*, which highlights racial and ethnic mixture beyond Hispanics and Africans) helps denote the hybridity and diversity of Latino/a culture. Scholars who think positively of *mulatez* often use it as a starting point to undermine oppressive identity politics that attempt to divide peoples of color under the gaze of White supremacy. These scholars argue that having a mixed starting point further challenges the ability of Whites to define bodies and minds, and also keeps White supremacist categories from frustrating liberative dialog.

Other scholars see *mulatez* as potentially oppressive in that it may harbor anti-Black sentiments that are rooted in colonial racial reasoning. These scholars believe that *mulatez* is often applied by Latino/as who are closer to White and therefore benefit from the pigmentation politics of White supremacy. In this line of thought, the application of *mulatez* and the denotation of racial and ethnic mixing are not about solidarity with other oppressed peoples, but about being closer, because of miscegenation, to the White racial and ethnic ideal. Here, it is believed that those who use *mulatez* may have internalized the mental and physical oppression of European colonists and therefore seek the perpetuation of racism for their own benefit.

As a third way, some thinkers withhold loyalty to either accepting or rejecting *mulatez*. These scholars believe *mulatez* (and *mestizaje*) to be important in its ability to bring peoples of color together, but are also leery of the danger of enveloping all Latino/as into a monolithic vacuum. The vital point here is that the presence and effect of Africans on Latina/o culture survive to the present. In the same way that African religiosity challenged the imperial religion of Iberian colonizers, the legacy of this resistance continues to problematize racial and ethnic reasoning that has its basis in White supremacist structures. The amazing and confounding truth is that the gods of African culture and religion continue to persist. For those who seek a "pure" race or ethnicity of any kind, these gods, in the malleable tradition of African religiosity, continue to challenge any normative racial and ethnic reasoning.

Ben Sanders III

References and Further Reading

De La Torre, Miguel A. "Rethinking Mulatez." *Rethinking Latino(a) Religion and Identity*, ed. Miguel A. De La Torre and Gaston Espinosa (Cleveland, OH: Pilgrim Press, 2006).

Gonzalez, Michelle A. *Afro-Cuban Theology: Religion, Race, Culture and Identity* (Orlando, FL: University Press of Florida, 2006).

Franklin, John Hope, and Alfred A. Moss Jr. *From Slavery to Freedom: A History of African Americans*, 8th ed. (New York: Alfred A. Knopf, 2006).

Klein, Herbert S. *African Slavery in Latin America and the Caribbean* (New York: Oxford University Press, 1986).

Mbiti, John S. *African Religions & Philosophy*, 2nd ed. (Portsmouth, NH: Heinemann, 1990).

Raboteau, Albert J. *Slave Religion: The "Invisible Institution" in the Antebellum South* (New York: Oxford University Press, 2004).

West, Cornel. *Prophesy Deliverance!: An Afro-American Revolutionary Christianity*, Anniversary ed. (Louisville, KY: Westminster John Knox Press, 2002).

AJIACO CHRISTIANITY

An ajiaco (ají, African name for an Amerindian ingredient plus the Spanish suffix -aco) is a Cuban indigenous stew made from readily available native root vegetables and chunks of meat. As the stew cooks, the ingredients partially disintegrate yet retain their distinct identity and flavor. New and perhaps different ingredients are added as the ajiaco is consumed. Thus each serving of stew has a unique and unpredictable combination of flavors. In Hispanic religious discourse, "ajiaco" signifies less a particular essence than the unfinished status and cultural and ethnic unpredictability of the Cuban people. Amerindians, Africans, Chinese, Spanish, and Anglo-Saxons are some of the ingredients that have undergone rearrangement and change on the cooking fire that is the island of Cuba.

Historical Development

Fernando Ortiz, the Cuban legend and polyglot intellectual, was the first to use ajiaco as a metaphor for cubanidad (the distinctive Cuban identity). Ortiz emphasizes that since Cuba is an ajiaco, la cubanidad is not found in the fusion of different cultures' lineages dissolved into Cuba but in the continual and complex process of formation, disintegration, and reintegration within the dynamic Cuban cultural milieu (Ortiz 1940, 169). Ajiaco is the concretization of Ortiz's abstract notion of transculturación, a neologism stressing the transitional and fluid nature of the Cuban condition. Over and against the hegemonic concept of "acculturation," which only names the phenomenon of acquiring a new culture, Ortiz proposes three phases of cultural contact in Cuba: (1) deculturation, the loss of certain cultural elements; (2) acculturation, acquisition of parts of another culture; and (3) neoculturation, the creation of new cultural elements through the amalgamation of the two cultures. For Ortiz, not only does ajiaco offer a more appropriate, complete, and precise description of Cuban culture, but it also functions as an anticolonial rhetorical tactic, replacing the externally imposed metaphor of a melting pot or crisol. Though the metaphors are close, ajiaco is preferred because it is a "native" word derived within Cuba. Hence, as the culinary emblem of Cuba, ajiaco forms a concrete and distinctly Cuban image of constantly changing cultural configurations of Cuban society.

Characteristics

Religious scholars, more notably Miguel A. De La Torre, have adopted and reformulated ajiaco as an attempt to accurately describe the complex multiracial Cuban identity. Until its introduction, Hispanic religious discourse had only two terms to metaphorically describe the heterogeneity of Latino/a identity: mestizaje and mulatez. Mestizaje refers to the mixing of indigenous and Spanish heritages. It is most often used for Latino/as from Mexico, Central America, and most of South America. The second term, mulatez, refers to the mixing of African and Spanish cultures. Scholars use mulatez to describe Hispanics descended from areas of continued African presence: the Caribbean islands, the coastal areas of Columbia and Venezuela, and Brazil. However, mulatez derives from the root word mulo or mule. Despite the attempts by academics to fabricate a more positive meaning, "mulatez" remains a racist term. A mule is the sterile result of breeding a horse and a donkey. In contrast, ajiaco is a hearty and life-giving food that nourishes and sustains the

community from its own indigenous roots (De La Torre 2003, 17). Over and against monolithic, pan-Latino/a identities, Ajiaco Christianity insists on the distinctiveness and varieties of Latino/a experiences of Hispanics from various countries of origin, in particular the Cuban experience. In the tradition of Ortiz, the adoption of ajiaco becomes symbolic resistance to hegemonic imposition of identity from the outside, even from within the Hispanic community, in the ongoing attempt to define the nature of what it means to theologize from a Cuban perspective.

Like the stew for which it is named, Ajiaco Christianity takes exogenous ingredients and "cooks" them into new and unexpected permutations. Ajiaco Christianity contains elements from postmodern and postcolonial theories as well as liberation theology. Like postmodernity, ajiaco recognizes itself as a social construct and celebrates multivalent diversity, rather than modernity's insistence on homogenization. Consistent with the radical critique of modernity's assumptions of identity and culture, Ajiaco Christianity deconstructs Cuban identity to debunk the social construction of machismo and the sexism, racism, and classism inherent in it. As a postcolonial theory, Ajiaco Christianity situates religious discourse in the colonial context of mass trauma and challenges the normalizing authority given to Spanish and Anglo roots. As a liberation theology, Ajiaco Christianity emphasizes orthopraxis over orthodoxy and counteracts postmodernity's paralyzing plurality through the unifying principle of liberating praxis (De La Torre 1999, 22–27).

Ajiaco Christianity does not refer to a specific Cuban religiosity. Instead it constitutes a Cuban ethical response toward reconciliation, in particular of Resident and Exilic Cubans, the Cubans allá (over there) and those aquí (here). Ajiaco Christianity draws on the tradition of the Hebrew prophets calling on all, not just Cubans, to cooperate with God to bring about reconciliation. Like the Hebrews, Exilic Cubans resist reconciliation, aligning themselves with the dominant powers. Identifying the refusal to reconcile as the central Cuban sin, Ajiaco Christianity alters the liberationist equation. Instead of salvation or liberation leading to reconciliation, salvation and liberation are synonymous with reconciliation (De La Torre 1999, 18–19).

A Preliminary Assessment

How useful is the rubric of Ajiaco Christianity to the overall project of Hispanic Religion Studies? Michelle A. Gonzalez has argued that ajiaco, despite insistence to the contrary, is as artificial an academic construction as mestizo or mulatez. In addition, she questions the real-world applicability of the term, since no one refers to themselves as ajiaco (Gonzalez 2006, 28). On the other hand, "ajiaco" successfully describes the existential space of a multicultural people, the inheritors of five broad cultural traditions, a reality masked by the use of either mestizo or mulatez. Just as discussions from distinctly Mexican or Puerto Rican perspectives have enriched the varieties of Latino/a religions, "ajiaco" adds to the Latino/a religious discourse by enabling discussion of Cuban religious identity on Cuban terms. More broadly "ajiaco" moves beyond questions of identity by providing a way to deconstruct oppressive social structures

and reveal racist assumptions within the Latino/a community.

Rodolfo J. Hernández-Díaz

References and Further Reading

De La Torre, Miguel A. *Ajiaco Christianity: Toward an Exilic Cuban Ethic of Reconciliation* (Ph.D. diss., Temple University, Philadelphia, 1999).

De La Torre, Miguel A. *La Lucha for Cuba: Religion and Politics on the Streets of Miami* (Berkeley: University of California Press, 2003).

Gonzalez, Michelle A. *Afro-Cuban Theology: Religion, Race, Culture, and Identity* (Gainesville: University Press of Florida, 2006).

Ortiz, Fernando. "Los factores humanos de la cubanidad." *Revista bimestre cubana* 21 (1940): 161–186.

Ortiz, Fernando. *Contrapunteo cubano del tabaco y el azúcar* [Cuban Counterpoint: Tobacco and Sugar], trans. H. D. Onís. 1st American ed. (New York: A. A. Knopf, 1947).

Pérez Firmat, Gustavo. "The Cuban Condition: Translation and Identity in Modern Cuban Literature." *Cambridge Studies in Latin American and Iberian Literature* (Cambridge, England: Cambridge University Press, 1989).

ALCANCE VICTORIA

Alcance Victoria's goal is to assist drug addicts, gang members, and prostitutes by keeping them off the street and out of prison. They attempt to achieve this goal through the proclamation of the life-transforming power of Jesus Christ. Founded in 1967 by Sonny Arguinzoni in East Los Angeles, Alcance Victoria, better known today as Victory Outreach, has become an international inner-city ministry phenomenon.

The Legacy of Sonny Arguinzoni

Sonny Arguinzoni, the son of Puerto Rican immigrants, was a heroin addict, gang member, and ex-convict. According to his autobiography and personal "testimony" entitled *Sonny*, at the age of 21 he was cured of his six-year addiction to heroine and converted to Christ when he came into contact with ex-gang leader Nicky Cruz and Teen Challenge, the ministry of David Wilkerson. In 1962, Sonny left New York to attend the Latin American Bible Institute (LABI) of the Assemblies of God in La Puente, California. While in school, Sonny continued to work with Teen Challenge and quickly became discouraged by local churches that refused to embrace the ex-drug addicts and gang members that he brought along with him. Undaunted, Sonny started a new ministry that specifically targeted society's rejects (Arguinzoni 1987).

In 1967, Arguinzoni and his small band of disciples purchased a small church in a drug- and gang-infested section of East Los Angeles and began what was then called "Victory Temple Addicts Church." Since 1967, Alcance Victoria (Victory Outreach) has grown from a single inner-city church to a worldwide network of over 600 churches and ministries with locations across the United States and 30 countries throughout Latin America, Europe, Africa, and Asia. According to information available on the church's official Web site (www .victoryoutreach.org), more than 10,000 drug addicts and alcoholics go through their intensive rehabilitation program each year. They claim that seven out of ten drug addicts who participate in their boot-camp program kick their habits.

Approximately 40,000 people attend services each Sunday at one of 250 Victory Outreach (VO) churches in the United States. Each local VO church strives to promote a positive image in the community and instills self-respect and dignity in its members. While most VO churches have between 100 and 300 members, some congregations are larger. For instance, VO churches in San Diego and San Jose, California, have more than a thousand members. The mother church in La Puente, California, now led by Sonny Arguinzoni Jr. has over 4,000 members.

More Than a Drug-Rehabilitation Program

Since 1967, Victory Outreach has become more than drug-rehabilitation or gang-prevention programs. VO is a comprehensive outreach and discipleship ministry that spans the globe. Programs such as "Mighty Men of Valor" and "United Women in Ministry" help members live out their faith. "Victory Outreach International Bible Institute" provides biblical, spiritual, and theological training to its members. "Urban Training Centers" (UTC) provides extensive one- and two-year training programs for young adults wanting to go into full-time ministry.

Victory Outreach is now training a new generation of young people referred to as "God's Anointed Now Generation" (GANG). Many of those involved in GANG and the UTC are the children of ex-addicts converted through VO. Many of these young men and women have gone on to start group recovery homes, drug treatment centers, urban intervention programs, churches, prison visitation outreaches, and family counseling centers

In his book entitled *Internalizing the Vision*, the unofficial ministry manual for VO, Pastor Sonny insists that boldness is one of the secrets to the movement's success. "Because of our boldness, we are able to move into the worst neighborhoods of some of the world's roughest cities with aggressiveness and dedication and effectiveness" (1995, 76–77). Another key to the success of VO is an emphasis on leadership development within the context of the local church, short-circuiting the traditional role of preaching schools, Bible colleges, and seminaries in most Protestant and Evangelical denominations. Two factors drive this unique strategy. On the one hand, the vast majority of the promising pastoral candidates in VO would not qualify for admission to most preaching schools and Bible colleges. On the other hand, leaders at VO have learned from experience that would-be pastors must first earn their credentials in the local church, where the would-be pastors are given opportunities to develop preaching and pastoral skills under the direction and supervision of a local pastor.

Born in the Barrio

Victory Outreach is unique in that it specifically targets the inner city, drug addicts, ex-convicts, gang members, alcoholics, prostitutes, and other social outcasts. As one might expect, VO is a multiethnic and interracial movement. Still, an outside observer would quickly notice that the overwhelming majority of the movement's members are second-and third-generation English-dominant Latino/as. Nevertheless, VO resists referring to itself as a Chicano or Latina/o Pentecostal church, even though the demographics, including the overwhelming number of Latino pastors throughout the movement, cannot be easily overlooked. For example, seven of the denomination's eight elders, including Pastor Sonny are Latinos as are 75 percent of the 39 regional pastors.

Conclusion

Pastor Sonny and VO have been recognized for their ongoing efforts and commitment to combat drug addiction and gang violence by a growing list of law-enforcement agencies as well as local, state, and federal officials, including former presidents George H. W. Bush, and William J. Clinton. In anticipation of Victory Outreach's 40th anniversary in 2007, President George W. Bush sent Pastor Sonny a special note thanking him for his involvement and support with the mission of making the United States a better place to live.

In *Treasures Out of Darkness*, an anecdotal history of VO, Pastor Sonny acknowledges that many people today have a hard time believing that God still performs miracles. He insists that Victory Outreach is proof that God does. Since 1967, the approach of VO has transformed lives from addiction, gang violence, and self-destructive behavior.

Daniel A. Rodriguez

References and Further Reading

Arguinzoni, Sonny. *Sonny* (San Dimas, CA: Vision Multimedia, 1987).

———. *Internalizing the Vision* (San Dimas, CA: Vision Multimedia, 1995).

———. *Treasures Out of Darkness*, 2nd ed. (San Dimas, CA: Vision Multimedia, 2000).

ALIENATION

From the Gulf of Mexico to the Pacific Ocean runs a 1,833-mile border that separates Latin America from the United States. This artificial line, created immediately after the U.S. territorial conquest of northern Mexico that ended with the Mexican-American War (1846–1848), is more than just a border separating countries. The creation of this border, along with the Spanish-American War (1898), the consequences of which was the territorial conquest of Puerto Rico, resulted with the borders crossing over Mexicans and Puerto Ricans living on their own lands—making them and their descendants aliens in their homelands. For this reason, many Hispanics see these artificial borders as a scar where the First and Third Worlds rub up against each other.

There are millions of Latino/as who live in cities that are located along this artificial line. But the U.S. borderlands are more than a geographical reality; they are also the existential reality of Latina/o alienation. A Hispanic does not need to reside along the 1,833-mile border to experience the alienation of living on the borders. Regardless of where Latino/as live or how they or their ancestors ended up within the U.S. borders, Hispanics live with the alienation caused by borders. These are the borders that separate Hispanics from Euro-Americans.

Slum neighborhood built up near maquiladoras *(border factories) owned and operated by foreigners, Chihuahua City, Mexico (opposite El Paso, Texas). (Time & Life Pictures/Getty Images)*

Regardless of their proximity to the militarized 1,833-mile line separating the United States from Latin America, these borders exist in every state, county, city, town, and village throughout the United States. The invisible walls are as real in New York City; Washington, D.C.; Omaha, Nebraska; and Chapel Hill, North Carolina, as are the visible walls in Chula Vista, California; Douglas, Arizona; or El Paso, Texas. To be a Latina/o living anywhere in the United States is to live alienated, to constantly live on the border, that is, the border that separates them from privilege, power, and whiteness.

To live on the borders throughout the United States means that Hispanics live in a state of alienation that keeps them separated from the benefits and fruits that society has to offer its inhabitants. Latino/as who demand a share of the benefits and fruits of society are asking for neither charity nor some sort of handout, but rather for what belongs to them. Through their labor (usually cheaply paid labor) they have contributed for centuries to the wealth building of this nation. Yet exclusion from the product of their labor occurs mainly because Hispanics are perceived by the dominant Euro-American culture as not belonging, as unwelcome aliens. They are seen as inferior partly due to the pervasive race-conscious U.S. culture. For centuries Euro-Americans have been taught to equate non-Whites, specifically mixed-race persons, as inferior. Seen derogatorily as "half-breeds," a mixture of races and ethnicities (Caucasian, African, Amerindian, or any combination thereof) has historically meant, and continues to mean, limited access to education and social services.

Alienated from the wealth they produce due in part to many Latina/os being seen as inferior due to their mixture (specifically racial mixture), it should not be surprising that many Hispanics cluster in the lower stratum of the economy, receiving the lowest weekly wages of any major group in the labor market. Hispanic poverty is often understood by the dominant Euro-American culture as being a choice made by Latina/os or the consequences of lacking a Euro-American Protestant work ethic. They are usually stereotyped as lazy, backward, and mentally underdeveloped. If this is true, then the only hope for Hispanics would rest with the generosity of Euro-Americans who might attempt aid by providing food, affirmative action, or charity. Instead of blaming those made victims for their condition, it is important to understand that Hispanic poverty exists due to economic forces that cause the prosperity of some to be rooted in the poverty of many. As the wealth of the rich grows, so too does the number of those falling into poverty, making the former dependent on the latter. Thus the main consequence that Hispanics living in the borderlands face is alienation, not only from the goods they produce, but from the dominant culture itself.

To exist in the social location called the borderlands means that Latina/os construct religious perspectives from the location of imposed alienation, marginality, and disenfranchisement. The spirituality that emerges from the borderlands is one that is contextual, where the everyday experience and struggle for the survival and life of the disenfranchised becomes the subject and source of religious reflection. For example, the God who is understood and worshiped in the borderlands is a God who became human and still continues to enflesh Godself in the everyday lives and experiences of the alienated. It is these alienated people who are crucified each day so that those whom society empowers can enjoy their privileged space. This salvific experience of God, in the here and now, is experienced by the alienated in their daily struggles for humanization.

The theological perspectives arising from the space caused by the alienation of Latino/as are not only salvific for the Hispanics who live throughout the U.S. borderlands, but they are salvific for the dominant Euro-American culture that erected the borders in the first place. A preferential option is made for the religious understandings and interpretations of the alienated and disenfranchised (in our case the residents of the borderlands) not because they are better Christians, nor because they are more intelligent. A preferential option for borderland spirituality is made because, unlike the dominant Euro-American culture that sees reality only through their privileged social location, Hispanics—in order to survive—must be aware of the reality of the dominant Euro-American culture as well as their own. This double consciousness, to use a W. E. B. Du Bois term, places Hispanics (and other marginalized groups) in the position of being capable of having a better grasp on reality because they can perceive it from both the perspective of privilege (due to their need to survive in that world) and their own marginality, while those of the dominant culture have no need or reason to make themselves aware of the perspectives of those existing on their underside.

The theological and spiritual perspectives that develop in the Hispanic borderland space of alienation serve as a salvific religious contribution made to the dominant Euro-American culture. A clearer understanding of the Good News emerges through the debunking of pervasive emphasis Euro-Americans place on a personal piety that justifies their power and privilege. From the alienation of Latina/os emerges an evangelical message of salvation for those who worship the false idols of power and privilege masked as Euro-American Christianity.

Miguel A. De La Torre

References and Further Reading

Abalos, David T. *Latinos in the United States: The Sacred and the Political*, 2nd ed. (Notre Dame, IN: University of Notre Dame Press, 2007).

De La Torre, Miguel A. "Living on the Borders." *The Ecumenical Review* 59, no. 2–3 (April/July 2007): 214–220.

Rodríguez, Havidán, Rogelio Sáenz, and Cecilia Menjívar, eds. *Latinas/os in the United States: Changing the Face of América* (New York: Springer, 2008).

ALTARS AND SHRINES

The tradition of altar or shrine making, or "an ordered arrangement of objects with symbolic meaning" (McMann, 1998:9) with the intent of bridging the physical and the spiritual realms, has its roots for Latinos/as among the ancient indigenous cultures of Latin America, the Caribbean, Africa, and the medieval cultures of European Catholicism. In Mexico, the Toltecs (950–1200 CE) of central Mexico, maintained small shrines or altars dedicated to specific deities in the privacy of domestic space. The Mexica or Aztecs (1200–1521 CE) continued the domestic tradition with small alcoves designed for an effigy of a deity and a container for burnt offerings. Among the Toltec, Mexica, and Maya, large stones with flat surfaces suitable for the burning of oblations served as public altars. Monumental temples or ceremonial platforms commonly referred to as pyramids were dedicated to specific deities where elaborate public rituals took place on the highest level of the temples. These sites served as the sacred center or *axis mundi* of densely populated urban areas. As an example, in Tenochitlan, the Mexica capitol, two colossal temple platforms, one dedicated to Tlaloc, the rain god, and Huitzilopochtli, the god of war, were erected for the necessary oblations and sacrifices required for these central deities. The size and grandeur of these temple platforms were consciously located along the horizon of the natural sacred mountains surrounding the urban areas. In this manner, humans constructed a continuum with the natural sacred environment. According to David Carrasco, the temple dedicated to Tlaloc also represented a "mountain of sustenance" or "mythic mountain that was the source of abundance, rain, seeds, corn, food" (1990, 167). Oftentimes, buried within the temple structures were sacred bundles holding the remains of powerful leaders, animal bones, or other items deemed essential to the religious and political identity of the society. The temple platform with its public altar located in the core of a society served as the central marker for a state religion while also maintaining the essential balance between humanity and sacred cosmic forces.

Indigenous peoples continued their practices of altar making after the period of contact, collision, and convergence with European colonizing powers by accommodating, but at the same time influencing, Catholic practices. During the early colonial period Catholic missionaries demanded the destruction of the public temples or axis mundi. In their places rose the baroque architecture of Catholic churches constructed from the recycling of "pyramid" stones and the forced labor of indigenous peoples. Within these churches, numerous altars dedicated to the Christian God, his mother, and canonized martyrs offered a new axis mundi to native and mestizo communities. The sacred bundles would be replaced by the tabernacle holding the body of Christ, with admittance to the new sacred center requiring the rite of baptism. Native neophytes, however, would often be restricted to attending worship services in the open atriums outside the inner sanctuary. The practice of home altar making would continue for native populations most likely in adherence to tradition, but also now as a strategy to resist the marginalization experienced in the new state religion.

Despite the efforts of church officials to curtail the importance of home altars for native peoples, these sites of spiritual vitality persisted, but with Christian symbols supplanting native iconography. However, for colonized indigenous and mestizo populations, the complexity of nepantla (a Nahua term meaning "in the middle") began to be visualized in religious iconography especially during the first century of contact. Indigenous and mestizo altars revealed the emerging synthesized nature of Latin American Catholicism with a symbol system incorporating indigenous and Christian elements in one object. For example, a cross with the crucified body of Jesus surrounded by the moon and sun, or a crucifix made of corn husks, connected

OUR LADY OF CHARITY SHRINE

In 1966, Cuban refugees funded and built a shrine on Biscayne Bay in Miami, Florida, for La Virgen de la Caridad, the Cuban patroness. On September 8, 1961, her feast day, a statue of la Virgen, a replica of the one in Cobre, was smuggled out of Cuba in a suitcase to an awaiting crowd of over 25,000 Cubans congregated at a stadium. The tent-like shrine built to house the statue serves as both a political and sacred space. The shrine is situated with its back toward Cuba so that prayers offered by the faithful face the island. The statue faces the ocean to serve as a beacon for Cubans coming to the United States. Behind the altar is a mural merging religious and patriotic themes. Behind the shrine are the busts of Cuban patriots José Martí and Father Félix Varela. Under the altar is a molded stone composed of the soil of all Cuba's provinces and the ocean water retrieved from a raft that sailed to the United States, a voyage that claimed 15 lives. The six columns sustaining the mantle and the six-sided golden cone-shaped roof represent the six provinces. The priest's chair was made from a Cuban palm.

—MAD

the Christian deity to the sacred cosmic forces and sacred food of Mesoamerican indigenous religions (Carrasco, 1995). Perhaps, the syncretic image par excellence is that of Our Lady of Guadalupe, as she incorporates the cosmic sacredness of the sun, the moon, and the stars within her Catholic representation of the divine Madonna.

Elite Spanish and *criollo* families constructed home chapels for private worship with elaborate altars dedicated to patron saints or the Madonna. The tradition of altar making and the construction of public shrines at pilgrimage sites had long been a tradition in medieval Catholic Europe. In the "New World" the public display of venerated Catholic icons reinforced a collective religious and emerging national identity. But Spanish and mestizo populations consistently appropriated the traditions and beliefs of local native populations partly to supplant native traditions and partly to acquire the miraculous efficacy of

native knowledge. For example, in the northern frontiers, Spanish and mestizo settlers constructed an adobe church on land held sacred by the Tewa people in the valley of Chimayo, New Mexico. Pilgrimage to the adobe shrine to experience the healing properties of the sacred dirt remains a central Mexican Catholic practice today. Or at Chalma, 115 kilometers from Mexico City, missionaries built a church in 1683 dedicated to Our Lord of Chalma along a riverbank where native pilgrims sought healing from the natural spring water flowing in a nearby cave. There they honored the deity, Ozteotl. Today Chalma is the most visited shrine in Mexico after the shrine to Our Lady of Guadalupe.

The most popular shrine and pilgrimage site appearing during the colonial period remains at Tepeyac in the central valley of Mexico. It is here that the presence of Tonantzin, the revered mother, had long been worshipped by the Nahua people. With the chaos and violence of the Spanish invasion, a new understanding emerged about the divine female presence at work in the "New World" ensuring the survival of native and mestizo peoples. Out of the colonial chaos appeared the image and story of Our Lady of Guadalupe, the divine mestiza mother. A shrine dedicated to her in 1536 atop the sacred mountain of Tepeyac remains the most visited shrine in all of the Americas. This sacred site includes two other churches, one being the more modern basilica built in 1976 that holds the original image of Our Lady of Guadalupe.

The curtailment of church authorities in Latin America during periods of revolution and independence from European powers in the nineteenth century increased the importance of domestic shrines where families could continue their prayers and rituals. Legislation often prohibited the display of holy images in public spaces as societies moved toward secularization. As noted by historian William H. Beezley, the solution "was to move holy images inside churches and other buildings, including homes (1997, 96). Anticlericalism and church-state conflict continued throughout the century, resulting in a decline of clergy and functioning churches. The *rezadora* or female prayer leader took on a central role in the maintenance and transmission of the faith in the nineteenth century. In rural communities, the virtual absence of clergy made the rezadora and the *curanderas/os*, or specialized healers, extremely significant. *Parteras*, or midwives, oftentimes baptized the newborn in the absence of male clergy. These varieties of spiritual work most likely took place around the home altar.

In Mexico during the last decade of the nineteenth century a reinstatement

of church vitality occurred with a new cadre of priests inspired by the ideals of social action. The papacy's approval of *Rerum Novarum* in 1895, with its concern for action over doctrine, served to increase the number of priests, churches, and church attendance. Yet, the home altar remained a central site for the practice of personal and familial devotions. Developments in printing and lithography, making images and prayer cards readily available, helped to embellish the art and content of home altars. Likewise, public shrines honoring patron saints, the Madonna, and Jesus Christ proliferated. Today, Mexico retains these sacred markers even in urban areas, where religious statues and small shrines can often be found overlooking busy intersections.

With the contested annexation of one-half of Mexico by the United States in 1848, Mexican Catholics became members of the U.S. Roman Catholic Church overnight. Overt discrimination, culturally insensitive European clergy, and bishops allocating unequal monetary resources for new Mexican American dioceses created a distance between Spanish-speaking communities and the institutional church. For example, Bishop Thaddues Amat of the Monterey–Los Angeles diocese published three decrees between 1862 and 1876 prohibiting Mexican popular devotions such as public reenactments of biblical stories, as well as funeral processions. The public display of Mexican Catholicism was found to be offensive to "clerical sensitivities" (Engh 1994, 91). In response, the home altar tradition was again renewed in its importance for the preservation of the faith among Mexican Catholic families. During the mid-twentieth century, as part of ecclesial efforts to universalize and modernize Catholic worship, Mexican American Catholics often succumbed to the pressure to seize domestic altar making and other popular traditions. Numerous devotees, however, continued the tradition that celebrates spirituality beyond the boundaries of institutionalized religion and signifies a resilient Latina/o spirituality that is usually centered on the divine female. The tradition of home altars is now a widely accepted expression of one's faith across ethnic and even religious lines. Texts such as *Altars and Icons: Sacred Spaces in Everyday Life* by Jean McMann and *Beautiful Necessity: The Art and Meaning of Women's Altars* by Kay Turner attest to the multicultural practice of altar or shrine making. As more of the U.S. population finds spirituality important, but church attendance less so, the desire for sacred space in one's home will inevitably rise.

Constructing Altars

Through the arrangement of symbols, photographs, candles, and icons, all imbued with meaning and preserving memory, altars connect the spiritual world with the physical world, the living with the dead, the past with the present, and the altar maker with the viewer. As Ramón Gutiérrez writes, "[On] home altars the photographs, trinkets, and mementos construct family histories that visually record one's relations to a lineage and clan" (1997, 39). Or, altars with a conscious arrangement of meaningful objects, might simply express the altar makers' spiritual understandings and offer the space that connects the mortal with the immortal. Altars become sites preserving special memories as they invite the viewer to remember and to

simultaneously be mindful of the present. Through the symbols, images, and/or texts arranged on a tabletop, dresser, or simple shelf, altars convey family history, personal, spiritual, and political identities.

Altars can take a variety of forms as there are few rules for constructing an altar other than the intentional arrangement of objects, symbols, and/or images imbued with meaning, a sense of balance in the arrangement of the objects, and choosing a privileged space for the altar. The latter can be anywhere from the top of a television set in the main living area to a secluded corner in one's bedroom. Altars are located not only in living spaces but also in public spaces like businesses, restaurants, grocery stores, bars, and even on the dashboards of vehicles. A central purpose of the altar in a public space is to announce a spiritual presence overseeing the business at hand. The sacred and the secular are fused and joined within the tradition of altar making.

Once created, altars or shrines become passive or active expressions. A passive altar is created at one moment in time, but with little subsequent interaction between the altar and the altar maker. Its presence marks the environment as special, but the energy around the altar becomes static. In contrast, an active altar is created and interaction between the altar and the altar maker continues. The space is cleaned regularly, fresh or new flowers are purchased, candles are lit, objects are added, removed, or rearranged, prayers are said, or silent reflections occur. In this manner, the altar emits energy that moves, and over time the altar takes on a life of its own. As one altar maker explains, "I meditate here in the morning ... then I bow ...

and I feel a difference ... in my being when I do that" (cited in McMann 1998, 35). Another altar maker who has maintained her altar for over 50 years states, "It's an ancient tradition, and you can't get away from it, wherever you go ... mi *altarcito* helps me to live" (cited in Turner 1999, 41).

Contemporary altars range from traditional to more abstract expressions, from personal and private creations to public and communal works of art. Because of the lack of rules governing altars, they represent fluid expressions of ever-changing personal and social identities. Latinos/as inherit a rich legacy of creating sacred spaces for spiritual and psychic nourishment.

Other Types of Altars

For Latino/a Protestants, the construction of home altars with symbols other than a cross and the Bible are rare because Protestant Christianity traditionally prohibits the display of icons or the practice of praying through material objects. Rather, *el altar familiar*, the family altar, takes the form of time and space set aside for Bible study and prayer. In contrast, Latinos/as practicing Santería or Lucumí regularly construct elaborate altars as part of their ritual practices of making oblations to deities and the ancestors. Material religion takes on primary importance in this tradition.

Depending on the orisha or sacred spirit being honored, a santería's altar will contain food and drink offerings, richly colored fabrics designating the orisha, elaborately decorated ceramic pots holding the *ashé* or spiritual power of the orisha, ritual instruments to call forth ancestors and spirits, and images of the orisha, at times a statue of a Christian saint that conceals the identity of the orisha.

Contemporary Chicana artists such as Amalia Mesa-Baines, Ofelia Esparza, and Yreina Cervantez have influenced significantly the reclamation of altar making as a central expression of Chicana and Latina spirituality. For Latinas who have left organized religions, but also for those who remain, altars provide the space for women to create and express what for them has ultimate meaning. For women, the act of altar making reinforces their agency to name the sacred. In religions and cultures that remain male dominant, the act of women deciding for themselves what and who represents the sacred holds revolutionary potential. Ofelia Esparza, who resides in East Los Angeles, is a third-generation altar maker. Learning the tradition from her grandmother, Ofelia now teaches the tradition to students of all ages and she exhibits her altars nationally and internationally. Cultural workers and artists like Ofelia Esparza have tremendously influenced the maintenance of the tradition across the United States and in the process sustain the "matriarchal core" of Latino/a religiosity (Díaz-Stevens 1994, 245). While men also partake in the creation of shrines or altars, women tend to dominate this aspect of Latino/a religiosity. Young male artists, however, such as Rigo Maldonado of Los Angeles are paving the way for men to participate more publicly in maintaining the tradition.

During the height of the Chicano movement in the early 1970s, Chicana artists including Ofelia Esparza, Amalia Mesa-Baines, Linda Vallejo, Esther Hernandez, and many others revived the tradition of altar making among Chicano/a communities. During the political turmoil of the late 1960s and early 1970s, artists understood the dire need to offer strategies of empowerment and healing to Chicano peoples affected by police brutality, inadequate housing, medical care, and poor education. In 1972, the tradition of *Días de muertos*, with the creation of altars or *ofrendas* for the dead at its ritual center, was offered to communities in the main urban centers of California: Los Angeles, San Francisco, and Sacramento. Quickly Chicano communities embraced the tradition of creating sacred space and laying out gifts for the dead. By 1978, the art of altar making and its healing properties was revived in the United States. The tradition of altar making, particularly around Days of the Dead, can now be found throughout the nation, in museums, cultural centers, schools, libraries, homes, and even churches. The power of remembering, of honoring, and of communing through the sacred center of the altar renews relationships between the living and the dead. In the process, the family, the group, and the community are renewed and empowered.

Street shrine on Janitzio Island, Mexico. (William Perry/Dreamstime)

Shrines

It is quite common now to see small or large altars or shrines located in popular businesses such as restaurants. In San Antonio, Texas, in the popular restaurant Mi Tierra, a larger than life altar honors the spirit and memory of Selena, the Chicana "Queen of Tejano music" who died tragically in 1995 at the young age of 24. This type of shrine keeps her spirit and accomplishments alive in the public memory and also serves as a teaching tool for those who did not know about this amazing young artist. Similarly, street shrines located near the scene of fatal accidents have become common-

place in the United States. By using candles, flowers, pictures, and even items of affection (stuffed animals), this tradition enables the living to spontaneously create sacred space marking the tragic passing of a soul. Humans have the need to memorialize tragedy as part of the grieving process, and the altar facilitates this innate desire.

Shrines constructed at the gravesites of historical healers like Teresa de Urrea (*La Santa de Cabora*), Don Pedro Jaramillo, and El Niño Fidencio offer vivid reminders of the deep spirituality embedded in the history and land along the border regions. All three of these healers played a significant role in the physical and spiritual well-being of Mexican communities in the late nineteenth and early twentieth centuries. The tradition of creating public shrines in their honor not only keeps their memory alive for later generations but also validates the role of *curanderismo*, a healing method that emerged from the mixture of cultures and medical practices in colonial Latin America.

Teresa de Urrea, born in 1873 in Sinaloa, Mexico, to an indigenous Tehueco mother and a mestizo father, would rise to international fame due to her healing abilities and commitment to serving the poor and marginalized. By the age of 17, Teresa had trained with a traditional healer or *curandera* in medicinal plants, and then experienced an emotional trauma (possibly an attempted rape), fell into a coma for 12 days only to awaken with extremely powerful healing and psychic abilities. Her profession as a healer and her progressive politics eventually took her into the United States where she was commissioned to tour with a medical company. In 1906, in Clifton, Arizona, Teresa's own body succumbed to tuberculosis. It is reported that 400 people attended her funeral. Today her unmarked grave in a hilly cemetery in Clifton draws the attention of townsfolk and outsiders who continue to be intrigued by her healing powers. Simple offerings can regularly be found at her gravesite that is marked only with a wrought iron fence, yet the scent of roses emanating from her grave is frequently reported.

Don Pedro Jaramillo, who was born in 1829 in Guadalajara, Jalisco, Mexico, rose to fame for his extraordinary healing powers. Born impoverished, Jaramillo experienced divine intervention for his own health and went on to establish himself as an immensely popular *curandero* near Falfurrias, Texas, in 1881. It is said that 500 people at a time would camp on his ranch waiting to be healed. Don Pedro would never charge for his work and always found a way to feed the many people who sought his help. The shrine dedicated to Don Pedro is located in a small cemetery near Falfurrias. Pilgrims find their way to the small brick building painted white that houses his grave, headstone, a small altar, a life-sized statue of the healer, a table for candles, and a bulletin board for the many messages that the faithful leave behind. Weekends are the busiest time at the shrine with pilgrims able to purchase sacred memorabilia of the healer at the nearby Don Pedrito Store.

The shrine and pilgrimage site of Niño Fidencio in Espinazo, Nuevo León, Mexico, is perhaps the largest of the three shrines briefly discussed here. José Fidencio Constantino Síntora was born in Iramuco, Guanajuato, in 1898. By the age of eight, he was already known to have set his mother's arm after she broke it in a fall. He would become a skilled midwife and *curandero*, using herbal medicine, mud, and at times broken glass in his treatments. He is known to have cured blindness, insanity, and paralysis. Like Jaramillo, he set up his clinic on land that could accommodate hundreds of pilgrims at one time with the apex of his career occurring during the late 1920s and early 1930s. The location of his work was in Espinazo, Nuevo León, where he was working as a kitchen helper and where he received what he believed to be instructions from God to heal others. His fame as a healer quickly grew with his public career lasting only 10 years. Today, a shrine at Espinazo where he lived, cured, and is buried attracts thousands of devotees from both sides of the border especially on October 17, his birth date, and October 19, his death date, and March 19, the day of Saint Joseph, his patron saint. According to folklorist James S. Griffith, the numerous pilgrims "visit the various sacred sites; the pirulito tree where Fidencio received his defining vision, the hill where he would meditate, the *charquito* or pond where he would treat lepers. Above all, they visit the hacienda containing the room where he worked, where he saw Jesus walking, and which is the site of his tomb" (Griffith 2003, 138). At Espinazo, a powerful healer is remembered, a history is told, and a legacy is passed on through the tradition of shrine making.

Lara Medina

References and Further Reading

Beezley, William H. "Home Altars; Private Reflections of Public Life." *Home Altars of Mexico*, ed. Dana Salvo (Albuquerque: University of New Mexico Press, 1997).

Carrasco, Davíd. *Religions of Mesoamerica: Cosmovision and Ceremonial Centers* (Prospect Heights, IL: Waveland Press, 1998).

———. "Jaguar Christians in the Contact Zone." *Enigmatic Powers: Syncretism with African and Indigenous Peoples' Religions Among Latinos*, ed. Anthony M. Stevens-Arroyo and Andres I. Pérez y Mena (New York: Bildner Center for Western Hemisphere Studies, 1995).

Díaz-Stevens, Ana María. "Latinas and the Church." *Hispanic Catholic Culture in the U.S.: Issues and Concerns*, ed. Jay P. Dolan and Allan Figueroa Deck, S.J. (Notre Dame, IN: University of Notre Dame Press, 1994).

Engh, Michael E., S.J. "From *Frontera* Faith to Roman Rubrics: Altering Hispanic Religious Customs in Los Angeles, 1855–1880." *U.S. Catholic Historian* 12, no. 4 (1994).

Griffith, James S. *Folk Saints of the Borderlands: Victims, Bandits, and Healers* (Tucson, AZ: Rio Nuevo Publishers, 2003).

McMann, Jean. *Altars and Icons: Sacred Spaces in Everyday Life* (San Francisco: Chronicle Books, 1998).

Turner, Kay. *Beautiful Necessity: The Art and Meaning of Women's Altars* (New York: Thames and Hudson, 1999).

ANONYMOUS SANTERÍA

The term "anonymous Santería" was coined by Miguel A. De La Torre as a response to the earlier theological concept developed by the Jesuit theologian Karl Rahner known as "anonymous Christianity." Rahner attempted to create an ecumenical environment for dialogue between Christians and members of other faiths. Moving beyond the concept that salvation can occur only within the church, specifically the Catholic Church, Rahner makes it possible for other religions to have a salvific quality. For Rahner, believers of non-Christian faiths have not made a self-willed decision to avoid accepting the "true" faith of God as revealed in Jesus Christ. Rather, as people of good will, they too could find God because the revelation of God's work can be found in all non-Christian religions. For Rahner, all religions contain God's grace, a gratuitous gift on account of Christ.

For this reason, all non-Christian religions should be recognized by Christians as a lawful religion without denying the error or depravity which that religion might contain. Those who have never heard of the Gospel or those who have rejected the revelation of Jesus Christ will still be saved. Because salvation can only occur through Christ, Rahner develops the concept of anonymous Christianity to show how Jews, Muslims,

Hindus, and others are saved by Christ regardless of their acknowledgement or acceptance of Christ's grace. This was one of the important theological concepts informing the Second Vatican Council. For those who belong to other faith traditions, for example Santería, the notion that santera/os are saved through Christian theology can be perceived as being somewhat paternalistic and/or presumptuous. In a very real sense, the faith of others is denigrated through the concept that they are really Christians regardless who or what they venerate or regardless whether they know it or not.

Although Rahner developed the concept of "anonymous Christianity" to provide a theological understanding that explains how non-Christians are saved through Christ, the idea of anonymous Santería developed to show how believers of this particular religion can worship or participate in other religions absent of inconsistencies. For followers of Santería, there is no such thing as absolute truth. No religion has a monopoly on absolute truth; rather all religions contain truth. When all that is was created, the supreme deity Olodumare distributed the wisdom upon which creation relied for everything. Therefore, the Christian, the Jew, the Muslim, the Hindu, the Buddhist, in effect every religious person regardless of the faith tradition, contains a piece of the truth in his/her sacred writings, in his/her worldview, and in his/her holy rituals. Believers of Santería neither condemn nor attempt to evoke the wrath of other religious faiths, but rather attempt to learn from other faiths.

What holds all these different faiths together is the concept of *ashé*. Ashé can be understood as the substance or cosmic energy undergirding every aspect

of existence that becomes the power, grace, blood, and life force of all reality. The blood of living creatures, the movement of the wind, and the elements of plants, fire, and moving water expend ashé. Because everything that exists contains ashé and all religions contain truths, certain universality exists within Santería. All of the orishas (the quasi-deities) are manifested in other religions, a type of "Anonymous Santería."

The incorporation and assimilation of new deities is possible and at times necessary within Santería. For example, the Virgin Mary, Mother of God among Catholics, can be understood as being the European manifestation of Obatalá, the creator of the world. Praying before a Catholic statue of the Virgin Mary is understood as praying to the orisha Obatalá signified by the statue. Catholics who venerate Our Lady of Mercy lack the "knowledge" about the real power behind the Catholic symbol. If the believer were Hindu, then Obatalá could easily be understood as Brahma the creator.

Because of anonymous Santería, worshipers are able to participate in other religious traditions. In fact, on certain occasions Santería requires that their members be baptized within the Catholic Church and attend the masses for the dead. Others attend church to honor the feast days of the Saints worshipped in Santería or to obtain holy water for incarnations. Anonymous Santería allows the follower of Santería to worship in another faith tradition without feeling any incongruency because ashé flows through all world religions. In short, anonymous Santería means that every human who worships some deity or cosmic force within their respective religious tradition is in reality worshiping

the orisha that particular deity or force signifies.

Miguel A. De La Torre

References and Further Reading

De La Torre, Miguel A. *Santería: The Beliefs and Rituals of a Growing Religion in America* (Grand Rapids, MI: Wm. B. Eerdmans Publishing Co., 2004).

Rahner, Karl. *Theological Investigations*, trans. David Bourke (London: Darton, Longman & Todd, 1973).

———. *Foundations of Christian Faith: Introduction to the Idea of Christianity*, trans. William V. Dych (New York: Seabury, 1978).

ASIANS

Asian Latino/as are frequently unrecognized and unacknowledged as a cultural and social category in the United States despite the growing number of Latina/os identifying with Asian heritage (2000 U.S. Census). For the first time, the 2000 Census allowed the public to select more than one racial category. The term "Hispanic" is not a racial category but a cultural tie that allows members to choose a racial category (e.g., White, Black, or Asian). In 2000, there were 35,305,818 people who self-identified as Hispanic and then chose a racial category as follows: 16,907,852 White, 710,753 Black, 119,829 Asian, and 45,326 American Indian. From the Asian perspective, 15 percent self-identified as multiracial. When Asians self-identified with their "other" heritage, 52 percent chose White, 6 percent identified with Blacks, 8 percent with Native Hawaiians, and 15 percent with Latina/os and "other races." Almost 249,000 Asians identified with Hispanic compared to 119,829 Hispanics who identified with Asian heritage. In order to understand Asian Latina/os mestizaje or miscegenation, we need to examine the historical context in which political and economic factors influenced individuals to immigrate to the United States, by either choice or force.

Japanese Latin Americans

In 1895, the Japanese government encouraged and provided legal authorization for Japanese citizens to migrate to the United States and Latin American countries, such as Peru, Mexico, Chile, and Argentina, to serve as a source of labor for economic and political advances. This was done to stimulate the Japanese economy and obtain the social changes that resulted from migration. As early as 1868, the first Japanese emigrants arrived in Hawaii, the United States, Canada, Mexico, Peru, Brazil, Chile, and Argentina. American recruiters were in search of cheap labor between 1890 and 1930 when 273,000 agricultural laborers, students, domestics, and entrepreneurs came to the United States from Japan. Similar emigration patterns began with the first Japanese migration to Peru in 1899 when 790 Japanese emigrants arrived at Callao. The reasons for emigration varied from difficult economic prospects due to the impact of the Sino-Japanese War, to shipping companies and emigration agents seeking to profit from the surplus of skilled farmers.

The Peruvian government supported their emigration because workers were needed in cotton and sugar fields. Migration was more attractive to the Japanese laborer since Peru welcomed the skilled laborer and opportunities existed for upward mobility in agriculture. The Japanese laborer mastered the Spanish language and Peruvian culture to advance him- or herself. By 1940, approximately 80 percent of the Peruvian Japanese were living in the Lima-Callao metropolitan area. During that time, Japanese numbered 17,598 and represented 28.08 percent of the foreign population living in Peru. In the United States, more than 100,000 Japanese had moved from rural areas to cities and were in commercial enterprises.

Similar to other first-generation immigrants arriving in Peru, the Japanese intended to work, save their earnings, and return to Japan. Many Japanese stayed in Peru, as did other immigrants, and created the Central Japanese Association of Peru (CJAP) as well as athletic organizations and other groups. Japanese migration included entire family units as opposed to the Peruvian Chinese colony that was 95 percent male. Typically, Japanese married second-generation Japanese or had a bride sent from Japan to Peru. Local Peruvians criticized them for defying "Peruvianization" because they would not intermarry with the existing population. Japanese community and cultural pride led to establishing the first of 50 Japanese language elementary schools in 1908. The Japanese immigrants retained many facets of their culture, including language, music, games, and dietary preferences. However, there was an immersion in Spanish-Catholic life.

In Peru, as in the United States, there was an anti-Japanese sentiment that began to replace the Peruvian dislike of the Chinese. The Japanese had taken control of agricultural zones and urban areas, and this led to protest over monopoly and unfair competition. In 1934, Peru denounced a four-year treaty of friendship, commerce, and legislation that required 80 percent of any work force be native Peruvians. Quotas were set for imported cotton goods. In 1936, the Peruvian government established immigration quotas and regulations that targeted the Japanese. For example, late birth registrations were quickly annulled.

Anti-Japanese sentiment grew and resulted in the Peruvian race riots of 1940. The Japanese Consulate recorded that 620 households and businesses were negatively affected, and a total of $6 million (U.S. dollar value) was lost in Lima. As a result, the Japanese were repatriated to Japan because they were unable to recover. Following the riots, even children would shout at Japanese people and call them "chino macaco." "Chino" means Chinese and "macaco" was used to indicate a "slave." This term had been used previously to demean the Chinese people who arrived in Peru as "semi-slaves" from the Portuguese colony of Macao. The Chinese had been sold to Peruvian mine operators and owners of large haciendas. Since then, "chino" has been used as a general term to refer to Asians when differentiation of Chinese from Japanese descent is difficult. The term "chino macaco" was typically used by the uneducated, but following the riots it was used as a racial epithet on a daily basis. Almost a week and a half after the riots, a great earthquake struck Peru. Most of the people who had participated in the riots were devout Catholics. They interpreted the earthquake as an omen or expression of anger on the part of the Lord for their violent behavior, and they began to repent. The earthquake tended to decrease some of the anti-Japanese sentiment that was intensifying in Peru during 1940.

On December 7, 1941, Japan was at war with the United States. After the attack on Pearl Harbor, Panamanian and American officials agreed to the internment of Japanese people. The Panamanian government allowed for the Panamanian Japanese to be exchanged for citizens of the Western Hemisphere held by Japan. The United States provided a blacklist, also known as the Proclaimed List of Certain Blocked Nationals. The list focused on economic strangulation through government-sponsored boycott of successful business owners or leaders in Italian, German, and Japanese communities in the United States, Canada, and Latin America. Seiichi Higashide, a first-generation Japanese Peruvian recalls that in his group there were 29 Japanese on the list, five or six naturalized Peruvians, and two had been born in Peru. Germans were also detained in the military concentration camp located in Panama.

Single Japanese men or married men without their families left Peru and were taken to concentration camps in Santa Fe, New Mexico, and Camp Kennedy located in Crystal City, Texas. Some families were split up, some were repatriated to Japan, while others were interned in separate concentration camps and never reunited with their families. The Peruvian government did not allow the return of deported Japanese during the Pacific War. Japanese Americans were detained and placed in 10 relocation centers in California, Oregon, and Washington. Thousands of Japanese Nisei (U.S. citizens) and Issei (first generation) served in the American Armed Forces during World War II to prove their loyalty to the country.

By the end of 1945, 20 to 30 percent of the 112,000 Japanese American internees remained in camps. Peru provided 84 percent of the total number of Japanese internees; other Japanese came from Panama, Bolivia, Nicaragua, and El Salvador. Brazil had the largest number of Japanese in South America but did not report any Japanese for deportation. Mexico moved its Japanese to inland areas and did not take a hard policy on deportation. Argentina and Chile remained neutral to the war until the end and did not deport their Japanese to the United States.

Japanese families that had been forced illegally by the U.S. government to reside in concentration camps were considered illegal immigrants to the United States post–World War II. Many Japanese were persuaded to return to Japan. With the issuance of Order No. 2663 on September 12, 1945, the U.S. government formally announced that all Japanese were to be removed from the Western Hemisphere. Higashide, an Issei, remembers that Wayne M. Collins, an attorney from San Francisco, was involved in efforts to restore U.S. citizenship to Japanese Americans who had been misled into renouncing their citizenship while detained in the camps. On June 26, 1946, Collins filed a writ of *habeas corpus* on behalf of the 364 Japanese from Peru in the Federal Circuit Court in San Francisco. The court approved a restricted parole while a decision was made for the Japanese from Peru, and a guarantor or sponsor for a provisional release was needed before they could leave the concentration camps. Seabrook Farms, a large food processing company located in southern New Jersey became the guarantor that provided work for many detainees. Many

Japanese had to start from nothing as a result of this injustice.

In 1952, naturalization laws allowed first-generation Asian immigrants to become naturalized U.S. citizens. In 1954, "illegal entrants" from Central and South America were formally given visas and the right to acquire permanent residency in the United States (as were other new immigrants). Immigrants no longer had to face the constant fear of being deported. Higashide shares that his children were involved in the redress movement that fought for numerous resolutions for World War II (WWII) internment of Japanese Americans. In 1970, Japanese American employees of the State of California received retirement credit for time spent in detention camps. In 1990, President George H. W. Bush presented a signed apology to three elderly Japanese Americans for wrongful imprisonment and compensation for pain and suffering during WWII. These elderly Japanese Americans each received a check for $20,000.

The Japanese Peruvians continue to negotiate their sense of identity, religion, language, social networks, and politics within the Japanese, Peruvian, and American cultures. Similarly, Japanese Mexican Americans face constant struggles between cultures and within each self-identified ethnic group. For example, consider a Mexican-born second-generation Japanese descendant who lived in the heart and capital of Mexico, and became a resident of California at the age of 12. She remembers her childhood in Mexico and tells her experience as an American citizen proud of her Japanese heritage. She describes her spiritual growth and religious practices:

My grandparents from both sides of my family came from Japan and migrated to Mexico before World War II. Both my mother and father had Japanese parents but were born and raised in Mexico. In Mexico, I felt very Mexican but with an Asian look. I went to a private school, El Liceo Mexicano Japones, which is a Japanese-Mexican integrated school. I was enrolled in the Mexican section, where all classes were in Spanish and 1 class was in Japanese. At that time, I identified more with Mexicans than with Japanese. I felt more racism in Mexico, in the form of people staring and looking at me weird and saying things like, "Ahi viene la chinita" [here comes the little Chinese girl]. The prejudice mostly came from uneducated people. I noticed it more when I was in places like the tiangis [farmer's market].

Now, living in the United States, I see the prejudice from the other side ... I now have to prove my identity as a Mexican, to get the same treatment from Mexicans as another Mexican. Mexicans are nice to me when I speak Spanish. People other than Mexican [in the United States] are surprised when I speak Spanish. They are totally accepting and see me with admiration and interest. I still feel very Mexican, but not as strongly as before ... I like the aspects of Mexican culture but I don't like the prejudices from Mexicans. It seems that some Mexicans (especially those less educated) feel the need to treat others badly (i.e., the people they perceive as non-Mexicans) as a kind of payback for the bad treatment they themselves may have received in this country because of their Mexican/Latino background. Or perhaps by treating each other better than they treat non-Mexicans (or those whom they think are not Mexican), they somehow feel like they're "beating the system" or helping society make up for what it hasn't given them but they feel they deserve. In surveys, I now tend to check the Asian or Asian-American boxes more than Hispanic category.

In Mexico, I don't remember seeing many Japanese Mexicans practicing Buddhism. I only remember my uncle praying at his Buddhist altar, bell, and incense at home. In Mexico, Japanese people seemed more Catholic. I did my first communion with other kids that also had both [Japanese and Mexican culture]. Our parents (2nd generation Japanese Mexican) embraced the Mexican culture, but also wanted us to know our own Japanese heritage and culture. When I first moved to California, our family visited the Japanese Buddhist temple. I felt weird . . . we had a double barrier . . . we were new to the community and couldn't communicate [not yet fully fluent in English]. I thought all Japanese people (at the temple) spoke only Japanese; but now that I have come back to the temple in recent years, I realize that all the people at the temple speak English and hardly any of them speak the Japanese language. It is a close-knit community. I now seek out Buddhist religion more than Catholicism. It seems more true about how I feel about life. I want my daughter to learn about Japanese culture. (Anonymous interview given the author, 2007)

Mexican Filipinos

The population of the Philippine Islands has always been diverse with the earliest settlers being dark-skinned *Negritos* or *Aetas*. From the 1500s forward, the Chinese have resided in the Philippine Islands as a separate group as well as intermarrying and creating a class of Chinese *mestizos* (mixed blood). Spain ruled the Philippine Islands for 300 years and converted the majority of the population to Roman Catholicism. Spaniards born in the Islands were called *Filipinos,* even though there was little intermarrying between Spaniards and the indigenous population. Filipinos revolted against the Spaniards and declared independence in 1898. But U.S. President William McKinley claimed the Islands instead of supporting the Philippines in their struggle for independence.

In 1903, through the *pensionado program*, the U.S. government provided Filipino students with scholarships for education in the United States. In exchange, they were to work for the government in the Philippines. *Pensionado* stories became a legend. Large numbers of Filipinos proved their capabilities to Americans and Filipinos, thus countering the notions that Filipinos were savages. During the 1920s and 1930s most Filipinos lived on the West Coast and worked in restaurants, in hotels, in private clubs, and as personal servants. During this time Filipinos faced de facto segregation. They were discriminated against and prevented from entering their professions after completing their education. As a result, many resorted to labor in low working-class jobs. Children born in the United States to Filipino immigrants were U.S. citizens. But before WWII, regardless of the number of years of residency in the United States, Philippine-born Filipinos were ineligible for naturalization. Prior to WWII, many Filipinos enlisted as officers in the U.S. Army and as messmen and musicians in the U.S. Navy.

By 1922, there were 5,018 Filipinos that constituted 5 percent of the enlisted force of the navy. The Tydings-McDuffie Act of 1934 promised the Philippines independence after 10 years, but immediately restricted immigration from the Philippines to 50 per quota. The Luce-Celler Bill passed in July 2, 1946, by the U.S. government granted access to naturalization for all remaining Filipinos who came before the Tydings-McDuffie Act; thus 10,764 Filipinos became U.S. citizens.

Finally, on July 4, 1946, the Philippine independence was celebrated. Under the War Brides Act of 1945 and the Fiancée Act of 1946, 118,000 Filipina wives and children, as well as fiancées of U.S. servicemen, entered the United States without a visa or passport. After the Immigration and Nationality Act of 1965, the purpose for migration was to relieve occupational shortages and achieve family reunification. During the 10 years after the 1965 Act, over 230,000 Filipinos migrated to the United States. By the mid-1970s doctors in the United States were no longer in short supply and the U.S. immigration law no longer welcomed foreign medical graduates from the Philippines.

This historical review of immigration and intermarriages that started in the Philippine Islands, and later in Hawaii, shows that most Filipinos ended up residing on the West Coast, where a mestizo identity was formed. Today, border towns between the United States and Mexico, specifically San Diego, have many Mexican Filipino residents. Mexican Filipino identity is thus complex. Many have Spanish surnames as a result of the Spanish conquest and brown complexions as a result of African, Indian, and Chinese roots or intermarriages with other ethnic groups (e.g., Mexicans, Hondurans, Salvadorians). Ethnic studies scholar Rudy Guevarra calls his own identity "Mexipino" or "Mexipina," a multiethnic identity of people from Mexican and Filipino descent. Other terms have been used in the past by others of this mixed heritage that include *Chicapino, Chicaflip, Mexiflip, or Flipsican, Chicano,* and

Pinoy. The last two terms refer to a political identity adopted by young Mexican Americans and Filipina/o Americans during the Civil Rights Movement.

Contemporary Mexican Filipinos utilize *Chicapino,* yet Guevarra argues that Mexipino is a more positive and inclusive self-identifying term that represents the generations born in the late 1960s and early 1970s and earlier. Guevarra interviewed Mexipinos and Mexipinas in San Diego who described having the "best of both worlds," where food, religion, struggles, and prejudices were very similar among Filipinos and Mexicans, which increased tolerance and open-mindedness toward other cultures. Some Filipino Mexicans struggle with an "ambiguous identity," as often they are perceived as Mexican, Hawaiian, Middle Eastern, or Polynesian. Filipinos and Mexicans share histories of colonial conquest by Spain and conversion to Catholicism, de facto segregation, discrimination, and prejudice that continue into the present.

Chinese Cubans

Miguel A. De La Torre describes in his work how Asian laborers were brought to Cuba as "indentured" servants during the late nineteenth century. The landowner's purpose was to obtain domesticated slaves as an alternative to African slaves. Chinese laborers were brought on ships that ironically had previously brought African slaves to Cuba. Many died in the long journey through what he calls "the Pacific Middle Passage." The Spanish frigate *Gravina* transported 352 Chinese laborers, of which 82 arrived at La Habana. In 1847, the first 206 Chinese laborers were brought to Cuba and that number grew to 300,000 by 1939. During that time, the word "coolie" was used in a derogatory way to refer to the Chinese laborer and described the social location of oppression. The word *coolie* is composed of two Chinese characters, *Coo* and *lee* meaning "suffering with pain" and "laborer," and describes the terrible treatment and working conditions that were similar to those experienced by slaves.

By 1874, 3 percent of the Cuban population was Chinese. Because of the terrible working conditions, between 1850 and 1860, 340 people per million committed suicide. More specifically, 92.5 percent of suicides were committed by Chinese laborers. The rate of suicide was the highest in the world. The illusion that Chinese were brought as "indentured" servants with a contract to work for eight years is elusive since they were treated worse than slaves. Many Chinese laborers were forced to leave their homes, deceived about the type of contract work they would do and the country to which they would be taken.

In many cases, Asian overseers were Black. Chinese laborers viewed Cuban Blacks as intellectually inferior to them due to their illiteracy, since the majority of Chinese were literate. Cuban structures of White supremacy placed the Chinese laborer under the same hierarchy as the African slaves. The sugar fields demanded a male work force; therefore, there were few Chinese women. Social and legal laws were enforced with regard to intermarriages or miscegenation of Africans or Whites with Asians.

A large wave of Chinese Cubans, along with other Cubans, fled the Island for the United States after Fidel Castro came to power in 1959. Many of these immigrants established themselves and their small businesses and restaurants in Miami and Los Angeles, as well as in New Jersey. Mike Yip, owner of the restaurant *La Caridad* in New York, was born in Cuba of Chinese parents, and he fluently speaks Spanish, Cantonese, and English. Cristina Garcia, a Cuban American writer, describes in her novel, *Monkey Hunting*, the multigenerational story of Chen Pan, a Chinese immigrant's experience as a *coolie* who develops a relationship with a mulatto former slave. Pan's great-grandson abandons Cuba after the 1959 socialist uprising and ends up fighting for the United States in the Vietnam War.

Punjabi Mexican Americans

The first period of immigration was between 1899 and 1914 when 6,800 Punjabi men, including Hindu and Muslim, but mostly Sikh, arrived in California to work the land. Punjabis primarily migrated to Canada and the United States as a result of increased population pressure, subdivision of land, rural debt, status, and adventure. As Punjabi immigration increased, prejudice arose, and rejection rates increased in Canada and the United States. Before 1907, fewer than 10 percent were rejected, and in 1909, 1911, and 1913 more than 50 percent of applicants were rejected. One strategy that Punjabi men used was to enter through the Philippines legally, for it was a U.S. colony at that time. In 1913, a judge ruled that a man legally admitted through the Philippines could still be detained and deported rather than admitted legally to the United States. The Immigration Act of 1917 "barred Asiatic Zone," and had literary provisions that excluded many Punjabi due to their illiteracy.

Initially, Punjabis settled in California, Washington, Texas, Arizona, Utah, and Colorado. Punjabis helped develop cotton in Cautillo, Texas, but major efforts took place in cultivating cotton in California's Imperial Valley. By 1919, Punjabis had leased 32,380 acres in the Imperial Valley, which was more than one-third of all California land leased and owned by Punjabis. This was accomplished by utilizing relatives or friends to hold land on a man's behalf. The earliest Punjabi settlement was in 1909 in the Imperial Valley. This is also where the first Punjabi-Mexican marriage took place in 1913. By 1920, the population in the Imperial Valley was 40 percent female, the minority being immigrant women. During this time, 37 percent of women were foreign born, representing 72 percent born in Mexico and 28 percent in Japan. Forty-three percent were American Black. There were two Chinese female and no Indian female residents. Many men returned to their countries for brides or sent for them (e.g., "mail order brides" and "picture brides").

Because of the strict immigration laws prior to 1965, many Punjabi men were unable to bring their wives and children from India. California had antimiscegenation laws prohibiting marriages between people of different races, and Punjabis were classified as non-White. Therefore, a marriage with a White woman had the strongest prejudice. The first intermarriages were between working-class Mexican women and wealthy, prominent Punjabi men. These early marriages caused conflict between the Mexican men and the Punjabis. In spite of rising interracial conflicts, Punjabi-Mexican marriages continued. A positive reason for a Punjabi to marry a Mexican woman was that then matches could be arranged for Punjabi friends or relatives with female relatives.

Not until 1933, with an Imperial Valley County indictment of some Punjabis and Anglos conspiring to evade the Alien Land Laws, did some Punjabi men begin to secure their land by marrying Mexican women to hold land under her name for her husband. In the 1940s, a common strategy used to secure land was to put land under their children's names as U.S. citizens and use a guardianship to continue controlling the land. As a result, many Punjabi men spent time working the land, while the women were responsible for instilling the language, culture, and religion to their children. Children's names reflected the dual heritage of Sikh men using "Singh" as a last name combined with Spanish first names, as in Maria Jesusita Singh or Jose Akbar Khan. Children were raised Catholic, spoke Spanish, and followed Indian customs only when men died. Sikh and Hindu men were cremated and all of the appropriate death rituals were performed. A picture was sometimes taken of the dead body of an Indian man in his casket and sent to his family in India. However, many of the pictures did not depict men wearing the customary turbans.

Sons typically worked with fathers on the land and learned the Punjabi work language. For the most part, Punjabi Mexican children did not speak Punjabi but understood it. The majority of children self-identified as "Indian" or "East Indian." Punjabi Mexican American children were segregated from White children and attended different schools with Chinese, Korean, Japanese, and Black children. Restaurants were also segregated by groups of immigrants who were also discriminated against. A reaction to this discrimination was that

Mexicans, Japanese, and Punjabi opened restaurants and barbershops to serve everyone.

The Luce-Celler Bill enabled Punjabi men to become citizens, which in turn brought the connection back to India. In 1965, the Immigration and Naturalization Act enabled families to reunite, but at the same time it brought risks and instability to existing Punjabi Mexican families. Upon arriving in the United States, new Indian immigrants discriminated against and denigrated the Hispanic ancestry within the Punjabi community, thus alienating descendants from Punjabi and the Indian heritage. More recently, few Punjabi Mexicans honor and celebrate their heritage through commemorations and the naming of local roads after prominent people as in "Singh Road."

Compared to the Imperial Valley, Phoenix is a cosmopolitan area that has expanded to an urban and suburban area where others rarely identify Punjabi Mexicans as Hindus or Spanish Pakistanis. The northern Californian descendants of Punjabi pioneers from Yuba City are hesitant to participate in the annual Yuba Sikh Parade, yet they still hold their annual Christmas Dance, which is open to all descendants of Punjabi pioneers. Discrimination exists relating to religious practices involving temple traditions that Punjabi pioneers and second-generation families followed compared to strict traditional Indian customs of new immigrants, which were not practiced or are unfamiliar to previous generations.

Time Line

1798 Alien Enemy Act permitted the apprehension and internment of nationals of states at war with the United States.

1882 Chinese Exclusion Act prohibits the entrance and citizenship of Chinese laborers; intended to last 10 years, it was extended to 1902.

1898 The Treaty of Paris ends the Spanish-American War and cedes the Philippines to the United States.

1907 Gentlemen's Agreement is issued by Theodore Roosevelt where the Japanese government refuses to issue passports for laborers immigrating to the United States but the agreement allows departure to Hawaii.

1913 Alien Land Act is signed into law in California, Washington, Oregon, Idaho, Montana, Arizona, New Mexico, Nebraska, Texas, Kansas, Louisiana, Missouri, and Minnesota. A person is not eligible for U.S. citizenship and prohibited the purchase of land for agricultural purposes but may lease property for no more than three years.

1917 Immigration Act or "barred Asiatic Zone" prohibited Asian immigrants and included literary provisions.

1924 Immigration Law or National Origins Act excluded immigration of all Asian laborers (including Punjabis and Indians) with the exception of Filipinos, recognized as U.S. nationals.

1934 The Tydings-McDuffie Act promised the Philippines independence after 10 years but immediately restricted immigration to 50 per quota.

1935 The Repatriation Act allocated funds for transport of Filipinos who chose to return to the Philippines.

1942 Internment in concentration camps of Japanese Americans and Japanese residing in Latin America.

1945 The War Brides Act allowed for wives and children of U.S. servicemen to enter the United States without a visa or passport.

1946 The Fiancée Act allowed for fiancées of U.S. servicemen to enter the United States.

1946 The Luce-Celler Bill allowed naturalization of all remaining immigrants before the 1934 Act.

1952 The Immigration and Nationality Act granted access to eligible immigrants to apply for U.S. citizenship.

1965 The Immigration Act (reversed the 1924 act) allowed Asian immigrants into the United States without restrictions or quota.

1965 The Great Grape Strike was led by Filipino and Mexican American labor leaders, who fought for higher wages and better working conditions for farm workers in California, among other states.

Sarah J. Rangel-Sanchez

References and Further Reading

De La Torre, Miguel A. *La Lucha for Cuba: Religion and Politics on the Streets of Miami* (Berkeley: University of California Press, 2003).

Guevarra, Rudy P. "Burritos and Bangoong: Mexipinos and Multiethnic Identity in San Diego, California." *Crossing Lines: Race and Mixed Race Across the Geohistorical Divide*, ed. Marc Coronado, Rudy P. Guevarra, Jeffrey Moniz, and Laura F. Szanto (Santa Barbara: Multiethnic Student Outreach and Center for Chicano Studies, University of California, Santa Barbara, 2003).

Higashide, Seiichi. *Adios to Tears: The Memoirs of a Japanese-Peruvian Internee in U.S. Concentration Camps* (Seattle: University of Washington Press, 2000).

Leonard, Karen I. *Making Ethnic Choices: California's Punjabi Mexican Americans* (Philadelphia: Temple University Press, 1992).

Min, Pyong Gap, and Jung Ha Kim, eds. *Religions in Asian America: Building Faith Communities* (Walnut Creek, CA: Rowman & Littlefield Publishers, 2002).

Oboler, Suzanne, and Deena J. Gonzalez, eds. *The Oxford Encyclopedia of Latinos and Latinas in the United States*, vol. 1 (Oxford: Oxford University Press, 2005).

ASSIMILATION

The online *Encyclopedia Britannica* (2007) definition of assimilation is "the process whereby individuals or groups of differing ethnic heritage are absorbed into the dominant culture of a society. Usually they are immigrants or hitherto isolated minorities who, through contact and participation in the larger culture, gradually give up most of their former culture traits and take on the new traits." In *Introduction to the Science of Sociology* (1921, reprinted 1969), R. E. Park and E. Burgess provide a definition for assimilation that does not assume a majority and minority dichotomy. According to them, assimilation is "a process of interpenetration and fusion in which persons and groups acquire the memories, sentiments, and attitudes of other persons or groups, and, by sharing their experience and history, are incorporated with them in a common cultural life" (735). Assimilation is also included in this encyclopedia of Latino/a religious experiences because of issues related to the Hispanic experience in the United States, specifically questions about how they should be a part of this country in the future. A secondary reason for considering assimilation is because of the role religion, particularly Protestantism, has played in Latina/o assimilation patterns.

LADINO

"Ladino" is an ethnic category typically used in contrast with the category of "Indian" that characterizes the Spanish-speaking populations of southern Mexico and Guatemala in particular. In its most popular use, the term refers to persons who abandon their indigenous language, dress, and other cultural practices while assimilating into the dominant Spanish-speaking culture. Both "Ladino" and "Indian" are more correctly understood as cultural rather than racial categories. The process of "Ladinization" can occur in a single generation when rural "Indian" parents move to the city and seek to hasten assimilation into the dominant economic and cultural system by not training their children in their mother tongue and folkways. "Ladino" can be applied to persons from different social classes and can represent different levels of cultural assimilation, ranging from poor Spanish-speaking peasants to wealthy, powerful, small-town merchants to persons that continue to flee rural poverty and seek economic opportunity in marginal urban communities. A similar diversity exists within the "Indian" community. As a dualistic model of ethnic classification, the terms "Ladino" and "Indian" are broadly used in public discourse. But for decades, historians, sociologists, ethnographers, and anthropologists have questioned such reductionist categories since they ignore or hide the rich and complex sociocultural diversity present in Guatemalan society.

—FCG

To understand the role assimilation has played in the U.S. Latino/a experience, it is important to review how assimilation has been interpreted and prescribed in discussions about the larger U.S. immigrant experience, paying attention to the role Protestantism has played in that process. This will set the framework for analyzing Latino/a assimilation patterns, understanding the current debate on the role of Hispanics in U.S. society, and considering how the migratory patterns of the globalized environment redefine the issues.

In his classic work on the subject, *Assimilation in American Life: The Role of Race, Religion, and National Origins*, Milton Gordon describes the experience of immigrants in the United States through the middle of the twentieth century. Gordon summarizes his understanding of the development of ethnic identity in the American experience, defines the

concept of assimilation by describing various "types" or stages of assimilation, presents various theories of assimilation in the United States, and then presents his perspective of how various cultural and ethnic groups interact in this country. His work is important here because of the complexity of what is called assimilation and his description of the various theories of how assimilation is happening or should happen in the United States.

Gordon describes seven types or stages of assimilation. *Cultural assimilation*, or acculturation, is the process of adaptation by which one group takes on cultural patterns from another group, usually a group with less power from a more powerful culture. Acculturation has to do with learning how to fit into the other culture and may or may not affect the other stages. This process can go from partial adaptation within the framework of the weaker culture to full adoption of the patterns of the dominant culture. *Structural assimilation* is the large-scale entrance into the institutions of the dominant culture. The members of the weak group are able to participate in the social, economic, and political structures of the dominant group. *Marital assimilation*, or amalgamation, is large-scale intermarriage. As various cultural groups interact, marriage across cultural and ethnic lines becomes common, unless the process is stigmatized directly or indirectly. *Identificational assimilation* is the development of a common sense of peoplehood among the various cultural groups based exclusively on the dominant culture. The weak group begins losing its clearly defined sense of separate identity. *Attitude receptional assimilation* is the absence of prejudice toward the assimilated group. This level of assimilation assumes an attitude shift in the dominant or host culture. The dominant culture no longer encourages separation by putting down the weak group. *Behavior receptional assimilation* is the absence of discrimination. Not only have attitudes changed, but the actions of the dominant culture no longer create barriers toward the minority culture. *Civic assimilation* is the absence of value or power conflict. The weak group no longer feels the need to "defend" itself or "protect" its rights. The need for protection of a clearly identifiable group identity has all but disappeared.

These various types of assimilation are stages in a process in which assimilation is complete if the weak group goes through all the stages of the process. Gordon states that "not only is the assimilation process mainly a matter of degree, but, obviously, each of the states or subprocesses distinguished above may take place in varying degrees." Throughout the book the author describes ethnic groups that have gone through the entire process, groups that are "in process," groups that have gone through parts of the process, but not others, and groups that are essentially separated and are not fully "assimilating" into majority culture, though they may be somewhat acculturated.

Gordon then describes the three principal goal systems in the U.S. experience. Each of these describes ideological perspectives that are prescriptive, describing how their proponents assume the various cultural groups are, or should be, part of U.S. society. The *Anglo conformity* model assumes that all people should adopt the culture, language, and institutions that came from England. In this perspective, the United States is a country that was formed with cultural values and norms brought by the English immigrants. It assumes that immigrants from other parts of the world are welcomed if they adopt U.S. Anglo culture. Historically, people who have held this perspective have assumed that only immigrants from "White" Protestant European countries would be able to fully assimilate into U.S. Anglo culture. According to Gordon, this was the majority view held in the United States, particularly during the early years of the country's history and through most of the nineteenth century.

The second perspective, the *melting pot*, is a more generous and idealistic form of the Anglo conformity model. This view began to take shape as the type of immigrant to the United States began to change in the middle of the nineteenth century. As the national, religious, and cultural backgrounds of the European immigrants began to change, the melting pot theory began to take hold of the U.S. imagination. Like the Anglo conformity model, the melting pot perspective also assumes the eventual disappearance of specific ethnic communities. But it proposes that the assimilation process among peoples is creating a new reality where none of the previous groups fully define the new culture, but that all of the groups assimilate into each other, creating a new reality, a U.S. culture.

This perspective was popularized in the early twentieth century by Israel Zangwill's drama, *The Melting Pot*. This perspective captured the imagination of many people, including U.S. presidents such as Woodrow Wilson and Theodore Roosevelt. Through much of the first half of the twentieth century this perspective competed with the Anglo conformity concept as the principal ideological construct for defining what the United States should look like.

According to Gordon, the third major theoretical model, *cultural pluralism*, has existed early in the U.S. experience. Before it became an explicit theory or perspective for life in the United States, it was either practiced by various ethnic groups or imposed on them. Some European immigrants attempted to both produce cultural enclaves and be a part of the larger civic life of the United States. They established their own schools, churches, and other cultural institutions, even as they identified themselves as citizens of the United States. On the other hand, some ethnic groups like Native Americans, African Americans, and other non-European peoples were not allowed into the "melting pot" and were forced to develop their own separate cultural institutions.

This perspective was also defined in the public square at the beginning of the twentieth century through the work and publications of Horace Kallen. In 1915 he published two articles with the title "Democracy Versus the Melting Pot" in *The Nation* magazine. He argued against Anglo conformity or the melting pot as useful descriptions of what was happening in the United States or as worthy ideals for the future. In this work, and in his later writings, Kallen argued that cultural pluralism fits the American ideal and enriches U.S. society.

Gordon goes on to argue that cultural pluralism is not a sufficient definition of what is happening in U.S. society. In the 1960s, Gordon sees that there is much cultural assimilation in the United States. People tend to adopt U.S. cultural patterns across ethnic, race, and religious lines. Nonetheless, there continues to be profound structural pluralism, defined by religion (Protestant, Catholic, and Jewish) and by race (Black) or what he calls "quasi-racial" groups (Puerto Ricans and Mexican Americans). Even though groups tend to acculturate toward common cultural norms, they are not fully assimilating and disappearing as distinct ethnic communities. In summary, he argues that the United States is the following:

> A multiple melting pot in which acculturation for all groups beyond the first generation of immigrants, without eliminating all value conflict, has been massive and decisive, but in which structural separation on the basis of race and religion—structural pluralism, as we have called it—emerges as the dominant sociological condition. (1964, 234–235)

This statement describes Gordon's understanding of the situation in the United States. He is concerned that the United States does not have clearly defined guidelines about what it wants as a country or about the implications of following any of the models he describes. From his perspective, intercultural relations in the United States seems like a racehorse with blinders. It has no idea where it is or where it is going, but it is moving very rapidly.

Though the book provides a very useful introduction to the issue, it also leaves out some crucial issues related to intercultural relations and assimilation issues within the United States. Gordon does not address the impact of government policies on some of the ethnic minority groups or on current migration patterns. He only describes the current reality that he is experiencing. Therefore, he recognizes that Native Americans are in an "odd" position, yet neglects the fact that U.S. government policies have over the years destroyed native cultures. He also addresses the issues of discrimination against African Americans, but ignores the historical issues of slavery, legal discrimination, and ongoing double standards in education and public services. In relation to Puerto Ricans or Mexican Americans, he does not deal with the conquests of Puerto Rico or of the Southwest, the migratory patterns from Latin America created by U.S. political or economic policies, and the impact of these actions on Latino/as cultures. By not addressing these issues, he recognizes the problem of discrimination, but does not address the crucial structural issues that continue to maintain a relationship where the majority continues to negatively impact, while maintaining separation from, the cultures of the "racial" or quasi-racial minorities in the United States.

Religion became an important factor in Hispanic assimilation patterns and perspectives during the nineteenth century. Many U.S. Protestants became concerned by the changing immigration patterns, which included a growing number of Catholics from Europe. These Protestants were convinced that these new immigrants would not, or could not, assimilate into the social structures of the young country. They responded to this situation politically, socially, and religiously. On the religious front many Protestant denominations developed missionary strategies to evangelize the new Catholic immigrants from Europe. When the United States conquered the Southwest from Mexico in 1848 some of these same denominations sent missionaries to evangelize the Mexican Catholics who remained in the region and were now legally U.S. citizens.

The Protestant missionaries that evangelized the Mexicans of the Southwest closely linked the roles of evangelization and of Americanization. They were convinced that Mexican Catholics could never be good U.S. citizens unless they both became Protestants and adopted U.S. cultural patterns. Throughout the late nineteenth century and well into the twentieth century, the missionaries and mission agencies that worked in the region described their task in terms of making the Mexicans good Christians and good U.S. citizens. The U.S. Protestant churches no longer describe their tasks in these terms. But to this day, many Protestant mission efforts among new Latina/o immigrants begin with issues related to cultural adaptation, such as teaching English or skills specific to the U.S. environment.

During the nineteenth century many Catholic immigrants worked very hard to demonstrate that Catholics could be good "Americans." The Catholic Church

SECRETARIAT FOR HISPANIC AFFAIRS OF THE UNITED STATES CONFERENCE OF CATHOLIC BISHOPS

United States Conference of Catholic Bishops (USCCB) was created in 1974, although it traces its roots to 1945. Its mission was to aid in the integration rather than the assimilation of Hispanics into the U.S. Catholic Church. The Secretariat had been instrumental in planning and implementing the last five Hispanic national Encuentros, promoting the "National Pastoral Plan for Hispanic Ministry," and assisting in the New Evangelization and ministry efforts, including the founding of the National Catholic Association of Diocesan Directors for Hispanic Ministry (NCADDHM 1991), which survives it. The executive director of the Secretariat has always been lay and Hispanic, important achievements in a Church still dominated by non-Hispanic, White (mainly clerical) leadership. The two directors have been Pablo Sedillo (1970–1991) and Ronaldo Cruz (1991–2007). The staff has raised millions of dollars for important studies and publications, including their newsletter *En Marcha*. In 2007 the USCCB reorganized, and the duties of this Secretariat and others were folded into the Committee on Cultural Diversity in the Church. Many observers see its closing as extremely unwise, although it reflects a general retreat by the bishops, especially away from extradiocesan structures that serve Hispanics.

—KGD

seemed to be working toward the twin tasks of keeping their people in the fold and also proving that they "fit" in U.S. society. This meant that the Catholic Church was often involved in Americanization efforts. When the American Catholic Church took over ecclesiastical jurisdiction for the Catholics of the Southwest, the Church sent priests and nuns who questioned the faith and practices of the Mexicans and sought to get them to accept a form of Catholicism that looked more like the Catholicism practiced by U.S. Catholics. Most Mexican priests were removed and replaced by those more acceptable to the U.S. hierarchy. The Catholic Church also set up schools, like the Protestants, to help "acculturate" and "Americanize" the Mexicans. Because of these actions, many Mexican Catholics in the Southwest felt alienated from the U.S. Catholic Church until well into the twentieth century.

This has created a unique situation for both Latino/a Catholics and Protestants. Some Hispanics assimilated into the larger Catholic or Protestant communities in the United States. But because they are part of both quasi-racial and distinct religious groups, they sometimes seem to fit better in one or the other and sometimes do not clearly seem to fit in either. For example, Latina/o Protestant converts seemed to participate in cultural assimilation by becoming Protestant, but they continue to be structurally separated because they are Latino/as. Also, many new Hispanic immigrants are already Protestants, but they are bringing faith expressions with them that do not easily fit within the U.S. Protestant world. Hispanic Catholics face a similar situation in which they are now almost 40 percent of the total Catholic population in the United States, the largest single ethnic community in the Catholic Church, but they are treated as a "minority" group within the Church and are very underrepresented in church structures and leadership.

A 2007 Pew study of religion among Latino/as (*Changing Faiths: Latinos and the Transformation of American Religion*) seems to indicate that religious identity is a marker of both acculturation and ethnoreligious identity maintenance. According to the study, Hispanics are more likely to become Protestant the more generations that they have been in the United States. This seems to be a sign of acculturation. But the study also indicated that a large majority of both Catholic and Protestant Latina/os continue to worship in churches that have a clear Latino/a identity even after several generations. These results would seem to indicate that because Hispanics include both religious and quasi-racial differences with the majority, it is possible that Latina/os are remaining structurally separate even if they seem to acculturate religiously. Other studies seem to indicate that Latino/a Protestants are developing and maintaining a clearly defined ethnoreligious identity, even though it is under constant pressure from an assimilating U.S. Protestantism and it has a minority status within the larger U.S. Hispanic community.

When Latina/os are measured by Gordon's seven categories of assimilation, one sees both signs of assimilation and signs of cultural identity maintenance. Latino/as do learn how to function within the cultural norms of the majority. Most learn English and a significant minority no longer speak Spanish. There is a significant level of participation in the structures of majority culture and intermarriage. One can find Hispanics for whom their ethnic background is merely

part of their history and has no impact on how they live their lives or how they perceive their future in the United States. As individuals they seem to be at the seventh stage in Gordon's description. They experience no power or value conflict between themselves and majority culture.

This is not, however, the experience of Latino/as as a group, or of the vast majority of Hispanics as individuals. For most Latinos cultural adaptation has not necessarily meant full-scale cultural adoption. There are clearly identifiable cultural traits that are Latina/o, but uniquely adapted to the U.S. reality. In many cases Hispanics are now merely adopting the traits of the majority. They also seem to include reworking traditionally Hispanic cultural traits so that they are functional in a different environment. The use of Spanish is growing in the United States, not as a "foreign" language, but as part of the U.S. experience. Spanish language media's continued reinforcement of the use of Spanish and popular dialects, such as Spanglish or Tex-Mex, reflect not only adaptation but also the development of new forms of communication. Latina/os are intermarrying, but the cultural movement of those marriages is not always toward majority culture. Latino/as from various national and ethnic backgrounds are intermarrying, expanding, and enriching U.S. Hispanic cultural identity.

In Gordon's model all of this is a description of structural pluralism. Latino/as are a quasi-racial community, in that they are considered similar to racial groups (Whites, African Americans, Native Americans, Asians, and others), though Latina/os can be a part of any of these "races." Like other racial groups, they are acculturating but are also

A parishioner attends services at La Casa del Carpintero Church, with a bilingual Bible on a seat in the foreground, July 2007. The Hispanic church began offering English-language services in an effort to integrate second- and third-generation Hispanics, and keep families together. (AP Photo/ Nam Y. Huh)

developing and maintaining a separate ethnic and cultural identity. This is a reflection of the complexities of intercultural, interethnic, and interracial relations within the racialized reality of the United States.

Nonetheless, structural pluralism does not seem to be a sufficient description of the Latina/o experience. Earlier generations of Hispanics maintained a fairly separate cultural and ethnic identity throughout the nineteenth century and well into the twentieth century with only limited cultural adaptation. Today Latina/os seem to be both acculturating

and strengthening a separate cultural and ethnic identity. Many Latino/as are clearly bicultural people, living in the midst of both Hispanic and majority cultures, knowing how to shift between them. They are also navigating between these cultures and the other minority cultures in the United States. New waves of immigrants from Latin America are reinforcing this complex intercultural interaction.

The cultural influences that impact Latina/os are not unidirectional. Hispanics are drawn toward majority culture, but also toward some of the other minority cultures in the United States. They are impacted by the globalization of Latin American and Spanish cultures. Latina/os are drawn in various directions simultaneously, and many choose to define themselves in the spaces between these influences and not merely in relationship to one cultural "pole" or another.

This seems to indicate that Hispanics are developing a polycentric identity; in other words, they are learning to work within more than one cultural reality simultaneously. Whereas Gordon's model seems to assume unidirectional and inevitable movement, the Latino/a experience seems to be more complex. Latina/os are involved in multifaceted processes in which they are being changed by the U.S. experience, but in which they are also expanding and enriching a distinct identity, even as they are also challenging majority culture to reexamine how it looks at itself and at other cultural minority groups in the United States.

Latino/a experiences with assimilation and identity maintenance are occurring within the larger ideological debate about what intercultural relationships in the United States should look like. It is here that Gordon's analogy of intercultural relations as a racehorse with blinders might need to be updated. It seems as if the horse has been spooked and is not only running faster than in the 1960s but may be trying to run in several directions simultaneously.

The issues raised by Gordon's description are particularly pertinent because of the current debate in the United States about how Latino/as are participating in and being incorporated into U.S. society. The specific discussions and political tensions related to immigration reform and the calls to declare English the official language of the United States both point to uneasiness within majority culture over the growing influence of a distinct Latina/o subculture within the United States.

Gordon's description of the various ideological paradigms (Anglo conformity, melting pot, and cultural pluralism) that has informed the issue is important because much of the current debate assumes that people in the United States have always had a common understanding of the issue and that Hispanics are coming to impose something that has not traditionally been a part of how the United States understands itself. But as Gordon clearly demonstrates, there has never been just one model or prescription for how ethnic groups participate in majority society, even though the Anglo conformity model has been the one with the broader support over the years.

One person who has framed the debate for many people is Harvard professor Samuel Huntington. In his book *Who Are We? Challenges to America's National Identity*, he argues that "historically America has thus been a nation of immigration and assimilation, and

assimilation has meant Americanization" (2004, 184). He sees this as the "great American success story," which is being threatened by Latino/a immigration.

Huntington quotes Gordon's book when addressing the question of cultural assimilation (acculturation) in the United States, and his definition of Americanization seems to fit with Gordon's understanding of acculturation. But Huntington then jumps over the complexities of full assimilation described by Gordon. He uses the term "acculturation" (stage no. 1 in Gordon's model) and makes it synonymous to "full assimilation" (all 7 stages).

His usage of Gordon's descriptions is also problematic because Huntington's description of the American experience is based on a modified version of the Anglo-conformity model. According to Huntington, all previous immigrants have assimilated into the culture established by the original British settlers, including "the English language, Christianity; religious commitment . . . the rule of law . . ., and the dissenting Protestant values of individualism" (Huntington 2004, xvi). Even though Anglo-Americans are no longer the principal portion of the U.S. population, "the Anglo-Protestant culture of their settler forebears [*sic*] survived for three hundred years as the paramount defining element of American identity" (Huntington 2004, 58). Huntington claims that the success of the United States has been based on the fact that all immigrants have assimilated following an Anglo conformity model.

Yet Gordon describes a much more complex situation. According to him, there have been three major theories and prescriptions of the American cultural experience: the Anglo conformity, melting pot, and cultural pluralism models. All three are ideals that have a long history in the United States. But Gordon demonstrates that none of them are fully descriptive of the American reality and opts for what he calls structural pluralism, a combination of acculturation and the long-term existence of clearly defined quasi-racial groups. Huntington implies that he is building on Gordon's understanding, but he ignores this crucial part of Gordon's basic premise.

Based on the Anglo-conformity model and prescription for the United States, Samuel Huntington sees Latino/as as a threat to the national identity of the country. The concept of multiculturalism that has developed in the latter part of the twentieth century has encouraged Hispanics to maintain their culture and their language. This tendency has been strengthened by the latest wave of immigrants from Latin America. According to Huntington, Latina/os are not following previous patterns—they are creating a cultural bifurcation in the areas where they are concentrated. He describes the Cuban influence in Miami and the Mexican American influence in the Southwest as examples of places where "Hispanization" is taking place. He ends his chapter on Hispanics with the following warning:

> The continuation of high levels of Mexican and Hispanic immigration plus the low rates of assimilation of these immigrants into American society and culture could eventually change America into a country of two languages, two cultures, and two peoples. This will not only transform America. It will also have deep consequences for Hispanics, who will be in America but not of it. Lionel Sosa ends his book, *The Americano Dream*, of advice to aspiring Hispanic entrepreneurs,

with the words: "The Americano dream! It exists, it is realistic, and it is there for all of us to share." He is wrong. There is no Americano dream. There is only the American dream created by an Anglo-Protestant society. Mexican-Americans will share in that dream and in that society only if they dream in English. (Huntington 2004, 256)

Linda Chavez in her book *Out of the Barrio* works from the same assumptions when she calls Latino/as to assimilate into U.S. culture. Chavez assumes that the future success of Hispanics in the United States depends on their willingness to let go of Latina/o culture, acculturating and eventually fully assimilating into majority culture.

Based on an Anglo-conformity prescription for the United States and for Latino/as in particular, issues like immigration reform, bilingual education, Spanish language media, and the borderland culture are all interpreted as threats to the national identity of the country. The Hispanic experience is interpreted in light of an Anglo-conformity understanding of European immigration, and Latina/os are found wanting.

Neither Huntington nor Chavez acknowledges the long-term existence of different interpretative models of the U.S. intercultural experience. But that is part of the difficulty in the current national debate. If one reads the U.S. experience only through the grid of an Anglo-conformity model (or the melting pot), then the problem and the "threat" lies with those who have not fit in the past and who do not fit today. But if one recognizes that there are other interpretative and prescriptive models, then the debate changes fundamentally. The lingering question is whether there will be room in the debate to recognize the other models or whether Gordon's racehorse will continue running with blinders.

Assimilation, as it is commonly used in popular parlance, seems like an incomplete term to describe the relationship between Latina/os and majority culture in the United States. It describes a part of the story, but leaves out crucial details that affect the discussion. Cultural assimilation (acculturation) may also be insufficient because it does not necessarily distinguish between cultural adaptation and cultural adoption. They are useful terms when used as descriptors the way Gordon uses them. But because their usage is both descriptive and prescriptive and the working definition of these terms tends to vary according to the prescriptive perspective of the user, we need more information than these terms provide if we are to adequately define the U.S. Hispanic experience.

First of all, if one only speaks of assimilation or acculturation in relationship to ethnic minorities, one presents an inadequate picture of intercultural relations in the history of the United States. Gordon's work acknowledges the existence of the minority groups and their continual separate identity, but does not adequately address how the quasi-racial groups became a part of the country and why they continue to exist. The U.S. territorial expansion and interventions in Latin America are not seen as factors that influence how minority groups do, or should, participate in U.S. society. There is no questioning of the forced destruction of peoples and cultures, of forced migration, or of the economic and political actions that influence current migratory patterns. By not acknowledging the nonvoluntary or "semi-voluntary" migration or

participation of many minority groups in the United States, descriptions that only address assimilation patterns do not adequately describe the intercultural relations between majority cultures and minority groups.

The terms also tend to be inadequate because they are usually tied to a definition of assimilation that assumes the majority in the United States sets the assumptions and prescriptions for all groups. Intercultural relationships are defined in relationship to the majority culture. The interactions between minority groups, the increasing cultural diversity because of structural pluralism, and the impact of globalization on the survival and growth of minority cultures are not given a significant role in the descriptions or prescriptions of U.S. cultural interaction. Minority groups are merely seen as those that will assimilate and are not given a voice in the decision of how to be a part of the United States.

Not only are the prescriptions completely linked to the majority, they are also unidirectional. The assumption is that assimilation works in a single direction (toward the majority) and that it is permanent in that direction. This understanding does not take into account the growing multidirectional influence of globalized culture or the resurgence of localized ethnic identities in the midst of the global village. Globalization and worldwide migration are creating new patterns of intercultural interaction. Cultural movement is going in various directions at the same time.

Many Latino/as live out of a polycentric cultural identity in which the various cultural influences are kept in tension. People find ways to negotiate between cultures, to adapt to and not merely adopt cultural influences, and to live various cultural identities simultaneously. This way of living intercultural life is not only related to majority culture, but also to other cultural minority groups. It is creating new types of cultural interactions in which the traditional ways of defining assimilation in the United States may not be sufficient to adequately describe what is happening.

Clearly individual Hispanics are assimilating and acculturating to majority culture in the United States. But Latino/as continue to develop as a clearly defined quasi-racial group in the country. They are also interacting with majority culture and with other cultural minorities in ways that cannot easily be defined in light of these terms. It is yet to be seen whether any of Gordon's terms (Anglo conformity, melting pot, cultural pluralism, or structural pluralism) will be completely adequate to define the multifaceted and polycentric reality being lived by millions of Latina/os (and other minority peoples) in the United States. It is even less clear whether any of these interpretative models will ever be accepted as a common framework for intercultural relations in this country. So Gordon's racehorse keeps galloping, still unable to figure out where it is going.

Juan Martinez Guerra

References and Further Reading

Changing Faiths: Latinos and the Transformation of American Religion. A joint survey by the Pew Hispanic Project and the Pew Forum on Religion & Public Life, 2007. http://pewforum.org/surveys/hispanic/.

Chavez, Linda. *Out of the Barrio: Toward a New Politics of Hispanic Assimilation* (New York: Basic Books, 1992).

Gordon Milton M. *Assimilation in American Life: The Role of Race, Religion, and National Origins* (New York: Oxford University Press, 1964).

Huntington, Samuel. *Who Are We? The Challenges to America's National Identity* (New York: Simon & Schuster, 2004).

Sánchez-Walsh, Arlene. *Latino Pentecostal Identity: Evangelical Faith, Self, and Society* (New York: Columbia University Press, 2003).

AZTLÁN

Aztlán has both a symbolic and literal significance. Aztlán, the land of herons or land of whiteness, is believed to be the place of origin of the Aztecs before traveling south to present-day Mexico. According to the *Códice Boturini*, a collection of Indian documents gathered between 1736 and 1743 by Lorenzo Boturini Benaduci, the Aztecs left Aztlán and arrived in Chapultepec, but fell under the subjugation of the Culhuacanos. Hernando Alvarado Tezozómoc also wrote in 1609 a history of the Aztecs in his *Crónica Mexicáyotl*. Tezozómoc dates the Aztec departure from Aztlán to 1069 due to a conflict between leaders. Upon some ritual desecration of religious objects that offended individuals within the camp, Chalchiuhtlatónac, son of the deceased king Moctezuma, along with the Mexica, leaves Aztlán.

The decision to leave was not easy, especially in view of the richness of Aztlán, which is described in terms reminiscent of the biblical myth of the Garden of Eden or Paradise. Nonetheless, Huitzilopochtli, a deity, instructs and guides the Aztecs on their journey southward to the promised land where the Aztecs will establish an empire and exercise dominion over many people.

From the preceding account one can assume that Aztlán exists north of present-day Mexico City. It is sometimes referred to as Chicomóztoc, the place of the seven caves, and is described as being surrounded by water. This physical description has led many to deduce the actual location of Aztlán. Boturini, for example, argues that Aztlán is located in the Gulf of California. Nineteenth-century colonial historiographer José Fernando Ramírez states that the region of Lake Chalco in the valley of Mexico is the most probable locale for Aztlán. Nineteenth-century biogeographist Alexander von Humboldt, however, asserts that the modern states of Oregon, Idaho, and Wyoming are the original location of Aztlán. Scholars such as Alfredo Chavero take up the most popular argument that the Pacific coast, the state of Nayarit in Mexico, is the place of origin of the Aztecs. However, there are some scholars such as historian Francesco Saverio Clavijero who maintain that Aztlán must have been located north of the Colorado River. While questions about the historical Aztlán abound and the possibilities are numerous, there is no overwhelming evidence to suggest that one or any of the above alternatives is, without a doubt, the actual location of Aztlán. Regardless of the unknown location of Aztlán, there is little doubt as to the symbolic meaning of Aztlán.

It is often maintained that Aztlán came into public and political use during the National Chicano Youth Liberation Conference that was held in 1969 in Denver, Colorado. However, there is some indication that the notion of Aztlán had been employed for public and political purposes prior to 1969. With the ending of the Mexican-American War in 1848 much of northern Mexico was ceded to the United States of America. Included among this land was New Mexico, which would eventually become a state in 1912. According to the Guadalupe Hidalgo Treaty of 1848, Mexicans who remained in the ceded land for a year following the ratification of the treaty would be considered citizens of the United States of America. Along with their newly given citizenship, Mexicans would maintain control of land they legally received from the Spanish empire in the form of land grants. The predicament for the U.S. government was that there were too many Mexicans in the territory of New Mexico and few immigrants of European descent. If the territory of New Mexico had become a state, then the newly established citizens would be able to exercise political influence in the state. What was needed was the presence of U.S. immigrants to overcome the political sway of those who resided in the territory longer than they. William G. Ritch, secretary of the Territory of New Mexico and president of the New Mexico Bureau of Immigration, provided the means for attracting more people to the territory of New Mexico.

In 1885 Ritch published *Aztlán: The History, Resources and Attraction of New Mexico*. Ritch maintained that Moctezuma had lived in northern Mexico, or, rather, New Mexico and Arizona, prior to traveling and conquering tribes in southern Mexico. Ritch argued that Pueblo Indian myths mentioned that Moctezuma had been born at the pueblo of Santa Fe. New Mexico, therefore, was part of Aztlán.

The appeal of Aztlán in *Aztlán: The History, Resources and Attractions of New Mexico* was to establish the presence of unlimited resources in the territory of New Mexico. Among these

PLAN ESPIRITUAL DE AZTLÁN

The manifesto articulated at the 1969 Chicano National Liberation Youth Conference, Denver, Colorado, established Aztlán as the symbolic "Chicano Nation." The plan declared that "before all our brothers in the bronze continent, we are a nation, we are a union of free pueblos, we are *Aztlán*." It created a geographic allegiance to Aztlán, a love of being Chicano, loyalty to a people, public spirit, civic engagement and rejection of White society. The articulation embraced anticolonialist thought, appreciation for the pre-Cuauhtemoc, and a separatist discourse. The unity of the "free pueblos" was over and against the exploitive "gabacho," though it did not account for internal differences of race, economic status, political views, and assimilation within the Mexican community and it was not inclusive of other Latin Americans or of indigenous people outside the Mexica. Eventually these flaws led to the demise of the Chicano movement and the La Raza Unida political party. Currently, the emphasis has shifted to a view that Aztlán is not a geographic place to be reconquered or the egalitarian, pacifist utopia left behind. Instead, Aztlán is a symbolic claim for the rights of the disenfranchised and dispossessed, a commitment to the creation of a new social order.

—MVS

resources were minerals of all sorts, including, but not limited to, copper, silver, and gold. Ritch also stated that the climate was such that it allowed farming all year, which would yield high profits. Not to exclude personal interest in moving to Aztlán, Ritch argued that moving to the territory would have positive health benefits. In addition to mentioning the near absence of heart disease, nervous trouble, venereal disease, and asthma, Ritch claimed that individuals with consumption, a pulmonary disease, would become healthy after breathing the air in Santa Fe. The myth of Aztlán, consequently, became the means for attracting individuals to the territory of New Mexico. Attraction to Aztlán, however, was limited to the physical land, rather than a psychological fascination. The latter would not take place until 1968, and would reach a pinnacle with the Mexican American civil rights movement. To understand the psychological,

identity, and political impact of Aztlán, it is necessary to describe the state of confusion that many Mexican Americans experienced prior to the Chicano movement.

As stated above, the Guadalupe Hidalgo Treaty granted American citizenship to all Mexicans who remained in the territory of New Mexico after 1848. The difficulty that would arise with such a treaty is that citizenship was a birthright and was tied to race, which continued until 1940. Prior to 1940 only those individuals who could be classified as White could be considered as citizens. Yet, Mexicans were not White, but they did have citizenship, which was in contrast to Blacks. Mexicans, consequently, did not fit within the Black/White dichotomy and challenged the accepted inclusive/exclusive tool that benefited both Whites and Blacks. For example, in *re Rodriguez*, the Texas federal court decided in 1897 that

Mexicans, because of the Guadalupe Hidalgo Treaty, were citizens. However, Mexicans were not to be considered as White from a scientific perspective; nonetheless, the court did establish a basis for considering Mexicans as White. Although Mexicans had a legal right to claim their citizenship in the United States of America, many were unable to exercise their rights as citizens. Groups such as the League of United Latin American Citizens (LULAC) argued they had experienced discrimination because they were unable to exercise their due rights and benefits of citizens.

Confusion concerning their identity would become entrenched with the National Origin Act passed by the U.S. Congress in 1924. This act confined immigration to Europeans and resulted in over 500,000 Mexicans being forcibly returned to Mexico. It is estimated that over half of those who were deported were U.S. citizens. Thirty years later in 1954, in order to further expel Mexicans from the United States, Attorney General Herbert Brownell launched "Operation Wetback." This resulted in over 3.8 million individuals being deported to Mexico. The vast majority did not receive a deportation hearing. Both the National Origin Act and Operation Wetback created doubt in the Mexican mind as to whether they would ever be part of American society. Being neither White nor Black, many Mexicans identified, on a limited basis, with Mexico of old.

Pachucos, individuals who rejected any White identity, racial and social assimilation, downplayed the notion that race should be used as the means of identity. For instance, in 1968 following the East Los Angeles student walkouts, 13 individuals were arrested and charged with conspiracy, a felony charge, to commit the crimes of "disturbing the peace, failing to disperse, and trespassing on school grounds." These individuals hired Oscar "Zeta" Acosta, who would later become a prominent Chicano lawyer, to defend in the case known as the "East L.A. Thirteen." Prior to accepting this case, Acosta had been working for the Black Civil Rights Movement, but left when leaders of the Black Civil Rights Movement failed to see that civil rights also included Mexicans. Mexicans would, then, have to fend for themselves in their plight for justice and identity. However, a platform for justice and identity was needed, which Aztlán could provide.

Unable to identify with either White or Black, many Mexican Americans began to appeal to Aztlán as an identity marker. In 1968 the prominent Chicano poet Alurista began appealing to Aztlán in a class for Chicanos at San Diego State University. Yet, it was not until 1969 when the National Chicano Youth Liberation Conference was held in Denver, Colorado, that Aztlán became a prominent identity symbol for Chicanos and many Mexican Americans. Both Alurista and Rodolfo "Corky" Gonzales, prominent leaders of the Chicano movement, developed "El Plan Espiritual de Aztlán," which would become the basis for Chicano self-consciousness and self-determination. Chicanos will, at times, identify themselves as Aztlán, but this is mostly done to create a historical consciousness. Differences between the usage of "Chicano" to identify those individuals or group of people who were involved in the struggle for Mexican American rights and "Aztlán" ought to be maintained as will be shown in the following paragraphs.

At a time when Mexican Americans were undergoing an identity crisis, Chicano leaders adopted the notion of Aztlán as the place that Chicanos could identify with and give them a sense of belonging. Identification with Aztlán occurs when Chicanos realize they are heirs of a powerful empire that once ruled southern Mexico. Chicanos identify themselves with neither their Mexican heritage nor American society. Instead, ethnic distinctiveness is achieved by identifying with the ancient civilization of the Aztecs. This entails the acceptance of their Indian and indigenous past as a source of pride, dignity, and self-respect. Identity also occurs when Chicanos suppose that the southwestern part of the United States was once the land that belonged to the Aztecs. There is then, a factual and tangible aspect to Aztlán. Chicanos claim to be living in the same place where the Aztecs once lived. Finally, the Chicano consciousness derived from Aztlán moves beyond the psychological arena into the political field. Chicanos claim rights to improved housing, better education, sustainable employment, along with self-determination and self-defense by appealing to Aztlán.

At the core of *El Plan Espiritual de Aztlán* is a line of reasoning that appeals to Chicano nationalism as the means for accomplishing political organization and action. The paradox of nationalism in *El Plan Espiritual de Aztlán* is the nonexistence of a Chicano nation. However, the genius of making the case for nationalism is that Chicanos are given a politically identifying marker that is in contrast to both Mexicans and Americans. Removed from Mexico by a national border and unable to assimilate into American culture, Chicanos are united by a common nationalism that is Aztlán.

The notion of Aztlán is not limited to a particular group of people such as those who belong to a particular religion, political party, and economic class. Chicano nationalism unites all divisions within the Chicano populace because all individuals, regardless of religion, political leanings, and economic status, are Aztlán. Of course, this is an ideal that is to be striven for and not a reality that existed at the time that *El Plan Espiritual de Aztlán* was drafted. The ideological aspect of the hoped for unity found within Chicano nationalism is especially clear from the failure of the *Congreso de Aztlán* in 1972, a proposed national Chicano political party that pitted Rodolfo "Corky" Gonzales and José Angel Gutiérrez, a comparatively new Chicano leader from Texas, against one another. Gutiérrez defeated Gonzales to become the president of the *La Raza Unida Party* (LRUP). LRUP had arisen in several states but had no national organization. Gonzales's hopes were to become the chairman/president of LRUP. Gutiérrez, recognizing that no one was running against Gonzales, decided to give up his position as moderator of the national LRUP convention held in El Paso, Texas, so he could oppose Gonzales. Following the announcement that Gutiérrez had defeated Gonzales, the latter made a public address admonishing those present of the importance of unity. However, the desired goal of a national organizational structure failed to become a reality due to the different personalities among the leaders of the Chicano movement.

Regardless of the lack of achieving a national Chicano political party, the notion of Aztlán remains a prominent and influential concept for the Chicano movement. For instance, in 1969 at the University of California at Santa Barbara, with the assistance of Alurista, the *Movimiento Estudiantil Chicano de Aztlán* (M.E.Ch.A.) was founded and organized. Among the many goals of M.E.Ch.A. is the education of young people so that they develop self-determination, self-consciousness, and political awareness. M.E.Ch.A. also seeks to promote cultural identity that rejects assimilation and advances educational, socioeconomical, and political empowerment. Moving away from the nationalism that is put forward in the *El Plan Espiritual de Aztlán,* M.E.Ch.A. adopts a philosophical stance and seeks to include all people regardless of race. It is possible for an individual to be a Chicano or Chicana and not be a descendant of *El Quinto Sol*, or, rather, Aztlán. Nonetheless, the ultimate goal of this organization is being in the service of the people of Aztlán through education.

Aztlán, then, has undergone an evolutionary process. Prior to the Chicano movement, Aztlán was primarily identified with a specific location, even if several scholars ranged in ideas of the exact location. During the Chicano movement in the late 1960s and early 1970s, Aztlán took on a psychological dimension when Chicanos identified with the indigenous Aztec race. This is especially evident in Anaya's text, *Heart of Aztlán*. For Anaya, Aztlán is to be found within the individual who is experiencing oppression and injustice. Aztlán is found in the heart of the one who seeks to exist in a land that belongs to him, but is a stranger in the culture of that land.

There were some, such as Reies López Tijerina, a Chicano leader who was concerned with the land grants in New Mexico, who identified Aztlán with a specific location, i.e., New Mexico. Of the four most prominent Chicano leaders, César Chávez, Rodolfo "Corky" Gonzales, José Angel Gutiérrez, and Reies López Tijerina, Tijerina was the most militant. This militancy, of course, is in contrast to the nonviolence articulated by César Chávez.

For some, Aztlán is the historical reality of a land that the ancient Aztec civilization once inhabited. For others, Aztlán is identification with the Aztec people, which is in contrast to both Mexican and American society. Many, however, consider Aztlán as a means to give a group of people, mostly Chicanas and Chicanos—those who struggle politically for the dignity of Mexican Americans—a sense of belonging, self-determination, self-consciousness, and political empowerment.

Dieties

Coatlicue

Coatlicue, or Snake Skirt, was the Aztec progenitor of celestial bodies and Mother Goddess of warrior god Huitzilopochtli (God of the Sun and War), Coyolxauhqui (Moon Goddess), Quetzalcoatl (the Feathered Serpent God), and Xolotl (Lord of the Underworld and the God of Lightning). Coatlicue was the personification of duality. She is visually represented as a fearsome bare-breasted warrior goddess dressed in a netted skirt decorated with rattlesnakes, human hearts, and skulls. She was venerated in two festivals. The spring ritual was called Tozozontli and celebrated the first fruits of the season, which occurred during the rainy season, culminating with sacrificial offerings and the flaying of skins to be placed in a cave. The autumn ritual, Quecholli, focused on hunting and culminated with the sacrifice of a woman impersonating Coatlicue. Agriculture, fertility, hunting, and sacrifice played key mythical roles in Coatlicue's symbolism. Huitzilopochtli was born after she was virginally impregnated when a ball of feathers fell from the sky and landed on her bosom. Her mythology evolved over time and one of her representations is Tonatzin, the Good Mother. After the Spanish conquest, the pre-Hispanic cult of Tonatzin fused with the Catholic veneration of the Virgin de Guadalupe.

—FAO

Coyolxauhqui

Coyolxauhqui, a principal female deity in the Aztec pantheon and daughter of Coatlicue, the mother of the gods, and the sister of Huitzilopochtli, the central warrior deity. In Aztec mythology, two feathers miraculously impregnated Coatlicue as she swept the temple atop the sacred mountain, Coatepec. Upon hearing of the pregnancy of her aged mother, Coyolxauhqui convinced her 400 brothers, the stars, to kill their mother. As Coatlicue lay dying, she gave birth to a fully grown Huitzilopochtli, who quickly dismembered Coyolxauhqui with a fiery serpent known as Xiuhcoatl and banished her brothers. Coyolxauhqui's limbs tumbled down the sacred mountain. The Xiuhcoatl wielded by Huitzilopochtli represents the fiery rays of the sun dispelling the forces of darkness. Coyolxauhqui is often identified with the moon overpowered by the solar deity. In the late twentieth century, Chicana feminist writers and artists began reconstructing

this mythology of Coyolxauhqui's violent murder as it mirrors the misogyny present in patriarchal cultures that seek to obliterate women's autonomy, intellect, and creativity. Writers, visual artists, and performance artists work to reconstruct a mythology with Coyolxauhqui rising from her ashes and transforming herself into the moon, lighting our way through the darkness of patriarchy, racism, and homophobia.

—LM

Huitzilopochtli

The most important of the Aztec deities, Huitzilopochtli, is the war deity of the Aztecs, whose name means "hummingbird of the south" honoring warriors who die in battle and women who die in childbirth, returning as hummingbirds from the south. Huitzilopochtli guided the Azteca, now calling themselves Mexica, to Tenochtitlan from their home in Aztlan by looking for the place in Lake Texcoco where he had thrown his nephew Copil's heart when the boy challenged Huitzilopochtli. From Copil's heart had grown the prickly pear nopal with its beautiful red fruit, and perched on it was an eagle eating a sacred serpent, an image on the present-day Mexican flag. The Toxcatl Panquetzaliztli, or "lifting of the banners," ceremony in Huitzilopochtli's honor is celebrated in contemporary times, without warrior sacrifices, during December by parading the traditional amaranth seed and honey effigy of Huitzilopochtli through the village as people fight to take the effigy away from danzante warriors. Danza Azteca banners are honored with decorations of Cuetlaxochitl, or poinsettias, original Mexica flowers. The celebration ends with eating of the amaranth effigy. Because of its similarity to Christian mass, the ceremony was banned after European contact until recently and replaced by the Nativity Posadas.

—*MVS*

Mayahuel

In the Aztec tradition, Mayahuel is the female deity who represents the maguey cactus. Mayahuel was a sleeping maiden, guarded by her fierce Tzitzimitl grandmother in the sky with the other tzitzimime stars that do battle against the sun and moon every dawn and dusk. Quetzalcoatl persuades Mayahuel to come to Anahuac. Discovering Mayahuel gone, her grandmother descends to Anahuac with all the tzitzimime in search of Mayahuel. The pair hide as a forked tree, each of them one branch. When her grandmother and the tzitzimime recognize Mayahuel, they savagely tear the branch apart, devouring it. Once the tzitzimime return to the sky, Queztalcoatl returns to his actual form and sadly buries the gnawed bones of Mayahuel, from which come the first maguey. Mayahuel is represented as a 400-breasted image who feeds her children, the lunar and terrestrial guardians of plenty and the harvest called Centzon Totochtin, or Four Hundred Rabbits, pulque, the rich nectar of the maguey. Mayahuel became associated with all healing plants through *La Virgen de Remedios*, when the lost statue left by Cortes at the Temple Pyramid of Quetzalcoatl at Cholula was found under a maguey by Juan Ce Cuautli, bridging European and indigenous faith traditions.

—*MVS*
Santiago O. Piñón

References and Further Reading

Alurista. *Floricanto en Aztlán* (Los Angeles: Chicano Studies Center, University of California, 1971).

Anaya, Rudolfo A. *Heart of Aztlán* (Albuquerque: University of New Mexico Press, 1976).

Boturini, Lorenzo Benaduccie. *Crónica mexicana, Teoamóxtli, o Libro que contiene todo lo interesante á usos, costumbres, religion, política y literatura de los antiguos indios tultecas y mexicanos, redactado de un antiguo codice inedito del caballero Boturini* (Mexico City, Mexico: M. Ontiveros, 1821–1822).

Chavero, Alfredo. *Las Aztecas O Mexicas: Fundacion de le Ciudad de Mexico* (Mexico City, Mexico: Impresa Universitaria, 1955).

Elizondo, Virgil. *The Future Is Mestizo* (Bloomington, IN: Meyer-Stone Books, 1988).

Garcia, Juan Ramon. *Operation Wetback: The Mass Deportation of Mexican Undocumented Workers in 1954* (Westport, CT: Greenwood Press, 1980).

Guerrero, Andres G. *A Chicano Theology* (New York: Orbis Books, 1987).

Humboldt, Alexander von. *Essay on New Spain* (Baltimore: Wane & O'Reilly, 1813).

Orozco y Berra, Manuel, ed. *Codice Ramirez* (Mexico City, Mexico: Editorial Leyenda, 1944).

———. *Historia Antigua y de La Conquista de Mexico* (Mexico City, Mexico: Editorial Porrua, S.A., 1960).

Rendon, Armando B. *Chicano Manifesto: The History and Aspirations of the Second Largest Minority in America* (Berkeley, CA: Ollin and Associates, Inc., 1971).

Ritch, William G. *Aztlán: The History, Resources and Attractions of New Mexico* (Boston: D. Lothrop and Co., 1885).

Rosales, F. Arturo. *Chicano: The History of the Mexican American Civil Rights Movement* (Houston: Arte Publico Press, 1997).

Tezozómoc, Fernando. *Cronica Mexicayotl* (Mexico City, Mexico: Imprensa Universitaria, 1949).

Tijerina, Reies. *They Called Me "King Tiger": My Struggle for the Land and Our Rights* (Houston: Arte Publico Press, 2000).

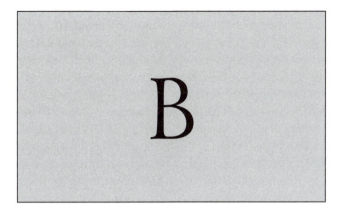

BASE COMMUNITIES

Base Communities (BCs) denote a domestic model of church that developed in Latin America starting in the 1950s, but that is now practiced around the world under various names, including house churches. Also called Basic Ecclesial Communities from the Spanish term "Comunidades Eclesiales de Base," the groups are local contextual expressions of the Church, as differentiated from church movements that operate under a specific charism or service. BCs are rooted in home meetings and are led by lay leaders, having in common rituals of shared prayer and reflection on the Word of God. They are generally mission oriented toward active involvement in society so as to transform unjust social structures. The groups have found great success in poor social settings, and it is estimated that there are over 1 million groups active in Latin America alone. It is there that they take on an ecclesiology based primarily on the work of Liberation theologians, especially following

their biblical concept of the "Preferential Option for the Poor." In addition, North American and Protestant models of the Hispanic domestic church have also arisen.

Historical Development

The earliest prayer services of Christians were not held in church buildings, since these had not yet been constructed, but were gatherings of the faithful in private homes (1 Corinthians 16:19; Romans 16:3–5). The believers in Jesus Christ came together to pray, share the Eucharist, and support one another while witnessing to the Holy Spirit active in their lives. These household churches were quite vibrant from the beginning of the apostolic period until the fourth century. They would have coexisted together with a developing hierarchically ordered ministry of bishops, priests, and deacons, which was in place by 110 CE, and which was slowly developing into a structured ministry. When the Roman Emperor Constantine proclaimed the Edict of Milan in

313 CE, Christians ceased being persecuted. Confiscated properties were restored and new churches were built upon ruins of old temples. The private home services of the Apostolic period became less familiar as ministers had to cope with large numbers of the converts coming to the basilicas for worship.

The parish model of Church began to develop in the latter part of the Patristic era, taking some of its shape from the legal practices of the Roman Empire. The sacramental structures of parish life were in place by the Middle Ages. Parishes came to be identified with the community cared for by a pastor in a specific neighborhood or territory, and dioceses became the larger territory cared for by the local bishop. The communion of local churches was united under the leadership of the Church of Rome.

In modern times, the parish model has shown weaknesses, especially in the Church of Latin America, due to the shortage of clergy and also to the huge number of people migrating to cities. Both clergy and lay leaders have been asking themselves how the life-giving spirit of the early Church, so tangibly felt in tightly knit communities, could be recreated in new ecclesial models. It was in this desire for renewal that the grassroots experience of BCs was born.

In the late 1950s, the Church of Latin America turned its efforts toward creating smaller and more vibrant groupings of the faithful. The experiments were supported by the updating of ecclesial life and doctrinal formulations called forth by the Second Vatican Council (1962–1965). At the meeting of the Latin American Bishops Conference (CELAM) in Medellín in 1968, the experience of "Comunidades Eclesiales de Base" received strong support, being called "the first and fundamental ecclesiastical nucleus," and "the initial cell of the ecclesiastical structures." These grassroots ecclesial groupings were also supported by the CELAM meeting in Puebla in 1979, although concern was voiced about the lack of training of lay leaders and the need to incorporate the BCs more closely to diocesan and parish structures. The CELAM meeting in Santo Domingo in 1992 cautioned that BCs should remain in communion with their parish and their bishop, as well as avoid ideological and political manipulation. The Latin American Episcopal Conference continues to give legitimacy to BCs when they are integrated into the parish, the diocese, and the universal Church. They can be especially helpful to the apostolate in areas where priests are few or where parishes are too large to be personable. Many groups are now active in the United States, Africa, Europe, and Asia. In North America BCs have been a key aspect of most Hispanic evangelization efforts, and also in parish RENEW programs.

Latino/a Protestant denominations have had great success with this ecclesial model, sometimes calling them "house churches." While less justice oriented than their Catholic counterparts, Protestant BCs have given a sense of vitality and community to their congregations, especially to denominations that appear to be losing membership. All of these different models of grassroots churches have served to renew and reconceptualize the structures of modern Christianity, calling believers to a closer fidelity to what it means to be baptized, while making their spirituality and ministry more alive and dynamic.

Theological Concepts

An important biblical concept for any BC-type ministry is *ekklesia*, the Greek word for Church. In ancient secular circles it denoted any grouping of people, but in the New Testament it was used to identify the early Christian communities. While the word *ekklesia* is largely absent from the Gospels, St. Paul used the term about 60 times in his epistles. The word sometimes refers to a community in a specific place (a house church) and sometimes to a group of churches in a region. The house churches of Paul are specifically mentioned in his epistles, such as the church in the house of Aquila and Prisca (1 Corinthians 16:19). They consisted of more than just immediate family members and servants; they included other believers in the area who joined those who worshiped there, such as the house of Gaius, which was in Corinth (Romans 16:23). Because of their small size, the house churches were places for personally focused catechesis and discipleship, where one could experience the liturgy and be educated in the mission of Christ. These types of settings are particularly useful when it comes to supporting the metanoia of the newly converted so that they remain in communion with the Holy Spirit and avoid their old ways (1 Corinthians 6:11).

An innovative development of *ekklesia* is the theological idea of "Ecclesiogenesis." This "birthing of a new Church" has to do with the structural changes that are inherent when one highlights the BCs as a community of communities that form the parish. Here the laity, who are the leaders of these small church groups, take a role as sharers in Christ's priestly office (1 Peter 2:9), a service that flows from their baptism. In areas of priestless parishes, this "starting the church again" is the sign of a shift in ecclesiological models that shows the reception of the teachings of Vatican II. It was at this council that the theological focus turned toward the contemporary understanding of Church as the People of God (1 Peter 2:10). Incorporated within the ordained ministry of the deaconate, presbyterate and episcopate, the grassroots leadership of BCs highlights the lay axis of Church organization, more so than the clerical axis. This genesis of lay leadership, in areas where ministry was once the privilege of the ordained, signifies diverse models of Church.

Another important theological concept for BC ministry is *koinonia*, meaning community of voluntary sharing or partnerships. The early Church gatherings were places for partaking of a sacred meal, where the baptized were characterized by their concern for one another. They sold their possessions, distributing the proceeds as any had need while keeping everything in common (Acts 2:42–47). These early communities acted as places for religious fellowship with strong temporal and supratemporal senses of meaning. As members of an earthly and a heavenly community, the baptized could proclaim that Christ was the head of both realities.

Hispanics have offered considerable contributions to BCs due to their cultural values of community and their interest in close personal groupings. As a people, they are well suited to a *koinonia* ecclesiological model. Latina/os emphasize sociocentric and organic structures, where the family and the group form the fundamental units of society. Hispanics also mine key aspects of their identity from their memberships. This cultural perspective is markedly different from that of mainstream U.S. society, which has been described as egocentric and contractual. Instead of an emphasis on the individual, Latino/a society is more concerned with the communal. Maturity is not so much a process of individuation, where one distances oneself from others, but rather is more a process of accepting interdependence. This cultural fact of Hispanic society in general and Hispanic churches in particular supports the ecclesiology of BCs, which strives to re-create the early Church sociodynamics. For this reason, North American diocesan leaders have used BCs to target and attract Hispanic people to evangelization projects. The BCs draw their strength from Latina/os' formation of kinships and also their desire to have a sense of community in large anonymous urban centers.

The social mission of the Church is also an integral aspect of the practice of BCs. Lay members are empowered to link the Bible to their concrete situation and determine a praxis to undertake. The BCs of Latin America have traditionally shown an emphasis on working for social justice and achieving structural change in secular society. Since the reality of Latin America is represented by a majority of people who are poor, BCs have used "see, judge, and act" methodologies to reflect on their situation and improve social conditions. Following the experience of Liberation theologians, the communities critically examine their own local situations with an eye toward liberating all those burdened by structural sin and injustice.

It is to the masses of marginalized people that the theological and biblical concept of the Preferential Option for the Poor can offer some liberation. Throughout the Bible one finds a common theme, which shows the love

that God had for the little ones (Matthew 1:25–30; Luke 6:20–25). The Hebrew term *anawim*, or the poor of Yahweh, is especially poignant (Zephaniah 2:3; Isaiah 41:17). Official Vatican statements have supported God's predilection for the poor as consistent with the continuous thread found throughout the social doctrine of the Church. The same documents have criticized the option when it supports the exclusion of the physically non-poor from ministry, thus leaning toward promoting a Marxist type of class struggle. Nevertheless, the teachings of Christ's special love for the poor gives the Latin American BCs more than their counterparts in other areas, a unifying concern for social justice. The poor also include the different marginalized groups such as the elderly and the sick, refugees and migrants, etc. This broader vision of pastoral service ensures that the Kingdom of God remains the primary focus of the proclamation of the Good News of Christ (Luke 4:18).

Ritual Structures

There are no formal rituals of BCs, yet the gatherings have some structures in common. Under the umbrella of a larger parish, the smaller group BC meetings are almost always held in homes. Times are chosen that are convenient to the participants, which is usually in the evenings. Isolated rural Catholic groups sometimes meet on Sundays when there are no priests available to celebrate the Eucharist. Generally, the people who come together know each other very well and can greet each other by name. These face-to-face interactions are part of the patterns of intimacy that can develop for most groups, giving them a familiar and neighborly feel. Eight to twelve people is considered an appropriate size, since larger numbers can lose the faith-sharing dynamic so important to the BC. There is usually a coordinator for each group, who has met previously with other coordinators in the parish or deanery to plan future meetings under a larger pastoral plan or theme. The meeting begins with moments for prayer and song. A major part of the evening is dedicated to reflection on Scripture, usually the readings of the following Sunday. Many groups use published lectionary-based guides to explore scripture together. All the attendants have a chance to share what they feel God is saying to them. There is usually time to reflect on another chosen topic or teaching, and some groups have specific questions that have been previously prepared. Depending on the tenor of the group, the reflections can remain at a spiritual level, as they often do in the RENEW and post-RENEW programs of North America, or lean toward social justice issues as they often do in less economically developed areas. The meeting ends with time for refreshments and socializing, since fellowship and the nurturing of friendships are so important to the building up of the Church.

Key Figures

Important people in the theory and dissemination of BCs include Jose Marins, a Brazilian priest who has written and traveled extensively since the 1970s speaking for and animating groups throughout the world. One of his hallmark concerns is that BCs should be seen and promoted as the Church itself at the smallest level. Leonardo Boff, a former Brazilian priest, has also been a strong proponent of BCs. He envisions them as reversing hierarchical structures and rigid clerical versus lay distinctions. Boff sees this rebirthing of the Catholic Church through BCs as a way to replace parishes and reinvent a new ecclesiology from the grassroots. Fr. Bernard J. Lee, S.M., is an important writer on the theology and practice of BCs in the United States. He differentiates Catholic BCs under these headings: General type of small Christian communities, Hispanic/Latino communities, Charismatic communities, Call to Action communities, and Eucharist-centered communities. Regardless of their typology, he sees BCs as Spirit-led associations that are reshaping the modern parish.

Leopoldo Perez

References and Further Reading

Boff, Leonardo. *Ecclesiologenesis: The Base Communities Reinvent the Church* (Maryknoll, NY: Orbis Books, 1986).

Lee, Bernard J., William V. D'Antonio, Virgil Elizondo, et al. *Catholic Experience of Small Christian Communities* (New York: Paulist Press, 2000).

Loreto Maniz, Cecilia. *Coping with Poverty: Pentecostals and Christian Base Communities in Brazil* (Philadelphia: Temple University Press, 1994).

Marins, Jose, et al. *Basic Ecclesial Community: Church from the Roots* (Quito: Imprenta Del Colegio Tecnico don Bosco, 1980).

Vandenakker, John Paul. *Small Christian Communities and the Parish* (Kansas City: Sheed and Ward, 1994).

BIBLE INSTITUTES

The beginnings of Bible institutes can be traced to what Lawrence A. Cremin identified as the metropolitan period (1876–1980) of educational developments in the United States. During the earlier part of this period, Protestantism was facing the challenges of addressing modernism and industrialism. Two different Christian views arose to address this challenge. The first was an emergent social Christianity. This perspective saw the church as responsible for bringing Christian values to bear on the industrial order. The second Christian view was a fundamentalist one. It viewed the world as a sinking vessel from which its passengers could be saved only through immediate conversion. Hence, the church's mission was an evangelistic one with a more personal pietistic focus. It was out of the fundamentalist perspective that the Bible institute movement emerged. Dwight L. Moody pioneered three major educational strategies: the Bible conference, which focused on renewal through Bible study; the Student Volunteer Movement, which recruited college graduates for services as domestic and foreign missionaries; and the Bible institute, which became a training school for persons who would carry out ministries in local congregations and on the urban streets.

The Development of Bible Institutes

Bible institutes offered a precollegial education and were not constrained by the traditions of degree-granting institutions. The school was only for older laypersons who had been denied the opportunities of study but who had knowledge of the Scriptures and experience in the areas of gospel music and evangelizing individuals. The school equipped these persons to do ministry in their churches and in the poorest and forgotten places of the urban areas. Under the leadership of Reuben Torrey, James M. Gray, and Clarence H. Benson, the Bible institute became a major center of orthodox evangelical Christian education. Between the years of 1886 and 1915, 32 Bible institutes were organized.

One of the Bible institutes that was organized during this time and that still continues to operate is the Latin American Bible Institute in La Puente, California (www.labi.edu). Alice E. Luce was a missionary of the Church Missionary Society. After working in Texas she launched out on her own to the Pacific coast to take up missionary work among the expatriate Mexicans in Los Angeles, leaving behind the work undertaken by Henry Ball in Texas. As a part of that work, in 1926, she began the Latin American Bible Institute (LABI) in San Diego. She also contributed educational materials and the curriculum to an institute with the same name that Henry Ball had begun at the same time in Texas. Both institutes continue to operate as a part of the Assemblies of God Higher Education Institutions.

In 1935 LABI moved to nearby La Mesa, California, in 1941 to East Los Angeles and to its present site in La Puente in 1947. The school offered on-site and correspondence courses. Today the school offers a three-year ordination track and a two-year missionary track. It has a bilingual curriculum and reaches up to four generations of Latino/a leaders. It has many extension programs that reach across the nation. Students have the option of using up to one-third of their credits toward a bachelor's degree at denominational colleges and universities.

Some Bible institutes have evolved into evangelical institutions of higher learning, such as Biola University and Gordon College. At the time they were established, their emphasis was the training of laypersons, both men and women, for Christian service. They saw their work as complementary to the seminaries.

In 1990 the Association for Hispanic Theological Education (AETH) was formed to create a network of Hispanic Bible institutes across denominations, their teachers, Hispanic theological programs at seminaries, and Hispanic seminary professors. The organization linked all manner of formal and informal theological education programs across the United States, Canada, and Puerto Rico. It addresses the needs of Bible institutes as its focus and has provided training for its teachers, presidents, deans, and librarians. AETH has offered instruction on fund-raising and other administrative tasks. Most importantly, it has begun to create its own texts in Spanish written by Hispanic scholars. Currently there are several series of texts on the Bible and on other major curricular subject matters that have been published in partnership with publishers that had not previously been supplying these institutions. AETH has served as a way of not only networking the Hispanic Bible institutes but of helping to create partnerships between them and other organizations and institutions that would have otherwise not known how to gain access to the institutes. According to the National Survey of Hispanic/Latino Theological Education, the proportion of Hispanic religious leaders who had attended Bible institutes and lay ministry formation programs is approximately 47 and 53 percent, respectively.

The Educational Purpose

The aim of the institutes is to train consecrated men and women, both lay and clergy, for qualified ministry. Many of the participants are already engaged in ministry. These institutions are affordable, flexible, and efficient. They are therefore accessible as compared to more costly seminaries and divinity schools. Also, they are grassroots institutions headed by leaders indigenous to the community they serve and are typically small and in urban areas.

The Bible institute is an adult education model where one works full-time during the day at a secular job and studies in the evening. Classes are structured to accommodate the needs of its participants, many of whom are bivocational pastors pursuing a secular job for financial stability while serving as part-time, oftentimes unpaid ministers in a church. In this setting persons are educated while in the context of their ministry. This model provides theological training for pastors without college education. It does so in Spanish, the first language of the participants. Each of these characteristics makes the institute and lay ministry program the most accessible theological education institutions to Hispanic pastors and lay leaders. Courses are designed for both the clergy and the laity, although sometimes there are courses specifically geared toward the pastors' needs. This is why the institute model is used by the Hispanic mainline churches as well.

Types of Bible Institutes

The Center for Urban Theological Studies (CUTS) in Philadelphia has identified three types of Bible institutes. The first type is the independent Bible institute.

These institutes tend to promote a particular theological or doctrinal perspective, and many are fundamentalist or dispensational. The second type is developed by and connected to church judicatories with the purpose of grounding persons in their faith and preparing them for different areas of ministry in their local congregations. The purpose of these institutes is to inform or indoctrinate students in an understanding of their faith heritage. These are usually a three- to four-year program of study.

A third type of Bible institute is that established in a local congregation for its own membership with the purpose of discipling or training new members and leaders so that they may become involved more fully in the mission of their congregations. An institute may emerge when the mission and theology of the church are being evaluated and revamped. The pastor, usually a charismatic leader, articulates the new vision and prepares leaders for it through the institute. This helps to manage conflict between the old and new visions since those attending the Bible institute are exposed to a new understanding in a positive environment where it can be discussed and eventually appropriated at each one's pace. The project originates in the personal and ministerial pilgrimage of a visionary pastor whose encounter with the realities of ministering in the Hispanic community drives him/her to seek ways to contextualize the ministry.

Enrollment

Those who enroll in any of these types of Bible institutes need to be members of a local church. It is a provision of the church at large to provide an environment of nurture for the walk of faith and for ministry involvement. Many are already involved in ministry. Since a large percentage of the Hispanic population is very young, it is not unusual to have teenagers attend Bible institutes. Larger institutes such as LABI provide classes in English to accommodate the second generation who have received all their formal education in English. These young persons must meet the demands of both their public school education as well as the institute.

Cost

Institutes are affordable institutions with tuition costs ranging from $25.00 to $250.00 a semester. They are efficient, low-cost operations where most of the staff are volunteers or part-time personnel with very modest stipends who serve local churches in other capacities. Building facilities are supplied by the host church at no cost. There is usually no formal budget.

Teachers

Instructors at Bible institutes are many times graduates of institutes who will pass on what they have learned to the next groups. This is in keeping with the biblical principle found in II Timothy 2:2 of faithful persons passing on what they have received to others. This is what makes up the parochial nature of these institutes and would present a challenge if an outside entity were to attempt to make any changes in the structure or curriculum of these institutes since the knowledge continues to be recycled through this means. These characteristics reflect aspects of an oral culture.

Pedagogy

Institutes use teachers who may or may not have the educational credentials required by accredited schools. Their wisdom is passed on through the sharing of ministerial experiences. It is these experiences coupled with the book knowledge that provide the skills and preparation needed for ministry. It also creates an action or reflection model for learning theology.

Curriculum

Curricula at Bible institutes are varied; some follow a generic evangelical template that includes general knowledge of the scriptures and practical skills. In the area of biblical knowledge, one acquires a panoramic view of the Bible that includes archaeology and history with the purpose of seeing the Bible in the light of its historical context. One also studies the relationship between the Old and New Testaments and learns to locate key passages. The study of biblical periods and how the plan of salvation is reflected in each period and in biblical doctrine is also stressed. In the area of skills for ministry, one studies homiletics, pastoral counseling, pedagogy, and evangelism. Other curricula follow a Moody Institute model or come from the Evangelical Training Association (ETA).

Bible institute curricula are prepared for a wide audience and are not contextualized for any particular group. They are strong in theological content but lack a ministry reflection learning component. This is where the work of AETH is responding by writing curriculum that is more contextualized. The material assists institutes to develop a philosophy of education that helps persons be critical of their theological traditions in light of the realities of the communities where they minister. This is a qualitative change since it integrates the evangelistic church mission with an understanding of the social dimension of sin and therefore a need to acquire skills in addressing the injustices of social structures as a part of the ministry.

A Summary of Pressing Needs

Networking meetings among the Bible institutes revealed that Bible institutes need library and information services, coalition building or networking between institutes, and technical and administrative support in areas of computerization of information resources and academic record keeping. This could include the development of a Web site with all of its component parts, faculty enrichment or continuing in-service education, enlarging fund-raising capacity, strengthening institutional identity and standing that includes a clear, well-articulated mission statement, and credit recognition. Currently, some of the institutes related to their judicatories are accredited by an undergraduate institution within the denomination. This means that at graduation from the institute, a person has credits toward an undergraduate degree.

Lay Ministry Formation Programs

The Lay Ministry Formation Programs of the Catholic Church could be considered the Catholic counterpart to Bible institutes. In 1980 the pastoral statement *Called and Gifted* first recognized the increasing number of laymen and laywomen responding as volunteers and part-time workers to serve on pastoral councils and other advisory boards. Others were undertaking new roles as special ministers of communion, lectors, catechists, pastoral assistants, and missionaries. This group of laity was preparing themselves professionally to work in the Church, and the bishops recognized them by giving them the name "ecclesial ministers." In 1995, a pastoral statement on the laity entitled *Called and Gifted for the New Millennium* provided a more complete description of lay ministries. The bishops pledged to do further study of the issues concerning this group and their relationship to the bishops and other ordained ministers and to develop a theology concerning lay ministry in the Church in the United States.

In 1997 at the University of Dayton, a theological colloquium was held entitled "Toward a Theology of Ecclesial Lay Ministry." The goals of the colloquium were threefold. They were as follows: (1) to articulate a theology of ecclesial lay ministry that emerged from the experience of lay ministry, (2) to recommend future action that would foster the development of this ministry, and (3) to model effective collaboration between bishops and academic and pastoral theologians.

In the summer of 2001 the Center for Applied Research in the Apostolate (CARA) conducted a comprehensive study of Hispanic ministry at the diocesan level in the United States. Leadership training was one of the issues addressed. One dimension of this is the Lay Ministry Formation Programs. The Secretariat for Laity of the U.S. Catholic Bishops reports that Hispanics comprise 4.4 percent of lay ecclesial students and 23 percent are lay ministry students. This clearly shows a disproportionate representation of Hispanics in this group since Hispanics are reported to comprise one-third of all U.S. Catholics.

Types of Preparation Programs

There are four distinct programs that prepare lay ecclesial ministers:

1. Diocesan formation programs that are multiyear programs and offer certificates.
2. Diocesan formation programs that are affiliated with a college, university, or seminary and offer certificates and degrees, sometimes through distance learning.
3. Academic programs at institutions that offer certificates, undergraduate and graduate degrees, and some ministerial formation.
4. Nondegree programs sponsored by independent Catholic organizations.

In 1998, of the 287 programs reporting the language they used, 41 used English and Spanish, and 12 used Spanish only.

The Federation of Pastoral Institutes (Federación de Institutos Pastorales— FIP) was formed in 1985 at the Mexican American Cultural Center and the Southwest Pastoral Institute in order to create a collaborative system, to design a common vision, and to share experiences with the purpose of enriching each other. The federation currently includes 23 member institutes from different dioceses. They publish the *Bilingual Manual Guide* and *Concepts and Practical Instruments for Pastoral Institutes.*

Curriculum

The programs have not been standardized. The content and format of the curriculum varies according to the needs of preparation of persons attending the program. Usually the program takes three to four years. Besides the course work, there is a practical component overseen by a supervisor of practical ministry. Spiritual direction is also part of the program for a discernment of call period of approximately six months to one year. Retreat experiences may be included in this period of discernment. Courses include the study of the scriptures, church history, pastoral ministry, social justice, liturgy and the sacraments, and morality or ethics. This is designed to provide persons with the skills for analyzing and critiquing economic and political systems and for engaging the world as persons of faith. Critics of the present programs claim that they do not always bring persons to a socially active faith but that the focus is more on evangelization.

Cost

The financing of the preparation for lay ministers is one of the challenges facing the Catholic Church. It is particularly difficult for poorer communities with fewer economic resources, where the prospective students enter the programs with greater educational needs.

A Summary of Pressing Needs

The Association of Graduate Programs in Ministry (AGPIM) was founded in 1987 as an organization of Roman Catholic graduate programs with focus on the preparation of laypersons for ministry. In 1999 the number of such programs was 104. The AGPIM and the committee of the National Association for Lay Ministry have been in dialogue with the subcommittee on ecclesial lay ministry. The issues they have identified for discussion and action are the following:

1. Concern about the financing of ministry education for lay students.
2. Challenges of educating seminarians and lay ministry students together (desirable as a preparation for the practice of collaborative ministry, this sometimes raises concerns about maintaining priestly identity).
3. Necessity of preparing for the entire Church both ordained and lay ministers who are aware and affirming of all cultures.
4. Hope that dioceses might help the graduate schools with spiritual formation and related screening.

The committees have also been working on creating competency standards and a certification process, but these attempts are still relatively new.

The training programs that serve the Hispanic constituency of the Catholic Church comprise only 18.5 percent of all the programs. Bible institutes, on the other hand, serve the majority of the training needs of the Protestant context. The issues of cost and curriculum are similar in both traditions as are the needs for certification. The Hispanic programs of both traditions have organized (FIP and AETH) in order to network and provide for themselves a way to share resources and address common concerns.

Elizabeth Conde-Frazier

References and Further Reading

Conde-Frazier, Elizabeth. *Hispanic Bible Institutes: A Community of Theological Construction* (Scranton PA: University of Scranton Press, 2004).

Davis, Kenneth, and Edwin I. Hernández. *Reconstructing the Sacred Tower: Challenge and Promise of Latino/a Theological Education* (Scranton, PA: University of Scranton Press, 2003).

DeVries, Paul. "New York . . . The Bible Institute Capitol?" *Religion and Contemporary New York City*, ed. Tony Carnes (New York: New York University Press, 1998).

Thigpen, Jonathan N. "A Brief History of the Bible Institute Movement in America." *Journal of Adult Training*, no. 1 (1994).

Together in God's Service: Toward a Theology of Ecclesial Lay Ministry (Washington, DC: National Conference of Catholic Bishops, Subcommittee on Lay Ministry, Committee on Lay Ministry, 1998).

BLACK LEGEND

After listening to the famous sermon on Job by Fray Antonio de Montesinos on Christmas Day 1511, Bartolomé de Las Casas underwent a conversion experience. This led to his lifelong work on combating the conditions of slavery being experienced by the indigenous peoples and the violence they underwent at the hands of the Spanish conquistadors. In order to raise the Spanish Crown's consciousness concerning the atrocities being committed, Las Casas set out to document the kinds of abuses that the indigenous peoples were subjected to by the conquistadors. He published the record of these atrocities under the title *A Very Short Account of the Destruction of the Indies*. In order to illustrate the violence against the indigenous inhabitants, Las Casas used some of the engravings by Theodorus DeBry, even though DeBry never visited the Americas. As a response to many of the complaints by Las Casas, the Spanish Crown issued the *Nuevas Leyes de España* (the New Laws of Spain), which created important mechanisms that tried to protect the indigenous peoples from being abused. For example, the *encomiendas* (forced labor) were abolished despite great opposition from the Criollos (children of Spaniards born in the Americas). Las Casas's record of Spanish atrocities against the indigenous peoples of the Americas would eventually tarnish every Spanish imperial attempt from the sixteenth through the eighteenth centuries, and came to be commonly known as the source of the "Black Legend."

Although used in various contexts, the Black Legend was originally used as propaganda by the Protestant Dutch in the sixteenth century. First coined by Julián Juderías y Loyot, the "Black Legend" is a distortion of Las Casas's

Bartolomé de Las Casas, a sixteenth-century Spanish historian, was the earliest crusader for human rights in the New World. (Library of Congress)

writings by Anglo and Dutch Protestants. Carlos I of Spain (also known as Carlos V) dedicated much of his time and money to combat England, France, Italy, Flanders, Germany, and Hungary. Tired, he abdicated the throne to his son Phillip II, whose government was characterized by sustaining the Spanish (Habsburg Dynasty) Empire against the lower countries of Belgium and Holland. The Dutch rebels contributed intentionally to the creation of the Black Legend in their efforts to discredit the Spanish Crown. The devastation against the indigenous peoples as narrated by Las Casas, they claimed, was comparable to the ravages of Fernando Álvarez de Toledo, third Duke of Alba and his successors, as they suppressed the rebellion in the Netherlands by creating what came to be known as the "Blood Court." As part of their attempt to free Holland from Spain, the rebels reprinted translated editions of Las Casas's *Very Short Account* no less than 33 times between 1578 and 1648, more than all other European countries combined.

The suppression of the Dutch rebels was also connected to Spain's war against Protestantism. In order to counter the spread of Protestantism in Spanish imperial territories, the Catholic inquisition sometimes resorted to violent measures. This provoked the fabrication of the Spanish Inquisition as cruel and bloodthirsty. Images of moats, dungeons, chains, cries, and rooms of torture accompanied such descriptions, creating a sense of extreme fanaticism and evil. This also contributed to the creation of the myth of thousands of Jews, Muslims, Protestants, and non-Catholics being tortured and murdered in the dungeons of the institution by Dominican friars.

These notions of the Spanish as inherently cruel, superstitious, and tyrannical soon became part of the Black Legend.

During the sixteenth century, the Black Legend was used by the British to oppose Spanish imperialism in the Americas while justifying their own form of colonialization. They highlighted the cruelty in the ways the Spanish conquered the Americas and defended their territories. They constructed an image of the Spanish as superstitious obscurantists, opposed to spiritual progress and intellectual pursuits. They also accused them of tyranny because of the way they imposed control over the lives of Spaniards in the "New World." Later in the nineteenth century the Black Legend played an important role in the British attempts at discrediting and delegitimizing the Spanish presence in the Americas. In the twentieth century it has also been part of the Protestant-Catholic tensions created by Anglo North American Protestant missionaries to Latin America.

The nineteenth century's ethos against Spanish imperialism contributed to and fueled the efforts for the independence of the Americas. Simón Bolívar's famous manifesto for independence drew from the Black Legend in order to find legitimacy in the cause of independence. In his famous *Carta de Jamaica* (Letter from Jamaica, 1815), Bolívar argues for the removal of the yoke of the Spanish Crown upon the Americanos (Spanish Criollos). For him, the Americanos were oppressed by the Spanish empire despite their double citizenship. Highlighting the emergence of the conscience of the Criollo, he claimed that such violence against its citizens was similar to the initial violence of the Spanish conquistadors against the indigenous peoples, as recorded by Las Casas. As such, the moral responsibility of the Americanos was to rid themselves of Spain and become independent republics.

In his attempt at setting the record straight, Rómulo Carbia insists that the Black Legend is an exaggeration of Las Casas's account of the destruction of the indigenous regions by the Spaniards. Accusing Las Casas of being dishonest and providing wrong information, he claims the latter never saw some of the things he wrote but heard them from Montesinos and other friars. His attempt at depicting Spain in a less violent light has given rise to what is commonly known as the "White Legend," which is an attempt of Spanish authors to paint a more positive picture of Spain's imperial history.

Néstor Medina

References and Further Reading

Juderías y Loyot, Julián. *La leyenda negra y la verdad histórica, contribución al estudio del concepto de España en Europa, de las causas de este concepto y de la tolerancia religiosa y política en los países civilizados* (Madrid: Rev. de Arch, 1914).

Carbia, Rómulo D. *Historia de la Leyenda Negra Hispanoamericana*. Prologue by Rafael Gambra (Buenos Aires, Argentina: Ediciones Nueva Hispanidad, 2000).

Las Casas, Bartolomé de. *A Short Account of the Destruction of the Indies*, ed. and trans. Nigel Griffin (New York: Penguin Books, 1992).

Reyes Govea, Juan. *El mestizo, la nación y el nacionalismo Mexicano* (Chihuahua, México: Ediciones del Gobierno del Estado de Chihuahua, 1992).

BORDER SAINTS

The term "border saints" refers to a phenomenon of folk saint devotions that has acquired a distinctive popularity along the U.S.-Mexican border. Traditionally, a saint has been a person whose life of holiness has been celebrated by some faiths, primarily by the Catholic Church. Veneration of unorthodox saints, or "folk saints," on the other hand, usually emerges from folkloric devotional practices that are not necessarily recognized by the official church. A border saint is an example of a folk saint, whose life is celebrated in the borderlands, a sociopolitical and cultural space of human tensions and struggles, and whose intercessory mediation is widely sought by immigrants and devotees on both sides of the U.S.-Mexican border. The fame of these popular saints and the faith of their devotees has transcended the borderlands to other Latin American countries.

The most popular folk saints are Don Pedro Jaramillo (1829–1907), Jesús Malverde (1870–1909), Teresa Urrea (1873–1906), Pancho Villa (1878–1923), El Niño Fidencio (1898–1938), and Juan Soldado (1914–1938). Some consider Saint Toribio Romo González (1900–1928) the only Catholic orthodox border saint. In a top-down approach, the primary criterion for the orthodox canonization, or official acknowledgement and declaration of someone's sainthood, is the recognition of someone's virtuous and exemplary Christian life. In reaction to this perceived exclusivist right to define holiness and elitist notion of sanctity, the populace has defined "Robin Hood," revolutionary, miraculous, and antiestablishment behaviors as worthy of celebration and veneration, especially

Pancho Villa was one of the great revolutionary heroes of the Americas. A general in the epic struggle of the Mexican Revolution of 1910, Villa took on a legendary importance in Mexico for his social ideals and daring military exploits. Today he remains an easily recognizable symbol of Mexican nationalism and social justice. (Library of Congress)

when these are characterized as criminal, deviant, sinful, and superstitious by the powerful elites of police, military, government, medicine, and Church.

Don Pedro Jaramillo, also known as Don Pedrito or the Healer of Los Olmos, was born in Guadalajara, Jalisco, and died at Paisano, Texas. According to legend, when his mother became very ill, Don Pedrito prayed for his mother's recovery, but when she died he decided to leave Mexico. He crossed the border into Texas in 1881 and settled on Los Olmos ("The Elms") ranch, near present-day Falfurrias. He immediately earned a reputation as a healer. As many as 500 people would come to see him at one time, often camping at Los Olmos Creek, waiting to see him for the miraculous healing of many types of physical ailments. Devotion to Don Pedrito is widely celebrated in northern Mexico and in southern Texas. His shrine is located at a grave site near Falfurrias, Texas.

Jesús Juárez Maso, also known as Jesús Malverde, was probably born in the area around Culiacán, Sinaloa. According to some accounts, he was a bandit who helped the poor by robbing the wealthy. Some say that he was betrayed by a close confidant or comrade and allegedly some henchmen cut off his feet and dragged him to collect a monetary reward. After his death, his body was reportedly left hanging from a mesquite tree as a warning to others. His main shrine is located in Culiacan, Sinaloa, and is frequently visited by people who attribute miraculous healings to his intercession. He is known as the patron saint of drug traffickers, especially in the northern region of Mexico.

Teresa Urrea, also known as Teresita or La Santa de Cabora, was born in the state of Sinaloa, an area then densely populated by Mexican Indians, during the rule of Mexican dictator Porfirio Díaz. Protesting the dictatorial mistreatment of Indians by President Díaz and fearing political persecution, her family had to flee Mexico, and they crossed the border in June 1892 into Nogales, Arizona. Her arrival in the United States attracted a great deal of public attention. Risking deportation, her family unsuccessfully applied for citizenship in Tucson. Teresita earned a reputation as a healer and traveled extensively to other

U.S. states, including California and Illinois. She earned a reputation as a strong political advocate for the rights of Indians in Mexico. She died in Clifton, Arizona.

Doroteo Arango, or Pancho Villa, was born in the Rancho de la Coyotada in Durango. About the age of 16, Doroteo became a bandit and later got involved in the Mexican Revolution. He earned a reputation as a brave revolutionary, and many considered him a friend of the poor and an enemy of the wealthy and powerful. During his life he also gained fame as a great general and fearless warrior. One of the most celebrated events of his life is a military raid he led across the border into Columbus, New Mexico, on March 9, 1916. The United States ordered a punitive expedition into Mexico for his capture, and he became an instant hero of the Mexican people. He was assassinated on July 20, 1923, by a group of political enemies. His tomb and shrine are located in the city of Parral, Chihuahua, where one can find numerous petitions on scraps of paper. In his lifetime as a popular revolutionary, he was vilified by his enemies for being a ruthless criminal; as a folk saint, he is now venerated by his devotees for being a compassionate intercessor.

José Fidencio Constantino Síntora, or Niño Fidencio, was born in Iramuco, Guanajuato. His mother died when he was young, and he was considered by his followers to have been an orphan left to care for himself from a very early age. At five or six years of age, he was living alone in a shack caring for a younger brother when he apparently had an apparition of Jesus Christ who gave him a book that included many cures and recipes to be made from plants and herbs. At the age of 13, he moved to the family hacienda at Espinazo, Nuevo León, where he stayed until his death. He started using herbal remedies and became a famous curandero. The peak of his notoriety as a healer was in the late 1920s and early 1930s when even the Mexican president, Plutarco Elías Calles, came to see him for healing. His shrine at Espinazo attracts thousands of devotees every year.

Juan Castillo Morales, or Juan Soldado, was originally from Ixtaltepec, Oaxaca. He moved to the border city of Tijuana with his family at an early age. On February 13, 1938, while he was a military recruit at the local garrison, he was implicated in the rape and death of an eight-year-old girl named Olga Consuelo Camacho Martínez. He was arrested and shot by the police without a trial. He immediately became a cause célèbre. People reported having visions at the site of his death and erected a shrine at his grave. This has become a place of miraculous healing for devotees. He is considered the patron of border crossers or people who attempt to cross the U.S.-Mexican border without legal documents.

Saint Toribio Romo González was born in Jalisco and was ordained a priest. He was shot to death by federal soldiers during the bloody, anticlerical Cristero War. He was laid to rest in the town of Santa Ana de Guadalupe, which has become one of the fastest growing religious shrines in the country. Many immigrants visit his shrine to thank Saint Toribio for miracles performed on their journey to the United States. He has been called the Patron Saint of Immigrants.

Fernando A. Ortiz

References and Further Reading

Griffith, James S. *Folk Saints of the Borderlands: Victims, Bandits and Healers* (Tucson, AZ: Rio Nuevo, 2003).

Griffith, James S. *Saints of the Southwest* (Tucson, AZ: Rio Nuevo, 2000).

Macklin, Barbara J., and Ross Crumrine. "Three North Mexican Folk Saint Movements." *Comparative Studies in Society and History* 15 (1973): 89–105.

Octavec, Eileen. *Answered Prayers. Miracles and Milagros along the Border* (Tucson: University of Arizona Press, 1995).

Ortiz, Fernando A., and Kenneth G. Davis. "Latino/a Folk Saints and Marian Devotions: Indigenous Alternative Healing Practices." *Mestizo Indigenous Healing Practices: A Handbook*, ed. J. Velasquez and Brian M. McNeill (New York: Routledge Publishers, Inc., 2008).

BORDERLANDS

"Borderlands religions" refers to the varied religious traditions ranging from the preconquest indigenous practices to Catholicism imposed by the Spaniards in the sixteenth century, resulting in the mixture, or mestizaje, of religious expression found at the beginning of the nineteenth century when Mexico got its independence from Spain. When the northern half of Mexico became part of the United States, there was yet another set of religious practices imported by Protestant Euro-American immigrants to the newly acquired Southwest. "Borderlands religions" exists as its own category (rather than, say, Mexican religions or southwestern religions)—a result of at least two sets of conditions: first, sociopolitical and historical realities of the border region; and second, philosophical, theoretical, and theological frameworks that emerge from and through those realities. The borderlands are where two or more worlds come together and forge oppressive, violent, and divisive relationships between those who are defined as "us/insiders" versus "them/outsiders." But borderlands are also a place where intense creativity, fluidity, and empowerment can flourish. In other words, the conditions of the borderlands religions yield neither completely negative nor completely positive results but, rather, a combination of both. Borderlands religions reflect the complex historical, political, economic, and cultural relations of power. Moreover, borderlands religions include traditions ranging from Roman Catholicism, pre-Columbian indigenous practices, mainline Protestant, Pentecostal, Mormon, as well as variations of the above.

The peculiar historical experiences take place in, near, and around the geographic national marker known as the U.S.-Mexican border established with the signing of the Treaty of Guadalupe Hidalgo ending the U.S.-Mexican War in 1848. The border dividing the United States from Mexico serves as a reminder of Mexico's loss of over half of its national territory to the United States. Those who remained on the north side of the border would grapple with issues of national, ethnic, cultural, political, and religious identity that continue to inform their experiences. Those who found themselves south of the Mexican border would be forever inextricably tied to the United States, either by intimate familial bonds or through the political, social, and economic relationship between the two nations. Both religious and nonreligious experiences comprise borderlands characteristics. Results of

---

TREATY OF GUADALUPE HIDALGO

Signed on February 2, 1848, the Treaty of Guadalupe Hidalgo officially ended the Mexican-American War of 1846–1848. It is named after a city located north of Mexico City where President Antonio López de Santa Anna and his government took refuge during the military campaigns of September 1847 when U.S. forces captured their capital. Mexico ceded 55 percent of its territory to the United States, including modern-day Arizona, California, Colorado, New Mexico, Nevada, Texas, Utah, and Wyoming. Although managing people and resources across these vast northern territories was difficult for Mexico's government, later generations criticized the treaty's terms as unfair and detrimental to Mexico's future economic development. The United States paid Mexico $15 million in compensation for war damages. The American negotiators further agreed to protect the property and civil rights of Mexican nationals living within the boundaries of lands ceded to the United States in the treaty, a promise later ignored as land and property disputes swept across the American Southwest. Mexico's loss of ancestral farming and grazing lands had a profound impact upon Hispanic American religious cultures throughout the southwestern U.S., *Hispano-Mexican* communities that fought for independence from Spain and then after the Mexican-American War had to live as foreigners in their ancestral lands.

—AH

---

the war included dispossession of Mexican Americans' land rights, discrimination through legal means such as English language–only forms of communication, and extralegal and vigilante law enforcement. Lynchings of Mexicans (men and women) were not uncommon for actions that threatened the unquestionable power of the White world. Due process and other rights were consistently denied to Mexicans under U.S. control. Imbalance of political and social power between Euro-Americans and Mexicans was virtually always in favor of Euro-Americans, with the few exceptions of Mexican Americans with enough wealth to negotiate for limited power and rights. Since violence is, and has been, part of the daily experience for most Mexicans around the borderlands, it is important to understand the roots of the clashing of worlds and cultures: the conquest of Mexico by Spain.

The tumultuous history of the borderlands does not begin and end with U.S.-Mexican relations, however. The first of the historical world clashes took place when the heterogeneous, multilingual, multiethnic populations of Mesoamerica came into contact with Hernán Cortez in 1512. Since the Spaniards' arrival to the Americas, there has been a constant negotiation between seemingly incompatible religious practices and worldviews, namely indigenous and European religious practices. One of the most important examples of the contact is epitomized by the apparition of La Virgen de Guadalupe in 1531 to the recently Christianized Nahuatl-speaking man, Juan Diego. In the midst of violent and bloody battles of conquest between the Conquistadores and the native peoples of Mesoamerica, Guadalupe appeared on the hill of Tepeyac, where, for centuries, indigenous peoples had made pilgrimages to honor Tonatzin/Coatlicue, the feminine goddesses of the Mexica-Aztec pantheon.

To some, her appearance served as evidence of Christianity taking hold in the Americas. Yet to others, she served as a symbol of the vanquishing of pre-Colombian religious practices. Yet, typical of borderlands religions, Guadalupe served neither as the complete end of Mexica practices nor as the total takeover by Spanish Christianity. She served as a bridge between two worlds. The fact that indigenous communities bonded with her could signify that they accepted the newly imposed faith and gave up their old ways deemed diabolical and worthy of punishment. Or, they may have accepted her only on the surface to remain safe from punishment, all the while worshipping their own deities in their hearts and minds.

Situated within borderlands religions, though, Guadalupe has become a symbol of what is commonly referred to as syncretism, or mestizaje. Syncretism is used to describe the coming together of two distinct religious systems to form a new hybrid, or mixed religiosity. Typically, syncretism is the result of a colonial relationship between a powerful, Christian European tradition and a subjugated population of indigenous peoples. Equally typical is that the religion of the colonizing nation or culture becomes the more commonly practiced at the expense of that of the colonized, or conquered. In other words, the European Christianity is imposed and ultimately defined as superior to any indigenous traditions. Because of this imbalance of power, some scholars have begun to use the term "nepantla" instead of "syncretism" to describe religiosity in the borderlands.

The term "nepantla" comes from the Nahuatl language meaning "in the middle, or the middle place." Leading scholar of Mesoamerica Miguel Leon-Portilla interprets nepantla as a place of confusion and ambiguity brought on by the violence and chaos of conquest. Chicana scholar Lara Medina suggests that nepantla presumes agency, not confusion. Moreover, there is, according to Medina, "[a] duality within nepantla, a transparent side where there is clarity and self-determination, and a shadow side, where diversity confuses and creates disorientation"; in addition, "nepantla is a multifaceted psychic spiritual space composed of complementary opposites: obscurity and clarity" (2006, 253–254). By going beyond the understanding of nepantla as merely "torn between ways" into a place of "in-betweenness," it becomes a place from which peoples and communities can reconcile fundamentally conflicting cosmologies and epistemologies through spirituality.

The continuing importance of La Virgen de Guadalupe reflects the phenomenon of nepantla that began with the conquest of Mexico by the Spaniards. Daily devotion to the symbol is a reminder of the adaptability and flexibility of a people under centuries of oppression and power negotiations. Nepantla spirituality has continued to inform the beliefs, practices, and survival strategies in the borderlands through today. The appearance of La Virgen and the initial experiences of nepantla occurred during the colonial period in Mexican history. These events, nevertheless, inform the next major sociopolitical event: the U.S.-Mexican War and cessation of the Southwest.

At least a decade prior to the signing of the Treaty of Guadalupe Hidalgo, the United States was expanding its national boundaries in all directions. The doctrine of Manifest Destiny provided the social, political, economic, and religious justification for U.S. expansion. Manifest Destiny was the belief that God had granted the United States superior capacity to control the land, its natural resources, and those who resided in it. After the initial choque (crash, clash) of the U.S.-Mexican War established the physical border, a series of other borders were established as well. The division between Euro-American Protestants and Mexican Catholics, commonly referred to as "Romanists," was perhaps one of the most formative divisions between 1848 and 1940.

There was a steady influx of Methodist, Baptist, and Presbyterian missionaries who viewed the region as lost in the old ways of Mexico and who were in need of the enlightened, rational, "true" Word of God through the Bible and through education. For some Mexicans in the border region, their Catholic parishes provided a safe haven or protection from the predominantly Euro-American and English-speaking world into which they had just been thrown. Spanish-speaking Catholics found their faith communities to be the last refuge in which there was a sense of common culture remaining intact after the United States took over their land.

For others, however, the Protestant missionaries brought a new source of spirituality that was unfulfilled by the Catholic community. Conversion stories focused on the spiritual, God had called them to leave the Catholic Church and join the Protestant mission. Others were exposed to the new faith through institutions established by the mainline denominations in the region. In New Mexico, for example, very few Hispanos had access to even the most basic educational opportunities. The Catholic Church, when it did provide education, charged exorbitant fees that only the most affluent of society could afford. Many Mexicans who desired to be acknowledged and treated as citizens took advantage of the opportunities presented to them despite the risk of losing "traditions" of Mexican and Catholic culture. Methodists Thomas and Emily Harwood established schools for boys and girls in New Mexico. The Presbyterian Menaul School is still in operation today in Albuquerque.

Settlement houses along the U.S.-Mexico border were established to take in recent migrants who needed health care or English language classes. Many of these institutions were also centers in which Americanization programs were taught. Part of the mission of the Protestant work was to instill distinctively American values and habits in conjunction with the religious component. Many Mexicans who relied on the services of the missionaries became deeply committed to the newly imported religious practices and continue to work in and with their Protestant congregations today.

Certain parallels can be drawn between the Spaniards' imposition of Catholicism on indigenous peoples in Mesoamerica. Certainly, the relations between Spaniards and Native peoples were shaped by violence, subjugation, and the forced conversion to Christianity. However, what has emerged from that initial contact is a dynamic and fluid religiosity. Of course, most historians would say it is debatable whether Euro-Americans were as brutal as the

Spaniards in their treatment of the conquered population and in their views on the necessity of religious conversion. Definitely, the tactics and strategies were different for Mexican Americans, but the ultimate need for the assertion of power is what drove both Spaniards and Euro-Americans.

In the case of the missionary attitudes toward Mexicans in the newly formed Southwest, that assertion of power was identifying and negating the beliefs of the conquered community. U.S. discourse made certain to narrowly define categories that oppose each other, called binary or dichotomous categories. These binaries set up rigid boundaries between categories such as Black-White; male-female; Catholic-Protestant; and citizen-foreigner. Americanization programs along with Protestant sponsored institutions created divisions between themselves as White Anglo-Saxon Protestants believed their mission was to make Mexicans in their own image. Mexicans were assumed to be Catholic and therefore superstitious as well as under the spell of local Catholic priests. So the conversion was not forced by sword, but by converting to Protestantism; Mexicans would ultimately be choosing the superior, more heavenly religious tradition.

Theoretical Foundations

A main argument of borderlands theory is that systems of meaning are not closed or fixed but, by nature of existing in the borderlands, are shifting. The physical location of the U.S.-Mexico border informs the theoretical and theological understandings of borderlands. One important contribution by borderlands theory has been its invocation of the border as metaphor. Borderlands theories

take into account that nobody can be completely one thing or the other, but are inherently variations of the two. Especially in terms of religious practices, there has been a blending of traditions for over 500 years; La Virgen symbolizes both European Christianity and indigenous respect for feminine deities. Then again, when the U.S.-Mexican contact takes place, Mexicans who converted to the quintessentially Euro-American Protestantism held on to language and culture and adapted the new tradition to their own context. Neither group transformed completely, but transformed and coalesced based on their own community's needs. They were somewhere in between Catholic Mexican and Euro-American, between citizen and foreigner. By looking to the spaces between the categories listed above, borderlands theory provides both a method and a theoretical framework that can potentially decolonize the epistemologies and cosmologies that have undergone silencing and repression under various structures of domination.

A borderland is the "emotional residue" caused by an unnatural boundary that defines what is "us" and "them." The border, according to novelist and scholar Gloria Anzaldúa, is "una herida abierta," where the "third world grates up against the first and bleeds." Anzaldúa's work has nevertheless been groundbreaking and invaluable for the theorizing of issues of identity in terms of class, race, gender, sexuality, nationalism, and religion. In *Borderlands/La Frontera: The New Mestiza*, the reader is confronted with the physical dimensions of life in the geographical space of the U.S.-Mexico border as well as the psychological, emotional, spiritual, and sexual borderlands that emerge as a result of the border. Borderlands theories destabilize binary categories such as Mexican-American, Black-White, queer-straight, male-female, sacred-profane, and history-myth. Scholars such as Anzaldúa and Chela Sandoval make use of their own experiences of discrimination, marginalization, sexism, homophobia, racism, and classism to develop theories and produce works of art and poetry. This method pushes the reader to interrogate the ways in which the divisions have caused harm.

Borderlands theory gets deployed in disciplines outside of theology and religion as well. Particularly, the field of Chicano/a studies has been developed by rereading history or, rather, redefining historiographic methodology that has relied on primary documents to tell the "truth" of what happened in the past. Borderlands theory disrupts the notion of a unilinear concept of time, and instead offers readings and interpretations of historical actors in cyclical and relational methods. Borderlands theorist and historian Emma Perez argues that the "decolonial imaginary" can help to disrupt the nationalist historiography of Chicano history by unearthing the ways in which history has been written on the body of Chicanas. The relegation of Chicana stories to the backdrop of men's lives is not only due to racism of Euro-American historical method, but also due to the inability of some Chicano scholars to acknowledge the simultaneity of oppressions, borderlands of experience that shape Chicana lives.

Scholar Luis León's discussion of the "religious poetics" in the borderlands as being informed by and informing nepantla spirituality is important in highlighting the role of borderlands theory in terms of religious studies. By arguing that culture is religious, not that religion is cultural, León's framing of the practices found in the Victory Outreach communities in Los Angeles, and the performance art of El Vez, points to the varied ways in which religion and culture intersect and operate in borderlands. Borderlands religions in the Latino/a community are a dynamic, fluid, and adaptable set of practices. Their symbols and meanings change over time, depending on the circumstances in which those communities live, pray, eat, and die. The ancestors took what they could use and strategized for survival in a world of violence, oppression, and chaos; they transformed it into something beautiful and a source of strength. Latina/os will continue to do so because we all live in the borderlands.

Adriana Pilar Nieto

References and Further Reading

Anzaldúa, Gloria. *Borderlands/La Frontera: the New Mestiza* (San Francisco: Aunt Lute Books, 1987).

Barton, Paul. *Hispanic Methodists, Presbyterians, and Baptists in Texas* (Austin: University of Texas Press, 2006).

De La Torre, Miguel A. "Living on the Borders," *The Ecumenical Review* 59, no. 2–3 (April/July 2007): 214–220.

Elizondo, Virgilio. *Galilean Journey: The Mexican American Promise* (New York: Orbis, 1983, 2000).

León, Luis D. *La Llorona's Children: Religion, Life, and Death in the U.S.-Mexico Borderlands* (Berkeley: University of California Press, 2004).

Leon-Portilla, Miguel. *Aztec Thought and Culture: A Study of the Ancient Nahuatl Mind*, trans. Jack Emory Davis (Norman: University of Oklahoma Press, 1971).

Medina, Lara. "Nepantla Spirituality: Negotiating Multiple Religious Identities among U.S. Latanas." *Rethinking Latino (a) Religion and Identity*, ed. Miguel A. De La Torre and Gastón Espinosa (Cleveland: Pilgrim Press, 2006).

Sandoval, Chela. *Methodology of the Oppressed* (Minneapolis: University of Minnesota Press, 2000).

BUDDHISM

Buddhism within Latino/a communities stems from the cross-fertilization between Hispanic and Buddhist cultures, principally due to three modes of transmission: import, export, or baggage. These modes, conceptualized by U.S. Buddhist scholar Jan Nattier, illustrate the varying movements between Buddhist communities and the U.S. culture. The term "Buddhism" is a Western construction used to describe the teachings and practices derived from the life experience of a man born Siddhartha Gautama in the fifth century BCE. His keen observations and rigorous reflections brought him the distinction of becoming "Awake" or "The Enlightened One" (Buddha), claiming complete awareness of reality and truth.

Buddhism does not have a centralized system to promulgate and safeguard its teachings, nor does it have a strong sense of orthodoxy. Rather, as the Buddha instructed his disciples in his final moments to "Be your own lamps," stress is placed on the individual quest for truth. Subsequent to the Buddha's life, various communities and traditions have developed, stressing particular aspects from his life. Through the immigration of peoples and cross-cultural marriage, particularly among Austronesian, European, and American cultures beginning in the sixteenth century, Hispanic Asian cultures developed. Hispanic Buddhist

communities developed from these influences, and some individuals within contemporary Latino/a communities have practiced Buddhist philosophy and meditation techniques, particularly to manage their own experiences of suffering and marginalization.

Development of Hispanic American Buddhist Cultures

The development of Buddhism within the context of the United States includes the conflagration of various cultures, in this case Asian cultures with European and indigenous Mesoamerican cultures. Chinese and Japanese peoples were attracted to the California Gold Rush of 1849 and soon began to settle and develop their own religious communities by bringing their religious practice with them and beginning to root it in American soil. This mode of transmission represents the "baggage" manner through which Buddhism became part of U.S. culture. By the beginning of the twentieth century, hundreds of Buddhist centers were established along the western coast of the United States.

A second manner through which Buddhism developed in the United States is characterized as the "import" mode, exemplified in two ways. First, in 1893, Theravada Buddhist teachers accepted the invitation of organizers of Chicago's Parliament of World's Religions (held concurrently with the World Columbian Exposition to celebrate the United States' technological expertise in the modern world). Both organizers and participants were impressed with the presentation of Buddhism by the Theravada monks, who articulated a practice of peace, justice, and morality within a doctrine of "absence," wherein impermanence characterized all of reality, even to notions of the individual self and the divine. Through this invitation and reception by U.S. citizens of Theravada Buddhist teachings, the U.S. scholarly community entered into dialogue with Buddhist philosophical concepts.

Second, even earlier in the nineteenth century, New England intellectuals discussed the meaning of Asian religious scriptures, including Buddhist texts, and brought Buddhist thought into U.S. intellectual culture, although this was certainly separate from any practice within exclusively Buddhist communities. Both of these instances exemplify Buddhist teaching and practice being invited by interested U.S. parties, "imported" for consumption through either practice or incorporation into intellectual systems—philosophical or political—by academics. The third mode of transmission is exemplified by Nichiren Buddhists, who promulgate a type of Buddhism begun in the thirteenth century and stress practice and study, including sharing of their understandings with others. However, the "export" nature of this Buddhism is disputed among scholars, particularly the degree of this tradition's "evangelical" practice.

Particular American Hispanic Buddhist Communities

Although less than 1 percent of all American Hispanics are Buddhist, Latina/o Buddhists are developing a presence in the United States that engages their Buddhist practice with their experience of suffering and marginalization. A number of Hispanic American Buddhists participate in society while striving to heal the scars that such marginalization inflicts, managing their mestizo Catholic/Christian origins with their Buddhist practice, and finding an organic partnership between the two traditions with little contradiction.

The Shambhala Meditation Center of San Antonio, Texas, began in 1992 through the efforts of interested adherents, led by Elisa Gonzalez. This center has the distinction throughout its history of being led by women directors, with several American Hispanic teachers making efforts to teach this tradition of Buddhism to all economic groups in Spanish and English. A Spanish-speaking Vajrayana study group is presently in existence on the Westside of San Antonio, one of the least economically advantaged of all urban areas in the United States.

Raised as a Catholic in San Antonio, Elisa Gonzalez was drawn to raising religious and philosophical questions about reality and meaning. She became interested in the Buddhist tradition because of its encouragement of such questions, a quality she did not find within her practice of Catholicism. Although she found Catholicism to emphasize compassion and service, qualities that she would find resonating with Buddhism as well, her experience of the Catholic tradition discouraged the questioning of its doctrine and tradition. Upon returning from the University of the Americas in Mexico City, she moved to Seattle for work considerations and there began what was to be a 20-year study and exploration period of Buddhism. She was exposed to a variety of teachers, most of whom were from the Western/U.S. culture. There she endeavored to be instructed by an Asian teacher, immersed in the Buddhist culture and sensibilities. Her quest led her to various Vajradhatus and Dharmadhatus (meditation centers), and finally to Chögyam Trungpa Rinpoche, a Buddhist instructor and founder of Shambhala Buddhism. This type of Buddhism had been in development over several years by Trungpa as an effort to make this Buddhist tradition accessible to secular Western students. Elisa Gonzalez entered a three-month training program, equivalent to seminary training in Christian traditions, and returned to San Antonio to offer training.

San Antonio proved to be ripe for Buddhist development, as interested study groups began to rise oriented toward a variety of traditions—Theravada, Vajrayana, Tibetan, and Zen Buddhism. Many of these native San Antonians had Christian foundations and understood themselves to be religious individuals. The particular dimension of their religious sensibilities stressed the questioning aspects of their tradition, the impetus to think creatively and question presuppositions and teachings. This sensibility was not encouraged in their experience of Christianity; instead, heavy reliance on doctrine as expressed through their schooling and faith practice discouraged questioning. These religious seekers began to find in Buddhism not only an appreciation for religious questions, but a rigorous standard for seeing reality clearly, without reliance on simplistic answers or appeal to divine mystery.

These seekers, American Hispanics among them, found within Buddhism a concerted effort to localize ultimate meaning and truth within the individual, and to laden on this individual responsibility for discerning reality within her/his particular situation. This self-responsibility refrained from understanding or experiencing the self as victimized. Instead, Buddhist practitioners accepted the reality of their situation and endeavored to put their awareness into practice. Change is possible in the present moment, particularly if that moment is perceived as painful, by coming to a fuller awareness of the entire situation that is the cause of such pain and suffering. Through the Buddhist perspective, the search for external happiness is not realistic, a search that is itself fraught with pain and anguish. In the particular teaching from the Rinpoche, Elisa Gonzalez understood suffering as the result of confusion stemming from the "Three Poisons": Ignorance, Passion, and Aggression.

Through the efforts and development of the San Antonio Meditation Center, it was recognized by Sakyong Mipham Rinpoche (firstborn son of Chögyam Trungpa Rinpoche who had died in 1987) as a Shambhala Center in 1992, based upon teachings of personal enlightenment and societal transformation. A number of lay teachers have developed to the point that they serve as missionaries to South American countries, using their language and cultural skills to develop lay Tibetan Buddhist communities in Chile and Argentina.

Because of the diversity among American Hispanics, there is no one model of the American Buddhist experience. This diversity cuts across race, ethnicity, cultural, and economic classifications, including those who embrace the experience of marginalization with the larger American culture and articulate meaning from this place of isolation and pain. It includes those who are not sensitive to this experience, but rather consider their ethnic and cultural heritages complementary, without pain and conflict.

José Luis Reissig grew up in Buenos Aires, Argentina, and associated with like-minded young political dissidents, critical of his country's governmental policies. He was incarcerated periodically, during which time he experienced pain as many of his associates were tortured by the government. His disgust of oppressive military regimes grew more acute. He came to the United States at the age of 19 for study, became aware of Buddhist principles, and subsequently received Buddhist training in England by an English teacher. Through Buddhist dharma, José came to understand that the world cannot realistically be divided into two classes—those with and those without power—and also that such considerations do not remove individuals from political responsibility. In this Mahayana Buddhist tradition, the concept of *karuna* (compassion) is developed by practicing a type of compassion foreign to many Judeo-Christian cultures and political analysis. That is, compassion shared toward another is actually compassion extended to one's self, indeed, the entire world, as all share the same reality in the ever-changing cosmos. *Karuna* is the practice of an awareness of an interrelatedness of all reality, not an awareness of a constant struggle between two opposing realities. Instead, compassion is shown toward all who have the capacity for pain.

Because of the proximity of Mexico and Latin America to the United States, a significant amount of communication has occurred between the various political entities. Since the early 1970s, American Hispanics have imported Buddhist teaching from Mexico, and American Hispanics have exported their Buddhist tradition and practice to Mexican and Latin American communities.

Japanese Zen priest Ejo Takata Roshi instructed a group of young American Hispanic students inclined toward a broad range of spiritual traditions and practice. These instructions included meditation on death, a common practice in Zen Buddhism, calling to the individual's perception the impermanence of reality, particularly personal existence. This experience resonated with Latino/as through their own cultural traditions of death, its common presence and inevitability, and helped them conceptualize Buddhist notions of change and reality.

Other American Hispanic Buddhists have experienced the life of impoverished Tzeltal communities in Mexico and endeavored to consider impermanence within that context. These American Hispanic Buddhists found it difficult to reconcile the perceptions of their world outside of that community—comfortable, even excessive—with persistent poverty and oppression. In the comfortable, developed world, pain is indeed impermanent; in the oppressive political reality of many impoverished communities, pain has a permanence not experienced by many Latino/a adherents. In addition, the Hispanic experience of that community brought them to an encounter with a fullness and appreciation of life, even within that oppressive political state, that challenged their own experience of life, wherein there are numerous facile attachments, no real physical need or want, and so much unrest.

Nichiren Buddhism, another tradition that has found many Hispanic adherents, differentiates itself in many ways. Among these differentiations is the stress placed on recitation of a simple verse, individually and communally, as well as civic and political engagement. There is also an evangelical dimension with

Nichiren Buddhism, wherein adherents are called upon to practice some degree of recruitment of new members by attending Nichiren Buddhist centers and events. A number of small Nichiren Buddhist groups have developed among Hispanics; among the most prominent is Puerto Rican musician Nestor Torres.

Oswald John Nira

References and Further Reading

Baldoquín, Hilda Gutiérrez, ed. *Dharma, Color, and Culture: New Voices in Western Buddhism* (Berkeley, CA: Parallax Press, 2004).

Eck, Diana. *A New Religious America: How a "Christian Country" Has Become the World's Most Religiously Diverse Nation* (New York: HarperSanFrancisco, 2002).

Hanh, Thich Nhat. *The Heart of Buddha's Teaching* (New York: Broadway Books, 1999).

Reissig, José. "CEMVE: Círculo para la Enzenañza de Meditación Vipassana en Español: An Association to Promote the Teaching of Vipassana in Spanish-Speaking Communities." *Turning Wheel: The Journal of Socially Engaged Buddhism* (Summer 2001).

Zubizarreta, Rosa. "El Latinismo y sus Bellos Colores: Voices of Latina and Latino Buddhists." *Turning Wheel: The Journal of Socially Engaged Buddhism* (Summer 2001).

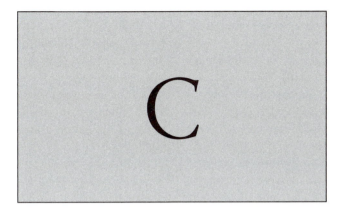

CATHOLIC CHARISMATIC MOVEMENT

The Catholic Charismatic movement is a transparish and transnational Catholic lay movement where the people believe in the practice of the spiritual gifts listed in Romans 12, Ephesians 4, and I Corinthians 12 and 14. These spiritual gifts (charismata) include pastoring, evangelism, exhortation, giving, leadership, mercy, service, teaching, administration, discernment, faith, healing, helps, knowledge, and others. Catholic Charismatics stress having a personal conversion experience with Jesus Christ as their savior and lord, adhering to the spiritual disciplines, and practicing the spiritual gifts. They believe that the purpose of the spiritual gifts is to build up and edify the Church. For this reason, they are often very involved in lay ministry in the parish, help lead worship and prayer groups, and often assist the priests in other aspects of lay spiritual formation.

Latino/a Catholic Charismatics differ from classical Pentecostals in three respects. First, they do not believe that speaking in tongues is the initial, physical evidence of the baptism with the Holy Spirit—also called the Initial Evidence Theory, a view held by the Assemblies of God and other classical Pentecostal denominations. Second, they see themselves in the vanguard of Catholic evangelization and renewal rather than as a Trojan horse for Pentecostalism—a charge that has been leveled at them in the past. They are first and foremost Catholics, who also believe in the practice of the spiritual gifts. Many midweek services are officiated by the parish priest. In many respects, the Catholic Charismatic movement has served as a bulwark against the growth of the Latina/o Protestant Pentecostal movement. And third, their movement tends to be lay driven and led by women. It is a place where women can exercise lay leadership roles in the church and in society through their outreach programs to the community.

The exact origins of the U.S. Latino/a Catholic Charismatic movement are uncertain. The four primary sources appear to be the following: (1) the U.S. Catholic Charismatic Renewal (CCR) in the 1960s; (2) the Catholic Charismatic movement in Columbia and Latin America as early as 1967; (3) Glenn and Marilynn Kramar and their Charisma in Missions movement begun in California in 1972; and (4) Latina/o Catholics who became Pentecostal and eventually returned to Catholicism, but remained Pentecostal in theology and orientation. One of the primary catalysts in the development of the U.S. Latino Catholic Charismatic movement is Marilynn Kramar and the movement she founded called Charisma in Missions.

Charisma in Missions is a Catholic Charismatic missionary and evangelization society founded by Marilynn Kramar (1939–) in Los Angeles. A former Assemblies of God missionary-evangelist to Columbia from 1967 to 1972, Kramar converted to Roman Catholicism in 1972 in the wake of Vatican II and a greater openness to the gifts of the Holy Spirit as a result of the Catholic Charismatic Renewal. She was licensed as an Assemblies of God missionary-evangelist. She and her husband served as the last non-national superintendents of the Assemblies of God work in Columbia from 1967 to 1970. They returned to California in 1972, where they decided to convert to the Roman Catholic Church. That same year, at the urging to Cardinal Timothy Manning of Los Angeles, Marilynn and Glenn Kramar founded Charisma in Missions, a Catholic international lay-missionary evangelization society. Glenn

eventually left the movement and Marilynn assumed leadership. Many women and men, especially Esther Garzón, assisted her.

Although international in scope, the three primary goals of Charisma in Missions are to reach alienated Latino/a Catholics, to train evangelizers to work in the Spanish-speaking community, and to bring about "spiritual renewal" and "reformation" within the Catholic Church. Kramar stated that the Bible and Vatican II "outlined our mission in the church—to rattle new life into dry bones within the household of God. . . . Our job was to evangelize baptized Catholics who either didn't fully understand or were not actively involved in the life of faith." In 1975, she began leading the International Latin Encounter for Renewal and Evangelization, better known as the Latin Encounter (Encuentro Latino). The annual Encuentro Latino has grown in attendance from 600 in 1975 to an estimated 20,000 in 2003. They have a mailing list of 70,000 Latinos throughout the United States, Mexico, and Latin America. They sponsor Youth Encounters, rallies, and faith campaigns, and a missionary institute of proclaimers (school of evangelism), spiritual growth seminars, women's ministries, and children's ministries. At their headquarters in the Los Angeles area, they run various programs and events through venues like CharisBooks, CharisTapes, CharisMedia, and CharisPublications. They also sponsor a television program. They have generated over 2 million cassette tapes related to their ministry.

Their international headquarters is named the Porciuncula (after St. Francis) and was founded in 1982 with the pastoral blessing of Cardinal Timothy

---

CURSILLO

The Cursillo de Cristiandad is a weekend experience meant to evangelize individuals through an affective encounter with Jesus Christ, self, and neighbor. It began in 1944 as a week-long course held by the Catholic Action movement. This short course, or Cursillo in Spanish, was used to prepare lay leaders for pilgrimages to the Shrine of Santiago (St. James) at Compostela, Spain. Now it is used to assist people with the pilgrimage of life. At the age of 26, Eduardo Bonnín and a few friends turned the Cursillo for pilgrim leaders into a weekend experience that sought a profound conversion in the cotidiano (day-to-day life) of its participants. The experience soon became a movement of apostolic action and spread to Latin America and then to over 60 nations. The Cursillo is not meant to be either a course or a retreat; rather it is an "Encounter" with the mysteries of the kerygma (core of the Gospel) through a renewal of the sacraments of Christian initiation: Baptism, Confirmation, and Eucharist. To ensure that this conversion would continue to develop and mature, participants are encouraged to join small communities based on the three pillars of Christian life: prayer, study, and action.

—GCG

Manning. Between 2,000 and 3,000 people attend services, programs, workshops, and events every week. Like their Pentecostal brethren, they believe in the practice of the spiritual gifts listed in I Corinthians 12 and 14, such as healing, performing miracles, pastoring, evangelizing, serving, performing works, speaking in tongues, interpreting tongues, prophesying, and helping. They also emphasize personal conversion and spiritual renewal with Jesus Christ, divine healing, and community empowerment and renewal. Despite their emphasis on conversion and the spiritual gifts, they are staunchly Catholic and see themselves in the vanguard of Catholic spiritual renewal. They hold tremendous reverence and respect for Our Lady of Guadalupe and the Virgin Mary in general. They often refer to their meetings as prayer services because prayer is central to the movement. The movement is lay-driven. Their prayer services are often led by women and attended by younger adults. Their emphasis on enthusiastic worship and music services has contributed to a renewal of Sunday and weekly masses as many members of the movement often serve the priest in other capacities in the parish.

Charisma in Missions has been a major catalyst in spreading the Pentecostal/Charismatic movement and spirituality among Latino/a Catholics in the United States, Mexico, and throughout Latin America. They have been joined in their work by other Latino priests and leaders like Emmy Canales and Noel Diaz of *El Sembrador*, Horacio Trujillo of Arizona, and others have also had a tremendous impact on the U.S. Latina/o Catholic Charismatic community.

The movement has witnessed phenomenal growth. The Hispanic Churches in American Public Life national survey, directed by Father Virgilio Elizondo, Jesse Miranda, Gastón Espinosa, and Harry Pachon of the Tomás Rivera Policy Institute along with several other Pew

Charitable Trusts, found that over 22 percent of all Latinos (10.1 million in 2008) in the United States self-identified as Catholic Charismatic. In Bishop Gerald R. Barnes's *Hispanic Ministry at the Turn of the Millennium: A Report of the Bishop's Committee on Hispanic Affairs*, they reported that the Charismatic movement was active in 36 percent of all Hispanic-serving parishes, thus making it more common than either the Cursillo (31 percent) or Christian Base Communities (13 percent).

Gastón Espinosa

References and Further Reading

Espinosa, Gastón. "The Pentecostalization of Latin American and U.S. Latino Christianity." *Pneuma: The Journal for the Society of Pentecostal Studies* 26, no. 2 (Fall 2004): 262–292.

Peterson, Anna, and Manuel Vasquez. "Upwards, Never Down": The Catholic Charismatic Renewal in Transnational Perspective." *Christianity, Social Change, and Globalization in the Americas*, ed. Anna L. Peterson, Manuel A. Vasquez, and Philip J. Williams (Piscataway, NJ: Rutgers University Press, 2001).

Synan, Vinson. *The Holiness-Pentecostal Tradition: Charismatic Movements in the Twentieth Century* (Grand Rapids, MI: Eerdmans Publishing Company, 1997).

CATHOLICISM

The expression "Latino/a Catholicism" refers to a vast and diverse tradition within the Catholic Church in the United States, with evident roots and plentiful parallels in Latin America. Most demographic projections state that by 2035 Latino/as will be at least half of all Catholics in the United States. They already are, when added to their Latin American counterparts, the largest cultural group within the world's entire Catholic population. Latino/a Catholicism, however, is quite different from European and European-American Catholicism.

Clarifying What Is Understood by "Latino/a Catholicism"

Latina/o Catholics generally share in a tradition of Catholic Christianity that assumes the following: (1) the normative centrality of the Bible; (2) the acceptance of the doctrinal definitions of the ecumenical councils; (3) the apostolic succession of bishops; (4) the preeminent role of the liturgy and sacraments; and (5) the indispensable hermeneutic and sacramental role of the Church. Nevertheless, there is no doubt that the most frequent religious universe among U.S. Latino/as is "popular Catholicism." This is the case among all of the different cultural communities (Mexican and Mexican American, Puerto Rican, Cuban American, etc.). Certainly, many Latino/as participate in the "official" tradition, but both numerically and culturally the symbolic universe of the popular version of the religion is by far the more widespread and commanding of the two. It can be argued that, first of all, popular Catholicism is the manner in and through which most Latino/as are Catholic; and second, that this popular Catholicism is a key matrix of all Latina/o cultures.

If forced to attempt a nearly impossible general description of such a diverse phenomenon as Latino/a popular Catholicism, we might say that it incorporates at least the following elements: (1) it focuses

Worshipers attend a service at the Cathedral of Our Lady of the Angels in Los Angeles. (David Butow/Corbis Saba)

and centers on Christ, and especially his humanness; (2) it has great admiration for and devotion to Mary (and secondarily the saints); (3) it is led by the laity (especially older women) and focuses on the faith and life issues of lay Catholics, with little interest in the concerns of the clergy; (4) it is family-centered (hence, not parish-centered or individualistic); (5) it is symbolic, affective, communal, and public in its expressions of faith and of the sacred; (6) it "performs" (rather than "explains") its beliefs and doctrines; (7) it greatly appreciates wisdom, and the role of the *sensus fidelium* (literally the "sense of the faithful" where the doctrines and church teachings are developed "from the ground up" with the faithful masses guided by the Holy Spirit); (8) it seems to mistrust authoritarian ("clericalized," or "institutionalized") approaches to Christianity; and (9) it distinguishes

communal solidarity and compassion (especially toward the poor) as the two most important Christian virtues and ethical demands. With significant consequences for the interpretation of Christianity, the socioculturally marginalized are by far the majority of Latina/o Catholics.

It seems that Latino/a Catholicism cannot be properly understood apart from its history. Its beliefs and practices did not develop only as a result of general inner- or intra-Catholic Christian events, but also shares in worldwide Christian history and basic doctrines. Latino/a Catholicism's shape and contents are especially the consequence of historical confrontations with the realities of conquest, annexation, marginalization, and religiocultural invasions.

This history encompasses the Christianity of what today is Spain, as it uniquely developed in the Iberian

Peninsula through the patristic and medieval periods. This earlier Christianity was brought to the Americas after 1492, preached to the natives and the slaves, and survived among the vast majority of people even after reforms of the Council of Trent.

Colonial Heritage

Spanish politics (e.g., the "royal patronage" over the Church, etc.) kept most of Trent's reforms away from most natives, slaves, *mulatos*, and *mestizos*. The legal prohibitions against non-White clergy furthered the distance between the reformed Catholicism of Trent (which has come to be identified with modern Roman Catholicism) and the people's Catholicism (which preceded Trent to the Americas, and which brought with it 1,500 years of earlier Christian tradition).

The religion taken to be "normative" Christianity, in the early colonial period, was Catholic Christianity in its medieval, Iberian, pre-Tridentine (pre–Council of Trent), village version. It was this religion that was reinterpreted by the native and slave populations (and later by mestizos and mulatos) in their attempt to make cultural and religious sense out of their conquest and vanquishment.

This "interpreted" Catholic Christianity was perceived, late in colonial times, to be in need of reevangelization. Mestizos and mulatos were by then fast becoming the majority of the population, and it was through and to them that the new catechetical efforts were channeled. This allowed for some elements of reevangelization to reach Amerindians and Blacks, but the latter groups' religion remained basically as it had been. Among Blacks and Amerindians, of course, some non-Christian traditional religions (or vestiges of these religions) survived and continue today.

The late colonial reevangelization mainly reached the mestizos (although by comparison fewer mulatos). This allowed mestizos to further interpret the new messages being presented through the prism of their inherited popular, medieval, pre-Tridentine, village Catholicism (which was still seen by them as normative). This latest reinterpretation slowly became the Catholic norm for the mixed-race majority. It was this religion, for all practical purposes, that was the only Catholicism acceptable by most people during the period of the (nineteenth century) independence movements.

A split can be clearly detected at the start of the nineteenth century, which has widened since. The "official" (Tridentine) Christianity of the bishops and of the social elites, presenting itself as the sole valid norm, was distinct from the "popular" Christianity (pre-Tridentine) of the vast majority of the population. This popular Christianity also claimed to be the valid norm, though it acknowledged the existence of what it called the "clerical" version.

By the time pro-independence movements broke out in the nineteenth century, the bearers of official Catholicism had become the main pillars of Spain's colonial rule (and therefore, inimical to the anticolonial forces). The other strand of Catholicism, the popular version that the ecclesiastical and social elites deplored, was the religion of the independentists (or at least openly allied with them).

It became commonplace to find the symbols of popular Catholicism used as gathering banners for the people against Spain. The people (and some of the local parish clergy) fighting Spain appealed to God, to the Virgin, to the faith, and to religious symbols of the majority in order to demonstrate that God was indeed on their side. After independence (or after the U.S. occupation in the case of Puerto Rico), what had been official colonial Catholicism soon identified itself with *criollo* elite interests, while most mestizos and mulatos (and also an increasing number of Amerindians and Blacks) still claimed popular religion as theirs. Therefore, even after Spain's defeat, the "dual-level" Catholicism of the late colonial period was preserved. And the link between the two versions of the religion was maintained due to the mestizos' and mulatos' gift for cultural reinterpretation. After some mestizos and mulatos finally entered the clergy and rose through its ranks, popular Catholicism began to receive partial acceptability from the postindependence ecclesiastical hierarchy. This belated acceptability, however, had its price.

During most of the postindependence period in Mexico, and during the colonial nineteenth century in Puerto Rico and in Cuba, the Church hierarchy started participating in some key rites of popular Catholicism. Whether the bishops (and other clergy) suspected these rites to be syncretic or superstitious did not seem as important as the fact that these rituals were "Catholic." They were a sacred, public link between the hierarchy and the people, recognized as such by all.

19th Century: Independence, Occupation, and Annexation

The maintenance of this sacred and public link became very important during the nineteenth century. The institutions of the Church came increasingly under attack by growing intellectual elite (criolla, mestiza, and mulata) that was influenced by the European currents of modern thought. The Enlightenment had arrived in the Americas with an anti-Church zeal. The ecclesiastical hierarchy, apparently sensing the danger, saw in popular Catholicism an ally and tool in the Church's defense strategy. The natives, slaves, mestizos, and mulatos, for centuries marginalized from the official institutions of Catholicism, were now courted and their version of Catholic Christianity blessed.

On the other hand, the intellectual elites—in typical nineteenth-century rationalist style—had no use for the Church and its economic and political power, and condemned popular Catholicism as obscurantist ignorance. They thought that popular religion prevented the people from achieving higher levels of educational and material development. Intellectuals of the nineteenth century, in Mexico and the Antilles, in their disdain for Church and ignorance, fomented a strategic alliance (necessarily clothed in "acceptable" theological and pastoral language) between the ecclesiastical hierarchy and the masses of people.

Nineteenth-century official and popular Catholicisms (plural!) confronted the same enemy in Mexico and the Antilles, and they joined forces. But by then the official brand of the religion was also imbued with the mentality of the post-Reformation and of the Enlightenment. It was only a matter of time before the rationalist intellectuals and the Church establishment would discover a sufficiently "reasonable" dialogue, and then turn their respective sights and disdain onto popular Catholicism.

The intellectual elites of the nineteenth century have—100 years later—

SAN FERNANDO CATHEDRAL

The San Fernando Cathedral is located in San Antonio, Texas, and is the oldest cathedral sanctuary continuously in use within what is now the continental United States. Established in 1731 as a local parish on the northern frontier of New Spain, San Fernando's predominantly Hispanic, working-class congregants have worshiped God in the same church sanctuary under the flags of Spain, Mexico, the Republic of Texas, the United States, the Confederate States of America, and then the United States again. Pope Pius IX established the Catholic diocese of San Antonio in 1874 and designated San Fernando as its cathedral; Pope Pius XI established the archdiocese of San Antonio in 1926, making San Fernando a metropolitan cathedral and further enhancing its prominence as a center of Hispanic Catholicism. Amidst all the ecclesiastical, political, and social changes in San Antonio, San Fernando parishioners have celebrated the practices of their religious and cultural heritage. Successive generations of parishioners shaped and developed their religious traditions to suit new historical contexts and needs, particularly their public devotion to Our Lady of Guadalupe and to Jesus in his birth, passion, and death. This rich heritage has made San Fernando a source for various contemporary studies of Latino theology and religion.

—TM

---

either lost their influence or have (most probably) transformed themselves into other ideological or political shapes and adopted new names. Much of modern-day education, business, politics, etc., in Mexico and in the Antilles, as well as among U.S. Latino/as, depend on the new versions of the rationalist mentality. The powerful elites of the Right, as well as most of the Left, share the same basic worldview that sees the people's religion as an unfortunate (or at best, folkloric) vestige of the past. In their common view, the best use of popular religious symbol is its instrumentalization. Most U.S. Latino/a conservative Protestants typically misunderstand popular Catholicism, or misinterpret it as a proselytizing argument.

The nineteenth century saw the U.S. purchase of Florida and the U.S. military conquest and annexation of Mexico's northern half. Florida's Latino/a Catholics, mostly gathered in the cities of St. Augustine and Pensacola, chose one of two paths when the purchase from Spain occurred: a few decided to stay in the new American territory, while most elected to leave Florida and settle in Spanish Cuba. It would not be until several decades later when large communities of Cuban Catholics settled again in the peninsula, fleeing the increasingly repressive Spanish colonial authorities in Cuba. The new settlers established themselves in Tampa and Key West. Smaller groups of Cubans went to Philadelphia and New York. There are indications that in Tampa and Key West there were some forms of Latina/o popular religion during the last decades of the nineteenth century. One must be very careful on this point because of the religious apathy that accompanied much of the Cuban nineteenth century.

The Southwest, however, had a different story than Florida. The lands from Texas to California were annexed by the

United States after military intervention, and many Mexican towns and villages were occupied. Some of these had been founded three centuries before, and the presence of Catholicism in them was as old.

The "dual-level" Christianity of Mexico had also become part of the religious life of the Southwest (these lands were still, after all, part of Mexico). Here, however, popular Catholicism seems to have had so heavy an influence that even the local ecclesiastical establishment—too weak to claim power on its own—had to actively promote it, thereby publicly linking it to the clergy. The same fundamental reasons of defense and buffer, evident in the rest of Mexico at that time, were operative in the northern frontier as the clergy allied itself with the symbols of popular religion. The new American Southwest had been Mexico's remote northern border outpost. Not many of the Mexican progressive elites of the period would have chosen to leave the big cities in the south and come to settle the northern frontier. Even the few residents who pretended to belong to these elites were numerically insignificant and ultimately powerless.

Popular Catholicism remained the de facto religion of the vast majority of the population. Its shape, functions, and sociodoctrinal developmental process paralleled the rest of Mexico. In other words, the popular Christianity that preceded the American annexations was at its core the pre-Tridentine *traditio*. It was mestizo, but in this case because mestizos were the ones who mainly settled here. This religion assumed as normative the Catholicism that had been interpreted by earlier "popular" generations in southern Mexico. However, the

reevangelization efforts, so important during much of the late colonial period, had little effect in the lands from Texas to California.

But then came the American military conquest and subsequent annexations. For the first time Latino/a Catholicism faced the Reformation and a type of Christianity that was not Catholic. The confrontation happened between, on one side, an anti-Catholic Protestant nation, increasingly aware of its military might and apparently convinced of its moral superiority (its "Manifest Destiny"), and, on the other side, a conquered people, suddenly and violently deprived of right and land, whose religion had long roots in the medieval past that the new conquerors loathed. The Catholicism of the people was not the post-Tridentine reformed version, by now common in Catholic Europe and in the eastern American states. The people's religion and culture had assumed as self-evident that truth was "Catholic." But after the U.S. territorial annexations, to be Catholic in Florida and the Southwest was to be poor and conquered. Furthermore, the religion of the people was soon going to face another confrontation—the arrival of post-Tridentine reformed Catholics.

After Trent and the Reformation Arrive

The implementation of the decrees and doctrines of the Council of Trent had been very selective in Spanish America. Tridentine Catholicism, arriving at least a century after the conquest, became identified mostly with the Spaniards and White criollos, and limited to their social circles. There were so few Protestants in Spain's colonies that the European urgency for reform seemed foreign. One result, as we have seen, was the preservation of *pre*-Tridentine Christianity in the Western Hemisphere. The "reevangelization" of the late colonial period attempted to bring Tridentine Catholicism to the people, but only with very limited success. By then even the official religion was undergoing a profound change that would eventually lead to the centralizing Romanization started by Pius IX and continued by most of his successors (that would drastically transform the face of worldwide Catholicism).

Latino/as were forced to deal with the Church of Trent immediately after the American military occupation and territorial annexation of Florida and of the northern half of Mexico. The people's Catholicism, fundamentally untouched by the Tridentine reforms, suddenly confronted a new type of Catholic Church that seemed always on the defensive, that emphasized doctrinal knowledge (and guilt) over experience and affect, and that emphatically devalued lay participation. Worst of all, this "new" Church supported the American conquest of the Southwest and treated the majority of Catholics (in the conquered lands) as second-class Catholics and citizens. Therefore, Latina/o Catholicism in the United States at the start of the twenty-first century is displaying the effects and consequences of this first century and a half of confrontations with post-Tridentine Roman Christianity, with the American heirs of the Protestant Reformation, and with the modern world (culturally disseminated mainly by the Calvinist and Roman theological traditions).

Today we can understand why the Catholicism of the American eastern states appeared to be on the defensive. It was. And perhaps this in turn led to American Catholics' perceiving public, popular Latino/a Catholicism as superstition in need of correction and catechesis. Compounding this perception, however, was the growing influence and control of the Irish in the U.S. Church, especially when we know that many of the Irish became racially motivated opponents of the Mexicans in the annexed lands. The American (specifically Irish) Catholics' need for acceptance and respect in the wider U.S. society led many to conceive of Latina/o religion as an added weight they did not want to carry, as well as a source of embarrassment for their reformed Tridentine Church.

Some of the public social celebrations of popular Catholicism were soon transformed into more private family expressions. The new Church was organized according to the ecclesiastical patterns developed in the eastern states. Although most Catholics in the Southwest were Latino/a, their participation and leadership in the institutions of religion were drastically diminished and often avoided. The people's alternative seems to have been withdrawal into the universe of popular Catholicism—it was theirs, and it made familiar sense of God and Christianity. By taking refuge in this religious world, Latino/as were also preserving one of the most important roots of their cultural identity as well as their very ancient type of Christianity.

However, for the new European-American ecclesiastical establishment in the Southwest, Latina/o flight into traditional religion implied that the new, "White" Catholic elites could ignore Latino/a Christianity and further emphasize, to the Protestant majority, that

PATRICIO FERNANDEZ FLORES (1929–)

Patricio Fernandez Flores was born on July 26, 1929, in Ganado, Texas, the seventh of nine children to Patricio and Trinidad Fernandez de Flores. He dropped out of high school at the age of 14 due to his father's illness and worked in the cotton fields to help support his family. He returned to high school and graduated at the age of 19 from the Christian Brothers' Kirwan High School. Patricio Flores was ordained a priest in the Roman Catholic Church on May 26, 1956. He became the nation's first Mexican American bishop on May 5, 1970. This humble bishop greatly lives his motto "Laborabo non mihi sed omnibus"—"I will work not for myself but for others." He co-founded both PADRES, an organization of Hispanic priests whose purpose was to call attention to issues concerning Hispanics in the church, and MACC, the Mexican American Cultural Center in San Antonio, Texas. This founder of the National Hispanic Scholarship fund remains the only archbishop to professionally make a record album. The proceeds from the sales were used to raise funds for MACC. In 2003, he was honored by the San Antonio Spurs basketball team with a championship ring. At the time of his retirement in 2005, Patricio Fernandez Flores was the country's longest-reigning archbishop.

—NDA

Latina/o Catholicism was "not really Catholic"—only a marginal anachronism from the past in need of instruction. Because of racist and other cultural biases, European American Catholics had, thereby, assumed as true and valid the Protestant Reformation's premise that pre-Tridentine Christianity was deviant.

As long as those dominant in the Catholic Church in the Southwest doctrinally and pastorally ignored Latino/as, and as long as the latter maintained some ritual links with parishes and continued to identify themselves as Catholics, Latina/os could keep their popular Catholicism with only occasional hierarchical interference. Some local Latino/as even joined the ranks of the clergy, but their meager numbers and lack of real institutional influence did not alter the fundamentally ritual (i.e., "devotional") relationship that existed between priests and people since the colonial days.

After the 1960s: the Impacts of Modernity, Vatican II, and Social Movements

This uneasy truce between the official European American (mostly Irish) Church and Latino/a popular Catholicism, however, started to unravel with the Second Vatican Council (1963–1965) and the social and cultural movements of the 1960s and 1970s. The council's call for increased lay participation and leadership, and its many other reforms of the Church, added to the civil rights, farm labor, and Chicano/a movements, and helped create a cultural atmosphere in which the dominance and certainties of the White European-American clergy began to be questioned by Latina/o Catholics.

Several elements of the contemporary world came together to present a growing challenge to the ecclesiastically dominant. There is, for example, the influence that decades of access to European American mass media have had on the sacral worldview underlying and sustaining much of Latino/a Catholicism. There too are the efforts of public education in communicating the values and worldview of modernity. It is difficult to imagine how the long exposure to European American society (heir to the Calvinist religious tradition, imbued of individualism, and increasingly secularized) could not have affected the very foundations and premises of the Latina/o religious and communal universe. The growth of urbanization and of a city-based job market after World War II began to deeply impact the stable, rural-based traditional extended family and community relationships so fundamental to Latino/a religion. Finally, the upsurge of immigration (to American cities) from Mexico and the Antilles added huge concentrations of unrelated Latino/a nuclear families in large metropolitan areas. This immigrant wave (which has not ended) brings people who are not accustomed to being treated as foreigners in their societies or Church.

The poverty, discrimination, and consequences thereof suffered by so many generations of Latina/os seem to have socially justified, in the eyes of the larger society, the perpetuation of the marginal role of the Latino/a populations. The dominant ideology has long attempted to explain and "prove" the supposed reasons for this marginal status. Needless to say, sadly and precisely as a symptom of their social vulnerability, some Latino/as have internalized the "proofs" put forth by the dominant ideology, thereby becoming willing agents of society's continued marginalization of their own people.

Regrettably, the European American Catholic Church frequently and uncritically assumed these ideological justifications, thereby reaffirming the "validity" of society's arguments of prejudice within its own ecclesiastical milieu. The Church and its clergy many times became a willing accomplice in the promotion of Latino/a internalization of the dominant ideology, and in the preservation and justification of the structures of dominance.

Demographics (and probably not the evident long-standing pastoral need) have finally begun to make the European American Church take notice. The European American Catholics who have actively and repeatedly, as well as out of conviction, sided with the ecclesial and sociocultural needs of Latino/a Catholics are and have been, unfortunately, only a minority in the Church.

Whatever the motive, the alternatives offered today by official Catholicism ("progressive" or "conservative") to U.S. Latina/os seem clear and are certainly not new. They become religiously "Americanized" or face the continued onslaught of accusations of ignorance and superstition, followed by pastoral activity geared to "correctly" educate in "real" Roman Christianity. The American Church's attempts at understanding Latino/a Catholicism have frequently seemed to be motivated by the hope of the early and definitive demise of that which is specifically "Latina/o" in Latino/a Catholicism.

The current trend at "multiculturalizing" the American Church perhaps conceals the obvious, and not surprising, fact that those who set the pastoral agendas, determine the doctrinal parameters, and direct the implementation strategies for the so-called "multicultural"

LAS HERMANAS

The organization known as Las Hermanas (the sisters) began in 1971 when 50, mainly Latina, religious women and nuns, were gathered by Gloria Gallardo, S.H.G., and Gregoria Ortega, O.L.V.M. These women primarily gathered to discuss how to better serve the needs of Spanish-speaking Catholics in the United States of America. The national organization of Las Hermanas was formed through a charter granted by the state of Texas on February 22, 1972. Four goals were set at the initial meeting. These four goals would direct the organization for over three decades: (1) to activate leadership among themselves and the laity; (2) to effect social change; (3) to contribute to the cultural renewal of La Raza; and (4) to educate their Anglo-dominant congregations on the needs of Spanish-speaking communities. Originally, membership to Las Hermanas was open only to native Spanish-speaking Hispanic sisters. Yet, early in its history, all Latina Catholic women were allowed to join, regardless of country of origin. Las Hermanas has played integral roles in influencing policy decisions for major ecclesial bodies and in establishing the Mexican American Cultural Center in San Antonio, Texas. Las Hermanas published a quarterly newsletter called *Informes* and has been a strong supporter of the United Farmworkers.

—NDA

dioceses and parishes of the future are still the European- American Catholics. Therefore, even this apparently well-intentioned effort at cultural diversity does not question the structures of dominance or the unspoken premise that U.S. Latino/a Catholicism to the degree that it is distinctly Latino/a must be left behind.

The U.S. Latina/o responses to the alternatives offered by the European American Church have been creative attempts at religious and cultural survival. There is still, for example, the learned pattern of flight into the traditional religious universe. Some Latino/as (perhaps the majority among a certain age group, and among many recent immigrants) do choose to perpetuate the forms and vision of pre-Tridentine Catholicism. They are probably not aware of its having been the official religion until a few centuries ago, nor are they familiar with the long history of Christianity that preceded the Reformation. For them, simply, this is their Catholicism, their way of being Christian, and that reason suffices.

There have been other responses to the official Church's alternatives. These alternatives have been, in different ways and to varying degrees, culturally optimizing paths for preserving traditional religion and its sustaining worldview vis-à-vis the always encroaching world of modernity and post-Tridentine Catholicism. These newer responses are compromises with a European American reality perceived as, at best, overwhelming or, at worst, dangerously invasive.

It may be argued that nonparochial lay movements and associations, such as the *Cursillos de Cristiandad* or even the traditional *cofradías* and other post-Vatican II *movimientos*, have allowed for the formation of an alternative

ENCUENTROS

Encuentros or meetings refer to national consultative gatherings of Hispanic Catholics called by their bishops usually preceded by a previous, grassroots consultation. Each Encuentro sought greater representation so as to make specific recommendations. The first occurred in 1972, the second in 1977, and the third in 1985, which resulted in the "National Pastoral Plan for Hispanic Ministry." That "Plan" was updated by the document proceeding from the fourth Encuentro (2000), "Encuentro and Mission." The last Encuentro, held in 2006, was especially for youth and young adults. However, the process itself is more important than the initiatives (usually underfunded) or documents (sometimes disregarded) that they engendered. The consultations provided for a remarkably democratic consultation within a hierarchic church and increased representation of all Hispanic groups, both genders, every age cohort, as well as a wide variety of socioeconomic sectors. This created national networking among Hispanics first begun by groups such as the cursillo, but through the Encuentros much expanded, connected to the bishops, and sustained over time. Thus, many see the Encuentro process as a defining feature of U.S. Hispanic Catholic ministry after the Second Vatican Council.

—KGD

Latino/a Church within the broader community of Catholicism. This Latina/o Church has often acted, for all practical purposes, as parallel parish and diocese, permitting a high degree of participation and leadership to Latino/as otherwise marginalized from the European American–controlled parishes and dioceses. Through the acceptance of varying degrees of preferably nonintrusive institutional links to the hierarchy, Latina/os managed to preserve a considerable degree of autonomy within their lay movements.

A close examination of the latter would show how deep the influence is of the symbols and the worldview of popular Catholicism on these movements. Acts of public piety, for example, are consistently encouraged, praised, and performed. Some of the associations have been specifically established for the purpose of preserving traditional forms of devotion and communal prayer.

Through this lay-led, parallel Catholicism, Latino/as have managed to preserve and reinterpret significant elements of their shared worldview, together with their emphasis on family and community. The movements have also served as important vehicles for the dissemination of many of the doctrinal contents of popular Catholicism, though sufficiently adapted (and concealed) in forms acceptable to the modern ecclesiastical realities.

The European American Church's reaction to the Latino/a lay movements and associations has been frequently adverse, demanding that local (i.e., mostly White European American) clergy exercise control over the people's alternative Catholic "spaces." Increasingly perceived by many Latina/os as the institution's sociological need to control, the Church's reactions have at times been understood by the people as one more battle in the European American

PADRES

Priests Associated for Education, Social, and Religious Rights (PADRES) is the English name for the organization known as Padres Asociados para Derechos Religiosos Educativos y Sociales. Founded in February 1970 in Tucson, Arizona, 25 native Chicano priests created PADRES as a specialized organization to maximize their responsibilities in the struggle for social justice. Rapidly growing in membership and importance, PADRES developed a clear set of recommendations for social justice action on behalf of Latino/as. At the same time, it promoted education in church leadership skills that linked this social justice mission with the emerging Theology of Liberation. Finally, it motivated a growing cohort of Latino priests nationwide to support each other in ministry by developing a set of common goals. Evidence that Latino priests were capable leaders encouraged ordinaries to appoint PADRES members as bishops. PADRES contributed to implementing Encuentro decisions by providing progressive church leadership, often receiving substantial grants for its work. At the same time, PADRES altered its rules to allow non-Mexican Latino members. In 1976, the annual meeting was held in New York City with the specific goal of inviting the existing Association of Hispanic Priests (ASH) to join with PADRES, a merger accomplished some 15 years later.

—ASA

clergy's relentless struggle to dismantle Latino/a religion. It is important to note that as Latina/o popular Catholicism attempts to survive by somehow adapting to post-Tridentine Roman Catholicism, it has begun to modify and reinterpret the doctrinal contents and symbols that have traditionally distinguished it.

The most telling example of the contemporary reinterpretation of symbols and contents refers to the Bible. It is highly inaccurate to think that western Christianity did not know the Bible before Trent and the Reformation. In the European villages, where most people lived and did not know how to read, and where medieval culture was very much alive, the Bible's contents were presented graphically through art, *autos sacramentales*, storytelling, and preaching. The same was true in pre-Tridentine colonial Christianity in the Americas. The Bible was known at the popular level, but

through performed or visual symbol and the spoken word, not through reading the printed page because most Christians were illiterate. In others words, the Bible was known in late medieval Europe and early colonial Americas as it was known in early Christianity.

However, as the literacy rate increased, the direct reading of the text of the Bible became widespread. There is no doubt that, after Vatican II, the Church's insistence on biblical reading was heeded by Latina/o Catholics. The increased numbers of Latino/a Protestants have also been a strong influence. Whatever the reasons for this scriptural awakening, the written text of the Bible has been taken out of the hands and control of the ecclesiastical institution and is now being interpreted by the people. Interestingly, this increase in familiarity with the sacred texts of Christians does not seem to have decidedly contributed

NATIONAL ASSOCIATION OF HISPANIC PRIESTS OF THE USA

Established in 1990, the National Association of Hispanic Priests (ANHS) was founded to provide fraternity and support for the approximately 2,500 Latino Catholic priests within the United States. Known in Spanish as *La Asociación Nacional de Sacerdotes Hispanos, EE.UU.*, ANHS is an organization that collaborates with bishops and the laity to implement the National Plan for Hispanic Ministry and to develop approaches for meaningful ministries among Latino priests. The main activity of the organization is to hold an annual national conference, where a specific aspect of the priestly ministry is studied from a Hispanic perspective. The conference attempts to provide a national forum where the personal experiences of Latino priests are shared in the hope of developing a common vision that will help in understanding and solving the problems that arise in different Latina/o communities and among Hispanic priests. Additionally, the Association stands ready to take official positions on social justice with respect to the problems that affect priests and their Latina/o communities. To this end, ANHS attempts to be the official voice of Latino priests belonging to the organization.

—MAD

to the exodus of many Latina/os from Catholic Christianity. Their departure, say most significant studies, can be directly explained by White European American pastoral and institutional disregard of Latino/as in the U.S. Catholic Church. It seems, in fact, that increased familiarity with the Bible among Latina/o Catholics is strengthening the symbols and fundamental worldview of popular Catholicism through a new process of reinterpretation, this time biblical.

There is another common response to the either/or alternatives offered to Latino/a Catholicism. This is Pentecostalism. Latina/o Pentecostalism has shown itself an important, culturally acceptable vehicle for the preservation of the pre-Tridentine and premodern religious worldview. Although obviously and consciously rejecting many medieval and colonial Catholic symbols and practices, Pentecostalism has managed to hold on to the very "sacramental," symbolic ethos and worldview that made pre-

Reformation Christianity possible. Many of these symbols have been "reformed" and some modern ones added, but the fundamental structures and premises of the traditionally religious Latino/a worldview have basically remained within Pentecostalism.

One cannot understand the current popularity of the Catholic charismatic movement among Latina/os, or the ever-increasing number of Pentecostal churches in the *barrios*, without realizing the seemingly crucial role of cultural and religious preservation that the Pentecostal movement in its Catholic or Protestant versions is playing. It is well documented that the growth of the charismatic or Pentecostal communities is in direct relation to people's perceived sense of threat or invasion at the hands of modernity. In these studies, the Christian Churches of any denomination that appear more allied to the modern worldview and against the traditional religious and communal relations, will suffer considerable

UNITED STATES CONFERENCE OF CATHOLIC BISHOPS

The United States Conference of Catholic Bishops (USCCB) traces its roots to World War I. Then called the National Catholic War Council, it secured monies and developed programs for the spiritual and temporal care of the U.S. military. It has since turned its concern toward the general welfare of the country—with particular emphasis on the Catholic Church—and has changed its name periodically to reflect its vision. The USCCB includes over 45 departments, ranging from evangelization, family, social justice, and liturgy, and 16 committees. Bishops chair the committees, and laity staffs the departments. U.S. Bishop's ministry of Hispanics began through the leadership of San Antonio Archbishop Robert E. Lucey, who organized an office for the Spanish-speaking people in 1945. The National Catholic Welfare Council (a former name of the USCCB) would later include this office within its Social Development department. This office evolved into the Secretariat of Hispanic Affairs in 1974 and would organize three national *Encuentros* (1972, 1977, 1986) developing pastoral leadership and collaboration between the Hispanic faithful and U.S. bishops. The collaborative discussions from the *Encuentros* would be the source for the bishops' "National Pastoral Plan for Hispanic Ministry" in 1987.

—*OJN*

numerical losses. It is, therefore, highly ironic that the Roman Catholic Church, which engaged in the ideological battles that followed the Reformation supposedly on the side of tradition, should now be an uncritical bearer of the Reformation's and modernity's theological premises vis-à-vis pre-Tridentine Latina/o Catholicism. It almost seems that the contemporary confrontation of Latino/a Catholicism with the European American Roman Catholic Church is the modern version of the sixteenth-century Reformation that Latina/o religion never had to face. This time, however, it is official Roman Catholicism that has taken the side of the Protestant reformers, arguing through similar logic and with surprisingly similar doctrinal assumptions. Unfortunately, Latino/a Catholicism had been robbed (by the consequences of military occupation, territorial annexations, prejudice, and poverty) of most

theological and institutional means of defense and self-affirmation needed in this new Reformation.

There are, evidently, many Latina/o individuals across the country who participate in the life of the official Roman Catholic Church. There are Latino/a Catholics who are very well educated in theology, who are successful in ministry, ordained or not, and who are respected leaders of their faith communities. There are even a few Latino/a diocesan bishops, and a few auxiliary bishops. But all of these individuals, taken together do not alter the fact that popular Catholicism remains the manner in and through which most Latina/os are Catholic.

The Shape of the Future?

Arguably, the day will come when a majority of U.S. Latino/as will be less "popular" in their Catholicism. Will this

---

ACHTUS

The Academy of Catholic Hispanic Theologians of the United States (ACHTUS) was founded in 1988 in Ruidoso, New Mexico. A forum for the distinctive theological scholarship emerging from Latino/as, ACHTUS ensures agency for the growing number of Catholic Latina/o theologians and the Hispanic communities they accompany by promoting research and critical theological reflection within the context of U.S. Hispanic experiences and by privileging *teología de conjunto* as a method for engagement. Through membership categories and annual colloquia, ACHTUS creates and sustains professional networks of Catholic Latina/o theologians in conversation with non-Latino/a theologians engaged in U.S. Hispanic religious experience, as well as with Latino/a Protestant theologians and Hispanic scholars in other academic disciplines. In response to the marginalization of Latino/a perspectives in the theological mainstream, ACHTUS established the *Journal of Hispanic/Latino Theology* in 1993, with founding editor Orlando Espín. After 10 printed volumes of quarterly issues, in 2006, the journal was reconstituted online as the *Electronic Journal of Hispanic/Latino Theology* under the direction of the second editor Jean-Pierre Ruiz. One of the largest Catholic professional theological associations in the world, ACHTUS confers two awards, the *Virgilio Elizondo Award* and the *ACHTUS Award,* in recognition of those individuals and institutions that advance the mission of the Academy.

—CMN

---

transformation imply that their Latina/o cultural and religious specificity or identity will be lost? Will the future show that the European American "religious invasion" will have finally succeeded? The answer to these questions is probably "no," if present trends continue. The demographic growth of Latino/as will make it impossible for the European American Church to remain what it is. It too will be changed. In other words, the future will probably bring a profound and thorough cultural mestizaje or mulataje, and a new style of American Catholicism will develop.

It is important to note that there are clear, although mostly local, early indications of what this future Catholic mestizaje or mulataje might look like. There are signs that Latina/os are beginning to take ownership of the U.S. Catholic Church as their own, as well as to exert pressure on the White dominant structures and demand changes. New organizations have been established that will have, and have begun to have, deep impact on mainstream American Catholicism: the National Catholic Council on Hispanic Ministry, the Academy of Catholic Hispanic Theologians of the United States, and the *Instituto de Liturgia Hispana*, among others. A respected theological quarterly, the *Journal of Hispanic/Latino Theology*, founded in 1993, continues to bring Latino/a Catholic scholarship to a growing academic public.

The relentless confrontation of Latina/o popular Catholicism with the White U.S. Catholic denominational power structures and policies, plus the equally relentless struggle with and need for understanding Latino/as who have become identified with other forms of Christianity, have impacted and will continue to impact Latina/o Catholicism. Given the current and foreseeable social, cultural, and political U.S. context, the resulting transformations within Latino/a Catholicism will probably lead to the stabilization of the present rates of denominational/religious affiliations among Latina/os but with the "unchurched," not the "secular," becoming the unexpected yet fastest growing Latino/a religious group.

Latino/a Catholicism will continue because it is too important religiously and culturally. It is the modern heir of the long Christian tradition of Iberia, begun during the apostolic period, developed during the unique medieval history of the peninsula, brought to and planted in the Americas with the establishment of the Spanish and Portuguese colonial empires, surviving mostly unaffected by the Reformation and Trent. However, since the nineteenth-century U.S. military occupation and territorial annexations of Florida and the Southwest, Latina/o Catholicism has been repeatedly confronted by Protestant Christianity and Tridentine Catholicism, thus being forced into a complex process of sociocultural change that is provoking a significant religious transformation. Given current and projected demographic realities, it can be assumed that Latino/a Catholicism will become more intertwined with the American Catholic Church, as the latter discovers among Latina/os its main or only chance of relevant survival while both are changed into an internally diverse complex whose contours are still unclear.

Orlando O. Espín

References and Further Reading

Espín, Orlando O. *The Faith of the People: Theological Reflections on Popular Catholicism* (Maryknoll, NY: Orbis Books, 1997).

Espín, Orlando O. *Grace and Humanness: Theological Reflections Because of Culture* (Maryknoll, NY: Orbis Books, 2007).

Goizueta, Roberto S. *Caminemos con Jesús: Toward a Hispanic/Latino Theology of Accompaniment* (Maryknoll, NY: Orbis Books, 1995).

Matovina, Timothy, and Gary Riebe-Estrella, eds. *Horizons of the Sacred: Mexican Traditions in U.S. Catholicism* (Ithaca, NY: Cornell University Press, 2002).

Nanko-Fernández, Carmen M. "¡Cuidado! The Church Who Cares and Pastoral Hostility." *New Theology Review* 19, no. 1 (2006): 24–33.

Nanko-Fernández, Carmen M. "We Are Not Your Diversity, We Are the Church!: Ecclesiological Reflections from the Marginalized Many." *Perspectivas* 10 (2006).

Sandoval, Moisés. *On the Move: A History of the Hispanic Church in the United States*, 2nd ed. (Maryknoll, NY: Orbis Books, 2006).

CELAM

Consejo Episcopal Latinoamericano or Conference of Latin American Bishops (CELAM) was established in 1956 in Rio de Janeiro, Brazil, with statutes approved in 1974, representing 22 Catholic bishops' conferences of Latin America and the Caribbean. Its aim is to coordinate the work of the Catholic Church in the Americas, focusing on the adaptations of the Second Vatican Council (1962–1965) to promote creative strategies for spreading the Catholic faith, as well as the spiritual, social, political, and economic needs of the Latino/a people. General conferences at Medellín, Colombia (1968), Puebla, Mexico (1979), Santo Domingo, Dominican Republic (1992), and Aparecida, Brazil (2007) resulted in affirming the Church's "preferential option for the poor," the concept of "structural sin," "ecclesial base communities" (*comunidades eclesiales de base*), and the theological/pastoral method "to see, to judge, to act."

At Medellín it was explained that the Church's preferential option for the poor meant that the Church "must favor any honest effort to promote the transformation and elevation of the poor and of all those who live in sub-human social conditions." This entails, "not supporting systems and structures that hide and support serious and oppressive inequalities [structures of sin] between the social classes and the citizens of a country." This is best accomplished through small reflection groups (ecclesial base communities), especially in rural and slum city areas, where the poor can reflect through the method "see–judge–act" on their daily reality in light of the word of God. This will aid them in the process of personal conversion and salvation through a communal living of faith and love as well as empowering them to work for the transformation of the structures of sin into more just and humane structures that promote and support the well-being of all the members of society, especially of the social and material outcasts of society.

With CELAM headquartered in Medellín there were established departments, publications, and training centers throughout the continent. Research centers and intellectual networking became common among the different pastoral agents throughout the Americas. Based in Bogotá (Colombia), CELAM pushed the Second Vatican Council toward a more progressive stance. During the next four years, CELAM prepared the Medellín Conference officially supporting the liberation theology founded by Dominican friar Gustavo Gutiérrez in his 1972 essay, *A Theology of Liberation: History, Politics and Salvation.*

CELAM support to liberation theology was frowned upon by the Vatican, with Pope Paul VI trying to slow the movement after the 1962-1965 Council. Cardinal Antonio Samoré, in charge of relations between the Roman Curia and the CELAM as the leader of the Pontifical Commission for Latin America, was ordered to put an end to this orientation. With Bishop Alfonso López Trujillo's election in 1972 as general secretary of CELAM, conservatives gained control of this organization, as well as of the Roman Curia. López Trujillo stayed CELAM's general secretary until 1984. However, at the 1979 CELAM's Conference of Puebla, conservative reorientation of the CELAM was met by strong opposition from the progressive part of the clergy, which defined the concept of a preferential option for the poor. But with the election of Pope John Paul II, conservatives took control of both the Roman Curia and the CELAM. Cardinal Joseph Ratzinger, now Pope Benedict XVI, was charged with bringing back the Vatican's authority in the Third World. In 1984 and 1986, the Vatican twice condemned liberation theology, accusing it of Marxist influence. In his travel to Managua, Nicaragua, John Paul II harshly condemned what he called the "popular Church" rooted in the ecclesial base communities and spoke against the Nicaraguan clergy's tendencies to support the Sandinistas. Cardinal Óscar Andrés Rodríguez Maradiaga was CELAM's general secretary from 1995 to 1999, and Cardinal Luis Aponte Martínez was general secretary. Bishop Raymundo Damasceno Assis is the current general secretary (2008).

Medellín (1968)

When the first sketches of a theology of liberation appeared at the end of the 1960s and beginning of the 1970s, several "liberationist" options for an urgently needed basic structural change in Latin American society seemed possible. In the meantime, something similar to a coupe within the Latin American Catholic hierarchy was taking place. After CELAM's conference in Medellín in 1968, the new liberationist pastoral and theological ideas quickly spread to the entire Church in Latin American and the Caribbean. Medellín ushered in a new spirit directed toward the preferential option of the poor. In essence, this special preference called on the Church to strive for social justice in concert with, and on behalf of, the poverty stricken. Medellín called for the defense of the rights of the oppressed; a recognition of the plight of the poorest segments of the population; the development of ecclesial base communities (CEBs); a correction of prices for Third World products to ensure just terms for raw material exports; and a denunciation of the unjust actions of world powers perpetrated against weak nations. This was a radical condemnation of most Latin American governments of the time and the international economic system that had for nearly five centuries been, at the very least, tacitly supported by the traditional

Roman Catholic hierarchy. Every year hundreds of clergy and religious attended the training courses offered by CELAM's liberationist instructors. However, the general attitude of questioning that followed the Second Vatican Council led to public confrontations between groups of liberationist priests, the religious, and most bishops. The reaction of the hierarchy was inevitable.

However, there were contrary movements even with the Vatican. The encyclical *Octogesima Adveniens* of Pope Paul VI in 1971 reflected the impact of liberation theology on the official social teaching of the Church. Noticing the increasing interest of Catholics in socialism, Paul VI abstained from issuing condemnations and simply urged caution and discernment. That same year a worldwide Synod of Bishops that took place in Rome recognized that the efforts for social justice are a "constituent dimension" of the teaching of the Gospel. That action, which they explicitly called "liberation," was central and nonperipheral to the mission of the Church. Hence, while liberation theology was provoking controversy within Catholicism, some of its central tenets were becoming official Church positions, especially through the work of certain sectors of CELAM and the documents produced by its general conferences.

Puebla (1979)

The gathering of CELAM in Mexico in 1979 can be seen as the struggle between the three different established paradigms among the Latin American and Caribbean bishops. On one side were the "conservatives," who emphasized hierarchical authority and doctrinal orthodoxy. This group consciously fought liberation theology because it perceived a blatant Marxism in its theologizing and praxis. On the other end was the liberationist group whose force lay in the ecclesial base communities and who insisted that the Church had to adopt a lifestyle in agreement with its service function. Not only were abuses denounced but also the structures that caused them, and sometimes the capitalist system as a whole. Both groups represented the tendencies of the minorities. To the largest group belonged those who could be called "centrist," whose main preoccupation was the unity of the Church. With the conservatives, this group shared its preoccupation for ecclesiastical authority, and with the liberationists, a conviction on the necessity to defend human rights, at least in extreme circumstances. These figures played the main role in directing the Puebla conference, while the conservatives and liberationists exercised pressure by changing words, adding some passages, and objecting to others.

The extremely long final document that was produced at Puebla was not very convincing. The liberationists congratulated themselves because there were no condemnations included. The document used occasionally strong language to denounce existing injustices. The general tone, however, stayed developmentalist, not liberationist. For example, the bishops frequently requested greater "participation and communion" in the Church and society instead of liberation from unjust ecclesial and political structures. These words composed clearly a new type of terminology to replace the vocabulary of liberation. Each one of the three tendencies could find positive elements. What Puebla called the preference for the poor was probably the most

positive element for the liberationist side. The conservatives could also find many citable phrases and complete subjects, especially the frequent condemnations of Marxism and violence, as well as the affirmation of hierarchical authority. The centrists could indicate the insistence on "the properly religious" role of the Church. Since in the Puebla document three types of analysis and theology coexisted, it was clear that the tensions would continue within the Church.

Santo Domingo (1992)

At Santo Domingo, far more than at the preceding CELAM conclaves, the Vatican's Curia sought to impose its will—an effort that met with considerable, but not total, success. The curial representatives seemed bent on limiting the autonomy of the bishops' conferences of Latin America and minimizing the kind of collegiality that had been forcefully affirmed by the Second Vatican Council. Yet, the document reaffirmed some of the liberationists' emphases, particularly "the preferential option for the poor . . . as solemnly proclaimed at Medellin and Puebla." That option is now described as "evangelical," no doubt in deference to John Paul II's call for a new evangelization. But it is also termed "irrevocable." Breaking little new ground, the document is essentially a holding action. Liberationists can take heart that the document is not retrogressive; it does not betray Medellín and Puebla. It reendorses the ecclesial base communities. Above all, it recapitulates the preferential option for the poor—not in the sentimental sense of extending charity to the poor, but in the sense of being in solidarity with them and helping empower them to determine their own destiny. It also singles out for "special denunciation" acts of violence against the rights of children, women, and "the poorest groups in society—peasants, indigenous people and Afro-Americans."

Aparecida (2007)

From an historical perspective, one can argue that in the meeting of CELAM that took place in Medellín, in 1968, liberation theology made its début, that Puebla, in 1979, was its watermark, and Santo Domingo, in 1992, its Waterloo. Aparecida, in 2007, was to a certain extent the separating of liberation theology's wheat from its chaff. The project of Aparecida is ambitious. It is nothing less than a radical inversion of the ecclesiastical system. In accordance with the Aparecida project, everything is going to be oriented toward the all-encompassing evangelizing mission of the Church.

In the first place, Aparecida decided to return to the method of Medellín and Puebla, that is, to the scheme see–judge–act of liberation theology abandoned at Santo Domingo. There is a very strong insistence on that continuity. This continuity with Medellín and Puebla is especially made manifest in two of its fundamental subjects: the option for the poor and the ecclesial base communities. These were precisely the two subjects that had been attacked or that dealt with indifference, as being things of the past, especially in the years preceding the conference.

Aparecida explicitly speaks about the ecclesial base communities recognizing that they were the signal for the option for the poor. There is also recognition that these base communities were not able to develop despite their value, and that several bishops had placed

Pope Benedict XVI presides over Mass at the opening of the fifth general meeting of CELAM (Latin American bishops' conference) in front of Brazil's most famous shrine on May 13, 2007, in Aparecida, Brazil. (Getty Images)

restrictions upon them. Now the bishops want to raise those restrictions and give new life to those communities. Aparecida also renews the option for the poor. There is a certain accent of repentance and a consciousness that that option had lost its urgency in the pastoral work of the Church in the Americas: it was no longer lived as a priority. Aparecida enumerates the new categories of the poor that arose or have developed in the past decades: women, youth, the destitute, the unemployed, migrants, displaced peoples, landless farmers, child prostitutes, victims of abortion, drug addicts, the mentally challenged, victims of incurable diseases, the lonely, the kidnapped, victims of violence, the elderly, and prisoners. In other words, not only those who suffer exploitation and oppression but all those who are socially excluded are now included within the Church's preferential option for the poor. Finally, Aparecida assumes contemporary challenges: ecology and environmental problems, and the need for an urban pastoral. The program for urban pastoral is quite complete and defines tasks that are going to demand the collaboration of millions of formed people. Hence, this is evident in the document's heavy emphasis on the disciple-missionary character of all the baptized. Therefore, there are also some calls to change the way the Church is to work for justice.

Because of the unprecedented advances as well as setbacks in the post-1978 wave of democratization in Latin America, from a region dominated by authoritarian regimes to one in which openly authoritarian regimes are the rare exception, an impetus to the thought that a political solution to the problems beseeching this part of the world became possible. Hence Aparecida makes a special call to those laymen and laywomen in decision-making positions to embrace the cause of the poor and realize their political apostolate based on the principles of the social doctrine of the Church.

CELAM's Impact on U.S. Hispanics

U.S. Latino/a theologians have appropriated many of the key insights of CELAM's documents as well as liberation theology and transformed them to develop a theology that would sink its roots in, respond to, and accompany the faith experience of the Hispanic communities in the United States. One of the key concepts that has been appropriated from CELAM and its ecclesial base communities with its theological/pastoral method is the notion of *teología de conjunto* (collaborative theology). This process implies a method that stresses direct involvement and analysis of reality as necessary first steps to the author's option to theologize from within the Latina/o social and pastoral context. *Pastoral de conjunto* (collaborative pastoral ministry) ensures that Hispanic theologizing is grounded in human experience, especially the experience of oppression. U.S. Latino/a theology attempts to give a voice to the voiceless. As members of the community, in the pastoral de conjunto theologians also see themselves as *mestizos*, as both Americans and Latinos, articulating their own theology, much like CELAM's attempt to inculturate the adaptations of the Second Vatican Council to the promotion of creative strategies for spreading the faith as well as to the material needs of the Hispanic people in the Americas. Therefore, inspired by CELAM, especially its ecclesial base community model, U.S. Latina/o theologizing aspires to be communal, inclusive, dialogical, and liberating. U.S. Latino/a theology realizes that only through communal dialogue, an inclusive dialogue based on praxis, are persons able to discern and live out—from a grassroots level—what truly foments integral liberation for each participant. This teología de conjunto pays close attention to *lo cotidiano* (daily living)—the daily experience of hope and suffering in "human relations lived in the home, in social institutions, at work, in culture, and in religion." Lo cotidiano, in this sense, radically critiques today's social models, which dehumanize and polarize persons.

Hence, U.S. Latino/a theology, influenced by the theology that has arisen from CELAM, seeks not only equality of opportunity (a "piece of the pie") but most importantly an equality of outcome —a new rational daily life. All the baptized, as agents of social justice, are called to guarantee the participation of all members of society, especially the marginalized (preferential option for the poor), in the transformation of the structures of exclusion that daily keep people from actively and communally participating in the common good. This is done by protecting *la dignidad* (dignity) of all, especially the outcasts, through the daily struggle for human rights and through *accompañamiento* (accompaniment) or solidarity at every *momento* (moment) or historical experience of mestizaje (cultural/racial mixing)—the daily experience of being a new people (mestizaje), product of a violent past and present—a resurrected body that still bears the marks of the passion.

Alejandro Crosthwaite

References and Further Reading

Berryman, Phillip. *Liberation Theology: The Essential Facts About the Revolutionary Movement in Latin America and Beyond* (New York: Pantheon Books, 1987).

Espín, Orlando O., and Miguel H. Díaz, eds. *From the Heart of Our People: Latino/a Explorations in Catholic Systematic Theology* (Maryknoll, NY: Orbis Press, 1999).

Deck, Allan Figueroa, ed. *Frontiers of Hispanic Theology in the United States* (Maryknoll, NY: Orbis Books, 1992).

Hennelly, Alfred T., ed. *Santo Domingo & Beyond: Documents: Documents & Commentaries from the Historic Meeting of the Latin American Bishops' Conference* (Maryknoll, NY: Orbis Press, 1993).

CENTRAL AMERICANS

The label "Central Americans" is highly contested for a number of reasons. For some, Central America refers to the short and narrow strip of land uniting North and South America that encompasses the countries of Guatemala, El Salvador, Honduras, Nicaragua, and Costa Rica. In Central America this is the most generally accepted definition because neither Belize nor Panama existed upon the formation of the "Federal Republic of Central America," a short-lived union created after most of the region gained independence from Spain in the nineteenth century. For others the label includes the countries of Belize and Panama after these gained their independence from Britain in 1981 and from Colombia in 1903, respectively. And yet for others, who wish to distinguish between the Anglo and Latin American portions of the continent, Central America includes Mexico, or at least the southern regions of Chiapas, Campeche, Quintana Roo, Tabasco, and Yucatán. For the purpose of this entry, Central Americans will refer to the groups of peoples living in the United States who were born in the countries of Belize, Guatemala, El Salvador, Honduras, Nicaragua, Costa Rica, and Panama. It also means children whose parents came from those countries and people who self-identify as Central Americans.

Similarly, to speak about the religious expressions and culture of Central Americans is a misnomer, as the population encompassed by this label are diverse, culturally and ethnically heterogeneous, with different histories, sociopolitical realities, religious traditions, practices, and customs. Internally, each of these countries are also richly diverse, and populated by peoples with different ethnocultural groups and religious traditions, many of which are represented among the Central American population of the United States. Each of these groups migrated into the United States at different points in the history of their countries and for various reasons. So it is impossible to make generalized statements about such richly diverse populations. Here, the intention is to merely touch the surface of these complex, ethnic, and culturally colorful populations, each of which deserves fuller individual attention.

Immigration Background

The Central American populations are recent phenomena in the United States. It is only within the past 40 years that the majority have arrived. While several patterns of migration can be identified with each of these populations, it is impossible to know exactly which country Central Americans came from prior to 1960. Until then the United States kept only general statistical information lumping them together. Guatemalans, Salvadorans, and Nicaraguans share some of these patterns as their countries suffered internal armed strife, which resulted in the migration of large numbers of peoples during the 1970s to late 1980s and then the 1990s. Belize, Costa Rica, and Panama share in common the lower numbers of immigrants present in the United States, and, including

Honduras, most have arrived since the late 1980s to the present.

Divided by war, some of the first migrants from Guatemala left when the democratically elected president Jacobo Arbenz was overthrown by a military coup aided by the CIA in 1954. He was followed by the dictatorship of Carlos Castillo Armas. His military repressive regime resulted in the renewal of internal armed conflict unseen since the 1940s decade. A second wave of immigrants into the United States took place as a result of the 1976 devastating earthquake that ravaged the country. The number of immigrants to the United States increased dramatically during the decade of the 1980s, which coincided with the worst years of repression during the time when countless Guatemalans left the country. Many of them sought refuge from the war in neighboring Mexico, and many made the journey to the United States. During the 1970s, those emigrating were primarily Ladinos (*mestizos/as*), but during the 1980s the majority of those emigrating from Guatemala were indigenous. After the peace accord—that brought to an end over 35 years of civil war—was signed in 1992, many thought that migration of Guatemalans would slow down and even cease, but instead, migration increased to its highest levels during the second half of the 1990s. Different from the migrants of the 1980s, these last waves of migrants left Guatemala for primarily economic reasons. In 2000, it was estimated that 1,811,676 Guatemalans lived in the United States.

Salvadorans also experienced their period of military repression and rampant violation of human rights by death squads. The years of repression can be traced as far back as 1932, the year of *La matanza* (the massacre), which singled out the indigenous population, virtually eradicating it. The rebellions that took place in the following years inaugurated an extended period of civil war between the repressive military governments and the guerrilla forces. By the 1960s, many Salvadorans had moved to Honduras, but after the soccer war with Honduras in 1969, many were forced to return to El Salvador, while others left the country and migrated to the United States.

It would not be until the 1980s that immigration into the United States increased dramatically as many Salvadorans fled the country because of the heightened military repression and death squads. Approximately half of the refugees made it to neighboring refugee camps in Honduras, Costa Rica, Nicaragua, and Mexico. The other half left for the United States and Canada. After the signing of the peace accord in 1990, El Salvador's economy and society was left in shambles. High levels of unemployment, increase in crime, and extreme poverty have been contributing factors in the migration of countless Salvadorans since the 1990s. With the exception of the 1986 "legalization" of refugees who entered the United States in 1982, just like Guatemalans, Salvadorans received little sympathy from the U.S. Reagan administration; most immigrants from El Salvador and Guatemala were denied legal status by U.S. immigration. In 1990 the American Baptist Churches (AMS) launched a lawsuit against the Immigration and Naturalization Services (INS) for biased treatment of Salvadoran refugees during the 1980s. The settlement prompted the reopening of many cases of Salvadoran refugees that had been denied, and to approve new ones in greater number. In 1991 Congress

awarded Temporary Protected Status (TPS) to those Salvadorans who had been in the United States since 1990. It is estimated that there are well over a million documented Salvadorans in the United States.

Distinct from the other Central American people, Nicaraguans tended to migrate in two directions, Costa Rica and the United States. From the mid-nineteenth century to the 1970s, the exclusive destination of Nicaraguan migrants was Costa Rica. During the 1980s, which is marked by the years of the Contra War, Nicaraguans turned to the United States. Once the war ended, Costa Rica became, once again, the primary destination of Nicaraguans. There are records which document that since the 1890s Nicaraguans have been migrating to the United States, although the numbers are not significant. In the decade 1910–1920 a recorded 17,000 Nicaraguans migrated to the United States because of the demand for labor during World War I. During the decade 1967–1976 a recorded 7,500 Nicaraguans migrated to the United States, most of whom reported to be White, and women outnumbered men almost by one-third. Immigration into the United States increased dramatically immediately after the revolution that ousted the U.S.-backed Dictator Anastasio Somosa. As many as 20,000 Nicaraguans left the country during this period. A second large wave entered the United States during the early 1980s, many of whom were industrialists. But the largest wave, one which accounts for most Nicaraguans in the United States, occurred from 1984 to the present, during the "Contra War," the open Reagan's administration financing of the anti-Sandinista insurgency. After signing the peace accord in 1987, migration took on a new meaning. During the 1990s, Nicaraguans migrating to the United States because of economic reasons or in search of new work opportunities rose to unprecedented heights. In 2001 many undocumented Nicaraguans were granted TPS as a result of the destructive aftermath of Hurricane Mitch. According to the 2000 Census information, there are as many as 266,848 documented Nicaraguans in the United States.

Not characterized by war or armed strife, Hondurans have migrated into the United States since the 1960s, settling mostly in the areas surrounding the city of Chicago. It was not until 1975 that emigration from Honduras to the United States became more pronounced. It was during the period of the 1980s that the United States established a military based in Honduras to support the illegally funded Contra War against the Sandinista government in Nicaragua. During the 1980s social unrest, rampant violation of human rights in the country, and extreme levels of poverty forced many Hondurans to migrate to the United States. This number has steadily risen since then. The 1990 Census recorded that most Hondurans were of working age and concentrated in the farming, forestry, and fishing sectors. In the aftermath of Hurricane Mitch, large numbers of Hondurans migrated to the United States, and in the year 2000 they received TPS scheduled to expire on July 5, 2001. Today, an estimated 600,000 Hondurans live in the United States, most of whom are undocumented.

Costa Ricans have not had to flee the political situation in their country, so they do not display the same patterns of migration as Guatemalans, Salvadorans, Nicaraguans, and Hondurans. They share more in common with Belizeans and their neighboring Panamanians. Most Costa Ricans have not left their country because of extreme economic circumstances, and very few have tried to enter the United States without proper documentation. In other words, waves of Costa Rican immigrants are not readily detectable. And they are not present in the United States in large numbers. By the mid-1980s there were only 26,639 Costa Ricans in the United States. Most Costa Ricans migrate because of marriage, study, and jobs and trades for which they were enlisted in their home country.

There are also no identifiably large waves of Panamanian immigration into the United States. Different from other Central Americans, Panamanians have a long-standing presence in the United States. Records show that by the 1830s, 44 Panamanians arrived in the United States. By the turn of the twentieth century 1,000 more arrived each year until World War I when it tapered off. By 1940 there were 7,000 Panamanians listed in the U.S. records. A very small number of Panamanians entered the United States during the 1960s, but by the 1970s they constituted one of the largest groups of Central Americans in the United States. Most of them were non-Whites and most were women. By 1990 there were 86,000 Panamanians in the United States.

There is very little information about Belizeans in the United States. This may be related to several factors: (1) Belizeans are often considered part of the Caribbean population; (2) the label of Belize was not adopted until 1973—prior to 1973 the country was known as British Honduras and considered a disputed territory between Britain and Guatemala;

and (3) it was not until 1981 that Belizeans gained their independence from Britain. These factors help explain why there are no records of Belizean migration prior to the early 1980s. Their numbers are small, but by 1984 there were 55,000 recorded residing in the United States and by 1988 this number had climbed to 65,000.

When considering the Central American population, one must note these are fairly young populations, most ranging between 20 and 50 years of age. They tend to gravitate to the urban centers where there are other Latina/o populations, particularly New York, Los Angeles, Chicago, Miami, New Jersey, Houston, and Washington. They vary in the ways they settle in the United States and in how they keep ties with their countries of origin. Since the 1990s there has been a steady flow of Central Americans into the United States, and no accurate count can be made because a large portion of these immigrants are undocumented. Their communities continue to grow in numbers not only because of the influx of recent arrivals, but because many are having children so that second and even third generations are emerging.

Culture and Folklore

There is great internal ethnic and cultural diversity among the Central American nations and populations in the United States. These communities are not homogeneous. For example, although the large majority of Belizeans are Creole, there are also smaller numbers of Indian and Chinese groups who arrived in the region during the nineteenth century as indentured laborers. There are some Hindi people who migrated into Belize during the 1960s, and some Chinese who

migrated from Hong Kong and Taiwan during the 1980s. Another large group among Belizeans is the Garinagu, or Garifuna, people (the descendants of the mixture of Caribbean indigenous peoples and Africans who did not want to be slaves and were expulsed from the Island of St. Vincent and arrived to Belize during the 1880s). One can find among Belizeans a good number of Mopan and Q'eqchi' Mayans who migrated from Mexico during the Caste War in the Yucatán Peninsula (1847–1901) and from Guatemala because of the systematic persecution of indigenous peoples during the 1970s and 1980s. Arabs are another group found among Belizeans. Usually identified as Turks, Lebanese, and Syrians, these people are actually Palestinians. This mosaic of ethnic and cultural background contributes to the creation of a multicultural ethos among Belizeans. English is the common language, but with all the immigrants from Guatemala, Mexico, and El Salvador, many also speak Spanish. Because of their ethnocultural diversity, it is not uncommon to find Belizean people who speak other languages depending on the region they are from, such as Garinagu, the language of the Garifuna and Mayan languages.

Of all the Central American countries, Guatemala has the largest concentrations of Mayans. There are 23 indigenous groups in Guatemala, in addition to the large dominant Ladinos (*mestizos/as*) population. Among them one can also find Garinagu peoples of the Atlantic coast, the Xinca people (an indigenous group unique to Guatemala), and other small groups such as Palestinians, Jews, Chinese, and Germans. This is clearly reflected in the Guatemalan population in the United States where the Maya

VIRGEN DE SUYAPA

In 1925, Pope Pius XII declared Nuestra Señora de Suyapa as the patron saint of Honduras, making February 3 her feast day. A statue of her is kept in Suyapa, a suburb of the capital city Tegucigalpa. Although several versions of the story of the statue's discovery exist, the most common concerns a laborer named Alejandro Colindres. During the mid-eighteenth century, while returning home after clearing a cornfield, Colindres was overtaken by nightfall. He decided to sleep outside, but when he lay down, he noticed a sharp pain. He reached for the object and tossed it away, but when he lay down again, he again felt the object. He removed it, but this time, instead of tossing it, he stored it. Come morning, he discovered he had been sleeping on a wooden statue of a dark-image Virgin, which stood a little over two inches tall. He took the statue home where it stayed for the next 20 years. By 1768, the statue began to garner public attention and was credited for occurring miracles. By 1777, a chapel was built to house the statue. Today she is venerated by Hondurans in their homeland and in the United States.

—*MAD*

communities are noticeably diverse, including peoples of Quiché, Mam, Kaq'chik'el, Chuj, Jacaltec, and Acatec ethnic and cultural roots. The largest numbers of Mayan people among Guatemalans in the United States are the Chujes, Quichés, and Kanjobals. For this reason, although Spanish is the official language in the country, among the Guatemalan population residing within the United States, Mayan groups still preserve their indigenous languages. One also encounters the language of the Garifuna population. These indigenous peoples preserve their cultures and traditions, such as the *baile de las máscaras*. The women wear the *huipíl* (typical women's attire) and men wear their traditional costumes. They continue to make many of their traditional dishes such as *pepián*, *tamales*, and *chuchitos*.

Most of the Salvadorans in the United States are culturally Ladino/as. They identify themselves with the Spanish culture they inherited from their Spanish ancestors. Although there are indigenous peoples from El Salvador, culturally most of them have been assimilated into the dominant Ladino culture, and for all Spanish is their native language. Small pockets of indigenous peoples that preserve their customs still remain. The most well-known is the community of Panchimalco, just outside of San Salvador, and they are *Pupil*, a nomadic tribe of the Nahua people from central Mexico. Salvadorans in the United States are an insular group, and because of the ways they organize their communities, often with their own doctors, banks, and social clubs, many do not learn English. One important aspect of Salvadoran culture is its cuisine. It is not difficult to find in the Salvadoran communities in the United States the famous *pupusas*, along with *tortillas*, *curtido*, *salpicón*, *y chicha*.

Hondurans in the United States are diverse; although the majority of the population is Ladino/as, there are African descendants, culturally Ladino/as, among them. There are also many of Ch'orti', Pech, Tolupan, or Xicaque,

Lenca, Miskito (Chibchan), and Sumo or Mayangna people (who display more commonalities with indigenous communities of Costa Rica, Panama, and Colombia). One also finds Garinagu and West Indian peoples who came as indentured laborers from Jamaica and Haiti, as well as growing Palestinian Arab and Jewish sectors. As a result of the military base that the United States built in Honduras during the 1980s, many Chinese, Ryukyuan Japanese, Filipino, and Vietnamese came as contract laborers and stayed in the country. It does not come as a surprise that, while Spanish is the common spoken language of Hondurans, the people from the island of Bahia, for example, speak Pidgin English. The indigenous and Garinagu languages are also found among the Honduran population of the United States. Among other cultural elements distinct to Honduran people is the Chatuye, the typical music of the Garinagu people characterized by fast drums and percussion beat. Among the distinctive Honduran dishes one finds the tamale, the *mondongo*, *atol*, and among the Garinagu fried fish and mashed plantain are popular foods.

The Garinagu people can be found among the Nicaraguan population in the United States. The majority of the population is Ladina/o, but other smaller groups such as the Chinese, Palestinian Arabic (who arrived to Honduras during the 1980s), Sumo, Rama, Miskito, and Afro-Caribbean also color the ethnic and cultural landscape of the Nicaraguan people. More than in any other of the Central American peoples, baseball is one of the most popular sports and pastimes played by the population. The *tortilla*, *Nacatamal, tamal*, and desserts called *almibares* represent only a small sample of the rich menu of Nicaraguan delicacies.

As already indicated, Costa Ricans and Panamanians in the United States do not represent large numbers, and often they tend to disappear in the English-speaking dominant culture. Indeed, both groups have indigenous and African presences, but most have been assimilated into the Ladino/a culture, and it is difficult to untangle their unique cultural elements. Some of the cultural distinctions of these communities are the *Punto Guanacastero*, which is the marimba rhythm original from the province of Guanacaste in Costa Rica, and the *Tamborito*, the folkloric music of Panama. One can also find blues and jazz among them. Panama distinguishes itself because, as Nicaragua, baseball dominates as the popular national sport. It is not too difficult to find places where one can taste various Panamanian dishes such as *sancocho*, *ceviche*, *carimanolas*, *tortillas*, and *chica fuerte* as a favorite beverage.

Part of the cultural ethos of Central Americans is a sense of sadness and nostalgia, which is communicated through music. The communities are deeply androcentric, and oftentimes men have the last word in the home. But things are changing because of their new contexts and different laws that help prevent abuse against women, and women are entering the labor force contributing to the well-being of the family. Moreover, for Central Americans food is not just sustenance; it is a sociocultural event. It is an opportunity to share one's life with relatives and friends. So when Central Americans get together, they must have their typical meals as part of the celebration. Food connects them to the good memories of their birth countries and gives them a sense of identity, so Central American products are imported or made locally in order to supply the demand.

Contrary to the Anglo emphasis on the nuclear home, great value is given to the extended family. Like many other ethnocultural groups, Central Americans mark the passage of time by way of relationships like *compadrazgo*, which is established when friends become the godparents of each other's children. They also celebrate the *quinceañera*, which is the celebration of the 15th birthday of one's daughter, and represents the passage from being a child to becoming a woman. Many Central Americans in the United States still believe their countries' folklore stories like *la Siguanaba, la Siguamonta, la Llorona, el Cadejo*, the *evil eye* spell, and *el Cipitio*. In many places of the United States they gather together to celebrate the day of independence from Spain, which, with the exception of Belize and Panama, took place the same day on September 15, 1821. Like most ethnic and cultural groups that migrate, Central Americans maintain close ties to their country of origin. Many establish transnational relations traveling back and forth between the United States and their birth countries by way of sending remittances, visiting for extended periods of time, and establishing small businesses.

One of the most recent negative sociocultural phenomena is the rapid growth of street gangs that originated in the United States but have spread rapidly in the Central American countries, the most affected of which are Guatemala, Salvador, and Honduras. The *Mara Salvatrucha* or MS-13 and the 18th Street Gang are transforming Central American communities as most gang members are from El Salvador, Guatemala, and Honduras, with small pockets of other Central Americans. Because many of these young Central Americans were deported back to their countries as a U.S. strategic fight against gang-related crimes, these gangs have shown extraordinary resilience as they have imported into their birth countries the U.S. style of gang crime, and maintain close ties to their U.S. counterparts. These gangs are the latest expression in the increasing phenomenon of Central American transnationalism.

Religion

Central Americans are profoundly religious and spiritual people. Their entire lives are permeated by religious symbols and practices. It is difficult to know the distribution of religious allegiances among them. In studying them, one must keep in mind that while a majority of the population is of Catholic background, followed by significant Protestant and evangelical presences, a number of other religious traditions are taking hold of the Central American population. Evangelicals does not refer to the type of evangelicalism as practiced in the United States. While there is great influence because of historical missionary activity and socioreligious impact, Central American evangelicals refer to nondenominational congregations that share more in common with Pentecostals.

Despite the small size of the Belizean enclaves, one can find Baha'i, Buddhist, Muslim, Jewish, and Rastafarian believers among them. In the Creole of Belize one can find practitioners of Obeah (a type of folk ritual that resembles Palo, Voodoo, and Santería). The majority of the people are Catholics, and the Protestants are largely United Methodists and Anglicans, as a result of the British influence in the region. There are small numbers of Baptists, Salvation Army,

Elementary school students with paper crowns march in the annual Three Kings Day Parade (Dia de los Reyes) *on January 5, 2006, in East Harlem, New York City. (AFP/Getty Images)*

German and Swiss Mennonites, and growing Pentecostal groups as a result of large missionary activity from the United States during the 1980s. Also, because of recent missionary activity, there are some Jehovah's Witnesses and Mormons (The Church of Jesus Christ of Latter-day Saints).

The small communities of Panamanians are quite diverse. Mormons, Jehovah's Witnesses, and Seventh-day Adventists are growing among them. There are Jews and Muslims, as well as Baha'i, and Chinese practicing Buddhism. Again the majority identify themselves with Catholicism. Protestants are very diverse and can be traced to direct U.S. presence in Panama for almost 100 years since the original leasing of

the Panama Canal area in 1903. Among Protestants one can find Lutherans, Southern Methodists, United Methodists, Presbyterians, and Unitarians. The Methodist Church in the Caribbean and the Americas (MCCA) is also present. A number of Baptist and Evangelical churches—the latter among the people of lower social and economic stratum—are making ground.

Among Costa Ricans, many claim to have no religion. Although largely Catholic, there is a growing Protestant population of Methodists, Baptists, Episcopalians, and Evangelicals. The Unification Church, Seventh-day Adventists, Jehovah's Witnesses, and Mormons are also present. Among other religions one encounters are Judaism, Islam, Taoism,

Baha'i, Scientology, Hare Krishna, and Tenrikyo. Although there are pockets of Beechy Amish communities and Quakers who migrated into Costa Rica as Conscientious Objectors, there is little trace they can be found among the Costa Rican people in the United States.

In Nicaragua, three-quarters of the population is Catholic. This is reflected among the Nicaraguans in the United States. There are also contingents of Protestant people such as Moravian, Episcopalian, Amish-Mennonites, Evangelicals, Mormons, and Jehovah's Witnesses, as well as some who claim to have no religious affiliation. The Baha'i faith is present, along with Muslims, Jews, the church of Scientology, and some syncretistic Garinagu religious expressions like Obeah.

Among the Garinagu of Honduras, Obeah and African folk religions honoring their ancestors are practiced. A significant portion of Hondurans in the United States are evangelicals. Growing rapidly, most Evangelical converts are ex-Catholics. Other Protestants among them are the Episcopalians and Lutherans. Few belong to the Greek Orthodox tradition. One can also find Mormons, Jehovah's Witnesses, and small concentrations of Muslims and Jewish peoples.

Although Catholicism is the predominant religious expression among Salvadorans, Protestantism has been present among them since the turn of the twentieth century, by way of the Central American Mission (CAM) that arrived in 1896. Not much later the Seventh-day Adventists and the Assemblies of God began doing missionary work. During the times of the economic depression of the 1930s growth dropped, but since 1960-1970, the years of heaviest military repression in El Salvador, Protestants grew exponentially. Thus, among Salvadorans, Catholics and Protestants are the largest groups, but there are other religions expressed such as Hare Krishna, Mormons, Jews, and Muslims, which constitute sizable minorities.

Guatemalans in the United States are not any less diverse than other Central American groups. The unique characteristic of Guatemalans is that a large percentage of them are of Evangelical background. The largest Evangelical churches are Prince of Peace, Assemblies of God, Elim, and a myriad of independent churches. Protestantism became possible in Guatemala because of anti-Catholic sentiments during the tenure of Rafael Cabrera (1844–1848), which limited the political and economic influence of the Catholic Church, and the connections made by the liberal dictator Justo Rufino Barrios, who opened the door for the Presbyterian Church to enter Guatemala in 1871. Presbyterianism did not succeed among the Ladino/a population and by the 1930s it was hardly popular. Among the Mayans, because of the Q'eqchi' and Kaq'chik'el translations of the Bible by the middle of the twentieth century, Presbyterians started to multiply. By 1945 Presbyterian churches had their own indigenous leaders. The Nazarene churches started to advance among the Q'eqchi' and Kaq'chik'el communities and by 1977, three out of every four ascribed to the Nazarene church. Another reason Protestants have grown relates to the 1976 earthquake in Guatemala, during which time the membership jumped 14 percent in the Protestant churches that provided food, furnished temporary housing, and helped reestablish the communities. Despite its large Protestant and Catholic sectors, among Guatemalans one will also find Mormons, Muslims,

Jews, and Jehovah's Witnesses. Based on the 1995 "Agreement on the Identity and Rights of Indigenous Peoples," which has not yet been fully implemented in Guatemala, the indigenous religious ancestral practices, and syncretistic expressions are once again emerging. These religious traditions are found among the various Guatemalan communities in the United States.

The majority of the Central American population in the United States identifies with the Catholic tradition, and there are large sectors of Protestants, mainly Evangelicals, among them. Christianity continues to be the prevalent religious expression attested to in some of the celebrations and holidays like Christmas and Easter week. Even more noticeable are the celebrations of the patron saint feasts like *La purísima* among Nicaraguans, celebrated from the last day of November to December 7, and concludes with one night of shouting (*noche de gritería*). Costa Ricans celebrate *La Virgen de los Ángeles*, and *el rosario del niño* on December 25. The indigenous communities from Totonicapán, Guatemala, often travel from the United States to San Cristobal, to celebrate *la fiesta de Santiago*, the patron saint of the region. Kanjobal Mayans from Los Angeles and southern Florida celebrate the feast of the patron saint of San Miguel Acatán on September 29 every year. The first week of August of every year is the most important national and religious festival for Salvadorans. During this time they honor Christ the Savior, El Salvador's namesake and patron savior of the world. Salvadoran communities in the United States celebrate this day with processions, fireworks, and community-oriented activities like sports and carnival rides.

Other religious celebrations relate more directly to the ancestral indigenous practices and religious feasts such as *Los hombres de maíz*. This is connected to the Popol Vuh, the Mayan sacred book narrating the creation of humanity out of corn. Particularly among the communities with a greater amount of indigenous people, there are tensions between indigenous religious practices and Christian ones. Traditionally Protestants, and more specifically Evangelicals, have been extremely intolerant of any type of syncretic religious expression claiming that the indigenous religious practices are some kind of witchcraft or devil worship. But even among Evangelicals and Catholics many Mayan believers secretly practice Mayan rituals.

It is worth noting that among Catholics issues of social justice are of major importance, a shift in the attitude of the Central American Catholic churches that can be traced back to the resolutions by the Second Vatican Council. In some of the mainstream Protestant religions, issues of social justice also play an important role. But among the recent Evangelical communities, the message of an afterlife salvation, packaged with a middle-class cultural ethos and work ethic, which minimizes the role and responsibilities of the state for its citizens is a perfect recipe for supporting conservative governments, as well as for adopting a gospel of prosperity by which financial wealth is seen as the result of one's good relationship with God. It is in this way that Central American Evangelicals in the United States, with the exception of some pockets of Nicaraguans, do not engage in direct political activity such as participating in political parties. Moreover, despite the large numbers of Protestants and Evangelicals among Central Americans in the United States, ecumenical conversations are rare, as people are also committed to the national expressions of the denomination to which they belong.

Néstor Medina

References and Further Reading

Berryman, Phillip. *Stubborn Hope: Religion, Politics, and Revolution in Central America* (New York: Orbis Books, 1994).

Garrard-Burnett, Virginia. *Living in the New Jerusalem: Protestantism in Guatemala* (Austin: University of Texas Press, 1998).

Medina, Andrés, ed. *La etnografía de Mesoamérica meridional y el área circuncaribe* (Mexico City, México: Universidad Nacional Autónoma de México, Instituto de Investigaciones Antropológicas, 1996).

Nepstad, Sharon Erickson. *Convictions of the Soul: Religion, Culture, and Agency in the Central America Solidarity Movement* (New York: Oxford University Press, 2004).

Samandú, Luis E. *Protestantismos y procesos sociales en Centro América* (San José, Costa Rica: Editorial Universidad Centroamericana, 1991).

Stoll, David. *Is Latin America Turning Protestant?* (Berkeley: University of California Press, 1990).

CHÁVEZ, CÉSAR (1927–1993)

César Chávez is widely acknowledged as the most important Mexican American civil rights activist of the twentieth century. His efforts to improve the lives of migrant farmworkers were guided by a religious and moral vision that was shaped by a variety of influences: the

César Chávez organized the first effective migrant worker union in the United States. His political skill and his unswerving dedication to one of society's most unprotected sectors made him a popular hero. (Library of Congress)

popular religion of his forebearers, his formal engagement with Catholicism and its social teachings, the Ghandian principle of nonviolence, and a preferential option for the poor.

The son of Mexican immigrants, Chávez was born on a small farm outside Yuma, Arizona. His family lost their farm during the Depression, compelling them to move to California in search of work as migrant farmworkers. Because of his family's ongoing search for work, Chávez reportedly attended 65 different elementary schools, and he never graduated from high school. His lack of formal education did not, however, lessen his desire to assist people like his parents and fellow farmworkers.

In the early 1950s, Chávez joined forces with labor organizers Fred Ross

UNITED FARM WORKERS UNION (UFW)

The United Farm Workers Union was established by Filipino and Mexican agricultural workers in California to confront the agribusiness power hold in the rural areas of that state. The union, while led by César Chávez, organized a successful international grape boycott in 1965. A major reason for the success of UFW was due to Chávez's ability to merge religious themes and symbols. Chávez used religious symbols like la Virgen de Guadalupe and religious acts like fasting to bring unity to the union. The grape boycott was able to reduce the international consumption of grapes by almost 25 percent, thus placing enough pressure on California grape growers to enter into collective bargaining. But by 1973, a massive campaign was launched against UFW by the Teamsters, agribusiness, and the Nixon administration. Violence was used to try to break UFW. Over 3,600 UFW members and supporters were arrested, many were beaten, and at least two were killed. Influenced by Ghandi's nonviolence religious movement, UFW refused to answer in like-kind.

—MAD

and Saul Alinsky through his involvement with the Community Service Organization (CSO). Chávez registered Mexican Americans to vote and helped them interact with government agencies. He rose to prominence within the organization, becoming its national director. After 10 years of a stable salary with the CSO, Chávez resigned in order to form the National Farm Workers Association (NFWA), which later became the United Farm Workers of America (UFW). For three decades, Chávez committed his life to the plight of impoverished laborers. He paid himself a salary of $5 a week.

The UFW came to national prominence in 1965 when Chávez led the first of many strikes against growers. In 1968, he championed the UFW's most successful campaign, urging Americans not to buy California table grapes until growers agreed to union contracts. Within this three-year period, Chávez helped transform a local coalition of 1,700 farmworking families into a national grape boycott observed by some 17 million Americans.

Chávez 's political activism owed much to his personal piety, but his religious and moral vision extended far beyond his own sacrificial action. He was particularly dedicated to the practice of nonviolence, as demonstrated by Mohandas Gandhi and Martin Luther King Jr. In 1968, the UFW commitment to nonviolence was challenged from within, and some members began to advocate violent tactics as they grew increasingly impatient with growers and the government. When faced with this dissension among the ranks, Chávez remained steadfast. "You cannot justify what you want for *La Raza,* for the people," he said, "and in the same breath destroy one life." Furthermore, knowing the commitment to nonviolence had been violated, Chávez undertook a penitential fast for 25 days to help restore the integrity of the movement. Chávez's fast—the first of three major ones—represented a turning point for the union and the movement. It marked an important political and spiritual crossroads for Chávez and for the proponents of *la causa* ("the struggle").

Fasting was just one element of popular religious practice utilized by Chávez. Chávez and the UFW mobilized several other popular religious practices and symbols of the community in the service of defending worker dignity. Other examples include the symbol of *La Virgen de Guadalupe*, often carried during marches; a 300-mile penitential pilgrimage from Delano to Sacramento; prayer vigils along the picket line; and political and comedic skits performed by *El Teatro Campesino*, the union theater troop, that emphasized the innate dignity of the farmworkers.

The union of the spiritual and the political is also seen in the fact that Chávez fostered a "community of inclusion." The range of people who participated in *la causa* was impressive and included Catholics and Protestants, Mexicans and Anglos, Filipinos and African Americans, Jews and Muslims, the working poor and the middle class, intellectuals and the unlettered, secular humanists and committed Christians. Chávez's commitment to an inclusive community is captured, for example, by his willingness to welcome students active in the Free Speech and Civil Rights movements. "At the beginning, I was warned not to take the volunteers, but I was never afraid of the students," Chávez recounts. "If it were nothing but farmworkers, we'd only have about 30 percent of all the ideas that we have. There would be no cross-fertilization, no growing. It's beautiful to work with other groups, other ideas, and other customs. It's like the wood is laminated."

Arguably more than any other Latino/a figure of the twentieth century, Chávez embodied the spiritual and political vision of a people. Chávez's life, according to scholar Frederick Dalton, was "liberation theology embodied, a life of sacrificial service and nonviolent action for the sake of human dignity and justice in solidarity with the poor." This commitment to human dignity and justice is nowhere better seen than in Chávez's famous "Letter from Delano," written in 1969 on Good Friday. The letter, which was reprinted in the *National Catholic Reporter* and the *Christian Century*, is addressed to the president of the California Grape and Tree Fruit League, Mr. E. L. Barr. Chávez writes:

> You must understand—I must make you understand—that our membership and the hopes and aspirations of the hundreds of thousands of the poor and dispossessed that have been raised on our account are, above all, human beings, no better and no worse than any other cross-section of human society; we are not saints because we are poor, but by the same measure neither are we immoral. We are men and women who have suffered and endured much, and not only because of our abject poverty but because we have been kept poor. The colors of our skins, the languages of our cultural and native origins, the lack of formal education, the exclusion from the democratic process, the numbers of our men slain in recent wars—all these burdens generation after generation have sought to demoralize us, to break our human spirit. But God knows that we are not beasts of burden, agricultural implements or rented slaves; we are men. And mark this well, Mr. Barr, we are men locked in a death struggle against man's inhumanity to man in the industry that you represent. And this struggle itself

gives meaning to our life and ennobles our dying. (Dalton 1993, 78–79)

Christopher Tirres

References and Further Reading

Dalton, Frederick John. *The Moral Vision of César Chávez* (Maryknoll, NY: Orbis Books, 2003).

Ferriss, Susan, and Ricardo Sandoval. *The Fight in the Fields: Cesar Chavez and the Farmworkers Movement*, ed. Diana Hembree (New York: Harcourt Brace & Company, 1997).

Griswold del Castillo, Richard, and Richard A. García. *César Chávez: A Triumph of Spirit* (Norman: University of Oklahoma Press, 1995).

León, Luis. "César Chávez and Mexican American Civil Religion." *Latino Religions and Civic Activism in the United States*, ed. Gastón Espinosa, Virgilio Elizondo, and Jesse Miranda (Oxford: Oxford University Press, 2005).

Lloyd-Moffett, Stephen R. "The Mysticism and Social Action of César Chávez." *Latino Religions and Civic Activism in the United States*, ed. Gastón Espinosa, Virgilio Elizondo, and Jesse Miranda (Oxford: Oxford University Press, 2005).

CHICANO THEOLOGY

Chicano Theology is a theology that emerges from the experience of Mexican Americans who are born and raised in the United States. For Chicana/os, it becomes a theological response to what they consider to be an occupied America. Reies López Tijerina, Episcopalian minister and Chicano land-rights activist of the 1960s in New Mexico, summed up the sentiments of many Chicana/os when he stated that for Chicano/as, the United States is their Babylon.

The Treaty of Guadalupe Hidalgo (1848), which brought an end to the Mexican-American War, was supposed to guarantee and secure the rights of Mexicans who discovered that the borders crossed them. Twelve years after signing the treaty, the United States violated its terms, just as the United States unilaterally voided earlier treaties signed with Native Americans. Both Native Americans and the Chicano/as were treated similar to the Israelites under Babylon's aggression. Corky González, who founded the Crusade for Justice in Denver, Colorado, captured this sentiment when he said that as Chicana/os living in the United States: "We have gone everywhere to windup nowhere."

Chicana/o Theology can be understood as a theology of captivity. Because Chicano/as are not treated as equals by the dominant Euro-American culture, oppressive structures are formed in their churches, their schools, their jobs, and their jails and prisons. Chicana/o Theology believes that those in power within the United States, as well as other industrialized nations, are not ignorant of the reality suffered by the dispossessed. Rather, they are aware of the existing imperialistic structures but choose not to change the prevailing systems because of the benefits and privilege derived from them.

Chicano/a Theology has many elements that are not germane to other theologies developed throughout the Third World. It is a synthesis of the world of affluence and the world of poverty with a corazón (heart) Latina/o. This heart identifies with the struggles of the Third World, but their presence within the United States provides understanding for the oppressive acts committed by the First World.

Another element that Chicano/a Theology confesses is a maternal understanding of God. The Lady of Guadalupe appeared to Saint Juan Diego, a poor Native American in Mexico, rather than a rich Spaniard. Because she appeared as a poor indigenous woman, many Mexicans hold a special place in their hearts for her, especially because of the important role played by mothers within Chicano/a culture. As a symbol of identity, the Virgin of Guadalupe becomes an important ingredient to Chicana/o consciousness.

A third element of Chicana/o Theology is that it outlines the identity of Chicana/os. The lure to assimilate into the dominant culture is powerful. This assimilation process has wreaked havoc among Chicana/os because it divides them from their identity. Advocates of a Chicano/a Theology believe that this process of assimilation has been the goal implemented by the dominant culture through the religious institutions and secular schools that service Chicano/as. The danger of assimilation is that it attempts to erase the collective memory of Aztlán. The ancestors of the Chicana/os have always inhabited the lands that would come to be known as the Southwestern United States. They did not come to the United States; the United States came to Aztlán only to hold the descendants of the original inhabitants, today's Chicana/os, captives on their own land. As dangerous as colonizing the taken land is, more so is colonizing the Chicana/o's mind. Though their response to the Euro-American seizing of another's land, Chicano/a Theology offers the world a different paradigm, specifically, not to hoard material things, but rather to share

them. In this sense it becomes a prophetic theology that condemns private property as constructed by Western imperialism. In essence, a Chicano/a Theology is a theology that attempts to dismantle the present social structures based on land ownership.

A fourth element of a Chicano/a theology is the concept of leadership and organization. Chicana/o Theology insists that the leadership of the Chicano/a movement can never compromise the struggles and hopes of its people, not just for their sake but also the sake of their oppressors. It is within the organizations created by the oppressed that oppressors find liberation from Mammon. It is important that Chicana/os teach unconditional self-love in order that the oppressed can learn to love themselves and others unconditionally. Love of enemies becomes the ultimate expression of unconditional self-love. Chicana/o Theology directs leaders to empower their constituents to organize themselves for justice and peace at whatever cost, even to the point of death.

Ideally, the leadership of the Chicano/a Movement in the United States understands both the world of the oppressor and the world of the oppressed. Having a fuller grasp of reality provides greater insight into the problems and challenges faced by Chicana/os. Thus they are in a better position to develop possible solutions. Chicano/a Theology maintains that the problems faced by the oppressed were created by the structures fostered by oppressors for the purpose of maintaining and advancing their power and privilege. Seldom are Chicano/as consulted prior to implementing social or economic policies that directly affect them. Ironically, it is the powerless that can offer the dominant culture liberation from having to live up to a false conscience of superiority.

Another concept of Chicana/o Theology resides in the coexistence of the person and the community. The focus of Chicano/a thought is the person, not material—"person" here understood as an extension of community. Rugged individualism is rejected as part of the assimilation process that subordinates the community to the individual. As important as the individual is, the community comes first. Finally, Chicano/a Theology is centered on needs of the oppressed. As Jesus would say, the last shall be first, and the one losing his/her life will win it. It is from this perspective that the wider world is understood.

Andrés Quetzalcóatl Gonzalés Guerrero

References and Further Reading

Acuña, Rodolfo. *Occupied America: The Chicano's Struggle Toward Liberation* (San Francisco: Cantfield Press, 1972).

Elizondo, Virgilio. *La Morenita: Evangelizer of the Americas* (San Antonio: Mexican American Cultural Center, 1980).

Freire, Paulo. *Pedagogy of the Oppressed*, trans. Myra Bergman Ramos (New York: Seabury Press, 1974).

Guerrero, Andrés Gonzalés, Jr. *A Chicano Theology* (New York: Orbis Press, 1987).

CHICANO/A MOVEMENT

The Chicano Movement emerged in the late 1960s and early 1970s on college and high school campuses, in urban barrios, and in rural communities across the Southwest United States, coalescing a new generation of activism. Inspired by the influence of an emergent youth culture and the turbulent voices of social change reflected in the free speech movement, Black Civil Rights Movement, Antiwar Movement, and an emerging feminist movement, young Mexican Americans sought to confront the racism of the dominant culture. They chose new organizing strategies, articulated their own vision, and confronted the "Establishment" of both an older generation of Mexican Americans and the Anglo power structure.

The term "Chicano/a" identifies people of Mexican heritage in the United States. As the term adopted by the Movement, it represented a political consciousness that asserted the right to full participation in U.S. society without surrendering their Mexican heritage and identity, rejecting what they saw as the more assimilationist identity reflected in the usage of the term "Mexican American." Additionally, the terms "Hispanic" and "Latina/o" both refer collectively to peoples from all Latin American heritages. While these terms are sometimes used interchangeably with the term "Chicana/o" or any other specific ethnic identity, this is grossly inaccurate. Most people who identify as Latino/a or Hispanic would usually first identify themselves by their particular ethnicity or national heritage.

The War on Poverty and the Vietnam Era GI Bill begun in 1966 helped to create a significant Mexican American presence on college campuses in the mid-1960s, especially in California. Mexican American college enrollment surged just as student activity on campuses across the country radicalized. Mexican American campus activists, many of whom came from poverty, began to make connections between the Civil Rights Movement and the Antiwar Movement and the poverty, social

REIES LÓPEZ TIJERINA (1926–)

Along with César Chávez, Rodolfo "Corky" Gonzales, and José Angel Gutiérrez, Reies López Tijerina is considered one of the four founding fathers of the Chicano movement. Tijerina is the most militant of the four, interested mainly in land grants of New Mexico. On September 10, 1926, in Fall City, Texas, Tijerina was born to a farmworking family. As an ordained minister of the Assemblies of God, Tijerina used his oratorical skills as a preacher to become a popular voice in New Mexico during the 1960s. Tijerina helped establish *La Alianza Federal de las Mercedes* (The Federal Land-Grant Alliance) to address land-grant questions. In 1967, Tijerina called his group to convene at the town of Coyote to make plans to reinhabit the Republic of San Joaquin del Rio Chama—Echo Amphitheater in Kit Carson National Forest, which they had done the previous year. Eventually, Tijerina and his group would raid the courthouse in search of the county attorney who violated the civil rights of the Alianza. Two police officers were shot and two hostages were taken, albeit the latter without Tijerina's knowledge. Although becoming nonmilitant in his later years, Tijerina and his group demonstrated that Chicanos were willing to resort to violence if forced.

—SOP

isolation, and political marginalization of their own communities.

Leaders as diverse as César Chávez (United Farm Workers, UFW), Reies López Tijerina (Alianza Federal de Mercedes), Rudolfo "Corky" Gonzáles (Crusade for Justice), and José Angel Gutiérrez (Raza Unida Party) organized local communities around a broad agenda of issues, including labor, land, education, economic development, and voting rights. Student walkouts on high school campuses in cities like Los Angeles, Denver, and Tempe (Arizona), and emerging student organizations on college campuses spread the grassroots movement.

Chicano/a activists disagreed on priorities and strategies, but were unified in seeking radical social change. They rejected the accommodationist and assimilationist politics of earlier generations, asserting claims for a distinct identity in U.S. politics and culture.

The militancy of *movimiento* rhetoric met resistance within the Mexican American community, where established leaders critiqued the strategies and ideology, including use of the term "Chicano/a." They also met forceful opposition from law enforcement that often resulted in violent encounters from riots to rural gun battles. The death of Ruben Salazar, a Los Angeles journalist, in the aftermath of the Chicano Moratorium was a galvanizing moment. The August 1970 national day of protest, following two earlier actions in Los Angeles, drew an estimated 30,000 protestors to Laguna Park in East Los Angeles. Violence erupted when police decided to put an early end to the rally and tried to force the crowd to leave. Salazar was one of three people killed by police. His reporting of police brutality and support for the Chicano Movement in Los Angeles led many to suspect he had been targeted.

TEATRO CAMPESINO

El Teatro Campesino was founded by Luis Valdez in 1965 as an organizing tool of the United Farm Workers (UFW) and contributed significantly to the development of the nationalist Chicana/o identity of the movement. The ensemble theater drew on the rich oral tradition of Mexican and Chicana/o culture. A collective development process and improvisation created short *actos* (acts) to dramatize the themes of the union struggle, often with a dramatic humor that reflected the influence of the comedic style of Cantínflas. Laughter became a powerful political tool, proclaiming the worker's truth and making oppressive bosses, politicians, and other symbols of authority laughable. In the 1970s, El Teatro Campesino left its affiliation with the UFW and became an active voice of the Chicano Movement, expressing the Chicana/o critique of cultural assimilation and political accommodation. It contributed to the strong identity of Chicanisma/o with its indigenous, non-European roots and working-class culture, and employed the bilingualism of Chicana/o youth. It also reflected the male dominance of the movement. Women's roles in Teatro productions were typically very traditional. Female members of the ensemble, like women in many parts of the movement, subverted their feminist critique to the seemingly more pressing goals of the cause.

—TCS

The movement grew out of disparate roots and never agreed on a common agenda or ideology, yet it gave birth to a new sense of identity that empowered the Mexican American community, asserting the fundamental claim that one did not have to surrender language, heritage, or culture to claim the rights of citizenship, to participate in the economic and political life of the nation. César Chávez, for example, never identified the UFW with the Chicano Movement, but young Chicanas/os were inspired by the UFW to believe change was possible. *El Movimiento* confronted racism and racial self-hate, asserting pride in the Indian-*mestizo* physical features and cultural roots. The Chicana/os of the 1960s proclaimed "brown is beautiful" and advocated a strong sense of cultural nationalism. Chicanos asserted pride in the very things that made them suspect in a racialized culture—claiming not only the beauty and strength of Chicanisma/o over and against the prejudices of the dominant White culture but also claiming their right to belong. The use of Spanish in the context of English emerged as an intentional statement of *mestizo/a* identity and sense of place in the dominant culture.

The early movement was extremely male dominated. The leaders of the movement had been socialized in a very patriarchal and homophobic culture. As they asserted the right to express their own identity from within that culture in the public arena, they did not critique those values. Yet the movement gave impetus to a generation of Chicana feminist activists and writers, such as Marta Cotera, Anna Nieto-Gómez, Norma Alarcón, Gloria Anzaldúa, and Cherríe Moraga. Marta Cotera organized the first national Chicana conference in Houston in 1971, but it would be a second generation of Chicana students on college campuses in the late 1970s who would speak to the issues of Chicana feminism and demand change to include their perspective in Chicano Studies programs.

Leadership of *El Movimiento* emerged from different streams: labor and community organizers, many working through agencies and programs of the War on Poverty, voting rights, and student activists. Some had first organized with Black civil rights groups. Maria Varela joined the National Student Association, working alongside the Student Nonviolent Coordinating Committee (SNCC). She would later join the Alianza in New Mexico. Carlos Muñoz joined SNCC as a student at California State University at Los Angeles and would later become a major figure in the student movement. César Chávez learned from and modeled the strategies of the UFW on the nonviolent model of Martin Luther King Jr.

From Local Organizing to National Movement, Leaders of El Movimiento

César Chávez gained national prominence as a union organizer. He remained focused on the UFW, not attending any of the national Chicano/a conferences or protests, nor linking the farmworker struggle to a larger Chicano cause. Still, he was an inspiration for the movement. Many of the students on college campuses had come from farmworker families who represented the poorest and most vulnerable of the Chicano community. Chávez expressed a demand for justice and goals for a better future that transcended the immediate goals of union organizing.

Chávez trained in grassroots organizing with the Industrial Areas Foundation

(IAF), led by populist Saul Alinsky, and was inspired by the social justice teachings of the Roman Catholic tradition. Gil Padilla and Dolores Huerta joined the effort early and were key organizers. All three began their careers working to improve conditions for migrant workers through the Community Services Organization (CSO). Dolores Huerta had lobbied in Sacramento for legislative reform. All three became convinced that a union was needed to effect real change.

A strike in 1965 and the march to Sacramento in 1966 brought national attention to the growing union. Without a strike fund, the UFW turned to outside sources for aid. One of the first organizations to respond was the California Migrant Ministry. Union leadership intentionally employed religious symbols, in large part to stave off the potential for violence that historically plagued union organizing. Workers were admonished in strike meetings that anyone who used violence would have to leave the strike. Although local clergy in Delano were not supportive at first, the union actively sought church involvement, building a strong interdenominational coalition of supporters. Mass or prayer services were held before strike activities. "*De Colores*," the theme song of the Roman Catholic Cursillo program, became a theme song of the union. Strikers displayed banners of La Virgen de Guadalupe, the Huelga flag.

Reies López Tijerina, a Pentecostal preacher, organized *hispanos* in northern New Mexico to reclaim lands lost to the Anglo occupation. He articulated the rationale for Chicano nationalism, grounded in the experience of conquest and the broken promises of the 1848 Treaty of Guadalupe Hidalgo. This treaty guaranteed Mexicans north of the Rio

Reies López Tijerina gestures during a speech in Albuquerque, New Mexico, in 1972. Tijerina and the Alianza Federal de Pueblos Libres, *the organization he founded in 1963, demanded that the U.S. government recognize the provisions of the 1848 Treaty of Guadalupe Hidalgo. They contend the government reneged on the treaty, which settled the U.S.-Mexican War and, in essence, stole nearly 100 million acres of land from Chicano ancestors from Texas and California. (Bettmann/Corbis)*

Grande all the rights of citizens of the United States, including the right to their property, the right to maintain the Spanish language, and the right to practice their own religious traditions.

The *Alianza Federal de Mercedes*'s (Federal Alliance of Land Grants) stated objective of regaining land grant properties for the descendents of the Spanish and Mexican colonists was doomed to fail, but in its short-lived rise to national prominence it spotlighted the severe poverty of northern New Mexico and the *Hispano* communities in particular. Land once held in common by villagers for farming and ranching, now controlled by the U.S. Forest Service, was the primary target of Alianza efforts. In the mid-1960s the Forest Service enacted greater restrictions, banning access for grazing milk cows and draft horses needed by small *Hispano* farmers. The Alianza began by seeking remedy through the courts and governmental actions. In July 1966, the group marched from Abiquiu to the capitol in Santa Fe to demand an investigation of their claims that the Treaty of Guadalupe had been abrogated, calling for a commission to investigate their claims.

Met with resistance, the Alianza moved to more direct action and began plans to occupy a campground in the Kit Carson National Forest. This action was largely ignored by government officials. Eventually, five *Aliancistas* were arrested. The confrontational rhetoric provoked open hostility from Anglos in the region, even though then Governor David Cargo expressed sympathy with their cause. High emotions and media frenzy helped to escalate events. Alianza organizers were accused of being communist. The movement ultimately was short-lived, its energy dissipated by legal charges and court cases, but it inspired Chicano/a activists' appeal to nationalist/ separatist notions of an historical homeland—Atzlán.

Rudolfo "Corky" Gonzales, a Democratic Party leader heavily involved in the Denver War on Poverty, co-chaired the Mexican American contingent of the Poor People's March with Reies López Tijerina in 1968. He became disenchanted with local party politics as indifferent to Mexican American poverty and formed the Crusade for Justice as a grassroots organization. Author of the epic poem, "*Yo Soy Joaquin*," which became an anthem of the movement, he helped define cultural nationalism and articulated a vision of liberation rooted in the mythic return to Atzlán. His "El Plan de Barrio" proposed a self-sufficient economically developed barrio, with public housing for Chicano/as only, bilingual education, barrio economic development, and restitution of land to descendants of *Hispana/o* colonists in Colorado and New Mexico.

Gonzáles connected with the emerging youth movement in Denver, where high school students walked out in 1968 after a teacher made derogatory statements in class. Their action grew to a three-day protest. Twenty-five people were arrested, including Gonzalez, who told rallying students they were the leaders of the revolution; they were making history.

The Denver protests drew national headlines. Gonzales called for the National Chicano Liberation Youth Conference in March 1969. More than 1,000 people from across the country gathered in Denver. The largest contingent came from California. Participants described the conference as an intense celebration of Chicanisma/o. It produced *El Plan Espiritual de Atzlán*—a separatist response to "Gringo" occupation and oppression—and gave birth to the idea of a national day of protest against the Vietnam War—what would become the 1970 Chicano Moratorium in East Los Angeles.

The conference also sparked one of the earliest expressions of Chicana feminism. Women at the conference organized their own workshop. They condemned the sexism of the movement and asserted that women's liberation would have to follow the men. Male speakers at the conference attributed feminism to the CIA—a scheme to undermine the movement—or simply attributed it to the incursion of Anglo culture and refused the report from the women's workshop. Although the male leadership of the crusade hushed up the women's criticism at the conference, they did not silence the emerging feminist voice of *El Movimiento*. Women took the ideas from the women's workshop back to their communities. Marta Cotera, for example, went from Denver to organize in Texas. A Raza Unida Party activist, she organized Chicana feminist meetings in Houston in 1971 and 1972.

Shortly after the Denver conference, students from California met at the University of California, Santa Barbara (UCSB), where they called for college curricula that served the community. They outlined a design for implementing Chicano Studies programs throughout the UC system. This meeting also led to the organization of MECHA (*El Movimiento Estudiantil de Atzlán*). "Chicano" became "canonized" at this meeting as the term identifying the movement. The term has had varied popularity in the Mexican American community, but has remained in use by political activists, in academia, in Ethnic Studies programs, and in student organizations.

José Angel Gutiérrez was one of the founders of MAYO, the Mexican American Youth Organization. Organized in San Antonio in 1967, it was the precursor of La Raza Unida Party (LRUP). Gutiérrez was a driving force behind the organizing in Crystal City, which galvanized support for LRUP. Impatient with the slow and costly process of seeking redress through the courts, MAYO made significant strides organizing student walkouts and boycotts across Texas to protest segregation and advocate for bilingual education in public schools.

Crystal City typified many communities in South Texas—Mexican Americans were 80 percent of the population, yet most lived in extreme poverty. A very small percentage of middle-class Mexican Americans owned small businesses or worked in civil service. An Anglo-dominant power structure excluded Mexican Americans from political power and controlled the local economy. Organizing began in the high school where Chicana/o students protested their exclusion in extracurricular activities. Their efforts grew, gaining community-wide support and advocates from across the

state. In January 1970, the school board conceded to many of their demands. This success launched the development of La Raza Unida, a significant third-party movement, as the Chicano/a community organized through LRUP to gain political control of local government in Crystal City also.

Early success in Texas led to chapters of LRUP across the Southwest and California. Although most local chapters were not successful in getting candidates elected, LRUP brought greater visibility to the issues of the Chicano Movement—the need for education reform, the need for economic development, and the reality of racism toward Mexican Americans. The growth of LRUP would give the Chicano Movement a national voice on the political scene and give Chicano/as greater bargaining power within both traditional political parties. The increased participation and representation of Mexican Americans in state and local government is one of the legacies of the Chicano Movement.

The Chicano Movement helped change the way U.S. history is written in textbooks across the country. It created new directions in scholarship and saw a growing Mexican American middle class emerge, able to take advantage of opportunities created by Affirmative Action. It has also seen the backlash in the English-Only Movement and the aggressive anti-immigrant politics of the 1990s and 2000s. The legacy of the movement may also be seen in the incursion of Chicana/o identity and culture in the larger cultural landscape and consciousness—from popular music and media to the contributions of Chicana/o artists, poets, scholars, and theologians.

Teresa Chávez Sauceda

References and Further Reading

Broyles-González, Yolanda. *El Teatro Campesino: Theater in the Chicano Movement* (Austin: University of Texas Press, 1994).

De La Torre, Adela, and Beatríz M. Pesquera. *Building with Our Hands: New Directions in Chicana Studies* (Berkeley and Los Angeles: University of California Press, 1993).

Muñoz, Carlos. *Youth, Identity, Power: The Chicano Movement* (New York: Verso, 2007).

Noriega, Chon A., Eric R. Avila, Karen Mary Davalos, Chela Sandoval, and Rafael Pérez-Torres, eds. *The Chicano Studies Reader: An Anthology of Aztlán, 1970–2000* (Los Angeles: University of California Press, 2001).

Rosales, F. Arturo. *Chicano! The History of the Mexican American Civil Rights Movement*, 2nd ed. (Houston, TX: Arte Publico Press, University of Houston, 1997).

COMUNIDAD

Comunidad is the Spanish word for community, derived from the Latin *communis*, which refers to "common sharing." This entry considers comunidad, understood as a unique theological term that cannot simply be interchanged with its seeming English equivalent "community." The term "comunidad" refers to the experience of Latino/as religious sharing that embodies their history and culture and considers their vibrant spirituality. Both of the terms, "community" and "comunidad," emerge from and embody the same classic theological principles. This entry explores this foundational theology of community, but primarily highlights comunidad as manifested in the mid-twentieth century to the present and in Latin America and the United States.

A secular understanding of community refers to multifaceted relations of people who share common values, beliefs, and responsibilities in any number of human structures and relationships such as family, neighborhood, or country. Depending on the level of personal commitment, these relations determine the level of engagement. Consider that in a single day a person may relate to a marriage partner, family members, co-workers, bowling team members, and parishioners they pray with at a local church. These various and multifaceted relationships help form identity and provide meaning to the individual as well as the group.

Theologically, all Christian communities are recognized by their shared belief in Jesus Christ. The early Christian communities were also known by their sharing of a common life and efforts toward mutual love. Thus charity remains at the heart of any authentic and vibrant Christian community.

Theologian Roberto Goizueta theologizes about the meaning and implications of comunidad for Latina/os. He recalls the history of oppression endured by Hispanics that has forged a shared communal experience of suffering. This oppression continues in the present, in Central and Latin America, and in the United States, particularly with the immigrant community. This comunidad is inclusive of all who participate in acts of Christian charity as well as spiritual solidarity with compassion for the poor and suffering. The term "accompaniment" articulates this experience of a Latino/a shared journey. Goizueta understands communal accompaniment to be "an active solidarity with the poor.

In the face of intransigent political obstacles to liberation, the process of accompanying the poor in their everyday struggles is seen as the foundation of more expressly or overtly sociopolitical forms of liberation." Moreover, comunidad is the Christian experience of a grassroots faith journey lived out day by day (*lo cotidiano*). Accompaniment is "walking with" the others in all the joys and sorrows of daily life. It is a moving blend of both the spiritual and the cultural expressions of the Latino/a's inclination for communal sharing.

The tragedy of one family, such as the death of a family member, is transformed into a collective experience when an entire comunidad shares the burden of suffering as well as assisting one another. Such experiences express the significance of all accompaniment, which is the implicated understanding as well as the living reality of Christ's passion in comunidad. The suffering of Christ and that of the comunidad are one. Latino/a scholars also apply "accompaniment" to the common experience of celebration at the Liturgy and expression of popular religiosity. For the Latino/a comunidad Holy Week Liturgies with their processions and feast days, like the Day of the Dead and the Feast of Our Lady of Guadalupe, are cultural and spiritual experiences, shared and passionately celebrated by all with music and food.

Goizueta makes these observations. Most Hispanics would tend to identify comunidad less with the institutional and hierarchical Church than with their local parish. The Latina/o finds her/his identity and home within this comunidad in relationship with those she or he finds there. The comunidad is the extension of the family, a place of warmth and safety. Traditionally, Latino/a communities consist of immigrants and the children of immigrants bonded not only by faith but by common language and their shared immigrant experience. The dynamic flux of these communities gathers together Latino/as of various cultural traditions at varying stages of their acculturation. The inherent sense of accompaniment that is central to Hispanic culture exists in contrast to the individualistic anthropology that is dominant in U.S. culture.

In the broader theology spectrum, community as fundamental to Christianity possesses a complexity of meanings and encompasses overlapping theological arenas. These theological disciplines all systematically reflect upon and enrich the Church's understanding of community. For example, biblical theology considers the origin and nature of the first Christian communities; ecclesiology understands both the universal Church as well as the local community as base ecclesial communities; ecumenism envisions a theological reality where all Christians join in full communion; spirituality theology articulates the praxis of the Christian life.

The biblical understanding of community begins in the Hebrew Scripture and has its roots in the nature of God's relationship with the Hebrew people. Many individuals were bonded together as one people by way of their "covenant" with God. The Hebrews' relationship with God was a collective covenant, or, as theologian Bernard J. Lee. clarifies, "There were no private covenants with Yahweh."

He also explains that in the Christian Scripture it is important to distinguish between Church and community. In the Act of the Apostles the term *ekklēsia* is used, which comes from the Greek verb

Cristina Vazquez celebrates her fifteenth birthday with a lavish celebration called a Quinceanera. *The custom is a celebration of the young girl (*la Quinceanera*), and a recognition of her journey from childhood to maturity. The celebration highlights God, family, friends, music, food, and dance. (Najlah Feanny/Corbis)*

kalio meaning "to call" or "convoke." In classical usage, *ekklēsia* refers to the assembly of the people, called together to deliberate on a problem of a public nature (Acts 19:29–40). The gatherings of Christians took place in private houses until the fourth century, meaning that the term *ekklēsia* referred to a gathering of people and not to a church building (*domus ecclesiae*). This clearly differs from the common notion of church today as either a building or an institution.

In the Gospels, Jesus forms a community of 12 apostles, whom he loves, instructs, and patiently mentors into future pastors of the first primitive Christian communities. Moreover, Jesus' ministry is founded upon his efforts to form an extended community of disciples.

These members included rich and poor, men and women, Jews and Greeks. Some of these first communities' members shared a common life, offering their possessions for the good of the community. Certainly there were also more generic Christian communities, where members retained their possessions and homes and continued living their respective lives. All early community members were spiritually transformed in their way, sharing a common faith that bonded them together in the person of Jesus.

From John's Gospel a theology of community emerges as Jesus gathers his flock through self-sacrifice (John 10:1–15). Various Johnanne theological allegories suggest the importance of community, for example, the allegory of the vine and the branches (John 15:15). These allegories correspond theologically to the Pauline teaching that Church is the Body of Christ. Pauline theology depicts Christians as part of the Body of Christ, each with her/his specific role, working in harmony with one another. No part or member can exist without the other; all work together to form the Body of Christ.

Religion scholar R. E. Whitson recalls the two doctrinal theological principles that define and affirm Christian community. First, the Trinity is the primary and perfect community. God is a dynamic community of three persons: Father, Son, and Spirit, united as One. Thus, implicit in the principle of humans as "created in God's image and likeness" emerges a theological anthropology of the human person as relational in character—as God exists in community, so too human existence necessitates relationships with others. Though the Father, Son, and Spirit exist in perfect communion, they also retain their individual personhood. Likewise, people have innate individuality essential to their personhood. A healthy community affirms and cultivates both the individual and collective identity. Thus Trinitarian doctrine establishes a community as a complex dynamic that is relational and individual in nature. The second doctrinal premise is the incarnation. In the person of Jesus Christ, divinity and humanity are joined, thus establishing a unique communion between God and humankind. Jesus Christ is the unifying center of all creation. In Jesus Christ, salvation is extended to all through the miracle of this union of divinity and humanity.

No other experience of comunidad has had more impact than the Latin American manifestation of Christian Base Communities. Marcello de C. Azevedo traces the origin of these communities not to Latin America, as one would suppose, but to the 1950s and 1960s in Europe, especially in France and Italy. Initially these communities were attempts to establish an alternate model of church that was neither hierarchically nor institutionally centered. Distinctive forms of these communities developed apart from Latin America in other Third World countries such as the Philippines, Zaire, and Mozambique. Efforts were made in the late 1970s and 1980s to establish these communities among Latino/as in southern California, Texas, and New Mexico.

Originally these communal initiatives were called "basic ecclesial communities," "CEBs," or "*comunidades de base.*" "Base" refers to the communities' place at the bottom of both ecclesial and social structures. After the General Assembly of Latin American bishops met in Medellín, Colombia, in 1968, these communities began to consolidate. Presently there are thousands of these groups in Latin America, though exact numbers remain undetermined. Azevedo notes that in Brazil alone, which has the largest number of CEBs, it is estimated that in 2007 there were as many as 70,000 or 80,000.

Various factors gave rise to the emergence of these CEBs. The theological movements and new methodologies of the twentieth century came to fruition in the Second Vatican Council in the early 1960s. Rather than solely reflecting upon doctrinal principle, the Council considered "the signs of the times." Thus the Council engaged the vital concerns of the laity with a newfound theological anthropology that emphasized social and economic justice in a modern world.

These movements brought fresh and pertinent meaning to what the Council now understood as contemporary evangelization.

For the poor in Latin America, modernization was simply an extension of their long history of oppression that had now taken the form of political and social injustice and economic dominance by the first world powers. The modern oppression that continued in Latin America meant ongoing discrimination, marginalization, and poverty. Liberation Theology employed the Council's methodology and applied its rearticulated evangelism to the Latin American people. It boldly placed the suffering of the poor at the center of its reflection. Thus Liberation Theology emerged as a font of original and relevant theology empowering the poor, for the most part, at a distance from the institutional church. Ordinary people formed small communities and found themselves empowered not only by one another but by ongoing reflection on scripture. These groups identified their oppressive condition with biblical narratives, such as the Hebrew enslavement in the book of Exodus. Furthermore, these groups naturally cultivated lay leadership and the importance of the immediacy of their individual and communal needs. This communal empowerment was a radical shift from traditional privatized or devotional spiritualities of the past. Azevedo writes of his experiences in Brazil: "These are communities. They want to recover the Judeo-Christian tradition of living faith in a public way, not a privatized way; of defying, through solidarity, the individualist and competitive character imposed by the contemporary culture; of transcending the privatistic spiritually centered solely on the individual person

that has prevailed for the past five centuries."

Other important and timely theological contributions to the CEBs came from bishops' conferences held in Latin America. This entry can offer only a listing of these important conferences: Medellín (1968) and Puebla (1979), as well as the Protestant assemblies of CLAI (Latin American Council of Churches) in Lima (1982), Sao Paulo (1988), and Concepcíon (1995).

If CEBs offer the most original contemporary expression of community, ecumenism advances a visionary union of presently divided Christian traditions. The premise of ecumenism comes from John's Gospels, where Jesus instructs "that they [my disciples] may be one just as we are" (John 17:11). Perhaps even more compelling is Jesus' explanation that the unity of Jesus Christ's disciples gives witness that He is the savior of the world. In contradistinction, the greatest scandal of Christianity is its disaccord. Though ecumenical efforts began in the first part of the twentieth century, for Roman Catholics the Second Vatican Council initiated the importance of ecumenical relationships. The Council offered a new understanding that Christian unity was not an appendage but an essential to Roman Catholic ecclesiology. Ecumenism envisions "full communion" between major Christian traditions, though it is impossible at this time to articulate how this might come about or what it might look like. Thus, ecumenism is a theology as well as a practice of communal hope, Christians of various traditions compelled by their common faith in Jesus Christ to courageously engage in dialogue that advances their unity. Theological dialogue between various Christian traditions is the means employed by ecumenists. Formal theological dialogues are conducted on a local, national, and international level. They engage in discourse to understand and advance not only theological accord between these traditions, but meaningful relations between Christian traditions that are still divided by significant theological, historical, and practical differences. Scholar Jeffrey Gross clarifies that "This [dialogue] is effected not by compromise, but by common biblical and historical study." The goal, he writes, is to "find a ground of truth which transcends historical division."

With regard to the ecumenical movement in Latin America, Gross makes this observation: "The ecumenical movement in Latin America is complicated by a preponderance of evangelical and Pentecostal Christians there who are more dominant and less ecumenical than the historical churches with whom the Church is in dialogue."

It is important to consider the emergence of Latino/a theologians from various Protestant as well as Catholic traditions who work together in an academic context to articulate a shared Hispanic theology. More notable has been the cooperative theological reflection of Hispanic Christian traditions, Catholic and Protestant, in the work of the Academy of Catholic Hispanic Theologians (ACTUS). The Asociacíon para la Educacíon Teológica Hispana (AETH) carries out a similar theological mission in the Protestant tradition and has always been open to Catholic participation and membership. Joint theological mentoring has been sponsored by Hispanic Theological Initiatives (HTI).

Rafael Luévano

References and Further Reading

Azevedo, Marcello. "Base Communities." *The Dictionary of Catholic Social Thought*, ed. Judith A. Dwyer (Collegeville, MN: The Liturgical Press, 1994).

———. *Basic Ecclesial Communities in Brazil: The Challenge of a New Way of Being Church* (Washington, DC: Georgetown University Press, 1987).

Boff, Leonardo. *Ecclesiogenesis: The Base Communities Reinvent the Church* (Maryknoll, NY: Orbis Books, 1986).

Goizueta, Roberto. "Accompaniment." *Dictionary of Third World Theologies*, ed. Virginaa Fabella and R. S. Sugirtharajah (Maryknoll, NY: Orbis Books, 2000).

———. *Caminemos Con Jesús: Towards a Hispanic/Latino Theology of Accompaniment* (Maryknoll, NY: Orbis Books, 2005).

Gross, Jeff. "Ecumenism." *The Dictionary of Theology* (Collegeville, MN: The Liturgical Press, 1987).

Whiteson, R. E. "Community." *The New Catholic Encyclopedia*, 2nd ed. (Gale, MI: The Catholic University of America, 2003).

CONQUISTADORES

The Castilian term *Conquistadores* signifies the "conquerors" that sailed from Spain to the Americas, Asia, Africa, and the Pacific in search of land and wealth. The term originated in Spain during the Middle Ages to identify the knights, mercenaries, and soldiers who fought against the Moors in the Spanish Reconquest (*Reconquista*) from the late 700s to the defeat of the Islamic Caliphate of Granada by the unified monarchy of King Ferdinand II of Aragon and Queen

LA MALINCHE (1498?–1540?)

La Malinche was the indigenous woman who became Hernán Cortés's interpreter, local guide, and mistress who bore him a son during the Spanish conquest of Mexico from 1519 to 1525. Her Nahuatl birth name was probably "Malintzin" or "Malinal." She is also known by her Christian baptismal name, Doña Marina. After her father died, her mother remarried and had a son. Malinche was given away as a slave by her step-father who favored her half-brother as heir. The Cacique of Tabasco gave her along with 19 other slave girls to Cortés. Her knowledge of Nahuatl, and the Mayan languages of Yucatan, as well as a rapid mastery of Castilian allowed Cortés to build the alliances he needed with other local tribes before invading the Aztec capital at Tenochtitlan. She is revered as the mother of the first mestizo of Spanish and Aztec blood, yet vilified as the traitor who helped Cortés and the Conquistadors. Malinche's life yields two highly contested stories: an archetypal tale as one of the first indigenous converts to Christianity and mother of the Mexican people, and a painfully ambiguous story of betrayal resulting from her collaboration with the Spanish forces who destroyed the Aztec civilization and enslaved its people.

—AH

Isabel I of Castile on January 2, 1492. Throughout the Spanish Reconquest, knightly "conquerors," much like the Conquistadors of the sixteenth and seventeenth centuries, became the subject of heroic tales portraying their romanticized chivalry and service to the nation. Ironically, 1492 was also the year Christopher Columbus journeyed across the Atlantic Ocean in search of a westward trade route to Japan, China, and India. Although he mistook the continents of North America and South America for Asia and the East Indies, these previously unknown lands became the stage on which the Conquistadors played out their quest for gold and power. Among the peoples of Latin America, the Caribbean and Philippine Islands, and the Hispanic American Southwest, the men known as *Conquistadores* represent Spain's exploration and exploitation of the Western Hemisphere, as well as the ambivalence with which many people from these regions still regard the legacies of Spanish conquest and colonization.

The myth of the Spanish Conquistadors is inextricably tied to the chivalric militancy and territorial ambitions of feudalism, which was the political system that governed territorial, social, and military relations in Medieval Europe. As "soldiers for hire" such men found ample opportunity for collecting the "spoils-of-war" amidst the land disputes that were common in Europe before the rise of modern nation-states like Spain, France, and England. Within the prescriptions of the "feudal contract," relations between high ranking nobles (lords) and the lower nobility (vassals) were based on the exchange of surplus land for armed service and protection by the lesser nobles and their sons, who, in turn, benefited greatly from the fertile lands and resources they received from their upper-class patrons and allies. Kinship ties also figured prominently in this

REQUERIMIENTO

The Castilian term "requerimiento" means "requirement." It also signified Spain's imperial "demand" for control of the territories, resources, and labor of indigenous peoples. It originated in a legal document written in 1510 by Spanish jurist and royal advisor Juan López de Palacios Rubios of the Council of Castile, who argued for Spain's and Rome's political and religious dominion over all indigenous lands and peoples. Designed to be read to native leaders before conquest or battle, the document claimed universal rule for St. Peter's successors as "heads of the entire human race" who, by the will of God, governed the spiritual realm until the end of the world. It then alluded to a Papal Bull, signed by Alexander VI in 1493, giving the monarchs of Castile and Aragon control of all islands and lands across the world's oceans. This was followed by strict orders to convert to Christianity, or suffer the penalties of war, enslavement, and total loss of sovereignty for resistance, thus blaming the natives for the violence of their impending Spanish conquest. Very few indigenous tribes accepted the document's terms when read to them before battle. Requerimiento was severely criticized by Bartolomé de las Casas as illegal and immoral according to Christian ideals.

—AH

system, which led to frequent "feuds" over disputed lands, entangling alliances, and inheritance rights.

As Spain became modern Europe's earliest unified nation-state between 1474 and 1492, a surplus of Spanish males trained in the arts of war and the politics of the feudal system became problematic for the new nation. Reports of unknown lands discovered by Columbus and tales of vast wealth and resources waiting to be claimed in the Americas inspired many older and younger men across Spain to transfer their feudal and militaristic concerns to the lands across the Atlantic. In 1493, the Spanish monarchy established the *encomienda* system on the Caribbean island of Hispaniola, and the following year received papal approval for this forced labor policy, which was basically a modification of the old feudal system of lordship over a specified area of land and over the peasants living on the property. In this case,

the recently conquered indigenous tribes were treated as the new peasant class and forced into slave labor. Unlike earlier feudal arrangements, the Spanish Crown retained strict ownership rights over the new land and its native laborers through the encomienda system, but granted rights of "trusteeship" for these properties to Conquistadors and colonists.

The earliest Conquistador leaders were known as *Adelantados*, a term denoting "one who pushes forward" or the "advance man" who arrives in the name of the monarchy. This term originated in the frontier wars of the Spanish Reconquest when the territories of the Iberian Peninsula often changed hands between Muslim and Christian overlords. "Adelantado" also served as the official title of the first military governors in many of the Spanish colonies. The conquest of the "New World" provided these men and their families, who knew no way of life outside these outdated

MANIFEST DESTINY

The notion of "Manifest Destiny" first appeared in John L. O'Sullivan's 1839 newspaper essay, "The Great Nation of Futurity." Fusing romantic nationalism with ideas of unlimited economic progress, he set the tone for an increasingly captivating national myth that influenced American politics from 1840 to the early 1900s. Proponents believed the Anglo-Saxon races that founded the American colonies were destined by God to settle the entire continent, developing its natural resources and spreading liberty, democracy, and Protestant Christianity. The 1840s were the myth's defining moment when the United States confronted Great Britain over the disputed Oregon Territory, and then ignited the Mexican-American War by annexing Texas and later gaining 55 percent of Mexico's territory through the Treaty of Guadalupe Hidalgo. Besides westward expansionism, the doctrine's racial overtones influenced the conquest and removal of Native Americans from their lands. Pundits were declaring the frontier closed when Chicago's 1893 World's Columbian Exposition opened. The fair, which celebrated American progress alongside the 400th anniversary of Columbus's voyages, generated a reassessment of America's destiny in the world. This growing global view of Manifest Destiny culminated with the seizure of Cuba, Puerto Rico, Guam, and the Philippines during the 1898 Spanish-American War. Today "Manifest Destiny" is understood as the ideology behind U.S. imperialism.

—AH

feudalistic and military traditions, with renewed possibilities for territorial and economic expansion while serving under the banner of the Spanish Crown and sharing the spoils of conquest with their royal landlords back in Spain. Conquistadors were especially motivated by the promise of accumulating wealth, such as gold, silver, trade goods, and spices, and also by the power and prestige that came with military success in the service of the Spanish Crown and building an empire. Spreading the Christian faith among the natives was also an integral aspect of the Spanish colonial enterprise. The exploits of the Conquistadors made Spain the most powerful and richest nation in European history.

Key Figures

While hundreds of commanders and soldiers participated in Spain's conquest of the Americas from 1492 to the subjugation of Upper and Lower California in the late 1700s, some figures amassed such enormous wealth and power that their exploits stand out among all the others. The four *Conquistadores* best known among scholars and the general public are Christopher Columbus (1451–1506), Hernán Cortés (1485–1547), Francisco Pizarro (ca. 1471–1541), and Francisco de Orellana (1511–1546).

After setting sail from the port of Palos in southern Spain on August 3, 1492, Christopher Columbus's beleaguered flotilla of three small ships made landfall somewhere in the Bahamas on October 12, 1492, at a place the natives called Guanahani, which he renamed San Salvador. Columbus visited and named about four more islands after Guanahani. The expedition arrived in

After the first transatlantic crossing, Christopher Columbus lands in the Caribbean. In contracting with Christopher Columbus, the Spanish crown authorized Columbus to discover and conquer non-Christian lands. (National Archives)

Cuba by October 28 and then moved on to the neighboring island of Hispaniola in November. On Christmas Eve Columbus lost his flagship on a reef off the coast of Cuba and ordered his men to build a fort with the wooden remains of the ship. Columbus and his men were awestruck at the natural beauty and pristine conditions of the islands they renamed, charted, and claimed for Spain. By January 1493, it was clear to him and his fellow commanders that they needed to get back to Spain in order to realize their hope of returning with a much larger and well-equipped expedition. On March 15, 1493, Columbus and his two remaining ships returned to their home port of Palos. Columbus led three more voyages to the Caribbean and Central

America over the next ten years before returning to Spain severely ill and nearly blind. He died convinced that he had found a sea route to Asia.

As news of Columbus's Atlantic crossing spread quickly around Spain and beyond, it became clear that the European world, and the lives of the indigenous peoples of the Americas, would never be the same again. Some historians interpret Columbus's voyages from 1492 to 1504 as the beginning of the "Age of the Conquistadors," while other scholars place that responsibility in the hands of Hernán Cortés who conquered the Aztec Empire of Mexico in 1521. Francisco Pizarro, who in 1533 conquered the Inca Empire that once spanned the areas of modern Peru,

---

VIRGEN DE LOS REMEDIOS

Mayahuel became associated with healing plants through *La Virgen de Remedios*, for the statue Cortés left behind after pillaging the Temple Pyramid of Quetzalcoatl at Cholula, Puebla, Mexico, where a mural depicts pulque drinkers. Spaniards escaped a night attack by inhabitants, attributing their escape to the *Virgen*, *La Conquistadora*, building a church to the *Virgen de Los Remedios* over the temple. The statue was lost for 20 years until the *Virgen* appeared to Juan Ce Cuautli, One Eagle, as he walked along the road, recognizing her as the Virgen who fought alongside the Spanish on *La Noche Triste*. He finally went to the place she instructed, finding the lost statue under a maguey cactus. The statue returned repeatedly to the maguey until he built a hermitage to her in Michoacan. *La Virgen* was used again by the Royalist troops in the Mexican War for Independence. Between September 1 and 8, thousands make an annual pilgrimage to the basilica of the *Virgen*, in San Bartolo Naucalpan, enjoying fireworks, dances, food, and elaborate church and indigenous ceremonies, while in San Francisco, California, Xiuhcoatl Danza Azteca sponsors a *velación* and danza, honoring Mayahuel, *La Virgen de Los Remedios*.

—MVS

Bolivia, Chile, and Ecuador, had sailed from Panama several times since the 1520s in search of the legendary city of gold known as *El Dorado*. The quest for this mythical city motivated a considerable number of the expeditions and campaigns led by the Conquistadors. *El Dorado* was made famous by Pizarro's cousin and top lieutenant, Francisco de Orellana, who explored the Amazon River from the interior all the way to the Atlantic Ocean in search of gold and new territories. Despite his vast wealth and influence with the Spanish Crown, Pizarro had to fight a disastrous civil war against his own people, and he was assassinated in July 1541 by rival Conquistador Diego de Almagro.

Since the 1992 Quincentenary of Columbus's first voyage to the Americas, the motivations and violent deeds of the Conquistadors have been interpreted very differently outside of Spain. In many parts of Latin America today the Conquistadors are viewed as invaders and criminals, while in northern New Mexico and southern Colorado reside *Hispano* families who still remember their Conquistador origins by celebrating this heritage each year in local festivals honoring their Spanish ancestors and Roman Catholic traditions.

Time Line

The following time line summarizes some of the major Conquistador figures and events relating to the Hispanic American religious cultures and regions covered throughout this encyclopedia.

1492   Christopher Columbus's first voyage.

1496   Columbus's brother, Diego, establishes first permanent Spanish colony at Santo Domingo on the island of Hispaniola.

1509   Juan Ponce de Leon, who fought in the overthrow of the Muslim Caliphate of Granada in 1492 and

SAN MIGUEL COLONY

In 1523, King Carlos V of Spain granted permission to Lucas Vásquez de Ayllón to establish a settlement on the North American coast for the express purpose of bringing the Catholic faith to the inhabitants of the land. In 1526, Ayllón set out from Hispaniola and founded the colony of San Miguel de Guadalupe, the first European colony in North America. San Miguel, which was settled with about 600 individuals, was located near the vicinity of Jamestown, the English colony that would be founded nearly a century later. Here, for the first time on what was to become the United States, a chapel was built, a Spanish Mass given, and the first Thanksgiving dinner shared. But life in San Miguel was difficult, claiming the lives of many, including Ayllón. The colony finally failed after a cold winter marked by slave revolts, Indian attacks, and mutiny. San Miguel was eventually abandoned and the surviving 150 people returned to Hispaniola.

—*MAD*

accompanied Columbus on his second voyage, conquers the island of Puerto Rico and becomes its first governor. In 1513 he explores the coast of Florida in search of further conquest and the mythical "Fountain of Youth." He dies in Cuba in 1521 from wounds received while fighting against the Indians in Florida.

1510–1513
Vasco Nuñez de Balboa reaches the Pacific Ocean, claims it for Spain, and establishes the first Spanish colony in Panama.

1511 Father Bartolomé de Las Casas begins preaching in Santo Domingo against the abuses of Spain's colonial administration, and he teaches that the Christian faith is incompatible with the cruelty and violence inflicted on the Indians.

1511–1515
Diego Velázquez de Cuéllar conquers Cuba, becomes its first governor, and establishes the city of Havana as a base of operations for future Spanish expansion campaigns to North America, the Caribbean, and Central America.

1517 Francisco Hernández de Córdoba explores the Yucatan Peninsula and begins the conquest of the coastal Mayan cities whose pyramids remind him of the "wonders of Egypt."

1519–1521
Cortés conquers Aztec Empire in Mexico.

1521 Ferdinand Magellan claims the Philippine Islands for Spain.

1526 Lucas Vásquez de Ayllón sails from Santo Domingo and founds the colony of San Miguel on the coast of South Carolina, near the site where the English would found the Jamestown colony 100 years later. His expedition included about 600 colonists, and the first ever use of African slave labor in North America. He explores the coastlines of Georgia, the Carolinas, and discovers Chesapeake Bay. The expedition ends in total failure when a mere 150 surviving colonists return to Santo Domingo after Ayllon's death.

1528 Panfilo de Narvaez and Alvar Nuñez Cabeza de Vaca land in Florida with the intention of exploring and conquering what is now the southwestern

United States. The expedition falls apart after a series of misfortunes and battles with Indians. Cabeza de Vaca and a few others survive by living among various indigenous tribes while wandering through the Southwest until reaching a Spanish outpost in Mexico by 1536.

1533 Pizarro conquers Inca Empire in South America.

1535 Antonio de Mendoza appointed first Viceroy of New Spain by King Charles V of Spain. Mexico becomes center of Spanish colonial rule in the Western Hemisphere.

1537–1542

Hernando De Soto, who served with Pizarro in the conquest of Peru, is named governor of Cuba and later granted a contract by King Charles V to conquer, pacify, and colonize North America. The expedition costs De Soto his reputation and his life, and ends in total failure in 1543.

1539–1540

Inspired by wealth looted from the Aztecs and Incas, Francisco Vásquez de Coronado explores the American Southwest in search of the legendary "Seven Cities of Gold," also known as *Cibola*.

1541–1542

Coronado explores New Mexico, Kansas, Oklahoma, Arizona, Texas, and the Grand Canyon in search of *Quivira*, another legendary city believed to have been as wealthy as those of the Aztecs and Incas.

1542 Juan Rodriguez Cabrillo explores the coast of California and claims the region for Spain. He dies of an infection before returning to Mexico and the expedition records are lost.

1544 Coronado is found guilty of atrocities against the Indians and of misrepresenting the wealth of the American Southwest, and he is removed from his post as governor of New Galicia in northern Mexico.

1552 Father Bartolomé de Las Casas publishes *A Brief Account of the Destruction of the Indies*. The book angers many among the Spanish colonial leaders and the Conquistador ranks, but the Spanish monarchy ignores the book.

1565 King Philip II of Spain orders the conquest of the islands discovered by Magellan in 1521. The Conquistador and Adelantado, Miguel López de Legazpi, invades and colonizes the Philippine Islands, which he names in honor of the king, and, which Spain controls until the conclusion of the Spanish-American War of 1898.

1565 Pedro Menéndez de Aviles founds the city of Saint Augustine in Florida, as a Spanish fortress guarding the sea lanes against pirates and European rivals disrupting annual convoys of Spanish galleons transporting gold and silver from the Aztec and Inca Empires and from the mining operations in Mexico, Peru, and Chile. Saint Augustine becomes the oldest permanent European settlement in North America and the oldest city in the United States.

1595 King Phillip II of Spain authorizes Juan de Oñate to conquer and colonize the upper Rio Grande region and the territory of New Mexico.

1598 Oñate claims all of New Mexico beyond the Rio Grande for Spain and serves as the first governor of the Province of New Mexico, establishing his capital city at San Juan de Los Caballeros, near present-day Santa Fe.

1606–1613

King Phillip III of Spain accuses Oñate of atrocities against the Acoma Indians and of exaggerating the

---

JUNÍPERO SERRA (1713–1784)

Born Miguel José Serra in 1713 on Spain's island of Mallorca, Serra joined the Franciscan Order at age 16 and took the name of St. Francis's companion, Junípero. He taught philosophy until age 36, when he left Spain for missionary work in Mexico. Serra arrived at Vera Cruz in 1750 and traveled by foot to Mexico City to fulfill a religious vow at the shrine of Our Lady of Guadalupe. For 17 years he preached and converted Indians along Mexico's Sierra Gorda and in the coastal villages and mining camps. Following the expulsion of the Jesuits from New Spain, Serra was appointed "Father President" of the Baja California missions in 1767, a post that later included the nine Franciscan missions he founded across Alta California. In 1769 Serra joined Governor Gaspar de Portolá's expedition to colonize New California, the last Conquistador campaign. In July Serra founded the first Franciscan mission at San Diego on the Camino Real road connecting the Spanish settlements along California's coast. Native Americans and some U.S. historians remain critical of Serra's complicity in Spain's conquest of California's Indian peoples. Serra died in 1784 and was beatified in 1988 by Pope John Paul II.

—AH

---

wealth of New Mexico. He is recalled to Mexico City and then banished from the colonies.

1610 Pedro de Peralta founds the city of Santa Fe in New Mexico, which then becomes the administrative, military, and missionary capital of Spain's colonial efforts in the American Southwest until Mexican independence from Spain in 1821.

1680 Harsh and oppressive living conditions provoke a native uprising that expels Spanish colonists from Santa Fe during the Pueblo Indian Revolt.

1692 Calling upon the old themes of the Spanish Reconquest, Don Diego de Vargas recaptures Santa Fe and restores Spanish colonial rule in New Mexico.

1727 Pedro de Rivera dispatched by the king of Spain to investigate fiscal abuse and waste in New Spain, Texas, and the American Southwest. His report recommends a shift from imperial expansion to the consolidation of lands and peoples already under Spanish rule. Given the growing world power of England and France, the Crown implements Rivera's recommendations.

1769 The last Conquistador campaign, led by Governor Gaspar de Portolá and the Franciscan Father Junípero Serra, sets off to colonize Nueva California and founds a series of Catholic Missions along the Camino Real beginning at San Diego Bay and continuing northward to San Francisco Bay.

Although praised through the centuries for their bravery and fantastic discoveries, posterity has recorded and judged the actions of the Conquistadors, and the Spanish monarchs who hired and empowered them to undertake these military campaigns, with a mixture of fame and infamy. Alongside the old naïve themes of "exploration," "discovery," and "adventure," a new generation of historical studies and educational materials on the "Age of the Conquistadors" today emphasizes themes of "liberation" and "justice" for the indigenous peoples and former colonial nations that were enslaved and exploited during the "Conquest of the Americas," cultures and nations that in complex ways still struggle with the legacies of colonialism.

Albert Hernández

References and Further Reading

Diaz del Castillo, Bernal. *The Discovery and Conquest of Mexico: 1517–1521* (Cambridge, MA: Da Capo Press, 2003).

Cañizares-Esguerra, Jorge. *Puritan Conquistadors: Iberianizing the Atlantic, 1550–1700* (Stanford University Press, 2006).

Chavez, Thomas E. *Quest for Quivira: Spanish Explorers on the Great Plains, 1540–1821* (Tucson, AZ: Southwest Parks and Monuments Association, 1992).

Greenblatt, Stephen. *Marvelous Possessions: The Wonder of the New World* (Chicago: University of Chicago Press, 1991).

Restall, Matthew. *Seven Myths of the Spanish Conquest* (New York: Oxford University Press, 2003).

Weber, David J. *The Spanish Frontier in North America* (New Haven, CT: Yale University Press, 1992).

Wood, Michael. *Conquistadors* (Berkeley: University of California Press, 2001).

CONVERSION

Conversion is the religious process of exchanging one's beliefs system for another. Usually, it encompasses the movement away from one's faith tradition and embraces the beliefs and doctrine of a different group. Although most Hispanics, according to a 2007 study conducted by the Pew Hispanic Center, continue to practice and participate within the same faith tradition of their birth (82 percent), a growing minority, almost one out of every five Latina/os (18 percent), has changed faith affiliation or has ceased identifying with any faith tradition. Many factors are in play when a person changes religious affiliation. The primary reason given among Hispanics was a desire to experience a closer relationship with God (83 percent). Inspiration of a certain pastor (35 percent), a response to a deep personal crisis (26 percent), and a result of marriage (14 percent) are the other reasons most often given for Hispanic conversions.

Because most Latina/o Christians are Catholic (70 percent), it should not be surprising that a large number of converts were former Catholics. As the Pew study shows, for every Latina/o who converts to Catholicism, four leave it. However, this does not necessarily mean that the numbers of Hispanic Catholics are decreasing—quite the contrary. If the conversion rate over the past quarter century continues, the overall Catholic population will decline from 68 percent in 2006 to 61 percent in 2030. Yet, over that same period, the proportion of Catholics who are Latina/o will increase from 33 percent to 41 percent.

Of the 18 percent of all Hispanics who converted, 13 of the 18 percent were former Catholics and 3 percent were former Protestants (the remaining 2 percent indicated no religious affiliation or were from a non-Christian tradition). For Hispanic evangelical converts from Catholicism, one in three stated a lack of excitement with the Catholic Mass as a primary motivation. While almost half of all converts from Catholicism were at odds with the Church's teaching on divorce and on whether women or married men could be priests, only 7 percent

CONVERSOS

In 1391, Spain engaged in the first mass conversion of Jews. Many converted to Christianity, others simply fled. By 1492, Jews, as well as Muslims, were expelled from Spain. Those who stayed and converted, along with their descendants, were collectively called converses (converts). Pejoratively they were referred to as marranos. Among those who were converses were Christopher Columbus (suspected), several of his crew, the conquistador Pedrarias de Ávila, and the cleric Bartolomé de las Casas. While some converses embraced their new faith, others continued to secretly practice their former faith under the veneer of Christianity. They were called crypto-Jews or secret Jews. The expulsion of Jews and the start of Spain's colonial project in the Americas coincided. Many converses immigrated to the so-called New World seeking safer havens. Even those who sincerely converted still feared the Inquisition quest and punishment of crypto-Jews. Those who immigrated to Mexico still thought it would be safer to be as far as possible from the imperial center. Many migrated to the farthest reaches of the empire, far from the reaches of the Catholic Church and the Mexican Inquisition. Specifically, they migrated to the lands that would become Texas and New Mexico. Understanding the Southwestern Hispanic culture requires a serious consideration of Jewish influences. Since the 1960s, many Latina/os have rediscovered their Jewish roots with some returning to the faith of their ancestors.

—MAD

listed these disagreements as reasons for their conversion.

It is important to note that Hispanics are not necessarily leaving Catholicism to become Protestants. According to research conducted by Gastón Espinosa, a substantial number are converting to Jehovah's Witness and Mormon traditions. This is not necessarily a new phenomenon, but rather has its roots in the 1920s. Today, Jehovah's Witness have more than 2,200 Spanish-speaking congregations, making them the largest non-Catholic Christian tradition among Hispanics. They have the highest conversion rate among Latina/o immigrants compared to any other non-Catholic tradition. Meanwhile, Mormons rank eighth among the Hispanic's largest religious traditions.

The decision to convert encompasses many reasons, making it impossible to

pinpoint the determining factor. Nevertheless, it appears that conversion occurs more frequently among Latina/os born in the United States and among those who are more fluent in English. The 2007 Pew study shows that 14 percent of those whose primary language was Spanish converted, 20 percent of those who were bilingual converted, and 26 percent of those whose primary language was English converted. It appears that assimilation plays a role. Moving to the United States and learning English is somewhat associated with changes in religious affiliation. Although national origins do not seem to influence conversions, there exists one noteworthy exception. Puerto Ricans have a higher disproportionate number of converts (31 percent).

It is important to note that 28 percent of converts, according to the Pew study, moved away from all religious affiliation. Most of those who moved toward secularism were Catholics (39 percent of all Hispanics who claim to be secular). Latina/o seculars who were former Protestants represented 15 percent of those self-identifying as such. Those who converted to secularism had several characteristics in common. Most notable is that they are economically better off than the rest of the Hispanic population. About a third of them earned in excess of $50,000 annually, compared with only 17 percent of all Latino/as. Also, about 20 percent of them had a college diploma, compared with 10 percent of all Hispanics. Finally, more than half of them are U.S. born (54 percent) and the dominant language they speak is English or they are bilingual (68 percent).

Miguel A. De La Torre

References and Further Reading

Espinosa, Gastón. "Methodological Reflections on Latino Social Science Research." *Rethinking Latino(a) Religion and Identity*, ed. Miguel A. De La Torre and Gastón Espinosa (Cleveland, OH: Pilgrim Press, 2006).

Pew Hispanic Center. *Changing Faiths: Latinos and the Transformation of American Religion* (Washington DC: Pew Forum on Religion and Public Life, 2007).

LO COTIDIANO

Daily lived experience, lo cotidiano, is a privileged source or *locus theologicus* in the scholarship of a number of U.S. Latino/a theologians. In general, the term refers to the ordinary, in all its particularities, and for Latina/o theologians it invites critical analysis of the multiple factors that impact and shape daily living. The complexity of lo cotidiano as a site of both sin and grace is explored from a variety of perspectives and serves as ground for liberative praxis. Attention to the daily is focused through various concrete lenses, including but not limited to mestizaje/mulatez; diasporas/migrations; las luchas/struggles endemic to poverty, oppression, injustice, colonization; experiences of women; popular religion and liturgy; spirituality; popular culture. While this category is prevalent in a number of Latino/a theologians, it is worth noting its development in seminal and influential scholarship by Ada María Isasi-Díaz, María Pilar Aquino, Orlando Espín, and Roberto Goizueta.

The significance of vida cotidiana, the everyday life, is especially evident in the works of Latina theologians. For Ada María Isasi-Díaz, lo cotidiano is central to mujerista theology. She finds the daily to be descriptively, hermeneutically, and epistemologically significant as it pertains to the lived experience of grassroots Latinas. Descriptively, lo cotidiano entails such factors as race, class, and gender, as well as relational interactions, faith expressions, and experiences of authority. Hermeneutically, lo cotidiano serves as an interpretive lens through which reality, in terms of actions, relationships, discourses, norms, and social roles are perceived and evaluated. Epistemologically, lo cotidiano gives credence to the ways of knowing and expressing rooted in Latinas' efforts to make sense out of their living and circumstances. For Isasi-Díaz, the use of lo cotidiano as a theological source exposes knowledge in general and theological knowledge in particular as being fragmentary, biased, and provisional, and this affirms its use as an act of subversion. However she

LOCUS THEOLOGICUS

The term *locus theologicus* means a source for theology that includes but is not limited to the sociopolitical, cultural, economic, and gender contexts taken into account in theological tasks. The term is based upon Aristotlian *topoi* introduced by the Spanish Dominican Melchior Cano (1509?–1560) in *De locis theologicis*. As Meza states, Cano adopted the *locus* tradition to give further authority to Catholic doctrine over three other schools of thought: reformers like Martin Luther and their scripturally based assertions; mystics like Teresa of Avila and their subjective religious experience; and humanists like Lorenzo Valla and their academic skepticism. Liberation Theologies introduced the primacy of the life of the poor as sources for theologies. Both Protestant and Catholic Hispanic Theologies add a mutual accountability between theologian and community in theologizing. The primary place for these theologies comes from lo cotidiano, daily lived experiences of Latino/a communities in the United States of America. In using lo cotidiano as a primary source for theological tasks, theologians are not to speak for others but rather to listen and rearticulate theologically the lived experiences of communities of accountability. Whenever possible a theologian should allow community members to articulate their own theologies based upon various contexts.

—NDA

contends that lo cotidiano must also function as a catalyst for structural change in the face of all that is contrary to the kinship constitutive of the Reign or kin-dom of God.

María Pilar Aquino asserts that Latina thought is explicitly theological when it focuses critical reflection on daily practices as sustained by liberating visions and Christian tradition. She attributes salvific value to daily life, in so much as the presence of God is experienced through the struggles of the people for justice, humanization, and a better quality of life. At the same time lo cotidiano encourages participation in a transformation with eschatological significance.

For Orlando Espín, the birthing place of an authentically Latino/a theology of grace is the foundational experience of daily life, as it exists and is lived. Espín is careful not to reduce lo cotidiano to living that occurs primarily within the private or domestic sphere and

acknowledges the impact on daily life of such macro factors as violence, poverty, global economics, information technology, politics, education, and media. For Espín, popular religion is a key hermeneut of daily experience. The scholarship of Roberto Goizueta continues in this vein, in his development of the metaphor of accompaniment to describe the interactive relationship between human and divine as expressed through popular religious practices. In these ritualized moments daily living is affirmed as the locus of divine presence, and all that denies life is resisted.

Latino/a theologies are part of a greater stream of scholarship that attends to critical analysis of the daily. Among some of the pioneering influences in this area are the works of Agnes Heller, *Historia y vida cotidiana* (1972), *Sociología de la vida cotidiana* (1977), *La revolucíon de la vida cotidiana* (1982); Michel de Certeau, *The Practice of Everyday*

Life (1984); and Teresa de Barbieri, *Mujeres y vida cotidiana* (1984).

Carmen M. Nanko-Fernández

References and Further Reading

Aquino, María Pilar. *Our Cry for Life* (Maryknoll, NY: Orbis Books, 1993).

———. "The Collective 'Discovery of Our Own Power." *Hispanic Latino Theology: Challenge and Promise*, ed. Ada María Isasi-Díaz and Fernando F. Segovia (Minneapolis: Fortress, 1996).

Goizueta, Roberto. *Caminemos con Jesús: Toward a Hispanic/Latino Theology of Accompaniment* (Maryknoll, NY: Orbis Books, 1995).

Cavazos-González, Gilberto. "La Cotidianidad Divina: A Latin@ Method for Spirituality." *Journal of Hispanic/Latino Theology*. http://www.latinotheology.org/.

Espín, Orlando O., and Miguel Díaz, eds. *From the Heart of Our People: Latino/a Explorations in Catholic Systematic Theology* (Maryknoll, NY: Orbis Books, 1999).

Isasi-Díaz, Ada María. "Lo Cotidiano: A Key Element of Mujerista Theology." *Journal of Hispanic/Latino Theology* 10, no. 1 (August 2002): 5–17.

———. *Mujerista Theology: A Theology for the Twenty-first Century* (Maryknoll, NY: Orbis Books, 1996).

Martell-Otero, Loida I. "Lo Cotidiano: Finding God in the Spaces of the Everyday." http://www.thewitness.org/archive/dec2000/locotid.html.

CUBAN AMERICANS

Cuban Americans account for approximately 1.3 million U.S. residents who trace their ethnic and cultural origins back to the island of Cuba. Cubans migrated intermittently to the Southeastern United States as political and economic conditions fluctuated throughout the nineteenth century. Although American presidents from Thomas Jefferson to James Buchanan entertained dreams of either annexing Cuba or purchasing it from Spain, the Cuban Revolution of January 1959 motivated thousands of Cubans to leave their homeland and seek asylum in the United States as political exiles. Today Cuban Americans comprise the third largest group of Hispanics living in the United States after Mexican Americans and Puerto Ricans, who, respectively, rank first and second among Latino/a demographic patterns. The highest concentrations of Cuban American residents are in the urban areas surrounding Union City, New Jersey, and Miami, Florida. As a result of Cuba's strategic location between Latin America and North America, and the economic and political successes of exilic Cubans and their American-born offspring, Cuban Americans are an important and vibrant community within the context of Hispanic American religious cultures.

Historical Development

During his first voyage, Christopher Columbus (1451–1506) landed somewhere along the northeast coast of Cuba on October 28, 1492. He was seeking a sea route to China and new territories for the Spanish Crown. In 1494, during his second voyage, Columbus explored Cuba's southeastern and western coasts while still searching for mainland China. The Native inhabitants, known as Taínos and Siboneyes, told Columbus that Cuba was the largest "island" in the area, but he persisted in his misguided hunch that it was the coast of China. The Natives also informed him their homeland lacked

HATUEY

Hatuey is a sixteenth-century *cacique* (chieftain) whose resistance to the Spanish colonizers made him a modern symbol of Cuban resistance, specifically against foreign powers—first Spain, then after the Revolution for Independence, the United States. He created in eastern Cuba a loose confederation of Native Americans whose military objective was to resist the invading colonizers. For three months he carried out a style of guerrilla warfare against the Spaniards. By 1511, Cuba's first Spanish governor, Diego Velázquez, led an expedition intent on capturing the renegade chieftain and pacifying the island. Once in custody, Hatuey was condemned to death so as to serve as an example for others. Before Hatuey was to be burned at the stake, a Franciscan friar attempted to convert him to the Christian faith with the promise of heaven and the threat of hell. Hatuey is reported to have asked if Christians went to heaven. When the friar answered in the affirmative, Hatuey rejected Christianity, retorting that he had no desire to go to a heaven where he would see such cruel people.

—MAD

the riches of other nearby islands. Mesmerized by Cuba's pristine magnificence, a Cuban legend claims Columbus said that this was the most beautiful land human eyes had ever seen. Soon other Spanish navigators explored the Cuban coastline and confirmed it was an island. As news of its natural beauty and protected harbors reached Spain, Cuba caught the attention of Conquistadors and Adelantados seeking ever-increasing personal wealth while expanding the Spanish Empire. Surviving copies of an early sixteenth-century Royal Charter, signed by King Ferdinand of Aragon and Queen Isabel of Castile, decrees the island's name as *Fernandina,* but the newcomers preferred the Native name for the island, *Cubanacan,* which they shortened to *Cuba.*

Motivated by exaggerated reports of the island's wealth and resources, the Spanish Monarchy issued orders for the conquest and colonization of Cuba in May 1509. Cuba's first Spanish governor, Diego Velázquez de Cuéllar (1465–1524), arrived in 1511. Cuba remained under Spanish domination for almost four centuries until the end of the Spanish-American War. In the process of looking for the gold exaggeratedly attributed to both Cuba's natural resources and its Native peoples, the Spaniards attacked, enslaved, and exploited the Indians until violence and disease nearly wiped out their presence throughout the island. Velázquez established Santiago de Cuba as his capital city on the island's southeast coast, and established the main Roman Catholic Bishopric for the growing Spanish Empire of the Caribbean at Baracoa. He also founded the cities of Bayamo, Santiago de Cuba, Sancti Spiritus, Trinidad, and the famous naval port at San Cristobal de La Habana, which would one day become the island's capital city. Given its strategic location in the Caribbean Sea, Cuba served for centuries as the Spanish Empire's forward base of operations for colonial military deployment to the Americas. It was from here that

Spain, under Velázquez's leadership, launched its Conquistador explorations and invasions of Mexico, Florida, Central America, the Southeastern United States, and finally Peru. During the first several decades of the sixteenth century, and before the establishment of the viceroy of New Spain, Cuba's governor was the most powerful Spanish colonial leader in the Western Hemisphere.

However, Cuba's importance in the region diminished after the Spanish conquest of Mexico and Peru dominated the transfer of plundered wealth and the flow of trade goods from the colonies back to Spain. As colonial competition between Spain and its western European rivals increased, Cuba's strategic position as the gateway to the Americas became a handicap for Spain. From 1538 to about 1796 France, England, and Holland provoked naval confrontations aimed at disrupting Spanish shipping, which included invading or briefly occupying Cuba. In the 1600s corsairs, pirates, and buccaneers repeatedly attacked Cuban ports until naval stability and the protection of trade routes were restored in the Caribbean and Central Atlantic regions by the early 1700s.

Spanish colonists and their Cuban-born offspring, known as *criollos* or Creoles, felt abandoned and isolated from Spain during the two centuries of piracy and foreign naval interference in Cuba. Despite lingering territorial conflicts with England and France, the eighteenth and nineteenth centuries witnessed the largest colonial population increases in Cuba. By 1700, however, less than 3,000 Natives survived in Cuba. In the late 1500s large numbers of African slaves were brought to the island to work on the sugar and tobacco plantations. As the balance of population in Cuba

between "Whites" and "Blacks" shifted over time, the Spanish Crown and the governor of Cuba often enticed new waves of "White" Spanish settlers from the Canary Islands, Andalucía, Galicia, and Catalonia to settle in Cuba. The *Isleños* (Islanders) from the Canaries and the Galicians from northern Spain accounted for the largest percentages among these settlers. Hence, Cuba's racial demographics became predominantly White versus "mulatto" or Black as in other Spanish colonies, a demographic trait that persists among Cuban Americans living in the United States as well as among the population of today's Cuban nationals. This racialized colonial policy, known as *blanqueamiento* (whitening), alleviated economic pressures back in Spain and the Canaries by providing new land and employment opportunities for farmers, laborers, and families willing to migrate to Cuba.

However, while most of Spain's colonies in Central and South America were in open revolt during the early 1800s, the constant influx of new settlers arriving in Cuba from Spain and its territories generated a relatively loyal colonial populace. Hence, the idea of a Cuban independence movement emerged gradually after the Enlightenment among Creole intellectuals, teachers, literary writers, and statesmen like Father Felix Varela (1788–1853), José Antonio Saco (1797–1879), José de La Luz y Caballero (1800–1862), and Narciso López (1797–1851). Several of these individuals were graduates of the Royal College and Seminary of San Carlos in Havana, which was founded in 1773 after the expulsion of the Jesuits from the Spanish colonies.

Felix Varela was a Roman Catholic priest and renowned university professor who embraced liberalism and advocated for Cuba's complete separation from Spain. When colonial authorities ordered his arrest for fomenting revolt, Varela left Cuba for the United States and founded a newspaper in New York City, *El Habanero*, which he secretly distributed in Cuba, and which became both a forum and a vehicle for spreading the ideals of Cuban independence among those living on the island as well as abroad. Contemporary Cuban Roman Catholics, living in Cuba and the United States, have suggested that Father Felix Varela's extraordinary life of ministry, teaching, and service against despotism and oppression is worthy of being considered for canonization.

The final break among the Cuban-born Creole class erupted on October 10, 1868, when Carlos Manuel de Céspedes proclaimed and led the *Grito de Yara*, meaning the rallying "Cry of Yara," which launched the so-called "Ten Years' War" against Spanish domination. For his efforts on behalf of liberty and the rule of law, he became known in Cuban history as the "Father of the Nation." Unfortunately, Spain responded with about 200,000 troops and a naval blockade of the island until the war ended in 1878. On the other hand, some historians interpret the struggle for Cuban independence as a war that lasted for over 30 years because revolutionary movements and Spain's oppression of democratic partisans did not cease until after the 1898 Spanish-American War.

During the 1800s and early 1900s Cubans experienced a fascination with the United States at the imaginative intersection of democratic idealism and economic opportunity. Cuban Americans are fiercely independent and entrepreneurial, an economic and sociopolitical characteristic forged through Cuba's protracted nineteenth-century independence struggles and the people's fascination with their large and powerful northern neighbor. Nineteenth-century Cuban intellectuals, whose colonial ancestors were self-reliant farmers, laborers, and plantation owners disturbed by the increasing abuses of Spain's colonial administration of their homeland, were also influenced by the ideals of Jeffersonian democracy and Abraham Lincoln. Freedom (*libertad*), personal integrity and self-determination, and valor against tyranny are central themes in the writings of the Cuban "Apostle of Independence," José Martí. Many Cuban Americans also have nineteenth-century roots in southeastern U.S. cities, like Tampa, Key West, or Saint Augustine, dating back to the era when Florida was still a Spanish possession. Some Cuban Americans claim ancestry in New Orleans originating in the years when trade between Cuba and Louisiana was essential for French interests in North America. When Vicente Martinez Ybor founded a cigar company in the late 1800s near Tampa, Florida, the area became the site of a thriving Cuban American immigrant community. Today Ybor City claims many fourth- and fifth-generation Cuban Americans. Some Cuban Americans also have great-grandparents who for business reasons lived temporarily as far north as New York City and Philadelphia during the mid-1800s. Many nineteenth-century Cuban visionaries of liberty, like Félix Varela and Narciso López, sought refuge in the United States after Spanish colonial authorities ordered their incarceration or execution.

Among the most illustrious figures in Cuban history is the poet, journalist, and

Considered by many Cubans to be their national hero, José Martí led the fight for independence from Spain. He was killed in battle with Spanish troops in 1895. (Library of Congress)

revolutionary leader José Martí (1853–1895). Martí was a first-generation Cuban Creole whose father was from Catalonia, Spain, and whose mother was from the Canary Islands. He is highly revered among both contemporary Cuban Americans in the United States and Cuban nationals back on the island. At 16 years of age he published a revolutionary newspaper, *La Patria Libre* (*The Free Nation*). Before reaching the age of 20, Martí already had been arrested for anti-Spanish activities, and in 1871 he was deported to Spain for his public efforts on behalf of Cuban independence. He lived much of his adult life as an exile who passionately loved his homeland and advocated for improved living conditions and justice throughout Latin America. In 1881 Martí settled in New York City, among a growing community of Cuban exiles and first-generation Cuban Americans, where he wrote some of his major essays, books, and poems. By 1892 Martí was convinced that Cuba's only hope of gaining independence from Spain, and avoiding annexation through rising U.S. imperial ambitions, was to accelerate the planning and implementation of an open revolt in Cuba against Spain. He soon formed the Cuban Revolutionary Party in New York City, which mobilized anti-Spanish leaders and forces back on the island for a revolt that began on February 24, 1895. Martí was tragically killed at the Battle of Dos Rio on May 19, 1895, but the War of Independence he inspired achieved numerous victories before the intervention of U.S. forces in Cuba three years after his death in the Spanish-American War.

After several years of American military occupation, Washington conceded Cuban independence. Unfortunately, the ratification of the infamous Platt Amendment to the Cuban Constitution of 1901 by both the U.S. Congress and the Cuban Senate, gave the United States the right to intervene in Cuban affairs as deemed necessary. On May 20, 1902, General Leonard Wood handed control of the island over to Cuba's first president, Tomás Estrada Palma (1832–1908), who had succeeded José Martí in 1895 as leader of the Cuban Revolutionary Party. Despite the general mood of optimism throughout Cuba, many former leaders and soldiers who had fought in the War of Independence saw the Platt Amendment as an undermining of Cuban political and economic autonomy.

Cuba was the last of the Spanish colonies in the Western Hemisphere to gain independence, and then remained under the influence of U.S. foreign policy and economic development interests from the early 1900s until the Cuban Revolution of Fidel Castro ousted President Fulgencio Batista from power on January 1, 1959. Cuban American ambivalence toward the United States, the use of the English language, and adoption of U.S. citizenship produce a complex web of regret for allowing repeated American interference in Cuban affairs during the twentieth century juxtaposed with genuine appreciation for the nation and people who welcomed Cubans with open arms throughout the 1960s as Fidel Castro moved his people toward Communism and an alliance with the Soviet Union (USSR). Castro's move toward the Russians during the Cold War resulted in decades of Cuban economic and military dependence on Soviet bloc countries until the dissolution of the Soviet Union in December 1991.

Although there were small communities of Cuban Americans living in Tampa, Key West, New Orleans, and New York City before 1959, the vast majority of Cuban Americans trace their U.S. residency or birth to four successive waves of immigration after 1960. The first wave began when Castro seized power on New Year's Day of 1959 and lasted until shortly after the Cuban Missile Crisis of October 1962. With the United States and the USSR pushing each other to the brink of nuclear war over Cuba, tensions between Havana and Washington led to the cancellation of all cultural exchange visits, exit visas, and the imposition of travel restrictions to and from the island. When it was over, the first wave of the exodus accounted for over 280,000 residents leaving Cuba from 1959 to 1962. The second wave began in 1965 and ended in 1973. It was the result of Washington and the Castro

regime negotiating a temporary airlift of people from Cuba to Florida, which at one point transported about 1,000 people per week to Miami International Airport and over 273,000 Cubans of all ages by the time the flights concluded. Not all of the Cubans in this second wave decided to live in South Florida. Some settled in Union City, New Jersey, others went to Chicago, and some became residents of New York City or its surrounding districts. Finally, the third wave of Cuban immigration was the result of an incident at the Peruvian Embassy in Havana when about 10,000 people stormed the embassy on Easter Sunday in April 1980 and asked for political asylum. After several very tense days, the Cuban government gave permission for those staying at the Peruvian Embassy to leave Cuba, along with anyone else who wanted to leave the country permanently. For Cuban exiles on the U.S. mainland this was, at first, like a gift from heaven. From April 15 to October 31, 1980, over 125,000 Cubans were picked up in boats by relatives, or by opportunistic private ferrymen, who crossed the 90 miles of open seas separating Key West, Florida, from the Port of Mariel in Cuba. The migration came to be known as the "Mariel Boatlift" or the "Mariel Exodus," and had both positive and negative repercussions for Cuban Americans already living in the United States.

Finally, the "*Balsero* (Cuban Rafters) Crisis of 1994" almost became a repeat of the 1980 Mariel Exodus as some people stormed foreign embassies in Cuba, while thousands of others attempted to flee the island on makeshift rafts and unsafe boats in desperate hopes that either the Gulf Stream current would carry them to Florida's shores, or that the U.S. Coast Guard might rescue them

FÉLIX VARELA Y MORALES (1788–1853)

Félix Varela y Morales was beatified by Pope John Paul II, who referred to Father Varela as "the foundation-stone of the Cuban national identity … the best synthesis one could find of Christian faith and Cuban culture." If canonized, he will be the first Cuban-born saint. Varela was ordained a priest by his 23rd birth date and elected as a delegate to the Spanish Parliament in 1822. He proposed two bills, the first abolishing slavery and the second calling for an autonomous Cuba. He became the first person of importance to make a serious call for Cuban independence while a delegate. These political views endangered his life, forcing him to seek exile in the United States in 1823. There he worked with the poor and published a paper dedicated to science, literature, politics, and faith. He published many articles dealing with human rights, religious tolerance, the importance of education, and the need for cooperation between English and Spanish speaking communities. By 1837, he was named vicar general of the New York Diocese. He spent the majority of his life in the United States, dying in Saint Augustine, Florida. In 1997 the U.S. Postal Service issued a 32-cent stamp honoring Varela.

—MAD

before being lost at sea. That summer, over a four-day period in late August, a fleet of 16 Coast Guard cutters picked up over 8,000 Cuban rafters. The single day rescue record for that year was 3,253 people. Some scholars identify this crisis as the fourth wave of Cuban immigration to the United States, while others interpret it as part of the smaller scale post-1980 Cuban migration pattern. Although the Cuban Rafter Crisis of 1994 was settled by an agreement between Fidel Castro and President William Clinton, the *balsero* phenomenon has not entirely ceased even as foreign economic investment and development in Cuba increased during the 1990s and the first decade of the twenty-first century. The *balseros'* dream of finding a better life in the United States is not just about economic and political hope, but indicates an integral characteristic of Cuban American spirituality founded on the principles of human dignity and personal liberty reminiscent of how Cuba's "Apostle of Independence," José Martí,

believed very passionately that people simply love liberty and were intended by their Creator to live free of oppression and exploitation. This sentiment is also echoed in Roman Catholic social justice and liberation teachings about "human flourishing," for in order to become all that God's love and mercy intended for each person, then personal liberty and dignity is a vital aspect of one's relationship with his or her Creator.

Ideals of liberty along with spiritualized sentiments about life in the United States versus the effects of Communism on individuals, children, families, and society were at the root of the international custody battle over Elián Gonzalez, the six-year-old boy who became the most famous Cuban rafter ever found drifting along the Florida coast. He was found by fishermen on Thanksgiving Day 1999 while hanging on to an inner tube after his mother and ten others had drowned at sea attempting the crossing from Cuba through the Florida Straits. The fishermen turned him over to the

U.S. Coast Guard who then handed him over to officials of the Immigration and Naturalization Service. Relatives of Elián's mother from Miami's Cuban community claimed the boy and took him into their home, but his father, Juan Miguel Gonzalez-Quintana, soon contacted the family and informed them that the boy was taken from Cuba without his knowledge or consent. The Cuban American side of the family in Miami refused to let Elián return to Cuba. They argued that Elián would have a much better life in the United States without the propaganda and indoctrination of Communism. This set off a five-month custody struggle that eventually involved both sides of the family along with the Clinton administration, the Castro regime, and leaders of the Cuban American community in Miami. Elián's Miami relatives applied on his behalf to the 11th Circuit Court in Atlanta for political asylum, but were turned down because he was just six years old and required his father's approval. Attorney General Janet Reno ordered Elián's return to his father and family in Cuba and set a firm deadline for his Miami relatives to obey the order. When the deadline passed without compliance, a team of armed officers from the U.S. Border Patrol stormed the house in Miami and seized Elián during Easter weekend on April 22, 2000. After Elián was reunited with his father and grandparents in Cuba, he became a symbol of nationalism for Fidel Castro, who attended the boy's birthday each year until stepping down from power due to declining health on February 24, 2008. In June 2008 Elián Gonzalez officially joined the Cuban Communist Party and acknowledged his continued appreciation for Fidel Castro's support on his behalf, while Cuban Americans in the United States responded sternly to the contrived and propagandistic tone of such reports from Cuba's news agency.

Elián's dramatic rescue on Thanksgiving Day 1999, and his mother's courageous sacrifice of her own life at sea to save her son, together with the tense events of Holy Week 2000 that culminated in the boy's return to Cuba, heightened the religious idealization and spiritual themes of the entire incident among the Cuban American exile community. Some compared Elián's inner tube experience to the infant Moses being set adrift on the Nile in a basket and suggested that Elián's story would somehow bring down Castro's regime just as Moses had freed the Hebrews from the bondage of Pharaoh. For some Cuban Americans the incident reactivated memories of their own childhood departures from Cuba without their parents during the 1960s, or through the U.S. government and Roman Catholic Archdiocese of Miami sponsored *Operation Pedro Pan* (Peter Pan), which transferred over 14,000 unaccompanied Cuban children on freedom flights to the United States from December 1960 through late October 1962. Liberty and spirituality are inextricably bound in the conscience of Cuban Americans in ways that transcend their particular denominational affiliation, whether Roman Catholic, Protestant, or Pentecostal, as well as transcending the generational categories of the exilic versus American-born members of their community.

Key Concepts, Ritual Structures, and Institutions

Cuban Americans identify predominantly as Roman Catholic. However, as exemplified by historic assimilation

VIRGEN DEL COBRE

In 1971, the Cuban community of Miami had a chapel consecrated to the memory of la Virgen de la Caridad del Cobre, an image of María that had been exiled from Cuba in 1961. This image remembers the Mother of Christ as the Virgin of Charity from the town of Cobre, Cuba. The original image was discovered in the sixteenth century by an African child, Juan Moreno, and two indigenous children, Juan and Rodrigo de Hoyos. They are remembered as *los tres Juanes* (the three Johns). Their story relates that after a storm, the image was found floating on a wooden plank at sea. The plank contained the inscription "I am the Virgin of Charity," and the cloth dress worn by the small statue was completely dry. A chapel was built for the statue near the site of its recovery, but eventually the statue began to disappear at night, indicating that it wanted to be moved to Cobre. Another chapel was built for it in Cobre but again it kept disappearing at night, until it appeared to a little girl atop a nearby mountain (*Sierra Maestra*). Another chapel was built, and the statue finally found a home in Cuba and the hearts of the Cuban people.

—GCG

patterns among numerous U.S. immigrant groups, a growing number of Cuban Americans are finding faith and fellowship in other Christian denominations such as Southern Baptists, the United Methodist Church, the Presbyterian Church, and Pentecostalism. There is also a percentage of Jewish Cuban Americans known among the South Florida community by their ethnic nickname, *Jewbans*. Given the historic syncretism of racial, cultural, and religious beliefs fostered throughout the Spanish colonies, many Cuban Americans, regardless of their Christian denominational affiliations, honor and practice the traditions of *Santería*, which originated in Cuba, other Caribbean colonies, and Brazil as a mixture of West African traditional *Yoruba* religion with the worship of Catholic saints and spiritual beings known as *orisha*. Also known as the "Rule of Lukumi," or "The Way of the Saints," Santería influenced the Creole class in colonial Cuba and became an important part of both Cuban and Afro-Caribbean religious culture. Since certain rituals involve animal sacrifice, Cuban American practitioners of Santería were often accused of health code and animal rights violations until the U.S. Supreme Court ruled in 1993 that a law passed by the City of Hialeah, Florida, restricting the practices of Santería and its animal sacrifice rituals was unconstitutional.

One of the most beloved religious traditions among Cuban Americans is their historic veneration of *Nuestra Señora de La Caridad de El Cobre* (Our Lady of Charity), Cuba's patroness whose legendary story dates back to the early 1600s. According to the story two Native brothers of Taino ancestry, Rodrigo and Diego de Hoyos accompanied by a Black slave boy, Juan Moreno, were searching for salt in a boat on the Bay of Nipe, near the island's northwestern tip, when a statue of the Virgin Mary miraculously floating on a piece of wood appeared to them. They were amazed that despite the rough seas, the Virgin's feet and robes were dry. Upon hearing of this apparition, the Spanish Captain of the Mines of *El Cobre*, Francisco Sanchez de Moya, ordered the construction of a shrine to Our Lady of Charity, which sparked a wave of pilgrimage to the site. The region's prosperity increased to the point that the Captain relaxed certain policies toward the Native and African slaves under his charge, which led to the Virgin's legendary association with both charity and freedom. Over the next three centuries Cuba's Virgin patroness became a symbol of the motherland, as well as of benevolence and liberty. By 1968 Miami's Cuban exile community began raising funds to build the present-day Shrine of Our Lady of Charity at a waterfront site on Biscayne Bay facing out toward the Atlantic. Contemporary Cuban Americans have interpreted the Virgin of Charity's story as that of the first Cuban rafter, and as a symbol of hope against tyranny and liberty for all Cubans.

Biblical themes have also functioned as an integral and sustaining aspect of the Cuban American exile and immigration experience. While Cuban American families have embraced typical U.S. holidays like the Fourth of July or Thanksgiving Day in November, the most revered day on the calendar for Cuban Americans is the annual Christmas Eve feast, known as *Noche Buena* (The Good Night), consisting of a traditional meal of roasted pork marinated in a special sauce, called *mojo*, served alongside yucca and plantains, and different variations of rice and black beans. Throughout the Cuban migration waves, and in recognition of solemn hopes for returning to their homeland, Cuban

American exiles and their American born offspring began the tradition of offering a short prayer, or a toast of sangria wine, with the words, "Next Year in Cuba," derived from the biblical story of Passover and traditional sayings during the Hebrew Diaspora experience, "Next Year in Jerusalem." Indeed, biblical themes of exile, such as allusions to the "Babylonian Captivity" as a metaphor for the plight of the Cuban people or references to biblical ideals about hospitality to strangers, are derived from the lessons of the Jewish Diaspora, on which Spain also left its mark in the same year as Columbus discovered Cuba. Many older Cuban Americans, who arrived in the United States during the first and second waves of the Cuban exodus, have fond memories of the support and compassion they received as new arrivals from Jewish Americans, and still appreciate how these gestures fostered healthy relationships between Cuban exiles and Jewish American communities in urban areas like New York City and Miami Beach.

In the Iberian-Spanish tradition Christmas is not the day set aside for exchanging gifts. Instead, this celebratory role is assigned to the visit of the Three Wise Kings, who brought gifts to the infant Jesus on January 6 of the Christian liturgical calendar, which became the feast day for gift giving and family celebration. When Fidel Castro banned Cubans from celebrating the feast day in 1971, Miami's Cuban American exile community responded by founding the annual *Parada y Festival de Los Reyes Magos* (Three Kings Day Parade and Festival), which draws over 500,000 people each January along Miami's "Little Havana" parade route, and has become one of the top Hispanic

American religious celebrations in the United States. The political circumstances that led to the establishment of this parade and festival in 1971 further exemplify the characteristic mentioned above about the comingling of religious traditions with both personal and spiritual aspirations for the liberty and dignity of the Cuban people.

The foremost Cuban exile organization in the United States is the Miami-based Cuban American National Foundation (CANF), whose Web site describes its mission statement as conducting and supporting the scores of activities aimed at advancing human rights in Cuba, educating public opinion on the plight of the Cuban people, dispelling prejudice and intolerance against Cuban Americans, and promoting culture and creative achievement among the Cuban people. CANF has worked since its founding in the 1970s fostering national and international dialogue about Cuban concerns and influencing the executive and legislative branches of government in Washington on behalf of Cuban American concerns. Despite complaints from some sectors of the U.S. government and corporate America seeking normalized relations with Cuba for economic gain, the organization's emphasis on humanitarian assistance, educational programs, and legal support of Cuban religious and dissident leaders earned CANF the widespread support of the Cuban American community.

One of the most significant yet little known aspects of the Cuban American community is the vital role played by Cuban exile private schools and professional educators from the mid-1960s to the present. Many of these Cuban private schools began operating in the United States after their founders either

migrated to Miami or were expelled from Cuba by the Communists. Among these schools we find institutions like Dr. Gil Beltran's *La Luz School,* or the highly successful chain of day-care centers and schools founded by Demetrio Perez Jr., the *Lincoln-Marti Schools.* Cuba's famous all-male Roman Catholic, Jesuit institution, *Colegio de Belen* (Belen School), was founded in 1854 in Havana by a Royal Charter from the Spanish Crown. Although among its high school alumni we find Fidel Castro, the Jesuit Fathers fled the religious oppression of Cuban Communism and relocated the school to Miami in 1961 as the *Belen Jesuit Preparatory School*, which today has an enrollment exceeding 1,200 students in grades 6 through 12. Hard work, scholarship, good conduct and citizenship, and religious values form the core of the curriculum at each of these schools. By providing standard and affordable K-through-12 educational programs for South Florida's Cuban and Latin American immigrant families, these Cuban American private schools have served as vehicles for assimilation and acculturation into U.S. society while instilling a sense of shared memory and deep respect for their Cuban cultural or religious roots among Cuban American, and other Hispanic American, youths residing in South Florida.

While Cuban American communities existed in several U.S. cities prior to 1959, it is estimated that these Cuban enclaves in New York City, Tampa, Key West, Miami, and New Orleans totaled less than 40,000 residents. Hence the post-1959 migration waves of Cubans moving to the United States account for the vast majority of Cubans who either became naturalized U.S. citizens or were born in this country after their parents' arrival in the United States. Transitioning from their native island to the United States in the aftermath of a revolutionary crisis, and then living through the Cuban Missile Crisis, first-generation Cubans faced the challenge of rebuilding their financial and professional lives while redefining their religious and cultural identities. Second-generation Cuban Americans have struggled with identity in the context of what it means to be a fully bicultural American while honoring the memories, assumptions, and hopes of their parents and raising their own much more assimilated families. As the third generation of Cuban Americans reaches adulthood, it will be interesting to witness how they deal with the pressures of continued assimilation to White, North American identity roles, personal religiosity and denominational affiliation, and the cultural memories of first- or second-generation Cuban Americans.

Albert Hernández

References and Further Reading

Antón, Alex, and Roger E. Hernández. *Cubans in America: A Vibrant History of a People in Exile* (New York: Kensington Books, 2003).

Conde, Yvonne. *Operation Pedro Pan: The Untold Exodus of 14,048 Cuban Children* (New York: Routledge, 1999).

De La Torre, Miguel A. *La Lucha for Cuba: Religion and Politics on the Streets of Miami* (Berkeley: University of California Press, 2003).

De La Torre, Miguel A. *Santeria: The Beliefs and Rituals of a Growing Religion in America* (Grand Rapids, MI: William B. Eerdmans, 2004).

De La Torre, Miguel A. *The Quest for the Cuban Christ: A Historical Search* (Gainesville: University Press of Florida, 2002).

Diaz, Guarione M. *The Cuban American Experience: Issues, Perceptions, and Realities* (St. Louis: Reedy Press, 2007).

Fernández, Alfredo. *Adrift: The Cuban Raft People* (Houston: Arte Publico Press, 2000).

Fernández Soneira, Teresa. *Cuba: Historia de la Educación Católica, 1582–1961.* 2 vols. (Miami: Ediciones Universal, 1997).

Firmat, Gustavo Perez. *Next Year in Cuba: A Cubano's Coming of Age in America* (New York: Doubleday Anchor Books, 1995).

Firmat, Gustavo Perez. *Life on the Hyphen: The Cuban-American Way* (Austin: University of Texas Press, 1994).

Grenier, Guillermo J., and Lisandro Perez. *The Legacy of Exile: Cubans in the United States* (Boston: Allyn and Bacon, 2003).

Herrera, Andrea O. *Remembering Cuba: Legacy of a Diaspora* (Austin: University of Texas Press, 2001).

Llanes, José. *Cuban Americans: Masters of Survival* (Cambridge, MA: Abt Books, 1982).

Poyo, Gerald E. *Cuban Catholics in the United States, 1960–1980* (Notre Dame, IN: University of Notre Dame Press, 2007).

CUBAN REVOLUTION

For Cuban Americans, specifically those living in Miami, Florida, the 1959 Cuban Revolution led by Fidel Castro was a traumatic experience that contributed to a collective identity. The underlying impulse of this revolution was not fidelity to some Marxist ideology; rather, the Cuban Revolution was a response to the radical economic and political changes that occurred on the island of Cuba throughout the twentieth century—changes that affected all aspects of Cuban culture. How Christianity came to be understood and portrayed also underwent several transformations throughout and since the revolution, impacting the religiosity of those Cubans who stayed on the island and those who came to the United States as refugees.

Probably the most significant event of the Revolution, which began the merging of the political with the sacred, occurred on January 8, 1959. Just seven days after the triumph of the Revolution, Fidel Castro gave his first national speech from Camp Columbia. At the moment Castro called for unity and peace, a white dove landed on his shoulder. For Christians, it was as if Castro assumed the role of Jesus, who also underwent a similar experience of a descending dove shortly after his baptism. But this religiously charged symbolism did not just start with Castro's speech calling for unity; during the Revolution, both Catholic and Protestant chaplains and leaders actively served with the guerilla forces. It is important to note that two early martyrs of the Revolution were Frank and Josué Pais, Baptists who were killed by Batista's soldiers for leading an uprising in Santiago. Also, individuals like Esteban Hernandez, a Presbyterian, were tortured and killed by Batista's police. These religious leaders were targeted because the houses of several Protestant leaders served as underground headquarters for the Revolution.

Catholic leaders also took part in the insurrection, most evident in the activities of Father Sardiñas who served as chaplain to the rebel army and was promoted to the rank of *comandante*. Also, Father Madrigal served as treasurer for the July 26 Movement, and Father Chabebe would relay coded messages to the rebel forces through his religious radio program. Although the church hierarchy remained silent during the insurgence, a significantly large percentage of Catholics, like the martyred Catholic student leader José Antonio Echevarría, participated in the uprising.

While some Protestants and Catholics chose to live out their faith through the Revolution, others, specifically foreign U.S. missionaries, saw the Revolution as a threat to the basic teachings of Christianity. While at first pleased with the new government's initiatives to end gambling, prostitution, and political corruption, early optimism gave way to disillusionment as the new regime took a more leftist tilt. Months after the 1959 Revolution, these missionaries returned to the United States, followed by many Cuban pastors and their middle-class congregations. The departure of these Christians almost brought the Protestant church to extinction. Although entire congregations disappeared, finding salvation in U.S. exile, those who stayed tended to reject the Revolution, becoming a social space for political resistance. Catholics, as well as Protestants, became engaged in counterrevolutionary activities, openly supporting and praising the United States, the hegemonic power intent on ending the Revolution and reestablishing its authority on the island.

For many Christians, Cuba needed to be "saved" from godless communism. On Christmas 1960, Archbishop Pérez Serantes (a critic of the former Batista regime) wrote a pastoral letter that presented Cubans with an ultimatum, titled "With Christ or Against Christ." In his letter, the archbishop laid out the existing dichotomy in eschatological tones, "The battle is to wrestle between Christ and the Anti-Christ. Choose, then, each to who they prefer to have as Chief."

Shortly after the failed U.S.-backed Bay of Pigs invasion, the Castro regime nationalized all church schools and declared most foreign clergy *persona non grata*. These drastic actions were taken in response to three Spanish priests and at least one minister (Methodist) who participated as chaplains during the April 1961 invasion. One of the priests, Father Ismael de Lugo, was to read a communiqué to the Cuban population: "The liberating forces have disembarked on Cuba's beaches. We come in the name of God. ...The assault brigade is made up of thousands of Cubans who are all Christians and Catholics. Our struggle is that of those who believe in God against the atheists. ...Have faith, since the victory is ours, because God is with us and the Virgin of Charity cannot abandon her children. ...Long live Christ the King! Long live our glorious Patron Saint!"

Several months after the failed invasion, on September 8 (the day of La Virgen del Cobre), 1961, the most notable protest against the Revolution occurred. An anticommunist march (riot) began at the Cathedral of La Habana, by the auxiliary archbishop, Eduardo Boza Masvidal, the Revolution's most outspoken critic. About 4,000 faithful participated in the march. Church forces clashed with revolutionary supporters, resulting in several injuries and the death of a passing 17-year-old. Within two days, priests were rounded up, and on September 17, 135 priests, along with Monsignor Boza Masvidal were expelled from the country (he went on to form the "Unión de Cubanos en el Exilio"—Union of Cubans in Exile). Additionally, all religious acts outside of the church became illegal.

At the end of that momentous year, on December 1, 1961, Castro declared himself to be a Marxist-Leninist, sending further shock waves throughout churches in Cuba, as well as the rest of Latin America. It was now official: a supposedly Catholic nation had fallen into the hands of an atheist communist regime. Because Catholics viewed communism as incongruent with Christianity, due mainly to the encyclical *Divini Redemptoris*, no room existed for dialogue. Cubans were forced to choose between "Roma o Moscú."

To remain in power, Castro had to decisively deal with these nonconforming Christians. The proclamation that was supposed to be read by the priest involved in the Bay of Pigs invasion, and the participation of churches in protests against the Revolution, led Castro to believe that an organized strategy existed among Christians to overthrow the Revolution. In his speech concerning the September 8 showdown between the government and the church, Castro laid out his argument.

[The counterrevolutionaries] want to paint the Revolution as an enemy of religion, as if that had anything to do with the things that interest the Revolution. ...The doctrine of Christ was a doctrine that found an echo among the slaves, among the humble people. It was persecuted by the aristocracy, by the dominant classes. These gentlemen, in contemporary times, completely abandoned the essence of the Christian doctrine, dedicated themselves to taking religion as an instrument to hide all the vices and all the defects of the present dominant classes, forgetting about the slaves of today, the workers, the peasants without land. These gentlemen separated themselves from the interests of the exploited masses, and from the humble masses, in order to carry religion on a silver platter to the great exploiters, to the dominant classes. They divorced themselves from the people, and they prostituted the essence of primitive Christianity.

Those Christian leaders who refused to conform to the Revolution faced expulsion. They were denied the right to run religious-based schools, thus deeply cutting into their ability to raise funds. Also, the churches' formerly private media became nationalized. Church members were routinely watched by the government, and many bishops, priests, and ministers were placed under house arrest. It was illegal for Christians to be members of the Communist Party, the only route to economic advancement. Furthermore, they were denied high-level government and university positions. No sociopolitical or economic reason existed to remain a Christian. Many, mostly the middle class, chose flight, rather than fight, creating a brain-drain on the island and further weakening the churches' power bases.

Those who neither left nor forsook their faith faced persecution. Between 1965 and 1968, thousands of artists, intellectuals, hippies, university students, and homosexuals were abducted by the State Secret Police and interned, without trial, in Military Units for Assistance to Production (UMAP), reeducation labor camps. Also interned were Jehovah's Witnesses, Gideonists, and Catholic or Protestant activists. Even the Nicaraguan priest, Ernest Cardenal, who had been friendly to the Castro regime, criticized the Cuban government in its treatment of Christians in his book *En Cuba*. With churches decimated, silence became

essential to self-preservation. Thus began an era of "internal exile."

With time, tensions between the church and government subsided. As the church ceased to challenge Castro's authority, tolerance for religion re-emerged. The Catholic Church in particular began the reconciliation process under the leadership of Cesare Zacchi, the Vatican's emissary appointed in 1962. He was quick to criticize prerevolutionary Cuba and the clergy who abandoned Cuba while praising Castro's social reforms. By April 10, 1969, a decisive break with the past occurred when the Catholic Church published the Cuban bishop's letter denouncing the U.S. embargo. Influenced by the theological developments occurring elsewhere in Latin America, specifically liberation theology, the Catholic Church, for the first time, committed itself to work for the development of Cuba without condemning the ideology of the regime.

Castro reciprocated by establishing a Christian-Marxist dialogue. Castro was influenced by priests such as Camilio Torres, who in 1966 ceased to say the mass to join the peoples' struggle in carrying out a revolution in Columbia. The 1979 success of Nicaragua's Sandinista Revolution, where Catholic clerics partook in the struggle against Somoza and assumed governmental positions, further impacted Castro's attitudes toward religion.

Protestants also sought a rapprochement. In 1977 the Confession of Faith of the Presbyterian-Reformed Church declared, "The Church lives joyfully in the midst of the socialist revolution." Baptist minister Jesse Jackson visited Cuba in 1984, at which time Fidel Castro gave a televised speech from the pulpit of a Protestant church flanked by church

Pastoral visit of Pope John Paul II to Cuba on January 24, 1998. (Gianni Giansanti/Sygma/ Corbis)

leaders. Additionally, the 1985 publication of Castro's bestseller *Fidel y la religión* (*Fidel and Religion*) began a public dialogue concerning areas of cooperation between Marxist and what Castro called "honest" Christians.

Today, Cuba is experiencing a spiritual revival. The fastest-growing churches (excluding those that practice Santería) are Pentecostal. The Bible has become the top seller, and seminaries like the one in Mantanzas have seen an increase in enrollment. Catholic churches have witnessed a renewal in popularity as thousands attend open-air masses inspired by the pope's 1998 visit. As Cuba entered the negative economic period known as the "special period," caused by the collapse of world communism, church pews are beginning to fill. After years of absence, Christians are returning, bringing with them the experience of secularism. Some are Marxists who have never been churched. These new parishioners are more critical, more questioning, and more demanding. This revival has created a meeting ground for those who have been opposed to the Revolution and those who have served it. Since the Revolution, Cuba's churches have evolved into an indigenous expression of faith. The breakage with the United States and the effects of the embargo have isolated the Cuban Christian community, forcing it to find its own expression of religiosity. Regardless of these churches' political views, ranging from accommodation to aloofness toward the Revolution, the Cubanization of church has been a century-long process.

Miguel A. De La Torre

References and Further Reading

De La Torre, Miguel A. *La Lucha for Cuba: Religion and Politics on the Streets of Miami* (Berkeley: University of California Press, 2003).

———. *The Quest for the Cuban Christ: A Historical Search* (Tampa: University Press of Florida, 2002).

Kirk, John M. *Between God and the Party: Religion and Politics in Revolutionary Cuba* (Tampa: University Presses of Florida, 1988).

Maza, Manuel P. *The Cuban Catholic Church: True Struggles and False Dilemmas* (master's diss., Georgetown University, Washington, DC, 1982).

CULTURAL ANTHROPOLOGY

Anthropology is generally divided into four fields: archaeological, physical or biological, linguistic, and sociocultural. Cultural anthropology falls in the last category and studies all aspects of human behavior and thought. Most cultural anthropologists carry out fieldwork and write ethnographies about a particular culture. The modern concept of a distinct discipline of cultural anthropology did not emerge until after the eighteenth-century Enlightenment when the social sciences were separated from the natural sciences. Some scholars in France and England suggested that society should be considered its own natural system with its own laws. Charles Montesquieu (1669-1755) attempted to discover the laws of social life in eighteenth-century France by comparing political institutions and religious beliefs as social behavior. The school of moral philosophers, Adam Smith (1723–1790) and Adam Ferguson (1723–1816), argued that "primitive" societies could offer clues about the history of "higher" societies. While Adam Smith argued that capitalism improved people's wealth, a nineteenth-century German theorist, Karl Marx (1818–1883), argued that the market created inequalities and that social systems were inherently unstable. These two positions were reflected in the foundational work of French sociologist Emile Durkheim (1858–1917) and German sociologist Max Weber (1864–1920). While Durkheim's social theory emphasizes stability or the maintenance of society, Karl Marx and Max Weber's ideas explore the stratification of society (between the bourgeoisie and proletariat classes) and the process of how a society changes. In other words, Durkheim focused on a stable social structure within society, while Marx and Weber examined social process.

The field of anthropology was dominated by Europeans and North Americans who traveled to observe indigenous cultures. In one of the early ethnographic studies of the poor in Latin America, Oscar Lewis follows one family's migration from a rural village into Mexico City in his classic work: *The Children of Sanchez*. Appropriating Sigmund Freud, Lewis offers a psychosocial view into the violent world of suffering, deprivation, infidelity, delinquency, corruption, police brutality, and cruelty of the poor to the poor. Through a series of in-depth interviews, Lewis also captures intense feelings of human warmth, joy, individuality, love, and hope for a better life among the urban poor.

Another important work, *The Devil and Commodity Fetishism in South America*, by Michael Taussig, applies Marxist Theory to analyze the

PERSONALISMO

Personalismo is a Spanish term from *persona* (person) and the suffix *-ismo* (-ism), which linguistically refers to a distinctive interpersonal style that places a unique emphasis on the human person. Other examples of interpersonal "isms" are familism and altruism. It is considered a core value dimension of Latino/a cultures and it is conceptualized affectively, cognitively, and behaviorally. It affectively prescribes for people to be interpersonally warm and affectionate. Cultural anthropologists note that this "cultural script" is part of a cultural worldview characteristic of highly collectivistic and relational cultures that value people over tasks, things, and time. Latina/os engage in several verbal and nonverbal behaviors to show personable traits. They prefer face-to-face contact, personal close and informal attention, shaking hands when greeting someone, and hugging to express closeness and rapport, and formal and informal forms of address (*usted* versus *tú*, respectively). As part of the cultural interpersonal ethos, personalismo is cross-situational and expressed in a variety of settings. A Spanish-speaking religious minister would express personalismo by exhibiting *simpatía* (friendly affection) and inspiring *confianza* (trust) and *respecto* (respect). The religious audience, in turn, would demonstrate personalismo by addressing the religious leader as *usted* and demonstrating culturally appropriate manners (*bien educado*).

—FAO

introduction of capitalism into native Bolivian culture. When colonialism enslaved the indigenous as plantation workers and miners, and converted land into a commodity, Taussig argues that the locals fetishized nature to understand why so many lives are being taken by the new system. Taussig concluded that working in the mountain mines becomes tantamount to selling one's soul to the devil.

In another historical study, Ruth Burns researched the archives of a Roman Catholic convent in Cuzco, Peru, at the time of the conquest to determine what role it played in introducing colonialism. She found that the orphanage raised the mixed-race offspring of Spanish *encomenderos* and Inca princesses with a Spanish mentality—thus training the new *meztizo* elite. The convent introduced the capitalistic values of private property, commodification, and banking with interest, and became the largest financial institution in colonial Peru.

In spite of these sympathetic ethnographies, the field was largely dominated by anthropologists of European descent. In the 1970s Octavio Romano (1923–2005), a native of Mexico City, became a pioneer Chicano anthropologist who claimed that social scientists were not immune from the general American pattern of blaming the victim. He criticized ethnographies that reinforced the stereotypes of the Latino/a people as being underachievers, fatalistic, traditional, and emotional. He challenged the social scientist notions developed in the 1950s and 1960s as reflecting the institutional racism and domination of society at large. Romano began a journal entitled "El Grito," which gave voice to emerging Chicana/o social scientists who advocated a decolonialized, antiracist anthropology and opened the door for research on contemporary Latino/a concerns such as health care, education, criminalization, identity, and immigration.

A. Paredes also criticized Anglo anthropologists, but took a more moderate and more constructive view. He argued that ethnographies about Hispanics were not overtly prejudiced; rather they perpetuated subtle unconscious stereotypes through some mistranslations and by taking literally what people mean figuratively. Paredes urges ethnographers to move beyond stereotypes by acquiring a deep knowledge of the language, social relations, and the context.

Appropriating the work of postcolonial studies, Renato Rosaldo critiqued the rigid "us and them" separation between the ethnographer and the native, noting the significant interpretative power involved in writing about another people (*Culture and Truth: The Remaking of Social Analysis* 1989). José David Saldivar also emphasized the importance of native participation in his research along the Texas-Mexico border (*Border Matters* 1997). Rodolfo Torres, Louis Miron, and Jonathan Xavier Inda have examined the differences between being a citizen and respecting one's culture as a Hispanic American in the Cultural Citizen Project (*Race, Identity and Citizenship* 1999).

Cultural anthropology has historically been understood as an objective social science, but more recently anthropologists have acknowledged the subjective nature of the discipline. A researcher often cannot remain neutral and can impact the very same conditions that one is studying, thus giving birth to the field of applied anthropology. The field of applied anthropology does not simply observe phenomena from an objective distance, but rather seeks to educate the public through publications and documentaries to address the problem at hand.

Philip Wingeier-Rayo

References and Further Reading

Burns, Ruth. *Colonial Habits: Convents and the Spiritual Economy of Cuzcu, Peru* (Durham, NC: Duke University Press, 1999).

Hendry, Joy. *Other People's Worlds: An Introduction to Cultural and Social Anthropology* (New York: New York University Press, 1999).

Layton, Robert. *An Introduction to Theory in Anthropology* (New York: Cambridge University Press, 1997).

Lewis, Oscar. *The Children of Sanchez: Autobiography of a Mexican Family* (New York: Vintage Books, 1961).

Paredes, A. *A Texas-Mexicano Cancionero: Folksongs of the Lower Border* (Urbana: University of Illinois Press, 1977).

Pew Hispanic Center. *Changing Faiths: Latinos and the Transformation of American Religion* (May 2007). http://pewhispanic.org/reports/report.php?ReportID=75

Scheper-Hughes, Nancy. *Death Without Weeping: The Violence of Everyday Life in Brazil* (Berkeley: University of California Press, 1992).

Torres, Rodolfo, ed. *Race, Identity and Citizenship, The Cultural Citizen Project* (Boston: Blackwell Publishing, 1999).

Taussig, Michael. *The Devil and Commodity Fetishism in South America* (Chapel Hill: University of North Carolina Press, 1980).

CURANDERISMO

Curanderismo is a therapeutic approach to healthful living and healing, particularly common among Hispanic Christians of indigenous and mestizo ancestry. Contemporary interest has been influenced by the modern cultural anthropology, psychiatry, psychology, and medicine, as well as changing multicultural demographics.

There are at least four historical sources in the development of *curanderismo*: (1) The Judeo-Christian belief recorded in the Bible (Numbers 21:9; 2 Kings 5:10–14; James 5:14) attesting to God's power to heal, as well as God's use of chosen people as instruments of such supernatural cures. Apparently, believers also used certain natural remedies, such as the Balm of Gilead (Jeremiah 8:22; 46:11), the fig poultice prescribed by Isaiah to cure Hezekiah's boil (Isaiah 38:21), and the oil and wine of the Good Samaritan (Luke 10:25–37). (2) Christian Europeans, particularly the Spaniards, who came to the Americas with medical beliefs that had also been influenced by the Hippocratic theory of the four humors of the body (blood, phlegm, black bile, and yellow bile balanced correctly between hot, cold, wet, and dry); such had been inherited from the Greeks, and preserved and added to by the Arabs (including Avenzoar and Averroes who built on the work of the Persian Avicenna). (3) Indigenous peoples of the Americas contributed their own extensive knowledge of local herbs and their medicinal applications through brews and poultices, as well as surgical techniques using obsidian and thorns. (4) Curanderismo developed alongside witchcraft (which seeks to exert human control over the supernatural), *Santería*

(which performs possession of practitioners by spirits), and later Spiritism (whose mediums communicate with spirits such as famed healers), as well as the modern Christian charismatic/Pentecostal movements. All these belief systems have exerted a conceptual and practical influence on curanderismo. Contemporary *botánicas*, for instance, often stock supplies, equipment, and books used by all these approaches to healing.

Curanderismo, therefore, is a venerable, but evolving, healing tradition rather than a modern health fad with quack claims. There are practitioners (called *curanderos* or *curanderas*, male and female healers, respectively) who are quacks, just as there are ministers and medical doctors who are charlatans. While effective and ethically responsible curandera/os do not usually have diplomas or belong to professional organizations, there are indicators of their credibility and healing competence.

The most effective curandera/os are not ill-intentioned in their practice. They do not charge a fixed fee, but accept free-will offerings. They demonstrate considerable dedication to their profession, even when this requires sacrifice and/or defying traditional gender roles. They attribute their supernatural abilities and magico-religious interventions to God. They usually recount how they received their gift of healing. They also strive for a therapeutic alliance with patients by being accessible and collaborative with the family of the patient throughout the healing process, from diagnosis through termination. Finally, they are profoundly knowledgeable of, and widely admired by, the community they serve.

Patients and practitioners in curanderismo access modern medicine and use it

BOTÁNICA

Botánica is an herb store, also known as *yerbería*, that offers a wide variety of medicinal remedies that include herbal extracts, vitamins, and potions, alongside folk religious items such as rosaries, cards, crucifixes, amulets, statues, and cards with incantations to Catholic saints and other folk. An herbal vender at this store is called a *yerbero* or *yerbatero* and may be considered a folk healer by the community or simply a provider of medicinal products for other curanderos. In Latino folk healing, a botánica is part of an ancient herbolary tradition that attributes curative powers to herbs. The natives of the Americas cultivated vast gardens of medicinal plants. The Aztec manuscript *Libellus de Medicinalibus Indorum Herbis* (Little Book of the Medicinal Herbs of the Indians), for example, is a classic ancient pre-Hispanic herbal codex that describes the medicinal use of 150 indigenous herbs in Mexico used by Mesoamerican populations. In folk indigenous traditions, disease is often seen as an imbalance in the physical and spiritual realms, and herbs are believed to restore health. Hispanics often resort to herb shops because they often trust natural remedies as well as conventional medicine, and botánicas offer culturally meaningful items with attributed curative and spiritual powers.

—NSM

in an alternative or complementary manner. Curanderismo survives in part because so many Hispanics cannot access the modern medical system. Many lack the financial means or insurance necessary to meet its high and ever-rising costs. Others find language barriers. Transportation and child care are often obstacles. Another difficulty, however, is the clash of cultures.

Science by definition is universal but often, therefore, impersonal. Medical practitioners, for example, may operate from a specific cultural frame of reference that can be ethnocentric, biased, and insensitive. When the ethnicity of a medical professional is very different from that of its patient, such differences might lead to resistance and mistrust by the patient; hence, a visit to a neighborhood curandero/a may be experienced as therapeutic, while the experience at the distant and impersonal hospital may be traumatic.

Healing is often attributed to the curandera/o's ability to effectively deal with subjectively expressed symptoms, especially when such symptoms are framed in layman's terms. Note the distinction some cross-cultural psychiatrists have made between illness and disease. Whereas illness refers to the subjective experience of being sick (symptoms, suffering, help seeking, side effects of treatment, social stigma, explanations of causes), disease refers to the diagnosis given by the doctor or healer. Western-trained doctors focus primarily on diagnosing and alleviating symptoms, whereas a curandera/o's approach is more holistic and culturally sensitive, paying special attention to the subjectively expressed symptoms.

Curandera/os usually practice in the community they serve and thus are typically well integrated into their patients' neighborhood. Therefore, curandero/as generally share the client's cultural

EL NIÑO FIDENCIO (1898–1938)

José Fidencio Constantino Síntora began life as a conventional Catholic in Guanajuato, Mexico. During the Mexican Revolution his fame as a healer spread, especially after reportedly gaining the support of President Calles. Although many Catholics still venerate him, during his life he was in conflict with Church leaders as well as medical doctors. But as his standing with such authorities decreased, his popularity with the subaltern increased. People knew him to live simply, even sacrificially, and devote himself totally to healing. Certainly typological, he exemplifies the way curanderos cross religious, class, and gender lines. Although some curanderos do not marry, Fidencio appears to have been celibate, perhaps transgender, almost asexual. The designation "el Niño" connotes prepubescent innocence as well as his childlike demeanor. El Niño did not practice espiritismo and, although he gathered disciples, it does not appear that he intended to found a church, much less a personality cult although both developed. His decade-long public career ended with his death after which a cult developed with strong Spiritist tendencies now recognized as a religion by the Mexican government and located in Espinazo.

—*FAO & KGD*

experiences, geographic location, socio-economic status, class, language, religion, and beliefs regarding the causes of symptoms. The place of healing is usually a private home, which often includes a waiting area and a room for private consultation. This is mirrored in popular movies such as *La Bamba*, *Mi Familia*, *El Norte*, and *Tortillas Again*, which portray these characteristics of curanderismo. In these movies, healers usually share wisdom with their clients and perform rituals to protect them from evil spirits, to cleanse them from harmful influences, and to heal them from unknown maladies.

These movies demonstrate that both Hispanic patients and curandera/os value the benefits and contributions of conventional scientific medicine. However, they often also experience a medical culture of clinical coldness, bureaucracy, and exclusive dependence on technology with little respect for communal or spiritual values, as well as an emphasis on individual patient rights to the exclusion of family. Medical practices and models are closely monitored by cost-effective managed care and the concepts of efficiency. When supposedly informed by objectivity, such medical interventions can reduce people to just their symptoms and ignore important cultural clues. Too often these medical practices and models complicate and aggravate, rather than improve, Hispanics' health concerns. Frequently, modern health care appears to mirror only the prosperity-driven, individualistic, self-interested, even self-isolation aspects of U.S. culture. Such a medical system is one that Hispanics may find physiologically healthful but also experience as culturally unhelpful.

Hence, many Hispanics may use a continuum of care. The range of health-seeking behaviors may begin with a family member (usually female) diagnosing

DON PEDRITO JARAMILLO (1829–1907)

Don Pedrito Jaramillo was known as the healer of Los Olmos, Texas, from 1881 to 1907, and was probably the most orthodox of the famous curanderos. He has never been the object of ecclesiastical censure or even much clergy criticism. Likewise, the medical profession did not oppose him. His appellation helps explain why. "Don" is an honorific title expressing respect while Pedrito is the affectionate diminutive of Pedro. Hence "Don Pedrito" expresses both the love and honor this humble man gained by his selfless service in the name of God. A shrine and store near Falfurrias, Texas, help maintain and perpetuate veneration through candles, prayer cards, poems, prints, and statues not unlike more conventional Catholic pilgrimage sites. Although there are numerous versions of his reception of the healing gift as well as many stories of its efficacy, they follow the conventions of curanderos. The gift came from God rather than through study, and since it was freely given, it was shared without fixed charge. Healing was holistic: Don Pedrito prescribed prayer and penance as well as plants and poultices. And he both suffered the common doubts about his healing gift and enjoyed the grateful respect of admirers.

—*FAO & KGD*

a disease or injury and assessing her ability to treat it. Normally, her attention, advice, home remedies, or over-the-counter medicines are sufficient. However, if she decides that the illness or injury is beyond her ability to treat, she may consult family and friends. As the circle widens, concerns about the medical health care system arise, and also causes and cures might be discussed. Culturally specific syndromes such as fright (*susto*), impacted bowels (*empacho*), excessive bile (*bilis*), extreme jealousy (*envidia*), the evil eye (*mal de ojo*), or suspicion of hexes (*hechizo*) might lead the family to consult a curandero/a first. Alternately, patients may attempt to access modern medicine first, and if it is found wanting or frustrating, then a curandera/o might also be consulted.

As with medical doctors, some curandera/os are generalists. Others claim to follow in the healing tradition of a particularly famous past curandero, such as Don Pedrito Jaramillo or el Niño Fidencio. Still others specialize in a particular area, for instance, herbalists, midwives, and those who set bones or massage muscles. But all share certain cultural beliefs and attitudes toward health and life that are holistic, ecological, and natural. Health is not understood in purely organic or biological terms. Rather, well-being is considered a balance among and between the physical, emotional, social, and spiritual aspects of the human. These might be considered the four cardinal points that interact to bring about harmony and health, which constitute central tenets in the healing worldview of curandero/as.

The physical dimensions of health are addressed through proper hygiene, rest, diet, and exercise, as well as purges, massages, and herbs. These therapeutic recommendations usually have psychological as well as physical implications, and they opt for the integration of body

TERESA URREA (1873–1906)

Teresa Urrea, also known as Teresita or La Santa de Cabora, was born on October 15, 1873, in a hacienda, located in a Tehueco Indian village in the Mexican state of Sinaloa. She was baptized under the name of Maria Rebecca Chávez and was the illegitimate daughter of Tomás Urrea (Don Tomás), a wealthy hacienda owner and Cayetana Chávez, a 14-year-old Tehuecan Indian. The Tehueco, Yaqui, and Mayo refer to Mexican indigenous tribes inhabiting the coastal states of Sonora and Sinaloa. At 16, her father invited her to live with him at his hacienda where she came under the apprenticeship of an Indian woman named Huila, a curandera and servant of Don Tomás, from whom she learned the use of herbs and other healing rituals. In 1880 Don Tomás moved to Cabora, Sonora, with his family to escape political reprisals from the Mexican dictator Porfirio Díaz. During the first months at Cabora, Teresa fell into a cataleptic state. After recovery she began performing healings by laying her hands on the sick and earned a reputation as a prodigious healer and revolutionary advocate for Indian rights. She died in 1906 at the age of 33 in Clifton, Arizona.

—FAO

with mind. Cleansing rituals (*limpias*) are often performed to restore the body's balance and to remove unwanted supernatural influences. Certain emotions are often proscribed, such as worry, ambition, and envy. Other emotions are prescribed, including honor, modesty, respect, and dignity. Balanced, complementary, and harmonious social relationships are encouraged; therefore, questions concerning family and community are often part of the curandero's diagnostic interview with patients. Of course, prayer, penance, and amends are ways of maintaining or restoring spiritual, as well as emotional and social, wholeness; they are often part of any cure.

To the patient and the curandero/a, their practices are considered a seamless and integrated approach to health care. They understand the continuum they use, from home care and curandera/os to medical doctors, clinics, and hospitals. However, too many doctors and pharma-

cists do not appreciate these alternative treatments their patients might be practicing with whatever medicine or therapy such health professionals have approved. Medical professional resistance to others' healing practices may result from limited knowledge, biased attitudes, perceived incompatibilities, misinformed opinions, and lack of exposure to non-Western modalities of healing and treatment. This limitation in professional medical knowledge and practice may lead to counterproductive outcomes. For these reasons, more and more professionals now study curanderismo, and some attempt to learn from its ritual structure, such as the four health management patterns suggested below.

First, a culturally sensitive environment might relieve patient anxiety and facilitate therapeutic rapport. Instead of a stark office, a calming space with nondenominational Christian imagery (e.g., angels rather than saints), candles, incense, flowers, and fountain might be

Curandero "Don Pedrito" seated outside a frame building, San Antonio, Texas, 1894. (University of Texas, Institute of Texan Cultures at San Antonio)

used. Family and curandero/a altars usually include such religious imagery, as well as symbols for earth, wind, fire, and water.

Second, a professional must gain cultural entree. Like priests, psychologists, and medical doctors, curandera/os must undergo lengthy training and experiential practice that includes understanding both indigenous and religious beliefs. Knowing the language and its nuances for respect with intimacy, as well as speaking the idiom of dedication and compassion, is essential. Self-confidence without arrogance and a willingness to speak of her or his healing vocation in a respectful tone are culturally congruent ways of gaining wisdom credentials. A ceremony of greeting and small talk, questions about family and friends, all build bridges of confidence. Comfort

with silence, closed eyes, even manipulating cultural props such as lighting incense help create an invitation to active speaking and listening. If typical herbs or oils are present, verbal suggestions that the patient touch and discuss them may lead to helpful information, reassure the patient, or aid her or him to externalize and articulate fears. All these rites of introduction allow for a culturally congruent diagnosis leading to a holistic or organic treatment of the person, not just the disease.

Third, diagnosis and treatment plans must include more than just the assessment of physiological symptoms reported by the individual patient, but rather also address how the patient's condition has affected her or his family and community. What emotions does illness, loss, or injury evoke? What are the customary ways in which an extended family and community help restore members to health? Here questions of finances may arise, and social workers might prove helpful. All these dimensions are critical to holistic health care, and proper attention to them reinforces treatment. These therapeutic interventions highlight the importance of the family and the community, which often provide considerable emotional support and facilitate healing, as well as the role of faith in treatment.

Fourth, one might ask how the patient could reinterpret this new situation through religious narrative. People construct their experiences of illness in certain ways based on their religious and cultural learning. Through ritualized practices, clients may be able to reconstruct their subjective experiences of symptoms and conceptualizations of illness. What rituals (psychodrama) is the patient using to restore spiritual harmony? So long as they are practical, proportionate, and unlikely to cause harm, they may be encouraged. Competent clergy could be recommended.

This ritual structure paralleling curanderismo or even in concert with curandero and curanderas reverently approaches the patient not as an individual with a problem, but as a person who initiates or accelerates the social, emotional, and spiritual forces of a cultural community in ways that promote the health and harmony of everyone involved. The patient is a change agent, not just the object of others' interventions. This approach to healing, like the holistic approach to health, is empowering. The ritual structures of curanderismo provide culturally congruent observances that bring meaning to confusion, thus promoting psycho-somatic health; proffers emotional coherence to frightening anomie, thus helping the weak feel capable; marshals the power of social solidarity, thus averting debilitating isolation; and brings spiritual balance to a life on the edge, thus snatching hope from despair. In any language, this may prove curative, but in Spanish it is called "curanderismo."

Fernando A. Ortiz and Kenneth G. Davis

References and Further Reading

Kieve, Ari. *Curanderismo: Mexican American Folk Psychiatry* (New York: Free Press, 1968).

Trotter, Robert T., and Juan Antonio Chavira. *Curanderismo: Mexican American Folk Healing* (Athens and London, GE: University of Georgia Press, 1997).

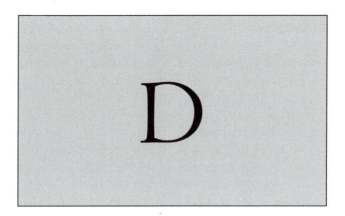

DEMOGRAPHICS

The demographic shifts occurring within Latino/a religious affiliation in the United States are at the root of a major debate. Sociologist Andrew Greeley of the University of Chicago has argued that the Catholic Church is experiencing mass defections of Latina/o Catholics to Evangelical and Mainline Protestantism. The Hispanic Churches in American Public Life (HCAPL) National Survey refined and revised this finding and argued that although Roman Catholicism is witnessing mass defections, it is still nonetheless experiencing unprecedented numerical growth and has remained relatively stable over the past two decades. Catholic defections are not only benefiting Evangelicals and Mainline Protestants, but also Pentecostals, Alternative Christian groups like the Jehovah's Witnesses, Mormons, and Seventh-day Adventists, world religions, and metaphysical traditions. In short, the U.S. Latino/a religious marketplace, while predominantly Christian, is also becoming increasingly denominationally and religiously pluralistic. The day has long since passed when one could assume that to be Latina/o was to be Roman Catholic.

The findings in this entry are based on the *Hispanic Churches in American Public Life* research project directed and managed by Virgilio Elizondo of the University of Notre Dame, Jesse Miranda of Vanguard University, and Gastón Espinosa of Claremont McKenna College. This three-year study (1999–2002) was funded by a $1.3 million grant from the Pew Charitable Trusts. It fielded the HCAPL National Survey in the fall of 2000, one of the largest (n = 2,060) and most comprehensive bilingual surveys in history on U.S. Latina/o religions and politics.

Latino/a Catholic Religious Switching

Andrew Greeley ignited the public crisis over what he called "mass defections" when he wrote in *America* in 1989 that 60,000 Latino/as were defecting every year from Roman Catholicism to Protestantism. Drawing upon the General Social Survey (GSS) at the University of Chicago, he estimated that 1 million Latina/os had left the Catholic Church in the United States between 1972 and 1989. Nine years later he wrote in the same periodical that these defections had only grown worse, with as many as 600,000 Latinos leaving the Church annually. These defections resulted in the U.S. Latino/a Catholic population declining from 77 percent in 1972–1974 to 70 percent by the mid-1990s, he reported.

Greeley lamented that one out of seven Hispanics had left Catholicism in less than a quarter of a century and that if this "hemorrhaging" continued half of all American Hispanics would not be Catholic in 25 years. Far from being a sporadic episode in the story of American Catholicism, he warned that he saw no reason why these defections would not continue. He called these mass defections "an ecclesiastical failure of unprecedented proportions" and the "worst defection in the history of the Catholic Church in the United States." He ended his lament by chastising the Catholic hierarchy for its "dereliction of duty" and for its inability or unwillingness to stem the tide of these "cataclysmic" defections. Greeley's trumpet blast announcing the mass defections did not attract a single public response or an outcry from a single cardinal, archbishop, bishop, priest, or clergyman working with Hispanics, he claimed. He found this remarkable and indicative of the deep-seated problem facing American Catholicism.

The HCAPL national survey confirmed and refined some of Greeley's findings. The survey found that 70 percent of all U.S. Latino/a adults self-identified as Roman Catholic—the exact figure that Greeley found in 1997. However, it would be inaccurate to conclude that the U.S. Latina/o Catholic population has remained completely stable because the GSS survey only captured the attitudes of second- and third-generation English-speaking Latino/as—those most likely to be Protestant. The actual percentage of U.S. Latina/os that were Roman Catholic in 1997 was probably around 74 percent—the percent of immigrants that self-identified as Roman Catholic in the HCAPL national survey. Further evidence for mass defections include the fact that the percentage of Latino/a Catholics drops from 74 percent among the first generation to 62 percent by the third. At the same time, the percentage of Latina/o Protestants and other Christians simultaneously increases from one in six (15 percent) among the first generation to almost one in three (29 percent) by the third generation. Furthermore, although 800,000 U.S. Latino/as indicated that they "recently converted" or returned to Catholicism from another non-Catholic tradition, over 3.9 million Latina/os recently converted away from Catholicism. Thus for every one Latino/a that returned to Catholicism, four left it. Contrary to popular perception that vulnerable immigrants were falling prey to proselytizers, the HCAPL survey found that a clear majority of Latina/o converts were second- or third-generation U.S. citizens (57 percent).

Pentecostalization of U.S. Latino/a Christianity

Who benefited from the mass defections? Andrew Greeley argued Evangelical and Mainline Protestants were benefiting.

He went so far as to state that almost half of all Latino/a Protestants "belong to moderate or even liberal Protestant denominations." The HCAPL survey found that they were not the only traditions benefiting. The major surprise was that the Pentecostals were benefiting the most from these mass defections. In fact, we are witnessing the Pentecostalization of U.S. Latina/o Christianity. This may seem contrary to the findings of many other studies such as the Latino National Survey (LNS) and American Religious Identity Survey (ARIS), both of which argue that the percentage of Pentecostal Christians is relatively small.

However, they make two serious methodological oversights. First, they do not include Charismatics in their totals of Pentecostals. Second, they restrict Pentecostal identity only to those who self-identify as such or who attend a classical Pentecostal denomination like the Assemblies of God, the Foursquare, the Church of God, Cleveland, and the Church of God of Prophecy. They overlook the fact that the Pentecostal experience has entered into non-Pentecostal traditions and denominations of the Roman Catholic Church, Mainline Protestant traditions, and non-Pentecostal Evangelical traditions. They also overlook the fact that there are a very large number of Pentecostals who do not like the term "Pentecostal" because of the negative stereotype associated with the term (i.e., holy rollers) and that many prefer to be called "Charismatic," or just "Christian."

The evidence for the growth of the Pentecostal/Charismatic movement in Latino/a Protestantism is borne out in the HCAPL survey, which found that 64 percent of all U.S. Latina/o Protestants self-identified as Pentecostal or Charismatic or with a Pentecostal tradition. The Pentecostal movement has entered into non-Pentecostal traditions and is contributing to the Pentecostalization of U.S. Latino/a Christianity. The HCAPL survey found that 22 percent of U.S. Latina/o Catholics, 21 percent of U.S. Latino/a Mainline Protestants, and 51 percent of U.S. Latina/o evangelicals not attending a Pentecostal denomination self-identified as Pentecostal, Charismatic, or Spirit-filled. Thus the Pentecostal movement has moved outside the confines of the Pentecostal tradition and into other segments on Latino/a Christianity.

The Pentecostal movement has a number of distinctive teachings. For example, it teaches that people should be baptized in the Holy Spirit as evidenced by speaking in unknown tongues and they also affirm the practice of all of the spiritual sign gifts listed in I Corinthians 12 and 14. They are much closer to the African American rather than Euro-American Pentecostal experience because of their emphases on direct unmediated experience with God, prayer for divine healing, the practice of speaking and singing in tongues (aka singing in the Spirit), and their rather lengthy worship services, which can run two or three hours in duration. Many Latina/o Pentecostal traditions such as the Assemblies of God, Foursquare, Church of God of Prophecy, and others also allow women to go into the ordained and/or lay ministry.

Charismatics are those individuals who affirm and/or practice the spiritual gifts but choose to remain within their non-Pentecostal traditions to bring about spiritual renewal. The growth of the Latino/a Charismatic movement within the Catholic Church was confirmed in Bishop Gerald R. Barnes's *Hispanic*

Ministry at the Turn of the Millennium: A Report of the Bishop's Committee on Hispanic Affairs, which found that the Charismatic movement was active in 36 percent of all Hispanic-serving parishes, thus making it more common than either the *Cursillo* (31 percent) or Christian Base Communities (13 percent).

The Pentecostal movement has contributed to the growth of Latino/a Evangelicalism across denominations. Having a personal born-again experience with Jesus Christ is arguably the single most important distinction of Evangelical identity—especially in the U.S. Latina/o community. The growth of the Pentecostal experience is also contributing to the growth of born-again Christianity in non-Pentecostal and non-Evangelical traditions. The HCAPL survey found that 88 percent of U.S. Latino/a Protestants, 43 percent of Latina/o Mainline Protestants, and 26 percent of Latino/a Catholics chose to self-identify as "born-again" Christian. The growth of Protestantism was noted in Barnes's Report, which found that the percentage of diocesan directors who said that Protestant groups were affecting Hispanics to a "great extent" had increased from 12 percent in 1990 to 52 percent in 1998. The report also noted that Protestants were most effective with both the newest and poorest immigrants and middle-class Hispanics.

All of these findings refine Andrew Greeley's claim that half of all Latino/a Protestants "belong to moderate or even liberal Protestant denominations." In fact, the HCAPL survey found that Latina/o Mainline Protestants make up 14.8 percent of all Latino/a Protestants. This figure includes those who are also born again (43 percent) and Pentecostal, Charismatic, or Spirit-filled (21 percent).

All combined and across all religious traditions, 37 percent of all U.S. Latina/os reported being born-again Christian and 28 percent reported being Pentecostal, Charismatic, or Spirit-filled.

These figures are much higher than those given in past national surveys because most surveyors do not take into account that (a) the Pentecostal/Charismatic movement is a transdenominational phenomenon, (b) the proliferation of independent and nondenominational churches are more often than not either Evangelical/born-again and/or Pentecostal or Charismatic, and (c) that a significant percentage, if not a majority, of those Latino/as that self-identify as "other Christian," independent/nondenominational, something else, other religious tradition, no religious preference, and other religion actually self-identify as born-again Christian and/or as Pentecostal, Charismatic, or Spirit-filled.

Challenging the general perception that movement away from denominational Christianity signals secularization or decline in spirituality and confirming the trend in the growth of nondenominational Protestantism, we also found that the vast majority of those who did not self-identify with a particular denomination also self-identified as born again. This was true for those who self-identified as "other Christian" (77 percent), "independent/nondenominational" (75 percent), "something else" (52 percent), "other religious tradition or denomination" (52 percent), and even "other religion" (50 percent), and do not know/unspecified (48 percent). This finding was further confirmed by unusually high levels of church attendance (almost every week or more) for "other Christian" (71 percent), "independent/ nondenominational" (67 percent), "other religious tradition or denomination" (60 percent), "something else" (52 percent), "other religion" (40 percent), and do not know/unspecified (48 percent). Given that being born again is one of the defining marks of both Evangelical and Pentecostal Christianity, these data suggest that many Latina/o Evangelicals and Pentecostals are being inadvertently misclassified in other national surveys (both for Latino/as and for the general U.S. population) as practicing another religion or having no religious preference.

Explaining Latina/o Catholic Switching

How do we explain Latino/a Catholic defections? There are four factors that contribute to the mass defections. First, there are simply not enough parishes to effectively minister to the nation's 30 million Latino/a Catholics. Mary Gautier at the Center for Applied Research in the Apostolate (CARA) noted in 2003 that only 22 percent (4,224) of the nation's 47,511 Catholic parishes in the United States have an identified ministry to Latina/os. This means that 78 percent of all Catholic parishes do not have an identified ministry to Hispanics, despite the fact that they now constitute an estimated 40 percent of the U.S. Catholic Church.

Second, there are simply not enough Latino and Spanish-speaking priests to minister to the nation's 32 million Latina/o Catholics. According to Gautier, U.S. Latino/as make up 4 percent of all Catholic women religious, 5 percent of all priests, and 9 percent of all bishops, even though Latina/os make up almost 40 percent of the U.S. Church. Of the 47,511 priests in the United States in 2003, only 2,175 were Latino and of the

85,000 women religious, only 3,400 were Latina. There is only one Latino Catholic priest for every 11,500 Latinos in the United States, a rate that is actually higher in the United States than in Latin America where Brian H. Smith has noted the ratio is one priest for every 10,000 Catholics.

The shortage of priests is further complicated by the fact that more than two-thirds of all Latino priests were born and raised outside of the United States, such as Latin America or Spain. Many of them come from different cultural, class, and socioeconomic backgrounds than their U.S. parishioners. This has contributed to an often unspoken chasm between some foreign-born priests and their working-class U.S.-born parishioners. These factors have made it particularly difficult for Latin American–born priests to work with second- and third-generation inner-city Latino/a youth, influenced by hip-hop, rap music, and gang life. The clergy shortages and difficulties are not likely to go away anytime soon, as there were only 511 U.S. Latinos nationwide seeking vocations and attending Catholic seminaries. The numbers have since picked up a little, but not much. These factors along with reports that non-Hispanic priests are not prepared to work effectively with Hispanics and that continuing clergy education in Hispanic ministry for non-Hispanic priests and sisters is actually *declining,* make the low number of U.S.-born Latino clergy all the more acute.

Third, there has been a steady decline in the number of faith-based sociopolitical movements like Liberation Theology and Christian Base Communities (CBCs), despite interest in Catholic seminaries and universities. The Gerald Barnes's Bishop's Report found that only

13 percent of U.S. Catholic Hispanic-serving parishes sponsor CBCs and that their numbers appear to be declining. This is an important development because the CBCs have been some of the most vocal groups pressing the Church for more native clergy and Hispanic ministries.

Fourth, the most important external reason for the mass defections and religious switching is proselytism. As already noted, more than 3.9 million Latino/as had recently left the Catholic Church. At the local parish level, the Bishop's Report found that the percentage of diocesan directors who said that Protestant groups were affecting Hispanics to a "great extent" had increased from 12 percent in 1990 to 52 percent in 1998.

Alternative and Nondenominational Christianity, World Religions, and Metaphysical Traditions

The HCAPL survey found that Alternative Christians make up 3 percent of all U.S. Latino/as (44 million), 10 percent of all non-Catholics, and 13 percent of all non-Catholic Christians. The Jehovah's Witnesses and Mormons ranked as the first and eighth largest Christian traditions in the U.S. Latina/o community. There are more than 1 million Latino/a Jehovah's Witnesses and Mormons in the United States. The Jehovah's Witnesses are the largest single self-identified Non-Catholic Christian tradition in the United States, followed by three Pentecostal traditions—the Assemblies of God, the Pentecostal Church of God, and the Assembly of Christian Churches.

The impact of Alternative Christian traditions is not only evident with the growth of Latino/a Jehovah's Witnesses and Mormons, but also with other traditions such as the Seventh-day Adventists and the Oneness Pentecostals—the latter of which reject the doctrine of the Trinity and insist that true Christians must be baptized in Jesus' name only for salvation. Regardless of the "orthodoxy" of their theology, together Adventists and Oneness Pentecostals number approximately half a million people. These traditions not only represent the first, seventh, eighth, and ninth largest non-Catholic self-identified Christian religious traditions in the United States, but all combined they are more numerous than all Latino/a Mainline Protestants combined. They make up 15 percent of all non-Catholics and 20 percent of all non-Catholic Christians.

Another equally surprising finding was the number of Latina/os that identified with world religions, with metaphysical/occult traditions, and as nondenominational Protestants. The HCAPL survey found that only 1 percent of all U.S. Latinos are affiliated exclusively with a world religion or a non-Christian tradition. In fact, 93 percent of Latinos self-identify as Christian, when both denominational affiliation and born-again experience are used to mark religious identity. Although many have suggested that the lack of attraction to Judaism and Islam is due to an historic anti-Muslim and anti-Jewish apologetic birthed during Ferdinand and Isabella's *Reconquista* of Spain in the sixteenth century and brought over to Latin America by the Spanish conquistadores and Franciscan, Dominican, Augustinian, and Jesuit missionaries, the HCAPL survey found that some Latino/as are in fact embracing Islam, Judaism, and other Eastern religions. In fact, the most popular world religion among Latina/os is Buddhism, not Islam or Judaism. The HCAPL survey found that almost 1 percent of all U.S. Latino/a non-Catholics (10.6 million) self-identify as Buddhist. There are almost three times more Latino/a Buddhists than Latino Muslims or Jews. This may be largely due to the meditative and contemplative nature of Buddhism.

Although Latino/a interest in Islam was catapulted into the national spotlight with the arrest of *Al Qaeda* sympathizer José Padilla, Latino/a Muslims represent a comparatively small tradition. The HCAPL study found that 32,000 Latina/os self-identified as Muslim and another 21,000 self-identified as Jewish. While too few in number to make statistical generalizations, Latino/as also mentioned practicing Hinduism, Taoism, Paganism, Satanism, Spiritualism, Deism, mixed traditions, and Native American spiritual traditions. Despite their relatively small numbers, there are almost more Latino/a practitioners of world religions than all Latina/o Methodists, Presbyterians, and Disciples of Christ *combined*.

These numbers may not appear significant, but they represent real (if modest) movement toward religious pluralism in the Latino/a community. As significant as they are, they do not fully capture the growing diversity and pluralism. The HCAPL survey found that a significant number of Latina/os believe in the practice of metaphysical traditions like spiritism, *brujería* (witchcraft), and combinative popular Catholic healing traditions like *curanderismo*. The survey found that 17.1 percent of all U.S. Latinos believe in the practice of Spiritism,

curanderismo, brujería, or all of the above. When broken down individually, 2.5 percent of all Latinos said they believe in the practice of Spiritism, 1.7 percent believe in the practice of brujería, 1.3 percent believe in the practice of curanderismo, and 11.7 percent believe in the practice of all of the above. To put these numbers in comparative perspective, there are more Latino/as who believe in the practice of Spiritism than Jehovah's Witnesses or Assemblies of God practitioners and more people who believe in the practice of witchcraft than Latina/o Southern Baptists. All combined, 15.9 percent of the U.S. Latino/a national population indicated that they believe in the practice of one or more of these metaphysical traditions (excluding curanderismo), thus making them more numerous than all U.S. Latina/o Pentecostals and Evangelicals (excluding Protestant and Catholic Charismatics) at 15.4 percent. Whether or not this is simply an acknowledgement that these traditions exist, or is in fact an actual affirmation that they personally practice these traditions, is uncertain.

The growth of Protestantism, non-Christian traditions, and pluralism are contributing to an increasing number of Latino/as choosing to self-identify as nondenominational, as other, as something else, or as having no religious preference. For example, our survey found that almost 20 percent of Latina/o non-Catholics said they were "other Christian," "independent/nondenominational," "something else," "other religious tradition," "other religion," and "do not know/unspecified," had no religious preference, or were atheist or agnostic (only 0.37 percent). This may indicate a growing dissatisfaction with organized religion, diminishing status differences between denominations, high rates of religious mobility, increasingly porous denominational boundaries, or more than likely some combination of factors. However, it may also reveal the rise of nondenominational Evangelical Christianity because most of the people in this category also self-identified as born-again Christian. As noted in Chapter One of my co-edited book with Miguel A. De La Torre entitled *Rethinking Latino Religion and Identity* (Pilgrim Press 2006), the HCAPL survey found that the majority of those who reported being "other Christian" (77 percent), "independent/nondenominational" (75 percent), "something else" (52 percent), "other religious tradition" (52 percent), "other religion" (50 percent), and "do not know/unspecified" (48 percent) also stated that they were born-again Christian. This finding was further confirmed by high church attendance (almost every week or more) for those respondents that self-identified as "other Christian" (71 percent), "independent/nondenominational" (67 percent), "other religious tradition" (60 percent), "something else" (52 percent), "do not know/unspecified" (48 percent), and even "other religion" (50 percent). Given that being born again is one of the defining marks of both Evangelical and Pentecostal Christianity and that high church attendance is often related to participating in these religious traditions, these data may suggest that much of this growth does not indicate a movement away from religion at all but rather toward new kinds of independent and interdenominational religious traditions and transdenominational movements that have not yet been carefully tracked by scholars of religion.

All of these demographic shifts are contributing to a growing level of denominational and religious pluralism in the United States. Although the number of Catholics is at an all-time high, its market share of the U.S. Latina/o religious community is declining despite high Catholic birthrates and massive Catholic immigration from Latin America. If the border remains as porous as it is today, it is likely that the percentage of U.S. Latino/a Catholics may remain around 68 percent, while the number of Latina/o Catholics that defect to other religious traditions continues to grow. Regardless of the dynamics within the U.S. Latino/a community, there is little reason to doubt that the percentage of Latina/os that make up the U.S. Catholic Church will only continue to grow due to high birth and immigration rates. The day is not far off when Latino/as will hold a 51 percent majority of the American Catholic Church. While this will be a transformative moment for the U.S. Church, imagine what the future of American Catholicism would look like if 51 percent of all U.S. priests, bishops, and archbishops were Latino—that would be a truly revolutionary moment indeed. If the trends taking place today hold steady, then we are going to see not only the Latinization of the Roman Catholic Church in the twenty-first century but also the Latinization of American Christianity and U.S. society.

Gastón Espinosa

References and Further Reading

Espinosa, Gastón. "The Pentecostalization of Latin American and U.S. Latino Christianity." *Pneuma: The Journal for the*

Society of Pentecostal Studies 26, no. 2 (Fall 2004): 262–292.

———. "Methodological Reflections on Social Science Research on Latino Religions." *Rethinking Latino/a Religions and Identity*, ed. Miguel A. De La Torre and Gastón Espinosa (Cleveland, OH: Pilgrim Press, 2006).

———. "History and Theory in the Study of Mexican American Religions." *Rethinking Latino/a Religions and Identity*, ed. Miguel A. De La Torre and Gastón Espinosa (Cleveland, OH: Pilgrim Press, 2006).

Greeley, Andrew M. "Defection Among Hispanics," *America* (July 30, 1988): 61–62.

———. "Defection Among Hispanics (Updated), *America* 27 (September 1997): 12–13.

DÍA DE LOS MUERTOS

Día de los Muertos, or Day of the Dead, is a day of commemoration of family and friends who have died. In contemporary times, this commemoration takes place on November 2, to coincide with the Christian holy day of All Soul's Day. And yet, the commemoration is separate and distinct from the Christian holy day. The origin of the commemoration is sometimes attributed to Aztec or Nahuatl tradition, sometimes to postcolonial syncretism or a mixture of the indigenous Aztec/Nahuatl tradition with Christianity, and, in a more contemporary understanding, as a sign of Mexican national pride and as a Chicano sign of resistance, as well as indigenous precolonial pride. For some observers of the tradition, the commemoration remains a religious one, for others merely a cultural expression of identity, and for outsiders a kind of political recognition or even kitsch.

Prior to European contact, the Nahuatl-speaking people in the area now known as southern Texas, Mexico, and Central America as far south as Nicaragua marked the end of a temporal cycle beginning the 13th month of the Aztec solar calendar. Offerings to the dead were made between May and August, taking place between two zenith passages when the sun's shadow pointed north. Records of these traditions were written by postcolonial ethnographers who both interviewed indigenous people and interpreted glyphs and other records. In one commemoration during *Atemoztli*, the 16th month, the Aztecs made wooden images of the rain god, Tlaloc, which they covered with *tzoalli*, or amaranth seed dough, shaped in human form—with hearts, eyes, and teeth. The images were worshipped with music and then their breasts were opened with a *tzotzopaztli* or weaving sword and worshippers removed the hearts and struck off the heads. The body of seed dough was then divided up among the worshippers who ate the body with the words: "The god is eaten." Those who ate it were said to "keep the god."

Whether Christian tradition had influenced or transformed these Nahuatl traditions by the time ethnographers recorded some of this information is not clear. In postcolonial times, common food customs from Europe associated with All Saints' Day and All Souls' Day commemorations were common among the Pueblo and Zuni Nations in what became the southwestern United States, the Nahuatl Nation of what became parts of Mexico, and the Aymara Nation of the Andes. Whether this was merely a coinciding of similar traditions into an easy syncretism in which Nahuatl tradition of offerings to the dead during one time of year were combined with Christian holy days in another time of the year or whether this was a way of preserving indigenous tradition in the face of overwhelming European contact is not known with any certainty. Other elements of the commemorations such as public begging, food distribution, and noise making seem common to both European and indigenous practices. Again, which tradition influenced the other cannot be confirmed.

Today, Día de los Muertos is viewed as a commemoration beginning at sundown on November 1 and lasting until the dawn of November 2. During this time, the belief is that the spirits of those family members and friends who have died are able to visit the earth, enjoy the sight and scent of their favorite foods, drink, and other sensual pleasures such as cigarettes and cigars. Sometimes these spirits are said to communicate with the living.

The Aztec teachings about death and the afterlife are grounded in the tradition of Mictlan. According to the tradition, Mictlan or Chicunauhmictlan is the ninth level of the Aztec underworld. All souls of the dead are required to make this downward journey that takes four years and is an arduous one. The only ones who are not required to make this journey are those who die as warriors, women who die in childbirth, and those who die after being struck by lightening. The god of the dead, Mictlantecuhtli, and his spouse, Mictecacihuatl, live in a windowless house in this northernmost part of the underworld. Here they wait for the souls of the dead to return to them. The journey is a difficult one. First the dead have to cross the river Apanohuaya. The dead are buried with the dog

Techichi, who had to help them swim across the river. They emerge naked and then must pass between a pair of mountains, the Tepetl Monamictia, that crash into each other. The dead then must climb the mountain Iztepetl, which has a surface made of razor-sharp obsidian fragments. Each day contains a new test. Next, the dead must cross the *Cehuecayan*, eight freezing gorges with constant snowfall and the Itzehecayan, eight valleys with cutting winds. The dead then walk down a path where they are exposed to a flurry of arrows, the Temiminaloyan. Here they realize a jaguar has eaten their hearts. Finally, they come to a place "where the flags wave" where they would find Xochitonatl, a lizard who symbolized Tonantzin, the Earth that lets them know they are near the end and soon would return to the Earth, to become one again with Tonantzin, the Mother Earth where they began life and where they will become once again part of life energy.

The dead must make this journey to Mictlan because of the sacrifice made by the gods. Queztalcoatl, the feathered serpent, symbol of the sun, traveled to Mictlan to rescue the precious jade bones of the humans of previous ages to give life to a new era, the Fifth Sun, which is the era of contemporary times. The jade bones are the seed of new life. Mictlantecuhtli tested Quetzalcoatl by requiring Quetzalcoatl to parade four times around Mictlantecuhtl's throne of spiders and owls, blowing a conch shell that had no finger holes. Queztalcoatl was able to secure the aid of worms to bore the finger holes and bees to make the sound. Still, Mictlantecuhtli laid a trap for Queztzalcoatl into which he fell, shattering the jade bones into the different sizes of human beings. Yet he prevailed and with the other gods sprinkled the bones with blood to give them life. Because humans were born from the penance of the gods, they must endure the tests of Mictlan before returning again to give life. For those who continue to practice the Aztec or Nahuatl tradition, the ritual practices of Día de los Muertos are an opportunity to assist the dead in this terrible journey, replacing the amaranth seed dough effigies and related ceremony once used to commemorate the dead.

Because this commemoration occurs close to the Western and European holiday of Halloween, the Hallowed Eve on October 31 when the veil between the worlds was traditionally thought to be the thinnest, the move from a sacred tradition to a holiday tradition is also a coinciding event. The celebration of Halloween in Mexico and Central America has been met with mixed reception. For some, it is welcomed as simply one *fiesta* or festivity that gives honor to the dead or even a status symbol for those able to afford store-bought costumes. For others, it is seen as an intrusive, foreign, and even colonizing custom. In the United States, some immigrants refuse to adopt the custom of Halloween, just as some longtime U.S. resident Latino/as reject the celebration as a sign of resistance to a history of U.S. domination. For them, Día de los Muertos is a symbol of the cultural borderland in which they live that transforms their indigenous past and provides a postcolonial "border crossing" into the future. Adopting the commemoration intentionally is used to define and unite a community divided by a history of oppression, exploitation, and colonial domination. The commemoration becomes a cultural symbol of identity and, in some cases, radical Chicano activism.

Ritual Structures

Celebration of Día de los Muertos reflects the variations in its origins, religious tradition, and cultural symbolism. In most Christian communities, the commemoration and celebration is accepted as a part of popular religiosity—not part of the institutional church and thus not in conflict with it but, in fact, helpful to the prayer of the faithful. However, some Christian communities view the non-Christian origins of the tradition as problematic. For most Christian church communities, the commemorations take a form outside the established liturgical requirements of masses or prayers for the departed commemorating All Saints' Day and All Souls' Day during the month of November. Primarily, Día de los Muertos is a private or family tradition featuring home altars or, in some cases, altars at the cemetery gravestones of the departed. Some churches welcome altars on church grounds, usually not in the house of worship, and sponsor community days of fiesta. Some church communities embrace the range of syncretism and permit traditional Nahuatl ceremonies—including all-night vigils and danza at dawn on their premises. Where the tradition is primarily one of cultural identity, community centers, museums, and other public places sponsor altars together with storytelling, traditional Danza Azteca, food, and community-building events.

The altar is the focus of the commemoration whether located at home or in a public place. The ritual symbols express the coming together of indigenous and Christian elements of tradition, the *mestizaje*. The altar is covered with a white cloth symbolizing Christian baptism. Fragrant marigolds or *zempoalxochitl*, the indigenous symbol of truth, wisdom, beauty, and eternity adorn the altar, together with votive candles. The pictures, or if not available, favorite objects, of beloved family members and friends who have died are placed on the altar so that each one is unobstructed. Around these pictures and objects the family and friends place favorite foods, drink, or other favorite items that the dead might take pleasure in seeing again.

The preferred *ofrendas*, or offerings, are those with scent to them because the sense of smell, together with sight, is a pleasure the dead are traditionally thought to be able to enjoy. Additional ofrendas of sugar skulls and *pan de muertos*, a bread made especially for the commemoration, are also placed on the altar. These traditions are thought to be postcolonial adaptations of Nahuatl customs although no clear lines as to the time and space of these traditions is established. Sugar as a source of postcolonial industry is thought to be a replacement for the amaranth seed and dough effigies. The skull symbols seem related to iconography found among indigenous glyphs, although this iconography seems removed in time and place from traditions related to the known indigenous commemoration of the dead. On the most traditional altars, a *sauhmador*, or clay incense holder, is placed in the center, burning fragrant copal incense, to please the spirits of the dead and the living. Some traditional commemorations follow the sacred tradition by a journey to the cemetery to place flowers, food and drink ofrendas on the places of the dead. This is done so no one is forgotten. Some

*Dancers dressed as skeletons perform at a Day of the Dead Festival (*Día de los Muertos*) in Hollywood, California. (Jose Gil/Dreamstime)*

Christian churches will incorporate the journey to the cemetery or the altar into its All Souls' Day worship, sometimes following or preceding the church liturgy as a way to encourage the prayer of the community throughout the month of November.

If the altar is part of a traditional Danza Azteca ceremony, it will be used during an all-night *velación*, a vigil, of singing in Nahuatl and Spanish—including songs about both Aztec traditional stories and Christian narratives. Songs are led by mandolins, the instrument used to preserve many indigenous songs and drumbeats during postcolonial times when drums were banned. Families or Danza circles take turns choosing songs and leading a call-response round. The velación begins at sundown. Shortly after midnight, the participants take a break to enjoy food and drink. In some celebrations, tequila is passed around as homage to the maguey plant. Tobacco is also smoked ceremoniously. After the break, the participants continue singing as the flowers are prepared for a flower *limpia* that happens just before dawn. At dawn, the danzantes pray in danza form for the spirits as they depart back on their journey to Mictlan. When the ceremony ends, the altar is taken down. All candles and flowers are distributed to be used on home altars throughout the month of November until the candles are burned down, a resonance perhaps with the "keeping of the god" when the amaranth seed dough effigies were eaten in the past.

If the altar is one used in a community or public commemoration in a cultural way, these altars are usually adorned with marigolds, candles, and ofrendas that are pleasing. If the altar is in a place of business or school, it might include pictures of family and friends of that community. The altar will be set up sometime around November 1 and remain for the month of November. Cultural events, community education, and other events of the month would be centered around the altar. Despite the ambiguity regarding the origin, perhaps because of it, and the multivalent purposes of Día de los Muertos, its commemoration is a unifying experience for U.S. Latino/as that sometimes bridges time and space.

Marta Vides Saade

References and Further Reading

Aguilar-Moreno, Manuel. *Handbook to Life in the Aztec World* (New York: Oxford University Press, 2007).

Brandes, Stanley H. "Sugar, Colonialism, and Death: On the Origins of Mexico's Day of the Dead." *Comparative Studies in Society and History* 39, no. 2 (April 1997): 270–299.

Brandes, Stanley H. "Iconography in Mexico's Day of the Dean: Origins and Meaning." *Ethnohistory* 45, no. 2 (Spring 1998): 181–218.

Brandes, Stanley H. *Skulls to the Living, Bread to the Dead: The Day of the Dead in Mexico and Beyond* (Boston: Blackwell Publishing, 2006).

Carrasco, David, and Scott Sessions. *Daily Life of the Aztecs: People of the Sun and Earth* (Westport, CT: Greenwood Publishing Group, 1998).

Empereur, James L., and Eduardo Fernández. *La Vida Sacra: Contemporary Hispanic Sacramental Theology* (Lanham, MD: Rowman & Littlefield, 2006).

Leon, Luis D. *La Llorona's Children: Religion, Life and Death in the U.S.-Mexican Borderlands* (Berkeley: University of California Press, 2004).

Medina, Lara, and Gilbert R. Cadena. "Dia de los Muertos: Public Ritual, Community Renewal, and Popular Religion in Los Angeles." *Horizons of the Sacred: Mexican Traditions in U.S. Catholicism*, ed. Timothy Matovina and Gary Riebe-Estrella (New York: Cornell Press, 2002).

DIASPORA THEOLOGY

The word "diaspora" means dispersion, and it refers to the migration of people from a homeland and their resettlement in one or several host countries. One of the outcomes of migratory processes is the formation and development of diaspora people and communities in receiving countries. A *diasporic person* is anyone who left his/her native country and settled down provisionally or permanently in another country. This person: (a) claims some form of membership to the country of origin; (b) maintains a feeling of loyalty to the homeland; (c) reproduces cultural practices and identities related to the sending country; and (d) engages in some kind of transnational exchanges across borders. He/she might aspire or not to return to his/her homelands.

Diasporic people carry with them their cultural traditions, including their religions. They live out their religion in their homes, communities, and congregations. *Diaspora congregations* are religious communities of migrant peoples and their descendants who gather and organize to practice their religion and culture. These congregations foster religious and ethnic identities in continuity with the religious and cultural traditions of their countries of origin.

Apart from the religious functions, these congregations provide important

Mural of Our Lady of Guadalupe on a building in Santa Fe, New Mexico. (Louise Roach/ Dreamstime)

cultural and social services. They help migrants to maintain their cultural traditions and at the same time acculturate to the new country and its culture. Diaspora congregations provide informal and formal social and advocacy services, as well as engage in local and international practices of family support, community development, and human relief. They also can generate strategies of compliance or defiance in relation to social, economic, and political conditions and processes that might affect diaspora communities and congregations in the receiving country. Diasporic religious people practice, adapt, and interpret their religious faith and traditions in light of the experiences of becoming immigrant and minority groups in host countries.

Diaspora theology is the process and product of interpreting a religious faith that takes into account the social situation, experiences, needs, and interests of diasporic people, communities, and congregations. Diaspora theologians seek to discern the religious meaning and ethical guidelines of life in diaspora and for religious life in diaspora. Diaspora theologies express the religious vision, beliefs, values, and commitments that guide and sustain religious people and congregations living in diaspora.

Diaspora theologians explore and interpret the doctrinal and ethical beliefs and the spiritual practices of their religions in connection with the challenges, conflicts, and opportunities present in the diasporic context. They make proposals on how the divine is present and active on behalf of the diaspora community and in the life of the diasporic community of faith. They present religious visions on how to think and celebrate the faith, live morally, and act civically. Diaspora theologies are generated by

common faithful people, religious leaders, and professional theologians committed to the spiritual, cultural, and sociopolitical survival and development of their diasporic communities and congregations.

Hispanic Christians are major contributors to the presence of Christian diaspora theologies in the United States. Hispanic Catholic, Protestant, and Pentecostal theologians formulate interpretations of the Christian faith and lifestyle focusing on the way the Latino/a people experience their lives and faith as members of migrant and minority communities and congregations in the United States. They develop versions of the Christian faith and mission that address the spiritual, cultural, moral, political, and economic issues and struggles of Hispanic migrant communities and congregations. Latina/o diaspora theologies incorporate the religious insights coming from grassroots popular religion, the church theological and social doctrines, as well as the reflection of Hispanic professional theologians in the academy.

Latino/a diaspora theologies are developed mainly by first and 1.5 generation theologians (those who immigrated before or during their early teens) of the different communities of Latin American descent in the United States. These theologians are found among different Hispanic groups in the United States: Cubans, Mexicans, Puerto Ricans, Argentineans, and Venezuelans. For these theologians the experience and awareness of being a diasporic person and a member of a diaspora community and congregation become the focus of their theological and ethical reflection.

The theological work of these diaspora theologians tends to follow two perspectives. One is a panethnic perspective in which they join their voices in solidarity with Hispanics of other migrant groups and place the emphasis on common characteristics and aspirations across the diverse Latino/a communities. In this sense, diaspora theology is one form or expression of Hispanic theology. The other trend is more specific to the national and cultural group of origin. In this other sense, some of these theologies can also be classified as expressions of Cuban American, Puerto Rican, Mexican, etc., diaspora theologies.

Justo L. González and Fernando F. Segovia have made important and sophisticated contributions to a general understanding of Hispanic diaspora theology and hermeneutics. Both were born in Cuba and became U.S. naturalized citizens after exile. González is a Methodist church historian and theologian. Fernando Segovia is a Catholic New Testament scholar. Both are major contributors and interpreters to both Hispanic theology and Cuban American diaspora theology in the United States. Their writings give insight into the key themes of Hispanic diaspora theology.

González has identified five key themes in the theological reflection and biblical hermeneutics of Hispanic diaspora theology. The five "paradigms" that Hispanic theologians employ to describe the social and theological situation of Hispanics are the following: marginality; poverty; mestizaje and mulatez; exile and aliens; and solidarity.

González explores three aspects for each of these topics. First, each of these themes points to a negative dimension in the social situation and human condition of Hispanics as migrant and minority people in the United States. For example, they point to experiences such as the following: (a) exclusion from the centers of power; (b) high levels of poverty and under- and unemployment; (c) the rejection of mixed people of color in a White racist society; (d) the political and cultural subordination of foreigners; (e) the sense of homelessness and uprootedness.

Second, these themes are also interpreted in a positive dimension. For example, they speak of the options of Hispanics as follows: (a) to stand on the sidelines of dominant society in order to affirm and promote their cultural traditions; (b) to practice love, hospitality, and solidarity with the poor; (c) to produce and celebrate their racial and cultural hybridities; (d) to contribute to the economic, social, and cultural life in a multicultural society; and (e) to provide hospitality and care to new migrants.

Finally, each of these topics is interpreted theologically to reveal something about the presence, action, and demands of the divine in the experience and struggles of Latino/a diaspora communities and congregations. The God of the Christian gospel is a God who reveals and redeems in the marginal person of Jesus who lived and ministered among the poor for their spiritual and social liberation. God announces a preferential option for the poor in the Law and through the prophets, and demands love, hospitality, and justice for the poor and the stranger. This is a God who created a diverse cultural humanity and affirmed hybrid people in the incarnation of the Galilean Jesus, the ministry and message of the cultural mestizo apostle Paul, and the formation of a multicultural church and kingdom with people from all countries and cultures. God calls churches and nations to become inclusive, diverse, and hospitable communities that provide refuge, home, care, justice, and community for the poor, the stranger, and the destitute.

In several of his essays, the New Testament scholar Segovia has developed a "hermeneutics and theology of the Diaspora" or a "hermeneutics and theology of otherness and *mescolanza* (racial and cultural mixture)." According to Segovia, Hispanic Americans are members of diverse diaspora communities of Latin American and Caribbean descent whose migrations are partially the result of the imperial politics and economics of the United States in the American continent. The Hispanic experience in the United States is characterized by four dimensions: (a) otherness; (b) mixture or hybridity; (c) passion for life (commitment to a dream of freedom, life, dignity, and opportunity in a new home); and (d) struggle for freedom and justice (against discrimination, political powerlessness, economic deprivation, and educational marginalization).

At the center of the Hispanic social situation are the experiences of otherness and mixture. Hispanics become others in the United States because they are different in terms of cultural, national, and racial origins and in terms of power differential from the national majority group. By coming to the United States, diasporic Hispanics start living in between two sociocultural worlds: the worlds of the host land and the homeland. They are able to live and navigate between two worlds they know but belong only partially because they are considered strangers or others. At the same time, they experience "alienation" from these two worlds because they have different experiences, status, and identities from the majority groups in each context. Hispanics also come from countries with a history of racial and cultural mixtures of Amerindian, European, African, and Asian populations.

Because of this otherness and mixture, Hispanic diasporic people live in two worlds at the same time and in neither of those worlds completely. This experience makes them permanent strangers or others in their home and host lands. This "otherness" is construed negatively (indicated by the use of the quotation marks) by majority groups in the United States. Hispanics are called by names (Hispanic, Hispanic Americans) that they did not invent. Hispanics are also represented and treated negatively in both the United States and in many of their homelands. They become undesirable aliens or diminished "others."

Segovia's hermeneutics of otherness and mixture is geared to critique and challenge the ideologies and practices that make Hispanic Americans "others" in the United States and to advance a process of self-affirmation and liberation for Hispanics and for all. The key to reverse this negative "otherness" is to understand that this is a construct that can be reconstructed in a positive way. Segovia calls Hispanics to appropriate the status of being aliens or others and make it an identity and vocation for the liberation of all.

Turning this negative "otherness" into a positive otherness is what Segovia calls *engagement* and it involves three tasks. First, in the task of *self-appropriation* Hispanics revise and write their history from their own perspective, challenging the imperial versions of that history. Second, in an act of *self-*

definition they challenge the negative "otherness" imposed on them and articulate positively and militantly their aspirations, values, contributions, interests, and needs. Finally, Hispanics will engage in *self-direction* by developing visions and dreams for a just, inclusive, democratic, and liberating society for all. In doing all this, Hispanic Americans claim their mission or "manifest destiny" to embrace, speak out, and struggle out of their status as aliens (others and strangers) for the liberation of all.

Segovia's diaspora theology is geared to critique the United States for the following: (a) its imperial ideology of manifest destiny; (b) its ethnic-racial stratification system; (c) its Americanizing policy toward immigrants and conquered communities; and (d) the colonized mentality in minorities that consent with the bifurcated system of imperial center and margins. On the other hand, diaspora theology affirms the distinct presence and positive contributions of the diverse Latino/a communities in the United States.

Segovia's diaspora theology demands respect for the recognition of different identities among Hispanic Americans and respect for the identities of other groups in the nation. Diaspora theology should assist Hispanic Americans in struggling to survive and claim their political membership and rights in the new country. Latina/os should declare their manifest destiny as aliens who wish to be strangers no longer.

Segovia classifies his theology as an exercise in liberation theology for several reasons. First, it is concerned with the sociopolitical, racial, and economic liberation of all marginalized people, but in particular U.S. Hispanics. Second, as a postcolonial theology, it critiques the empire and its imperial theology and social and religious institutions. Instead, it argues for the freedom and rights of the margins for self-affirmation, self-definition, and self-direction in politics and theology (decolonization). Third, diaspora theology critiques as oppressive the Western and modern ideology and project of homogeneity, universality, objectivity, and essentialism. Instead, it affirms diversity and plurality as liberating ideals and goals for society, church, and theology.

Hispanic diaspora theologies share theological themes, hermeneutical strategies, and political goals with Asian American and African American diaspora theologies in the United States. All of these diaspora theologies are committed, in their own way and according to their historical experience, to struggle for the spiritual and cultural survival, the material and moral well-being, the economic and social development, and the advocacy for civil and human rights for their diasporic people, communities, and congregations and for the rest of the nation. They are convinced that their diaspora experience is not only a sociocultural condition. It is also a spiritual journey, an ethical vocation, and a cultural gift that can contribute to the formation and transformation of their new country into a more inclusive, just, free, and democratic society.

Luis Rivera-Rodriguez

References and Further Reading

De La Torre, Miguel A. *La Lucha for Cuba: Religion and Politics on the Streets of*

Miami (Berkeley: University of California Press, 2003).

González, Justo L. *Santa Biblia: The Bible through Hispanic Eyes* (Nashville: Abingdon Press, 1996).

Rivera, Luis R. "Towards a Diaspora Hermeneutics." *Character Ethics and the Old Testament: Moral Dimensions of Scripture*, ed. M. Daniel Carroll R. and Jacqueline E. Lapsley (Louisville: Westminster John Knox Press, 2007).

Segovia, Fernando F. *Decolonizing Biblical Studies: A View from the Margins* (Maryknoll, NY: Orbis Books, 2000).

————, ed. *Interpreting Beyond Borders* (Sheffield, England: Sheffield Academic Press, 2000).

Warner, Stephen, and Judith G. Wittner, eds. *Gatherings in Diaspora. Religious Communities and the New Immigration* (Philadelphia: Temple University Press, 1998).

DOMINICAN AMERICANS

The first great wave of Dominican immigrants to the United States took place in the 1960s and 1970s, as a result of the assassination of the dictator Rafael Leonidas Trujillo. These were years of political turmoil. The 1980s marked the beginning of the second wave of Dominicans to the United States. Economics, however, was the primary reason for this exodus. The large number of Dominicans who immigrated to the United States was concentrated mostly in New York City. Among the top 20 nations with immigrants in the City (1980-1989), the Dominican Republic was the highest. This continued for the next decade. Today, there are Dominican communities in almost every region of the country. Nationwide, the Dominican population in the United States rose from 520,121 in 1990 to 1,041,910 in 2000, making this group the fourth largest Hispanic group in the United States, after Mexicans, Puerto Ricans, and Cubans. At the current pace, it is estimated that prior to the year 2010, the Dominican population will overtake the Cuban population, making it the third largest Latina/o group in the country.

As economic migrants, Dominicans faced the same struggles that new immigrants often face: unemployment, formal educational and health access problems, fair housing, and societal discrimination. During the late 1980s in New York City, political gains were evident as new school board members were elected. In 1991, Guillermo Linares was elected to the City Council in New York City, becoming the first Dominican elected official in the United States. Today there are 23 Dominicans holding elected positions in the United States and Puerto Rico, including State Assembly, City Council, County legislator, State Representative, State Delegate, and County Commissioner titles. In 1997, the Dominican American National Round Table was established to advocate for the empowerment of Dominicans in the United States, Puerto Rico, and U.S. territories.

Economically, Dominicans in the United States are a heterogeneous group that represents low-wage blue-collar jobs as well as high-level professionals. In addition, the Dominican community has adopted an entrepreneurial spirit, generating jobs for new arrivals (bodegas, beauty parlors, restaurants, travel agencies, and supermarkets). In New York City, Dominican students constitute a vast majority in the City University system where the Dominican Studies Institute was established for the study of

The Dominican Day parade is held in New York City each August. The Alianza Dominicana, *with more than 350 employees, is the largest Dominican-directed service organization in the United States. (Pedro Antonio Tavarez)*

issues, problems, and research efforts related to the Dominican experience in the United States and abroad.

Dominicans maintain close relations with their native land. For example, monies sent back to the Dominican Republic by Dominican immigrants represent the second highest source of external funds for the nation after tourism income. Over three-quarters of these monies come from the United States and Puerto Rico. In what some scholars refer to as double loyalty, Dominicans in the United States are active participants in the political, social, and cultural life of their homeland. There is a constant transnational mobility in which Dominicans send their children to the island for vacations, visit periodically for family, cultural, and religious celebrations, and

participate in business ventures. Dominican families on the island also send relatives to the United States for periodic vacations, educational opportunities, and the seeking of citizenship status or economic gain. It is also established that in New York and other major cities, there are specific chapters of national political parties where political candidates seek support during national elections. Binational status (double citizenship) today allows Dominicans to vote abroad as well as in the United States.

The official religion of the Dominican Republic is Roman Catholicism, established by a concordat with the Vatican. It is estimated that more than 90 percent profess this faith. Recent surveys, however, indicate that 39.8 percent identify themselves as practicing. Upon

NUESTRA SEÑORA DE LA ALTAGRACIA

Nuestra Señora de la Altagracia, Our Lady of High Grace, is the patroness of the Dominican Republic. She is referred to by Dominicans as "Tatica from Higuey." The portrait of Altagracia was brought from Spain by the brothers Trejo at the beginning of the colonization process. They offered the icon to the parish church when they moved to Higuey where a shrine was erected in 1572. The portrait, which is only 33 centimeters wide by 45 centimeters high, is said to be a primitive work of the Spanish school. Experts date it to the end of the fifteenth century or the beginning of the sixteenth. The original icon was conspicuous for its simplicity, but in 1708 it was restored and embellished. The icon as it appears today is a depiction of the holy family and Jesus' birth. At the center of the picture is Mary, in a prayerful attitude, hands brought together, looking down on the child who lies asleep and naked on the straws. Altagracia's original feast day was August 15, but was changed on account of a victorious battle fought on January 21, 1691. The latter day is the one celebrated at present by the Dominican Community both on the Island and in the United States.

—*ASD*

immigration, Dominicans appear to continue this trend, and as in their native land a high percent practice popular religiosity, including Dominican Voodoo, Santería, or other African-based religious expressions. A common feature in Dominican neighborhoods is the Botánica—an alternative folk medicine retail store with spiritual emphases on healing remedies and religious health-care products. Dominicans are also present in mainline denominational churches; however, it is within the Pentecostal movement where there appears to be rapid and exponential growth.

An important feature that touches the identity of Dominicans in both the Caribbean and the United States is the game of baseball. This sport has become a significant economic gateway for young Dominicans. In 2007 in the United States, there were 77 professional players in both leagues and close to 50 percent or more of the rosters were composed of Dominicans for 11 of the teams. After the United States, the Dominican Republic produces more players than Puerto Rico, Cuba, or Venezuela.

Arelis M. Figueroa

References and Further Reading

Department of Planning. *The Newest New Yorkers 2000* (New York: Department of Planning, 2004).

Guarnizo, Luis E. "Los Dominicanyorks: The Making of a Binational Society." *The ANNALS of the American Academy of Political and Social Science* 533, (1994): 70–86.

Hernandez, Ramona, and Francisco L. Rivera-Batiz. *Dominicans in the United States: A Socioeconomic Profile, 2000. Dominican Research Monographs* (New York: The CUNY Dominican Studies Institute, October 6, 2003).

Hernandez, Ramona. *The Mobility of Workers under Advanced Capitalism.*

Dominican Migration to the United States. (New York: Columbia University Press, 2002).

Torres-Saillant, Silvio, and Ramona Hernandez. *The Dominican Americans* (Wesport, CT: Greenwood Press, 1998).

U.S. Department of State. "Dominican Republic." http://www.state.gov/g/drl/rls/irf/2007/90251.htm.

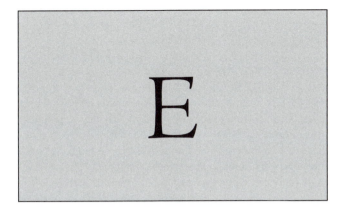

E

ECONOMICS

In the year 2000, the accumulated buying power of the Latino/a community was estimated to be $440 billion. By 2008, the purchasing power was expected to surpass $1 trillion. As impressive as these figures are, they mask the levels of poverty and inequality existing within the Hispanic community. Latina/os are 11 times more likely to live in poverty than Euro-Americans. They are also more likely to lack health insurance and pension plans. Hispanics' poverty rates are over twice the 2000 national rate of 11.9 percent. A poverty rate of 22.3 percent means that one out of every five Hispanics lives below the poverty level. This is substantially higher than the Euro-American poverty rate of 7.9 percent. In 2000, the Euro-American median household income of $44,232 was substantially higher than that of Hispanics at $33,455. Dominicans have the highest poverty rate (27.4 percent), followed by Puerto Ricans (24.8 percent), and Mexican Americans (23.3 percent). Cuban

Americans have the lowest poverty rate (14.3 percent) among Hispanics. A lack of English proficiency, lower skill levels, and low levels of human capital (i.e., education) contribute to the low income levels and the high poverty rates among Latina/os.

Within the Latino/a community, those who identify as Roman Catholics have the lowest socioeconomic status among all Christian religious traditions. According to a 2007 survey conducted by the Pew Hispanic Center, almost half (46 percent) of all Catholics have a household income under $30,000 a year, and only 14 percent have household incomes that exceed $50,000. Those who claim to be Evangelicals have a higher socioeconomic status than Catholics with 39 percent having household incomes that fall below $30,000 and 21 percent with household incomes over $50,000. Mainline Christians have the highest socioeconomic status with only 29 percent having a household income less than $30,000 and 24 percent with household incomes higher than $50,000. Those who claim

BARRIO

The Spanish word "barrio" means "neighborhood," "district," or "quarter." Linguistically, it is derived from the Arabic *barri* (outside, open country), referring to the Moorish quarters outside fortified cities. Urban terms such as barrio *colonia* (suburb) and *pueblo* (town) were brought to Latin American and other colonized countries by Spain. In the United States, the first barrios formed after the Mexican-American War (1846–1848), usually in the center of former Mexican pueblos and mission towns, where Mexicans were able to retain some land after the war. In the early 1900s, the two main Mexican American urban centers were El Paso and San Antonio, with the largest urban barrios in the Southwest. Other cities that developed large barrios are Santa Fe, Albuquerque, Las Vegas in New Mexico, and Durango, Pueblo, and Denver in Colorado. The barrio served as a social, cultural, political, and religious space for Latino/as to create networks of solidarity, support, and self-determination. However, the formation of barrios was often based on poor infrastructure in highly populated areas, usually on the periphery of downtowns and manufacturing zones. Home ownership was low due to poor wages, coupled with overcrowding and sanitation problems.

—FAO

to belong to another Christian tradition seem to be at a socioeconomic status that is closest to Catholics with 45 percent falling below $30,000 and only 11 percent of households earning in excess of $50,000.

Hispanics who comprise the most recent immigrants and have less proficiency in English represent the poorest segments of the community. They also tend to be more conservative on social issues. Nevertheless, Hispanics appear to take a more liberal view on economic issues, regardless of whether they are conservative on social issues or not. For example, 69 percent of all Latina/os, regardless of economic status, support publicly financed health insurance even if it means higher taxes. Nearly two-thirds of all Latino/as believe that poverty exists because government benefits and services are insufficient.

Because poverty is a major component of the Hispanic social location, a religious response to poverty exists.

Although there are multiple theological approaches to the poverty experienced by Hispanics, probably the two extreme points on the continuum are the prosperity gospel and liberation theology. The prosperity gospel relies more on self-reliance to reach God's desired blessing and plan for one's life. The liberationist approach attempts to dismantle existing social structures designed to enrich the dominant culture at the expense of Hispanics (and other peoples of color). Those who advocate a prosperity gospel tend to be theologically more conservative while liberationists tend to be theologically more liberal.

Prosperity Gospel

Among many Latino/as, specifically those who are either Pentecostal or charismatic, there is a belief that God's will is for believers to be blessed with health and wealth. The Pew Hispanic 2007 survey showed that 73 percent of all

Hispanics believe in the prosperity gospel, the highest among them being Protestant Pentecostals (86 percent), Protestant charismatics (73 percent), and Catholic charismatics (79 percent). The only thing preventing God's children from receiving these presents is their lack of faith. They simply do not believe strongly enough. This theological position is usually referred to as the Prosperity Gospel. Wealth indicates closeness to God, while poverty demonstrates a lack of faith. These Hispanic Christians adopt the tenet that they have a right to their riches, which represents a blessing from God. Yet critics insist that poverty among people of color, including Latina/os, is one of the major consequences of a society designed to privilege those within the dominant culture.

This form of theology assumes that anyone can "make it" in this country, regardless of race or ethnicity. The poor, those who fail, have no one to blame but themselves. Their poverty becomes a divine manifestation of God's rejection of them. In short, you can tell we are Christians by our blessings of health and wealth. The emphasis, then, is on assimilating to Eurocentric economic patterns in the hope that imitation will lead to greater financial security. Once again, critics dismiss prosperity theology because they claim it ignores *how* poverty is caused, specifically, how the racism and classism of the dominant culture must keep a segment of the population (usually of color) poor so that their culture can benefit and maintain its level of economic privilege.

Liberationist Theology

Those Latino/as who advocate a liberationist theology place oppression, including economic oppression, as central to Christian theological thought. In many respects, liberation theology is considered to be a theology of and from the poor. They insist that the wealth of some is directly related to the poverty of many. The present U.S. economic structures ensure that a disproportionate segment of the Latina/o population (as well other groups composed of people of color) do society's undesirable work, work that is usually dirty and/or dangerous. Within the United States, disproportionate numbers of Hispanics occupy menial, dead-end, underpaid jobs. But this labor pool of undereducated Hispanics is crucial because they provide profits for the industries that employ them, specifically agriculture and segments of the garment industry—industries whose profits are dependent on the economic exploitation of the poor. Second, the low wages paid to Hispanics subsidize Euro-American middle- and upper-class lifestyles by providing cheap labor in the form of domestic help such as nannies, gardeners, and maids. Additionally, because our present U.S. tax code is designed so that the poor pay a higher proportion of income and property taxes, Hispanics subsidize local and state government services that usually go to the more affluent White neighborhoods. Third, poverty creates jobs—not just dysfunctional jobs like drug dealers, production and sale of cheap liquor, pawn shops, and prostitutes—but respectable professional jobs in penology, criminology, public health work, social work, or the social sciences. Fourth, because Latino/as living in poverty can seldom afford new products, they extend the economic usefulness of goods by buying what others do not want—not just secondhand clothes and merchandise, but also expired food.

Migrant farmworkers pick strawberries along the coast of central California. (Heather Craig/Dreamstime)

Conclusion

Regardless of whether Latino/as believe in a prosperity gospel, or if they take a liberationist stance, or if they fall somewhere in between these two extremes, all agree that poverty is a major concern of the community. Poverty's impact upon the Hispanic community surpasses the basic need for finances. Poverty's definition can never be limited to simply a lack of money. The multiple consequences of poverty include, but are not limited to the greater likelihood of failed marriages; a higher susceptibility to illness, disease, and sickness because of the lack of adequate health care; a greater likelihood of physical and sexual abuse; a greater likelihood of having children who will neither go to college nor complete high school; a higher probability of conflict with law enforcement agencies; a greater chance of being a victim of a crime; a greater chance of living in ecologically hazardous areas; and, of course, a shorter life expectancy. Because poverty contributes to a debilitating lifestyle, robbing Latina/os of dignity and personhood, a religious response to economics exists.

Miguel A. De La Torre

References and Further Reading

Dávila, Alberto, Marie T. Mora, and Alma D. Hales. "Income, Earnings, and Poverty: A Portrait of Inequality Among Latinos/as in the United States." *Latinas/os in the United States: Changing the Face of América*, ed. Havidán Rodríguez, Rogelio Sáenz, and Cecilia Menjívar (New York: Springer, 2008).

Gans, Herbert J. "The Uses of Poverty: The Poor Pay All." *Down to Earth Sociology*, 3rd ed., ed. James M. Henslin (New York: The Free Press, 1991).

MEXICAN AMERICAN CULTURAL CENTER

The Mexican American Cultural Center (MACC) is a national pastoral and language institute for Hispanic and multicultural ministry in San Antonio, Texas. The dream of establishing a pastoral center for Mexican Americans emerged at a February 1971 PADRES retreat and workshop in Santa Fe, New Mexico. PADRES member Virgilio Elizondo served as MACC's founding president from 1972 to 1987; Las Hermanas and lay leaders joined Elizondo and other PADRES in establishing the Center. Elizondo's successors as MACC president were Father Rosendo Urrabazo, C.M.F. (1987–1993) and Sister María Elena González, R.S.M. (1993–2007), whose vision, leadership, and organizational skills enabled MACC to construct and dedicate a new facility. Though primarily focused on Mexican American Catholics, since its founding the faculty and staff at MACC have engaged in an ongoing ecumenical, interethnic effort to train leaders for cross-cultural work in a variety of contexts. MACC has played a leading role in advocating for Hispanic ministry and rights and publishing groundbreaking research about Latino liturgy, faith expressions, history, and theology. The Center's most far-reaching influence is the numerous participants formed and trained in MACC programs over the years, encompassing literally thousands of Catholic and Protestant leaders in Hispanic ministry at the parish, diocesan, regional, and national levels. Since 2007, the Center began evolving into the Mexican American Catholic College under the leadership of its new president, Arturo Chávez.

—TM

Pew Hispanic Center. *Changing Faiths: Latinos and the Transformation of American Religion* (Washington DC: Pew Forum on Religion and Public Life, 2007).

ECUMENISM

Hispanics come from many cultural, linguistic, and religious backgrounds. Religion historian Justo L. González speaks of "mixtures of cultures," race, language, and traditions with a common Latina/o cultural heritage. Priest and scholar Virgil Elizondo stresses the *mestizo* element as a hermeneutical tool to understand a history of colonization and a future of liberation. Mestizo is a concept originally imposed by the colonial discourse and used to justify racial discrimination. The term gradually moved from a pejorative usage to an affirming principle that values the formation of a new identity. It aims at constructing new racial and cultural exchanges for the Hispanic diaspora in the United States. The Latino/a label, as a visual way to convey both diversity and commonalities of Hispanic culture, reflects the richness and complexities of this situation.

Those who come from Central America have a strong indigenous heritage, which explains the "Maize culture" that is so pervasive in the region. The Caribbean people for the most part, have an indigenous Afro-Antillean and Spanish-Creole mixture. Mexicans and South Americans come from a strong indigenous heritage, mixed with European ancestry. Those who were born in the United States have Native American blood mixed with European and in many cases African American blood. A common denominator is the colonial history of conquest and colonization. It is a history of oppression and violence.

These differences are, with all its colonial and neocolonial influences, in a contradictory way, a blessing and a promise. A "Hispanic culture" that has both a colonial component and the blend of a new mestizo race and culture provides a hermeneutical principle to understand the historical roots of oppression and the eschatological dimension of liberation. This interconnection of race and culture is a key element in developing Latino/a theologies in the United States. In fact, the entire discussion on modernity and postmodernity in Latin America and the Caribbean relates to this colonial history. The same applies to the Mexican American experience in the Southwest of the United States.

Additionally, many Hispanics are pilgrims in a strange land, in a *diaspora,* defending their identities, reclaiming their place as "Hispanos and Hispanas," but discerning a political and social context, many times hostile. The United States is the new locus of their daily lives, transforming their cultural and religious experiences and providing new realities with new components, in language and educational models, in a searching and affirming process as people. Latino/as must recreate and reconstruct, in a different context, a new community with old and new components. In many communities this is the real tension: How can the *barrio* be re-created in a hostile and racist, excluding society? How can lives be reconstructed after torture, repression, and marginalization in their countries of origin? How can the immediate family and the extended family be maintained in a communal experience when individualism is so dominant in society at large? These are both problems and challenges. The barrio can be a creative space in larger cities of the United States, but also a repressive ghetto that marginalizes.

The next relevant issue is mission and unity. The ecumenical movement of the twentieth century and its predecessor, the missionary movement of the nineteenth century, has a long history in dealing with these two principles. Mission and unity are so intimately related that they constitute a paradigm for any ecumenical theology. The church is mission. Unity is God's mission to create a new humanity out of the division, barriers, and prejudices of the existing structures of church life and in society. Mission and unity need to be understood as part of a historical conflict and a search for an eschatological reconciliation in God's reign. In that tension, Latina/o churches struggle for peace, justice, and the integrity of creation, as a Christian fellowship, a sign of the salvation still to come, in real *koinonia* and *diakonia.* But Hispanic believers also stress the church as an apostolic community of faith, witnessing a visible unity in solidarity: A unity in diversity through a koinonia of mutual commitment.

Hispanic theologians Justo L. González, Virgil Elizondo, Ismael García, and Luis G. Pedraja emphasize this growing sense of unity as a process of social and cultural awareness, a common goal for justice. Religion scholars Edwin D. Aponte and Miguel A. De La Torre point to what they call a "New Ecumenism" where they claim that a productive theological discussion and a cross-fertilization of perceptions and ideas is already taking place among Hispanic religion scholars in spite of the checkered history of contacts between Catholics and Protestants. A testament to this New Ecumenism exists in the number of collaborative institutions (i.e., Hispanic Summer Program or the Hispanic Theological Initiative) and book projects where formal and informal dialogue on common matters of theology and pastoral concerns occur.

The reality of oppression, racial prejudice, economic marginalization, and the lack of educational opportunities are some of the issues that challenge Latino/as to political and social involvement. Here the growing sense of unity is seen as a search for a common vision that respects doctrinal differences in an ongoing ecumenical dialogue, particularly between Catholic and Protestant theologians and pastors. The church is experienced as a new extended family, struggling against brokenness and alienation, sharing in concrete solidarity, and affirming human dignity and ethical values. The growing sense of unity is also seen as a unity to resist, to promote solidarity with other minorities, and to provide a new sense of identity that includes the Spanish language and a dignity that affirms the hope for a better future in the midst of a dominant culture that marginalizes and excludes, searching for real reconciliation.

Hispanic Christians are challenged as a growing minority in the United States to continue witnessing in the public arena with an ecumenical spirit that promotes unity and affirms diversity. A real commitment to reconciliation will constitute a valuable contribution toward a new ecumenism in a divided society.

Carmelo E. Álvarez

References and Further Reading

De La Torre, Miguel, and Edwin David Aponte. *Introducing Latino/a Theologies* (Maryknoll, NY: Orbis Books, 2001).

Elizondo, Virgil. *The Future is Mestizo: Life When Cultures Meet* (Bloomington, IN: Meyer-Stone Books, 1988).

González, Justo L. *Mañana: Christian Theology from a Hispanic Perspective* (Nashville: Abingdon Press, 1990).

ENCOMIENDA

The Encomienda system in Spanish America was a structure theoretically based on the cooperation of the *encomendero* and of the *doctrinero*. The encomendero, usually a conquistador or his descendant, was entrusted (*encomendado*) with the integration of his Amerindian wards into the social and economic life of the Spanish Empire and helped the doctrinero (*teacher*) establish the cultural, moral, and religious patterns of Catholicism. This feudal social, political, economic, and religious system, as far as scholars know today, was created in May 1493, by the Crown of Castile who reserved the right to grant and remove the encomiendas as seen fit. It first appeared in the Viceroyalty of New Spain (Mexico) in the 1520s. The encomienda system is deeply entrenched in the history and culture of Latin America, and it is one of the most damaging institutions that the Spanish colonists implemented in the New World. The system came to signify the oppression and exploitation of Amerindians, although its originators did not set out with such intent, and it can be argued that it is at

BARTOLOMÉ DE LAS CASAS (1474–1566)

A Dominican priest, considered the earliest European advocate for indigenous rights, Father De Las Casas was also the first Catholic priest ordained in the Spanish colonies of the Americas. Born in Seville in 1474, his father served on Columbus's second voyage and brought him an Indian boy as a servant, a relationship that deepened his compassion for the natives. His father's earnings allowed him to study law at the prestigious University of Salamanca. Following Columbus's expulsion, Las Casas was legal advisor to Hispaniola's first two governors, Ovando and Velazquez. By 1511 Las Casas was preaching in Santo Domingo against the encomienda and *repartimiento* systems, and teaching that the Christian faith was incompatible with the exploitation and cruelty being unleashed upon the Indians. Critics argue that he offset colonial pressures on the Indian population by advocating the introduction of African slaves into Cuba and Hispaniola. He was appointed first bishop of Chiapas in southern Mexico, but returned to Spain permanently after clashing with the encomenderos. His *Brief Account of the Destruction of the Indies* (1552) angered many conquistadors and colonial entrepreneurs. He died in 1566 at age 93 after many years of lobbying the Spanish monarchy in Madrid for Indian's rights through the *New Laws of the Indies*.

—AH

the origin of much of the social, political, and economic injustices of the continent.

At the start of the system, the sole justification for the Spanish dominion over the Amerindians was to convert the natives to the Catholic faith. However, it quickly became an opportunity for the encomenderos to exploit and utilize the natives to their own greedy ends. This was because the Amerindians were required to pay the encomendero a tribute in return for protection and religious instruction. The encomienda system did not entail any land tenure by the encomendero; in fact, the land of the Amerindians was to remain in their possession, a right that was formally protected by the Crown. However, the encomenderos did often own land nearby their encomiendas and had natives working on plantations as well as at the local mines. Another interesting point is that the encomienda grant did not give the Spaniard the right

to exercise any political authority or jurisdiction over the natives. However, these distinctions were very difficult to enforce because there was an ocean between the rulers making the laws and the colonists in charge of the natives. As time passed, the conquerors of New Spain came to expect the encomiendas as their reward, so the practice became an institution and it eventually became tradition to divide newly conquered territories among the conquerors.

The necessity for the encomiendas arose out of the condition of the Amerindians when the Spanish first made contact with them. In essence, the Spanish believed the native population to be savage and pagan, so the major aim of the encomienda was to look after the welfare of the natives, as well as to educate and teach them about the Catholic faith and integrate them into society. The encomenderos were not allowed to mistreat the natives in any way, but at the same time, the natives were to be persuaded to abandon their ancient ways. Although the encomenderos were responsible for them, the Amerindians were not granted to the Spaniard for life, but only for two to three years at a time. It was during that time they were to be educated and protected by the encomendero. Furthermore, the local natives were not supposed to work for nothing; in fact, they were to be paid and supplied with the provisions they needed to live. At one point, the Crown even encouraged the Amerindians and Spanish to intermarry, so that they could "tame" the natives through constant and direct contact with the colonists. They also hoped this would help in their efforts to convert the natives to Christianity. However, what the encomienda actually accomplished was to ensure the colonists a large indentured work force.

Among all those preoccupied with the exploitation of the natives, there were also men who defended the Amerindians. One of the most prominent of those men working to better the lives of the native population was Dominican Bishop Bartolomé de Las Casas. Las Casas was a secular Catholic priest living in Cuba, with an encomienda of his own. However, he came to see the evils of the encomienda after hearing a sermon preached by Dominican Friar Antonio de Montesinos. Las Casas was sickened by what he heard and saw and soon repented. He then decided to dedicate the rest of his life to righting the wrongs committed against the natives as a Dominican friar. Las Casas also took to documenting the problems, and in his work, *A Very Brief Account of the Destruction of the Indies*, he detailed the extent of the abuses committed against the natives. Shortly,

because of Las Casas's persistence, his message about the terrible conditions in which the Amerindians lived reached the Crown's officials. The Crown stepped in and began regulating the situation through legislation, particularly the New Laws of 1542. However, upholding the New Laws that protected the Amerindians was a nearly impossible task in the Spanish colonies that was never quite mastered. Therefore, it could be said that the encomienda system was formalized under the New Laws, rather than abolished by it. So, although not everyone was blind to the transgressions against the indigenous population, these men were in the small minority and even the *Audiencia*, which was in place to correct the ills committed against the Amerindians, soon became filled with encomenderos, thus making the protection of the Amerindian population from exploitation and abuse an almost impossible task. The encomienda was generally replaced by the repartimiento throughout Spanish America after mid-sixteenth century.

At one point Las Casas claimed that some 15–20 million natives perished at the hands of the encomenderos. Now, these numbers have been disputed, and they may very well be off the mark, but historians have agreed upon Las Casas's other major claims on the mistreatment and abuse of the conquered indigenous population. The system set a precedent for the treatment and esteem for the indigenous population in the Americas, and the fight against it was an uphill battle that was never quite won. In fact, one could argue that the encomienda system never died off, that it merely evolved and took on new forms of oppression, exploitation, and injustice in the continent.

Alejandro Crosthwaite

References and Further Reading

Himmerich y Valencia, Robert. *The Enco-mendros of New Spain* (Austin: University of Texas Press, 1991).

Simpson, Lesley Byrd. *The Encomienda in New Spain* (Berkeley: University of California Press, 1950).

Thomas, Hugh. *Rivers of Gold* (New York: Random House, 2004).

Tindall, George Brown, and David E. Shi, eds. *America: A Narrative History*, 6th ed. (New York: W. W. Norton & Company, Inc., 1984).

ENVIRONMENTALISM

Environmentalism is a political, ethical, and social movement that endeavors to develop and defend the planet through changes to environmentally destructive human behavior, such as air pollutants, downstream dam impacts, mining operations, oil spills, and power plant wastes. "Environment" and "environmentalism" are now popular terms compared to a decade ago. "Go Green," "All Things Green," "Greening the Earth," and "Green Cars" exemplify the present trend. The "Green" phenomenon originated with the U.S. environmental movement of the 1800s. From the 1880s to the 1950s, most ecologists concentrated on the natural world (conservation and preservation of wildlife) without considering the extensive influences of human settlement and commerce. In the 1960s, the modern environmental movement emerged alongside the civil rights, women's, antiwar, and democracy movements. During this period environmentalists became concerned about air and water pollution, so they widened their vision to include all landscapes and

human activities. The environmental movement has evolved into the current diverse national and international organizations that are inclusive of the urban environment. These nongovernmental organizations (NGOs) differ in political ideology and efforts to influence environmental policy in the United States and other countries. Hispanics have joined the ranks of the environmental movement. As of 2001 the figures of the U.S. Census Bureau demonstrate that Hispanics have surpassed African Americans as the largest ethnic group; therefore, Latinas/os (U.S.-born and foreign-born) are important stakeholders in the future management of natural resources. Latina/o environmentalism manifested through Hispanic religious beliefs, attitudes, and activism, serve as predictors of their environmental ethos.

Environmental Belief and Behavior

With the exponential increase of Hispanics in the United States, the majority of these being immigrants from Latin America, Latino/a environmentalism has been the focus of quantitative and qualitative research measuring ethnic variation, regional attitudinal results, and the interplay of religion and politics. The New Ecological Paradigm (NEP) is a tool that assesses environmental behaviors such as environmental reading, household recycling, environmental group joining, and participation in nature-based outdoor recreation. Although the empirical analyses of Hispanic social practices at times conforms with the majority culture's (White) perceptions and interactions with the environment (e.g., outdoor recreation for U.S.-born Hispanics is more like Whites than other minorities), others argue that Anglo conformity is dependent on the level of Latina/o acculturation to White, middle-class values. Yet, foreign-born Hispanics embrace a different view of the natural world than Whites (nature separate individual and community); Latino/as see humanity as intimately connected to nature; absent are the romantic preservationist and human-nature dichotomy in their nature myths. Results have shown that Hispanics who are educated, are younger, and hold a liberal position or ideology tend to be more environmentally concerned than other Latina/os.

Civic Environmentalism

Although federal research (the U.S. Environmental Protection Agency convened two scientific panels in 1987 and 1990) ascertains the environmental health status of Hispanics (who fare worst or face significant threats in ambient air pollutions, worker exposure to chemicals, pollution indoors, and pollutants in drinking water), the lack of government funding in the end minimizes regulatory efforts. The considerable deficiency of political support and federal subsidies for environmental regulations has resulted in civic environmentalism—partnerships between local place-based communities who collaborate in innovative ways to develop modes of consensus and understanding to reach solutions. Latino/a communities have contributed across the country to civic responsibility to assist in "new modes of land use regulation," "regional planning for urban density," "neighborhood preservation," and "environmentally sustainable agriculture." In the early

Dolores Heurta, vice president of United Farm Workers, during a grape pickers' strike in 1968. (Time & Life Pictures/Getty Images)

1960s, Hispanics like César Chávez and Dolores Huerta in California founded the United Farm Workers movement and Ernesto Cortes organized Latino/a groups in the Southwest (Texas and California) for the Industrial Areas Foundation. These community organizations exemplify not only civic responsibility, but also express the relationship between Latina/o spirituality and political socioeconomic activism. In Chávez's case, the influence of Catholic spirituality is explicit. The UFW under his leadership used methods of boycotts, pilgrimages, and fasts all as part of the nonviolent protest tradition and Catholic social teaching and spirituality. Most of these groups work with mainly poor underprivileged church and religious communities to empower them to become active participants in decision-making forums to impact their communities.

Environmental Racism

In the 1980s, the environmental justice movement began in the United States in order to end environmental racism—it is common to find minorities living near waste centers, industrial plants, and highways, where exposure to large amounts of pollutants and environmental health hazards prevail compared to the rest of the privileged populace. In 1993, 80 percent of Hispanics lived in areas where one standard of air quality was unmet while 60 percent (two standards), 31 percent (three standards), and 15 percent (four standards) were unmet. The pollutants were ozone, carbon monoxide, suspended particulate matter, sulfur dioxide, lead, and nitrogen oxide known to cause lung damage, bronchitis, cancer, brain damage, asthma, respiratory tract problems, and damage to the cardiovascular, nervous, and pulmonary systems. Workers' exposure to chemicals and pesticides is another environmental issue and concern. In 1992, Latino/as comprised 71 percent of the agricultural workforce, while in the same year 11 percent of all occupational fatalities occurred among farm workers. Environmental racism is also seen clearly on the U.S.-Mexico border. The U.S. energy companies are an example of "environmental imperialists" who have found cheap labor and are EPA/OSHA regulation-free on the "borderlands." In 2002, across the California border into Mexicali, InterGen (owned by Shell Oil) built one of two large power plants where millions of Californians receive energy while Mexicans receive more pollution and experience more economic exploitation.

Eloy H. Nolivos

References and Further Reading

Hispanics and the Environment: Key Indicators (Washington, DC: National Coalition of Hispanic Health and Human Services Organizations, 1994).

Anderson, Joan B., and James Gerber. *Fifty Years of Change on the U.S.-Mexico Border: Growth, Development, and Quality of Life* (Austin: University of Texas Press, 2008).

Anzaldua, Gloria. *Boderlands/La Frontera: The New Mestiza* (San Francisco: Aunt Lute, 1987).

Burke, John Francis. *Mestizo Democracy: The Politics of Crossing Borders* (College Station: Texas A&M Press, 2002).

De La Torre, Miguel A. *Doing Christian Ethics from the Margins* (Maryknoll: Orbis Books, 2004).

ESPIRITISMO

Espiritismo (Spiritism), also known as Kardecism, originated in France during the mid-nineteenth century, when an educator named Hippolyte Léon Denizard Rivail became interested in psychical and other supernatural phenomenon. Through mediums, he questioned the spirits and codified their answers in a series of books (*Spiritist Codification*), which he wrote under the pseudonym Allan Kardec. According to Rivail, spiritism is a collection of principles based on every aspect of human knowledge, and, as such, it is applicable to philosophy, religion, science, ethics, and the social life. Rivail introduced the movement as a positive science that combined mysticism with Christian morality, scientism, and progressivist ideology. The spiritists adhere to a scientific philosophy that produces moral consequences. They do not conceive nor perceive their movement to be a religion. The movement's anticlerical views attracted many disenfranchised Catholics who held reservations toward institutionalized Christianity and the political power held by the Church. Many activists within radical social movements of the time, i.e., abolitionists and women suffragists, were attracted to spiritism for its progressive and individualist underpinnings. As a result, the initial adherents to the movement were from the middle and upper economic classes.

Spiritists believed that when God, the supreme intelligence and primary cause of all things, created the universe, God composed it of spirit and matter. Two worlds exist, one that is visible (the physical) and one that is invisible (the spiritual). Within the created universe, the living within the physical world can have contact with the dead and others within the realm of the spirit world. As humans, we have a physical body and a soul (or spirit). Thus we subsist in a reality composed of two planes of existence, a material world and the spiritual world that are continuously interacting. Humans can learn to communicate with spirits and to give and receive spiritual energies in order to achieve spiritual and physical health. To this end, spiritists employ human observation and experimentation in order to subject and explain the spiritual world.

Communicating with the spirits of the dead is not considered to be the product of magic or the supernatural. The spiritual world is a reality that can become subject to a rigorous scientific experimentation and observation. Spiritism belief in reincarnation can explain human suffering or happiness as the

consequences of previous lives due to a cause and effect, or karma. All humans upon death, that is the moment they cease being material entities and become spirits, seek advancement in the hierarchy of perfection in which they now exist. This process toward perfection is accomplished through light (enlightenment), which facilitates their reincarnation on this planet, as well as in other worlds. The spiritualist is able to provide light, helping the spirit of the dead move onto the next higher spiritual level of existence. Christ, who achieved the highest level of spiritual incarnation, becomes the model for the supreme virtue of love. To practice a Christianity based on love can ensure the individual a higher spiritual level of incarnation after he/she departs from this physical world.

Spiritism's teachings quickly became popular throughout all of Europe, eventually making a presence in Latin America during the 1850s. It took root in the Caribbean and Brazil under the name "espiritismo," the Spanish word for "spiritism." Although similar to the Mexican version, espiritualismo (spiritualism), there remain differences. Like their European counterparts, the original participants were intellectuals or from the middle and upper economic classes. As espiritismo spread throughout the Caribbean and Brazil, espiritistas gathered in small groups where they were assisted by a medium who was able to communicate with the spirits of the dead. The participants of these séances would usually sit around a table waiting for the spirits. A bridge from the physical world to the spirit world was established once the medium fell into a trance. At this point, solutions to whatever ailed the participants were communicated by the

Brazilian spiritist Osvaldo de Azeredo Coutinho performs a ritual with spirit-possessed girls. (Time & Life Pictures/Getty Images)

spirits through the medium. Through these practices, the practitioners were able to find a connection to their pre-Christian past of ancestral ghosts that encouraged different religious practices historically repressed by the official Catholic Church.

Throughout the Caribbean, specifically in Cuba and Puerto Rico, which were still colonies of the Spanish empire, freedom fighters found espiritismo to be an attractive alternative to the Catholic Church that remained loyal to the Spanish monarchy. Because political organizations that could challenge Spain's rule of the islands were suppressed, espiritismo provided a political space, as well as a spiritual space, for progressive liberal ideas to flourish. Intellectuals and revolutionaries discovered a pseudoreligious ideology that was based on and advocated science, modernity, and democracy.

Eventually, espiritismo made its way to urban groups that possessed lesser power and privilege. These marginalized communities turned to espiritismo for help and guidance with the daily struggles of life. Representing lower economic classes, Blacks, and the rural poor, they considered themselves Catholic even though they seldom visited a church or a priest. The practice of espiritismo did not seem to conflict with their Christian worldview. Devotees of African-based religious beliefs with long-standing practices of spiritual (orisha) possessions and ancestor worship found residence with espiritistas' practices. In most cases, espiritismo absorbed into its practices elements of Spanish folk religion, specifically herbalism, African religious practices, and Amerindian healing practices. Espiritismo also influenced African-based religious expressions like Candomblé, Umbanda, or Macumba in Brazil and Santería, Mayombe, or Palo in Cuba and Puerto Rico.

Espiritismo came to believe that there are good and evil spirits that can affect a person's health, wealth, love life, or luck. These spirits were believed to work under a specific saint or orisha to whom they belonged when they were alive. The roles of these saints or orishas became more prominent. The séances came to be called misas (masses), incorporating magic-based elements that were originally foreign to the spiritualism practiced by the middle and upper Eurocentric economic classes. These misas centered on an altar called a boveda espiritual or mesa blanca (white table). This simple altar or table with a white linen would have anywhere from one to nine glasses filled with cool water,

flowers with some sweet basil, a crucifix, incense and/or perfume, Kardec's book of prayers, and a lit candle. Home-based bovedas usually have a statue of a saint or saints (orishas) along with a talisman sacred to saint(s). Offerings are also usually left for the dead, i.e., food, candy, rum, cigars, etc. Each glass of water represents an ancestor and/or a spirit guide. By gazing at the water glasses and reciting certain prayers, the séance's medium can create an environment where he or she can be possessed by the dead.

Espiritismo became an important component of Santería. By the time espiritismo was introduced in the Caribbean, ancestor worship among the Cuban and Puerto Rican African slaves came to an end. Ancestor worship, as the name implies, is usually conducted within a particular extended family; however, slavery destroyed the family units, making it impossible to continue the veneration of the ancestors. Families fragmented due to slavery were unable to gather to carry out the rituals required for the reverence and respect due to the family ancestors. The introduction of espiritismo in the Spanish Caribbean made it possible to reintroduce ancestral worship to the African slaves, even though these new practices were Eurocentricly based. Nevertheless, the Spanish Caribbean–based manifestation of espiritismo differed from its European counterparts. The mediums who would now enter into their trances would rely on spirit guides who were African born but died during their enslavement. Some of these guides were among the original indigenous natives of the island, the Taínos people. This explains why many homes of devotees of Santería usually display a statue of a Native American (usually a U.S. Plains Indian) or of *el negrito Jose* (the little Black man Jose) somewhere in the santero/a's home, usually close to the family altar.

With time, all devotees of African-based religions throughout the Spanish Caribbean became espiritistas, even though not all spiritualists are devotees of the orishas. Worshippers of the orishas became dependent on several of the practices of espiritismo, augmenting their African-based rituals. Within Santería many of the invocations, prayers, paraphernalia, and rituals of espiritismo were appropriated, even though spiritualism's scientific and philosophical claims were either ignored or discarded. For example, when a member of the Santería community dies, a shrine is erected. Like the boveda espiritual or mesa blanca, it contains seven glasses of water with a cross and/or rosary beads inserted in the largest goblet. The water for these glasses can consist of herbal water, holy water from the Catholic Church, and/or a cologne known as Florida water (agua de florida). A photograph of the deceased, with fresh flowers, is prominently displayed on the table.

With the migration of Cubans and Puerto Ricans to the United States, so came the practices of espiritismo. For poor migrants trying to survive in a new country, espiritismo became the poor person's physical and mental health plan. Many go to a espiritista's misa as if they were going to a doctor or psychiatrist seeking a cure. Even today, espiritistas in the United States focus on the needs of the devotees, specifically in areas of love, work, and health. They attempt to deal proactively with the immediate concerns of the Hispanics seeking help.

Miguel A. De La Torre

References and Further Reading

De La Torre, Miguel A. *Santería the Beliefs and Rituals of a Growing Religion in America* (Grand Rapids, MI: Wm. B. Eerdmans Publishing Co., 2004).

Kardec, Allan. *¿Qué es espiritismo?* (Madrid, España: EDAF, 1986).

Morales Dorta, Jose. *Puerto Rican Espiritismo: Religion and Psychotherapy* (New York: Vantage, 1976).

ESPIRITUALISMO

There are several formative characteristics of Mexican spiritualism. First, though texts exist for its basis, it is mostly an oral tradition filled with contradictions and inconsistencies. Second, it is based in Mexico City, though it has spread throughout the United States. Third, and perhaps most importantly, while men are also devotees of the tradition, it is primarily in the hands of women. The Espiritualistas are members of churches or temples dedicated to the worship of God and the ancestral spirits who they believe exist in a loose hierarchy. Spiritualists believe they have received the gift of healing and therefore are obliged to heal others by acting as mediums for the intercession of the spirits. In this sense, all priests and "guides" or *guias* are also spiritual healers, a tradition known throughout Latin America and especially Mexico as *curanderismo*. The term "curanderismo" comes from the Spanish verb "curar," which means to heal or to cure. Healers are called curanderas and curanderos and operate mostly as community-based individuals. Most curanderas identify as Catholic; however, there is also a

A spiritual healer treats a believer in a candlelit room, Santa Ana, California. (National Geographic/Getty Images)

spiritual healing movement within Latina/o Protestant churches, especially among the Pentecostal.

Espiritualismo is institutionalized curanderismo that emphasizes the spiritual role in physical healing, but it also seeks to alleviate social disease and illness of many kinds. Espiritualistas generally do not identify as Christian, though some might: they call themselves Spiritualists. However, there is a distinct and grand role for Jesus Christ within their spiritual hierarchy, and many of the Catholic saints exact devotion within the tradition and manifest themselves in the bodies of believers to heal and speak prophecy like Aztec deities and ancestors. The Virgin of Guadalupe is regularly celebrated in Espiritualista temples, especially on her feast day,

December 12. Espiritualistas hold religious ceremonies called "catedras," resembling a Catholic mass, and some temples follow the Catholic liturgy—a sharp contrast from their North American counterparts who replicate the Protestant congregational model of local control. Yet, Espiritualismo's emphasis on moral "purity" suggests an association with the Holiness movements of the early twentieth century.

Popular healing practices involving channeling spirits, divine healing, and clairvoyance, are common in many traditions throughout Latin America such as Pentecostalism, Santería, Candomblé, and Espiritismo (Spiritism). Espiritualismo is most closely related to Espiritistas. The two traditions developed simultaneously during the nineteenth century throughout Europe and the Americas. Distinctive to espiritualismo, however, are its prophetic founders, particularly Roque Rojas Esparza (1812–1879), also known as Father Elias, and Damiana Oviedo, one of his first followers, who died in 1920 and about whom less is known. Espiritistas trace their origins to the French medium and teacher Léon Denizard Hippolyte Rivail, who published under the name Allan Kardec (1804–1869). Though both are mediumship-based traditions organized into churches, the two movements also differ for their teaching on reincarnation. Rojas condemned reincarnation and denounced espiritistas for teaching it. However, continuing revelation and religious poetics have amended that proscription in some espiritualista denominations, which now teach reincarnation. Mexican spiritualism also differs from American spiritualism, in that the former is hierarchical and resembles the structure of the Catholic Church.

In 1977, there were an estimated 8 million followers of espiritualismo, which does not include devotees in the United States. In 1981, ethnographers reported that there were over 1,000 espiritualista temples in Mexico and throughout Mexican American communities in the United States. Subsequent reports consistently indicate that the movement is growing, although exact numbers are unavailable. A 1996 film documentary produced for Mexican television claimed that there are "thousands" of temples in Mexico —at least one temple in every pueblo throughout the nation, and at least one in every colonia in Mexico City. Francisco I. Madero, president of Mexico (1911–1913), was an avowed espiritista. It is impossible to calculate the number precisely because the temples are largely hidden. There are at least three highly public espiritualista temples, each with several hundred members and many more "visitors" in East Los Angeles alone. There are numerous temples in Southern California and in Mexican American communities throughout the Southwestern United States. While the majority of Mexican spiritualists hail from the working classes, middle- and even upper-class individuals can be counted among espiritualista devotees.

While a survey of the foundational espiritualista texts reveals considerable linguistic patriarchy, women are the primary espiritualista agents, adopting its flexible spiritual revelations to serve their own needs. The Mexican scholarly literature, published mostly in Spanish, agrees that espiritualismo developed to empower women. Anthropologist Sylvia Echaniz estimates that in Mexico City nearly 80 percent of espiritualistas are women. Echaniz claims that espiritistas come from higher economic classes than do the espiritualistas, who draw from the most economically impoverished social population.

The largest espiritualista denomination is called Mediodia. Its main church in Mexico City boasts 10,000 members alone; however, based on my field work, this number seems exaggerated. On any typical Sunday, there are nearly 2,000 members attending the ceremony. Mediodia's leader is a woman. Mediodia has produced its own liturgy and texts, and all espiritualista movements adhere to Mediodia's Bible: *The Final Testament: Given by God to his Divine Chosen One the True Mexican Messiah Roque Rojas.*

Rojas's Final Testament claims to have been revealed during the years 1861–1869, in Mexico City—the city that espiritualistas expressly hold as their sacred center. The text contains Rojas's foundational teachings on the organization of temples, hierarchical structures, and eschatological predictions. It also contains the "Twenty-Two Precepts of Rojas," which constitute the basis of espiritualista theology. The precepts, including the preamble, read as follows:

IN MEXICO, SINCE THE FIRST OF SEPTEMBER OF 1866, THE WORD OF THE DIVINE LORD "JESUS OF NAZARETH" IS MANIFESTING BY WAY OF HUMAN INTELLIGENCE [CEREBRO], AS THE HOLY SPIRIT AND HE HAS ORDERED THAT WE MUST KNOW ALL OF THE COUNTRY'S VISITORS; THE LAW OF GOD AMPLIFIED IN THE 22 PRECEPTS AND PRACTICING THEM WILL BE AS AN ANTIDOTE TO THE TIMES THAT ARE GETTING CLOSER, THAT WILL BE A SCOURGE FOR HUMANITY, IN THE FORM OF GREAT WARS, PLAGUES, DROUGHTS, AND

EPIDEMICS. FOR THE TIME OF COMPLIANCE TO THE PROPHECIES OF SAINT JOHN, OF HIS BOOK OF REVELATIONS, THAT MARKS THIS ERA, HAS ARRIVED.

THE LAW IS THE FOLLOWING:

THE PRECEPTS OF MOSES, OF JESUS, AND OF THE SON OF MAN 1 SEPTEMBER 1866

1. Love God above everything created.
2. Do not judge your brother but ask him for justice.
3. Do not belong to, or love, a religion that does not practice love for God, charity for His sons, and the purity of Mary.
4. Love your parents next to God and your sons in the same manner; for the first, veneration and respect, and for the second, love and a good example, above all. If you do the contrary, you will be judged with vigor as authors of evil.
5. Do not judge or criticize anyone or testify falsely; if you do the Holy Spirit will judge you, because He will defend your cause only if it is just.
6. Do not work for money on Sunday; should you do so, repent, for this day belongs to God.
7. Do not possess the wife of another as your wife, or harm anyone.
8. Do not take what does not belong to you without permission of the owner, or practice usury. You are only permitted to gain an honest and legal interest on loans.
9. Do not drink intoxicating liquors.
10. Do not follow an occupation that will ruin you, or lower your morality and lead you into vice.
11. Do not enlist in a civil war dividing your brothers. You are only permitted to enlist in a foreign war when your government demands, and then you will act with the best of good will, because we are all brothers, sons of God.
12. Do not commit infanticide. If you do, you will be punished by God's law.
13. Do not abuse the poor or overwork them.
14. Do not curse anything created.
15. Do not treat with repulsion anyone suffering from a repugnant disease.
16. Do not judge or criticize any human being in public or private, which would cause their dishonor.
17. Do not leave your sons in strange hands, or do this only of necessity, and be sure the benefactors are well known for moral conduct and will take good care of the children.
18. Do not force children to work in places where they may learn of vices.
19. Do not relate to anyone any history or story of the following nature: devils; the condemned; witches; gnomes; evil spirits; miracles which are merely phenomena, astral occurrences which are not real, appearances of images that have no truth; false punishment; materialization; all of which is superficial and bad.
20. Do not rob, or keep stolen goods in your power.
21. Visit and console the sick whenever you can.
22. Do not kill your brother in thought, word, deed, or in civil war, or take his life in any manner.

Our guide Elias and spiritual Pastor Elias said: "My children, fulfill these 22 precepts and see my Father in all His splendor. Have charity and more charity for your brother, and give testimony of my Father."

The precepts are supplemented by Mediodia with the following narrative, written onto a pamphlet and distributed free of cost and without specific publication information:

> WHEN ASKED: WHO ARE THE ESPIRITUALISTAS: WE ARE TRINITARIAN BECAUSE WE BELIEVE IN THE HOLY TRINITY: GOD THE FATHER, GOD THE SON, AND GOD THE HOLY SPIRIT. . . . WE ARE MARIAN [MARIANOS] BECAUSE WE BELIEVE IN THE PURITY OF HOLY MARIA, MOTHER OF GOD, AND OUR MOTHER. . . . SPIRITUALISM MEANS THAT WE OPPOSE MATERIALISM AND THAT WITH OUR ACTS AND THOUGHTS WE ARE PREPARING THE PATH WHEREBY THOSE WHO WILL COMMUNICATE SPIRIT TO SPIRIT WITH GOD OUR FATHER MUST PASS. . . . GOD OUR FATHER IS INDOCTRINATING US BY WAY OF HUMAN UNDERSTANDING.

Additionally, when asked: "Who is God?" espiritualistas are instructed to respond that "GOD IS REASON, LOVE, CHARITY, AND FORGIVENESS." And finally, when asked what is the purpose of espiritualismo, the answer is "TO BENEFIT HUMAN KIND, STOP PRIDE, AND REJECT FANATICISM."

These explanatory narratives do not appear in the Final Testament. However, espiritualista leaders I spoke with agreed on these broad prescriptions—with the exception that some non-Mediodia temples (hereafter referred to as "independent" churches) place greater importance on the Virgin of Guadalupe. One anthropologist surmises that Guadalupe is not named by Mediodia specifically because the Catholic Church claims ownership of her. The female leader of an independent Mexico City congregation maintained that "Trinitarian Marian" refers to God, the Holy Spirit, and the Virgin of Guadalupe. Espiritualismo is closely related to Mexican nationalism; each temple marks and commemorates Mexican Independence, September 16, with religious ceremony.

Roque Rojas, founder of Espiritualismo, is said to be of Otomi Yaqui Indian heritage on his mother's side and is descended from Spanish Jews on his father's side. In his autobiography, Rojas identifies his parents by full name and identifies himself as a "legitimate son." He boasts that he was born in the "noble" and "faithful" city of Mexico, on August 16, 1812. He was also baptized a Catholic in Mexico City. When he was 11 his mother died, and he was placed in the care of the Mexico City Seminary, where for three years he studied to become a priest—a course he never completed.

He reports having two children, a boy and a girl. The boy, he tells us, died while an infant, and he provides no further information on the girl. Rojas creates nonetheless a genealogy, much like those found in the Bible. There is no question that the texts attributed to Rojas and collected and published as the Final Testament are meant to reproduce or mimic Jewish and Christian scriptures. In this case, text is mimetic; it is performative. After he was married, Rojas very likely worked as a low-level civil servant until the economy worsened and he lost his job. As a result, he and Guadalupe moved in with her parents—her father was a medical doctor in the colonia of Ixtapalapa, on the edge of Mexico City. Ixtapalapa is famous for its spectacular annual reenactment of Christ's passion. While living there, Rojas miraculously landed a job as a civil magistrate. The opportunity came as a result of a chance meeting on December 12 during a pilgrimage to the Guadalupe basilica and shrine church. Rojas claims to have become the judge of the Civil Registry of Ixtapalapa. It was in Ixtapalapa on the night of St. John, June 23, 1861, that, according to Rojas, God began to reveal to him that he was the Promised Elias of the Third Age. The revelations continued until "Resurrection Sunday," 1869. The "mystery" of his "church" was revealed as the central structure for the spiritual architecture of this new Third Age.

Rojas appointed 12 women and 12 men whom he called guias, or guides, as curators of his newly established 12 churches. Padre Elias's revelation, and the founding of the temples, are said to have initiated a new age, a Third Era that unfolds a millennial prophecy. Padre Elias taught that the history of the world is divided into three dispensations: The First Age (tiempo), the Mosaic Era, began with the Mosaic covenant, when Moses was harbinger of the divine word as established in the Old Testament. The Second Age began when Jesus Christ, Divine Teacher, accepted a covenant with his Father to redeem humanity, as described in the New Testament. The Third Age began with the full revelation of Roque Rojas in 1861, and it marks the arrival of God among humanity to "destroy idolatry, fanaticism, mysticism, and materialism." This age is called the Mexican Patriarchal Age of Elias, or the Age of Elias. The Third Era will last 2,000 years. Its end will mark the arrival of the New Era, or Age, and with it, a complete transformation of the world. This fourth and final era will begin in 3861, with Mexico City restored as the sacred center of the world. The world's population will congregate in Mexico City, and Roque Rojas will sit in judgment and governance over the totality.

Most converts to Espiritualismo had been initially attracted to churches for a physical healing. After receiving the gift of healing, they would return. Some espiritualistas also expressed disenchantment with the Catholic Church of their original baptism. They believed that the church was out of touch with the "real" issues affecting the people and was interested mostly in collecting money. As remarkable as it may seem, espiritualismo is a product of modern urban culture. It also contains key teachings found in parallel nineteenth-century contexts of rapid industrial growth, urbanization, and socioeconomic marginalization, most notably, a ban on alcohol and an admonishment toward "holiness." But it is also much more than that, and, in fact, because of its poetic theological character, its possibilities seem unlimited. However, one of espiritualismo's central discourses involves dispersion and reunification. Espiritualismo is intimately tied to the Mexican diaspora in the United States, to the healing of present-day troubles, and to the hope for a better time. All these beliefs are confirmed through a technology of the body. The body is the register for knowing the world, for confirming truth and goodness. Mostly, however, Espiritualismo is a product of a postcolonial reality. Espiritualismo is a borderlands tradition inasmuch as it blends Native myth and ritual with Catholic symbols, time, and other forms and sounds.

Luis D. León

References and Further Reading

Braude, Ann. *Radical Spirits: Spiritualism and Women's Rights in Nineteenth-Century America* (Boston: Beacon Press, 1989).

Echaniz, Sylvia Ortiz. *Una religiosidad popular: El espiritualismo trinitario mariano* (Mexico, D.F.: Instituto Nacional de Antropologia e Historia, 1990).

Finkler, Kaja. *Spiritualist Healers in Mexico: Successes and Failures of Alternative Therapeutics* (Salem, WI: Sheffield Publishing, 1994).

EVANGÉLICO/A

Evangélica/os consider themselves to be Protestants, and, in fact, within most mainline Protestant denominations there is an evangelical wing. But not all Protestants are evangélico/as. In a similar way, almost all Pentecostals consider themselves to be evangélico/as, even though not all evangélica/os are Pentecostals. Furthermore, evangélico/a is not simply the Spanish translation of the word "evangelical," for while similarities exist between Hispanic evangélica/os and Euro-American evangelicals, there are also divergences. Ergo, the term "evangélico/a" is a slippery one that may have different meanings depending on who is using it.

Like their Euro-American evangelical counterparts, Hispanic evangélica/os place an emphasis on being born again. To be born again, a term found in the biblical text (John 3:7), means that a public commitment to Jesus Christ is made. Neither good works nor church participation is enough to be saved from the penalty of sin, which is death. Usually the person seeking salvation will recite what has come to be called a "sinner's prayer." In the sinner's prayer, the person confesses his/her sins and his/her inability to bring about his/her own salvation. Each person recognizes that he/she is destined to remain lost in this life and destined for Hell in the next life. The only hope rests upon the mercies of God. For this reason, as per John 3:16, "God so loved the world that God gave God's only begotten Son, that whosoever believes in him shall not perish but have everlasting life." Only by asking Jesus to enter into his/her life and heart, can he/she be born into a new life where past sins are forgotten and forgiven as he/she becomes a new creature in Christ.

In short, only Jesus saves. All other religions or philosophies that refuse to recognize the Lordship of Christ are false paths that lead people to death and destruction. To be saved, and to care enough about the salvation of others who remain lost within this sinful world, propels the new believer to share the Good News of Jesus Christ with those still destined to spend an eternity in Hell. This Good News or Gospel is derived from the Greek word "euangelion," from which the term "evangélico/a" is derived. To be an evangélica/o is to be a believer in, and preacher of, the Gospel. It also requires the believer to live a life that is holy and pleasing to God, not that the believer is able to live a pious life through his/her own ability or will. After all, nothing good dwells among the sinful, even though the sinner may be forgiven. Only through Christ who lives in them can they live a life that brings honor to God. Usually, such a life is demonstrated by outward acts like being a teetotaler, abstaining from sex except in marriage, wearing conservative nonrevealing clothing, and not participating in

AMEN

AMEN stands for Alianza de Ministerios Evangélicos Nacionales or National Alliance of Evangelical Ministries. This Hispanic Protestant national organization was founded in 1994 when Jesse Miranda gathered 350 Hispanic leaders at Long Beach, California, under the financial support of the Pew Charitable Trusts. The organization claims to represent lay and clerical leaders from 27 denominations and 22 nationalities, as well as 77 religious ministries within the United States, Canada, Mexico, and Puerto Rico. The primary goal of this grassroots ecumenical organization is to promote unity among Hispanic Protestant churches and parachurch agencies and provide the central voice of Hispanic evangelicals in North America that can speak to the larger faith community. They speak out on issues that are considered important to the growing Latina/o evangelical community. AMEN was among the few Hispanic Christian organizations to have access to the George W. Bush administration.

—MAD

carnal activities like dancing. Bible reading and prayer, which bring the believer closer to God, become the new joyful activities in which to engage.

Historical Roots

U.S. Latino/as can trace their roots to Latin America where Roman Catholicism has historically been the official religion. During Spanish colonial venture, church and state, for all practical purposes, were united. The Church's allegiance was to the Spanish crown. Concern for the spread of Protestantism in Europe, and in an attempt to prevent its spread in Latin America, the Catholic Church and the Spanish colonial authorities banned the Bible throughout the colonies—a ban that lasted until the late 1700s. By the early 1800s, British and U.S. groups began sending Bibles to Latin America. European Protestant immigrants followed these Bibles and began to settle throughout Latin America during the early 1800s. As they made new homes for themselves, they brought their customs and traditions with them, including their religious beliefs and practices. Nevertheless, it is interesting to note that these new settlers were less concerned with proselytizing than they were with making new lives for themselves.

However, to be an evangelical is to go out into all the world and preach the gospel (euangelion) to every creature, as per the Great Commission of Mark 16:15. Originally, Euro-American evangelicals saw Asia and Africa as the mission fields that needed cultivation. Latin America garnered little attention. As missionary possibilities closed for them in these areas, they turned an eye toward Latin America. Although Latin America was technically Christian, albeit Catholic, many evangelicals did not then consider Catholics to be Christians, a bias that still exists among some evangelicals today. For some of those who felt a call to Latin America, they saw this calling as a holy mission to save Latin Americans from what they perceived to be the false religion of Roman Catholicism.

NUEVA ESPERANZA

In 1987 the Hispanic Clergy of Philadelphia and Vicinity (an organization of pastors and ministers founded in 1982) under the leadership of the Reverend Luis Cortés Jr. established Nueva Esperanza. This faith-based community development agency addressed various unmet needs of the Latino/a community of Philadelphia, especially as they were overlooked by local governmental and ecclesiastical entities. In 2002 Nueva Esperanza established Esperanza USA as its national subsidiary, complementing its local initiatives with national concerns and serving as an intermediary between government agencies and Hispanic faith- and community-based organizations. In 2007, both the Philadelphia initiatives of Nueva Esperanza and the national initiatives of Esperanza USA merged, creating Esperanza, possibly the most comprehensive Hispanic faith-based nonprofit 501(c)(3) corporation and development organization in the United States. Esperanza also describes itself as the largest Hispanic Evangelical network in the country. By nurturing Hispanic owned and operated institutions, Esperanza seeks to strengthen the familial, economic, and spiritual dimensions of Latino/a communities, specifically through community development (including assisting individuals and families to become homeowners), capacity building, workforce development, education (including Esperanza Academy Charter High School and Esperanza College of Eastern University), and public advocacy. Esperanza is the primary organizer and sponsor of the annual National Hispanic Prayer Breakfast and Conference.

—EDA

Because Roman Catholicism was loyal to the Spanish Empire and derived its political power from it, for Latin Americans to become Protestants was not only to reject the official state religion but also to reject the state. Not surprisingly, these missionary endeavors were supported by anticolonial revolutionary leaders who saw Protestantism as a progressive, capitalist alternative to Spanish rule. With time, the new Protestant religions proved to be as oppressive and as imperialistic as the former Catholic religion. This reality makes it difficult to pigeonhole evangélico/as into any one political camp. In some cases, Protestants pushed for revolutionary change, as in the case of Castro's Cuban Revolution that was supported by many evangélico ministers. At other times,

evangélico ministers supported a return to conservative authoritarian structures, as in their support to overthrow Salvador Allende in Chile.

The reasons for converting to a new faith, or a new way of practicing one's faith, are complex. Some convert out of a sense of religious fervor. For them, a conversion experience is very real and life changing. For others, conversion can be for the sake of self-interest. For some, the appeal of the evangélica/o lay in the array of social services they provided, especially in the neglected rural areas of Latin America. Evangélico/as started orphanages, created grade schools, distributed food and clothing, dispensed agricultural equipment and tools, established clinics, provided free vocational classes, and gave English-language instruction. Besides the material sustenance, evangélica/os offered an alternative moral system that implied modernity, prosperity, progress, and above all Americanism.

Still, it has been argued that missionary work was the vanguard of U.S. military activities; in effect, it was the spiritual dimension to Manifest Destiny. For example, the first Euro-American Protestant worship service held on the island of Cuba (excluding the brief English occupation in the 1700s) occurred on a U.S. gunboat in 1871 in La Habana Harbor, officiated by Bishop Benjamin Whipple, an Episcopalian. Sword and cross were merged as Euro-Americans attempted to save Latin Americans from their political and religious practices. These missionaries saw their role as agents for civilization, perceiving the Cuban as morally deficient and intellectually backward.

Yet, on that same island of Cuba, the first evangélica/o missionaries were not Euro-Americans, but fellow Cubans who were converted while living in the United States, mainly in Tampa and Key West, Florida. They returned to the island to partake in its struggle for autonomy from Spanish rule. In their return to Cuba, they brought their new faith with them. Thus Cuba, along with other Latin American countries, had two types of missionary activities—those orchestrated by Euro-American Mission Boards, and the returning natives who converted while away.

With time, these Latin American evangélico/as came to the United States. Some never left (original Mexican inhabitants of the southwestern United States), others were pushed here because of economic crises caused in their homelands due to U.S. foreign policies (Central Americans), others as a result of revolution (Cuba), and still others migrated as U.S. citizens (Puerto Ricans). Regardless of why a Hispanic U.S. presence exists, many brought the evangélica/o faith with them. Today, according to the 2007 study conducted by the Pew Hispanic Center, those who convert to an evangélico/a are more than likely to be Catholics. The reason for conversion has little to do with any negative views they may hold toward the Catholic Church, although a majority (61 percent) says they did not find the typical Mass to be lively or exciting. The reasons most given for becoming an evangélica/o are the following: (1) a desire to have a more direct and personal experience with God (90 percent); (2) inspiration by a certain pastor (42 percent); or (3) relief while undergoing a deep personal crisis (31 percent).

Demographics

There exists among Hispanics a difficulty in actually defining who is and who can be called an evangélico/a. This is evident in the 2007 Pew Hispanic Center survey, which revealed that among all Latina/o Christians, 39 percent self-identified as an evangélica/o or as being "born again." For those who are Protestants, 70 percent used these terms to describe themselves. Not surprisingly, many Hispanics use the terms "protestante" and "evangélico/a" interchangeably. But this is problematized when we note that the Pew survey also showed that among Catholics, 28 percent used the labels "born again" and "evangélica/o" for self-identification. While the term "evangelical" has historically been used to describe one type of Protestant, among Latino/as the terms "evangélico/a" and "born again" appear to be more

LUIS CORTÉS

The Reverend Luis Cortés Jr. is founder and president of Nueva Esperanza and Esperanza USA, faith-based organizations based in Philadelphia, Pennsylvania. Cortés is a nationally known Latino religious and social leader. A Puerto Rican from Spanish Harlem in New York City, Cortés attended City College and earned a Master of Divinity from Union Theological Seminary in New York, and a Master of Science in economic development from New Hampshire College. Cortés was awarded honorary doctorates of divinity from Moravian Theological Seminary and Palmer Theological Seminary. Both Nueva Esperanza and Esperanza USA emerged from the Hispanic Clergy of Philadelphia and Vicinity, which was founded in 1982 as a support group for Hispanic/Latino/a Protestant ministers in the Philadelphia area. In 2002, Nueva Esperanza, led by Cortés, established Esperanza USA as its national subsidiary at the first annual National Hispanic Prayer Breakfast. Esperanza USA seeks to strengthen Hispanic faith-based organizations through capacity-building, national programs addressing need, works as an intermediary with government agencies, and has provided over $10 million in grants and assistance nationally. Also through his initiative Esperanza College was established as a branch campus of Eastern University in partnership with Nueva Esperanza. In 2005 *Time* magazine named Cortés as one of the "25 Most Influential Evangelicals."

—EDA

inclusive. Both Protestants and Catholics seem to claim these titles, indicating that a lack of universal agreement exists as to what the term means and thus the difficult task of classification.

Nevertheless, if we were to solely define evangélica/os as Protestants who identify themselves as evangelical or born again, then only one in six (15 percent) Hispanics would consider themselves an evangélico/a. This 15 percent of the Hispanic population comprises 6 percent of the entire U.S. evangelical Protestant population. Of these evangélia/os, more than half are foreign born (55 percent); almost two-thirds use English as their primary language or are bilingual (63 percent); nearly two-thirds completed high school (64 percent); and only about 39 percent have a household income that falls below $30,000 per year (a slightly higher income than Hispanic Catholics). Of these evangélico/as, half

of all evangélica/os have Mexican roots (50 percent), followed by Puerto Ricans (16 percent), Central Americans (6 percent), and Cubans (6 percent). Because those with Mexican origins represent the majority of all U.S. Latino/as (63 percent), they hold a majority in all the different religious groupings. Still, Mexicans are more likely to be Catholic (74 percent), and Puerto Ricans, more so than any other Hispanic nationality, are more likely to be evangélica/os. If we look at the breakdown of evangélica/os along countries of origins, then 27 percent of all Puerto Ricans are evangélica/os, followed by Central Americans (22 percent), Cubans (14 percent), and Mexicans (12 percent).

Religious Activities

Evangélica/os, defined as Hispanic Protestants who self-identify as evangelical or born again, are more likely, according to the Pew Hispanic Center study, to say that religion is more important to them (85 percent) than Catholics (68 percent) or Mainline Protestants (65 percent). They are also more likely to attend weekly service (70 percent) and accept the Bible as God's literal word (76 percent) compared to Catholics (42 and 49 percent, respectively) or Mainline Protestants (36 and 44 percent, respectively). Evangélico/as are more likely to participate in monthly prayer groups (75 percent), read scripture weekly (78 percent), and share their faith with others at least once a month (79 percent). Catholics (31, 27, and 32 percent, respectively) and Mainline Protestants (47, 38, and 53 percent, respectively) are less likely to engage in these types of religious activities.

Political Views

The Pew study also discovered that evangélica/os are more likely (46 percent) than any other Hispanic religious group to describe themselves as conservatives. Yet when it comes to voting, 40 percent of evangélico/as are registered Republicans, while 41 percent are registered Democrats (5 percent Independent, 12 percent neither, and 3 percent both). To be a Hispanic conservative does not mean the same thing as being a Euro-American conservative. It is true that evangélica/os are overwhelmingly opposed to gay marriage (86 percent) and to abortion (77 percent), more so than Catholics. Still, unlike their Euro-American evangelical counterparts, evangélico/as are more liberal on economic issues. They favor government-guaranteed health care (70 percent vs 58 percent among Euro-American evangelicals); and they believe the poor have a hard life due to a lack of government services (57 percent vs 42 percent among Euro-American evangelicals). They are also more liberal concerning the justice system, with only 46 percent favoring the death penalty as opposed to 73 percent among Euro-American evangelicals.

Even though there may historically have existed a link between U.S. imperialism and evangelical movements throughout Latin America, it would be a mistake to simply assume that evangélica/os have culturally capitulated to Eurocentricism. There seems to be a progressive and revolutionary dimension to Hispanic evangelism that promotes radical social change and justice. The Good News is more than just eternal life; it also includes an abundant life in the here and now—a life free from the sins of ethnic discrimination and economic exploitation. It is therefore not surprising to find "conservative" evangélico/as at the forefront of fighting for immigration reform, universal health care, antidiscriminatory policies, just distribution of resources, and workers' rights.

Conclusion

The divine mission of evangélico/as is the proclamation of the Gospel message of salvation, which can only be found in Christ Jesus. The one who believes and is baptized will be saved, but the one who does not believe will be condemned for all eternity. Because eternal life and eternal death hang on the balance, the Christian discipleship of evangélica/os encompasses the responsibility of witnessing the message of salvation to the unbeliever so that they too, can hear,

---

NATIONAL HISPANIC CHRISTIAN LEADERSHIP CONFERENCE

In 1995, the Reverend Samuel Rodriguez, the Reverend Nick Garza, the Reverend Charlie Rivera, and others attempted to mobilize Latino/a evangelical church leaders in the various parts of the country with the hope of creating and coordinating a national Hispanic Evangelical ethos. Their efforts evolved along the model of the National Association of Evangelicals. The organization they founded, the National Hispanic Christian Leadership Conference (NHCLC) was organized to provide a unified voice for Latina/o born-again Christians of all Christian faith traditions within the United States. Today NHCLC is a board-governed association of Latina/o evangelical church leaders. They are committed to serving the Hispanic born-again Christian community within the United States and Puerto Rico across generational, country of origin, and denominational lines on issues pertaining to the family, immigration, economic mobility, education, political empowerment, social justice, and societal transformation. Their mission statement is as follows: "To lead the Hispanic born-again community in America for the purpose of transforming our culture, preserving our Judeo Christian Value System and building the spiritual, intellectual and social/political capital within the Hispanic American Community."

—MAD

---

be converted, and gain eternal life. Evangélico/as, like their Euro-American counterparts, understand the Great Commission to be Christ's calling of all believers, not just the professional ministers, to go and convert the world to the message and lordship of Christ.

Ironically, evangélica/os, like all other Hispanics, exist on the margins of the U.S. religiosity and are aware of the historical pressure placed on them to assimilate to an Euro-American evangelical norm. Much effort has been exerted by Euro-American evangelicals, especially within the political realm, for evangélica/os to fall in line and follow Euro-American evangelicals' lead on social issues. Yet Hispanic evangélico/as, like all other Latina/os, understand what it means to be seen as the ones who must convert from understanding the gospel through their own cultural symbols to the usage of what Euro-Americans consider to be their "superior and purer" cultural symbols.

Thus, while similarities exist between the Euro-American evangelical and the Hispanic evangélico/a, especially on the literal interpretation of the Bible, there are also differences. Because evangélica/os are part of a U.S.-marginalized ethnic community, they, unlike their Euro-American evangelical counterparts, are more receptive to some of the concepts that emerge from theologies of liberation. They may be among the more conservative religious groups when it comes to "moral" social issues, but they are as liberal, if not radical and revolutionary, on political and economic issues. You will find evangélica/os standing in solidarity with the poor and oppressed in the struggle for liberation advocating personal and social conversion to Christ.

Miguel A. De La Torre

References and Further Reading

Berryman, Philip. *Religion in the Megacity: Catholic and Protestant Portraits from Latin America* (Maryknoll: Orbis Books, 1996).

Costas, Orlando E. *Liberating News: A Theology of Contextual Evangelization* (Grand Rapids, MI: William B. Eerdmans Publishers, 1989).

Pew Hispanic Center. *Changing Faiths: Latinos and the Transformation of American Religion* (Washington, DC: Pew Forum on Religion and Public Life, 2007).

Traverzo Galarza, David. "Evangélicos/as." *Handbook of Latina/o Theologies*, ed. Edwin David Aponte and Miguel A. De La Torre (St. Louis: Chalice Press, 2006).

EXILIO

Exilio, or exile, is a frame for both the historical and lived experience of exile, as well as a biblical interpretation constructed by Latin Americans living in their country of origin or as part of a migration to the United States. This interpretation is used to explain and contextualize their experience. While the interpretation of the biblical narratives of exodus and exile were already part of theological and religious studies, the interpretation of biblical narratives in light of lived experience, and especially the social and historical experience of persons living outside the dominant social structure, is the contribution of Latin American Liberation Theology. The concept was introduced beginning in 1964 and developed by Latin American liberation theologians, notably Gustavo Gutiérrez of Peru. This methodology of Liberation Theology, which emphasizes the idea that a Christian community decides what action must be taken based on the lived experience of the poor, uses theology as critical reflection to ascertain the guidance scripture provides. The formulation of a theology based on the historical and liberating experience and narrative of exodus and exile began at a meeting of Latin American theologians in 1964 at Petrópolis, Brazil, and in subsequent meetings in Havana, Cuba, Bogotá, Bolivia, and Cuernavaca, Mexico leading up to the Medellín Conference of 1968 in Colombia.

The metaphor of exilio was initially used to describe the plight of poor, rural workers arising out of the economic and social concerns in Latin America excluded from the successes of the populist movements of the 1950s and 1960s that had improved the standard of living for middle class and urban workers, but had the effect of marginalizing or constructively exiling rural workers. The term was later adopted by Cuban exiles as a model to describe their experience upon arriving in the United States in successive and distinct waves commencing in 1959. Other immigrant waves, from Mexico in the late 1960s and Central America in the 1980s and 1990s, also considered themselves outsiders in a new land. By the early 1990s, even the Hispanic of the Southwest was described as "an exile who never left home."

The lived experience of exilio is not homogeneous. For Latin Americans in their home countries in Mexico and Central America, those who were unable to participate in the economic move to the middle class were constructively exiled from meaningful participation in the life of their home countries. For the indigenous population in parts of Mexico, as well as countries such as Nicaragua and

El Salvador, the obstacles were political, primarily due to ongoing decades of armed conflict. Immigrants from both Nicaragua and El Salvador included persons from different ideological perspectives, some of whom received political asylum or protected status in the United States. The Nicaraguan conservatives who supported the Somoza regime that lost the war in 1979 as well as earlier political refugees who were persecuted by the regime were included. Similarly, the Salvadoran refugees included political refugees who fled the repressive tactics of the government regime during a 20-year conflict that ended with peace accords in 1993, as well as a displaced middle class that could not sustain economic stability due to the conflicts.

For the Cubans who migrated to the United States, the experience of exile is also complex. It varied by waves that differed both in how people could leave Cuba or enter the United States and in the economic and ideological perspective of the migrating Cubans. Four waves came beginning in 1959 that add to the variation: the first wave was typically socially and fiscally conservative, educated, business leaders; the second wave was part of the Freedom Flights supported by the United States from 1965, and these were typically immediate or extended family of the first wave immigrants; the third wave, in 1980, was persons who were allowed to leave Cuba by boat, and at will, because the government considered them politically undesirable and generally less wealthy or educated, primarily working-class people with no family to assist them upon arrival; the fourth wave includes people who waited to migrate for various reasons and either have visas that became available in 1994 or came in boats that made it to dry land in the United States and were allowed to stay.

El exilio is not merely an experience of geographic landlessness, but includes disconnectedness and displacement. It becomes an in-between place to wait and hope for something better. That "something better" may shift. It can be a return to a paradise lost, or forward to connectedness to a promised land. In either case the experience of exilio preserves a separateness of history, culture, values, and experience. The variations within the exilio experience resonate in the richness of the exodus and exile metaphor.

Major Doctrinal Points

Rigorous analysis of the biblical narrative of the Exodus, including both exodus and exile is provocatively multivalent. The turn to the text by Gustavo Gutiérrez and others generated the attention of biblical scholars who provide a rich analysis of the scripture as literary source, on the textual level and of its social horizon. In reflecting critically on the lived experience of exilio, the biblical narrative of Exodus resonates with political liberation. Still, mere political liberation is not sufficient for the Christian community so the exile narrative becomes the metaphor for an internal morality.

For Gutiérrez, the Exodus is both a historical and liberating experience that is the basis of the link between creation and salvation. Creation is the work of God who saves and acts in history. Because humankind is the center of this creation story, the work of God is integrated into history being built by human efforts. The liberation from Egypt in the Exodus narrative is a historical fact that links the biblical theme of liberation with human effort. It becomes a human act of self-creation first through self-liberation in the exodus. Then subsequently, the gradual series of successes and failures during the exile ultimately raise the awareness of the Jewish people to recognize the internal roots of their oppression, to struggle against it and to perceive the profound sense of the liberation to which they were called. While liberation is a certainty, the end of the journey is to an unknown land. It is not a return to regain what was lost, but a moving forward within the spiritual impulse of the Covenant that occurred in a moment of disruption.

Biblical interpretation of the Exodus narrative, including the exile event, became an important spiritual center of Ecclesial Base Communities that arose in Latin America to respond to the spiritual needs of the poor and give them voice. To be authentic to the richness of the text requires attention both to the events of exodus and exile and to its literary character. The event is historical to the extent that something happened that resulted in the reality that Israel sprang to birth in Canaan out of bondage, by resistance to state oppression and a bold bid for self-determination. The story of this break for freedom is told from at least four successive perspectives. When these views are considered as a nuanced explanation of the process, the resonance of the exile metaphor with the various lived experiences of exilio by Latin Americans becomes clear. Biblical scholar Norman Gottwald synthesizes the widely scattered commentaries in an effort to create a robust understanding of the biblical text for those using it.

The first horizon is the one reported by the hypothetical participants of the events, though no one source is recoverable. The voices are several probably because the narrative was shaped by liturgical tradition. While this does not allow for a historically verified exodus, it does present the strong possibility, based on what is known about the historical time, that the "historical kernel" of the exodus traditions was a motley group of state slaves who employed stealth and cunning, along with stolen and captured weapons, and the assistance of nature's elements to make their break for freedom.

The second horizon is that of the similarly discontinuous accounts of the Israelite social revolutionaries and religious confederates in the highlands of Canaan in the twelfth and eleventh centuries. The importance of these accounts is the idea of the struggle as being a holy war, although the portrayal differs in style: a quietest account in which the agency of God in the exodus out of Egypt is heightened to the point that the people's participation is merely passive; or the holy war traditions of Joshua and Judges that place the Israelites squarely in the battlefield upon entrance into Canaan and victory over the Canaanites.

The third horizon is that of the Israelite tradition in monarchic times, which conceives the Israel of the exodus as a national entity in transit toward a secure state elsewhere in Canaan. The emphasis on God's deliverance and de-emphasis on the instrumental actions of the people are most likely due to the tradition's purpose in creating a liturgical mode that emphasized stability and order under a protective God, more suited to the ideological needs of a new state just as Israel entered that new rule. And finally, horizon four is that of the late exilic and postexilic restorers of Judah as a religious and cultural community that had lost its political independence. The priestly tradition emphasizes the transcendent source and empowerment of Israel with its distinctive unity. The purpose of the separation of religion and politics is to shape a Jewish identity that will outlive the loss of statehood. The lived experience of exilio is understood and actualized more fully within the spectrum of these biblical social horizons.

The danger of overemphasis of the exodus narrative to the exclusion of the exile narrative is contained in the difference of exegetical preferences of Protestants and Roman Catholic interpreters, that is, their choice of texts and commentary to use as authoritative text. For Protestants, the victory of the exodus without consideration of the exile during which the Israelites realized the need to be free from their own infidelities to God and God's law is a temptation to triumphalism, understood as a bias that the view of the people to be liberated is superior and to be regarded above all other interests, values, or beliefs. The danger of triumphalism's temptation in Latin America is a pragmatic justification for revolutionary violence as means to achieve the ends of freedom. Although the use of incendiary threats is a last resort threat by liberationists, the threat is real in Latin America and carries a high human cost. From outside the liberation movement, this violence may be indistinguishable from the terrorism that uses violence as a first resort. The danger in the United States is more subtle. Protestant churches questioned the triumphalism of civil religion in the United States during the 1930s Great Depression, which institutionalized a set of sacred beliefs about the nation that made ethical issues subordinate to the interests of the nation. In the radical 1960s, the mainline Protestant churches adopted progressive stances on civil rights issues and opened the way for a generation of Latin American leaders.

The Roman Catholic Church took an immigrant approach to recently arrived Latin Americans characterized by "national parishes" organized by identity, such as Mexican and Puerto Rican, and thought to be temporary until the English language and North American customs displaced those of countries of origin. Instead, these parishes became permanent because the identity of these Latin Americans was not that of immigrants but of Latin Americans in exilio, a colonized people entitled to cultural rights allowing them to maintain their heritage and sustain their culture. This resulted in an ecclesiastical form of Jim Crow when new churches were built for English speakers. As in the postexilic Exodus tradition, the hope of exilio included the ability to maintain unity even without statehood.

The liberation of the exodus is certain, but the outcome of the hope in exilio is not so certain. The hope transforms from the demand for equal standards of living of the Peruvians to political enfranchisement sufficient to change how people are governed; from the return home of the Cuban to creation of a stable political and economic foundation within the United States where Cuban identity can be preserved; from the repatriation of land of the Mexican indigenous or Central Americans to advocacy of a culture of reconciliation. Exilio has taken what some would describe as a postmodern turn in which exilio is that sacred hope and waiting within the separateness of a particular history, culture, values, and experience that transcends place, yet contains the surprise of the prophetic.

Ritual Structures

The ritual structures of exilio are those that maintain a distinctive religious identity apart from the loss of statehood or place such as the *mestizaje* resonance of Jesus as Galilean being from two places and having none on which to stand, similar to Mexican borderland experience and Amerindian experience with European contact familiar to so many living in exilio. Within this liturgical need for an identity that outlives loss of place, come traditions such as the December 12 celebration of the Virgin of Guadalupe, who is also Tonantzin, the Nahuatl-speaking lady who appeared to Juan Diego; or the Quinceñera, celebrating a young girl's coming of age at 15 years of age by a mass in many Mexican parishes, but nowhere in the Rites of the Catholic Church, and yet reminds one of the Xilonen, a Mexica coming-of-age ceremony celebrating the young girl's passage to womanhood with honor to the corn deity and likening the worth of the young woman to that of Xilonen.

Key Figures

Gustavo Gutiérrez is a Peruvian Roman Catholic who articulated the metaphors of exodus and exile in 1964 as a result of the collaborative efforts between Latin American theologians that began that year in Petrópolis, Brazil, and culminated in the Medellín Conference of 1968. Other contributors to this effort included Roman Catholic theologians such as Segundo Galilea, Juan Luis Segundo, and Lucio Gera, together with Protestant theologians such as Emilio Castro, Julio de Santa Ana, Rubem Alves, and José Míguez Bonino. The ideas from this work are most fully developed in Gutiérrez's 1971 book, *A Theology of Liberation*, still considered a key doctrinal text. Rubem Alves is a Presbyterian from Brazil who early on articulated the dangers of exodus without exile. Alves's work in *A Theology of Human Hope* (1969) and later in *Tomorrow's Child* (1972) includes his articulation of a "community of hope" necessary to maintain an alternative construction of the future more consistent with the prophetic character of scripture in the face of the inadequacy of liberal or Marxist solutions. Eminent biblical scholar Norman K. Gottwald noted the need for a robust scriptural interpretation of exodus and exile texts sufficient to support praxis methodology. His contributions to the dialogue making the Bible authentically relevant began with an edited volume in 1983, *The Bible and Liberation: Political and Social Hermeneutics*, which contains essays setting forth various approaches to Scripture from Asia, Latin America, South Africa, and North America. His own critical scholarly reflections in light of pastoral needs for interpretation are succinctly summarized in his article "The Exodus as Event and Process." Contemporary reflections on exile as relevant for Latin American theological reflection include several notable examples of pastoral applications as well as critiques.

In 1983, Virgilio Elizondo, a Mexican American, offered his concept of mestizaje in *Galilean Journey: The Mexican-American Promise* as an interpretation of the indigenous-European, mixed-race otherness of his lived experience on the Texas-Mexico border as being analogous to the outsider experience of Jesus of

Sign at a Boston pro-immigration rally reads "I was a stranger and you welcomed me (Matthew 25:35)." (Jorge Salcedo/Dreamstime)

Nazareth, a Galilean held in contempt by the Jews of Jerusalem. Roman Catholic Fernando F. Segovia explains this otherness in terms of place and journey in his early *Listening* article, "Two Places and No Place on Which to Stand: Mixture and Otherness in Hispanic American Theology," and more fully in his 1995 article, "Toward a Hermeneutics of the Diaspora: A Hermeneutics of Otherness and Engagement" in *Readings from This Place*. In 1995, Cuban Roberto Goizueta, offers a Roman Catholic pastoral theology of accompaniment as a comfort to the isolation and experience of division between culture and lands and even within the immigrant waves experienced by those living the exilio to the United States in his book, *Caminemos Con Jesús*. A Roman Catholic religious scholar, Cuban Ada Maria Isasi Díaz,

uses the experience of exile to critique the absence of women's experiences in Latin American liberation theology, as well as North American feminist theology in 1994, articulating a *mujerista* theology. In her 1996 book, *Mujerista Theology: A Theology for the Twenty First Century*, she describes exile as a way of life that includes injustice and oppression and demands the hope offered by a mujerista vision. Continuing this tradition of a hermeneutic of suspicion, in 2003, Cuban Miguel A. De La Torre coined the term "exilio" as a sacred space of waiting and hope. This place is not tied to the return to the promised land of the *Cuba de ayer*. Instead De La Torre offers an *ajiaco* Christianity of reconciliation that acknowledges the varied class and ethnic texture of Cubans in el exilio, including both elite and poor, as well as indigenous, Spanish, African, and Chinese Cubans. His reflections on *imago Dei* of Genesis, as countering the notion of the gods of the Babylonian exile who would hold people as subservient, indict the libertarian society of the exiled Cuban elite. He proposed the need to find reconciliation of the needs of Cubans in exilio that honors the *imago Dei* in all persons. The particularity of this history, this culture, these values, and this experience becomes prophetic and transcendent.

Marta Vides Saade

References and Further Reading

De La Torre, Miguel A. "Cubans in Babylon: Exodus and Exile." *Religion, Culture, and Tradition in the Caribbean*, ed. N. S. Murrell and H. Gossai (New York: Palgrave Macmillan, 2000).

Goizueta, Roberto. *Caminemos Con Jesús: Toward a Hispanic/Latino Theology of Accompaniment* (Maryknoll, NY: Orbis Books, 1995).

Gottwald, Norman K. "The Exodus as Event and Process: A Test Case in the Biblical Grounding of Liberation Theology." *The Future of Liberation Theology: Essays in Honor of Gustavo Gutiérrez*, ed. Marc H. Ellis and Otto Maduro (Maryknoll, NY: Orbis Books, 1989).

Gutiérrez, Gustavo. *A Theology of Liberation: History, Politics, and Salvation—15th Anniversary Edition* (Maryknoll, NY: Orbis Books, 1994).

Isasi-Díaz, Ada Maria. *Mujerista Theology: A Theology for the Twenty-First Century* (Maryknoll, NY: Orbis Books, 1996).

FAMILIA

Two sets of literature yield contrasting understandings of the Latino/a *familia*. On one side, a long tradition of Hispanic fictional literature is centered in the life of Latina/o families within the framework of paradigmatic personalities and shared traditional values. Sociological and anthropological literature, on the other hand, has cast a more complex and mutable understanding of the composition and nature of Latino/a households and its members. The ideational concept of *la familia* (familism) that has emerged from fictional literature conveys the idea that Hispanic families are essentially affiliate, extending the nuclear family through a set of relationships that are maintained across generations and geographic locations. Therefore, la familia is composed of parents, siblings, grandparents, aunts and uncles, cousins, and other relatives within an extended network of genetic kinship termed *parentesco*. The notion of "familia" is retained whether those relatives live within a household, close enough to nurture the relationships, or even at distant geographic locations, especially those who still live in the countries of familial origin.

The Latina/o familia could also affiliate individuals who have significant roles in the socializing activities of the nuclear family. Nonblood relatives who play a caring role for children can become *tios* or *tias* (uncles or aunts) and elderly people respected and appreciated by the nuclear family can turn into *abuelitos* (grandparents) by virtue of meaningful relationships. Nonrelatives are also incorporated into the social configuration of la familia through *compadrazgo* (godparentship) when they take upon themselves the responsibility to bear witness to a socioreligious rite of passage such as a baptism, a wedding, or a *quinceañera* (sweet 15). Godparents are considered part of la familia, and their deliberate participation within the family's life and the rearing of a child or adolescent is expected. Whether members of la familia are in close proximity to the

COMPADRAZGO

The Spanish term "compadrazgo" (godparenthood) refers to a system of fictive kinship resulting from ritual and contractual sponsorship. The structure of this cultural and religious institution consists of the godparents (padrinos), or sponsors, and the godchild (ahijado/a). The relationship between parents and godparents is very important (known as "padrinazgo"), and the participants usually address each other formally as compadre (male coparent) or comadre (female coparent), using the formal pronoun *usted* (you). Compadrazgo is found in many cultures, in both religious and secular forms. The Spanish system of godparenthood was introduced in Latin America and the Philippines by mendicant friars, who began the task of converting indigenous populations to Catholicism shortly after the conquest. The ideological and prescriptive components of Spanish godparenthood were established at the Council of Trent (1545–1563). Though theological and doctrinal aspects had been previously developed, with Tertullian using the word "sponsor" for the first time (second century) and the first recorded use of the term *patrinus* (godfather) in 752. In his *Summa*, Saint Thomas Aquinas explained the reasons for having sponsors and provided a summary of their duties. Compadrazgo can be sacramental and nonsacramental. Sacramental results from ritual and spiritual sponsorship at Baptism, Confirmation, First Communion, and Marriage. Nonsacramental forms of sponsorship are also varied and include special nonreligious occasions (graduations).

—*FAO & KGD*

nuclear family or far from it, the sense of familia is retained through high levels of communicative exchange and contact.

Family orientation and strong affective commitments to family life are part of the familial archetype that nurtures much of Latino/a literary fictional works and oral traditions. The archetype has also shaped the realm of values that define the social relations practiced within la familia. Some of the most prominent values are associated with gender roles and the preeminent issue of *machismo*. The traditional model situates women in the private sphere of the home assuming domestic responsibilities as the man is portrayed as the primary provider of financial support and family safety. Since women are particularly responsible for domestic affairs according to the traditional archetype, the roles accentuated are those of mother, teacher, caregiver, and helpmate. In turn, men are represented as particularly responsible for sustenance and safety affairs, thus their role as household administrators, overseers, protectors, and disciplinarians. Women, however, occupy the public space that constitutes the extended ecology of their domestic roles: the market, the school, the park, the health clinic, the church, government agencies offering social services, etc. Such public participation allows Latina women to exercise a great deal of decision making and influence in household matters. Because of the burden of balancing domestic work and public representation, women are acknowledged as central to the permanence of the household, especially as they grow older and those efforts are validated, by extension, in the achievements of family members. Although men and women share an expectation for improving the well-being of the family and its future prosperity, women are particularly expected to put family before their own needs and concerns. The fact that many literary works center in female characters and the history of their families shows the values associated with a "matristic" model of Hispanic households within a patriarchal family structure. These values are also derived from a strong devotion in Catholic Latino/a families to the Virgin Mary as *Madre de Dios*. Paradoxically, these Latina/o households maintain the tension between a matristic domestic model and one that encourages *machista* attitudes within gender relations. Machista attitudes are transmitted not only from man to man through role modeling but, interestingly enough, from mother to son. This places women in the position of reaffirming, at least symbolically, male role prerogatives. However, this tension should suffice to challenge the stereotype that Latinas are simply subservient and deferent to male members of the household. Gender roles attributed to Latino/a households also vary according to the country of origin with a more marked difference between Central American or Mexican women (lesser level of gender assertiveness) *and* Caribbean women (greater level of gender assertiveness).

Another value associated with the traditional notion of "la familia" is religious faith. While institutionalized religion and active participation in faith communities has always been part of the Hispanic family experience, la familia is seen as the primary place of religious nurture and formation. This is reinforced not only in household religious practices, such as table prayer, moral instruction, storytelling, and regulated behavior associated with belief and/or superstition, but also in the concrete display of religious symbols as part of the spatial representation of family values. It is common to find religious iconography in Latino/a Catholic households and some of this imagery is attached to family devotions. Most common representations are the Last Supper, Jesus' Crucifixion, the Sacred Heart, the Blessed Virgin in all its iconographic variations, and *La Sagrada Familia*, a depiction of Jesus, Joseph, and Mary that stresses the religious commitment to family. Although Hispanic Protestants have rejected the placement of religious iconography at home, they seek to represent their faith and its influence upon the household by a highly visible display of a Bible or even decorative objects with biblical verses inscribed in them.

For a Latino/a family the home constitutes a sacred space but not a private and closed one. Unexpected and unannounced visits are accommodated, participation of visitors in the family experience is expected, free movement throughout the house is allowed, and counsel from extended members of the family or neighbors on matters related to household management and child rearing are welcomed, as long as the sacredness of the space is acknowledged and respected. Religious sentiment is evident in the day-to-day interactions of Hispanic families that still hold some traditional religious expressions to communicate among their members. Children and young people will regularly ask for blessings while approaching older relatives (*la bendición*). Adult relatives will respond to this request saying "*Dios te bendiga*" (May God bless you). In many households, the inability or refusal of children and youth to ask for a blessing from older relatives is considered bad manners. Other common expressions demonstrate how deeply ingrained religious faith is within the fabric of Latino/a family life: "Gracias a Dios" (Thanks be to God), "Si Dios y la Virgen lo permiten" (If it is the will of God and the Virgin), "Ave Maria Santísima" (Holy Blessed Mary), "Como Dios Manda" (as God allows), "Alabado sea Dios" (May God be praised).

As the case of blessing requests makes evident, children should act in a deferential manner toward adults and show respect to all elders. This familiar attitude of *respeto* is carried out into other social organizations like the school and the church where children are expected to behave in a culturally prescribed manner. Children do not actively participate in family decision making, and their input in matters relating to the household and their own upbringing is rarely sought. Children, however, especially those of more recent immigrants, become social brokers between parents and the public sphere as they possess the capacities for both linguistic and cultural translation in the context of North American U.S. society. If lack of participation in household decision making places children in the periphery of the familiar unit, through education the immigrant children move into the center of the family unit as partners in the collective enterprise of acculturation. Hispanic children who are already acculturated and belong to families whose origins are within the continental United States will either stay in the periphery if the family has decided to hold to traditional parent-children values or will move to the center of participation according to the level of cultural assimilation attained by family members.

Another central value fostered by the family is that of *confianza* (trust), which allows nuclear families to extend the network of relationships beyond the nuclear family and direct blood relatives with ease. "Confianza" goes beyond relationships between individuals and forms the basis of reciprocity among Latino/a people and many social institutions. To have confianza means to approach social relations with the presupposition that if you foster respect, intimacy, and commitment toward other people and organizations, you can expect, in return, the support of these people and organizations. Reciprocated confianza can turn into friendship and friendship into *compadrazgo*, making confianza the basis upon which a person is incorporated into the extended family networks. In turn, confianza in social institutions and government organizations allows Latino/as to reach out with the expectation that they can reciprocate with loyalty and commitment (i.e., churches, schools, and work sites), obedient citizenship, and conformity to social norms. The value of confianza becomes an asset for new immigrant Hispanic families who need to respond to multiple institutions and organizations under the premise that many will hold more than one job and move from place to place, thus interacting with new neighbors, schools, and faith communities. In the eye of the non-Latino/a observer, such presumed confianza could be interpreted as *naiveté*, yet it is the core value that allows families to navigate effectively the ever-increasing relations of a family circle extended in time and space, as well as a diversified public sphere.

The fact that literary fiction about Latino/as can portray such a generalized and consistent understanding of traditional family values demonstrates that such literature is framed by the imaginary of familism that considers la familia to be the most important institution in the social organization of Hispanics. It is through la familia that a viable subsistence as a racialized minority within the U.S. context is guaranteed through household practices that allow Latina/os to connect to a familial support system transnationally and cross-generationally and to communicate effectively with the larger society. The generalization, however, stops there, and the task to unravel the heterogeneity of Latino/a family systems lies on the extensive literature of sociological analysis and field work.

It is expected from those working within the social scientific disciplines to see family systems reconstituted due to socioeconomic circumstances. Because of the newness of the receiving culture in the case of Latino/a immigrant families, or the shifts in racial relations in the case of U.S. "native" Hispanics, families encounter the challenge of adaptability, transiency, and flexibility. This challenge causes disruptions and reconstitutions of family structures even when some durable networks of relationships are kept. Economic demands upon the family produce a change in family expectations and challenges tight conceptions of gender relations as women are placed in the position of being co-providers or, in some cases, the sole providers of households. In turn, the level of acculturation of family members, and especially the generational gap that results from that acculturation, can fragment the venues of communication that are assumed to be part of the effective functioning of a family system. Other aspects adding to the diversification of Latino/a family structures and values are

intermarriage trends between Latina/os and members of other U.S. ethnic groups, social stratification and the place of Hispanic families in the class system, and education. As a result of these realities impinging upon the life of Latino/a families, sociologists have noted a shift from traditional nuclear and extended families to families with one parent, couples living in cohabitation, and single older people. An increase of single women heading families with children has become a tendency in Latina/o communities, and this has been attributed to divorce, single pregnancy, or the absence of the husband due to seasonal work far from home.

The family has also changed in terms of number of children per household since there is an increasing need to adapt family size to available financial resources and to the constraints of living space, which decreases once families move toward urban areas where the majority of jobs are to be found. There seems to be a consensus among social scientists that economic stressors could have an effect on the decline of the two parents and multiple children nuclear family and may also contribute to the poverty of some sectors of the Latino/a population. As a result of economic stressors, the Hispanic family will confront a serious decline of educational opportunity, communal social organization, and the well-being of children.

In addition, social scientists have underlined the fact that the family structure we call the Latina/o "familia" is affected by the patterns of emigration and acculturation of the diverse national and cultural groups that compose the socially labeled category of "Hispanics." Overall, Latino/as have been an economically disadvantaged community in the United States, although there has been improvement in social status over time due to increasing levels of education and occupational status. Cubans, for example, have posited high value on the education of family members, and for that reason are distinctive from Mexicans and Puerto Ricans who statistically hold lower educational levels than other racial groups, including African Americans and Native Americans. In contrast, Mexican and Puerto Rican men and women have comparable levels of education, while Cuban men have a slightly higher educational level than Cuban women. Demands for the education of Mexican and Puerto Rican women is similar to that of men in these groups as labor force participation of these women increased sharply between 1960 and 2000. Generally, labor force participation of women increases in single-headed households with children. As unmarried women with children face the economic challenges of family support, working outside home becomes a primary necessity. Although both married and unmarried Latinas with children work outside home, the most salient pattern is for Cuban and Mexican unmarried women to work at a higher rate than their married counterparts. The exception to this pattern is Puerto Rican and Dominican married women with children who are more likely to enter into the labor force than their unmarried counterparts. One reason for this exception is that Puerto Rican and Dominican women are likely to reside in the U.S. East Coast and in the Midwest where lower skilled jobs are declining. The difficulty of finding adequate jobs in this highly skilled market produces two household phenomena: husbands who cannot support families on their own and reduced employment opportunities

that discourage single mothers from job seeking. No doubt, these economic and job factors impinge upon the way the family acculturates to the U.S. context and requires the reevaluation of traditional values including child care (who raises the children), family headship (who makes decisions at home while the spouse works), gender roles (how household roles are divided among men and women, both children and adults), and the overall quality of family relationships.

Another issue that sociologists take into account when describing the complexities of the Hispanic familia is the effect of family values on nonimmigrant Latino/as who are fully assimilated into the U.S. culture and subsequent generations of immigrants who have acculturated positively into the cultural mainstream (although research with immigrant groups still dominate the sociological agenda). Those Latina/os who are assimilated by birth and acculturated through generations are likely to redefine the notion of "la familia" and its values by changing the trends of social stratification, gender role statuses, racial intermarriage, fertility, language use, and social commitments. However, a strong ethnic loyalty remains with an awareness of ethnic identification and the particular place of "la familia" as a centering institution and a relational metaphor within that identity.

José Irizarry

References and Further Reading

Caputo, Richard K., Daniel Hank, and Marvin B. Sussman. *Families on the Move: Migration, Emigration and Mobility* (New York: Routledge, 1994).

Crane, Ken. *Latino Churches: Faith, Family, and Ethnicity in the Second Generation* (El Paso, TX: LFB Scholarly Publishing, 2003).

Zambrana, Ruth E., ed. *Understanding Latino Families: Scholarship, Policy, and Practice* (Thousand Oaks, CA: Sage Publications, 1995).

FEMINISM

The growth and development of contemporary Latina (women from Latin America or of Latin American ancestry) feminist theories and Latina feminist theology is part of the larger history of Latinas/Chicanas (Mexican American women) in the United States and Latino/a social and political movements. Movements generally occur within particular time periods when large groups join forces on behalf of particular issues, i.e., civil rights movement, women's movement, etc. These movements are part of the history of political and social thought and have been the bases for some of the differences within feminism, liberation theology, Latino/a theology, and Latina feminist theology.

In the United States, Latina and Chicana feminists have challenged the use of the term "feminism" as it is explained by European and Euro-American women. "Feminism" is often described as the advocacy for equality and ending exclusion or limitations for women in society. For Latinas, their experiences of exclusion based on sex (also known as gender discrimination), class (based on their lower levels of income), and ethnicity/race require that they are advocates for more than gender equality. These distinctions are the bases of their separation from White feminists. The term "feminism" has come to refer to a largely Euro-American middle-class approach to the issues of gender/sexual equality.

Latin American liberation theology and Latino/a theology also have a certain shared history—the Spanish conquest and Native American heritage—as well as common approaches to the study of these fields, such as belief in the option for the poor. Theologies are philosophical explanations of how God is active within humanity and the world. Although similar, these two theologies are not versions of the same theology, as some scholars assume when they include only Latin American liberation theology in their historical surveys.

While these theological differences are more than can be explained here, some mention of key points of difference is in order. What it means to be U.S. Latino/a is quite different from what it means to be a Latin American living in Latin America. For many individuals who describe themselves as Latino or Latina (or Mexican American, Cuban American, Puerto Rican American, etc.) means they do not feel a part of mainstream U.S. culture. Some Latino/as do not speak English, so that the experience of being an outsider is an important part of their daily life. Being Latina/o means one has to identify one's or one's family's country of origin. Although the majority of Hispanics are native-born U.S. citizens, they often are treated as if they are immigrants. Being on the margins of U.S. society, the historical experience of the Spanish conquest and U.S. reconquest (of the Southwest), and the experience of being separated from their homeland (as in the case of Cuban Americans) are some of the reasons why Latino/a theology differs from Latin American liberation theology.

Along with these issues of cultural identity, certain aspects of feminist theology are part of the Latina/o theological approach, such as *lo cotidiano* (seeing God's activities within daily life), a hermeneutics of suspicion (shared with feminist theology and refers to reading the scriptures and writing theology with an awareness of the exclusion of women's experiences), the preferential option for the poor (shared with Latin American theology), and praxis methodology (also shared with Latin American liberation theology and refers to being in dialogue and committed to social justice action within local church communities). These similarities reveal the important role that being an outsider plays within the development of these theologies. Therefore, these elements of shared method are also of particular importance for Latina feminist theology. They validate Latinas' self-understanding and experiences as an important part of their "voice," which is their particular contribution within theology in general, and as an important critique within Latino/a theology.

The mere presence of Latinas among the scholars of the academy of theologians does not necessarily address the important role that feminist thinking needs to play within scholarship or writing of theology. While some Latino male theologians acknowledge the importance of Latina feminism, this does not mean that Latino theologians have engaged in the critical reading of feminist theories or feminist theologies.

One distinction among Latina feminist theologians María Pilar Aquino and Ada María Isasi-Díaz is the difference in their approach to the term "feminist." In *Mujerista Theology*, Cuban American

Isasi-Díaz describes her involvement with Euro-American feminists and the challenges she faced when she first voiced the experiences of Latinas. Her marginalization within the movement is why she chose not to name her theology "feminist." Coming from a different experience, Aquino was born and lived the first part of her life in Mexico. She, however, notes her experience of Latin American feminism and chooses to call herself a Latina feminist theologian. She argues that Latinas have the authority to claim the term "feminist" on the bases of their Latin American and Latina experiences. Aquino's experience of feminism arises out of Latin America and U.S. sociopolitical and ecclesial developments of feminism. She also challenges use of the term *mujerista* on the basis that there are no mujerista social, political, and/or church movements and active participants. Aquino's point is that the term "mujerista" implies that in the United States there are mujerista social, political, and/or church movements or active participants of these movements. Similarly, Latina feminist theologian Michelle Gonzalez responds to Aquino's point by noting there are no Latina feminist social, political, and/or church movements and active participants of these movements outside of the academia. Currently, beyond the question of the appropriate name for Latina feminist theology, they have not discussed any of the other differences in their theologies. This question is based on Aquino and Isasi-Díaz's similar, yet diverse, backgrounds and experiences, as well as their understanding of feminism and the important role of speaking with and for various ethnic or racial groups.

SOR JUANA INÉS DE LA CRUZ (1648–1695)

Sor Juana Inés de la Cruz is a prominent, complex, and fascinating figure in Mexican history. She was a nun, scholar, theologian, writer, poet, and defender of women's rights in a patriarchal society that limited women's development. Sor Juana had a brilliant mind. By age three, she knew how to read, and at seven years old, aware that only males had access to education, she wanted to attend the university dressed as a man. Instead, she had to stay home where fortunately she still acquired knowledge due to her grandfather's private library. As a teenager she went to live at the palace where the vicereine supported her writing career, and some years later she entered the convent. Although her motivations to enter the convent remain unclear, the religious life was compatible with her interest in learning and knowledge. During her years at the convent, she became a public figure recognized by her knowledge in religious and secular areas. The last years of her life were marked by a controversy with some members of the church's hierarchy when one of her writings was published without her authorization, and her position and right to knowledge came under attack. In response, she wrote a letter in which she defended vigorously women's right to intellectual pursuits.

—NOL

Latina/Chicana Feminism and Euro-American Feminists

Few Latinas were present in the early twentieth-century feminist movements. The reason for their limited participation is due, in part, to the suffragists' (early feminist equal rights leaders) antagonism toward the African American, Latina, and immigrant voting rights. Some suffragist leaders argued that only Euro-American women should be allowed to vote since they did not want African Americans and lower classes to have the right to govern them. Suffragists also rejected socialist causes out of fear that labor rights and socialism would hurt their push for women's right to vote. Their rejection of the concerns of women labor leaders and working-class women meant they did not include the poor, many of whom were Latinas and African American women. Although in 1920 women were granted the right to vote, many Latinas and African American women were not excluded on the basis of discrimination. They were unable to pay the poll tax, could not register to vote since registration was held in private homes where African Americans and Latino/as were not allowed, and were intimidated verbally and physically to register and vote. In 1974, President Lyndon Johnson signed the Voting Rights Act, which established their voting rights.

These tensions and differences within the feminist movement among Euro-Americans and women of color prevented a number of early Chicana leaders from identifying with the term "feminism." Chicanas and African American women disagreed with the feminist movement during the 1960s and 1970s, arguing that it was mainly designed to help Euro-American middle-class women who were seeking higher social status. Chicana feminists focused on class discrimination since the majority of Chicano/as were working-class or poor. They also identified with their brother Chicanos in a shared common ethnic identity. In general, the early ethnic minority women leaders had different cultural, social, and economic experiences than Euro-American women; therefore, they differed from early feminist thinkers in their understanding of the issues and the reasons for change.

In the 1970s and 1980s, Chicana writers Gloria Anzaldúa, Ana Castillo, Norma Alarcón, Marta Cotera, Cherríe Moraga, among others, developed some of the earliest writings of Chicana/Latina feminist thought. The early Chicana feminists were part of a larger movement who worked for the liberation and dreams of working-class and underrepresented groups of immigrants, Mexican Americans, and other Latino/as. While they believed their concerns were best expressed within the Chicano/a movement, many of them soon recognized the difficulties within this movement. Chicanos often relegated the women and their issues to second-class status. Chicanas noted the role of gender inequality and challenged the inequality of women within Chicano culture. The importance of a separate political struggle for change became a necessary aspect that established a Chicana movement.

While many Chicanas have maintained their identity and thinking within a Chicano/a framework, others have joined with Latinas from various Latin American heritages and nationalities to develop a Latina feminist theory. The development of a Latina identity, one that is not connected to a specific nationality, is growing stronger among second, third, and subsequent generations in the United States. For some of these women

who express their identity with reference to their regional differences, such as in the Southwest where the majority of Latino/as are from Mexico, Chicano/a studies and identity are often the most preferred identity and framework.

The majority of Latino/a studies academics select broader terms, "Latino" or "Latino/a," to identify their works while also defining their identity according to nationality. They describe their experience within the context of their ancestry and generation in the United States. Many Chicano/as explain their identity is connected to Mexico. They and their ancestors did not cross a border; rather, the border crossed them. While Chicano/as may identify and connect with the broader Latino/a perspective and academics, they choose to identify as Chicano/a to maintain their unique position in U.S. history.

A Latina Feminist Epistemology

The issue of difference, based on the intersection of gender, class, and ethnicity, is an important feature in a feminist epistemology, which is how one comes to interpret and understand the world and knowledge. This feminist way of coming to knowledge is one that is inclusive of Latinas' perspectives and voice. Latina feminist theologian Nancy Pineda-Madrid explains that a Latina feminist epistemology allows Latinas the opportunity to employ their own way of knowing or self-understanding, which ultimately supports their sense of dignity. In other words, unless people are empowered to employ their own epistemology—way of interpreting and understanding their world through their creation of knowledge—they will find themselves being defined by others and

CENTER FOR EMERGING FEMALE LEADERSHIP

In 1994, the Latino Pastoral Action Center (LPAC) introduced Latinas in Ministry (LIM) to the public via a small conference that was held for mostly Spanish dominant women in ministry. Some Latina progressive Pentecostals were honored at this event, including Pastor Aimee Cortese and Mama Leo. In its initial stages, the conference targeted only Latinas and the group was guided by Dr. Maria Perez y Gonzalez. LIM was an offshoot of a Black Women in Ministry project headed by the New York Mission Society, the oldest social service agency in New York. In 1996, when Rev. Dr. Elizabeth D. Rios started working for LPAC and due to the decline of participation from the initial parties involved with Latinas in Ministry, she began reorganizing the effort. In 1999, she renamed it the Center for Emerging Female Leadership (CEFL). The name CEFL emerged when after many conferences, and in an attempt to be more inclusive, Dr. Rios and her team noticed that most of the conference attendees were women of color. CEFL was created to discover and to give voice and visibility to emerging female leaders in church and society, particularly Latina women.

—EDR

easily used for the benefit of others, which ultimately could harm them. The acknowledgment of Latinas' experiences of discrimination is an important part of any inclusive and liberating epistemology. A Latina epistemology contributes to the overall development of Latinas because it promotes their voice, agency, resistance, and survival. Therefore, Latina feminist epistemology addresses the issues that are relevant not only for Latinas' self-understanding but also for developing Latino/a theology, because theology needs to be grounded in the experience of the individuals and not merely based on abstract theories or church teachings.

Latina feminist epistemology includes the analysis of both gender roles and class, as they are important in the development of women's power. Latina feminist epistemology includes the insights of European and Euro-American feminist interpretations that recognize the importance of women's experience as a basis of knowledge. Feminists also analyze the patterns of male control within society and academia. While Latina feminists, Alarcón, Anzaldúa, Castillo, and Moraga, accept feminist analysis, they also challenge Euro-American feminists who avoid discussions regarding issue differences. The feminist melting pot approach assumes that any position that supports Euro-American women automatically promotes the well-being of all women. This assumption is faulty since they do not see the concrete factors of race, class, sexual preference, etc., that affect women's status, particularly status for women of color. Alarcón notes the harm that feminist theories do that treat race and class as secondary to the analysis of female subordination. She challenges feminist analysis that does not address the gender inequalities of race and class due to lack of information and/or the feminist approach to race and class as an addition to their theories but is not included in their analyses since

MUXERISTA

"Muxerista" is a term that was used by Anita Tijerina Revilla to describe the ideology of Raza Womyn, a student organization at the University of California. In her book, *Muxerista Pedagogy: Raza Womyn Teaching Social Justice through Student Activism*, Revilla attempts to illustrate how Chicanas and Latinas struggle against racism, classism, sexism, and homophobia from the social location of being activist educators. They employ a methodology called Muxerista pedagogy that moves beyond Latina feminism and mujerista theology. Muxerista is a Latina/Raza-centered womanism where the "x" signifies an indigenous stance. Through student activism and leadership a Muxerista pedagogy provides a means of negotiating their cultural, gendered, and sexual identities in hopes of achieving transformational resistance to an environment hostile to their existence and presence. An attempt is made by Muxerista to expand, rather than limit, sexual identities. Rather than referring to themselves as lesbians or straight, the mostly undergraduate students of Raza Womyn prefer to self-identify themselves as "queer," "xueer," "bi-curious," or "straight for now." In essence, they refuse to fit or be defined by one category. Rather than an either/or they prefer to encompass everything at once, including the good and the bad.

—MAD

they do not challenge the reasons for these inequalities.

Furthermore, a Latina feminist epistemology challenges the primary focus within Euro-American feminism that questions male dominance but does not apply their approach to changing the ways that knowledge and power exist within society and academia. Euro-American feminism merely replaces male dominance with Euro-American female dominance. This way societal structures function is not questioned nor do they address the multiple ways women remain oppressed, i.e., lower wages, sexual harassment, domestic violence, etc. Pineda-Madrid persuasively argues that those approaches that promote societal change by merely adding more feminist women and issues into academic research are ignoring the heart of the problem. The prejudice within the academic world in the development of

research and writing are not addressed and, therefore, remain unchallenged.

Latina feminist epistemology, the way of understanding, necessarily focuses on the multiple aspects of Latinas' lives—gender, race, class, etc.—and analyzes those epistemologies that do not acknowledge the complexities of women's lives.

Latina Theology: Rooted in the Ordinary

Latina theologians—Aquino, Isasi-Díaz, and Jeanette Rodriguez (from the first generation)—argue that Latina theology must speak about the lives of ordinary Latinas if it is to have any meaning for Latinas. Being a woman of Latin American descent does not necessarily mean that she is a Latina theologian. Only those Latinas who employ insights and experiences of Latinas and are connected to *lo cotidiano* (daily lives) and the popular expressions of faith of Latino/as are able to claim the title of Latina theologian. Popular expressions of faith, also known as popular religion, are those practices that are home and/or culturally based traditions, which are sometimes but not necessarily accepted by religious leaders, pastors, priests, etc. These religious expressions, i.e., quinceañeras (Latina 15 birthday celebration), novenas to their patron saints such as novena to Our Lady of Guadalupe, La Posada, which is a Christmas novena, are an essential part of Latina theology, since they are rooted at the center of the people's lives and spirituality. Latino/a theology, in general, recognizes the value and importance of popular expressions of faith that reside at the crossroads of public and private experience.

Isasi-Díaz argues that the development of theology, which until recently was written by White males, is based on their experience. This long history of theology has silenced women's expression of their faith, wisdom, and experiences, and in particular the contributions from women of color. Therefore, she offers a creative method that combines feminist analysis, liberation praxis, and anthropology. While most theology is dependent on the insights of individual theologians, Isasi-Díaz's theological method builds upon the wisdom of Latinas, whom she studied through interviews about their spiritual and daily lives. Isasi-Díaz argues that theologians need to be a part of the community in which they study. Through their experiences women express their wisdom and define their own understanding of themselves and their world. These experiences are the bases for challenging those ideas that come from Christian tradition and society that are not relevant to their lives. Recognizing the lived reality of women, Isasi-Díaz explains the importance of popular religions, *lo cotidiano* (everyday life), *la lucha* (the struggle for justice), *permítanme hablar* (claiming their own voices), and argues that these are critical sources for theology.

A Hermeneutics of Suspicion

Upholding the importance of women's voices and the need to seek justice, Latino/a theologians, in general, promote a hermeneutic of suspicion, which is a healthy skepticism that always asks who benefits from this theology and/or institution, such as the church. Unlike Latin American liberation theologians, Catholic Latino/a theologians have tried to incorporate a Latina feminist perspective within their methodology from the beginning of the Association of Catholic Hispanic Theologians (ACHTUS) of the United States. Beginning with the initial years of ACHTUS, Aquino, Isasi-Díaz, and Rodriguez have been instrumental in promoting the inclusion of a hermeneutic of suspicion from a Latina feminist understanding. Nevertheless, these discussions do not mean that Latino/a theology is necessarily inclusive and that sexism, gender discrimination, is eliminated from the Latino/a theology and academia.

One disadvantage for Latino/a theology is the small numbers of Latina theologians, both Catholic and Protestant. Women find that getting a doctorate is a financial, psychological, and spiritual drain on their resources. Because of their few numbers, these Latina theologians carry added burdens because they must not only hold onto their positions in the university or seminary, they also are called upon to do additional work within academia to carry forward the voices of women. Hence, additional responsibilities of research, writing, presenting, and participation in community and educational committees are required of these already overworked women.

As a pioneer in constructing Latina feminist theology, *mujerista* theologian Isasi-Díaz has a distinctive method that uses a feminist hermeneutic of suspicion in the analysis of scripture, tradition, and ethical concepts. Isasi-Díaz coined the term "mujerista" and developed its meaning jointly with some of the Latinas whom she interviewed. Mujerista theology is inclusive of Latinas' voices as a means of empowerment so that the development of theology is not only based upon Latinas' lives, it also is the praxis of liberation from oppression. Isasi-Díaz argues that the purpose of this theology is to empower Latinas in their own lives to liberate them from the forces of economic, political, sexual, racial, and religious oppression.

Recognizing that women's voices, particularly Latinas' voices, have and continue to be silenced in the development of theology, Isasi-Díaz offers a creative method that combines feminist analysis, liberation praxis, and anthropology. Since most systematic theology is dependent upon the insights of individual theologians, Isasi-Díaz successfully claims—as shown through her use of ethnographic interviews—that her theology is not done in isolation but is built upon the wisdom of Latinas.

Latina feminist Aquino also writes feminist and liberation theology in solidarity with Latinas. Taking a hermeneutic of suspicion, Aquino addresses the sexism within scripture, tradition, theology, and the Catholic Church. Although she began her writing as a Latin American feminist theologian, Aquino explains in *From the Heart of the People* that Latin American liberation theology has not questioned the sexism that exists within liberation theology. Likewise, Aquino challenges Latin American theologians for their dismissive approach to Latino/a theology. Aquino notes that Latino/a theologians argue that their theology is different from Latin American theology because Latino/a theologians analyze not only economic and political dimensions but also racial, cultural, and aesthetic dimensions.

Aquino is both a feminist and a liberation theologian because her theology analyzes the sexism in the Catholic Church as a means of liberating the voices of women and their lives of oppression. Aquino stresses the importance of being connected to the lives of the poor as part of a theologian's responsibility to work for social justice. She explains that her theological principles are inclusive and promote equality. She sees that sexuality is a source of liberation, the daily experiences of life are a source of strength, and women's voices are the important sources and unique contributions of women. Aquino argues for a theological method that includes the primacy of desire, which is the expression of passion and life, an option for women and the poor. She argues that women will reclaim their voices, history, and place within the development of a theology that addresses the problems of oppression at all levels. Aquino has begun to describe the implications of this theology in her development of a Latina feminist theology of the Trinity, Christology, the Church, and Mary.

Latina theologian Rodríguez also explains that her theology is dependent on Latina's experience and she uses an interdisciplinary approach for understanding these experiences. In her book *Our Lady of Guadalupe: Faith and Empowerment among Mexican-American Women* she employs psychology and religious approaches based on the works of psychology by Jerome Frank, religious studies by William James, faith development by James Fowler, women studies by Carol Gilligan, and Chicano studies by Anzaldúa. Her most recent book, *Cultural Memory: Resistance, Faith, Identity*, was co-authored with anthropologist Ted Fortier. In this book the authors discuss cases of cultural memory, Mexican Americans, Yaqui Indians of Arizona, San Salvadoran church of the poor and martyrs, and Tzeltal Mayans of Chiapas, Mexico.

Rodriguez's ongoing work with Latinas and Latina groups as a clinical psychologist as well as a nationally recognized speaker on Latina feminist and liberation issues places her in contact with a variety of groups, which enables her writing and speaking to come from the voices of the women with whom she is in collaboration. She believes that Latinas have a common ground of understanding that is inclusive of their cultural heritage, i.e., language, customs, and ways of viewing and interacting in the world.

Ultimately, in developing a theological method—as Isasi-Díaz explains in mujerista theology and Pineda-Madrid, Aquino, and Rodriguez in Latina feminist theology—as one claims her voice, a Latina theologian either takes a stance for the liberation of her community or becomes a voice that is outside and separate from other Latinas. Therefore, the development of a theological method, as shown through this survey of these

women's methods, is a stance that has significant implications for potential good and harm that come in the development of one's method and voice.

Thus, Latina feminist and mujerista theologians employ a feminist hermeneutic in their theological method and have contributed to the use of a hermeneutic of suspicion in Latino/a theology in general. The importance of their insights and contributions are part of their leadership in ACHTUS and in their ongoing publications. They utilize a hermeneutic of suspicion that is critical of institutions and traditions that foster the dehumanizing effects of silence, poverty, and racism. These effects limit the lives of Latinas, within both church and society. Subsequently, the opportunity to articulate a theology that reflects these women's voices is an occasion for empowerment as an additional outcome of the women's faith practices, although empowerment is not the sole purpose of their beliefs and actions.

Praxis Methodology and Option for the Poor

Latino/a theology's emphasis on praxis methodology comes from its early relationship with Latin American liberation theology. The term "praxis" refers to actions on behalf of justice and liberation based on a preferential option for the poor and oppressed. In their critique of other theologies, Latin American liberation theologians and their colleagues, Latino/a theologians, and Latina feminist and mujerista theologians stress the importance of praxis. Their approach rejects the belief that faith is essentially an acceptance of church teachings and creeds. Rather, liberation theologians argue that true faith is focused on "knowledge and seeking to understand," yet this definition does not include living a Christian lifestyle. To be a follower of Christ is to love your neighbor as yourself and to seek justice. Thus, liberation and Latino/a theologians promote the importance of a praxis theology that is rooted in faith and one that reflects the daily faith practices of the Christian community, while seeking to live according to the scriptures.

Aquino argues for the necessity of a praxis-oriented theology. She maintains the need for a close relationship between theology and action for justice. Aquino also believes in the importance of seeking justice through the process of theology. In describing Latina feminist theology, Aquino believes that it is from the perspective of the poor and suffering that theology needs to work for the liberation of the poor and the emancipation of oppressed women. Seeking true liberation, she argues, means that Latina theologians advance a liberating action that encourages solidarity and community among women in order to promote a process for world peace and justice. Recognizing the importance of a praxis methodology, mujerista theologian Isasi-Díaz has a distinctive method. She locates mujerista theology within liberation theology, believing that mujerista theologians must be active members of the Latino/a community.

Isasi-Díaz has a four-step praxis method of mujerista theology: telling the women's stories, analyzing the women's reality, creating new ways of prayer and worship (liturgizing) to express their experiences as a means for empowerment, and defining ways to deal with oppression. Isasi-Díaz argues that the purpose of this theology is to empower Latinas in their own voices and to liberate them from the forces of economic, political, sexual, racial, and religious oppression.

Liturgizing these experiences among mujerista grassroots theologians is an important part of Isasi-Díaz's theology, and she is not alone. Rodriguez also employs rituals within her work with Latinas. Both of them see these expressions of prayer as an important part of empowerment of women. The value of ritual is the healing presence of sharing and naming their experiences within a space that is collaborative and spiritual. Praying together is important for the women as they bond together and share faith. This empowerment of women builds a sense of community and healing.

Latina feminism is often described as an outgrowth of European and Euro-American feminist movement within society and academia. The similarity of purpose and approach among Latinas/Chicanas with these feminists on issues has been the basis for some feminists to downplay the distinctive features of Latinas/Chicanas. Likewise, many in the academia assume that Latina/Chicana feminism comes directly from the larger feminist movement and relegates the Latina/Chicana experience as merely one example of the larger experience of women in general due to their second-class status in society. Reading the works of Latinas/Chicanas challenges these assumptions and the rush to a false sense of solidarity. Latina feminism and Latina feminist theology does have similarities of approach with feminism, but the assumption that no differences exist among them is the reason that Latina feminists and theologians strongly explain their position and challenge Euro-American feminists.

Theresa L. Torres

References and Further Reading

Alarcón, Norma. "Theoretical Subjects of This Bridge Called My Back and Anglo-American Feminism." *Making Face, Making Soul: Haciendo Caras,* ed. Gloria Anzaldúa (San Francisco: Aunt Lute Books, 1990).

Anzaldúa, Gloria. *Borderlands: La Frontera* (San Francisco: Aunt Lute Books, 1999).

Aquino, María Pilar. *Our Cry for Life: Feminist Theology from Latin America* (Maryknoll, NY: Orbis Books, 1993).

———. "Theological Method in U.S. Latino/a Theology." *From the Heart of the People,* ed. Orlando O. Espín and Miguel H. Díaz (Maryknoll, NY: Orbis Books, 1999).

Aquino, María Pilar, Daisy L. Machado, and Jeanette Rodriguez, eds. *A Reader in Latina Feminist Theology: Religion and Justice* (Austin: University of Texas Press, 2002).

García, Alma M. *Chicana Feminist Thought: The Basic Historical Writings* (New York: Routledge, 1997).

Gonzalez, Michelle. "Rethinking Latina Feminist Theologian." *Rethinking Latino(a) Religion and Identity,* ed. Miguel A. De La Torre and Gastón Espinosa (Cleveland: Pilgrim Press, 2006).

Isasi-Díaz, Ada María. *En la Lucha/In the Struggle: Elaborating a Mujerista Theology* (Minneapolis: Fortress Press, 1993).

———. *Mujerista Theology: A Theology for the Twenty-First Century* (Maryknoll, NY: Orbis Press, 1996).

Martell-Otero, Loida. "Women Doing Theology: Una Perspectiva Evangélica." *Apuntes* 14, no. 3 (1994): 67–85.

Peña, Milagros. "Border Crossings: Sociological Analysis and the Latina and Latino Religious Experience." *Journal of Hispanic/Latino Theology* 4, no. 3 (February 1997): 13–27.

Rodríguez, Jeannette. *Our Lady of Guadalupe: Faith and Empowerment among Mexican-American Women* (Austin: University of Texas Press, 1994).

———. *Cultural Memory: Resistance, Faith, and Identity* (Austin: University of Texas Press, 2007).

FIESTA

Understanding the concept of Fiesta is decisively important to understanding how Hispanics worship. Though centered on Latino/a liturgical celebrations in a parish setting or home worship, it is not confined to either place, but encompasses both the community and the home life of the people. Fiesta is a celebration of the relationship with God whose confinement to the private realm, as practiced in much of Western society, is resisted and rejected by Hispanics. The unabashedly public nature of Latina/o popular religiosity centers on the Fiesta, where God's revelatory presence in Hispanic worship spills out of the church and the home, and transforms public spaces, encompassing public squares, whole towns, and city neighborhoods. This most public and elaborate expression of how people understand themselves in relationship to God makes the Fiesta an outstanding example of the *sensus fidelium* (sense of the faithful) of the Christian faithful.

The Latino/a Fiesta is an amalgamation of Spanish, Indian, and African elements, all with long histories. Pedrito Maynard-Reid points out that the Fiesta directly benefits from the fact that these three cultures are cultures of passion, and that quality is intensified by their amalgamation into a public religiosity marked by passionate responses to the

SAN JUAN BAUTISTA FIESTA

The feast of Saint John the Baptist is June 24. In the Hispanic world it is celebrated with revelry as well as liturgical and popular religious rituals often lasting for a week. In Puerto Rico, where Saint John the Baptist is the patron saint of the island, it is observed in churches and with public celebrations in the town plazas. Thousands flock to the beaches to bathe and ask the patron for favors and good health. Because John was the baptizer of Jesus, it is believed that on his day all waters, especially sea water, are endowed with healing power. On June 29, 1950, the American Puerto Rican Saint John Day Observance was first celebrated in the Bronx. In 1953 the Archdiocese of New York adopted the already existing San Juan Fiesta as part of the pastoral outreach to the Hispanic community. The Fiesta came to symbolize both the faith and culture of the Puerto Rican in New York. Although it does not hold the popular appeal of the early years, the Fiesta continues to be celebrated in New York City on the closest Sunday to June 24.

—ASD

presence of God (2000, 179 and 181). This encounter of Spanish, Indian, and African cultures, while certainly not without conflict considering it occurred within a context of conquest and enslavement, nonetheless yielded surprising points of compatibility among the three groups that produced Hispanic religious practice, including the Fiesta.

It is typical to begin to trace the history of Fiesta with Spain because it was and remains an integral feature of Spanish religious and cultural life. Below the surface, the Latin American Fiesta is a product of a medieval, pre-Tridentine Spanish Christianity brought to America by the Spanish and untouched by the challenges brought by the reforms of the Protestant Reformation and the Catholic Reformation. The Spanish Conquest and the Protestant Reformation began at the same time. Protestants could not mount any significant challenge to Spanish America's allegiance to the Catholic faith because the Spanish ironically used Trent's reforms for the sole purpose of keeping out Protestant ideas, thus

maintaining (and never bothering to reform) the pre-Tridentine status quo. Orlando Espín argues that the pre-Tridentine religious world of the Spaniards "communicated their faith through symbol and rite, through devotions and liturgical practices," which encompassed daily life to the point "that the cycles and components of village life became fundamental transmitters of the Gospel message." Religious practice and the normative behavior expected of the Spaniard were one and the same so that "every dimension of daily life participated (or could participate) in the transmission and sustenance of Christianity" (1994, 317). Hispanic American culture is characterized still by many of these qualities, the most public of them being the Fiesta.

The Indian civilizations encountered and conquered by the Spanish were decimated, with some driven to extinction, but their influence nonetheless pervades Latino/a popular religion and the Fiesta itself. Maynard-Reid identifies two major influences. First, the Latina/o receives

VEJIGANTES

Vejigantes are colorful clown-like characters who for centuries have participated in Puerto Rico's carnivals. The term is derived from the Spanish word *vejiga*, which means bladder. Originally, a blown-up cow's bladder would be left to dry, then painted, and then filled with pebbles to make a rattling noise when shaken. While wearing this over the head, the Vejigante would chase children and women during the carnival, attempting to scare them. This practice is so old that it is mentioned in the 1605 classic *Don Quixote*. Today, rather than a dried cow's bladder, the mask is usually made of papier-mâché, complete with horns and fangs. Various Puerto Rican towns construct and adorn the Vejigante's masks differently. The custom's roots can be traced to the holy wars of Spain between the Christians and the Moors, with the Moors being represented by the Vejigantes. Saint James the Apostle is credited with leading the Spaniard Christians to victory. With the Spanish conquest of Puerto Rico, the custom was transformed by the African slaves brought to the island. Not allowed to pray to their own deities, slaves outwardly prayed to Saint James while inwardly praying to the African deity Saint James symbolized. Saint James came to be associated with the African deity Ogun, the Yoruban God of war, while the Vejigantes became the Christians.

—MAD

from the Indian a worldview that is wholly spiritual. All creation is suffused with divine presence. Second, the Western conception of community, understood as something formed by a collection of individuals coming together, is turned on its head. The individual received no identity apart from the community because the latter is entirely responsible for having brought the former into existence. A communal consciousness pervaded Indian life and a communal orientation directed all activities. Today, the Fiesta reveals these influences through its recognition of the all-pervasive and potent presence of God throughout creation and the life of the community. Of course, Hispanics do not reject individual identity and initiative (as demonstrated by their entrepreneurial acumen), but neither is the family nor the community impoverished by it. The Fiesta, with its curious mixture

of group planning and individual spontaneous behavior, and the communal celebration of individual milestones achieved in life by individual members of the community, all show how the individual and the community mutually maintain and strengthen the identity of each other.

Africans brought over as slaves by the Spanish and Portuguese to replace the labor lost by the decimated Indian population struggled to maintain their identity far from their native lands and under the worst conditions of forced labor. Music, dance, folklore, and the syncretism of Christianity with Yoruba religious beliefs found in much Hispanic religious practice, all carry an African pedigree. This last feature of African religious influence is controversial. Hispanic practice ranges from those who incorporate the African belief that spirits play a major role in life, but limit its influence to a belief in the active presence of the Holy Spirit alone, to others who freely and openly syncretize worship of African gods with Christian faith. *Santería* worship of African gods under the guise of Christian saints is perhaps the most prominent example of the latter. Despite criticisms leveled by many Christians against syncretistic practices, Latina/os incorporate these influences into the Fiesta nonetheless, celebrating the fact that they live in a spirit and/or Holy Spirit–filled world.

To understand the qualities of the Fiesta itself, one can begin with the fact that it is arguably *the* outstanding example of popular religion. The people put on the Fiesta by creating the *ambiente* (environment) for their praise and worship of God as a community. Establishing the proper ambiente, understood in this context as a worship environment, is of particular importance for the Fiesta. Ricardo Ramírez describes ambiente as a "human, deeply personal situation characterized by a hospitality, warmth and joy genuinely experienced . . . a festive setting in conjunction with a significant event." This significant event is the community's desire to worship God, which allows for the Fiesta to happen because it arises as "an extension of the *ambiente* of *la familia*, *el barrio* [the neighborhood] and the extended relationships of *compadrazgo* ([the] relationship between parents and their children's godparents) celebrated in sacrament" (1981, 33). Fixed barriers between private devotion and public praise and worship are nonexistent.

By virtue of its being a product of popular religion, the Fiesta discloses the fact that Latino/as hold a sacramental view of life. Miguel Díaz argues that Hispanic popular religion is populated with numerous symbols (the liturgy with its symbols, statues of Jesus, Mary, and Joseph, and other saints, religious processions, etc.) all of which serve to enable the people to encounter the divine reality made present by them (2001, 64–65). The plurality of popular expressions of religiosity erupts from the people themselves, contributing to the Fiesta. Through worship and praise of God's active participation in the life of the community and concern for each of its members, the Fiesta enables the community to construct a unique mode of encounter and communion with God.

Fiesta, as an example of popular religion, asserts the humanity of the Hispanic people. By extension it can serve also as a locus for resistance against attempts to dehumanize Latina/os through marginalization. Orlando Espín argues how popular religion is a locus for the most authentic expressions of Latino/a cultural identity and self-understanding as a people. Consequently, popular religious events like the Fiesta serve as a public display of the essentials of Hispanic cultural identity, which is not limited to the celebration of its many virtues but also the honest display of its vices. It also broadcasts a categorical rejection of attempts by those in the church and society who want to marginalize Hispanics as integral participants in the life of both (1992, 148–151).

Virgil Elizondo's argument that the Fiesta contains an eschatological dimension may come to some as a surprise, considering how, at first blush, the Fiesta celebrates the existing relationship between God and the community. The eschatological qualities of the Fiesta are decisively important because, in general, it reminds all involved of the irruption of God's presence and action in human history and that God's Kingdom is

TRES REYES MAGOS

In Hispanic tradition, the Three Kings are known as Melchor, Gaspar, and Baltasar. These are the names that Christian tradition has given to the astrologers mentioned in Matthew's Infancy Narrative. The Evangelist never mentions how many magi actually visited the baby Jesus; however, according to Matthew 2:1–12, the wise men from the East brought with them gifts of gold, frankincense, and myrrh. Over the years the number of magi varied, but in the seventh-century Christian tradition parceled out each gift to an individual wise man—three gifts, three magi. These magi came looking for a king, therefore tradition made them kings. Melchor (king of light) who brought gold was an old man and the Sultan of Arabia. Gaspar (treasurer) who brought frankincense was a youth and the Emperor of the Orient. Baltasar (God protect the king) was the middle-aged king of Ethiopia and he brought the myrrh. In the Middle Ages, the Three Magi Kings came to represent Europe, Asia, and Africa as well as the three ages of humanity: youth, adulthood, and old age. Instead of gold, incense, and myrrh, they bring toys and new clothes to good children. Their feast day was set for January 6 and is celebrated through gift giving within the Latino/a culture. In Miami, Florida, a large parade is held in the Cuban American community.

—GCG

coming into existence now and will attain complete fulfillment in the future. The specific eschatological message found in the Fiesta is twofold: first it is prophetic in that the Fiesta declares that the daily challenges and misery of life will not have the last word, but the maintenance of Latino/a identity as a people beloved of God will. In response to this prophetic message, the people are motivated to rally and begin anew the effort to cooperate with God's project in history. This project is the second aspect of the eschatological dimension of the Fiesta. It presents a foretaste of the world God will bring about, a world where the unique differences found among peoples will contribute to their unity as God's people instead of being marks of division (1992, 122–123). Hispanics, by virtue of their encompassing every racial category, possess a unique ability to communicate this eschatological message of human unity in God through their public celebrations of worship.

Roberto Goizueta argues that the Fiesta represents a theological anthropology with a decidedly different set of priorities from the dominant modern human anthropology. Modernity views human beings as agents who act to make something of their lives. The consequence is alienation from the life human beings make because it becomes a mere object for endless manipulation, instead of something that should be lived. Fiesta presents an alternative vision where human beings receive life as a gift from God. This gift is not meant to be an object of human manipulation, but something that motivates a human response of gratitude to God who, out of love, freely gave this gift of life (1999, 85–86, 90–91).

Goizueta warns that this idea of life lived as a gift from God must not be allowed to slip into sentimentality, in other words something akin to the experience of a simple exchange of presents. Being a gift from God, life possesses an irreducible, ontological value. Life is not something that human beings possess in order to do, make, or achieve something. The whole of life, by virtue of it being given to us by God encompasses human existence and activity. Human work, play, and identity are all grounded "in the prior constitutive relationship with the One who has loved us first" (1999, 95). God alone gives humanity the life that makes our work, our play, and our very existence possible.

This is why the Fiesta, observes Goizueta, is deliberately ambiguous. A common misconception of the Fiesta made by non-Hispanics is that it is solely a party, an event designed to escape temporarily from the daily duties and burdens of life. Certainly, the Fiesta does incorporate elements typically found in a party: food, drink, music, companionship, dancing, conversations, storytelling, joking about, and raucous laughter. However, the Fiesta is not designed to escape from the daily duties, burdens, and milestones of life. To the contrary, it remembers and incorporates into its proceedings the celebration of life, the play through which human beings enjoy life, *and* the commemoration of the work of life, reminding all gathered that it is a gift from God. The community is reminded that in response, the gift of life must be lived out with responsibility and joy, both in equal measure (1999, 90–91).

Manifold examples of the Fiesta exist. They include, but are not limited to, the Mexican Advent tradition of the *Posada*, which reenacts the pilgrimage of Mary and Joseph to Bethlehem, inviting the community to join in the pilgrimage and await the birth of Christ; the *quinceañera,* which honors the life and life experiences of young women passing from childhood to potential motherhood, without which the community cannot survive nor thrive; holidays such as the Feast of the Three Kings where the family, in its role as domestic church, commemorates that all life belongs to God; the *Dia de los Muertos* held on All Saints' Day (November 1), when living family members honor their ancestors; Holy Week liturgies and processions; *pastorelas,* which are plays commemorating God's salvific activity in human history; the administering of sacraments like baptism, Eucharist, and the anointing of the sick, whose ceremonies spill out from their core liturgical setting and encompass the community as a whole; and the veneration of saints. Fiestas that honor Mary merit special attention, in particular the Fiesta of Our Lady of Guadalupe, because her appearance is a clarion call from God that Hispanics are a new creation, a *mestizo* culture that unites the Spanish with the Indians (and by extension the other peoples they encountered) without destroying the identity of any group. Latino/a identity in all its rich variety is signified, through Mary, as being both a gift from God and a symbol of reconciliation of all peoples.

Fiesta is an activity of unity, which rejects as false dichotomies those persons or things that ought to be united as one. It unites private and public expressions of religion; it unites individuals with their communities; it unites the serious work of commemorating life in all its dimensions lived in God's presence with the celebration of the same; it is an expression of a Hispanic culture that, by its internal diversity, unites human cultures; it unites the present day with God's promised future; and through its sacramental vision and religiosity, it unites humanity with God.

Ramón Luzárraga

References and Further Reading

Díaz, Miguel H. *On Being Human: U.S. Hispanic and Rahnerian Perspectives* (Maryknoll, NY: Orbis Books, 2001).

Elizondo, Virgil P. "*Mestizaje* as a Locus of Theological Reflection." *Frontiers of Hispanic Theology in the United States*, ed. Alan Figueroa Deck, S.J. (Maryknoll, NY: Orbis Books, 1992).

Espín, Orlando O. "Grace and Humanness: A Hispanic Perspective." *We Are a People! Initiatives in Hispanic American Theology*, ed. Roberto S. Goizueta (Minneapolis: Fortress Press, 1992).

———. "Popular Catholicism among Latinos." *Hispanic Catholic Culture in the U.S.: Issues and Concerns*, ed. Jay P. Dolan and Alan Figueroa Deck, S.J. (Notre Dame, IN: University of Notre Dame Press, 1994).

Goizueta, Roberto S. "Fiesta: Life in the Subjunctive." *From the Heart of Our People*, ed. Orlando O. Espín and Miguel H. Díaz (Maryknoll, NY: Orbis Books, 1999).

Maynard-Reid, Pedrito U. *Diverse Worship: African-American, Caribbean & Hispanic Perspectives* (Downers Grove, IL: InterVarsity Press, 2000).

Ramirez, Ricardo. *Fiesta, Worship, and Family: Essays on Mexican-American Perception of Liturgy and Family Life* (San Antonio: Mexican-American Cultural Center, 1981).

G

GLBT

Following the sexual revolution of the 1960s, Americans felt more comfortable in openly discussing issues of sexuality. This, however, has not been true in every community. Among Latino/as, certain topics continue to be unmentionable, particularly the topic of homosexuality and religion. Although today homosexuality is no longer criminalized in Latin American countries, it is still perceived as unnatural by many religious groups.

Silence prevails around the subject of homosexuals of faith, particularly in Hispanic religious communities. In recent years, organizations, including the International Gay and Lesbian Human Rights Commission, Hispanic American Religion Group of the American Academy of Religion, and the Hispanic Theological Initiative, have provided platforms for discussion of the topic. To date, though, few open discussions about the topic among religious leaders have taken place.

Religion at large may be hostile toward gay, lesbian, bisexual, and transgender (GLBT) individuals; however, some religious communities welcome and celebrate gay identity. For instance, Espiritísmo, Santería, and other indigenous religious/spiritual practices are more open and accepting of homosexuality. Some denominations have GLBT organizations and openly welcome these individuals, such as the Other Sheep Multicultural Ministries, an organization founded in 1992 that has over 60 centers across six continents. Latina/os in general, including Hispanic GLBT, consider religion/spirituality an essential part of their lives and identity. Latino/as have historically been heavily influenced by Roman Catholic beliefs and, more recently, also by Protestantism.

Religion has greatly influenced Hispanic culture and the Latino/a notion of homosexuality. Traditional Hispanics hold rigid moral standards, strict gender roles, and fixed familial expectations. These expectations include getting

---

ELIAS GABRIEL GALVAN (1938–)

Born in San Juan Acozac, Puebla, Mexico, Elias Gabriel Galvan was the first U.S. Hispanic bishop elected in the United Methodist Church. He was also the first Hispanic president of the United Methodist Council of Bishops. Galvan received his higher education at California State University (B.A.) and the School of Theology at Claremont (Rel.D). He was elected to the episcopacy in 1984 by the Western Jurisdiction. While presiding over the Seattle Episcopal Area, he was involved in a controversy involving the removal and trial of an openly gay pastor, Rev. Karen Dammen. She was acquitted by an ecclesiastical jury of her peers on March 20, 2004. Shortly afterwards, Bishop Galvan published an open letter to the church opposing homophobia and urging reconciliation. He was assigned to the newly formed Desert Southwest Conference, Phoenix Episcopal Area. During his tenure, he was active in the formation of the National Plan for Hispanic Ministries and Methodists Associated to Represent the Cause of Hispanic Americans (MARCHA). He retired from the Episcopacy in 2004. He is currently serving as executive director of MARCHA.

—DFF

---

married, procreating, and continuing the family. Since homosexuality may disrupt the fulfillment of such expectations, it is often perceived as a threat to the core cultural values of the Latina/o community. Similarly, the Catholic Church and most organized religions support traditional family dynamics, promote sexuality in the service of procreation, and condemn homosexuality, considering it unnatural and its acts sinful.

In addition to procreation, other important values in the Latino/a culture are gender roles and machismo. For that reason, stigma accrues to a feminine man and a masculine woman, as they do not conform to gender expectations. Such strict gender guidelines lead to the use of terms such as "men who have sex with men," since men who engage in sexual behavior with other men may not consider themselves homosexuals or bisexuals, especially if they take the active role during sexual intercourse.

In general, Hispanic GLBT individuals find organized religion to be an oppressing factor in their coming out process, causing delays in the process or even in the decision to come out. Moreover, Latino/a communities seldom provide protection from homophobic prejudice to GLBT individuals. This is true in part because homosexuality may be perceived as a sin and their sexual acts interpreted as weakness of character that could or should be prevented.

Overall, regardless of their religious affiliation, those individuals who believe homosexuality is a choice tend to be less tolerant of homosexuality. Catholics and Protestants have been consistently identified as the faiths that are least tolerant of homosexuality, and who tend to hold negative attitudes toward homosexuality, more specifically toward sexual acts between individuals of the same gender.

For instance, the Vatican has actively condemned homosexuality, considers homosexuality immoral and against the natural law, and prohibits those who practice or support homosexuality from attending or teaching in a seminary. These beliefs are in part based on the literal interpretation of some biblical passages and the idea that sexual activity should only occur between a husband and a wife, and should be open to conception.

Tolerance of GLBT individuals in the Hispanic community may be granted as long as sexual identity remains invisible. For that reason many Hispanic GLBT men and women, specifically priests, ministers, and religious scholars, opt to keep their sexual identity a secret, in order to avoid the outcast status that would result from open acknowledgment of it. Such conflicting loyalties to both of their minority communities may cause Latina/o GLBT individuals to feel marginalized in both groups, leading them to compartmentalize themselves into two independent identities: the gay and the religious Latino/a. Feeling that they need to choose one or the other as these cannot coexist, GLBT Hispanics are faced with significant difficulties reconciling their religious (and therefore ethnic) identity with their sexual identity. Many live a life where they accept their homosexuality but at the same time believe it is a sin. Those who do achieve reconciliation seem to be able to achieve it through direct communication with God and not through organized religion.

At times, choosing to follow a conservative religion, such as Catholicism, involves not disclosing their sexual orientation, as well as dealing with the disparity between religious teaching and their lives, abstaining from sexual activity, and attempting to live a heterosexual life. The prohibitions of the church are a source of alienation that also separates them from their families. Religion is intrinsic to Hispanic family and community life, and therefore loss of religious support may result in the loss of family and community support. Given that Latino/as hold a collective worldview and heavily rely on external sources of support, such loss can often be a traumatic experience and affect the individual's sense of self. Strong ties with the family, culture, and the community support the Hispanic's healthy cultural and religious identification. Hence, such strong ties can provide Latina/o GLBTs with benefits such as a sense of belonging, heritage, values, and a strong sense of self.

In spite of the negative messages that most organized religions transmit to Hispanic GLBTs, there are potential benefits for these individuals in belonging to a religious group. Positive religious experiences may provide necessary support and encourage positive psychological wellbeing. Many Latino/a GBLT individuals find strength in religion/spirituality and employ prayers and other spiritual rituals to cope with difficult situations, including the coming out process.

Hector Luis Torres

References and Further Reading

Conner, Randy P. *Queering Creole Spiritual Traditions: Lesbian, Gay, Bisexual, and Trangender Participation in African-Inspired Traditions in the Americas* (New York: Harrington Park Press, 2004).

De La Torre, Miguel A. "Beyond Machismo: A Cuban Case Study." *Annual of the Society of Christian Ethics* 19 (1999): 213–233.

————, ed. *Out of the Shadows into the Light: Christianity and Homosexuality* (St. Louis: Chalice Press, 2009).

Lumsden, Ian. *Machos, Maricones and Gays: Cuba and Homosexuality* (Philadelphia: Temple University Press, 1996).

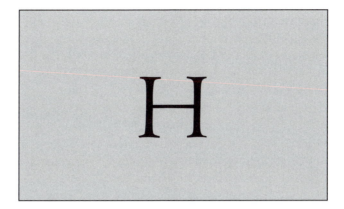

HEALTH CARE

The role of religion in health care among people who became known as Latina/os can be traced back to first encounters between the Spaniards and indigenous peoples in the Americas. Some of the Spanish chroniclers were interested in discovering new medicines, and so they collected as much information as possible about health practices. In general, health care and medicine were intertwined with an imperialistic study of subject peoples. This entry treats health care as a result of the triadic interactions of European, indigenous, and African traditions that are still being experienced among the pan-ethnic group we call Latino/as, and that includes Mexican Americans, Puerto Ricans, and Cuban Americans. Much of what will be discussed falls into the category of folk medicine that is derived from historical and traditional practices within Hispanic communities rather than from modern scientific methods of diagnosis and healing.

Historical Impulses in the Study of Hispanic Health Care

As the United States acquired formerly Spanish territories, there was an interest in knowing as much as possible about America's new imperial subjects. This is quite evident in the person of John G. Bourke, a captain in the United States Army who published in the 1890s some of the first formal studies of Mexican American health care practices and "superstitions" while stationed at Fort Ringgold, Texas. Bourke provided a catalogue of herbs and remedies along with the classification of illnesses such as *susto*, *empacho*, and *caida de mollera*, which are too often described without nuance by many researchers who study Mexican American health practices.

Bourke's studies also influenced the selection of the Lower Rio Grande of Texas as a primary laboratory for the study of Mexican American health practices. Bourke, as well as modern scholars, notes that at least six major traditions can be detected in Mexican

American curanderismo (folk healing), and these include Judeo-Christian, Arabic medicine, medieval and later European witchcraft, and Native American traditions. Given such disparate sources, it is difficult to speak of simply "indigenous" medicine.

Within the broader context of American society, the study of Latina/o health care has been included in studies of religious alternatives to conventional health care. Health care concerns have always shaped religion and vice versa. Some religious groups such as Seventh-day Adventists and Christian Science, may be seen, in part, as health care reform movements. As usual, whenever conventional health care is perceived to be deficient, new alternatives are proposed, and many of them are religious in nature.

Another impulse is more practical. Latinas/os have become a significant group in America, and modern medical personnel realize the importance of knowing the health care practices of their patients. This concern began in the late nineteenth century with Bourke, but since that time the Latina/o population has grown to over 40 million. Many doctors and nurses realize they must be educated in the role of religion in health care among Latina/os. Indeed, Latino/as can bring a host of illness classifications and ideas that are not familiar to Anglo practitioners.

A more recent impulse derives from efforts to show scientifically that religious factors can have positive effects on therapy. Some of the foremost representatives of this effort include D. B. Larson and Harold Koenig. These authors seek to reverse a disjunction between health care and religion that came into full force with the advent of "Germ theory" and powerful new scientific

therapies that made religion seemingly irrelevant. As we shall see, many of these studies of the effect of religion on health have bypassed Hispanic populations.

Explaining Illness

All health care systems usually include "etiology," the general name for ideas about the cause of illness. Here we distinguish between "disease," which refers to any modern biomedical classification, and "illness," which is any condition that a culture defines as abnormal. Thus, many "illnesses" among Mexican Americans are not recognized as "diseases" by a modern medical system. Likewise, many diseases are not recognized as illnesses by many Mexican Americans. For example, arteriosclerosis, when exhibiting no symptoms, may not even be acknowledged as an illness by Mexican Americans.

Among Mexican Americans, some of the best-known illnesses are mostly of "natural origin," especially as classified by Euro-American anthropologists. For example, some scholars note illnesses relating to dislocated organs (fallen fontanelle) or illnesses of emotional origin (susto). "Caída de mollera" (fallen fontanelle) is often manifested by an inability of a baby to breast-feed properly. "Empacho" refers to a wide variety of indigestive ailments, but often a bolus of food attached to the stomach walls is believed to be responsible for the illness. In part due to overemphasis on studying Mexican American folk traditions in South Texas, many anthropologists have missed the regional and sociolinguistic variation in the use of these terms.

Witchcraft (brujería) and magic are believed to cause illness. In the 1890s, John G. Bourke records this belief among the inhabitants of the Rio Grande Valley. One of the more common diagnoses attributed to witchcraft is mal de ojo (evil eye), which can be found in many cultures, ancient and modern. Belief that one is the victim of "bad magic" can help outline the moral and personal conflicts that explain why the patient, rather than someone else, has become ill.

Demons and gods can also cause illness. The biblical God, for example, is often seen as both the sender and healer of illnesses (Job 5:18). In Santería, fevers (and mishaps with fire) can be associated with Changó, the orisha associated with lightning and fire. In Pentecostal traditions, which we will discuss further below, what are otherwise perceived as natural diseases can also be attributed to demons. For example, it has been a common Pentecostal belief that demons are responsible for schizophrenia or psychosis, illnesses that modern medicine attributes to brain disorders.

Scientific medicine regards the issue of sin as irrelevant in etiology. However, sin and illness have been linked at least as far back as the third millennium BCE, judging by Mesopotamian sources. The biblical book of Deuteronomy (e.g., Chapter 28) makes a systematic link that may be reduced to two relationships: (1) Illness = sin; and (2) Sin = illness. That is to say, if one is sick, then one must have sinned. If one sins, then expect illness to occur. This sort of etiology was juxtaposed to that found in the biblical book of Job, in which illnesses can be caused by mysterious, yet divine factors other than sinning. In the New Testament, Jesus specifically disputes that sin is always related to illness (John 9:2), even if elsewhere he is portrayed as accepting this relationship (Mark 2:5–10).

Among Latina/os, the same tension exists in these opposing etiologies. Sins may be minimal social slights to more severe breaches of moral codes. Thus, Lydia Cabrera, the noted scholar of Santería, reports the case of a babalawo (a Santería priest) who was believed to be sick because he stole a peacock dedicated to Oshun, the orisha associated with love (1975, 45). Different folk healers may recognize an overlap between the Christian concept of sin and more "natural" factors (e.g., an imbalance of humors or disharmony with nature) in diagnosing an illness. As in the case of biblical stories, therapy may include seeking forgiveness from God or redressing perceived wrongs. As such, therapy serves social needs and may be subject to social controls.

Therapeutic Strategies

"Therapeutic strategies" refer to the concerted actions taken by a patient in order to receive healing. Such actions depend on religious presuppositions, economics, and other factors. Most health care systems develop a hierarchy of options. The first option is usually the least expensive and simplest remedy. If this option does not provide results, then more expensive or complicated treatments may be sought. In modern America, for example, one's first option for a headache may be to take the aspirin that sits on the nightstand. If headaches persist or become severe, then one may seek the help of a general doctor, and then a specialist.

In Latina/o subcultures, home remedies and self-help may include prayers and homemade remedies. Personal gardens may have yerba buena (mint), which is thought to cure a variety of

Vitamins, homeopathic medicines, and other products line the shelves at the shop of a curandero, or healer. (Stephanie Maze/Corbis)

ailments. Latino/as in the United States are just as likely as Anglos to have aspirin and other medicines bought over the counter at a local Anglo-owned pharmacy.

After simple self-help, the next step, especially among older or immigrant generations, may be to visit with a folk healer, usually called curanderos/curanderas among Mexican Americans. Determining the degree of utilization of these curanderos has been fraught with controversy. Some researchers have been criticized for regarding curanderos as characteristically widespread among Mexican Americans and/or for seeing them as the continuation of "primitive" superstition. Yet, one important survey completed in Southern California reports that less than 1 percent of 500 Mexican American households mentioned the use of folk healers. Indeed, one must heed generational and regional differences more than earlier researchers tended to do.

Curanderas/os have a range of skills and usually charge few, if any, fees. Some authors note that curanderas/os often resemble psychiatrists more than medical physicians. Mexican American curanderas/os can provide advice on everything from marital problems to preventive care. Giving advice on social and emotional problems is also common among consultants associated with "Spiritism" (see below) among Puerto Ricans in New York. Similar observations may be made about priests (babalawos) in Santería.

The most accomplished folk healers know plants very well. This was already reported by Bourke in the 1890s for Mexican Americans in the Rio Grande Valley. The "herbalist" tradition can also

YERBEROS

Yerberos (herbalists) are specialists who have learned the secrets of the herbs by which diseases and illnesses can be cured and evil diverted. Although most *curandero/as* and *santera/os* are yerberos, not all yerberos are religious faith leaders. Those who are not belong to a lower tier of folk healers. Nevertheless, the healing powers of yerberos are considered to be a gift from God. These yerberos understand herbs to be the most important ingredients within religious ritual, more important than sacrificial animals. Every plant is alive, infused with a magical force and protected by spiritual entities. As such, herbs and plants are able to heal body and/or soul. While a medical doctor might prescribe medicine that cures the physical, the yerbero also attempts to bring healing with the spiritual world. Yerberos can trace their roots to the ancient fusion of indigenous herbal medicine techniques (Native American in Central and South America and African in the Caribbean) and religious rituals. Still, not every yerbero is a practitioner of a religious tradition. Their approach to healing serves as an alternative to unaffordable conventional medical care. Because of the difficulty of obtaining wild plants and herbs in major industrial cities, the number of plants and herbs used has been greatly reduced. Yerberos participating in these forms of Hispanic folk medicine usually turn to the botánicas to obtain what is needed.

—*MAD*

be found among Afro-Caribbean traditions in Puerto Rican and Cuban American communities. At the same time, some older traditional specialties (e.g., hueseros/bone specialists) may be dying, according to surveys done by some medical anthropologists.

Therapy itself can take a wide range of forms. Curanderas/os can combine Christian prayer with nonofficial rituals, such as the Mexican American *barrida* ("sweeping"). The sweeping action of a broom, often made of special materials, is thought to act as a magnet that carries away any malady. It can also be seen as a form of sympathetic magic in which an action works by virtue of its imitation of the intended result. In Santería, one can combine more elaborate rituals, which may involve music, herbs, and the sacrifice of small animals.

Another aspect of therapy that is often overlooked by researchers is the role of art in healing. In cases of illness, many Mexican Americans paint special "retablos," or wooden boards. These retablos can be used in the petition for healing or as a thanksgiving offering after healing. Retablos characteristically include a picture of the patient along with an inscription detailing the scene or medical problem. Likewise, many crafted figurines may be used in Santería healing rituals. One may see that Santería healing rituals also have aesthetic dimensions that range from the placement of objects within the sacred space to the crafting of representations of the orishas.

Modern medical science may provide the next series of options, and economics is one of the most important factors in this selection. The relationship between folk healing and modern medical science is an uneasy one. Modern biomedicine is often viewed by religious believers to emphasize the physical at the expense of the spiritual dimensions of the human experience. The response of medical science toward folk healing may range from indifference to hostility. Recently, however, there are complementarian models that acknowledge that indigenous traditions have some merit.

Healer Cults

As has been the case through much of recorded history, many individuals rise to prominence as healers. U.S. Hispanics may have more than their fair share of such prominent miracle healers, and these include Don Pedro Jaramillo (d. 1907), who has been called the most famous healer in southwestern Mexican American history. Born in Mexico, he gained prominence when he moved to the Los Olmos Ranch in what is now Brooks County, Texas. Jaramillo also used a mixture of indigenous and Christian religious rituals.

Teresa Urrea was a woman whose fame as a healer at the turn of the century led to her being viewed as a political threat by many in U.S.-Mexico borderlands. Urrea also illustrates the extent to which gender is a crucial aspect of folk healing. Women form a relatively large proportion of folk healers among Mexican Americans and Puerto Ricans. This occupation can provide women with prestige and power that they may otherwise lack.

The healer who has inspired the most persistent new religious movement among some Mexican Americans is probably El Niño Fidencio, whose full name was José Fidencio Constantino Síntora. Reportedly born in 1898 in the state of Guanajuato, Mexico, he became renowned in the 1920s and 1930s for his reported healings in Espinazo, Nuevo León (Mexico). By the time of his death in 1938, El Niño ("The Child") spawned a whole "Fidencista" movement, part of which eventually became an official church in Mexico in 1993. Fidencista influence reaches into the United States, especially among Mexican Americans in the Southwest.

As Mexican Americans and other Latina/os grow and interact with Anglo culture, the traditions of Latino/a folk healers have lost some ground or have been recontextualized. Indeed, U.S. Hispanics may now be just as familiar with someone like James Van Praagh, the Anglo spiritist, or Deepak Chopra, who espouses Ayurvedic medical traditions of India. On the other hand, there is still much to be investigated. There may be dozens of healers who may be well known in smaller Latina/o communities, but unknown to a modern media that can create and market renowned healers on a massive scale.

Pentecostalism as a Health Care System

Pentecostalism, from its very beginnings, viewed healing as a central part of its mission. The history of this American-born movement is quite complex. The movement had at least two embryonic foci—one in the mountains of Appalachia, and the other in the urban landscapes of Los Angeles. Pentecostalism began as a sort of apocalyptic movement dissatisfied with the modernism that was perceived to be infecting mainstream churches.

The apocalyptic nature of Pentecostalism was also tied to the healing aspect, something illustrated by Acts 2:17–18 and Mark 16:17–18. Armed with such passages, Pentecostals emphasized that miraculous healings confirmed that the end of time was near, though eventually the apocalyptic aspect ceded to the idea that healing was simply a normal part of the Christian life. This attitude contrasted with many major Protestant churches, which saw miracles as restricted to the earliest "Apostolic Age." One of the earliest organized Pentecostal churches, the Church of God, had health care as part of its rationale for prohibiting the use of tobacco.

Many of the first Pentecostals among Spanish speakers certainly promoted healing as a central part of their message. For example, María Atkinson (1879–1963), who founded the Mexican branch of the Church of God, promoted the value of Pentecostal health care in a systematic manner. This was evident not only in her sermons but also in the banner that included the words "Jesus Heals" (Jesús sana) displayed at the altar in many of her services. Many of her early converts first visited her church, in part, because of their search for healing.

Spiritism as a Health Care System

Some scholars distinguish between "Spiritualism" and "Spiritism." The former is a general practice centered on a medium's ability to communicate with the dead for the benefit of paying clients. Spiritism is a specific movement that syncretizes Spiritualism, African, and Catholic traditions with the work of a Frenchman named Allan Kardec (1804–1865). Born Hippolyte Léon Denizard Rivail, Kardec was the author of influential spiritism treatises, including *The Book of Spirits* (1857) and *The Book of Mediums* (1861).

Puerto Ricans on the U.S. mainland, particularly in New York, are very familiar with Spiritism. Kardec's philosophy, which was brought to Puerto Rico by the 1890s, resonated at first with the White upper-income stratum in Puerto Rico. The upper classes turned to the French Spiritist beliefs, not wanting to identify themselves with the African and jíbaro (peasant) elements within their society. By practicing Spiritism, the elite legitimated the ancestor worship already thriving in Puerto Rico. Indeed, the idea of communicating with the dead existed among the indigenous Taíno, and in traditions brought from Africa.

In New York, Puerto Rican Spiritism began to mix with Cuban Santería. Much of the mixing took place through the interaction of Puerto Rican and Cuban musicians. Spiritism now provides a serious alternative to Protestant and Catholic traditions among New York Puerto Ricans. In New York City there are centros ("centers"), where practitioners gather. Sometimes these centros become the target of protests by Puerto Rican evangelicals who see them as centers for witchcraft. Pentecostalism and Afro-Caribbean Spiritism, in addition to being religious rivals sometimes, are also rivals in health care clienteles.

Santería as a Health Care System

Healing is a major concern of Santería. Santería is an adaptation of the religion of the Yoruba slaves, whose ancestors had a highly organized urban culture that can be traced back at least 1,000 years in Nigeria. The worship of African deities in the guise (or as equivalent to) Catholic saints ("santos") by the African slaves resulted in the word "Santería" being applied to the newly emerging religious tradition.

It is too simple to call the Yoruba religion polytheistic, as eventually all of the transcendent entities, called orishas, are but an aspect of the supreme God named Olodumare ("the Lord of all destinies"). The orishas may specialize in different illnesses. Babalu Ayé (identified with Saint Lazarus) is perhaps the orisha best known for specializing in the curing of diseases. But other orishas also have their roles in health care.

The year 1959 marked a turning point for Santería. Although Cubans had been coming to America since the nineteenth century, it was the Cuban revolution that resulted in hundreds of thousands of new Cuban immigrants to the United States, and particularly to South Florida. Santería thereby entered a new phase in a relatively new environment. In America, Santería was "desyncretized," meaning that it sought to reclaim its African origins. Animal sacrifice, which has been a part of many health care traditions since ancient times (see Leviticus 14:4–5) still plays a role in health care in Santería.

Perhaps the most important public gateway to the world of Santería in the United States is the botánica, a sort of Santería supermarket, which usually stocks the herbs and paraphernalia needed by practitioners. One may find cans of aerosol sprays marketed for their efficacy in love or other aspects important to everyday life. As such, the botánica represents the use of capitalistic marketing techniques by Santería. The multiplication of botánicas, especially in Miami and New York, reflects a more accessible attitude toward Santería in the United States.

Divination is probably one of the most recurrent services that a babalawo performs for his patients. Ifá, which relies on the casting of palm nuts or the reading of a necklace, is perhaps the most prominent form of divination. The procedures of Ifá aim to create a dialogue between the various configurations of the divining instruments and the client.

Any conflict between Afro-Caribbean religious traditions can also be seen, at least in part, as a conflict between health care systems. The competition may be economic, especially if practitioners in one system derive part of their livelihood from such consultations. The competition may also be for power, especially if one group deems their ideology as more "true" or the one that should have dominance. Indeed, many espirista consultations expend part of the time instructing patients not to go to an alternative system. Likewise, one often sees competition between scientific medicine and alternative health care, including that of Pentecostalism and Santería.

Science and Religion

Some medical researchers are renewing the study of the role of religion in health care. Some of these studies are practical attempts to see whether some religions create a healthier lifestyle. Other studies are motivated by the attempt to validate the efficacy of supernatural claims of specific religions. The scientific merits of such endeavors have been criticized by many scientists and scholars of religion. Nonetheless, the study of how religion can influence health is important regardless of whether one accepts supernatural assumptions or not. Are adherents of some religions healthier than adherents of other religions? If so, why? And, it is in this context that Latino/a health care is relevant. Such researchers have, by and large, neglected Latina/o populations. For example, the landmark tome published by Oxford Press, *Handbook of Religion and Health* (2001) bears only scant references to studies involving Hispanic religious traditions.

Many researchers who see the value of faith in health often cite studies that conclude churchgoers are healthier than nonchurchgoers. For example, some report that churchgoers have an average lower blood pressure (about 5 mm lower) than nonchurchgoers. Yet, in such studies "churchgoers" is a selective category that may reflect differences in socioeconomic status rather than church attendance. We can also ask if churches that emphasize healing attract the sicker individuals. If so, there would be a negative correlation between religion and health. These are the types of questions that still need to be answered in an exploration of the role of religion in health care among Hispanics.

Another problem is that the set of churches selected might not place much demand on members. Accordingly, it would be difficult to use such a set to generalize about the good effects of faith and "churchgoing." The churches used in these studies may indeed provide emotional support that may be regarded as positive. However, there are many other churches that can place demands on members that can cause emotional problems. By omitting such churches, researchers may be unscientifically selective in their samples. Indeed, Koenig, who is otherwise an advocate of the positive effects of religion on health, notes that groups that believe in suicide

(e.g., Jim Jones temple, Heaven's Gate cult) suffer obviously negative consequences to health.

Other scholars note that groups in which alternative therapies predominate over the use of conventional medical means suffer disproportionate mortality rates from diseases that are otherwise very treatable. Even some scholars generally positive toward African traditional health care reported that some Yoruba healers may use herbs that make mental illness worse. In short, much more comparative study needs to be done on religion and health.

Other writers would add that the efficacy of religion in curing disease may not be the most important role of religion. For example, some medical anthropologists have reported that the presence of symptoms can persist even among those reporting healing in Seattle, Washington. That is to say, patients would report being healed regardless of the status of their symptoms. Others also received conventional treatment along with religious therapy, and so it was not scientifically possible to eliminate the possibility that conventional treatment had brought about any healing.

Accordingly, there must be factors other than actual healing that attract patients to Pentecostalism and other alternative health care systems. Faith healing, even if it does not always produce desired effects, at least does not cost anything, or not as much as a conventional system that may be equally ineffective. Patients may perceive faith healing as an advantage simply because it is not as economically burdensome as conventional health care. In addition, a Pentecostal congregation may provide other means of emotional and social support that conventional health clinics or other denominations do not, at least from a patient's perception.

Conclusion

As is the case in many places and cultures, it is useful to think of health care among U.S. Latinas/os in terms of overlapping systems. Each system may stand alone. For example, Pentecostalism theoretically can stand alone as a complete health care system. Some Pentecostals may believe that they need not avail themselves of scientific health care if God can cure all illnesses without medical help. But, the majority of Pentecostals do not function in this manner, nor do believers in Cuban American Santería or Puerto Rican Spiritism. Most negotiate and interact with different health care systems to the point that we probably have to think of a larger super–health care system that encompasses both scientific medicine and folk medicine. This sort of interaction has been the case throughout history.

The need for an alternative health care system has never died out. We can see competing and/or overlapping systems from the dawn of writing until today. Certainly, scientific medicine has become more acceptable than ever. As Mexican Americans become more urbanized and move into higher income brackets, the old curanderismo has apparently yielded to more visits to conventional physicians. However, alternative medicine has not died completely; it has only taken new forms. In many communities, there may still be some links with traditional practices, but they are reinterpreted and recontextualized.

There are a number of trends that may intensify in the near future. One is a continued interaction in the health care systems of Hispanic subgroups in the United States. We already see that happening between Puerto Ricans and Cubans in New York City. The more Latina/o subgroups interact with each other, then the more Latino/as of one subgroup may feel comfortable using traditional healing traditions predominant in other subgroups. Many Hispanics are already clients of healing systems that are originally drawn from other parts of the globe (e.g., Ayurvedic medicine). Certain forms of folk healing may decline among more prosperous and assimilated Latina/os, though new forms will probably develop, especially as Central and South American groups become more prominent in the U.S. Latino/a religious experience. In any event, the complex configurations of etiologies and therapeutic strategies that are still evolving among Hispanics form a new and dynamic episode in the long history of the interaction of religion and health care.

Hector Avalos

References and Further Reading

Bourke, John G. "Popular Medicine, Customs, and Superstitions of the Rio Grande." *The Journal of American Folklore* 7 (1894): 119–146.

———. "Notes on the Language and Folk-Usage of the Rio Grande Valley." *The Journal of American Folklore* 9 (1896): 81–116.

Cabrera, Lydia. *El Monte* (Miami: Ediciones Universal, 1975).

Curry, Mary Cuthrell. "The Yoruba Religion in New York." *New York Glory: Religions in the City*, ed. Tony Carnes and Anna Karpathakis (New York: New York University Press, 2002).

De La Torre, Miguel. *Santería: The Beliefs and Rituals of a Growing Religion in America* (Grand Rapids, MI: Eerdmans, 2004).

Edgerton, Robert. *Sick Societies: Challenging the Myth of Primitive Harmony* (New York: Free Press, 1992).

Gardner, Dore, and Kay Turner. *Niño Fidencio: A Heart Thrown Open* (Albuquerque: Museum of New Mexico Museum Press, 1992).

Koenig, Harold, Michael E. McCullough, and David B. Larson, *Handbook of Religion and Health* (New York: Oxford, 2001).

Larson, D. B., H. Koenig, B. H. Kaplan, R. S. Greenberg, E. Logue, and H. A. Tyroler. "The Impact of Religion on Men's Blood Pressure." *Journal of Religion and Health* 28 (1989): 265–278.

Pattison, E. Mansell. "Ideological Support for the Marginal Middle Class: Faith Healing and Glossolalia." *Religious Movements in Contemporary America*, ed. Irving I. Zaretsky and Mark P. Leone (Princeton, NJ: Princeton University Press, 1974).

Perez y Mena, Andrés Isidoro. *Speaking with the Dead: Development of Afro-Latin Religion Among Puerto Ricans in the United States* (New York: AMS Press, 1991).

Roeder, Beatrice A. *Chicano Folk Medicine from Los Angeles, California* (Berkeley: University of California, 1988).

Trotter, Robert T., and Juan Antonio Chavira. *Curanderismo: Mexican American Folk Healing* (Athens: University of Georgia Press, 1997).

Wedel, Johan. *Santería Healing: A Journey into the Afro-Cuban World of Divinities, Spirits, and Sorcery* (Gainesville: University Press of Florida, 2004).

HERMENEUTICAL CIRCLE

The hermeneutical circle has become the focus of contemporary issues regarding interpretation of Scripture, especially as a methodology for theologies of liberation. It was initially used to describe the idea that any text must be understood as a whole by reference to its individual parts and also that each individual part must be understood by reference to the whole. The circle was to be found within the text and the tradition of which it was a part—its cultural, historical, and literary perspectives.

Later philosophers emphasized existential understanding, that is, the interplay between our self-understanding and our understanding of the world. Sometimes discussed as the fusion of horizons of the text and the interpreter, the focus is on the understanding the interpreter brings to the text from his/her perspective. At first, fusion of horizons included the concept that the perspective of text and interpreter, when brought together, would represent a fixed reality. Later, as critical philosophers of certain schools such as the Frankfurt school and post-structuralist philosophers questioned the idea of reality as fixed, the fusion of horizons was also viewed by some as the place where the interpreter was altered by the experience of the text, just as the text was altered by the interpreter's perspective.

Critics of some of the versions of hermeneutics challenged the idea that the text and interpreter could be altered without some mooring to a fixed reality. The theological emphasis is on the prophetic nature of the revelation made possible through the perspective of the interpreter and his/her lived experience. For Liberation Theologians, the emphasis is on those possibilities for liberation that the hermeneutical circle allows. For them, debates about the adequacy of the method used for interpretation of texts frame the debates about the meaning of liberation. Here lies the particular contribution of Hispanic American interpretation.

For liberation theologians, to do theology in a new way, a new method was also needed. Juan Luis Segundo, an Uruguayan Jesuit, is regarded as the first to articulate the need for rigor in the method of scriptural interpretation for the liberation movement. He synthesized the long-standing debates regarding interpretation in service of Liberation Theology. His insistence challenged the content of Latin American Liberation theology by its examination of interpretive method in reading the text.

For Segundo, the hermeneutical circle begins first with the interpreter's experience of reality, an experience that leads the interpreter to ideological suspicion —that is, a questioning of whether a view that permits persons to remain complacent in the face of human suffering is an adequate view of Scripture. Second, the interpreter takes his/her questions or suspicions, that is, the hermeneutical suspicions about interpretation, and applies them to scripture and understandings of theology as he/she knows them. Third, the combined new experience of lived reality and what must be the theological demand for justice brings the interpreter to a new perspective about the dominant interpretation that scripture or theological teachings must have left out. Liberation Theologians sometimes refer to this as the action of God in history because the interpreter is moved to some action as a result of this new understanding. Fourth, the interpreter creates a new interpretation consistent with his/her lived experience and the teachings of faith (Segundo 1976, 9).

This circle is open-ended and never-ending. It goes from self to text to self again, from lived experience of present history, including the action or *praxis*, inspired by reflection on the scripture and justice demands of theology, to past historical context. José Míguez Bonino describes this movement as one "between the text in its historicity and our own historical reading of it in obedience" (Míguez Bonino 1975: 102). Gustavo Gutiérrez describes the circle as

> from humanity to God and from God to humanity; from history to faith and from faith to history; from the human word to the word of the Lord and from the word of the Lord to the human word; from human love to the love of God and from the love of God to human love; from human justice to the holiness of God and from the holiness of God to human justice; from the poor to God and from God to the poor. (Gutiérrez 1977, 44)

The order in which the movement of the hermeneutical circle is described bears a relationship to the concern of the different theologians with assuring that some normative principles are present. For example, Bonino, Segundo, and others have been criticized because their movement permits violence in order to stop the suffering of some persons oppressed by others. Theologian Robert McAfee Brown cautions that the circle can be undermined by the following: (1) dehistoricizing the text so it becomes a "timeless truth" instead of a "timely perception"—thus permits complacency; (2) emphasis on the text's historical context to the extent that its contemporary impact is lost; (3) distortion of the text by reading in a contemporary historical situation anachronistically

(Brown 1978, 86). So he cautions that interpreters need to first, "keep alive back-and-forth tension between the text and ourselves, and second, to do so as communally as possible, since improbable individual interpretations can sometimes be corrected under the discipline of community judgment." Base Ecclesial Communities arose as the ritual way to realize this community judgment.

Ethicist Miguel De La Torre developed an ethical methodology for U.S. marginalized communities, especially Latina/os, based on the model of the hermeneutical circle. Moving beyond the traditional "seeing–judging–acting" circular framework, De La Torre expands the circle for the purpose of serving as a framework by which disenfranchised groups can engage in the doing of ethics. The first step in the hermeneutical circle De La Torre provides for ethics is observing. To observe is to conduct a historical analysis of the existing oppressive situation through the eyes of the disenfranchised to discover the causes of oppression. The next step is reflecting, which means applying whatever social analysis or critical theories can help provide insight as to the reasons for the existing oppressive structures. The third step is prayer. By prayer De La Torre means to communally apply theological and biblical principles for understanding the situation and discovering possible courses of action. The fourth step is to act, to implement praxis. The last and final step of the hermeneutical circle for ethics is reassessing. The new situation created by the praxis employed is observed, and thus begins again the circular progression.

Marta Vides Saade

References and Further Reading

Brown, Robert McAfee. *Theology in a New Key: Responding to Liberation Themes* (Louisville, KY: Westminster John Knox Press, 1978).

De La Torre, Miguel A. *Doing Christian Ethics from the Margins* (Maryknoll, NY: Orbis Books, 2004).

Gutiérrez, Gustavo. *Praxis of Liberation and Human Faith* (San Antonio: n.p., 1977).

Gutiérrez, Gustavo. *A Theology of Liberation: History, Politics, and Salvation—15th Anniversary Edition* (Maryknoll, NY: Orbis Books, 1994).

Míguez Bonino, José. *Revolutionary Theology Comes of Age* (London: S.P.C.K., University of Michigan, 1975).

Míguez Bonino, José. *Towards a Christian Political Ethics* (London: SCM, 1983).

Moylan, Tom. "Denunciation/Annunciation: The Radical Methodology of Liberation Theology." *Cultural Critique*, no. 20 (Winter 1991–1992): 33–64.

Schubeck, Thomas Louis, S.J. *Liberation Ethics: Sources, Models and Norms* (Minneapolis: Fortress Press, 1993).

Segundo, Juan Luis, S.J. *The Liberation of Theology* (Maryknoll, NY: Orbis Books, 1976).

HIP-HOP AND GRAFFITI

The seven elements of *deejaying* (playing records on turntables, cutting, scratching, sampling, etc.), *breaking* (b-boying, dancing), *emceeing* (rapping), *graffiti* (a form of inscription), *street knowledge*, *street fashion*, and *street entrepreneurialism* constitute hip-hop culture. These elements enable unique modes of expressions urban youth use to voice their life experiences. Religious imagery and themes appropriated in hip-hop culture add dimensions of depth to the search of meaning amidst the constant turmoil of inner-city life. The association of hip-hop culture with licentious lifestyles, misogynistic attitudes, drug use, and violence, expressed through rap lyrics, with vandalism and/ or turf gang markings of graffiti, obscure the existential force driving these arts. Beyond the glamorization of violence, licentiousness, or vandalism of private or public property, these arts express the challenges, vicissitudes, values, rituals, and hopes experienced by people, especially youth, living in urban centers often facing great odds.

Since the 1970s, Latino/as living in urban centers have made numerous contributions to the development of hip-hop culture. These contributions have gone unnoticed largely as a result of the racialization of these cultural and artistic performances as African American, thus relegating Latino/a rappers and graffiti artists to the margins, facing the pressure to adopt a Black identity. Recent attention to the role Latina/os play in the hip-hop culture promises to uncover their contributions to the development of this culture; specifically, an opportunity to assess the ways in which Latino/a religiosity has been appropriated by these art forms.

The significance of hip-hop and graffiti for the study of Hispanic religion is a complex one. Because of their content and their vehicles of expressions, these art forms blur the line between the secular and sacred through the indiscriminate inclusion of religious symbolism and ideas. The memorial aspects of graffiti murals offer a poignant example of how religious symbols are used in hip-hop culture. Through murals depicting the

deceased in poses reminiscent of saints, Christ, and other biblical images, but with the inclusion of personal items like jerseys and hats, graffiti murals sacralize the life of those deceased and place them in a sacred story of death and resurrection. The religious meaning of graffiti could be illuminated if compared to how *cuadros* and *retablos* function to express religious meaning and devotions.

Rapping as a form of musical expression may play a prophetic function within the Latino/a community. As a form of expression, rappers, through verbal sophistication and rhymes criticize the injustice they see in society with particular impact in urban settings and Latina/o daily living. Rappers often compare their words to prophetic speech that names the forces that oppress their community and speak words of the eventual defeat of the powerful. The rhymed construction of rap verses allows easy memorization potentially playing a didactic role much like evangelical *coritos* (praise songs) play a didactic role aiding scriptural memorization.

It is this blending of the secular with the religious in hip-hop culture that calls for sustained attention from the religious scholars. Hispanic religiosity's willingness to engage *lo popular* (the popular) could sustain the study of the ways in which the secular tone of hip-hop culture comes to be sacralized in the hands of their performers, and they serve as a mirror reflecting lives of our Latino/a inner-city community.

Elias Ortega-Aponte

References and Further Reading

Flores, Juan. *From Bomba to Hip-Hop: Puerto Rican Culture and Latino Identity*

(New York: Columbia University Press, 2000).

Laó-Montes, Agustín, ed. *Mambo Montage: The Latinization of New York* (New York: Columbia University Press, 2001).

Rivera, Raquel. *New York Ricans from the Hip-Hop Zone* (New York: Palgrave, 2003).

.

I

IDENTITY (LATINO/A VS. HISPANIC)

Any attempt to define the common identity of those grouped under the terms "Latina/o" or "Hispanic" raises a series of crucial issues. There are historical concerns related to how this group of people came into being, how they have sought to identify themselves, and how they became a part of the United States. There are political issues tied to the Hispanic experience, to race and ethnicity in the United States, and to how Latino/as should participate in broader U.S. society. There are questions related to the definition and popular use of the terms "Hispanic" and "Latino/a." All of these issues point to the complex process of identity formation among those who are called, or who call themselves, Latina/os or Hispanics.

Historically, the European conquest of what is now called Latin America sets the stage for the formation of a new people who carry in their veins the blood of the conquerors (Spanish or Portuguese), the conquered (native peoples), and those brought as slaves by the conquerors (Africans). Some of these peoples became a part of the United States because of the complex relationship between the United States and Latin America. Those called Hispanic or Latino/a are part of the United States because of the conquest of the Southwest (1848), the war with Spain (1898) that brought Puerto Rico and Cuba under U.S. influence or control, and the multiple twentieth-century political and economic interventions in Latin America. U.S. economic growth and influence in the region created and strengthened migratory labor patterns between the United States and Latin America, which resulted in changes in immigration laws in the United States, particularly in 1965 and 1986. Today's globalized economy has created new "pushes and pulls" in the region, broadening the circle of people who are migrating, temporarily or permanently, to the United States from Latin America.

LATINIDAD

Since the 1970s, Hispanic religious specialists have used "latinidad" in reference to their own Latino/a-ness. The term points to the cultural Latino/a essence out of which patterned expressions emerge as forms of life that are embodied, socially co-constructed, and transmitted in a given context. Thus latinidad is intrinsically tied to the understanding of cultural identity. What then is that Hispanic essence one is supposed to transmit? Latino/a religious specialists who subscribe to modern anthropology see latinidad as a concept that assumes that there is a universal core of unchanging characteristics that forms the essence of being Hispanic (e.g., language, land, race/ethnicity in correlation with religion). More recently, perspectives treat latinidad in relationship to cultural hybridity, which sees cultural matter as embodying historical-social consciousness but not fixating there, rather moving along to construct and negotiate meaning and identity as it encounters other distinct-cultural realities. Latinidad points to a style of engaging or a style of dancing with other cultural partners rather than a cultural essence. From this understanding, one can experience and express latinidad without being geographically connected to Latin America or speaking Spanish fluently but by being relationally connected with the Latin American consciousness, perhaps in the form of living as an exile or in a diaspora.

—OGJ

Before 1970 the various communities that today fall under the "Hispanic/Latino/a" umbrella in the United States self-identified based on their national heritage, i.e., Mexican, Puerto Rican, Cuban, or other. By 1970 many Mexican Americans adopted the term "Chicano" to differentiate between people from Mexico and those born and/or raised in the United States with historical links to Mexico and/or the pre-U.S. Southwest.

The year 1970 is important because the U.S. Census Bureau first used the term "Hispanic" in the census as an "umbrella" term for all of the peoples that had links to Spanish-speaking countries in Latin America. This decision raised many questions for those who were Hispanics. Some accepted the joint identity and began to point to the commonalities among Hispanics. For others the term was an outside imposition that

should be rejected. Some rejected it because they felt that they needed to name themselves, giving rise to the use of the term "Latino/a" as a self-identifier. Others rejected both terms and insisted that "Hispanic" (or "Latina/o") was an attempt to erase the national distinctions or the self-identifications that were developing (i.e., "I am Chicano, not Hispanic").

Both "Hispanic" and "Latino/a" are terms linked to the European conquest of the Americas and to the continuing European influence in the region. Both terms have been used to impose an identity, but both have also been part of the process of self-identification. This process recognizes a common history among Hispanics and Latino/as, but also seeks to address current issues. Both terms have a history that is both acceptable and questioned. Part of that history goes

TEJANO/AS

"Tejano" is the Spanish translation of Texan, one who is from the state of Texas. Different Tejanos, however, have different interpretations of what it means to be Tejano or Tejana. Tejanos are Hispanics born and raised in Texas. Some Tejana/o families have been in Texas prior to the arrival of the Europeans. Others came with the Spanish conquest. Other families migrated to Texas when it was still a part of Mexico, and still other Tejano/as are recent arrivals from various Hispanic countries. In any case, Tejana/os distinguish themselves from their non-Hispanic counterparts, the Texans. In 1835–1836 both Tejana/os and Texans fought for Independence from Mexico. Yet by 1845 the Tejano/as felt betrayed by the Texans when Texas was annexed by the United States. As a result the Tejano/a has a history of being doubly conquered, first by Spain and then by the United States. The Tejano is also a product of a double mestizaje (mixture): the Spanish-Native mestizaje and a cultural mestizaje that produces a variety of Tejano/as from the Chicano to the Mexican American to the Latina/o agringado. Tejana/os have their own variety of Mexican food and music, giving both their own Tejano/a flavor.

—*GCG*

back to 1492; others are tied to 1848 or to the U.S. Census Bureau decision to begin using the term "Hispanic" in 1970. The terms "Hispanic" and "Latino/a" are also tied to issues of immigration, the role of Spanish in the United States, and assimilation. These words are often connected with political preferences. Without an understanding of this complex set of issues, it becomes impossible to decide whether Latina/o or Hispanic best identifies the community or if neither of these terms is adequate to the task.

Over the last few years Latino/as have struggled with the issue of identity formation and the specific reasons for using either "Hispanic" or "Latino/a." Most published documents focus on the process of identity formation and touch on the specific issue of which term to use as part of their larger discussion. In *Hispanic Nation Culture, Politics, and the Construction of Identity* Geoffrey Fox argues for "Hispanic." He sees it as the less confrontational term, one favored by the "right" market-oriented wing of the broader pan-Hispanic movement. It is politically and racially neutral. From Fox's perspective, "Latina/o" is a more confrontational term used by the "left" as a challenge to the dominant U.S. cultural structure. "Latino/a" also offends some Hispanics because it seems like a bad dialect joke, because it is not "real" Spanish, nor "real" English.

David Abalos, in *Latinos in the United States: The Sacred and the Political*, advocates for "Latino/a" because "Hispanic" has been tied to the elitist preference for those with lighter skin, those who can demonstrate "pure" European blood. Latina/o is a broader term that recognizes the movement of peoples and the intermarriage between those of many different cultural and ethnic backgrounds (*mestizaje*) in the formation of those called Latino/as. From his perspective "Latina/o" also represents a growing political consciousness that has evolved from individual national identities to

Hispanic, and now to Latina/o. They were named by the Census Bureau in 1970, but now they are seeking to name themselves in a way that recognizes that they are not just descendants of White Europeans (Hispanics), but also of peoples of indigenous and African descent, and of peoples who have migrated to Latin America from other parts of the world.

Writers such as Arlene Dávila in *Latinos Inc.: The Marketing and Making of a People* and Juan González in *Harvest of Empire a History of Latinos in America*, use Latino in the title of their books, though both treat Latino/a and Hispanic as interchangeable. They wonder whether too much energy is being used in trying to define one term as better than the other. Ilan Stavans has used both in the titles of books he has written, *The Hispanic Condition* and *Latino USA: A Cartoon History*. Ed Morales in *Living in Spanglish: The Search for Latino Identity in America* prefers "Latino/a" over "Hispanic" because the latter is tied to assimilationists and the former to the reality of the mixed race heritage of Latino/as. His concern is that Latina/o is a static term and that the community needs a term that describes the dynamic linguistic, cultural, and "racial" movement that is the Latino/a community. He proposes Spanglish as the term that captures that movement.

Jorge Gracia has written a complete work on the subject. *Hispanic/Latino Identity: A Philosophical Perspective* approaches the question by defining the terms in their historical contexts. Gracia draws from the historical usage of each term and from the philosophical issues related to the efforts to develop a common identity among the peoples of Latin America. He addresses the larger processes of identity formation on the Iberian Peninsula, in Latin America, and among Hispanics in the United States. He sees these three efforts as intertwined because of common Spanish historical legacy, be it good or bad. Given this frame of reference, Gracia concludes that "Hispanic" is the appropriate term that unites each of these groups, which in fact share a common history and legacy.

Gracia himself acknowledges some people will tend to reject the term "Hispanic," in part, because of the historical "baggage" it carries. "Hispanic" is clearly representative of the Spanish conquest. Therefore, a different term, linked only to the American experience, should be used. "Latino/a" seems appropriate, except for the fact that it is also a term imposed by a European imperial power. France began talking about *Amerique Latine* during the rule of Napoleon III as a way of distinguishing between those areas of the Americas originally colonized by Europeans of Latin descent and those colonized by peoples from northern Europe. But the term was used to justify French intervention in the young republics of Latin America. Even though Latino/a refers to the American continent, its original referent is the "Latin" parts of Europe, not the Americas. Therefore, it is also a term that comes out of the conquest, though it is not as directly tied to Spain.

All of the authors mentioned point to the struggles faced in the process of Latino/a identity formation. Those under the Latino/a or Hispanic "umbrella" recognize a great amount of commonality, but find it difficult to decide which aspects of identity are most crucial. There are very real differences that further complicate any attempt to define this group as a homogeneous whole.

"Hispanic" places more of the emphasis on Spanish history. Latina/os began to exist as a people after the arrival of the Spaniards in the Americas and most of them now speak Spanish, or have ancestors who spoke Spanish. It is also true that some members of the community are relatively recent immigrants from Spain or are descendants of people who have not intermarried with native peoples or those of African background. "Hispanic" is also usually identified with those in the community who assume that they should seek to assimilate into U.S. society. Yet the fact that members of the community use "Hispanic" is recognition that there are things that differentiate them from others and commonalities that unite them, and these things deserve to be named and defined.

"Latino/a" is usually linked to more activist members of the community. Those who call themselves "Latina/o" feel that the community needs to name itself. This term clearly links the community to Latin America and, only indirectly, to Spain. Because "Latina/o" is most commonly linked to Latin America, and not the Latin regions of Europe, it seems better suited to identify the racial and ethnic mixes forged in the five centuries since the Europeans arrived in the Americas. Also, since the term as it is used today becomes a mixture of English and Spanish, it is uniquely "equipped" to define the bilingual, and multicultural U.S. Latino/a population.

Those who use either or both terms must recognize when they use them, they pick and choose their meanings. As they use "Latino/a" or "Hispanic" they often choose to downplay or ignore that both words carry the realities of European imperialism and a history of imposition. Each of these words carries a very negative connotation for some members of the community. Nonetheless, those negative realities are a crucial part of their formation as a people. Both terms have histories and implications for the present and the future.

As those who were named by U.S. government structures, they need to understand that their "naming" occurred within the larger issue of "race" in the United States. As they continued to form their own identity, they needed to recognize the role that ethnicity played in the question of the "American" identity and how ethnic minorities related and connected to each other pertaining to questions of assimilation and cultural pluralism.

Because neither "Hispanic" nor "Latino/a" is a racial term, they are caught within the larger U.S. race question. Should they define their experience more like "European Whites" or more like African Americans? Because of their various backgrounds, some of them fit into one category more than in the other. Many more seem to be in a status somewhere between the U.S. definitions of "White" and "Black," which makes it difficult to clearly "fit" within either category.

Hispanic ethnicity also raises the question of which model of cultural interaction they should follow in this country. Both those who call themselves Hispanic or Latina/o and take the time to defend these identity markers seem to point to a clearly identifiable group identity. But how should this ethnic minority group interact with the majority and with other ethnic minorities?

Those who strongly insist on using one term or the other usually have a clearly defined vision of the community and its future. That choice is an ideological decision, but is not one that can easily unite Hispanics. It is a sign of the strength of the Hispanic community that it can continue developing its identity without a name common to all.

Some argue for the use of Latino/Hispanic (or Hispanic/Latino) or the interchangeable use of both as a way forward. The goal of this usage is to focus on what unites the community, instead of on the differences. It is yet to be seen whether enough people will use the terms in this way or whether the exclusive uses are an inevitable part of the identity formation process.

Others will continue to argue for new terms as a way to move into the future. Given the polycentric identities that most Latino/as carry, it is unlikely that one term will ever satisfy everyone. Yet as they seek to identify themselves, they need the voices of all those who see themselves as a part of the community. This process could lead in many different directions. It may be possible, to some extent, to arrive at a common term or a combination of terms they all accept.

The process could lead Hispanics to conclude that one single term cannot identify all of them. Latino/a understanding of their histories and visions of the future might be so different that other terms will be chosen to focus on their differences. Hispanics might conclude that their identity is so complex that they need several terms to describe the various aspects of their common identity. In all likelihood identity formation will be part of a continuing conversation in which various members of the community participate at different levels, even as their identities continue to be reshaped by their new ethnic and cultural interactions in the globalized intercultural reality of the United States.

Juan Francisco Martinez

References and Further Reading

Abalos, David. *Latinos in the United States: The Sacred and the Political* (South Bend, IN: University of Notre Dame Press, 2007).

Dávila, Arlene. *Latinos Inc.: The Marketing and Making of a People* (Berkeley: University of California Press, 2001).

Fox, Geoffrey. *Hispanic Nation: Culture, Politics, and the Construction of Identity* (Tucson: University of Arizona Press, 1996).

González, Juan. *Harvest of Empire: A History of Latinos in America* (New York: Viking Press, 2001).

Gracia, Jorge. *Hispanic/Latino Identity: A Philosophical Perspective* (Boston: Blackwell Publishers, 2000).

Morales, Ed. *Living in Spanglish: The Search for Latino Identity in America* (Los Angelos, CA: Weekly Books, 2002).

Stavans, Ilan. *Hispanic Condition: The Power of a People* (New York: Harper Perennial, 2001).

Stavans, Ilan, and Lalo Alcaraz. *Latino USA: A Cartoon History* (New York: Basic Books, 2000).

IMMIGRATION

As social institutions, communities of faith serve preserving, integrative, and bridge-building roles vis-à-vis new and recent immigrants to the United States. Religious groups function as safe places that foster the preservation and expression of immigrants' religious traditions and practices from their countries of origin and in their own languages. Rites of passage, such as *quinceañeras* and presentation of children, or dramas, such as *posadas* and passion stories, are examples of Hispanic religious cultures that are safeguarded and passed on from one generation of immigrants to the next through church networks. Religious groups also aid immigrants to navigate through, survive, and advance in the new cultural, political, and economic climate of the adoptive nation. Through English as a Second Language (ESL) classes, immigration law services, job information, and educational opportunities, houses of worship play a public role in the transition and/or integration of immigrants into U.S. society.

Although contemporary voices increasingly speak of the role of religion in fostering a two-way bridge between immigrant and nonimmigrant groups where cultural exchange and networking leads to mutual learning, transformation, and enrichment, the language of integration from a historical perspective has been interpreted through a narrative of assimilation. In U.S. religious historiography, Daisy Machado has shown that the almost forgotten history of Mexican internal migration and dispersion in the Southwest through U.S. expansionist wars and treaties went hand in hand with the geographical and social marginalization of Mexicans but also with an Anglo Protestant missionary policy of assimilation of Mexicans through "Americanization." The Anglos' attitude of cultural and racial superiority vis-à-vis Mexicans, along with their religious self-understanding as a nation favored by God through the eschatological and political language of "manifest destiny," made Mexicans "strangers in their own lands" and also resulted in what is today a Mexican church with a "dearth of ministerial leadership, poor funding, and haphazard and uneven growth."

Immigration provides a lens for understanding and negotiating Hispanic American social location and identity in terms of resistance and engagement. Cuban American biblical and cultural critic Fernando Segovia has advanced the term "exile" as a category in U.S. Hispanic American theology to describe the social location of "otherness" immigrants experience in the adoptive nation. Although the word "exile" can be applied metaphorically to peoples colonized by the United States (i.e., Mexicans and Puerto Ricans) or minoritized by U.S. mainstream society (i.e., Latinos/as born in the United States), Segovia reserves the literal use for first-generation immigrants whose "diaspora" identity is one of "living in two worlds and no world at the same time." Instead of reading the Hispanic American experience of diaspora as an "allegorical antitype" of biblical themes such as the pilgrim people of God or the wandering followers of Jesus, the task of a "diaspora theology" demands unpacking what it means to be "in the world but not of it" through an ongoing deconstruction and construction regarding the world, the otherworld, and human-divine relations. Accordingly, diaspora theology can see the world as unjust but also as a potentially more just place; it sees the otherworld as bringing into question God's justice in the face of suffering, but without losing confidence that God hears and delivers the marginalized; therefore, a diasporic social location allows one to see divine-human relations in terms of the paradoxical character of the human religious experience of God as absence/presence, uncertainty/certainty, and limitation/power.

The experiences of marginality and questions of identity that immigrants face in a new nation, as well as the oppressive political conditions and socioeconomic factors that force them to

Our Lady of Guadalupe Parish, Salt Lake City, Utah, 1940s. (Utah History Research Center)

migrate in the first place, have shaped reflection on what it means to be a church in the United States. In the vein of cultural criticism, Professor of modern language Mark Griffin and Episcopal pastor Theron Walker use Richard Rodríguez's arguments in favor of the privatization of Latino cultures and their assimilation into a homogeneous or public U.S. "melting pot" as a metaphor and blueprint for the North American Christian church's caution against the increasing privatization of their faith and assimilation into "a uniform national culture in which communal traditions are exchanged for consumer choices." In contrast to ethnic immigrants' and churches' capitulations, respectively, to the U.S. melting pot and consumerist culture, the authors point to some Miami Cuban American discourses that propose "hyphenated identities." Yet these hybrid identities, in a sort of convenience arrangement, can lead to a withdrawal of the immigrant to ancestral ethnic roots (or "ghettoization") while paradoxically retaining consumerist values. Taking as a model Mexican American theologian Virgilio Elizondo's identification of Mexican Americans with Jesus' Galilean borderlands location, Griffin and Walker argue that the Christian church in the United States should become instead a "rooted diaspora" or "borderlands culture." Such an identity allows the church to best bridge the space between a merely privatized faith and an unacceptable absorption into the McWorld by taking up her prophetic denunciation of the hegemonic consumerism of U.S. society while doing so from a nonhegemonic stance as a "resident alien" church, which is never quite at home with the state of this world.

From a liberationist perspective informed in part by Jesuit theologian Jon Sobrino's ecclesiology, Harold Recinos reflects upon the painful experience and memory of Salvadoran refugees as "crucified peoples" and argues that their marginalized presence in the U.S. barrio serves as a locus from which the church can be reborn to become a vehicle for socioeconomic liberation. Traditional images of Christ as one who consoles those who suffer and as one who saves from sin and death justify models of being church that are only concerned with individual faith and personal salvation. A robust concern for the church's denunciation of the unjust social order and its transformation through bonds of fellowship arises out of insignificant places of divine revelation such as Israel and Galilee where God takes the side of the poor and from which God calls for a new social order. Recinos argues that, as a barrio people, Salvadoran Christians (and others like them) are in a divinely favored social location to lead the whole church in a rebirth so that her faith might rediscover or reacquaint itself with "the liberating historical consciousness it lacked." Through their active memory of Salvadoran "social martyrs"—their "religion of martyrology"—and its accompanying "ritualized symbols" such as Archbishop Oscar Romero, Jesuit priests, and the thousands of peoples killed during the civil wars in El Salvador, the barrio people can contribute to a "new church" characterized by a bond of solidarity with the poor, a prophetic and sacrificial love that unmasks oppressive social structures, and a responsible faith that leads to social transformation.

Orlando Espín looks at the global experience of immigration as a fundamental dogmatic category for the elaboration of a constructive contemporary Catholic ecclesiology. Taking as his point of departure the inescapable permeability of geographical political borders in an era of globalization characterized by the deterritorialization of capital, open labor markets, and the free exchange of goods, cultures, and ideas across borders, Espín argues that the church's "catholicity" can serve a prophetic role both in her affirmation and critique of globalization as a driving factor in the migration of peoples. Insofar as the labor and training demands of globalization create poverty and unjust social relations, catholicity upholds the God-given dignity and equality of humans who are excluded. When deterritorialization in a globalized economy homogenizes diverse peoples and cultures into a uniform market culture, catholicity affirms the value of all human cultures and envisions borders as social spaces of "exchange and encounter" where no culture is superior to the other and all can bear witness to the Gospel. The semantic field of the Nahuatl (Aztec) word *nepantlah* (literally, "in the middle"), with its connotations of "mutuality" and "reciprocity," serves to complement the language of catholicity with a more robust "welcoming" and "dialogical" orientation akin to the Hebrew Scriptures' call to welcome the stranger (alien or immigrant), the New Testament's witness to the love of the neediest neighbor "regardless of his/her virtues or lack thereof," and Catholic social teaching on the God-given moral right of people to migrate to take care of their needy families. Immigrants are suggestively portrayed as the privileged "sacrament" of the church's catholicity today through which God gives all Christians access to their catholic identity and, therefore, to what it means to be a pilgrim (migrant) church that is always on the move in this world and puts into question the world's ultimate claims.

In the area of textual studies, strategies for engaging in conversation on immigration from a biblical-theological framework or for reading biblical texts from an immigrant location and hermeneutical stance have been proposed. Biblical scholar Daniel Carroll R. shows that the Old Testament's teachings on the image of God in humans and on God's call for Israel to show openness to sojourners provide a biblical basis for a compassionate Christian attitude toward all immigrants. Although there is a diverse complexity and ambiguity in Old Testament texts dealing with sojourners or aliens, which requires an understanding of these texts' religious and sociological functions, biblical scholar Luis Rivera Rodríguez argues that through a "political hermeneutics" a number of Deuteronomist "values" can be gathered to affirm "the struggles and aspirations for justice and human rights of migrant workers around the world and in the U.S.A." Such values include judging rightly between peoples and giving a fair hearing to both citizen and resident aliens in the community, as well as refraining from depriving the resident alien of justice or from withholding fair wages from poor migrant workers. God calls Israel to love the stranger because they too were strangers in Egypt and curses those who oppress the alien, the orphan, and the widow. Carroll R. gathers from the ministry of Jesus—especially his unusually inclusive treatment of the Samaritan woman for a Jew of his time—an ethic of "compassion toward the outsider" for the church. There is a warning against uncritical

readings of Romans 13 (on submission to government authorities) that do not recognize the need and right to change laws that Christians believe might not deal fairly with their immigrant neighbors.

In the field of reader-oriented text criticism, and applying a hermeneutics of suspicion to the idea of an unbiased or neutral reader or text, Fernando Segovia calls for a "hermeneutics of the Diaspora" that takes seriously the immigrant bicultural location or "double otherness" of Hispanic American readers as they engage biblical texts. Although diaspora peoples fit neither in their country of origin nor in their adoptive one, and consequently are deprived of "self-definition," "self-appropriation," and "self-direction," they also inhabit a space of hybridity or *mezcolanza* ("hodgepodge") that enables them to be critical of both worlds and engage constructively their cultures, traditions, and values. A hermeneutics of "otherness" assumes an intercultural reading of texts that recognizes the need for readers not only to see themselves as "other" but also to distance themselves from the text in order to let it speak as "other" according to its own contexts and agendas. In the process, such hermeneutics becomes one of self-reflective "engagement" in which readers see themselves honestly as living texts who bring their own cultural matrixes into the biblical text even as they are shaped by it. An intercultural "filtering" or construction of reality moving back and forth from reader to text and vice versa fosters liberating dialogue with other interpreters of texts and openness to critical evaluations of readings. The goal of a hermeneutics of the diaspora that arises out of a Hispanic immigrant social location is to trade

SAN TORIBIO

In 2000, Pope John Paul II canonized Toribio Romo Gonzalez, a priest who was martyred by Mexican federal troops during the Cristero Wars. He was born on April 16, 1900, in Santa Ana de Guadalupe in the region of Jalisco. He was ordained a priest with a dispensation in 1921 because of his young age. During the uprising against Mexico's anti-Catholic government, he hid at a ranch, saying the Mass for local peasants. He was known for his sensitivity toward the poor. Betrayed by an informer, he was shot in the back on February 25, 1928. Since canonization, some immigrants crossing the Sonoran Desert to get to the United States have claimed that San Toribio has appeared to them, guiding their journey north. As a result, the Shrine of Saint Toribio, in Santa Ana de Guadalupe, draws many pilgrims from throughout Mexico who are preparing to make the hazardous crossing into the United States and are in need of spiritual protection. He has quickly become the patron saint of immigrants. In response to some of the harshest anti-immigrant laws in the nation, a second shrine is being built for him in Tulsa, Oklahoma, and is expected to be finished by 2009.

—*MAD*

oppressive universalizing metanarratives for "a manifest destiny of liberation and decolonization," which is characterized by a radical "contextualization" of all readers and texts that acknowledges their otherness and the possibility of their dialogical engagement with one another.

Immigration and immigrants call for a rethinking of approaches to pastoral theology (and praxis) and religious pedagogy. Catholic pastoral theologian Carmen Nanko-Fernández argues that immigrants challenge the church to think of its ministry as a form of "prophetic invitation" that fosters solidarity with immigrants by recovering the stories of their struggles. Typically such stories are either forgotten through a prevailing U.S. historical amnesia regarding its immigrant past or romanticized through cultural assimilation into the U.S. mainstream. The "prophetic invitation" also promotes solidarity with immigrants by bringing the U.S. mainstream church closer to the "edge" through exposure to the often unknown social teachings of

the Catholic church on the rights of migrants. Politicized rhetoric used commonly to refer to migrants as "aliens" or "illegals," as well as spiritualized or allegorical language used at times to speak of migration across borders as "passion/resurrection narratives," must undergo a process of humanization that bestows dignity upon migrants and does not relativize their concrete flesh-and-blood struggles. Drawing upon her teaching experience in Bible institutes serving immigrant populations, Elizabeth Conde-Frazier argues for a "culturally responsible" pedagogy that fosters partnerships between teacher and student through learning strategies of "intuitive reflection" that ultimately lead to concrete action in the interest of social justice. Religious education shaped after the immigrant experience of survival and invisibility in a new location should lead to collaborative and dialogical models of teaching and learning where participants think in a "conjunctive" way and are not mere receivers of knowledge but a living "theological resource." These pedagogical goals are mediated through an intentional process of critical appropriation of theological traditions in which the teacher serves as a facilitator of knowledge more than as "the interpreter or keeper of the doctrine or the tradition." Conde-Frazier's theological pedagogy as "an open-ended dialogical" process in which the Spirit always leads into all truth and as an emerging product of the community are, respectively, the pneumatological and epistemological underpinnings of her proposal. As loci of poverty and marginality, immigrant communities also bring to the classroom their suffering as a "hermeneutical insight" that challenges facilitators to allow participants not only to speak of the spiritual dimensions of their journeys but also of their sociopolitical dimensions. Drawing from Puerto-Rican theologian Samuel Solivan's language of *orthopathos* (right suffering), Conde-Frazier conceives religious education as the integration of critically appropriated theological knowledge or tradition that flows out especially from concrete suffering in life (*orthopathos*) and leads to concrete pastoral action in the interest of social transformation (*orthopraxis*).

Immigration promises a reshaping of the field of religious studies. Religion scholar Manuel Vásquez has argued that the diversity and fast growth of post-1965 migration to the United States has moved the study of religion from its privileged methodological foci on the hermeneutics of sacred texts and phenomenology of interiority (and subjectivity) toward a more historical and material approach that accounts fully for the social, political, economic, architectural, and technological aspects of "lived religion" as a legitimate source of religion. The study of post-1965 migration in the broader context of globalization and transnational networks where spaces across geographical borders are hyperfluid, cross-pollinated, reconfigured, and reimagined (also known as "de-territorialization" and "re-territorialization"), puts into question the field's assumptions supporting the denial of the "coevalness" (or common sharing of space and time) of immigrant societies of origin vis-à-vis the United States. A denial of coevalness supports disjunctive space discourses of margins versus center, readings of religion through a hermeneutics of impermeable "difference" from the "other," studies of religion that only see the religious in congregational structures but not outside of them, or one-size-fits-all or universalizing definitions of "religion." In contrast to these options, migration studies in a globalized world necessitate a thorough rehistoricizing and rematerializing of the traditional Eurocentric hermeneutical and phenomenological emphases in religion studies. This refocusing moves religious discourse toward a hermeneutics of "hybridity" ("border-crossing" and "transculturality") and a focus on lived religion in and outside of congregational networks.

Leopoldo A. Sánchez M.

References and Further Reading

Carroll R., M. Daniel. *Christians at the Border: Immigration, the Church, and the Bible* (Grand Rapids, MI: Baker, 2008).

Conde-Frazier, Elizabeth. "Religious Education in an Immigrant Community: A Case

Study." *Hispanic Christian Thought at the Dawn of the 21st Century: Apuntes in Honor of Justo L. González*, ed. Alvin Padilla, Roberto Goizueta, and Eldin Villafañe (Nashville: Abingdon, 2005).

De La Torre, Miguel. *Trails of Hope and Terror: Testimonies on Immigration* (Maryknoll, NY: Orbis Books, 2009).

Espín, Orlando O. "Immigration, Territory, and Globalization: Theological Reflections." *Journal of Hispanic/Latino Theology* 7, no. 3 (2000): 46–59.

Griffin, Mark, and Theron Walker. *Living on the Borders: What the Church Can Learn from Ethnic Immigrant Cultures* (Grand Rapids, MI: Brazos, 2004).

Machado, Daisy L. "Kingdom Building in the Borderlands: The Church and Manifest Destiny." *Hispanic/Latino Theology: Challenge and Promise*, ed. Ada María Isasi-Díaz and Fernando F. Segovia (Minneapolis: Fortress, 1996).

Nanko-Fernández, Carmen M. "Beyond Hospitality: Implications of Im/migration for Teología y Pastoral de Conjunto." *Perspectivas* 10 (2006): 51–62.

Recinos, Harold J. "The Barrio as the Locus of a New Church." *Hispanic/Latino Theology: Challenge and Promise*, ed. Ada María Isasi-Díaz and Fernando F. Segovia (Minneapolis: Fortress, 1996).

Rivera Rodríguez, Luis R. "Immigration and the Bible: Comments by a Diasporic Theologian." *Perspectivas* 10 (2006): 23–36.

Segovia, Fernando F. "In the World but Not of It: Exile as Locus for a Theology of the Diaspora." *Hispanic/Latino Theology: Challenge and Promise*, ed. Ada María Isasi-Díaz and Fernando F. Segovia (Minneapolis: Fortress, 1996).

Vásquez, Manuel A. "Historicizing and Materializing the Study of Religion: The Contribution of Migration Studies." *Immigrant Faiths: Transforming Religious Life in America*, ed. Karen I. Leonard, Alex Stepick, and Manuel A. Vásquez (Landham, MD: Altamira, 2005).

INSTITUTIONALIZED VIOLENCE

In recent decades Christian ethics has moved from an individualistic framework that emphasizes the subjective aspects of ethical problems to a social and political framework that stresses the institutional and collective aspects. Because of new theories related to socialization, the role of cultural expectations in the formation of the individual, gender and feminist theories, and ecological awareness—just to name a few—Christian ethics has moved from an individual realm to a social, cultural, and political one. This new understanding of human relations maintains that every individual is born within a social, communal, cultural, racial, familial, ecological, and sociopolitical environment to which he or she interacts and relates. What the individual does as a person relates closely to his or her surroundings and thus no action can be taken as isolated or detached from its context and reality.

This move from an individualistic to a communal ethics has emphasized the social as well as the personal dimensions of violence. Christian movements such as liberation theologies, feminists, environmentalists, and Latino/a theology in the United States are calling for both a change of hearts and minds of individuals and a transformation of the socioeconomic, cultural, and institutionalized causes of violence. They contend that the daily experience of violence in many societies, which affects their most vulnerable members, is closely related to the reality of socioeconomic injustice, ecological destruction, militarization of society, uneven distribution of wealth, poor access to education and health, poverty, unemployment, racism, gender inequality, and global economic policies that benefit only a small portion of the world's population. For all these reasons, they have approached violence both from the personal dimension as well as from socioeconomic and political dimension. They are criticizing and taking a stand not only against the persons committing violence, but also against the society and socioeconomic system that drive them to recurring violence.

The Medellín Conference

The Latin American Bishops Conference (CELAM) meeting in Medellín, Colombia, in 1968, made evident this shift in Christian theology for Latin America. While the conference was exclusively Catholic, its contribution to the debate on violence reached beyond Catholic theology. In its section on peace, the Medellín Conference recognized that violence is one of the gravest problems in the region. After reaffirming the church's commitment to peace, the document acknowledged that many regions in Latin America lived under a situation of institutionalized violence, created by agricultural and industrial business, national and international economic enterprises, and political and cultural domination. The Conference affirmed that as a result of this institutionalized violence entire populations lacked the basic human necessities and lived in a condition of dependency that impeded their social, cultural, and political participation, thus violating their most fundamental human rights. For this reason, the document maintained that underdevelopment and its sequels of marginalization, socioeconomic inequality,

oppression, armamentism, and neocolonial relations between poor and rich countries, was an unjust situation that conspired against peaceful alternatives.

For the Medellín Conference, this situation of institutionalized violence required urgent and audacious transformations. The Conference demanded from wealthy elites to accept and lead profound and necessary socioeconomic transformations in order to avoid violent revolutions and confrontations. It also called for peaceful resistance and citizen activism among the poor and the dispossessed. Finally, it reminded revolutionary groups that turning to violence created new injustices, engendered new inequalities, and economically ruined poor countries.

The Medellín Conference has transformed the ethical and theological approach to the phenomenon of violence on many fronts. First, it shifted the emphasis from an individual and subjective framework to a collective and social one. Violence in the household and in communities is related to violence perpetrated by corporations, governments, and global military agencies as they create social dislocation with their meager wages, reinforce the climate of social inequality and corruption in a nation, and set in motion cycles of violence by providing weapons to governments and belligerent groups.

Second, the Medellín Conference identified violence not as an isolated and random phenomenon but as part of a cycle. This cycle originates in the institutions and structures of society that, although operating in a legal framework, maintain an unjust order that creates the conditions for social dislocation and human alienation. In response, citizens recur to both social and political violence in the forms of crime, theft, gangs, guerrilla warfare, terrorist groups, domestic violence, and so forth, thus feeding the cycle of violence originating in these institutions.

Third, the Medellín Conference connected violence with injustice, stressing that peaceful societies are possible only when based on justice and equality. For this reason it stressed not only a change of hearts and minds of individuals, but also of institutions and structures that promote unjust relationships in society. Closely connected to this is its call for the political activism of religious groups to transform the sociopolitical and economics structure of society. The Conference sees as positive the religious involvement in political and economic actions in favor of the socially excluded such as education, political organization, citizen advocacy, peaceful and nonviolent protests, and socioeconomic alternatives.

Subsequent theological debates related to violence have approached this phenomenon utilizing the conceptual framework provided by Medellín, thus denouncing the personal as well as the institutional and structural dimension of the problem. The Puebla Conference of 1979 maintained that the violence in the region was generated and fomented by both the institutionalized violence of socioeconomic and political systems and the ideologies that utilize violence as a way of conquering power. The Santo Domingo Conference of 1992 denounced violence against children, women, and the poorest communities in the region: peasants, indigenous, and Afro-Americans. It also warned of a rising culture of death and violence that reaches families and societies through the media and television.

In the United States, Latina/o theologians have utilized the Medellín approach and have stressed institutional, racial, gender, and cultural aspects of the phenomenon. They have denounced racist discourses that promote violence against people of color, machista and male-chauvinistic practices that assume and promote male domination over women, and economic policies that affect the development of the poor and disposed within and outside the United States' border. They have also maintained a critical stand against the imperial, militaristic, and neocolonial practices of U.S. policies, and have critically engaged in solidarity with oppressed communities from around the world. In all, U.S. Latino/a theologies have criticized the racist history of violence in the United States while denouncing the neocolonial violent practices in American policies.

Defining Institutionalized Violence

Institutional violence is violence that is created, supported, and rooted in institutions and powerful groups to maintain an unequal, unjust, and repressive sociopolitical order that blocks the human development of its citizens, especially those considered as inferior, anormal, or threatening to the given order. Institutional violence is more than the inadequate distribution of a country's or community's resources. It presupposes an organization, justification, and normalization of unjust socioeconomic relationships in a given society through a legal and cultural framework that supports the mechanisms of justice and establishes a coercive force to maintain an unjust established order. This form of violence is maintained through a repressive framework that justifies its existence and incorporates its premises into the cultural, educational, and daily experiences of a given society. In this way, the system justifies the cycle of violence protecting the structures and the social groups that most benefit from it.

Four venues to understand institutionalized violence are the following.

(1) *Institutionalized violence and socioeconomic structures.* It is important to take into account socioeconomic structures and political systems when approaching the issue of violence. Sociopolitical and economic structures are violent when they selectively fulfill the human necessities of a given group of citizens at the expense of the majority of the population. When this occurs, the state becomes the original generator of violence in a given society, as it blocks its citizens from obtaining the basic social programs and political exercises to guarantee the fulfillment of their basic human necessities such as health, education, security, and employment. The sequels of violence in forms of petty crime, domestic violence, gangs, arms groups, violation of the basic laws, and other phenomena common in many areas of the world mirror an economic system that impedes the human development of the majority of its citizens and that often represses them when they claim constitutional and human rights.

(2) *Institutionalized violence and culture.* When approaching the phenomenon of violence, one must take into account its cultural aspects, as culture provides the material, spiritual, and intellectual elements of identity of a given society. Institutional violence has the danger of being transformed into a culture of

violence when society promotes values and attitudes that allow, empower, and even stimulate the use of violence as part of its cultural, material, and spiritual identity. When this occurs, societies celebrate and accept openly the use of violence to solve their daily conflicts and to provide a way of relating to themselves and to others. As a result, violence becomes a code of conduct that allows them to explain and make sense of their daily reality. More than a way of acting or a phenomenon, violence becomes a cultural point of reference that validates citizen's personal and social existence.

(3) *Institutionalized violence and history.* Institutional violence is in many ways the result of historical violence, for it is built upon historical dynamics of power exercised through its use. When violence has become part of the historical making of a given society, then that society's historical identity and institutions are violent. When approaching a violent phenomenon in a given society, it is important to study its historical roots as well as the historic dynamics that created and sustained it in the first place.

(4) *The role of ideologies and institutionalized violence.* Societies and human groups create ideological discourses that offer coherent explanations through concepts, symbols, images, and references necessary for the survival and organization of human groups. If culture gives humans a sense of belonging, ideologies provide them with the rational tools to explain their actions and behaviors. Yet many times ideologies are utilized to cover up group interests and particular policies, aiming toward benefiting a few and disregarding the well-being of the rest of society. When this occurs, social phenomena such as poverty, crime,

and human rights violations can be covered up by the subjective message of ideological discourses defending the status quo.

It is important to stress that societies with high levels of crime tend to utilize ideologies to defend and make sense of their situation. Violence, including non-institutionalized violence, is part of a social structure configured by social, economic, and political interests that builds upon ideological discourses to justify its existence. Many times these ideologies legitimize the use of force as a way to defend and maintain the position of powerful groups in society. These groups construct ideological discourses that dehumanize and almost bestialize the criminal and the outlaw, while avoiding any exploration of the socioeconomic, political, cultural, and environmental conditions that allow people to commit crime. Central American–based gang members in large U.S. cities, to cite an example, are blamed for most of the crime in the region, while the government ignores the conditions of poverty and cultural alienation these youths experience. Likewise, violence against suspected terrorists in the form of torture, annihilation, selective killings, and illegal detentions, in the United States and abroad, are often framed within discourses that defend these actions as necessary for the survival of the community or the interest of a given country.

Blind Spots of Institutional Violence

While the institutional approach to violence has contributed greatly to the interpretation of this phenomenon, the premises upon which this is built present some limitations. First, this approach relies on a socioeconomic and political analysis that is informed and built upon Marxist and post-Marxist theories. In this understanding, violence is the reflection of unjust economic structures, colonial relationships between poor and rich countries, social dislocation, lack of employment and education among the population, and so forth. To transform it and change the dynamics of violence in a given society, one has to change the socioeconomic realities that maintain it. The problem, however, is that a transformation of the socioeconomic realities does not entirely result in an automatic transformation of the realities of violence affecting societies. While a reduction of poverty affects the levels of crime in a given society, such correlation is not automatic, as the reality of crime in rich countries, such as the United States, points toward other complexities such as culture, race, sexual orientation, psychological conditions, and so forth.

Approaching violence only from the institutional and socioeconomic lens risks the possibility of overlooking other analyses to understand the complexities behind the phenomenon. Many times violence against women, nonheterosexual communities, people of color, to name a few, are subsumed under the categories of socioeconomic repression, and this, in turn, diminishes the possibilities of approaching all the layers related to the issue. For this reason, it is important to take into account not only the socioeconomic analysis, but also other cultural, gender, racial, and environmental frameworks to better understand the different levels and complexities of violent societies and actions.

Conclusion

Violence, in its social, political, and cultural forms, is a constant challenge to religious communities across the world. Civil wars, genocide, and refugee crises leave legacies of violence in societies that suffer from this phenomenon. Approaching it from an institutional point of view helps clarify the correlation and dialectic relationship between violence at home and violence in society. The daily experience of violence in many societies, which affects mostly the poor and oppressed, cannot be separated from socioeconomic and political structures that promote unequal distribution of wealth, militarization of society, poor access to education and health, poverty, and an uneven distribution of power among citizens. To promote peace, it is important to maintain an ethical stand that criticizes not only individual actions and subjective norms but also structural and socioeconomic realities that provide the material, historical, ideological, and cultural frameworks to exercise it.

Salvador A. Leavitt-Alcántara

References and Further Reading

Alvarenga, Patricia. *Cultura y etica de la violencia: El Salvador, 1880-1932* (San Jose, Costa Rica: EDUCA, 1996).

Conferencia General del Episcopado Latinoamericano. *Los Textos de Medellín y el proceso de cambio en America Latina: los documentos del CELAM, con las aprobaciones del Vaticano*, ed. UCA editors (San Salvador: UCA editores, 1971).

Dumas, F. Dabezies, ed. *Teología de la violencia* (Salamanca, España: Ediciones Sigueme, 1971).

Hinkelammert, Franz J. *The Ideological Weapons of Death: A Theological Critique of Capitalism* (Maryknoll, NY: Orbis Books, 1986).

Mananzan, Mary John, ed. *Women Resisting Violence: Spirituality for Life* (Maryknoll, NY: Orbis Books, 1996).

ISLAM

Within the Latino/a community, there are Hispanic Muslims. Although figures are obscure, and while some estimates range from a low of 20,000 to a high of 200,000, the latest and most conservative estimates by Islamic groups and leaders state that there are between 50,000 and 75,000 Latina/o Muslims in the United States. As of 2002, the Council on American-Islamic Relations established that Latina/o reversions constituted 6 percent of all Muslim conversion in this country. Most members of the Hispanic Islamic community are located, but not limited to, major metropolitan areas with large Latino/a populations, like New York, Chicago, and Los Angeles. While some reversions took place in the 1970s with the exposition of U.S. Latina/os to the Nation of Islam, the process of reversion among U.S. Latina/os at a larger scale is a recent phenomenon, specifically since September 11, 2001. The majority of U.S. Latina/os who have reverted are women and men between the ages of 15 and 35, most of whom have a college degree. Many of these reversions happened in school settings, work conversations, or through friendships. Most U.S. Latina/o Muslims described their reversion as a process or a search, an intellectual and spiritual journey that in some cases takes years, rather than an emotional conversion moment typified among Protestants and Pentecostals.

Multiple explanations for the growth of Islam among Latina/os during the past decade exist. Many express dissatisfaction and disillusionment with Christianity, specifically with the Catholic Church, for what they perceive to be a rigid hierarchical structure with what appears to be a polytheistic nature (concept of the Trinity). U.S. Latina/os who reverted to Islam claim that their new religion provides better explanations to the mysteries of God, as well as a closer and more direct contact with the Deity. For others, the aftermath of 9/11 spotlighted Islam, leading some U.S. Latina/os to search and research this religion that they found attractive. Some U.S. Latina/os saw in Islam a marginalized religion, and compared that marginalization to their own reality in the United States. This social commonality facilitated the process of reversion. Thus, the process of reversion among U.S. Latina/os should not only be understood as a religious process, but also as a social transformation.

As mentioned above, the growth of Islam among U.S. Latina/os is a fairly recent phenomenon; however, it has roots in Medieval Spain. U.S. Latina/os Muslims who have recently reverted, can claim a connection with over 700 years of Muslim (Moorish) rule in Spain (711–1492). This connection to the past helps explain and defend their reversion process as being neither new nor outside of the historical story of the Latino/a culture. However, some tend to romanticize the Moorish culture, not in its European and Western sense, but by tracing it back to northern Africa. The term "reversion" is specifically used by most U.S. Latina/o Muslims to focus on the aspect of "going

back" to their roots, not only religiously but also historically and culturally. Consequently, many do not see Islam as being outside of Latina/o culture, but rather as an intrinsic aspect of Hispanic heritage. Still, such explanations of reversion are viewed with suspicion and skepticism by the non-Muslim U.S. Latino community and by non-Hispanic Muslims.

The relationship between U.S. Latina/o Muslims and U.S. Latina/os and Muslims, in general, creates a sense of loss of identity and an anomie for the former. There are no specific *masjids* (mosques) just for Latina/os, compared to Latina/o churches within Christian groups. Hence, U.S. Latina/o Muslims attend the mosque with other Muslims, not taking into consideration their ethnicity or nationality, and the issues of language and culture become points of contention, even when there are multiple similarities. Because of this sense of anomie, U.S. Latina/o Muslims have been creating organizations in order to foster support groups. These organizations also bolster the spread of Islam among other U.S. Latina/os by producing Spanish translations of Islamic literature and work toward ensuring that language does not become an issue in the process of the *Dawah* (invitation to, sharing of Islam). These different organizations meet for social contact and educational purposes, engaging in their faith in both English and Spanish. For many participants of these activities, the group has become a family, since their own family does not necessarily share their religious experience. Some have even been marginalized and alienated for their reversion, specifically their turning away from Christianity. For women, it is more difficult because of wearing the *hijab* (women's head and body covering),

---

LADO

Latino American Dawah Organization (LADO) was founded in September 1997 by a handful of U.S. Latina/o Muslims in New York. Since then, LADO has become one of the most important and influential organizations among Latina/o Muslims in the United States. Created as a grassroots organization to promote Islam among Latina/os in the United States, it has developed into a national group with regional leadership. The group's mission is "to promote Islam among the Latino community within the United States by becoming better-educated Muslims and by working with like-minded Muslims." To fulfill this mission, LADO, during the past five years, has been at the forefront of education, support, and promotion by writing articles, giving presentations, translating materials, creating an online newsletter, and developing a Web site. The organization has also encouraged the establishment of local organizations in different cities across the United States. Through these initiatives, LADO has not only become a network among Latina/o Muslims in the United States, but also a liaison between the Latina/o Muslims and the general Muslim community. LADO promotes the education of Islam among Latina/os in the United States and educates the Muslim community regarding the perspective U.S. Latina/o reverts bring to Islam.

—HMV

---

as this piece of clothing becomes an obvious expression of their religion. Although their family members question their decision, U.S. Latina Muslims assert that they find in Islam more respect, rights, and privileges, even though some would accuse the religion of still being patriarchal. U.S. Latinas have expressed greater decision-making freedoms within Islam, especially regarding their clothing, which they see as being decided by women rather than imposed by men.

As of 2007, there are no major academic publications regarding this community, yet the presence of U.S. Latina/o Muslim organizations and groups are evident by their growth. There are local organizations in many cities across the United States, like the Los Angeles Latino Muslim Association, Latino Muslim of the Bay Area, California Latino Muslim Association, Chicago Association of Latino-American Muslims, Alianza Islámica (in New York) and PIEDAD (Propagación Islámica para la Educación de devoción a Ala' el Divino), which have Web sites with information and personal reversion stories. The largest and most recognized organization is LADO (Latino American Dawah Organization), founded in September 1997. LADO maintains a Web site, an online newsletter, and has regional chapters. Two of its founders, Juan Galván and Samantha Sánchez, are working on a book that will include reversion stories from Latina/o Muslims from across the United States.

This recent, growing presence of U.S. Latina/o Muslim is generating interest and concern, not only within the U.S. Latino/a community but also within the Muslim community in the United States, as both of these communities struggle to address the needs of this growing group among them. Meanwhile, U.S. Latina/o Muslims are striving to find their own space within both communities.

Hjamil A. Martínez-Vázquez

References and Further Reading

Cesari, Jocelyne. *When Islam and Democracy Meet: Muslim in Europe and in the United States* (New York: Palgrave Macmillan, 2004).

Lo, Mbaye. *Muslims in America: Race, Politics, and Community Building, Amana Islam in America Series* (Beltsville, MD: Amana Publications, 2004).

Martínez-Vázquez, Hjamil. "Finding Enlightenment: U.S. Latino/a's Journey to Islam." *The Journal of Latino-Latin American Studies* 3, no. 2 (Winter 2008): 57–71.

Sánchez, Samantha, and Juan Galván. "Latino Muslims: The Changing Face of Islam in America." *Islamic Horizons* (July/August 2002): 22–30.

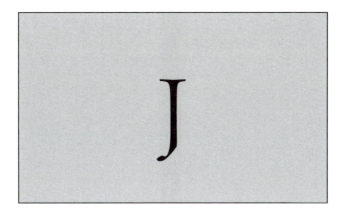

JEHOVAH'S WITNESSES

Jehovah's Witnesses are a religious organization founded in the United States toward the end of the nineteenth century, reaching a diversity of ethnic groups in more than 236 countries. Although many Christian groups consider Jehovah's Witnesses to be a sect, leading them to be classified as a "Para-Christian" group, their legal claims have helped them be recognized as a religious confession. They have been categorized as proselytes because of their aggressive style of evangelization: traveling from house to house, relating person to person, organizing themselves as a religious hierarchy, claiming to have a God-centered government. In terms of Hispanic involvement, in 2007 there was an estimated 2 million members from Spanish-speaking nations, exceeding Anglo-Saxons. Within the United States, there are more than 800,000 Latina/o adherents worshipping in more than 2,200 Spanish-speaking congregations. This makes Jehovah's Witnesses the largest non-Catholic Christian tradition among Hispanics in the United States, with the highest conversion rate among Hispanic immigrants than any other Latino/a non-Catholic tradition.

Their religious work is centered on sharing their beliefs through Bible studies and the teaching of basic principles of their faith through which they promote a strict code of unity in each of the countries evangelized. They consider themselves to possess a unique idea and revolutionary action when comparing themselves to other religious groups and when referring to their ideas, teachings, activities, practices, or personal conduct. They stress to maintain the same ethical code and Bible-centered message because of its universal message. They motivate members, both in Latin America and the world, to lead a moral and theocentric life as an answer to everything. The Kingdom of God is their solution, and each member is responsible before God for his/her actions.

While they trace their faith's roots to early Christian evangelists, the apostles,

Jehovah's Witness Kingdom Hall in Carpinteria, California. (Cynthia Odell)

most experts date the origin to 1870 in the United States, when Charles Taze Russell, son of a Presbyterian family, formed a Bible study group in Allegheny, Pittsburgh. His most predominant theme was the unfulfilled prophetic predictions of the end of the world, emphasizing the imminent war of Armageddon and coming of Christ. The *Watchtower*, originally known as *Zion's Watchtower and Herald of Christ's Presence*, was first published in July 1879. Today, there are 28,578,000 copies distributed monthly in 158 languages.

Russell, founder and first president (1870–1916), helped legally establish what is known today as "The Watch Tower Bible and Tract Society of Pennsylvania." This organization grew to obtain worldwide recognition by spreading its doctrine and beliefs, originally influenced by prophetic leaders of the Seventh-day Adventist. Russell copied their beliefs: the rejection of hell, an interest in apocalyptical prophecies, belief in the invisible return of Christ in 1874, and the destruction of the world in 1914, always emphasizing the war of Armageddon. The next leaders, Judge Rutherford (1916–1942), Nathan H. Knorr (1942–1977), Frederick Franz (1978–1992), Milton Henschel (1992–2000), and Don Adams (2000–present), gave continuity to Russell's work from their central offices located in Brooklyn, New York.

Other than language and climate differences, the Jehovah's Witnesses expansion within the Hispanic community is basically the same. Twenty-seven translators, based in Puerto Rico, representing 10 nationalities, mainly from Latin America and Spain, translate all the literature that is distributed worldwide from English to Spanish, even though there has never been a Hispanic representative in the Governing Body. They are represented in different committees through 114 branches around the world. The Hispanic community has weekly services at a meeting place called "Kingdom Hall," which is roughly equivalent to a Christian temple. Their leaders, referred to as elders, do not receive any special titles or monetary compensation. They go from house to house spreading their beliefs, such as the following: God is the Supreme Being, named Jehovah; the trinity is rejected as a pagan belief; Jesus is the first and greatest of God's creation and the human representation of the archangel Michael and is not the son of God, but he is the messiah and died for our sins. Christ's invisible second coming was in 1874 (later revised to 1914); the Holy Spirit is an active force associated with God; Jesus was not resurrected in body, but in spiritual essence, after establishing the Kingdom of God in Heaven, entrusted the "Watchtower" to administer the affairs of God on earth; the number of those going to heaven was 144,000. As their global membership grew, their belief changed to state that these "anointed ones" were going to heaven, including the main leaders. The rest of the membership is referred to as "The Great Crowd," the earthly class that must work with the 144,000 in order to be saved and live in paradise. There is no eternal hell. They prohibit practices that connote nationalism such as saluting the flag and military service, common celebrations such as birthdays, and religious or

national holidays. Christmas and Easter are considered pagan practices that are also prohibited.

There are specific differences based on the reality and needs of the people being evangelized. In the Hispanic communities in the United States, there are testimonies of immigrant families being reached and added to their membership. The Jehovah's Witnesses are helping people throughout Latin America and hundreds of immigrant families arriving in the United States, especially along the southwest border.

In the Caribbean, the offices in Puerto Rico and the Dominican Republic have been important. The work of the Kingdom in Puerto Rico began in 1932, when John Wahlberg, the only Witness living on the island, received a married couple from the United States to help him. The first Puerto Rican reached was Ambrosio Rosa in 1938. By 1944, the work gained intensity and spread to the U.S. Virgin Islands (1947) and the British Virgin Islands (1952) under the supervision of the Puerto Rico branch office. Four international assemblies have been celebrated in Puerto Rico (1967, 1973, 1978, and 1998). There is an estimated 28,000 witnesses who are supervised by the Puerto Rico branch office.

Virginia Loubriel-Chévere

References and Further Reading

Espinosa, Gastón. "Methodological Reflections on Latino Social Science Research." *Rethinking Latino(a) Religion and Identity*, ed. Miguel A. De La Torre and Gastón Espinosa (Cleveland: Pilgrim Press, 2006).

Mansferrer-Ken, Elio. *Sectas o Iglesias* (San Rafael, México, D.F.: Plaza y Valdés, 2000).

MARRANOS

The word "Marranos" is a derogatory term applied in medieval and early modern Spain and Portugal to Jewish converts to Christianity (*conversos*). These "New Christians" were believed to be living as Secret Jews (crypto-Jews), practicing their faith behind closed doors while receiving the Catholic sacraments. The origin of the word remains uncertain, but as used in Spain usually meant "pig" or "filthy" or "hypocrite." This abusive labeling increased across Spain after the mass conversions, anti-Semitic riots, and trials of Sephardic leaders in 1391 and 1481. King Ferdinand of Aragon and Queen Isabel of Castile signed the infamous 1492 Edict of Expulsion demanding that all Spanish Jews convert to Christianity or leave Spain without their possessions. Forced and clandestine departures became a frequent feature of Spanish Jewish life in the 1500s and 1600s. Marranos found better conditions among North Africa's Muslim nations and Turkey, while Protestant nations like England and the Netherlands became safe havens for *Marrano* and *converso* families fleeing the Inquisition. Conditions in Spain's colonies offered these New Christians a measure of independence far from the persecuting authorities of the mother country, and Marranos became part of the Hispanic American religious story by moving to places like New Spain (Central America), New Mexico, and California.

—AH

Moore, Donald T. *Las Doctrinas Sanas y las Sectas Malsanas, I, II y IV* (San Juan, PR: ABPR, 1986–1992; 1993–1996; 2000–2002).

Peters, Shawn F. *Judging Jehovah's Witnesses: Religious Persecution and the Dawn of the Rights Revolution* (Lawrence: The University Press of Kansas, 2000).

Watchtower Bible and Tract Society of New York. *Los Testigos de Jehová: Proclamadores del Reino de Dios* (Brooklyn, NY: WBTS, 1993).

JEWS

Hispanic Jews represent approximately 100,000 people in the United States, emigrating primarily from Europe, the Middle East, and Latin America since the late nineteenth century to the present. Hispanic Jewry is diverse in terms of origins (Sephardic or Ashkenazi), religious affiliation (Orthodox, Conservative, Reform), and nationality. Most Latin American Jews come from Argentina and Mexico. While there are thousands of Jewish people of Latin American descent in the United States, there are practically no Hispanic Jewish communities, and there is virtually no scholarly work on this subject. Latino/a scholars who study religion write about Catholicism or other Christian religions. Jewish scholars would have little reason to examine Hispanic populations. Most of the existing literature on Hispanic Jewry in the United States examines Sephardic Jewish communities and "crypto" Jews.

Sephardic Jews were Jews expelled from Spain in 1492. They settled in Europe, North Africa, and the Ottoman Empire. Many migrated to North and South America in the early twentieth century for political and economic

ANOUSIM

"Anous" is the Hebrew word for converts and their descendants forced into a different religious faith. "Anousim" refers to those born in Christian families, mainly Catholic, who rediscovered their Jewish identity. Anousim base their sense of identity on how their families practiced and preserved their Christian faith. For example, some of the basic tenets of Christianity (i.e., the Trinity or the Messiahship of Jesus) were rejected. Others noticed that their families followed certain customs and traditions (i.e., lighting candles on the Sabbath or following kosher dietary practices). Still others point to a family elder who reportedly has kept the family secrets alive, passing to the next generation their Jewish past, usually when on their deathbeds. Today, a large number of Hispanics from the Southwest, especially from New Mexico, believe that they are descendants of Jews forced to convert. But Jewish communities do not necessarily welcome the anousim. They require conversion if these Hispanics want to join their faith community. While some have formally converted, others are insulted at the request. For them, their families have maintained their Jewishness for centuries. In 1991, New Mexico's state historian, Stanley Hordes, founded the Society for Crypto-Judaic Studies to study and explore this phenomenon.

—MAD

reasons, and to the United States from Latin America in the twentieth century for similar reasons. Throughout their Diaspora, many have continued to speak their fifteenth-century Spanish, known as Ladino. Of the 4 million Jews in the United States, 40,000 are Sephardim.

Many "crypto Jews" live in the southwestern United States. They are descendants of Spanish Jews who converted to Catholicism during the Spanish Inquisition in the fifteenth century, but who maintained certain customs, such as lighting candles on Friday nights and not eating pork, not always realizing that those traditions were based in Judaism. Their descendants settled in the hinterland of the Spanish empire in today's Southwest during the sixteenth and seventeenth centuries. As a result of various studies conducted in observance of the Quincentenary in 1992, many families, who had lived as Catholics for generations, learned of their Jewish roots.

The first Jews in the United States were 23 Sephardic refugees from Catholic Brazil who came to New York in 1654. Anecdotal information suggests that most Jews who have come to the United States from Latin America self-identify as Jewish rather than Hispanic and are more likely to be involved in a Jewish community than in a Hispanic community. Even though most large U.S. cities have populations of Jews from Latin America, there are few Jewish Hispanic organizations. In Chicago, those who attend synagogue belong to various English-speaking congregations. Some get together over a specific issue, such as the bombing of the Israeli Embassy in Buenos Aires in 1992, or to help needy Jews in Latin America. Some are active in the equal rights struggles of Latino/a communities. In Los Angeles, 95 percent of Hispanic Jews self-identify as White/Caucasian and 1 percent as Hispanic; 90 percent marry into their faith. As in

---

JUBAN

The "Jubans" are the approximately 15,000 Cuban Jews of Miami whose families fled there in 1960 after the Cuban Revolution. Convinced that their stay would be a matter of weeks or months, they called their temporary setting Hotel Miami. After realizing that they would be there for a while, most settled in Miami Beach where Miami's Jews lived, not in the non-Jewish Cuban areas of Calle Ocho and Coral Gables. As Spanish-speaking refugees, they were not accepted by the established Miami Jewish community. Only one Miami rabbi offered assistance to the new arrivals. In 1961, they formed the Círculo cubano-hebreo, and in 1976, they built the Cuban Hebrew Congregation of Miami—Temple Beth Shmuel. In 1980, the Cuban Sephardim founded their own temple. The Cuban Jews continue to worship and socialize within the traditions they brought with them. Today they are a tricultural and trilingual community of Spanish, English, and Yiddish speakers. The oldest generation was born in Eastern Europe (Ashkenazi) or the Mediterranean (Sephardic), the second generation was born in Cuba, and the third in the United States.

—AA

---

other cities, they neither organize as a group nor gather when in the same organizations.

It is not surprising that Jews who come from Latin America identify as Jews, given the history of the lack of religious tolerance in Latin America, and the comparatively small size of the Latin American Jewish population. Between 1840 and 1942, 2,801,890 Jews came to the United States, while only 376,227 immigrated to all the countries in Latin America where the unity of church and state had existed since the fifteenth century. In contrast, in the United States, Jews enjoyed legal equality in a secular society. In Latin America, due to official religious intolerance, the Jewish population was small, but determined to maintain its Jewish identity. They did not assimilate to the national culture as easily as Jews in the United States. In Mexico, for example, there are 40,000 to 50,000 Jews, 95 percent of whom go to synagogue, 80–90 percent of their children attend Jewish schools, and only one in ten marries a non-Jew. On the other hand, many European Jews went to Latin America in the late 1930s after they were turned away by the United States.

In the United States today, there is one identifiable Jewish Hispanic community. The "Jewbans" are the approximately 15,000 Cuban Jews of Miami who settled there after the Cuban Revolution. As Spanish-speaking refugees, they were not accepted by the Miami Jewish community. In 1961, they formed the Círculo cubano-hebreo, and, in 1976, they built the Cuban Hebrew Congregation of Miami. The Cuban Jews continue to worship and socialize within their traditions. Anthropologist Ruth Behar jokes that all Jewbans have a relative named Moisés, eat Goya and Manischewitz products, and dance salsa at Bar Mitzvahs.

Some writers, such as Marjorie Agosín, Ilan Stavans, Ruth Behar, and Aurora

Levins Morales, treat the theme of their Latino Jewishness in their works. The songs of the Los Angeles rock group Los Hoodios reflect their Jewish/Latino heritage. The Jewish Identity Project in Los Angeles featured photographs that investigate the experiences of being Jewish and Latino, as well as Jewish and Black, and asks who is a Jew? Carlos Martini's documentary film, *Latino Jews: Journey to the Americas*, presents interviews with Latino Jews from Cuba, Puerto Rico, Chile, and Argentina.

There have been recent efforts to make connections between Latino and Jewish communities. For example, the American Jewish Committee recently named a director of Latino affairs. In her inauguration speech, Diana Siegel Vann, who is herself a Jewish Latina, stated: "Latino Jews such as myself can act as interpreters between both communities, both literally and figuratively, and hope to jointly identify venues for cooperation."

Anna Adams

References and Further Reading

Bettinger-Lopez, Caroline. *Cuban Jewish Journeys: Searching for Identity, Home and History in Miami* (Knoxville: University of Tennessee Press, 2000).

Cohen, Martin, and Abraham J. Peck, eds. *The Sephardim in the Americas: Studies in Culture and History* (Tuscaloosa: University of Alabama Press, 1993).

Elkin, Judith Laikin. *The Jews of Latin America* (New York: Holmes and Meier, 1998).

Jacobs, Janet Liebman. *Hidden Heritage: The Legacy of the Crypto Jews* (Berkeley: University of California Press, 2002).

Jenik, Ariel, and Judith Cichowolski de Jenik. *Jewish Spanglish: The Latin American Jewish Community of Los Angeles* (M.A. thesis, Hebrew Union College, 2005).

JUSTICE

Since the election of President Ronald Reagan, every subsequent administration, Democratic and Republican alike, has sought to reduce government costs by either privatizing or limiting state services such as welfare, public health, social security, and prisons. These new policies renewed a more intense debate about social justice in our society.

Christian churches have been proactive in this conversation, and like their secular counterparts they are not of one mind. The Roman Catholic Church and most mainline denominations have expressed strong opposition to the new policies. Their claim is that the proposed cuts in programs and services will unjustifiably increase human suffering, particularly among the poor, and as such they are unjust. They base their claim on the religious convictions that in the poor we find indications of our faithfulness to God's justice and that justice must be measured by how well the poorest members of society are doing. These Churches acknowledge their own responsibility for justice and express it through programs that provide generous assistance to the needy. However, they argue that charity is no substitute for justice and that Churches do not have either the material resources or the organizational capacity to effectively provide assistance to the poor. The resources and coordination provided by the state is indispensable for such assistance to be affective and just.

Evangelicals are divided on this issue. The evangelical Right have expressed support for the new policies. They encourage individuals to exercise more self-discipline and assume greater responsibility for their economic well-being. The state ought to get out of the business of social welfare and allow churches to provide such services through their different charitable organizations. Other Evangelicals assume a less legalistic attitude and want to coordinate efforts with the state to attend to the needs of citizens, which by no fault of their own had fallen into bad times. In their view, Jesus' compassion for the poor is the normative biblical mandate, placing all the faithful under the obligation to serve those in need.

Racial ethnic communities, while not of one mind as to what justice demands in our situation, do share a common concern about the economic burdens the proposed cuts in funding and services impose of their communities. They see how they negatively affect the life possibilities of their communities and how they significantly limit fair opportunities for them and their families to improve their lot.

As a people who have suffered much, Hispanics have much to contribute to the justice debate. Their experiences as native people during the formation and expansion of the country and their continued experiences as a migrant people seeking refuge from dehumanizing poverty, from political oppression and civil wars, and ecological degradation give them unique insights as to what constitutes a just and good society. Differences in social status and economic class, in residential status and their experience of immigration, cultural expression, and political and religious convictions, make it impossible to articulate *the* Hispanic view on justice. However, when one analyzes the language and the images used by most Hispanics when they address justice issues, one notices shared motifs that, in spite of their differences, are essential to their sense of justice.

The dominant notion of social justice within our society is predominantly utilitarian and defined in narrowly economic distributive terms. The debate on migration, for example, focuses on whether migrants represent a social gain or a social cost. If the former, they are welcomed; if the latter, they are to be refused entrance. Consideration of their human rights, the reunification of families, and hospitality to strangers at best take a second place. When Hispanics engage in justice talk, however, one notices a significant shift and enlargement of the scope of justice. While matters of economic distribution are important, justice considerations are expanded to include issues dealing with the following: (a) power and decision making, (b) cultural identity, and (c) the social division of labor.

The language of domination, exploitation, and liberation is ever present in Hispanic justice talk. Exploitation and domination point to the absence of justice; liberation points to the proactive pursuit of justice. Domination makes reference to those constraints that deny one's freedom and capacity to act in socially recognized settings. To be dominated is to be ruled by others without one's explicit consent whether within politics or at the work place. Exploitation entails being deprived of basic goods and services, as well as the education and/or training needed to acquire the knowledge and skills to fulfill ones self-realization. Domination and exploitation point to the fact that social reciprocity and mutuality are lacking in our society. It points to the unjust state of affairs where one social group disproportionately contributes to the freedom, well-being, power, and self-realization of another social group.

Liberation expresses the vision that justice goes beyond social reforms and necessitates a fundamental *restructuring of society*. It is the quest for all members of society to: (a) participate in the decision-making centers that establish the laws and procedures by which we organize our mutual dealings; (b) be actively included in the productive process, to have a say in the way labor is compensated; (c) have a fair opportunity to develop skills and talents so as to be recognized as a contributing member of society; and (d) be free to live in light of one's cultural heritage, which gives identity, meaning, and purpose. Inclusiveness, empowerment, and mutuality are the marks of a liberated society.

Dominant Motifs of the Hispanic Vision of Justice

Economic Justice. Hispanics experience oppression and domination most vividly through their marginal status within the social process of production and consumption. Being locked into the lowest economic strata of our society, deprived of work, continuously underemployed, and/or poorly remunerated for their work is the most obvious experience of injustice. The poverty and deprivation that results from this state of affairs is deeply rooted in the present social structure. Attempts to fix this condition by enacting a fairer distribution of goods and services has proven to be insufficient as well as a lost cause. The reformist policies that have led to the present cuts in goods and services enacted by conservative and liberal politicians have not forwarded

social equality. In fact, as everyone recognizes, the gap between the rich and the poor has significantly widened.

Of greater consequence is that the sought-after minimalist state, in its attempt to reduce social cost, has deprived people not only of access to basic goods and services, but also has limited their political access and possibilities. The distributive-reformist approach reduces citizens into depoliticized consumers, into a people incapable of questioning the economic process under which they live. The minimalist state assumes that as long as it delivers the consumer goods and services that most citizens crave, citizens are bound to be loyal and society will remain stable.

Latinos/as argue that when we look at the system from the margin, justice entails fundamental changes to the social structure. It must begin with the political empowerment of the poor and marginal, with the active participation of all citizens in the restructuring of the economic sphere. Welfare grants, even generous ones, will not solve the basic problems of the poor. The material goods and services received, while necessary, do not compensate for the loss of essential freedoms and rights. The real problem is not only the passivity, boredom, and sense of uselessness that comes from not having meaningful and well-remunerated work, but mostly the deprivation of the experience of being political agents. This is a violation of the democratic way of life. It deprives citizens of the experience of self-respect and recognition that comes from acting within publicly recognized settings. It also undermines the sense of self-worth that comes from assuming responsibilities for meaningful social tasks. Justice is a great challenge precisely because those in power are ultimately more willing to share their wealth and resources than to share their power. It is not that the better off are willing to readily share their wealth. Their "generosity" never takes place in the absence of significant struggle. However, dominant groups hold on much more tightly and struggle harder to oppose all efforts to restructure the configuration of power that cements their privileged position.

In the Hispanic vision of justice, the goal is for all social members to *be* more not just to *have* more. Clearly, one must *have* in order to *be*; however, our present consumerist culture, supported by the power of media, is making it harder for many to avoid making *having* the purpose of *being*. Justice seeks the formation of a community that relegates consumption to the purpose of creating citizens acting collectively and co-operatively for the obtainment of shared goals and the fulfillment and development of new talents and skills necessary to accomplish this task. Justice as "economic liberation" gives priority to the political. It seeks the right of all members of society to participate in those private and public centers of decision making that affect their lives in significant ways.

Social Justice. Hispanics, together with other racial ethnic minorities, are overrepresented in social tasks that, while socially necessary and useful, are neither desirable nor well remunerated. Most of the work they do is simple, overly repetitive, boring, dirty and brutish, and not conducive to nor require the development of diversified skills and talents. While at work they experience that they "belong to another," that they are followers of another's visions and commands. They are hardly ever consulted, much less granted the power of

decision making in matters regarding the various tasks they perform. They experience their work as contributing to the well-being of others more than contributing to their own self-development. This is what Hispanics mean when they say they are socially dominated and powerless.

Latinas/os argue that justice within a democratic society requires not only political democracy but also greater economic democracy. In as much as the workplace is organized by a system of rules used to discipline the behavior of producers, workers ought to have a say in the determination of these rules. This form of social democracy can only enhance the skills citizens need for political democracy. It is a way of creating more spaces and opportunities for self-determination, more spaces in which to be recognized as fellow citizens and as contributing members of the community.

Hispanic justice is particularly concerned with the systematic exclusion of racial ethnic people from those few privileged, high-paying, and socially recognized positions within our society. Latino/as are suspect of the claim that these privileged positions are distributed on the basis of *merit*. The dominant prejudicial and negative social attitudes toward Hispanics, together with the fact that they have not been consulted as to what constitutes merit, makes Hispanics distrust the specific criteria of merit being used to distribute those desirable social positions. Furthermore, the fact that most of these positions are overwhelmingly held by White males makes one suspect that there has been fair opportunity to compete for them. When a social procedure shows such a consistent imbalanced outcome, it reveals that there is something inadequate regarding the procedure itself; i.e., equality of opportunity is missing and the criteria of merit is biased.

Under this state of affairs, it should not come as a surprise that most Hispanics support Affirmative Action programs. They have no illusions that these programs will forward justice. Still, without Affirmative Action programs the condition of racial ethnic groups would be worse off than what it is presently. Ultimately these programs represent a minimalist approach that powerful conservative groups, in order to keep hold of their power and privilege, have been willing to grant those who have traditionally been excluded from equal opportunity. Racial ethnic groups accept them as a necessary evil, as the best they can do for the time being. At their best, Affirmative Action is necessary not so much to compensate for past discriminations but primordially to allow talented racial ethnic candidates to have an opportunity to show their skill and talents. It helps counteract the conscious and unconscious prejudices and biases of decision makers. The real challenge for minority groups and women is to continue their coordinated efforts, through coalition building and other political strategies, and remain vigilant and committed to the struggle to keep desirable social positions open for those who have traditionally been locked out.

The Cultural Dimension of Justice. The Latinos/as' vision of justice must create a space for the preservation of cultural values that provide a meaningful way of life for a given social group. Justice entails overcoming cultural imperialism and its attempts to devalue, make invisible, ridicule, and, if possible, eradicate the culture of the dominated social group. The struggle for cultural affirmation is not reactive to the entrenched resistance and prejudice that Euro-Americans have shown toward Hispanics. Hispanics tenaciously hold on to their cultural heritage and resist the ideology and politics of the melting pot because it has provided rich and abundant resources not just to survive but to thrive in the new land. It is not enough for them to limit their cultural expressions to the private sphere. They want to act privately and publicly in light of their cultural world views. To do anything else would be an act of self-denial.

They are not persuaded by the claim that in order to succeed, all citizens have to assimilate to the Euro-American way of life. Many have done so and their lot is not much improved. In place of the ideology of the melting pot, many Hispanics argue for the promotion and preservation of the unique cultural identities of different subgroups within society. Group solidarity and loyalty, more than conversion to individualism and abstract notions of human rights, continue to be, for Hispanics, the basis of what little empowerment they can achieve.

Latinos/as recognize that their social advancement is dependent on their capacity to negotiate a common life with the dominant culture. There are levels of integration, acculturation, and assimilation that are inevitable. As people who participate in two cultural systems, Hispanics will develop a new identity shaped by various forms of *double consciousness*. This is particularly true for future generations. What is not acceptable as a matter of justice are the demeaning stereotypes and overall negative images and attitudes propagated through the media and presented in the educational system, law enforcement agencies, and other governmental agencies that represent a form of domination through the misuse of power. These negative images result in attitudes of self-denial and of self-loathing that particularly affect Hispanic youth, and among Euro-Americans it promotes the kind of fear and aversion that nourishes attitudes and practices that are fundamentally cruel and unjust.

Political Justice. While many Hispanics make the cultural/identity dimension the center of their view of justice, there are others that give a priority to political justice. Politics takes priority because of how the economy and society is organized and because how multiculturalism and pluralism is structured is mostly a political decision. Just politics is democratic. Democracy provides the best means for individuals and groups to voice their needs, interests, and uniqueness. More importantly it enables citizens to develop habits of solidarity and the habit of thinking about their needs and interests in relation to the interests and the needs of others.

Sadly our society reduces politics to the private bargaining of interest groups and political bureaucrats. Those social groups with more economic resources have unequal access to those who wield political power and are better able to influence their policy options. Large sectors of society have limited capacity and occasions to present their views and interests, much less to have them acted upon. Interest group politics are inevitable, unduly favor the well-to-do, and disregard and ultimately undermine the rights of the oppressed. Even worse, interest group politics discourages public participation, generating within the larger community attitudes of cynical indifference.

Hispanics, with few significant exceptions, have not been able to invest their political capital and energy into national issues. Migration legislation has done much to encourage more attention to national issues and to motivate their participation. Still, most Latino/a politics focuses on pressing local concerns: jobs, housing, health care, better schools, voting registration, and the like. Latina/o politics is more a politics of resistance than a politics of seeking control over the main centers of decision making. It is a politics based more on community organizing, which aims at making the state and big businesses more accountable to the needs and concerns of the local community.

A just politics is democratic, and democracy entails among other things the empowerment, active participation, and recognition of the different social groups. The best way to foster justice within a society increasingly shaped by a plurality of social groups is to assure each social group representation in the process of decision making. This commitment to preserve group differences makes the Hispanic vision of justice somewhat incongruent with our society's interpretation of justice. The prevailing liberal notion of justice claims that no rights, benefits, nor special treatment ought to be connected to one's class, race, or gender. In fact, group differences are intrinsically prejudicial to those who do not belong to the group, and they limit the self-realization of individuals who belong to the group. The just and good society, therefore, is one in which all individuals are treated by the same standards, principles, and rules.

Latinos/as, on the contrary, claim that our society is, in fact, group structured and that, given the irreversible process of globalization under which we presently live, group affirmation is inevitable and will continue to increase. In this pluralistic group context, it is the lack of recognition of cultural differences that constitutes a violation of the principle of equal treatment. The claim is that affirming group differences does not in itself violate democracy. Democracy is diminished by the fact that within our society some groups are privileged and dominant over others. Hispanics, like other minority groups, have learned the hard way that to disregard group differences ultimately hurts the oppressed group and favors the dominant group. Formal claims of impartiality and equality sustain those complex social blinders that keep both the oppressed and the oppressor unaware of the concrete manifestations of group privilege. It shields the structure of privileges from critical public scrutiny. It is neither by surrendering one's cultural identity nor by striving for value commonness, but rather by group survival and *empowerment*, that more impartial and equal justice will be obtained. Social groups, contrary to the liberal view, are not something we contract into or can arbitrarily dismiss. Group membership is much more than an association for the sake of the satisfaction of needs, it is character forming. To a great extent they define who we are and provide our source of meaning and purpose. It makes no sense that justice calls us to neutralize these communal loyalties. Justice is more than individual rights, it is also being in solidarity with one's main community.

Justice requires commitment to the common good. The common good, from this perspective, is neither tyrannically substantive (all committed to the same end) nor purely individualistic and procedural (each individual doing what he or she thinks is good). The good we hold in common is the commitment that no one will be made marginal from the centers of decision making, nor forced to accept the ways of another group. It is a commitment to equal respect and inclusivity of the different groups. The common good entails a commitment to create more spaces and more occasions for this diversity of people to intermingle with each other without being coerced into a homogeneous pattern or whole. Within these spaces, social groups aim not only to affirm their interests but also to seek to engage with others, to mutually understand each other, and to form coalitions that are mutually beneficial and that enable them to find ways to share life together. When no one is left out or deprived of representation, and when all are empowered, group differences can be positive and liberating.

Concluding Remarks

"Hispanic" and "Latino/a" are the terms used by Spanish-speaking people from the Caribbean, Latin America, and Central America to describe the new identity being forged by people of these nations who have made the United States their permanent home. This new identity is not defined by their being oppressed, but by their struggle, in solidarity with others, to strive to overcome that which threatens their economic cultural, social, and political well-being. In this sense, the struggle for justice is an intrinsic dimension of the creation of that unique and original identity called Hispanic or Latino/a.

The formation and consolidation of this new identity is perceived most clearly in the urban centers of our nation where a plurality of Spanish-speaking people dwell together. The social and political realities of urban life have made them aware that only by creating coalitions and solidarity groups between themselves will they be successful in solving the challenges and concerns they confront. Living close to each other has facilitated the awareness of how they need and depend on each other to survive and to thrive. Shared experiences and proximity have created favorable conditions to transcend, without denying, national identity and to develop an awareness, sensitivity, and responsiveness to each other's needs.

Their vision of justice has been derived not only from the dynamics of their relationship with the dominant culture but also from the internal dynamics of the Hispanic community itself. While Hispanics see value in unity, they affirm the reality of group differences among themselves. They negotiate a common political struggle in pursuit of common goals without aiming at value and cultural commonness. "Hispanic" is a term that emphasizes solidarity, not uniformity.

The continuing struggle for the creation of a plurality of spaces for the affirmation of differences within a framework of equal rights shared by all is the vision of justice that integrates the larger historical project that feeds a new Hispanic identity and the contribution Hispanics can make to the national conversation about justice.

Ismael Garciá

References and Further Reading

De La Torre, Miguel A. *Doing Christian Ethics from the Margins* (Maryknoll, NY: Orbis Books, 2004).

Du Bois, W. E. B. *The Soul of Black Folk* (Greenwich, CT: Fawcett Publications, 1961).

Isasi-Diaz, Ada Maria. *En la Lucha: A Hispanic Women's Liberation Theology* (Minneapolis: Fortress Press, 1993).

Schlesinger, Arthur M., Jr. *The Disuniting of America* (New York: W. W. Norton & Company, 1992).

Segovia, Fernando. "Two Places and No Place in Which to Stand: Mixture and Otherness in Hispanic American Theology." *Listening: Journal of Religion and Culture* 27, no. 1 (1991).

West, Cornel. *Race Matters* (Boston: Beacon Press, 1993).

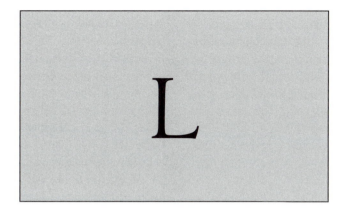

LANGUAGE

It is common to hear Spanish spoken throughout the United States. According to the 2005 census, of the estimated 268 million people age five and over, about 52 million (19 percent), or one in five, spoke a language other than English at home. Of this, over 32 million (12 percent) spoke Spanish. Over half of those who speak Spanish at home reported speaking English "very well." The West and South combined had about three times the number of Spanish speakers as the Northeast and Midwest combined. Many Latina/os speak a "pure" Spanish, some are bilingual, others speak Spanglish, while still others speak only English. In addition, caution must be taken that these are the only four choices available to Hispanics. There are those who are proficient in neither English nor Spanish, but rather converse in Cholo, Mayan, Náhuatl, or Pocho. Nevertheless, the prominence of Spanish to Latino/a identity has historically been and remains strong.

Language is more than a collection of words, it is a conveyor of concepts. For many Latino/as, identity is tied into speaking Spanish. To a certain extent, it holds together the Hispanic community, a community that encompasses many ethic groups and individuals whose residency in the United States dates back generations or just a few years. A Cuban, a Chicano/a, a Chilean, and a Costa Rican may trace their roots to different countries with a different racial, social, and political milieu, but more than likely they have one thing in common that allows them to be bounded together, their language. While other ethnic groups have consciously attempted to replace their native tongue with English, Hispanics have attempted to hold on to Spanish, passing it down to the next generation.

The reality of life in the United States is creating an environment where a new form of communication among Hispanics is developing—one that is neither Spanish nor English, yet is both Spanish and English. Hispanics are fragmented based on the length of time living in the United States and the degree of acculturation to the norms of the American culture. Latina/os, specifically the youth, who are caught in an in-between space between their parent's Hispanic worldview and that of the dominant Euro-American culture have developed their own language, which reflects the internal dialectic of these two cultures. Fragmented identity has led to a fragmented language. "Spanglish" becomes the verbal expression of a U.S. Hispanic space and expresses the attempt to *mestizar* the dominant Euro-American culture with the oppressed Hispanic reality. To an older generation of Latina/os, Spanglish becomes a corrupt vernacular of their mother tongue. In appearance, Spanglish seems to demonstrate neglectfulness, in effect a rejection of the Hispanic culture by Americanizing Spanish. But to the dominant culture, Spanglish is simply another example of linguistic deficiency, a humorous attempt to imitate the legitimate language of the land. In effect, both cultures rebuff their mutual product.

When a people are denied economic and cultural capital, a new way of expression is devised in the diverse setting of everyday life. Spanglish reflects the reality that forces Hispanics to live with one foot in the Latino/a world of their parents and the other foot in the present physical country where they reside. Rather than a rejection of both the Spanish and English cultures, an attempt is made to carve out a social space where Latina/os are distinguished both from their parents and from the dominant culture. The construction of Spanglish becomes a sociopolitical project toward the unification of "who they are" with "where they live." Spanglish represents the irremediable "two-ness" of cultures that dwells among Hispanics.

The ability to speak English, Spanish, or Spanglish seems to have an affect on Latino/a spirituality. According to a 2007 study conducted by the Pew Hispanic Center, a majority of Latino/a Catholics (55 percent) say that Spanish is their primary language, while a majority of evangelicals (63 percent) and mainline Protestants (73 percent) say that English is their primary language or that they are bilingual. Additionally, a majority of those who belong to other Christian faiths (61 percent) or are secular (63 percent) also said that English is their primary language or that they are bilingual.

It is interesting to note that conversion from one faith tradition to another is higher among English-speaking Latina/os than it is among Spanish speakers (and foreign born). Twenty-six percent of all Hispanics whose primary language is English converted. The conversion of those who are bilingual (20 percent) and those whose primary language is Spanish (14 percent) were lower. Even when other variables such as gender, generation, and education were taken into consideration, these rates of conversion persisted. The largest conversion rate among Latina/os who are English-dominant speakers occurred among those who converted to secularism. More than two-thirds (68 percent) of those who said that they became secular either are bilingual or have English as their primary language.

Among those who say that their primary language is Spanish, 75 percent also say that their religion is very important to them. Compare this to those whose primary language is English. For them, 59 percent said that religion is very important to them in their daily lives.

Likewise, for those with Spanish as their primary language, the vast majority, 83 percent, believe in a "prosperity gospel," which holds that God will bless them with financial rewards or with good health. But for those with English as their primary language, the majority is smaller, with only 54 percent believing in the prosperity gospel. Finally, those for whom Spanish is the primary language are more likely (60 percent) to believe in Jesus' Second Coming (his return to earth in their lifetime), than those for whom English is the primary language (43 percent).

It may appear obvious that foreign-born Hispanics and those for whom Spanish is the primary language would attend distinctly Latino/a churches with distinctive ethnic characteristics. But surprisingly, 70 percent of Hispanics who speak little or no Spanish also report attending such churches. Ergo, the Latino/a ethnic church phenomenon is not limited to those who speak only Spanish. Among Latina/o Catholics a majority reported that they prefer to attend a Mass in Spanish. In fact, 91 percent of Hispanic Catholic churchgoers state they attend Spanish language services. The numbers are also high for evangelicals (81 percent), mainline Protestants (67 percent), and other Christian traditions (86 percent). In short, language is an important factor in determining Latina/o religiosity; nevertheless, for the majority of Hispanics, regardless of language proficiency, God is worshiped in Spanish.

Miguel A. De La Torre

References and Further Reading

Pew Hispanic Center. *Changing Faiths: Latinos and the Transformation of American*

Religion (Washington, DC: Pew Forum on Religion and Public Life, 2007).

U.S. Census Bureau. http://www.census.gov/.

LATINA EVANGÉLICA THEOLOGY

Latina *evangélica* theology is a collaborative, incarnational, and constructive theological reflection done from the particular perspective of Latina Protestant women. As Latinas, they are part of the almost 47 million people who are of Mexican, Puerto Rican, Cuban, Dominican, Central American, and South American descent currently residing in the continental United States. "Latina" is not synonymous with "Latin American"—those who continue to reside in their countries of origin. To be Latina implies that one is adversely affected by sexism as well as the marginalization, cultural and linguistic discrimination, racism, colonialism, poverty, and adverse effects of globalization experienced by Latinos. First-generation Latinas and Latinos have further experienced the traumatic effects of im/migration, described by some scholars as a "Diaspora experience."

Latinas and Latinos are often called *mestiza/o* (hybridity), *nepantla* (literally, "the place in-between"), or *sata/o* (in Puerto Rico, refers to mixed-breed animals) to describe their distinctiveness as a people arising from the encounter of two or more cultural, biological, and/or religious groups. In the Americas, the encounter of European *conquistadores* —primarily from Spain and Portugal— with indigenous and African people resulted in a biological and cultural *mestizaje* that produced a particular religious worldview and spirituality: a popular

Catholicism that is foundationally Iberian Catholicism with Amerindian and African beliefs. This worldview retains an understanding that God is truly present in all things and all places in the daily (*cotidiano*) spaces of life.

At the beginning of the twentieth century and continuing through the present, European and U.S. Protestantism underwent the same process of mestizaje with the prevalent popular religious practices they encountered in the Spanish Americas and Caribbean. Native populations adopted the new faith in such a way that beliefs were either reinterpreted or transmuted to allow the new to coexist with older valued traditions. For example, new converts continued to use crucifixes or to exclaim *"Ave María Purísima"* (Hail Mary, most Pure), while allegedly eschewing all belief in the Virgin. Latinas and Latinos embraced their new faith with vigor, becoming ardent evangelizers of the Good News (*el evangelio*), and thus eventually identified themselves as people of this Good News—*evangélica/os*.

Protestants in many countries of the Spanish-speaking Americas to this day usually do not self-identify as *Protestantes*, since their goal is not to protest but rather to share el evangelio. Their Protestant foundation is evident in the evangélica affirmation of such important Reformation principles as *sola Scriptura*. They also agree with evangelicals that conversion is a "necessary" result of any real encounter with Jesus Christ. In particular, evangélica/os tend to stress the central role of the Holy Spirit for transformation and the importance of the community of faith as a base from which to carry out prophetic ministries "in the world." However, it is incorrect to translate the Spanish word as an

English equivalent of "evangelical," since evangélica does not have the same associated theological and sociopolitical implications. Furthermore, while evangelicals consider themselves distinct from "mainline" or "historic" Protestant denominations, evangélica/os apply the term solely to distinguish themselves from Roman Catholics. "Evangélica" can be defined as the lived faith of a popular Protestantism that distinctively retains elements of Latin American popular Catholicism, including indigenous and African spiritualities, as essential dimensions of its cultural and religious formation. It is a group that is fast becoming an important part of the larger U.S. Protestant Church.

Latina evangélicas are women who, conscious of their religious and cultural roots, construct new theological paradigms that contribute to the transformation of their communities and the liberation of Latinas and other oppressed women. They are an integral part of the grassroots church and other communities that nourish their faith and reflect in dialogue with those communities. They maintain a vital tension between affirming the life-giving aspects of evangélica beliefs and offering a prophetic critique of the traditions that contribute to the injustice against women in particular, and to oppressed communities in general. Insofar as they are rooted in the theological legacy they inherited from their *abuelas* and *abuelos*, theirs is not a "new" theology in academic or ecclesial circles. Rather, they represent a constructive and therefore distinctive perspective (Lozano-Díaz 2003, 38).

Evangélica theologians are just as diverse as the Latina community at large. They represent a variety of cultural, denominational, and professional backgrounds. They have contributed individually and collaboratively to a significant and growing corpus of scholarly work. The following is a brief description of some of the "first generation" evangélica scholars and their contributions. The first evangélica in the United States to graduate with a doctoral degree in theological studies, Cuban-born Daisy L. Machado, is a Christian Church (Disciples of Christ) ordained minister and church historian. She is also the first Latina evangélica to serve as dean of an Association of Theological Schools (ATS) accredited institution in the United States. She has written about Latinas and Latinos, particularly those located in the borderlands of the Southwest, who are often ignored in hegemonic historical narratives reflecting dominant perspectives. Elizabeth Conde-Frazier is a New York Puerto Rican evangélica and an American Baptist Churches/USA ordained minister. She completed her doctoral degree in practical theology and religious education. She has written extensively on the role of Bible institutes as a vehicle for training evangélica lay and pastoral leadership, and explored themes in spirituality and *testimonios* (witnessing). Zaida Maldonado Pérez is a Puerto Rican historical theologian raised in Pentecostal church traditions, but is presently a leader in the United Church of Christ. She has written on the Trinity as *familia*, the importance of the legacy of the early church for evangélicas/os, and the subversive role of martyrs in early Christianity. Mexican-born Nora Lozano-Díaz is a systematic theologian and member of the Cooperative Baptist Fellowship. She has constructed a Christology that seeks to counter the traditional views of passive suffering prevalent in Mexican and Mexican American

women, and she has revisited the importance of the Virgin of Guadalupe from an evangélica perspective. Loida I. Martell-Otero is a bicoastal Puerto Rican constructive theologian and an ordained American Baptist minister. One of the earliest contributors about the importance of evangélica theology, she has explored the incarnational dimensions of soteriology and Christology, and suggested *sata/o* as a more culturally appropriate metaphor for mestizaje from a Puerto Rican perspective.

These are not the only evangélica scholars who have made important contributions. Aida Besancon-Spencer, Esther Díaz-Bolet, Theresa Chavez Sauceda, Leticia Guardiola, and Awilda González-Tejera are just a few of the many women whose contributions are considered invaluable to evangélica constructive and liberative theologies. As more Latina evangélicas enter the ranks of professional academic pursuits, and their contributions continue to enrich the theological discourse, they will be an increasingly important voice in the Latino/a church, as well as in the larger ecclesial and academic community.

Loida I. Martell-Otero

References and Further Reading

Lozano-Díaz, Nora O. *Confronting Suffering: An Evangélica Theological Approach* (PhD diss., Drew University, 2003).

Maduro, Otto. "Notes Toward a Sociology of Latina/o Religious Empowerment." *Hispanic/ Latino Theology: Challenge and Promise*, ed. Ada Maria Isasi-Díaz and Fernando F. Segovia (Minneapolis: Fortress Press, 1996).

Martell-Otero, Loida I. "Women Doing Theology: Una Perspectiva Evangélica." *Apuntes* 14, no. 3 (Fall 1994): 67–85.

Martell-Otero, Loida I. *Liberating News: An Emerging U.S. Hispanic/Latina Soteriology of the Crossroads* (PhD diss., Fordham University, 2005).

Rodríguez, José David, and Loida I. Martell-Otero, eds. *Teología en Conjunto: A Collaborative Hispanic Protestant Theology* (Louisville, KY: Westminster/John Knox Press, 1997).

LITERATURE

As has been the case from the dawn of writing, U.S. Latino/a authors often express religious themes and attitudes in their literature. Although some scholars begin the history of U.S. Latino/a literature with the arrival of the Spaniards, we draw some very clear boundaries as follows: 1848 for Mexican American literature; 1898 for Puerto Rican literature; 1959 for Cuban American literature; and later for other groups. Overall, U.S. Latino/a literature reflects a triadic interaction among indigenous, Christian, and African religious traditions. The Christian tradition has been predominantly Catholic, with Protestant writers becoming a more recent phenomenon.

Mexican American Literature

Insofar as religious expression is concerned, three periods of Mexican American literature may be tentatively identified: "The Normative Religious" period (1848–1959) where most literary works still revered or supported the Catholic Church; "The Reactionary Religious" period (1959–1972), in which works began actively to criticize the Catholic Church; and "The Alternative Religious" period, (1972–present), wherein writers have consciously constructed alternative and systematic traditions that draw consciously from non-Christian religions.

The literature of Mexican Americans from our Normative Religious period (1848–1959) is still being recovered and categorized. Genres include corridos (short narrative poems set to music), and assorted devotional poetry and short stories. One of the exemplars of this period would be Fray Angélico Chávez (1910–1996), whose poetry and short stories (e.g., *New Mexico Triptych* 1940) portray the advent of Catholicism to the Americas and the Southwest as one of the greatest achievements of Christendom.

The Reactionary Religious period in Mexican American literature had a definite beginning with Jose Antonio Villarreal's *Pocho* (1959), which is often acknowledged as the first Chicano novel. The open criticism of the Catholic Church and its espousal of frank atheism by its protagonist were unprecedented in Mexican American literature.

After the significant changes in Catholic policy promulgated by Vatican II (1962–1965), many more Mexican American authors became quite critical of the Church. One of the most militant was the mysterious Oscar Zeta Acosta (1935–1974?), who assumed the alter ego of Buffalo Z. Brown in various novels, including his *Autobiography of a Brown Buffalo* (1972) and its sequel, *The Revolt of the Cockroach People* (1973), which discuss his rejection of Christianity and religion altogether.

The early 1970s mark a sort of golden age in Mexican American literature. Presses such as *Quinto Sol* were established to publish works by Mexican Americans. Especially notable is Tomás Rivera's *. . . And the Earth Did Not Devour Him* (1971), which tells a Job-like story of the miserable existence of

Chicanos in the fields, and the silence of God regarding their plight. However, for all of the criticism of Catholicism or religion, authors in this period usually do not construct alternative religious visions.

This changed with the publication of *Bless Me Ultima* by Rudolfo Anaya, a native of New Mexico. From its publication in 1972, we mark the beginning of the Alternative Religious period in which authors went beyond criticizing traditional Catholicism and began a systematic exploration and active construction of alternative religious traditions. In *Bless Me Ultima*, Tony Maréz, the main character, opts for a pantheistic religion that can mediate between a strict Catholicism represented by his mother, a skepticism represented by his father, and an indigenous tradition represented by Ultima, a curandera who lives with Tony's family.

The floruit of the Alternative Religious period in Mexican American literature may be seen in *Borderlands* (1987) by Gloria Anzaldúa (1942–2004), who constructs a woman-centered religion based on Nahuatl traditions. Another example is found in Ana Castillo's *So Far From God* (1993), which centers on a systematic critique of androcentric religions. For Castillo, religions must be judged according to how they serve the needs of women.

Some authors concentrated on how ordinary women navigated their Latino/a spirituality in American urban environments. John Rechy, an openly gay Mexican-American author, published *The Miraculous Day of Amália Goméz* (1991), which is about woman who struggles to find God in the midst of an urban life in Hollywood. Similarly, Maria Amparo Escandón's *Esperanza's Box of Saints* (1999) examines the life

of a woman who struggles to adjust Catholic theology to the realities she encounters as she moves from Mexico to the United States. Indeed, the religious lives of women were a hallmark of the religious themes in the Latino/a literature of the 1980s and 1990s.

Of course, not all books in this Alternative Religious period were intent on creating alternative systematic theologies. In Alejandro Morales' *Rag Doll Plagues* (1992) we find a science fiction genre used to express religious themes. Others concentrated on showing how religion helped maintain cohesive bonds in a Mexican Diaspora. For example, Victor Villaseñor's sprawling epic, *Rain of Gold* (1991), tells the story of the two sides of the author's semi-fictional family and its journey from Mexico to the United States.

Puerto Rican Literature

For the purposes of our survey, the Puerto Rican literature that is most significant was that published from 1898 to the present. It was in 1898 that the United States acquired Puerto Rico as one of its territories. In the U.S. mainland, Puerto Rican literati have mainly concentrated in the New York area and reflect closely the immigration patterns of most Puerto Ricans of the post–World War II era. Thus, our treatment of religion concentrates on the works published in the mainland since World War II.

As in the case of Mexican American literature, there is a mass of folk genres (e.g., boleros, plenas) of lyric poetry and song that have yet to be systematically categorized in terms of religious content. Although not published until 1977, *Memorias de Bernardo Vega* (Memoirs of Bernardo Vega), written originally in the late 1940s, has come to represent the period between World War I and World War II in the United States. Its attitude toward Catholicism does not seem to be very strong, but it is not hostile. With Jesús Colón (1901–1974), however, we find a more nonreligious and openly Marxist approach in *A Puerto Rican in New York* and *Other Sketches* (1961).

One of the most prominent differences of Mexican American literature is the prevalence of African religious traditions in Puerto Rican literature. Often this acceptance of African religious traditions is juxtaposed with a criticism of the Catholic Church, as in the work of Tato Laviera, reputed to be the best-selling Latino/a poet in America. His work *La Carreta Made a U-Turn* (1992) is a powerful jeremiad against organized Catholicism juxtaposed with a call to acknowledge African traditions. Some of the poems, in fact, form substitute African rituals for Catholic liturgical traditions.

Relations between Puerto Rican and Irish Catholics in New York have been a point of contention. One expression of these tense relations is found in Edward Rivera's "First Communion," a story that is part of a larger work, *Family Installments* (1982). "First Communion" is about a boy, Santos Malanguéz, and his transition from Puerto Rico to New York, where he learns about the various ways in which Puerto Ricans maintained their identity in an Irish-dominated parish.

It is to be expected that Jews and Puerto Ricans would interact in New York City in a manner that may not happen in many other places in the United States. Nicholasa Mohr has explored these relationships in a number of stories featured in her book *El Bronx*

Remembered (1986). Piri Thomas, one of the most salient of Nuyorican authors, exemplifies the experimentation of Latino/as with Islam in *Down These Mean Streets* (1967), while his later book *Savior, Savior, Hold My Hand* (1973) details his disillusionment with Pentecostalism.

The difficulty in finding books written by Protestants attests to the position of Protestantism in Puerto Rican culture (and in Latino/a culture). And although nearly a third of Puerto Ricans are now Protestant, one finds very few positive depictions of Protestantism. In fact, we find that Protestants are largely missing from the canon of U.S. Latino/a literature found in most anthologies of Latino/a literature. One omission is Nicky Cruz, whose book, *Run, Baby, Run* (1968), differs very little, on formal and content grounds, from what Piri Thomas writes. Despite the fact that Cruz probably outsells Piri Thomas, Cruz, who is vocally evangelical and criticizes non-Protestant religions, is not normally viewed as part of the canon in academia.

Ed Vega represents a more secularist approach in his writings. His book *The Comeback* (1985) is perhaps one of the most intricate and sardonic works in all of U.S. Latino/a literature. Vega's *The Comeback* is a literary expression of the idea that God and religion are products of the human imagination. In many ways, *The Comeback* mirrors Vega's rejection of his religious upbringing.

Puerto Rican literature also seems to have had more women writers earlier than Mexican American literature. These women include Julia de Burgos, Sandra María Estévez, Judith Ortiz Cofer, Aurora Levins Morales, and Esmeralda Santiago. Often, these women also comment on religion. For example, Judith Ortiz Cofer's poem, "Cada Dia" [Each

Day] in *Terms of Survival* (1976) offers a feminist and somewhat satirical version of the Lord's Prayer. In *Terms of Survival* one finds another poem, "Costumbre" [Custom], wherein she comments on how piety and hypocrisy mix in Puerto Rican culture. Aurora Levins Morales has alluded to the issues and problems of being Puerto Rican and Jewish in works such as *Getting Home Alive* (1986) and *Medicine Stories: History, Culture, and the Politics of Integrity* (1998).

Cuban American Literature

For Cuban American history, 1959 is a crucial date. In that year, Fidel Castro created a communist dictatorship, which led to the emigration of thousands of Cubans to the United States. Cuban American literature may be periodized easily into at least two phases: (1) the immigrant adult generation; and (2) younger immigrant and American-born generations. It is the second group that has produced the bulk of what is called Cuban American literature. A major theme involves the interplay between life and religion in Cuba and America. Also important is the role of race relations, a subject often suppressed in Cuba, but given new vigor by the role of race in the United States. Most Cuban American literature has been the domain of White Cubans. One of the works that integrates these themes is Cristina Garcia's *Dreaming in Cuban* (1992), which presents a multivalent view of Santería, one of the main African traditions brought to, and transformed in, Cuba.

But not all Cuban American literary attitudes toward religion are negative. The attitudes found in *Mr. Ives' Christmas* (1995) are quite positive toward the

Writer Oscar Hijuelos displays his new book, A Simple Habana Melody, *on June 18, 2002, in West Hollywood, California. Hijuelos won the Pulitzer Prize for the book* Mambo Kings. *(Getty Images)*

Catholic Church. *Mr. Ives' Christmas* was authored by Oscar Hijuelos, who was the first U.S. Latina/o author to have garnered a Pulitzer Prize (1990) for literature. Furthermore, Achy Obejas has opened up new paths in exploring a Latino/Cuban Jewish identity (e.g., *Days of Awe*, 2001). A more eclectic approach to religion is found in the works of Pulitzer Prize winning playwright Nilo Cruz.

Dominican Literature and Other Groups

Authors from other Latino/a subgroups, while still a minority, are increasingly producing significant works. The themes are quite similar to those found in

Mexican American, Puerto Rican, and Cuban American literature. For example, in *How the García Girls Lost Their Accents* (1991), Julia Alvarez, the Dominican American writer, illustrates how American consumerism replaces their Dominican Catholic traditions.

Central and South Americans still do not have a significant voice in Latino/a literature. In fact, some of the best-known works involving Central American characters are authored by Mexican American authors. One illustration is *In Search of Bernabé* (1993) written by Graciela Limón, a native of Los Angeles who worked in El Salvador. The plot of the book centers on a Salvadoran woman who seeks a son who was lost amidst the chaos that resulted from the assassination of Oscar Romero, the Archbishop of El Salvador. The book focuses on the political struggles of El Salvador, but alludes frequently to the Catholic milieu of Salvadoran culture. Similarly, in *Mother Tongue* (1994), Demetria Martinez, a Mexican American author, voices the real-life struggles of Salvadorans who are involved in the American church sanctuary movement for undocumented persons.

Conclusion

Latina/o literature reflects the religious experience of Latinas/os only partially. One significant reflection is the role of Catholicism in the U.S. Latino/a experience. Cultural differences are also reflected in literature as we compare Caribbean with Mexican American authors. Certainly, we find more evidence of the influence of African traditions in the works of Puerto Rican and Cuban writers. We find many allusions to Aztec

religious traditions in Mexican American literature.

However, many authors are part of the elite educated strata of Anglo-American society who hold PhDs. Many are academics. These are not the experiences of most Latinas/os. Nor is the general religious profile like that of most Latinas/os now. Although perhaps over 25 percent of Puerto Ricans are Protestant (and positive toward Protestantism), one will not find a quarter of all Puerto Rican authors writing positively about Protestantism.

From at least 1959 onward, we see in most Mexican American writers an antipathy toward organized religion. At the same time, many of these writers have emphasized individualism. This individualism is consistent with Anglo-American religious traditions. We also see a marked increase in tolerance toward non-Christian traditions, especially since Vatican II. The works of Laviera and García exemplify some of the diverse attitudes that Latinas/os have toward African religions.

There are still many areas unexplored in Latina/o religion and literature. There needs to be a more systematic study that integrates different genres (including folk songs, corridos, etc.) into a more synthetic study of religion and literature. Our periodizations need to be refined and perhaps even abandoned when more systematic study of all literary genres is completed. And, of course, we need more reliable demographic data on Latino/a religion so that we can gauge how Latinos compare with Latino/a authors. The future is difficult to predict, but certainly we can expect Central and South Americans to make their voices heard in U.S. Latino/a literature. Eclectic forms of religious literary expression, drawn from traditions all over the globe, may be the dominant trend for the foreseeable future.

Hector Avalos

References and Further Reading

Avalos, Hector. *Strangers in our Own Land: Religion in U.S. Latina/o Literature* (Nashville: Abingdon, 2005).

Borland, Isabel Alvarez. *Cuban-American Literature of Exile: From Person to Personas* (Charlottesville: University of Virginia Press, 1998).

Christian, B. Marie. *Belief in Dialogue: U.S. Latina Writers Confront Their Religious Heritage* (New York: Other Press, 2005).

Dalleo, Raphael, and Elena Machado. *The Latino/a Canon and the Emergence of Post-Sixties Literature* (New York: Palgrave Macmillan, 2007).

Kevane, Bridget. *Profane and Sacred: Latino/a American Writers Reveal the Interplay of the Secular and the Religious* (Lanham, MD: Rowman & Littlefield, 2008).

Menes, Orlando Ricardo. *Renaming Ecstasy: Latino/a Writing on the Sacred* (Tempe, AZ: Bilingual Press, 2004).

LA LUCHA

La lucha (the struggle) is an intrinsic element of Latina/o culture, influencing the way Latina/os learn, look at life, face life, and think about themselves. La lucha is a fundamental concept that captures and synthesizes a variety of Latina/o cultural insights, values, and ways of dealing with life. This dynamic, foundational concept is expressed in a variety of words and expressions, among them *bregar* for Puerto Ricans; *sí se puede* for Chicanas/os and Mexican Americans; and *resolver* for Cubans. La lucha takes on a particular meaning for Latina/os in the United States who historically have been and continue to be minoritized, marginalized, and exploited by the dominant group. Given the social, economic, political, and religious context of oppression in which the majority of Latina/os in the United States live, la lucha takes on a particular meaning, concerned not just with the efforts all living entails, but particularly with the struggle for liberation/fullness of life. La lucha, in this sense of struggle for liberation/fullness of life, is a concrete reality in the life of Latina/os in the United States, a first horizon in the way life is experienced and engaged.

La lucha is an element of the way Latina/os understand themselves—as social beings who struggle—not as an individualistic act but as a family affair, a community enterprise, a societal endeavor. La lucha is very much part of the way Latina/os come to know reality, being central to Latina/o experiences, and at the heart of the three-pronged process for acquiring knowledge: immersion in the material mediations of the reality one is learning; apprehending it, that is, grasping it as fully as possible; and, in the process of apprehending it, changing it. La lucha makes clear that to know reality is to change reality. La lucha also identifies the perspective from which Latina/os look at life; it is the grounding point of view of the perennial search for ways to struggle because not to struggle is to perish. La lucha likewise refers to reflective action on behalf of liberation/fullness of life, negating the erroneous idea that the oppressed do not have anything to contribute in the creation of a just world order. La lucha as a liberative praxis is not just any action, but one grounded in rational analysis and passionate intentionality, manifested in

Demonstrators in Washington, D.C., protest bill HR 4437, which blocks immigration from Latin American countries. (Richard Gunion/Dreamstime)

bodily exertion and desire for fullness of life. La lucha is a defining element of the historical project of all oppressed people in general and of Latina/os specifically: struggling for liberation/fullness of life.

Taking into account the deep sense of Latina/o communities in the United States that *la vida es la lucha* (to struggle is to live) *mujerista*/Latina/o theology has elaborated the different aspects of la lucha as a category that impinges on being, knowledge/meaning, perspective, and reflective action, proceeding then to develop ethical and theological perspectives grounded in such understandings.

From a mujerista/Latina/o ethical perspective, la lucha is a value, an option, and a virtue. As a value it is for Latina/os a face of "the good." To be involved in la lucha gives valuable meaning to Latina/os' everyday reality, which is why the elders in Latina/o communities insist that one must not reject la lucha, but rather gratefully embrace it. La lucha is also an ethical option: the oppressed are self-defining human agents deciding whether to engage in la lucha or to accommodate to oppression, succumbing to mere survival or choosing instead to struggle for fuller life. As a virtue la lucha is a habitual act, a daily way of living and understanding life. Because it is a central element of "the good" at the personal, communal, and societal level, Latina/os exert themselves to have la lucha at the center of their lives, guiding them every day.

From a mujerista/Latina/o Christian theological perspective, God is not removed from human reality but rather listens to the cries of the poor and the oppressed and contributes effectively to la lucha, to their struggle to escape captivity and slavery (i.e., Exodus) and oppressive human-made laws (i.e., Jesus' struggles with the Pharisees). In popular religious practices—a central element of Latina/o culture—God, as well as saints and ancestors, who are considered to be very close to the divine, join la lucha of the people to change oppressive structures that squelch fullness of life.

Theologically, la lucha makes concrete the "love one another" Gospel message, the command to "go into all nations" to proclaim justice, love, and peace—fullness of life for all. From a religious-theological perspective la lucha is the Christian endeavor to create the conditions needed for the fullness of redemption to become a reality in the world. In this sense la lucha incarnates the eschatological tension between the "yet, but not yet" of the fullness of Jesus' salvific life and message. It is through la lucha for fullness of life that Christians become full members of the kin-dom of God—of the family of God —for la lucha incarnates the Gospel command to feed the hungry, give water to the thirsty, clothe the naked, visit those in prison and the sick, and welcome the foreigner.

Ada María Isasi-Díaz

References and Further Reading

Díaz Quiñones, Arcadio. *El arte de bregar: ensayos* (San Juan, Puerto Rico: Ediciones Callejón, 2000).

Burke, Kevin. *The Ground Beneath the Cross —The Theology of Ignacio Ellacuría* (Washington, DC: Georgetown University Press, 2002).

Isasi-Díaz, Ada María. *La Lucha Continues— Mujerista Theology* (Maryknoll, NY: Orbis Books, 2004).

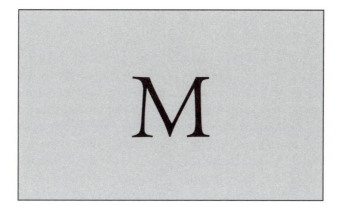

M

MACHISMO

The Spanish term "machismo" connotes emphatic masculinity, particularly in males, though it can also be applied to women (e.g., *marimacha*). Some sources trace its semantic roots to the Vulgar Latin *masclu*, *masculu*, or *masculus*, from where we derived "masculine," particularly as applied to animals and husbandry. An etymological hypothesis posits that it came from the arcane Portuguese *muacho*, from *mulus*, mule, with semantic emphasis on stubbornness and foolishness. The word entered English in the 1920s. It has also been introduced into other languages with the primary meaning of exaggerated masculinity (French *machisme*, Italian *maschilismo*). In Costa Rica and other parts of Central America, *macho* can also mean blond or light skinned. Some linguists in Nicaragua note that macho proceeds from the verbs *machar* and *machacar*, meaning "to pound, break, crush, hammer, beat, bruise, screw."

As a male ideology, machismo has existed in many cultures, with special salience in traditional Mediterranean cultures, especially in Spain from where derived the legend of Don Juan. In the legal system of Roman law in Latin Mediterranean societies, women were under one of the following three types of legal authority: *patria potestas* (paternal power), *manus* (subordination to a husband's legal power), or *tutela* (guardianship). *Patria potestas* is still prevalent in some Latin American countries where the men are considered as masters or heads of the households (*paterfamilias*) and have absolute authority and superiority over wife and children in virtually all legal and social situations. The sociocultural lineage of Latin American machismo is from Andalusian Spain and partly from the Saracen Moors who ruled southern Spain from 711 to 1492 CE. The confluence of Iberian, Roman, and Islamic cultures that merged in Spain evolved into a complicated code of chivalry and male honor with the rise of knighthood.

Spanish conquistadors introduced machismo through cultural and interracial interaction with American indigenous populations. The indigenous gender ideology was primarily based on a militaristic and patriarchal society where men were socialized to be warriors and women to be caretakers of the home subordinate to men. In the case of the Aztecs, for instance, the Spanish male ideology, especially in *donjuanismo*, the quintessence of Spanish machismo who was not interested in indigenous women per se, but only as tokens of his social and military dominance or conquering virility, reinforced Aztec warrior bravado.

As a stereotype, machismo has had a negative connotation, especially in the American popular culture, meaning, aggressive hypermasculinity, an obsession with status, power, and control at any cost, rigid self-sufficiency, misogynistic and domineering attitudes typically ascribed to authoritative husbands, patriarchal fathers, paternalistic landlords, and abusive womanizers. A traditional Hispanic saying embodying some of these attitudes is *La mujer en la casa, el hombre en la calle* (Woman in the home, man in the street), suggesting a strict differentiation of roles assigned by gender. Mexican folkloric glamorizing of machismo is often found in *corridos* (ballads) and *rancheras* (Mexican polkas) where vengeance, drinking, womanizing, banditry, and glorification of male sexual prowess are extolled. Hispanic popular images of this typical macho are personified in the Spanish *matador* (bullfighter), Mexican *charro* or cowboy, the Argentinean *gaucho*, often portrayed as tough (meaning unafraid and unemotional) and full of strength and virility, and the *caudillos* (military dictators)

with their bold and authoritarian *presidential machismo*, willing to use violence and oppression to achieve their ends.

A form of machismo some consider to be positive denotes a man as head of the household for an entire extended family, and this includes responsible and protective roles as well as the instillment of cultural values of *familismo*, *respeto* (respect), *dignidad* (dignity), *simpatia* (niceness), *confianza* (trust), and *personalismo*. *Familismo* refers to strong traditional family values that emphasize interdependence, affiliation, cooperation, reciprocity, and loyalty. *Simpatia* requires social politeness and smooth relations, which considers confrontations offensive and improper. Proper respect is due to all authority, and it is also displayed in relations with elders (e.g., parents). "Personalismo" refers to the trust and rapport that is established with others by developing warm, friendly, and personal relationships. Latino fathers often pride themselves on children who have developed these cultural values, which make them *bien educados* (well-educated). In this concept, being good providers, being hard workers, and silently suffering the consequences of both are part of being macho.

Chingón, *mandilón*, and *maricón* are three other important constructs in machismo discourse. The Chingón, from the verb *chingar*, which means to rape or to screw, is a macho type described by Octavio Paz in the *Labyrinth of Solitude*, and typifies the negative connotations of machismo. Some of the traits include a paternalistic attitude toward family and friends. The chingón does not show his emotions and uses his sexuality to feel virile and alive, thus acquiring manhood through sexual performance. The mandilón, on the other hand, is a male who wears the apron (*mandil*) instead of the pants, and it suggests a passive man dominated by his wife who has taken his wife's role. "Maricón" is a pejorative term used to describe the effeminate man or presumed homosexual. Also, the failure of men to perform such acts as drinking, fighting, assertiveness, and heterosexual promiscuity earns the label of maricón.

Marianismo is a female corollary to machismo, and it is a cultural or religious description of the ideal woman as self-abnegating mother. This concept is explained by the veneration of the Virgin Mary, the ideal symbol of virgin and mother, and it presumes that since women are spiritually superior to men, they are capable of enduring all suffering inflicted by macho men. It exalts femininity and childbearing capacity by emphasizing women's fated long-suffering or *hembrismo*, as well as the qualities of obedience, submission, fidelity, meekness, and humility. In traditional Latino societies, the macho is given the responsibility of defending family honor by protecting the virginity of wives, daughters, or sisters. These two polarities, *machismo* and marianismo, along with religion and traditional values have helped shape traditional gender role socialization in Latin America.

There is some evidence that secularization, new Catholic movements (such as Charismatics), as well as Protestantism are quite influential on contemporary gender roles. Since in almost any religion, gender roles and family are vital to its propagation, many scholars look especially to the role of men in family and society as a bellwether of current and future denominational affiliation.

Fernando A. Ortiz and Kenneth G. Davis

References and Further Reading

Aquino, Maria Pilar, Daisy Machado, and Jeanette Rodríguez, eds. *A Reader in Latina Feminist Theology: Religion and Justice* (Austin: University of Texas Press, 2002).

De La Torre, Miguel A. "Beyond Machismo: A Cuban Case Study." *The Annual of the Society of Christian Ethics* 19 (1999a): 213–233.

Gilmore, David. *Manhood in the Making: Cultural Concepts of Masculinity* (New Haven, CT: Yale University Press, 1990).

MARIAN DEVOTIONS

Devotion to Mary, the mother of Jesus, is historically attested in Christianity from around the second century CE. Devotion to Mary, the mother of Jesus, has been explained and justified on the grounds that she is the mother of the Savior. Devotion to Mary remains important in at least three main Christian traditions: Catholic (East and West), Orthodox, and Anglican. Other Christian traditions (since the sixteenth century) have accentuated either a disdain for such devotion or a discreet tolerance toward it. In *no* Christian church (Catholic, Protestant, Orthodox, or Anglican) is Marian devotion regarded as *necessary* to the church's self-understanding or its definition of Christianity. Doctrines regarding Mary cannot be confused with devotion to Mary. It is impossible to study any U.S. Latino/a cultural community and not encounter Marian devotion in one form or another.

Since at least the second century, prayers were directed to Mary asking for her intercession with God (and/or

Annual pilgrimage in honor of the Virgin of Guadalupe, from South San Francisco's All Souls Church to the preeminent sanctuary of San Francisco Catholicism at St. Mary's Cathedral. (Lonny Shavelson/Zuma/Corbis)

her Son). Devotion to her among Christians was very widespread by the time the Council of Ephesus (431 CE) taught that Mary was indeed the *Theotokos* (the "mother of God"). It seems that popular Marian devotion was a significant element in this Council's doctrinal discussions. After Ephesus there was an extraordinary increase in references to Mary in the (Eastern and Western) Christian Church's official liturgies and in popular prayers. In Western Christianity the devotion to Mary spread through the liturgies. The feast of the Assumption of Mary (called the "Dormition" in Eastern Christianity) has by far been the most popular Marian liturgical celebration during Christian history. This liturgical feast developed from an earlier, more general celebration of Mary during the

Christmas season. However, popular Marian devotions, although influenced by official liturgies (and vice versa), have historically been mostly local or regional.

During the Western Middle Ages there was a significant increase in Marian pious practices after the eleventh and twelfth centuries, with claims of miracles and apparitions increasing as well. There had been references to apparitions of Mary since the third century, but the second half of the Middle Ages saw growth in the number of such claims. Miracles attributed to Mary, or miraculous discoveries of her images, seemed to abound after the eleventh and twelfth centuries. Arguably, a number of social, cultural, and economic reasons helped shape this development—the eleventh and twelfth

JUAN DIEGO (1474–1548)

The figure of Juan Diego was declared a fabrication in 1996 by William Schulenburg, the Abbot of the Basilica of Nuestra Señora de Guadalupe in Mexico City. Because of this, the Vatican's Congregation for the Saints did a thorough investigation to verify his existence. The investigations revealed that he was born in 1474. His name was Cuatitlatoatzin (Eagle that speaks). He was a farmer and weaver of straw mats. He was married and may have had children. He and his wife (María Lucia) were among the very few natives who accepted Christianity. He was baptized in 1524 with the name Juan Diego, perhaps in honor of San Juan the evangelist whose symbol is the eagle and San Diego who was the first to proclaim the Gospel in Spain. In 1531, at age 57, he saw the Virgin Mary on the hill of Tepeyac and received her miraculous image in his tilma. He spent the rest of his life as sacristan at Guadalupe's Shrine where he would speak Guadalupe's message to visitors. More than 100,000 Nahuatls were baptized Christians because of Juan Diego's testimony. He died on May 30, 1548. Canonized in 2002, he is revered as the first Amerindian saint and lay evangelizer.

—*GCG*

centuries brought a critically important set of profound changes to Western Christianity. Religious reasons alone do not seem sufficient explanation, although these too played their part, as well as credulity and insufficient catechesis. Exaggerated claims, fabulous stories, and impossible miracles were common during the medieval period. Although sixteenth-century Protestant reformers opposed all forms of Marian devotions, the (Catholic) Council of Trent began a process of purification of Marian piety that was very much needed at the time. It took longer than most Council participants expected, but Marian devotional practices were "cleaned up" in most places, and most of the exaggerated claims contained. At the popular level, however, some fabulous stories and expectations continued (sometimes fueled by powerful social or ecclesiastical interests). Exaggerated Marian claims and practices are today not acceptable within mainstream Catholicism. In a parallel manner, exaggerated disdain for all Marian devotion is equally not acceptable today among most other Christian denominations (although sometimes the exaggerated disdain is fueled by powerful social or ecclesiastical interests).

During the period that immediately preceded the Catholic and Protestant Reformations, and historically coinciding with these, European Catholics discovered and conquered the Americas. With and after the conquest came the missionaries, who brought with them the usual Marian devotions from Europe. The specific practices that came to this side of the Atlantic often depended on the origins (home village, region) of the missionaries and colonizers. However, the most important Marian devotions in the Americas began here, such as *Guadalupe* in Mexico and *Caridad* in Cuba. It is well documented that Mary became popular and well accepted among the native populations and the African slaves during the centuries of Spanish and

GUADALUPANAS

The Guadalupanas are members of an association that promotes the cult of Our Lady of Guadalupe. Made up primarily of Latinas, the groups form within parishes, particularly in Latin America and the United States. The origins and history of this grassroots organization began in 1531 after the apparitions of the Virgin of Guadalupe. As early as 1578, Pope Gregory XIII granted indulgences to the Confraternity of Our Lady of Guadalupe at Tepeyac. Guadalupanas play a role in preserving Latino/a traditions of popular piety and teaching them to their children and the larger parish community. Their expression of popular religiosity takes many forms: the rosary, devotional altars to the Virgin, dramatic reenactment of the apparitions at Tepeyac, religious processions, and other public displays of devotion. There is a liturgical rite of initiation, in which new members are presented with special metals signifying their commitment to the Virgin and her cult. The central calendar event for Guadalupanas is December 12, the Feast of Our Lady of Guadalupe. Members meet throughout the year for prayer and the planning of this celebration. Generally, groups raise money for the festivities through bake sales and meals where Latino/a foods are served. In many parishes these meals have become important community socials events held after the Sunday Liturgies.

—RL

Portuguese rule. It is also clear that Marian devotional practices were instrumental in expanding colonial Christianity in the Americas. These devotions are still popular in Latin America and among U.S. Latino/as, and have become increasingly important to serious theological reflection on the *sensus fidelium*, on tradition, and on the poor's image of themselves and of God. Some (mostly U.S. Latino/a) theologians have begun to raise pneumatological questions as well.

Mary has become a symbol and instrument of empowerment for the poor in many places of Latin America and among many U.S. Latino/as. In many contexts Mary is deeply tied to issues of cultural identity and dignity, and to struggles for liberation. Although Marian piety and symbols have been used and abused by both church authorities and governments with serious alienating results, Mary does not seem to have lost a certain subversive character and role among the poor or disenfranchised. She has been and is, for the poor, a bearer of their culture, justice, and identity—to the extent that many Marian devotions could not be explained or understood otherwise (e.g., *Guadalupe, Caridad, San Juan de los Lagos*, etc.).

Claims of apparitions have continued in Catholic contexts throughout the world. Recent ones that have become popular are those that have centered on events at Fatima (in Portugal), Lourdes (in France), La Salette (also in France), Medjugorje (in Croatia), and others. However, apparitions or claims of apparitions occur on all continents. Apparitions and their "messages" have never been (and can never be) understood in Catholicism as necessary or as being anything but "private, pious recommendations" without *any* revelatory or obligatory character for the church or its members. No "message" could claim to bring a new revelation or anything that could be understood beyond the strictly pious. There is no obligation for Catholics to believe in apparitions or the possibility of apparitions (not even in those that church authorities might endorse). Sometimes Catholic church authorities may accept some devotional practices that could result from a claimed apparition (e.g., Lourdes); but other times church authorities can publicly reject the validity of all practices and claims made regarding an apparition (e.g., the *Virgen del Pozo* of Puerto Rico).

When Catholics refer to devotional Marian titles or names (i.e., "Our Lady of ..."), they are usually referring to devotions that were established either because of a claimed apparition or miracle (e.g., Fatima, Guadalupe), or because of a certain Christian virtue that Mary is said to exemplify (e.g., Charity, Mercy), or because of a specific devotional practice (e.g., the Rosary).

Were this entry to conclude here, the reader might think that Latino/a reflections on the history, development, and justifications of Marian devotions, or of the lack thereof, are still within the "expected" denominational bounds. However, a new current of discussion among Latino/a theologians has the potential for transforming what all Christians (Catholic, Protestant, Orthodox, and Anglican) think about Marian devotions. This new current can make significant potential contributions to ecumenical dialogues.

Some Latino/a theologians today have begun to raise possible connections between Mary of Nazareth and the Holy Spirit. More specifically: Is the focus of apparently Marian devotions *really* Mary, the mother of Jesus? The theological argument first acknowledges that the historical and sociological location of

Marian devotions have typically been among the poorer members of society, and thus among the most vulnerable and powerless. In other words, the more frequently "devout" have been those whose cultures and symbols have been more generally oppressed, more silenced, and more culturally invaded and persecuted. The theological argument further acknowledges that it is impossible to ignore the current powerful critique of most Christian evangelization and theology—for their historically androcentric ("male-centered") bias. It is further impossible to ignore the historically attested role played by generations of denominational leadership in shaping, justifying, and conforming the churches' assumptions and practices to the dominant culture's androcentric (and many other) biases.

Therefore, is it not possible for us today (asks the theological argument) to interpret Marian devotion as a historically "counter-androcentric" affirmation of the Holy Spirit, in and through subaltern cultural categories and symbols that the (denominationally and socially) dominant refused to associate with God? In other words, is it possible for us today to think that *who* has been and is being venerated in and through so-called "Marian" devotions is really not Mary of Nazareth but a Person of the Trinity—the Holy Spirit? Given the character, type, and texture of the devotion, and the expectations of the "devout" relationship with the One addressed in the devotion, is it possible to ask if this "One" is really Mary of Nazareth, or rather and more accurately the Holy Spirit (culturally portrayed in originally "Marian" cultural garb)? Understandably, many ministers and theologians (often still saturated by lingering androcentric biases) might rush to claim that the focus of these devotions is and must remain Mary of Nazareth—in their view "marianization" must remain because it justifies their support or disdain for the devotion. But the ministerial and theological attempts at "marianizing" the devotions cannot escape or dismiss the serious issues raised by some contemporary theologians. Why could the symbols and cultural categories historically associated with Mary in European Christianity not become associated with the Holy Spirit in the Americas? Why are the poor (among whom these devotions have traditionally thrived) bound to use or follow the dominant religious languages, symbols, explanations, or cultural categories? Because *all* human speech and claims about God are invariably and inescapably culturally bound (and, therefore, limited, imperfect, and created tools that will always fail to capture what is ultimately beyond all human understanding), it is necessary to conclude that *it is possible* to use feminine cultural categories and symbols (in this case those historically originating in devotions to Mary) for speech and claims about the Holy Spirit.

Orlando O. Espín

References and Further Reading

Espin, Orlando O. *The Faith of the People: Theological Reflections on Popular Catholicism* (Maryknoll, NY: Orbis Books, 1997).

Johnson, Elizabeth A. *Truly Our Sister: A Theology of Mary in the Communion of Saints* (New York: Continuum, 2006).

Tavard, George A. *The Thousand Faces of the Virgin Mary* (Collegeville, MN: Liturgical Press, 1996).

MARIANISMO

Because marianismo idealizes the social conditions Latinas find themselves in as normal, natural, and legitimate, it becomes a sexist paradigm based on a quasi-religious ideology by which Latin American women and U.S. Latinas have been denied their full humanity for generations. The introduction of Christianity within the Americas was a colonial project that maintained its structures of domination through the construction of gender roles. A dichotomy was introduced that divided labor along gender lines where men were defined as inhabiting the public sphere of economic and political production, while women inhabited the domestic sphere of household reproduction. To counter the aggressive and competitive immoral public sphere where men are required to operate, women provide a spiritual equilibrium within the serenity and security of the household.

Spanish Catholicism's emphasis on family unity and its communal ties to hierarchical structures helped create a spiritually based patriarchy. Catholicism contributed to the definition of what role women were to play within society through an idealized image of the Virgin Mary, hence the term "marianismo." Mary is presented as the best representation of the nature of women, and as such becomes the perfect role model for all women. Marianismo became the polar opposite of machismo. Through negative definition, machismo becomes what marianismo is not. Essentializing femaleness to the realm of passivity, chastity, and self-sacrifice meant that maleness must be understood as assertive, virile, and self-centered. Nevertheless, the male remains

ABUELITA THEOLOGY

Abuelita (little grandmother) theology, also known as "kitchen theology," refers to the transmission of religious beliefs, practices, and spirituality within the Hispanic family mainly through the women of the household. This theological expression looks toward the values of grandparents, specifically grandmothers, to confirm a present trajectory that is rooted in the past. The role of "abuelitas" preserves the religious practices of the family, such as preparing home altars, encouraging pilgrimages, celebrating the virgin or saint days, and spiritually cleansing, along with a host of other practices. Through the informal conversation that occurs within the space where women are usually relegated, the kitchen, a popular religious expression emerges and is preserved. The informal transmission of religious understandings to the next generation of mainly Latinas, who in turn teach the rest of the household, have led scholars to propose that Hispanic popular religiosity has a matriarchal core. There are some Latina religious scholars who would argue that abuelita theology is somewhat romanticized, masking the sexism within a Hispanic theology that relegates any contributions by Latinas both to the kitchen and to the abuelas, the grandmothers. In other words, can a young Latina at the university also make a contribution to Hispanic religious thought?

—MAD

responsible for providing and protecting his family. It would be an error to limit marianismo to Catholic families; as a sociopolitical phenomena within the Hispanic community, marianismo is also present within Protestant families, communities, and churches.

Proper female behavior is epitomized by a Virgin Mary mystique. Hispanic women are forced to choose one of two extremes. She exists within the dichotomy of virgin or whore—there exists no ambiguous space between these two extremes. As the ideal virgin, women are to be chaste, pure, and docile. Just as Mary submitted to God's will, and just as she was pure as signified by her virginity, so too are Latin American women and U.S. Latinas to accept God's will to be wives and mothers, living humble lives and always being willing to suffer for the sake of their families. The Latin American woman and the U.S. Latina exist for the sole purpose of

supporting their husbands and raising their children. She is the giver of care and pleasure, never the receiver. Although the husband is the absolute head of the household whose decisions are to be obeyed, she remains the sole nurturer of the children and the guardian of morality within the household. Her duty is to maintain and secure the honor and unity of her family. To work outside the home puts into question either her virtues or her husband's ability to be a man and provide for her, or both. Through her indiscretions, shame can be brought upon her husband and his family name.

In effect, marianismo reduces women to an object of male gallantry—an extension of the male ego. But even when husbands are callous, physically abusive, or engaged in extramarital affairs, marianismo provides women with the model of Mary who silently accepted her fate and suffering. Regardless of male behavior, women discover their value and purpose in being virgins, wives, or mothers. No other role or identity exists for her. To be or aspire to be independently minded, to be self-supporting, or to develop self-esteem is to forsake her traditional role.

Sex for women is for reproduction, not enjoyment. Because men desire to marry a "virgin María," who remains unsullied until he impregnates her, he needs and requires other sexual liaisons to satisfy his sexual appetite and prove his machismo. In a sense, rather than establishing strong families, marianismo encourages domination, aggressiveness, and a "cult of virility" that reinforces a machista culture detrimental to all women. Political scientist Evelyn Stevens wrote in 1973 a groundbreaking essay where she coined the term "marianismo." For Stevens, marianismo "teaches that women are semi divine, morally superior to and spiritually stronger than men." The force behind marianismo lies behind centuries of fertility goddesses who signified the ability of women to produce life. Although the social consequences of marianismo, according to Stevens, may have proven to be negative in the lives of women, women were still able to demonstrate spiritual authority in the home and society by emulating the characteristics of the Virgin Mary. In this fashion, women knew their place and role within society and were less prone to suffer identity crises. But the rise of Latina feminism in the late 1970s challenged Stevens's positive understanding of marianismo by emphasizing its structural patriarchy over the centuries through the use of sociological and anthropological analysis. Even though few today would insist on or advocate for structuring Hispanic

society around the concept of marianismo, its consequences and worldviews are still present within the Latina/o community.

Miguel A. De La Torre

References and Further Reading

Aquino, María Pilar, Daisy L. Machado, and Jeanette Rodríguez. *A Reader in Latina Feminist Theology: Religion and Justice* (Austin: University of Texas Press, 2002).

Gil, Rosa María, and Carmen Inoa Vázquez. *The María Paradox: How Lantinas Can Merge Old World Traditions with New World Self-Esteem* (New York: G. P. Putnam's Sons, 1996).

Morales-Gumundsson, Lourdes E., and Caleb Rosado. "Machismo, Marianismo and the SDA Church." *Spectrum Magazine* 25, no. 2 (December 1995): 19–28.

Stevens, Evelyn P. "Marianismo: The Other Face of Machismo in Latin America." *Female and Male in Latin America*, ed. Ann Pescatelo (Pittsburgh: University of Pittsburgh Press, 1973).

MATACHINES

The religious dance-drama of Los Matachines is an ancient tradition within the southwestern United States. These dances are shared by Latina/os and Native peoples. The influences of these dances can be traced to the European Middle Ages, specifically the Iberian Peninsular and the indigenous cultures of the Americas. Just as the sites where the religious dance-drama is produced are different, the 44 catalogued versions in the Americas also span diverse places from Pueblo, Colorado, to the deep rainforests of Belize.

Originally, the dance celebrated the conquest of the Moors who occupied the Iberian Peninsula between the years 711 and 1492. The influence of the Moors is evident from the costumes worn by the dance participants. Each dancer is appropriately masked with scarves that hide the lower part of their faces, as well as foreheads and eyes, called *fleco*. Upon the heads of the Matachines are mounted tall headdresses made of costly fabrics such as velvet and silk. These cupiles are decorated with silk ruffle borders, jeweled trinkets, and symbols. From the back of the headdresses hang long silk ribbons arranged in patterns that are pleasing to the eye. The masking of the hand is continued with many scarves that bedeck the dancers. Held within the right hand is a three-pronged wand called a *palma*. The palma represents the Trinitarian belief that God is one and three at the same time. In Europe, Saint Patrick explained the Trinity by holding the triple-leafed shamrock out to the Druids. In the Americas, this concept was reflected as the triune god Quetzalcoatl of Mexico who is lord of the air, lord of the land, and lord of the water at the same time.

In Europe, Los Matachines are reflected in the Italian commedia *dell'arte* as mattachinos. The people of England would certainly recognize their own beribboned "Morris Dancers" as "Moorish Dancers." As Los Matachines became an increasingly popular dance, much symbolism was attributed to them. They were figures to be seen only during feast days or during mid-winter mumming rituals. The dance was introduced to the native peoples in the hope of converting them to Christianity. It was changed and reinterpreted to incorporate local indigenous customs. As missionaries moved north toward what would

Matachines dance at San Ildefonso Pueblo, New Mexico. (Danny Lehman/Corbis)

become the United States, they brought the dance with them. The first documentation of the dance in what would be the United States occurred in San Juan Pueblo, New Mexico, in 1598.

New Mexico scholars such as the late Fray Angélico Chávez asked if it was possible that Los Matachines was originally only a form of social dance. Regardless, it is known that the oldest unbroken tradition of Los Matachines dancing that exists can be traced to the town of Bernalillo, New Mexico, where the dance has been performed for 315 straight years. The citizens of Bernalillo made a promise when they returned to their homes after the Pueblo Rebellion of 1680, that if their patron saint San Lorenzo were to keep them safe, they would dance in his honor every year.

Other scholars who have studied the dance have suggested that Los Matachines is a homoerotic dance, that is, a dance done by men for men, since female figures were not originally part of the dance. Just as female societies guarded their secrets, so did men's secret societies. The only female figure in the dance, an ogress called La Pirojundia, was always played by a man dressed as a woman. The word "pirojo" or "piroja" is an ancient word that refers to one having both male and female attributes. In this way the figure was assured of having both the strength of a man and the power of a woman.

As the history of the dance unfolded among the indigenous Native nations, more symbolism was added to it. The ancient ogres called *Abuelos*, were brought in to keep order in the dance as well as to call out the movements to the dancers. They played the role of dance monitors and were called *bastoneros*. Part of their duties included keeping the

dancers' ribbons arranged and keeping the spectators out of the arena. As the Abuelos took on the traits of trickster figures, they also teased the sacrificial bull of the dance. The bull is called *El Toro* while he is dancing and *El Capeo* whenever he is ritually castrated. He must bow low before the chief dancer called "Monarca" among the Spanish and "Monanca" among the Tiwa Natives. Monarca is easily recognized for he is the only dancer who wears solid white. It is only after the bull is felled that the ogress Pirojundia falls on the floor at his side and gives birth to a newborn abuelito who will become the spirit of the dance the following year. This action has been interpreted as a fertility rite.

Native influences on the Dance of Los Matachines also exist. For example, the participants, whose numbers vary according to their interpretations, carry masked rattles in their left hands. These rattles are highly decorated gourds. Also, they gird their waists with loincloths called tapa-rabos. The loincloths are decorated with ritual symbols known only to the dancers. Around their lower shins, they wear fancy leggings. The newest addition to the religious dance-drama is the little girl figure called La Malinche. Her name stems from the ancient records that say she was the paramour of the conquistador Hernán Cortez. In fact, in Belize, Los Matachines is known as "The Dance of Cortez" according to Maya Native Victor Choc.

Again, the symbolism attached to La Malinche depends on who is doing the interpretation. In Belize there are four Malinches who dance. In Bernalillo there are three. In Jémez there are two. In Arroyo Seco, there is only one. Depending on how she is seen, she can represent the waxing, full, and waning moon of the dawn, the full day, and the dusk. In the village of Tortugas she is the spirit of purity and she often wears attributes belonging to the Virgin of Guadalupe. The music of Los Matachines also varies in tenor and speed. It is usually played with guitar and violin among the Spanish villages and with ritual drum and rattle in Native villages. Today, Los Matachines dancers usually perform for free at local church fiestas paying homage to the church's particular patron saint.

Larry Torres

References and Further Reading

Rodriguez, Silvia. *The Matachines Dance, Ritual Symbolism and Interethnic Relations in the Upper Rio Grande Valley* (Albuquerque: University of New Mexico Press, 1996).

Romero, Brenda M. "Fariseos y Matachines en la Sierra Tarahumara: Entre la Pasión de Cristo, la Transgresión cómico-sexual y las Danzas de Conquista by Carlo Bonfiglioli," *Ethnomusicology* 44, no. 3 (Autumn 2000): 527–528.

Torres, Larry. *Six New Mexico Folkplays for the Advent Season* (Albuquerque: University of New Mexico Press, 1999).

MESTIZAJE

The term "mestizaje" generally refers to the process of biological and cultural mixing that occurs "after the violent and unequal encounter between cultures" (Garcia-Rivera 1995, 40). It is more commonly and specifically used, however, to refer to the mixture of Spanish and American Indian ancestry and cultures that marks Latin American and Latino/a history and identity, as a result of the arrival of Spanish colonizers in the Americas in the fifteenth century.

The origins of this Spanish and American Indian convergence can be traced back to the Spanish exploration and colonization of the Americas, beginning with Christopher Columbus's arrival in 1492. Columbus's discovery of a route from Europe to the Americas took place at a time when Spain was seeking to exploit resources from other lands in order to expand its colonial borders and to strengthen a faltering economy, and thus it served to open the way for other Spanish explorers and colonizers to sail to these areas. As a result of this deliberate takeover of these lands and of the subjugation of the native peoples that inhabited them, a good part of the territory that comprises the Americas, including much of Central and South America, Mexico, large segments of the Caribbean, and most of what is now the southern and western United States, eventually came to be claimed for Spain.

Among other effects, the Spanish colonial presence in these parts occasioned the appearance of people of mixed parentage and cultural heritage, and more specifically of Spanish and American Indian descent. Sexual encounters, both forced and consensual, between male Spanish colonizers and Native American women resulted in the births of large numbers of children with a Spanish father and a Native American mother. These children came to be known as *mestizos*. The truth is, however, that the Spanish colonial system generated other complex relationships—it occasioned the intermingling and fusion of at least three general and distinct groups of peoples and cultures in the Americas (i.e., the Spanish, Amerindian or Native

American, and African peoples and cultures). A full discussion of the Spanish colonial period and of the "making" or reinvention of the Americas is beyond the scope of this entry. However, it is both safe and necessary to say that what occurred over this period of American history was a violent and unequal encounter of peoples and cultures that was fundamentally motivated by imperial and socioeconomic interests.

Historians of the Spanish colonial period have established that much of the early Spanish interest in the "New World of the Americas" centered on mining and the profits that it could generate. The problem was, however, that development of these mines required a larger supply of labor than the Spanish colonizers were willing or able to provide on their own. For this reason, the conquered indigenous populations were generally forced into mining labor. But the oppressive labor conditions, meager diet, broken family life, and disease that were part of this harsh life of indenture under Spanish rule combined over time to bring about a significant decline in the native populations. And so, in order to replace or supplement the decreasing indigenous labor force, the Spaniards took to forcibly introducing large numbers of African slaves from the western coast of Africa to the Americas. The proximities of these groups of people in the Americas occasioned the emergence of a new cultural and even racial context as the Spanish, Native American, and African populations increasingly intermingled over time, creating large populations of peoples of mixed ancestry. In this forced encounter of peoples and cultures, three distinct groups of mixed populations came into being: first, the mestizos, who were persons of Spanish or Iberian and

American Indian parentage; second, the *mulattos*, who were persons of Spanish or Iberian and African descent; and third, the *zambo*, who were persons of African and indigenous or Native American derivation.

Evidence of this blending of peoples and cultures in the Americas abounds. Present-day Latin American and U.S. Latino/a populations have been especially marked by this history of biological and cultural fusion, however, and particularly by the reality or process of *mestizaje* and *mulatez*. Latino/a culture and identity does, in fact, often show itself to be the result of the blending of Spanish, Amerindian, and African lineages and cultures. Practically every dimension of the lives of present-day Latin Americans and U.S. Hispanics/Latinos shows a hint of this complex and syncretistic fusion in some way or another, from broad issues of race and religion to specifics of food, language, music, and most everything else in between.

Although it was originally coined to specify the blending of Spanish and Native American derivation and thus to denote the children of Spanish and American Indian parents, the term "mestizaje" has taken on a wider meaning in more recent usage. It is at times openly used to refer to the process of biological and cultural fusion itself, and is, therefore, sometimes used indiscriminately to speak of all forms of mixed parentage and cultural heritage that can be found within the Latin American and Latino/a population. In addition, the term has come to be used as a sort of philosophical and ideological or political concept in more recent Latin American and Latino/a literature. In this sense it has been used to contest racist Western notions of pure race and ethnic absolutism, to retrieve the indigenous element of Latin American and Latino/a cultural identity, to reclaim the mixed-race or mixed-cultural constituent of Latin American and Latino/a identity, or to open wider possibilities for the forging of new and potentially affirmative multiethnic identities.

An early move in the direction of the use of the idea of mestizaje as a broader philosophical and political construct can be found in the work of the Mexican philosopher, educator, and politician José Vasconcelos. In 1925 he wrote a treatise, *La Raza Cosmica/The Cosmic Race*, in which he gave an affirming and even celebratory reading of Mexican and Latin American mestizaje and used it to challenge Western theories of racial superiority and purity. To be sure, Vasconcelos was unable to break completely from the kind of Eurocentrism or Western elitism that he attempted to challenge, as he still tended to give priority to Iberian culture and to connect it too romantically or uncritically with modernization and the attainment of progress. Thus, it can be said that, even as he sought to reclaim the mixed-race and mixed-cultural identity of Mexicans as a unique source of creativity, he tended to look to Europe for inspiration and unintentionally to downgrade the aboriginal past or the indigenous component of Mexican and Latin American history and identity. Nevertheless, Vasconcelos's early work at least served to point up the possibilities of a more positive and expansive interpretation of the historical process and concept of mestizaje, moving the term away from the negative connotations it had elicited previously, for example, as a synonym for illegitimacy, half-breeds, mongrelization, and so on.

Interest in the idea of *mestizaje* has traveled north in recent years, gaining newfound recognition and reformulation in the writings of U.S. Chicano/a and Latino/a scholars and cultural critics such as Daniel Cooper Alarcon, Norma Alarcon, Guillermo Gómez Peña, Cherrie Moraga, Chon A. Noriega, Emma Perez, Chela Sandoval, and especially Gloria Anzaldúa. These writers and activists have both expanded and complicated the meanings and uses of the idea, by pointing variously to its potential usefulness in the demystification of boundaries and territorial borders, the accentuation of the fluidity and adaptability of cultures and identities, the complications of difference, the critique of essentialism, the countering of ethnic absolutism, and the conceptualization of multicultural convergence, as well as for the reclamation of hybridity or hybrid personal identities, nonlinear thought, and syncretistic constructs, among other things.

The concept of mestizaje has been of special interest to Latino/a religious scholars, and particularly to U.S. Hispanic theologians. Indeed, it is difficult, if not impossible, to find a work in Latina/o theology that does not refer to or make use of this concept in some way or another. Mexican American theologian Virgilio Elizondo was the first to attempt a theological interpretation of the lived mestizaje found among Mexican Americans and other Latino/as. In his two most renowned works to date, *Galilean Journey* and *The Future Is Mestizo*, he puts forward first a brief historical overview of the Mexican American experience, which he sees as being a product of two conquests—a Spanish conquest and later on a U.S. conquest; second, an affirmative rendering of the racial and cultural hybridity that constitutes the historical and cultural reality of Mexican Americans and the majority of U.S. Latino/as; and third, a comparison of the historical Jesus' marginal status, as a result of his coming from an out-of-the way and undistinguished Galilean rural town named Nazareth in first-century Palestine, and the experience of marginality that many Mexican Americans experience today. Elizondo suggests that persons of mixed heritage or culture have historically experienced a sense of cultural marginalization, not being accepted totally by either of the parent cultures that make up their identity. This was the case for Jesus, he intimates: Jesus was possibly not accepted totally by many Jews of his time, due to his origins from Galilee, nor by Gentiles, due to his Jewish lineage. Similarly, many Mexican Americans today feel that, as a result of their biculturality, they are neither totally a part of the dominant Anglo-American culture of the United States nor of the Mexican culture of Mexico. Yet just as the historical Jesus was able to come to terms with his status as a bicultural person, and just as he was able to generate new life for himself and others from the margins, Elizondo believes that similarly, Mexican Americans now find themselves in a unique position to advance a liberating mission not only for their own well-being but also for that of others. As he puts it, "as *mestizos* of the borderland between Anglo America and Latin America, Mexican Americans can be instrumental in bringing greater appreciation and unity between the peoples of the two Americas" (Elizondo 1983, 100). In short, as Elizondo sees it, the multivalent racial, cultural, and historical hybridity that characterizes the mestizo identity of

Mexican Americans and other Latino/as admits for much more than just pain and dislocation: It can also be a source of creativity, survival, and triumph, or, to put it in theological terms, of "redemption."

As the last few paragraphs demonstrate, the concept of mestizaje has found expanded use as both a celebratory and a critical construct in the works of varied recent Latin American and Latino/a and/or Chicana/o scholars, cultural analysts and critics, and activists. The interest in this concept attests to an emerging Latino/a sensibility that is willing to explore anew the phenomenon of pluralism in Latin America and in the U.S. Latino/a communities, and the significance of cultural hybridity or intercultural mixing both within the Latin American/Latino/a community and in the broader continental context. And the result of this sensible exploration has been the realization that the idea of mestizaje holds both resistive and liberatory possibilities: it can be invoked to resist purist and static ways of thinking about race, ethnicity, and identity; and to make known, uplift, or advance different forms of cultural mixing and interactive exchange.

Although the recent reformulations of mestizaje proffered by Latin American, Chicano/a, and Latina/o cultural analysts and critics carry great potential for the struggle against different kinds of injustice that are traceable to culture, it is possible to point to some problematic issues in regard to its recent use as a ubiquitous descriptive and strategic concept. Four points in particular are noteworthy. The first problem involves the use of the term "mestizaje" in a universalistic way or, in other words, in a way that refers to all modes of intercultural mixing. As noted earlier, the term "mestizaje" technically denotes the mixture of Amerindian and

Spanish lineage and culture. But at times one can note in some writings a tendency to use it in reference to the whole Latin American and Latino/a population or, in other words, to refer comprehensively to the different kinds of intercultural mixture that can be found among Latin Americans and U.S. Latino/as. The problem is that this penchant tends to brush aside and to cover up the African element that is to be found in the Latin American and Latino/a heritage. Latin Americans and Hispanics are more than just descendants of the Spanish conquistadores that colonized the Americas, and more than just descendants of the Native American/Amerindian peoples who had already been living in the Americas; they are often also the descendants of the peoples whom the Spanish brought from Africa to the Americas as slaves. Among certain groups of Latin Americans and U.S. Latino/as such as the Columbians, Venezuelans, Panamanians, and Caribbean Latino/as such as the Cubans, Dominicans, and Puerto Ricans, among others, the African component of the racial and cultural mélange fostered during the Spanish colonial period prevails. Thus, the use of the term mestizaje to refer indiscriminately to the ancestral and intercultural mixture that marks Latin American and Latino/a identity is at least shortsighted, and at worst exclusionary or racist. At the very least, the term *mulatez* should also be employed when referring to the phenomenon of intercultural mixture that is to be found in Latin America and among U.S. Latino/as.

A second potential issue is that the use of the concept of mestizaje may unintentionally bring with it assimilating, homogenizing, or unifying tendencies that can serve to whitewash the indigenous past and present that constitutes the Latin American and Latino/a reality, rather than helping us to acknowledge, retrieve, or uplift it. The point at issue is that the idea of mestizaje operates as an umbrella term—as a linguistic and representational construct that inherently tries to incorporate or lump together the histories, experiences, and idiosyncrasies of different groups of peoples. The problem that may arise with the prolonged and undifferentiating use of a concept such as mestizaje is that it could divert attention away from the varied realities, traditions, and/or populations to which it refers. It is in recognizing the actual specificity of the diverse identities, histories, experiences, and cultures of the population of peoples that encountered each other during the colonial period that we can begin to better understand our historical Latin American heritage. To accomplish this, it might be necessary to move away from homogenizing designators such as mestizaje, at least from time to time, in order to more seriously engage with and reexamine the specific character of the populations and cultures that have marked and continue to mark our Latin American and Latino/a actuality. In short, if Hispanics really do want to retrieve, reclaim, and honor the indigenous side of their heritage, they would do well from time to time to move beyond the cursory reach of homogenizing designators such as mestizaje to study the lives and ways, for example, of the Aztec, Inca, Purepecha, Mixtec, Zapotec, Huastecan, Mayan, and the many other indigenous peoples and societies that it subsumes.

A third issue concerns the possible use of the idea of mestizaje to conceal the reality of racism in the Latina/o past and present history. The notion that all share in the same mestizo/a ancestry or descent can be used by individuals and by state apparatuses, not so much to contest racist ways of thinking but rather to prop up the idea that racism does not or cannot abide in our midst because pure races do not even exist. And so, rather than serve as a critical device that aims to remedy racism and social inequality, the idea of mestizaje can in the hands of some serve to obscure the ugly history and reality of racism in our lands. The historical reality is that miscegenation in Latin America did not transpire in the context of nor did it result in the attainment of a level social and racial order. As Ilan Stavans puts it, "during the colonial period the racial hierarchy in the Americas was quite clear: Spaniards were at the top, Creoles (American-born, 'pure-blood' Spaniards) came second, with *mestizos* in third place, Indians in fourth, and blacks at the bottom" (Stavans 2007, 12). And it is unfortunate but true that remnants of this racialist hierarchical arrangement are still in evidence in Latin American and Latino/a communities today. It is important that the theorizing and deployment of the idea of mestizaje be done in the light of the social and racial hierarchies that shaped colonial society and that continue to exist today.

Finally, a fourth issue concerns a possible incongruence or paradox that surrounds the interpretation and deployment of the idea of mestizaje. It is notable that in some works the idea of mestizaje, and the intercultural mixture that it points to or represents, is set forth and celebrated as a process, occasion, realization, or form of identity that is unique to certain historical moments, cultural situations, and peoples, and, for this reason, is distinctively or potentially

significant. Moreover, it is assumed that the notion of mestizaje represents a liberatory source for good and change, and can or will only be invoked to offer a strategy of resistance and liberation. But some analysts of culture have found that mixture and combination is part and parcel of any cultural formation, and that it can be and has been produced in distinct ways (e.g., by way of the mingling of different cultures and the formation of new ones over time, by the history of conquest, by oppression and/or assimilatory pressures, by travel or migration, and so on). As noted before, the idea of mestizaje has, in fact, had pernicious connotations before and has also been used by state or governmental agencies and elites to cover up racism and inequality and, thus, to impede the furthering of justice. Rather than assuming its uniqueness and inevitable political or transgressive effect, theorists of mestizaje need to closely examine the specific historical and geographical situations in which it is historically produced and ideationally utilized, all the while allowing for the possibility of different types, views, and meanings of mestizaje.

Benjamin Valentin

References and Further Reading

Elizondo, Virgilio. *Galilean Journey: The Mexican-American Promise* (Maryknoll, NY: Orbis Books, 1983).

———. *The Future Is Mestizo: Life Where Cultures Meet* (Bloomington, IN: Meyer Stone Books, 1988).

Garcia-Rivera, Alex. *St. Martin de Porres: The "Little Stories" and the Semiotics of Culture* (Maryknoll, NY: Orbis Books, 1995).

Gibson, Charles. *Spain in America* (New York: Harper & Row, 1966).

Stavans, Ilan. *Latino History and Culture* (New York: HarperCollins, 2007).

Vasconcelos, José. *The Cosmic Race/La Raza Cosmica* (Baltimore: Johns Hopkins University Press, 1997).

MEXICAN AMERICANS

Mexican Americans of the twenty-first century, specifically their sociohistorical and cultural context, can be understood if we consider the impact of the conquest and colonization of the Southwest by the United States. Similarly, in order to understand the socioeconomic status of the Mexican Americans today, we must understand the legacy and effects of discrimination and cultural conflict that is part of the shared memory of Mexican-descent Latino/as. Unlike other immigrant groups from Europe and Asia who entered the United States by leaving an "old country" and crossing oceans, Mexican Americans did not become a part of American society through "voluntary immigration." Rather, like American Indians, Mexican Americans became an American ethnic minority through the direct conquest of their homelands in the Southwest. Chicano historians argue that this fact is of utmost importance in any effort to understand the contemporary status of Mexican Americans within American society. The period that brought the northern territories of Mexico under U.S. control begins in 1836 with the independence of Texas. It ends in 1853 with the Gadsden Purchase, which was negotiated five years after the signing of the Treaty of Guadalupe Hidalgo in 1848, marking the end of the Mexican-American War. By 1853 Mexico had lost more than half of its territory but remarkably less than 1 percent of its population. The United States, by adding over a million square miles, increased its territory by a third.

Dispossession and Occupational Dislocation of Mexican Americans, 1848–1900

Chicano historians have successfully argued that the decades following the signing of the Treaty of Guadalupe Hidalgo were formative in the history of Mexican Americans. This period is characterized as one of political, economic, and social marginalization. During the war and the decades that followed, a pattern of Mexican-Anglo relations was established characterized by racial hostility and violence. Anglo-Americans typically viewed Mexicans as inferior, as aliens whom they had beaten in a just war.

The loss of political influence by the Mexican population throughout the Southwest resulted in Anglo control of the judicial system, law enforcement agencies, elected political positions, and virtually all decision-making bodies. Mexicans also experienced economic and occupational displacement resulting from American attempts to divest them of their lands. The loss of their ranches and pueblo communal lands altered the nature of the economy, radically changed the land tenure system, and resulted in the economic exploitation of the Mexican people. Dispossessed and occupationally dislocated, by the late 1850s Mexicans began a steady migration to towns where they became landless laborers in the American capitalist economy and occupied a socioeconomic underclass.

VIRGEN DE GUADALUPE

Many people do not realize that there are two commemorations of Mary bearing the name of Guadalupe. The most famous is in Tepeyac in Mexico City and the other is in Guadalupe in Extremadura, Spain. Guadalupe de Tepeyac is a painting of María left miraculously on the tilma of a native Mesoamerican called Juan Diego Cuauhtlatoatzin in 1531, during the time of the Spanish conquest of America. María reportedly called herself Coatlalopeuh (she who conquers the snake) but to the Spanish Bishop the Nahuatl name sounded like Guadalupe. To the Spaniards, Guadalupe is a statue said to have been carved by St. Luke the Evangelist. It was found in Palestine, moved to Constantinople and eventually taken to Rome. From Rome it went to Sevilla as a gift to the Bishop by Pope Gregory the Great. When the Moors invaded Spain in 711, the statue was hidden along with proper documentation near the Guadalupe River. It remained hidden until 1252, when Mary appeared to Gil Cordero and revealed her statue's location.

Both of these images of María show her to be *morena* (dark skinned) and present the Mother of God as manifesting her Son's love and protection to oppressed peoples.

—GCG

As Anglo-Americans gained political and economic control of the Southwest, the Mexican pueblos were transformed into American cities where the earlier pastoral economy was replaced by an American capitalist economy. One important consequence of Americanization was the initiation of a process that has been described as the barrioization of the Mexican community, which entailed the formation of residentially and socially segregated Mexican barrios or neighborhoods.

The process of barrioization of the Mexican community was more than simple segregation and intertwined economic, social, and demographic forces. Barrioization meant the virtual elimination of the Mexican from the social and political life of the community at large. On the other hand, barrios offered Mexicans security and insulation from American influence and the forces of assimilation.

After the Southwest was acquired by the United States in the war with Mexico, the American Catholic Church assumed responsibility for the spiritual well-being of the newly created Mexican Americans. In *Mexican Americans and the Catholic Church, 1900–1965*, co-editor Gilberto Hinojosa observes that during the final half of the nineteenth century when Mexicans were being stripped of their lands, politically disenfranchised, and socially and economically marginalized, American ecclesiastical leaders offered little or no public protest. Driven by its desire to escape Anglo-Protestant anti-Catholic prejudice, the Roman Catholic hierarchy in the Southwest chose to cast its future with the new American political and economic system. In its desire to reap the benefits of joining the Anglo-American mainstream, the Roman Catholic Church in the Southwest became an active participant in the process of establishing

Anglo-American political and socioeconomic control over the Mexicans. To the conquered and marginalized Mexicans it appeared that their ancestral church was more concerned with gaining acceptability in mainstream American society than with serving or defending them, thereby appearing indifferent to the social and economic challenges facing the Mexican American community.

Church leaders who demonstrated little sympathy for Mexican Catholicism prohibited many traditional Mexican religious fiestas. They believed that the ceremonies, cults, and devotions of the unofficial, popular Catholicism of the Mexicans would tarnish the church's image in the eyes of the increasingly predominant Anglo-American society. The neglect of Mexican American Catholics was further evidenced by the church's preference for establishing strongholds in the newly developing urban areas of the Southwest where she was committed to serving mostly American and European immigrants, even though these were not the districts with the largest number of Catholics. An historical legacy was thereby established that downplayed the cultural and religious commitments and idiosyncrasies of the Mexican Catholic communities.

In self-defense, the Roman Catholic Church argues that difficulties with the language barrier, the mobility of the Mexican immigrant, deeply imbedded societal racism, the poverty of the Mexican worker, and a lack of Mexican or Spanish-speaking clergy generated innumerable pastoral problems. But historians insist that the so-called "Mexican problem" reflected the institutionalized racism experienced by Mexicans in a church that reinforced the marginalized and segregated position Mexicans occupied in American society.

In "The Mexican Catholic Community in California," Jeffrey Burns argues that in its ministry to Mexicans during the late nineteenth century, and among immigrants from Mexico in the early twentieth century, the church took as one of its duties the responsibility of ushering the Mexican-descent Catholic into mainstream American life. This was often done without a sufficiently critical attitude toward the Anglo-American society to which the church hoped the Mexican would assimilate, and without a sufficiently appreciative attitude toward the cultural and religious heritage of the Mexican immigrant. Church leaders believed the Mexican-descent Catholic needed to be assimilated to both the American way of life and the American Catholic way of life. In an era in which Americanism went unquestioned, the goal of Americanizing the Mexican was perceived as a positive good, the White Man's Burden. Assimilating and Americanizing the Mexican-descent Catholic was not an easy task for several reasons, not the least of which was the ambivalent attitude of Mexican Americans regarding Americanization. Other obstacles to acculturation and assimilation included proximity to the Mexican border, the demand for cheap exploitable Mexican labor, and the lack of immigration quotas, all of which contributed to a growing number of Mexican-American Catholics.

The Legacy of the Immigrant Generation, 1900–1940

As a result of the dispossession and occupational dislocation of Mexicans in the Southwest, Mexican immigration during the second half of the nineteenth century was modest in scale when compared to the twentieth century. However, economic and political pressures in Mexico exacerbated by a lengthy and bloody civil war (1910–1917) prompted many *Mexicanos* to migrate to "El Norte." At the same time, U.S. demands for cheap labor were growing, particularly for agriculture and related industries but also in mining and railroad related industries. The net result was that the economic interests in the Southwest found an abundant source of cheap and exploitable labor. Consequently, during the first three decades of the 20th Century more than 700,000 documented immigrants entered the United States from Mexico. These figures do not include the number of undocumented immigrants which some estimate was between 50,000 to 100,000 annually.

By the early 1920s Mexicans began to settle outside of the Southwest. Many were recruited by northern manufacturing interests: meat-packing plants and steel mills in the Chicago area; automobile assembly lines in Detroit; the steel industry in Ohio and Pennsylvania; and meat-packing plants in Kansas City. Others following the crops eventually arrived in the Northwest, the Mountain states, and even in the Southeast. By 1930 about 15 percent of the nation's Mexicans were living outside the Southwest.

Especially in the Southwest, immigration reinforced and underscored the existing Mexican American culture and gave it much of its specific shape and present-day content. Not only did the process of barrioization continue but so did the economic exploitation of the Mexican worker. The contract labor system, racial and gender wage differentials, and labor conflicts kept Mexican Americans underpaid and racially segregated

as an economic underclass with little hope of improvement.

The Great Depression of the 1930s was another defining moment for Mexican Americans. During the Depression, prejudices and social discrimination against Mexican Americans became more pronounced as a result of the economic competition between poor White migrants from the Dust Bowl and Mexican Americans in California. The Great Depression also engendered a collective social atmosphere of insecurity and fear as Mexican Americans were made to bear the guilt for many of the social and economic ills of the period. One creative response to the socioeconomic crisis was the demand for large-scale repatriation of Mexicans. The repatriation of more than 400,000 Mexicans, nearly half of whom were U.S. citizens, emphasized to Mexicans just how vulnerable they were to the actions of local, state, and federal officials. They were welcomed when there was a shortage of cheap labor, but when economic times were bad they were told to go back to Mexico.

The Legacy of the Mexican American Generation, 1940–1965

The Depression, Repatriation Program, and World War II revolutionized many aspects of social and economic life for Mexican Americans, especially in the Southwest. In his book *Becoming Mexican American*, George Sánchez notes that one major outcome of the Depression and repatriation programs of the 1930s was the rapid transformation of the barrio from a community dominated by the foreign-born *Mexicanos* to one centered around the native-born Mexican

Americans who were oriented toward greater participation in the American political and social scene. This orientation toward greater participation and integration was nurtured by American involvement in World War II.

In 1942 a manpower shortage created by the expansion of the U.S. armed forces and war-related industries prompted the United States and Mexico to initiate an informal program to allow manual laborers, known as *braceros*, to enter the United States to work. They labored in railroad construction and maintenance and in agriculture, two industries hardest hit by labor shortages. However, the Bracero Program and legal immigration did not meet all the manpower needs in the United States. As a result of these shortages, another group of Mexican workers, referred to as undocumented workers, as illegal immigrants or, metaphorically and pejoratively, as *mojados* (wetbacks), began to flow into the United States.

The Bracero Program and the steady flow of illegal immigrants were a mixed blessing for the Mexican American community in the two decades after World War II. On one hand they helped to reinforce and strengthen the traditional culture, but on the other hand they increased competition for jobs. The discrimination generated by the braceros and illegal aliens had negative effects on all Mexican-descent Latina/os, not the least of which included growing racial tensions with the dominant group. Two incidents that illustrate the growing racial tension in Los Angeles include the sensationalized "Sleepy Lagoon Case" of 1942 and the so-called "zoot-suit riots" of June 1943.

The wartime experiences of Mexican Americans profoundly altered their perspective and expectations. Because they fought and died as equals in disproportionately high numbers, Mexican Americans felt they were entitled to equal opportunities as loyal American citizens in civilian life. The G.I. Bill of Rights gave all veterans benefits such as educational subsidies and loans for businesses and housing, which highlighted discriminatory practices in education, labor, and housing. Veterans were instrumental in the founding and growth of a variety of Mexican American political organizations including the American G.I. Forum and the Mexican American Political Organization (MAPA). These organizations promoted civic and political action, helped to elect Mexicans to city councils throughout the Southwest, conducted voter registration drives, and fought against racial discrimination in schooling, police-community relations, housing, and employment.

As Mexican Americans moved into the cities in unprecedented numbers during the postwar years, and as more became middle class, they became increasingly dissatisfied with the limited and inferior roles assigned to them in American society. Incentive and strategies for expressing their dissatisfaction with institutional racism, discrimination, and inequality of opportunities in education, housing, and employment came from developments in the Black Civil Rights Movement during the late 1950s and early 1960s.

The Chicano and New Immigrant Generation, 1965–1985

In the late 1960s members of new organizations, including the Mexican American Youth Organization and *el Movimiento Estudiantil Chicano de*

Aztlan (MEChA), began to refer to themselves as "Chicanos" and formed part of a broad social movement variously described as *La Causa* or *El Movimiento*. The so-called Chicano generation came to realize that while it was even more acculturated than previous generations, it did not have any real prospects of escaping its virtually complete lower- and working-class status. Unity and cohesiveness of otherwise diverse elements within the Mexican American community was increased by employing the use of such politically charged terms as "Chicano" and *La Raza* as well as by emphasizing the distinctiveness of Chicano culture, norms, and values.

The steady flow of Mexican immigrants was a critical factor in the mobilization of *La Raza* in the 1960s and 1970s. One result of continued immigration was constant reinforcement of the traditional cultural patterns of their ancestral homeland. Continued reinforcement by newcomers from Mexico made it easier for Chicanos to exercise a choice concerning whether to embrace Anglo values and modes of behavior or to strengthen their ties to Chicano culture. Conversely, the constant flow of Mexican immigrants helped to perpetuate ethnic characteristics, which made Mexican Americans a highly visible minority. As a result, many Chicanos felt socially, as well as economically threatened by the influx of Mexican immigrants. The small but growing number of upwardly mobile middle-class Mexican Americans saw the newcomers as a threat to their hard-won prestige in the mainstream of American society where few in the dominant culture readily distinguished between "wetbacks" and middle-class Mexican Americans. Lower and working-class Mexican Americans saw the new wave of immigrants from Mexico and other Latin America countries as a threat to their economic stability as unskilled and semiskilled laborers in a postindustrial U.S. economy.

The Chicano movement of the late 1960s and 1970s facilitated a number of important concessions from the Anglo mainstream. Concessions such as bilingual education, Chicano studies programs, and affirmative action programs in higher education and employment practices created a setting from which a viable Mexican middle class could rise to local prominence. Another important concession was won in the *Cisneros* case of 1970, when the federal courts finally classified Mexican Americans as "an identifiable ethnic minority with a pattern of discrimination."

The political and social energy produced by the Chicano movement also inspired a generation of artists who would forever change the way mainstream America would perceive Mexican Americans. Chicano artists filled theatre, film, murals, paintings, and sculpture with social and political meanings, while dance, music, and literature celebrated the cultural heritage of *El Movimiento*. Thanks to the contributions of Chicano artists and victories won by Chicano political activists, Mexican Americans were able to maintain a high profile in American society throughout the 1970s.

Scholars observe that the Chicano movement also revitalized Mexican identity and culture, helping Mexican Americans redefine themselves in relation to both U.S. and Mexican societies. As the Civil Rights Movement and Antiwar Movements of the late 1960s and early 1970s gradually lost momentum, the Chicano movement also waned, but not before winning acceptance in many mainstream institutions and by making it possible for younger generations of Mexican Americans to enjoy the American dream.

In the 1960s and 1970s the Catholic Church experienced many significant changes resulting from the growing discontent among militant Chicanos and intensive proselytizing by Protestant groups, especially Evangelicals and Pentecostals. Important changes included the appointment of the first Mexican American bishops, the use of Spanish in mass, and a greater sensitivity to social issues of concern to Mexican Americans. There are several examples of the growing solidarity between the Catholic Church and the Chicano movement and Mexican American community during this period. Some priests and nuns openly supported United Farm Worker activities during the Delano grape strike. In an effort to raise awareness of the social problems facing Mexican Americans, a group of Chicano priests formed an organization named *Padres Asociados Para Derechos Religiosos, Educativos y Sociales* (PADRES), which was committed to bringing about social and economic changes in the barrio. An organization with similar goals and objectives named *Las Hermanas* (The Sisters) was started for nuns and laywomen in the Catholic Church.

The Mexican American Religious Experience since 1980

Just as the Chicano movement was beginning to lose momentum in the late 1970s, unprecedented numbers of immigrants from Mexico, but also from South America and especially Central America, began to flood into and beyond the Southwest. This dramatically affected the cultural and economic context of Mexican Americans in the final decades of the twentieth century. One of the most significant cultural developments of the past three decades has been the dramatic rise of the Hispanic, especially Mexican American, presence in evangelical and Protestant churches. According to figures published in 2007 by the Pew Hispanic Center in a study entitled "Changing Faiths: Latinos and the Transformation of American Religion," 68 percent of all Hispanics, including 74 percent of all Mexican-descent Latino/as identify themselves as Roman Catholic, representing approximately 33 percent of all Catholics in the United States. The same study found that 20 percent of all Latina/os, including 16 percent of all Mexican-descent Latino/as identify themselves as either evangelical or mainline Protestant (15 percent and 5 percent, respectively). Approximately 3 percent identified themselves as "other Christians," including Jehovah's Witnesses and Mormons, while 8 percent identified themselves as secular.

The 2007 Pew study also found that differences in religious identification among Latino/as coincide with important demographic characteristics, especially with nativity and country of origin. For example, foreign-born Hispanics are more likely than native-born Hispanics to be Roman Catholics (74 percent to 58 percent, respectively), and Mexicans were much more likely than other Latino/as to be Roman Catholic. In their study of Hispanics adults, the 2007 Pew study found that 18 percent of Latino/as say they have converted from one religion either to another or to no religion at all. Given the fact that most Hispanics are Catholic, it is not surprising that 70 percent of all Hispanic converts are

Mexican immigrants light votive candles during prayers at San Juan Basilica in McAllen, Texas. (Alison Wright/Corbis)

former Catholics. These figures are consistent with earlier studies. In 1988, figures reported by the Catholic Church suggested that between 1972 and 1987 more than 1 million Hispanics left their ancestral church to join Protestant denominations. Another study three years later suggested that more than 60,000 Hispanics were leaving the Catholic Church every year for Protestant denominations.

Catholic scholars maintain that a principal cause for the defection of Hispanics from the Catholic Church is that the church is not equipped or structured to meet the diverse needs of the growing number of Hispanic believers. They insist that the church lacks sufficient numbers of Spanish-speaking clergy who understand and appreciate the Latino/a community's diverse cultural and religious idiosyncrasies. Consequently,

Hispanic Catholics do not always find secure, inviting places of worship in their ancestral church. Experts also observe that the prevailing ministry paradigm places great emphasis on priestly office at the expense of an approach to ministry that stresses the call to equip and empower all believers for ministry. They argue that conservative Protestant groups that equip and empower Latina/os to assume real responsibility for a wide range of ministries are attracting large numbers of Hispanics. Additionally, Catholic scholars observe that as a general rule the Catholic Church does not offer the small, receptive, faith-sharing community context found elsewhere.

More militant Chicanos argue that the Catholic Church, historically preoccupied with either Americanizing the Mexican Americans or defending them against Protestant proselytism, has been insensitive to the need for social action on behalf of Mexican Americans. On the other hand, some church leaders point to the church's failure to acknowledge the diversity of persons of Latin American descent in the United States. They note that there is a lack of awareness of ethnic and social class distinctions. Instead, an undifferentiated "option for the poor" on the part of socially active clergy reveals a tendency to conceive of Hispanics only in terms of deficits or dysfunctions, which can lead Hispanics who happen to be upwardly mobile to regard themselves as outside the church's pastoral concerns.

In an article entitled "The Challenge of Evangelical/Pentecostal Christianity to Hispanic Catholicism," Allan Figueroa Deck, a Jesuit priest, traces the exodus of Hispanics from the Catholic Church since the nineteenth century. In the early nineteenth century, mainline Protestant churches attracted the greatest numbers of Hispanics. But since the turn of the last century, conservative Protestant groups, especially evangelical and Pentecostal churches have attracted the largest number of Hispanic converts. History reveals that while there have been priests sympathetic to Hispanic Catholics and their culture, the ecclesiastical hierarchy has historically chosen to defend the cause of the powerful, supporting the sociopolitical status quo. When Mexican American Catholics were not being marginalized or discriminated against in their ancestral church as the "White man's burden," they were the target of Americanization. Evangelicalism and Pentecostalism, on the other hand, have historically appealed to the working class, the poor, and the marginalized segments of the Hispanic community.

Today when one speaks of Hispanic Protestantism, one is not usually talking about mainline Protestant churches, but, rather, about some strain of evangelicalism and especially Pentecostalism. Hispanics, more than any other U.S. minority, are contributing to its revival and making evangelicalism, particularly in its Pentecostal manifestations, the fastest growing and arguably the most dynamic division of Christianity in the United States and in the world today. Evangelical and Pentecostal churches that attract growing numbers of Mexican Americans and other Latino/as are usually led by gifted, charismatic leaders from the community who seldom question the need to use Spanish in their ministry. They are also characterized by a respect for important idiosyncrasies of the local community and its natural, indigenous leadership. The success of evangelicals and Pentecostals is also credited to their insights into the diverse Hispanic presence and their willingness to respond creatively and energetically to that diverse presence.

Careful observers within the Catholic Church note that the "sects," as they are often referred to, do not only appeal to the poor, oppressed, and marginalized. They also appeal to the emerging Mexican American and Latino/a middle class. The sects appeal to the upwardly mobile because they provide a means of becoming responsible and respectable members of the American middle class without severing ties with their Latina/o roots and heritage. The Catholic Church's failure in this area has been to provide community and respectability for the upwardly mobile Hispanics. In other words, defection to the sects has social as well as economic payoffs for the Latina/o Catholics.

The affinity between Hispanic popular Catholicism and evangelical and Pentecostal Christianity is another characteristic that attracts a larger number of Latino/as. Catholic scholars affirm that popular Catholicism is the deeply rooted norm for most Hispanics. It is the existential Catholicism of most Latina/os, including Mexican Americans. It is mediated especially by grandmothers, mothers, and women in general. It is communicated orally and shuns the cognitive in its effort to appeal to the senses and the feelings. It does this through symbol and rite. The main qualities of popular Catholicism are the following: a concern for an immediate experience with God, a strong orientation toward the transcendent, an implicit belief in miracles, a practical orientation toward healing, and a tendency to personalize or individualize one's relationship with the divine. These qualities are notably absent in American Catholicism and mainline Protestantism. This is due to the antagonism between popular religion and modern rationality. Historically, Anglo-American Catholics have seen Hispanic popular religion as a problem to be uprooted, not a strength upon which to build.

Furthermore, the emphasis placed upon a direct and personal relationship with God is available in evangelical and Pentecostal churches in small faith-sharing contexts that affirm the communal thrust of Hispanic popular Catholicism while at the same time orienting Latino/as toward more self-determination. By providing the experiences described above, evangelical and Pentecostal churches become an effective bridge for Latin American Christianity, which is shaken to its core by the challenges of modernity. In other words, these new faith communities provide a new orientation for ordinary people seeking to deal with the stresses involved in the rapid changes brought about by immigration, urbanization, and secularization.

The preceding observations may leave the reader with the impression that most Hispanics have already or will soon abandon their ancestral church. This is certainly not the case. The majority of Latino/as, including 74 percent of Mexican-decent Latina/os, remain loyal Catholics, which raises a final question: Why do many Hispanics, especially Mexican Americans resist evangelical proselytizing efforts? Catholic scholars have identified three main sources of resistance. The principal source of resistance to evangelical Protestantism has to do with its intimate connection with the North American cultural ethos, especially the perceived individualism and consumerism. Furthermore, the more democratic, egalitarian ethos of Evangelicalism is somehow foreign to the hierarchical configuration of both the Hispanic family and society. Finally, profound cultural, social, and familial ruptures take place when a family member becomes a Protestant.

To say that most Mexican Americans are Catholic is not to describe a religious "preference"; it is a designation of cultural orientation. Especially in its popular form, Roman Catholicism is a symbol of ethnic solidarity. Yet Catholic scholars remind us that the main characteristic and appeal of evangelical and Pentecostal Christianity is its affinity with popular Catholicism. Mexican Americans respond favorably to a faith that is characterized by a clear affirmation of God's transcendence, strong convictions about God's will in matters of morality founded on biblical teaching, a confidence in God's power to work miracles and especially heal, and the possibility of establishing a personal relationship with God appropriate for a highly individualized modern world. Before being conquered, colonized, and marginalized by the dominant group in the United States and before being overwhelmed with the pressures of our modern, postindustrial urban society, these social and spiritual needs were met by popular Hispanic Catholicism. At the turn of the twenty-first century growing numbers of Mexican Americans and other Latino/as are now finding those needs met by evangelicalism and Pentecostalism.

Daniel A. Rodriguez

References and Further Reading

Acuña, Rodolfo. *Occupied America: A History of Chicanos*, 3rd ed. (New York: Harper and Row, 1988).

Burns, Jeffrey M. "The Mexican Catholic Community in California." *Mexican Americans and the Catholic Church, 1900–1965*, ed. Jay P. Dolan and Gilberto M. Hinojosa (Notre Dame, IN: University of Notre Dame, 1994).

Camarillo, Albert. *Chicanos in a Changing Society: From Mexican Pueblos to American Barrios in Santa Barbara and Southern California, 1848-1930* (Cambridge, MA: Harvard University, 1979).

Deck, Allan Figueroa. "The Challenge of Evangelical/Pentecostal Christianity to Hispanic Catholicism." *Hispanic Catholic Culture in the U. S.: Issues and Concerns*, ed. Jay P. Dolan and Allan Figueroa Deck (Notre Dame, IN: University of Notre Dame, 1995).

Griswold del Castillo, Richard, and Arnoldo de León. *North to Aztlán: A History of Mexican Americans in the United States* (New York: Twayne Publishers, 1996).

Hinojosa, Gilberto M. "Mexican American Faith Communities in the Southwest." *Mexican Americans and the Catholic Church, 1900–1965*, ed. Jay P. Dolan and Gilberto M. Hinojosa (Notre Dame, IN: University of Notre Dame, 1992).

McLemore, S. Dale, and Ricardo Romo. "The Origins and Development of the Mexican American People." *The Mexican American Experience: An Interdisciplinary Anthology*, ed. Rodolfo O. de la Garza, F. D. Bean, C. M. Bobjean, R. Romo, and R. Alvarez (Austin: University of Texas, 1985).

Meier, Matt S., and Feliciano Ribera. *Mexican Americans-American Mexicans: From Conquistadores to Chicanos* (New York: Hill and Wang, 1989).

Mirandé, Alfredo. *The Chicano Experience: An Alternate Perspective* (Notre Dame, IN: University of Notre Dame, 1985).

Pew Hispanic Center and Pew Forum on Religion & Public Life, "Changing Faiths: Latinos and the Transformation of American Religion." Available at http://pewforum.org/surveys/hispanic/ (April 25, 2007).

Sánchez, George J. *Becoming Mexican American* (New York: Oxford University, 1993).

MISSION SYSTEM

Within the Hispanic context, the mission system began with the arrival of the Spanish *conquistadores* to the Americas. On January 2, 1492, the Catholic *reconquista* in Spain finally recovered Granada from the Muslims. On March 31 of the same year, "The Decree of Expulsion" was signed, forcing the Jews to leave or renounce their faith. Although some historians argue that Granada was the final crusade, the Spanish conquest of the so-called New World, in many ways, follows the continual pattern of violent expansionism to fulfill a religious mission. On August 3 Christopher Columbus's fleet sought closer passage to India under the sponsorship of King Ferdinand and Queen Isabella. On October 12, 1492, Columbus spotted the Caribbean island of Guanahani thinking that this was a western island of India. The island was renamed San Salvador (Saint Savior) as an indication of the religious implications of his discovery. Columbus's main goal was the search for riches, but the Spanish crown felt a missionary obligation, so a priest was sent along during his second voyage.

The pope granted the Spanish a right already bestowed on the Portuguese *un derecho y el jus patronatus* or possession over newly discovered lands with the obligation to propagate the faith. It was the first time in history that the pope gave the double power to colonize and missionize to a state, thus mixing the temporal and the supernatural, the political and the ecclesial realms. In May 1493 the pope issued two bulls, *Inter Coetera* and *Eximiae Devotionis*, granting the rights of the newly discovered lands and their inhabitants to participate as members of the church in the benefits of the gospel. These bulls were part of Christendom—believing that the governors of a given conquered territory (kingdom) have the authority to convert their subjects.

Spanish explorers such as Juan Ponce de Leon and Vasco Núñez de Balboa continued to conquer the territories of Hispaniola, Cuba, Puerto Rico, Florida, and Panama early in the sixteenth century. These explorers reported back to Spain the sighting of riches. In response, the Spanish crown established the system of *encomiendas* to settle conquered territories. The prerequisite for settlement was the reading of the "Requirement," which stated that local people must acknowledge the dominion of the Catholic Church, the pope, and the king and permit the teaching of Christianity. Not always read in good faith, the Requirement was used to justify the seizure of property and the forcible conquest and the enslavement of women and children—citing the biblical example of the Israelite conquest of Jericho for justification.

Specifically, the encomiendas were land grants given in exchange for the Christianizing of the residents. Franciscan, Dominican, and the newly formed Jesuit Order often accompanied the settlers with the goal of converting the native inhabitants to Christianity, often with the sincere belief that participation in the Catholic sacraments—especially baptism—saved "heathens" from hell's torment.

Already having established colonies on the islands of Hispaniola and Cuba, Spaniard Hernán Cortez organized an expedition further west landing in Veracruz, Mexico, on Holy Thursday, 1521. Cortez's arrival coincided with the legend of Quetzalcoatl, the Aztec god who was believed would return shortly. Moctezuma sent a gift of gold to appease the expected gods—sparking Cortez's interest in visiting Tenochtitlan. More gold in the Aztec capital increased Cortez's insatiable desire to return and complete the conquest. Human sacrifices convinced the Spanish that the Aztecs were savages and must be "Christianized." The last Aztec emperor, Cuauhtemoc, surrendered at Tlatelolco, an Aztec holy site, on August 13, 1521. As a sign of domination, the same stones of the

Aztec pyramids were used to build the Santiago de Tlatelolco Catholic Church on top of the holy site. The Plaza of Tlatelolco, also known in Mexico City as the Plaza of Three Cultures, remains a symbol of the intersection of the Spanish and Aztec cultures and the birth of the mestizo (mixed) race.

A young lawyer, Cristobal de las Casas (1484–1566), accompanied Columbus on his third journey to the Americas and witnessed many atrocities committed by the Spanish against the native peoples. Shortly after coming to the so-called New World, he completed his studies to become a Dominican priest. Later, he was named bishop of southern Mexico. Fearing God's judgment against the Spanish, de las Casas wrote *A Brief Account of the Destruction of the Indies* to King Philip II. The book recorded the enslavement, cruel treatment, diseases, and death to which the native peoples were subjected. Some scholars estimate a decline from an original 16 million to about 1 million. In general de las Casas objected to the system of encomiendas, which assumed that the indigenous did not possess a rational soul, and thus had to be Christianized by force instead of convinced by reason.

The encomienda system was temporarily suspended in 1550–1551 when the King of Spain, Charles V, ordered a *junta*, a group of jurists and theologians, to examine whether or not the native peoples possessed a rational soul. De las Casas forced the issue to trial in what is known as the "Las Casas-Sepúlveda Controversy." Juan Ginés de Sepúlveda, a prominent humanist and Greek scholar, defended the encomienda system justifying violent means of evangelization. Despite losing the case, de las Casas raised important issues in Europe and the so-called New World about the interplay between missions, race, and colonialism. As a tribute to his struggle for human rights, de las Casas was named "Protectorate of the Indians." He was successful in shedding light on the Spaniards' cruel practices; nevertheless, he reportedly recommended that Africans were better suited as slaves—a position he later regretted.

As the Spanish colonialization expanded, explorers traveled from the early strongholds of Hispaniola, Cuba, and Mexico City to points north and south. Hernando de Soto sponsored an excursion by Francisco Pizarro from Panama to South America in 1531. There he found gold among the Inca civilization in what is today Peru. De Soto instantly became wealthy and was named ruler of Florida and Cuba in 1536; meanwhile Pizarro went on to have a career and success similar to Hernán Cortez, founding the new capital of Lima and conquering the Inca capital of Cuzco. In conjunction with the military expansion, the newly established Jesuit Order sent missionaries, establishing a mission in Cuzco. In addition to teaching the Christian faith, the mission acquired large tracts of land and introduced the concepts of private ownership, commodification, and banking. The mission housed an orphanage that raised the children of Spanish fathers and Inca princesses with Catholic teaching and a European mind-set. This new Creole class became the next ruling elites. Not surprisingly, the Indians were at the bottom of the new caste system.

Although the conquests in Mexico and South America brought immediate gold and silver to Spain, the expeditions in northern Mexico were not immediately successful. Juan de Grijalva explored the northern coast of the Gulf of Mexico in 1518 and 10 years later Alvar Nuñez Cabeza de Vaca, en route from Tampa Bay, was shipwrecked on the upper Texas coast. In 1540 Francisco Vasquez de Coronado explored further north through the Pueblo territories of Cibola, the Grand Canyon all the way to the Great Plains, finding small villages of nomadic tribes and buffalo, but no gold. Removed from the conquest of the central plateau, the northern region of New Spain was sparsely populated and apparently lacked the precious metals attracting European settlers further south.

Simultaneous to Hernán Cortez's conquest of Mexico was the start of the Protestant Reformation in Europe. On April 2, 1521, Martin Luther defended his 95 Theses against the Roman Catholic practice of indulgences at the Imperial Diet in Worms, Germany. Seemingly a world apart, these events would soon become entwined, as the Roman Catholic Church felt threatened by Luther's *Sola Scritura* doctrine and initiated a counter-Reformation campaign. These two competing beliefs soon encountered each other in the so-called New World with a German Lutheran settlement in Venezuela in 1532 and brief French Huguenot settlements in Brazil and Fort Caroline, Florida, in the 1550s and 1560s. Spanish captain Pedro Menendez de Avila momentarily eradicated the "Lutheran heresy" in Florida in 1556 by slitting the throat of a thousand "infidels" who did not confess the Catholic faith.

Hearing reports of French settlements further north and Protestant beliefs from Europe, the Spanish moved to defend their territory and the Catholic faith with the establishment of a chain of mission systems during the seventeenth and eighteenth centuries in what is today Texas, New Mexico, Arizona, and California. Seeing that it did not have enough Spanish soldiers or resources to secure such a vast region, mission systems seemed to be an ideal church-state partnership. The Crown decided to govern the region as a missionary province supporting the missions with an annual subsidy—a tithe of the taxes charged to the residents of the region. Although many priests shared a genuine desire to convert the Indians away from their indigenous beliefs to Christianity, the Spanish government supported this mission as a means of introducing Western civilization and bringing the native peoples under submission as subjects. In addition to teaching the tenets of the Christian faith, the missions served to teach the Spanish language, crafts, agriculture, law, and eventually European warfare.

The mission system is made up of three major institutions: the mission, the presidio, and the pueblo. The mission was the main institution consisting of the friars and the native population. The mission was within the fortified walls, but depended on the second institution, the presidio, for protection. The fort was located nearby and protected the mission from hostile groups such as noncooperative Indians or European rivals. The soldiers taught some defensive skills to cooperative residents while applying Spanish law to runaways and heretics. The third institution was the pueblo or civil community—made up of the surrounding residents. Many of the residents were ranchers or tradesman who did business with the mission.

Much more than a chapel, the mission system was a self-sufficient economic and military enterprise surrounded by fortified walls and gates. Inside the walls were the educational buildings, mills,

SAN DIEGO REVOLT

Christianity came to the U.S. West Coast in 1769 with the founding of a mission in what would be known as San Diego, California. Missionaries immediately began both the physical and the spiritual conquest of the indigenous people known as the Kumeyaay. By 1775, they baptized about 500 new converts. The Kumeyaay soon resented the presence of Spaniards for their conversion efforts, as well as the practice of the Spaniards to graze cattle on Indian lands, thus harming the Indian's agricultural activities. Accusations of rape of Indian women were also made. On November 5, 1775, a well-organized revolt against the mission took place, symbolizing the indigenous people's resistance to Spaniards and their religion. The mission was burned and the priest, Father Luis Jayme, and two others were killed. The revolt stopped missionary activities for at least a year and a half. But by 1777, with the arrival of Father Junípero Serra who rebuilt the mission, the missionary project was again reinstated. By 1797 the mission controlled over 50,000 acres and claim "winning" over 1,400 souls.

—MAD

storage buildings, trade shops, housing units for friars and Indians, and, of course, a chapel. Outside the walls were thousands of acres of land—that often was acquired from locals when loans could not be repaid—owned by the mission for cultivating and grazing cattle.

The friars governed the mission with a work ethic imported from the European monastical movement. A typical day started at 5:00 a.m. for morning worship, breakfast between 6:00 a.m. and 7:00 a.m., followed by four hours of manual labor, a midday meal, and rest. The afternoon consisted of another four hours of work, the evening meal, a period of religious instruction, and free time before bedtime.

In what is today the state of New Mexico, Franciscan friars were given control over their Indian converts. In the early seventeenth century, 50 churches were built by 26 friars. Tools and other hardware were paid by the Crown and sent by wagon train from Mexico City. Each mission received ten axes, three adzes, three spades, ten hoes, one medium-sized saw, one chisel, two augers, one plane, a large latch for the church door, two small locks, a dozen hinges, and 6,000 nails. Appropriating the adobe-style brick, the Native Americans worked together with the friars to build the self-enclosed missions.

A chain of Franciscan missions was established further west in what is today the state of California. Spanish penetration further west along the Alta California coast between Los Angeles and the current Mexico border was more difficult in the face of Indian resistance. One mission in the area of San Diego faced resistance to mass baptisms (at least 300 in a period of three months) from the local population and was attacked. Following an initial attack on the mission in 1769, the animosity continued after approximately 500 baptisms and in November 1775 the *Diegeños* (as the local residents were called) mounted a major attack on the mission. The Franciscans were taken by surprise even though there had been

Mission Santa Barbara was founded in 1786, the tenth of 21 Franciscan missions in California. (Salman Arif/Dreamstime)

warning signs. Father Luis Jayme said of the first attack: "No wonder the Indians here were bad when the mission was first founded. To begin with, they did not know why [the Spaniards] had come unless they intended to take their lands away from them."

The Roman Catholic mission system began to decline in Mexico during the war of independence from Spain in 1821, and in what is today the American Southwest after the annexation of Texas in 1845 and the ensuing Mexican-American War from 1846 to 1848. The missions remaining in Mexican territory were largely dismantled, and some were sold during Benito Juarez's rule as a result of the separation of church and state enacted by the 1857 Mexican Constitution.

During Roman Catholic control of colonial South America, the modern Protestant mission movement considered this region "Christianized," and all Protestant work was aimed at ex-patriots and conducted in English. U.S. citizen James Thompson preached the first Protestant sermon in South America in Buenos Aires in 1920 followed by immigrants from Europe establishing their own national churches. Following the Monroe Doctrine of 1823, Rev. Fountain E. Pitts traveled to Brazil, Uruguay, and Argentina and established the first English-speaking Methodist Society in Rio de Janeiro in 1835.

The first known Protestant sermon in Spanish was preached by Methodist John Francis Thomson on May 25, 1867 in Buenos Aires. After the Spanish colonial laws were rescinded in 1872–1873, Protestant missionary work was established in Spanish in Cuba, Puerto Rico, and Mexico. The Presbyterian Church

COLONIZATION ACT OF 1824

Spain, and later Mexico, had difficulty attracting settlers to their northern frontier, known today as the U.S. Southwest. The Colonization Act of 1824 was an attempt to liberalize land policy to attract settlers. Even Euro-Americans were encouraged to migrate to Texas and establish homesteads. As Mexican families moved to the frontier during the 1820s and 1830s, settling close to the missions, they found themselves in competition with the Franciscan missionaries. The Catholic Church held most of the land and laborers (in the form of Indians). Competition for these resources led to anticlericism (not for religious but economic reasons), resulting in 1833 with the Mexican Congress secularizing the missions, thus breaking the Church's hold on the area's resources. Nearly 8 million acres of lands held by the missions were granted or sold to Mexican officials, soldiers, and civilians (including women). These new landholders became a *ranchero/a* class. The Indians who were working under the "care" of missionaries were also emancipated, with most of those who worked at the missions receiving parcels of the mission's land. Unfortunately, Indian ownership of land lasted a short time. As they lost their land, they became workers at the estates of the new *ranchero/a* class.

—MAD

established missionary work in Mexico in December 1872. Methodists followed with the purchase of the first Protestant Church located at No. 5, Gante Street in downtown Mexico City, a former Franciscan monastery made available by President Benito Juarez's Constitutional Reformation. Former Catholic seminarian, Alejo Hernandez, fought for Juarez and later converted to Methodism to become the first ordained Mexican Protestant and pastored this congregation. Throughout Latin America, Protestants were perceived as being allies of liberalism, and liberal politicians welcomed Protestant missionary work. U.S. mainline denominations such as the Presbyterians, Methodists, Episcopalians, and Baptists started schools and hospitals along with church plants. Exiles from the early battles for Cuban independence fled to Key West and Tampa and found an ally in American Protestantism. Some were converted and returned to Cuba to start the first Protestant services in 1873. After U.S. military incursions into Latin America, for example, Teddy Roosevelt's "rough riders" 1898 intervention in the Spanish-American War in Cuba, Protestant mission work was often viewed as a "foreign" element. Other immigrants remained in the United States creating Hispanic communities in Florida, the Northeast, and the Southwest.

Protestant mission systems began in the United States among Hispanic communities after the establishment of mainline Home Missionary Societies in the 1860s. As the American frontier moved west after the Louisiana Purchase and the Mexican-American War, home missionaries ministered to Native American and Hispanic communities in the American Southwest to establish schools and plant churches—often in tension with the Roman Catholic traditions engrained in Mexican-American culture.

Philip Wingeier-Rayo

References and Further Reading

Barton, Paul. *Hispanic Methodists, Presbyterians, and Baptists in Texas* (Austin: University of Texas Press, 2006).

Bastian, Jean-Pierre. *La Mutación Religiosa de América Latina, Para una Sociología del Cambio Social en la Modernidad Periférica* (Mexico City, Mexico: Fondo de Cultura Económica, 1997, 2003).

Burns, Kathryn. *Colonial Habits: Currents and the Spiritual Economy of Cuzco, Peru* (Durham, NC: Duke University Press, 1999).

Lewis, Laura A. *Hall of Mirrors* (Durham, NC: Duke University Press, 2003).

Martinez, Juan Francisco. *Sea La Luz: The Making of Mexican Protestantism in the American Southwest 1829–1900* (Denton: University of North Texas Press, 2006).

Wingeier-Rayo, Philip. *Cuban Methodism: The Untold Story of Survival and Revival* (Lawrenceville, GA: Dolphins & Orchids, 2004, 2006).

Yohn, Susan Mitchell. *A Contest of Faiths: Missionary Women and Pluralism in the American Southwest* (Ithaca, NY: Cornell University Press, 1995).

MORMONS/LATTER-DAY SAINTS

Anglo-American visionary Joseph Smith founded Mormonism in the early nineteenth century. By far the religion's largest denomination—and the subject of this entry—is the Church of Jesus Christ of Latter-day Saints (hereafter LDS Church), headquartered in Salt Lake City and claiming 12 million members. Since the last quarter of the twentieth century, adherents have preferred to be called "Latter-day Saints," but "Mormon" is still a standard scholarly usage.

By 2005, some 200,000 Latino/a members of the LDS Church lived across the United States. Additionally, Mormonism affects Hispanic Americans by dint of the religion's political influence in Utah and other western states. Mormonism has unfolded on a transnational stage, with missionaries and immigrants playing important roles in the movement's history. Consequently, Hispanic American Mormon experience cannot be isolated from Mormonism in Mexico and elsewhere in Latin America. Because of rapid growth in Latin America, Spanish speakers are expected to overtake English speakers as the LDS Church's largest language group during the early 2010s. Thus Hispanic Americans are both the largest minority within Mormonism in the United States and part of the religion's rapidly up-and-coming new global majority.

Initial Mormon-Latino Contacts

For 15 years after the religion's founding in 1830, Mormons suffered recurring episodes of state-sanctioned as well as vigilante violence against them due to radical practices such as communitarianism, theocracy, and polygamy. After Joseph Smith was arrested and killed by a mob in 1844, the main body of Mormons fled U.S. borders, resettling in present-day Utah, which was then Mexican territory. As Chicano scholar Armando Solórzano has quipped, the Mormons were, in effect, illegal immigrants. The Mormon community at this time was composed mostly of Anglo-Americans and British immigrants, joined later by large numbers of Scandinavian converts.

Although Franciscans explored Utah in 1776, neither Spanish nor Mexican administrations established colonies there. The region was home to Uto-Aztecan speaking peoples; indeed, as early as the sixteenth century, a Utah site was proposed as the location of Aztlán, the Aztec homeland. Within a year of the Mormons' arrival, the United States annexed the Utah territory under the Treaty of Guadalupe Hidalgo. Mormons were uneasy about returning to life under the American government. They had, however, provided a battalion of 500 to fight in the Mexican-American War. Chicano scholars have interpreted the Mormon Battalion as an alliance with the U.S. policy of Manifest Destiny. That same policy, however, led to persecution of the Mormons as the federal government moved to assert control of the region by abolishing Mormon theocracy and polygamy.

During the second half of the nineteenth century, Mormons established colonies in Utah, Idaho, Nevada, and what had become the U.S.-Mexico borderlands in Arizona. They also launched their first missions to Latin America. Mormons had a particular interest in preaching to Native Americans and mestizos because of teachings from the Book of Mormon, which Joseph Smith claimed was a translation of lost scriptures written on golden plates by Israelites who had colonized the Americas in Old Testament times. The descendants of these people, called Lamanites, lapsed into barbarism, becoming the continent's indigenous peoples. The Book of Mormon prophesies that the Lamanites will convert and recover their former glory as a precursor to Christ's second coming. Down to the present, many Native American and mestizo Mormons proudly claim Lamanite identity, deriving from it a sense of extraordinary heritage and destiny.

After an abortive, poorly prepared 1852 mission to Chile, a Mexican mission was launched in the 1870s, attracting a few hundred converts by century's end. Among the fruits of this mission were the first Spanish translation of the Book of Mormon and the creation of colonies in Chihuahua and Sonora as havens for Anglo Mormon polygamists fleeing prosecution in the United States. The missionaries' work was interrupted by U.S. government efforts to confiscate church assets; by the Mexican Revolution, which also prompted Mormons to evacuate their Mexican colonies; and by the Mexican government's deportation of foreign ministers after the Cristero rebellion. Mexican Mormon congregations endured, however—on both sides of the border.

Beginnings of Hispanic American Mormonism

Withdrawing temporarily from Mexico during the Revolution, Anglo-American missionaries shifted their attention to Mexican Americans in Colorado and the border states from Texas to California. Around the same time, three sisters who had joined the church in Mexico—Augustina, Dolores, and Domitila Rivera—migrated to Salt Lake. There they launched missionary efforts among Hispanic Americans, who had been coming to Utah since the beginning of the twentieth century to work in industries created by the Mormons, such as sugar beet farming. The Rivera sisters were joined in 1920 by Juan Ramón Martínez, from New Mexico; Francisco Solano, a Spaniard who encountered Mormonism in South Africa; and Mexican-born Margarito Bautista. These six became the core of Mormonism's oldest continuously operating ethnic congregation in the United States, eventually called the Lucero Ward.

Outside Utah, proselytizing to Hispanic Americans continued under the Mexican Mission, which straddled the border until a separate Spanish American Mission was created for the United States in 1936. Eduardo Balderas, a Mexican native reared in Texas, was hired in 1939 as the church's first full-time translator, making many devotional texts available to Spanish-speaking Mormons in and out of the United States. The temple ceremonies, which convey esoteric instruction for the afterlife, were translated into Spanish in 1945, the first time that the century-old rites were administered in any language other than English. Hundreds of Mexican and Hispanic American Mormons gathered annually to perform the ceremonies at the church's Mesa, Arizona, temple, the only place the ceremonies were available in Spanish until the 1970s.

Especially for Hispanic Americans in Utah, membership in the LDS Church offered tangible benefits: spaces in which to socialize and preserve their culture, connections to White Mormon employers, and access to the church's welfare system. But Anglo Mormons' sense of racial privilege also bred a paternalistic attitude that kept Latina/o congregations and missions under Anglo leadership into the 1960s. During the 1930s, Margarito Bautista and others petitioned for a Mexican to head the Mexican Mission. When Anglo leaders rejected the petition, a third of the church's Mexican membership organized a separate denomination called the Third

Convention. Bautista and other Third Conventionists fused teachings about the destiny of the Lamanites with post-Revolutionary nationalistic fervor.

Growth and New Challenges

Mormon conversions in Latin America rose dramatically during the 1960s and 1970s, making that region the largest source of Mormon growth outside the United States throughout the second half of the twentieth century. Missionizing had begun in Argentina during the 1920s; by the 1960s, missionaries worked throughout Central and South America. In 1961, the first Latin American stake (analogous to a diocese) was created in Mexico City. The stake was initially headed by an Anglo, but within a few years that appointment passed to a Mexican, Agrícol Lozano. In 1983, Mexico City became the site of the first temple in Latin America; at century's end, the church had constructed nearly 25 temples and thousands of local meetinghouses to serve its 4.5 million Latin American members. By 2005, nine Spanish-surnamed individuals had served in the First and Second Quorums of Seventy, the lower tiers of the church's highest-ranking leadership. Also by that year, church membership in Mexico had reached 1 million, the greatest number of Mormons anywhere outside the United States.

In the United States, missionizing to Hispanic Americans expanded to the East Coast with the 1964 New York World's Fair. Immigration of Mormons from Latin America contributed to the continuing growth of the church's Latino/a membership in the United States. During the 1970s, the church helped Latin American Mormons fleeing political unrest in their countries of origin obtain U.S. visas and refugee status. In 1978, church president Spencer W. Kimball abolished the controversial policy of banning Mormons of Black African descent from holding church office or receiving temple ceremonies. This turning point cleared the way for Mormon growth among Black Spanish speakers, such as Dominicans.

Why did Mormonism appeal to Latino/as? Oral histories suggest that the church's emphasis on strengthening families and traditional gender roles appeals to many, as do prohibitions on alcohol and gambling, opportunities for local leadership in a lay-led church, and a middle-class ethos reflecting American corporate values. Also, Lamanite identity is important for many mestizo Mormons, particularly those who identify, for nationalist reasons, with pre-Columbian civilizations, notably Mexicans and Peruvians. Some Hispanic American Mormons developed a Chicano consciousness during the 1960s. Mormons in El Paso organized an Asociación Cultural México Americana in 1969 to voice concerns about discrimination and the predominance of Anglo culture in the church. Also in the late 1960s, Orlando Rivera, the Lucero Ward's first non-Anglo bishop, joined with a Catholic priest to found SOCIO, an organization that promoted Latino/a civil rights in Utah. Rivera was frustrated that Anglo church leaders, politically conservative by temperament, remained detached from the struggle for civil rights. Church leaders showed somewhat greater concern for Hispanic American exploitation during the 2000s. By then, according to newspaper reports, an estimated 30 percent of Utah's growing Latina/o population was Mormon.

Contemporary Issues

Ethnic Congregations. Since the mid-twentieth century, concern for organizational efficiency has led to the demise of ethnically or linguistically bounded missions, such as the Spanish American mission, in favor of geographically defined ones. Church policy has vacillated in its support for ethnic congregations in the United States, the greatest number of which are Spanish speaking. While Kimball enthusiastically supported such congregations, other Anglo leaders have favored integrating minorities into English-speaking wards. These leaders believe that cultural diversity must be managed to avoid compromising the unity of the international church or the integrity of its revealed message. Conservative anxieties about multiculturalism in the United States likely play a factor as well. Although church leaders have moved periodically since the 1970s toward disbanding ethnic congregations, in 2006 the number of Spanish-speaking units in the United States was at an all-time high of 600. In Los Angeles, entire Spanish-speaking stakes have been organized.

Anglo-Latino/a and Intra-Latina/o Tensions. For a century, Hispanic American Mormons have complained about unequal treatment from Anglo coreligionists—one reason that many Hispanic Americans prefer separate congregations. They have resented, for example, being pigeonholed as providers of ethnic food and dance for church socials. In addition, there are predictable intercultural misunderstandings: Anglos perceive Latino/as as disorganized, Latina/os perceive Anglos as cold, and so on. The drastically disproportionate number of Latina/os in the highest levels of

San Diego California Temple of The Church of Jesus Christ of Latter-day Saints. (Scott Prokop/Dreamstime)

church leadership is a likely source of future discontent. (All Latino/a leaders at that level have been Latin American natives, not Hispanic American.)

Within Hispanic American congregations, some have worried about a tendency for members to form cliques by nationality. Non-Mexicans have complained about Mexican dominance. Since 2002, the church has hosted annual celebrations of Latino/a cultures in its massive Salt Lake conference center. Drawing thousands of Hispanic American Mormons, these events aim to promote a sense of pan-Latina/o unity while showcasing different nationalities.

Immigration and Related Issues. The church has not voiced official positions on immigration reform or border security. However, Anglo-American Mormons tend to be politically conservative, and this has led Mormon lawmakers and voters in Utah, Arizona, and elsewhere to support initiatives such as English Only. Some conservative Mormons have called for church leaders to deny baptism or temple ceremonies to undocumented immigrants. The church has publicly rejected these proposals.

In 2002, the church launched a Hispanic Initiative that included creating a clinic and English classes for Salt Lake Latina/os. While the initiative is oriented toward assimilation, it represents an effort by Anglo Mormons to respond to the exploitation of Hispanic Americans. After Mexican president Vicente Fox held a 2006 meeting with LDS Church leaders in Salt Lake to discuss the church's work in Mexico and the situation of Mexican Mormons in Utah, CNN commentator Lou Dobbs accused the church of encouraging illegal immigration.

Challenges to Lamanite Identity. In the early 2000s, some Mormon intellectuals in the English-speaking world pointed out that DNA studies contradicted the long-standing Mormon belief that Native Americans were of Israelite descent. Other Mormon intellectuals responded to this challenge by proposing that the peoples described in the Book of Mormon occupied a much smaller territory than Mormons had traditionally believed and were eventually absorbed into indigenous populations. At stake in this debate is the plausibility of the Book of Mormon and, by extension, the authenticity of the religion's claim to revelation. Revising Lamanite identity allows Mormons to preserve faith in the Book of Mormon in the face of scientific counterevidence. However, that revision has been disturbing to some Latina/o Mormons whose own identities are bound up in statements by church leaders affirming that Native Americans and mestizos belong to the chosen Lamanite lineage. It is unclear how this dilemma will be resolved. Probably most Mormons in Latin America are unaware of these debates among English-speaking intellectuals. Hispanic Americans are more likely to encounter the debates.

Timeline

1830   Joseph Smith publishes the Book of Mormon.

1847   Mormon pioneers settle in Mexican territory (present-day Utah).

1920   The longest operating Hispanic American Mormon congregation, eventually known as the Lucero Ward, is founded.

1936   Margarito Bautista and other Mexican Mormons petition unsuccessfully for Mexican leadership.

1961   The first Latin American stake is organized in Mexico.

1966   Orlando Rivera becomes the first Hispanic American bishop of the Lucero Ward.

1969   Mormons in Texas found the Asociación Cultural México Americana to voice concerns about the dominance of Anglo culture in the church.

1978   Church president Spencer W. Kimball lifts restrictions on church members with Black African ancestry.

2002   Church leaders launch a Hispanic Initiative in Salt Lake City.

2004   The number of Mormons in Mexico reaches 1 million; about 200,000 Latino Mormons live in the United States.

John-Charles Duffy

References and Further Reading

Embry, Jessie L. *In His Own Language": Mormon Spanish Speaking Congregations in the United States* (Provo, UT: The Charles Redd Center for Western Studies, Brigham Young University, 1997).

Gurnon, Emily. "Minority Mormon: Latino and Latter-day Saint." *Christian Century* (February 16, 1994): 157–159.

Iber, Jorge. *Hispanics in the Mormon Zion, 1912–1999* (College Station: Texas A&M University Press, 2000).

Rivera, Orlando A. "Mormonism and the Chicano." *Mormonism: A Faith for All Cultures*, ed. F. LaMond Tullis (Provo, UT: Brigham Young University Press, 1978).

Solórzano, Armando. "Struggle over Memory: The Roots of the Mexican Americans in Utah, 1776 through the 1850s." *Aztlán* 23, no. 3 (Fall 1998): 81–117.

MOZARABIC RITE

The official name of this liturgical system centered at Toledo, Spain, is the

Hispano-Mozarabic Rite. Variously called the Old Spanish Rite, the Hispanic Rite, and more usually the Mozarabic Rite, the ancient rite of Spain is one of several Latin language liturgical systems that arose in the West in the first four centuries of the Christian era. Only three have survived to this day, the Roman, the Milanese, and the Spanish. Vatican II's openness to diversity in the liturgy was stated in the Decree on the Eastern Catholic Churches (1964) when it stated that all the rites celebrated by Catholics in East or West enjoy the same dignity and privileges as the Roman rite (*OE* 3). This led Cardinal Marcelo González Martín (Archbishop of Toledo 1972–1995) to renew the ancient Spanish rite's status and life. He formed a commission whose work resulted in updating and designating it as an alternate liturgy for all Catholics in Spain in 1988. Consequently, new liturgical books for the celebration of the Eucharist appeared in 1991. With permission the Eucharist in the Mozarabic Rite may be celebrated elsewhere, and it has been celebrated in the United States on seven occasions since its updating: five at Sacred Heart School of Theology (1999, 2000, 2001, 2003, and 2004); once in Chicago (Quigley Seminary, 1999); and once at Notre Dame University, South Bend, Indiana (2003). The liturgy is primarily celebrated in Latin, although an unofficial Spanish translation is occasionally used.

The importance of this rite for Latino/as in the United States is that when the Mozarabic rite was replaced as the primary liturgy for Spain by the Roman rite, many of the Mozarabic sacramental celebrations entered into the popular religious practices of peoples evangelized by Spanish missionaries throughout the world. These include such things as the

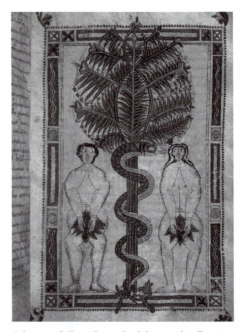

Adam and Eve, from the Manuscript Beato de Libeana, *tenth century. (The Art Archive/ Corbis)*

use of the *lazo* and *arras* at weddings, the presentation of children in the church, blessings on occasions of rites of passage such as *quince años* celebrations, and an approach to sacramentality that sees God's presence and blessing of creation and humankind everywhere. Events are marked by special blessings and celebrations, as well as by the use of *padrinos* (godparents). In addition, the high Christology of the liturgy is reflected in the popular approach to Jesus Christ as the God-Man who is exalted above all others. This spirituality lends itself to seeing the Virgin Mary and saints as mediators, for instance, and the establishment of shrines and home altars where God can be readily encountered by the faithful. Furthermore, liturgy is not to be confined to the Church building but is to be taken out on the streets to encourage the public manifestation of faith, a trait seen in the numbers of Latino/as who seek ashes on their foreheads on Ash Wednesday. The rite also has a notable penitential character, which is expressed in Hispanic popular religion through *mandas* and *promesas*, votive offerings, and practices such as *Via Crucis* processions.

The Mozarabic Rite is the principal liturgical system celebrated by Mozarabs, an ethnic group centered at Toledo. By the time Caracalla granted Roman citizenship to all residents of the empire (212 CE), the Romanization of the Hispanic peoples, and therefore also the citizens of Toledo, was completed in a legal sense. The adoption of Roman names, customs, and language took longer. Nonetheless, a large number of Iberians considered themselves Roman in many ways by the time of the Visigothic triumph in the fifth century, not least of all in their Christianity. Thus, it is appropriate to refer to them as Hispano-Romans. The growth of the Hispano-Roman church was exemplified in many ways by the renown of the Council of Elvira (c. 314) and the influence of one of its bishops, Hosius of Córdoba (d. 357), who as an advisor to the Emperor Constantine (d. 337) presided in the emperor's name at the Council of Nicaea (325). Certainly, the *acta* of the Hispano-Roman and Visigothic Councils of the fourth, fifth, and sixth centuries reveal a church in touch with the wider communion of Catholic Churches while especially adhering to the Apostolic See.

Present-day Mozarabs claim to form a community composed of the descendants of those Hispano-Roman and Visigothic Christians who held onto their faith despite the vicissitudes of Islamic invasion and the need to adapt culturally

to the dominant culture. Through the centuries they intermarried with subsequent conquerors and inhabitants of Toledo including Arabs, Berbers, Syrians, Castilians, Galicians, and French. During the more than 370 years of Islamic domination, they spoke Arabic and acquired the cultural characteristics of the dominant Arabic culture.

Since the reconquest of Toledo (1085), Mozarabs have blended in with the general Spanish populace. Over the course of time, many Mozarab families were subsumed into the dominant culture and disappeared as part of a distinct cultural group or forgot their origins. For long periods of time those who despite everything maintained their sense of identity have suffered marginalization and domination as well.

Mozarabs today speak modern-day Castilian, although at one time they spoke a particular Romance dialect. Economically they fall within various economic levels and socially rank in the upper-middle to the titled classes. Nonetheless, in language, appearance, dress, lifestyle, occupation, education, and religious practice they appear to differ little from the general population of Toledo.

The third and fourth centuries witnessed great development in the celebration of the Eucharist among Christians resulting in the formation of various liturgical families. Thus, the Latin West saw the rise of the Latin-language liturgies between the fifth and seventh centuries, and clearly there are significant affinities between the Mozarabic rite and the other Latin liturgies. This is especially true of the Roman and Gallican rites in terms of common evolution, structure, memorial, and soteriology.

The development of the Hispano-Mozarabic Rite was a slow process that had its greatest unfolding during the Visigothic era in the sixth and seventh centuries. The *acta* of the III and IV Councils of Toledo, conducted under the auspices of Kings Reccared (586–601) and Sisenand (631–636), give clear evidence of this. Three metropolitan sees had the greatest influence on the rite's development: Seville, Tarragona, and Toledo. Three bishops, Leander (c. 540–600), Isidore (c. 560–636), and Ildephonse of Toledo (c. 610–667), especially contributed to its formation. Notably, Toledo III (589) was presided over by Leander, whereas Toledo IV (633) was presided over by Isidore.

The *prenotanda* to the *Missale Hispano-Mozarabicum* (1991) indicate that various sociocultural factors contributed to the evolution of the rite. First of all there was the synthesis of Roman cultural values and organization particularly maintained in the highly Latinized zones of the peninsula. By the time the Visigoths triumphed in Spain, they had already absorbed many of the same Roman cultural values and patterns of organization. This helped form a solid cultural base of language and values that provided the Spanish church with the opportunity to develop its liturgy. Second, a relative religious peace was obtained through the official conversion of the Visigoths from the Arian to the Catholic faith. Third, the Visigothic court generated a Latin humanism that flourished in the work of the Iberian Fathers, such as Braulio of Zaragoza (d. 631). A creative period resulted in terms of arts and letters as well as the composition of music that contributed greatly to the liturgy. Fourth, the *acta* of several Visigothic councils reveal that great attention was paid to the celebration of the Eucharist. These councils attempted to provide some semblance of liturgical unity emanating from Toledo, the Visigothic capital. This was accomplished in some measure under Julian of Toledo (d. 690) who compiled the first liturgical texts into what later ages would identify as a sacramentary.

A commission established by Cardinal González Martín (1982) was charged with identifying and retrieving the structure of the Eucharist and its subsequent reformulation into the *Missale Hispano-Mozarabicum*. The commission based its work on what can only be identified as the ideal of a "classical period" in the development of the rite. Unfortunately, there has never been an ideal Roman or Hispano-Mozarabic period, for as is well known, the churches influenced one another on many levels and incorporated practices that suited their worship and held these as part of their treasure. Nonetheless, the classical period is seen as the fifth to seventh centuries when most of the euchological texts and musical compositions were formulated. This was the period just prior to the Islamic invasions of 711. It was also the period in which the Visigothic kingdom reached its apex. The seventh century in particular is seen as the period of highest creativity. Therefore, the updated rite as it appears in the *Missale Hispano-Mozarabicum* and the *Liber Commicus* (lectionary) reflects the texts of this period while excluding most of what was introduced between then and the Cisneros reform of the sixteenth century.

Once Toledo's ecclesiastical primacy was lost with the Islamic invasion, a significant group of Christians remaining there maintained their faith and celebrated as well as developed their liturgy. With great difficulty they continued to recopy their texts and add new prayer formulas, which would help them interpret the experience of domination and marginalization. Once Toledo had been retaken and the Roman rite imposed, the Mozarab community there continued to cling to its rite. The parishes of Santa Eulalia and Santas Justa y Rufina had their own schools of scribes that recopied the liturgical texts for their use. Thanks to these two parishes and their efforts to preserve their heritage, canon Alfonso Ortiz was able to compile the necessary manuscripts to form the core of the *Missale mixtum* (1500) of Cardinal Francisco Ximénez de Cisneros (1495–1517).

Over the centuries numerous factors have kept Toledo at the forefront of efforts to maintain the rite even though other places such as Salamanca and Plasencia have contributed to this effort. Specifically, Toledo regained its position as the primatial see with the reconquest in 1085. Later, Cardinal Cisneros established a Mozarabic chapel in the cathedral of Toledo in 1502, assuring the ancient Spanish liturgy a home where the rite could be conserved for posterity. Most recently, Cardinal González Martín's role as former president of the Spanish Episcopal Liturgical Commission and his interest in the rite have contributed to the latest efforts to conserve it. The efforts of the Mozarab community to preserve and promote the rite since the reconquest have helped maintain Toledo's leadership. These factors have borne fruit in the updating and reestablishment of the Hispano-Mozarabic Rite in the contemporary era.

Raúl Gómez-Ruiz

References and Further Reading

Burman, Thomas E. *Religious Polemic and the Intellectual History of the Mozarabs, c. 1050–1200*. Brill's Studies in Intellectual History 52 (Leiden: E. J. Brill, 1994).

Gómez-Ruiz, Raúl. *Mozarabs, Hispanics, and the Cross* (Maryknoll, NY: Orbis, 2007).

Isidore of Seville. *De ecclesiasticis officiis*, trans. Thomas L. Knoebel (Mahwah, NJ: Paulist Press, 2008).

Liber Commicus, 2 vols. (Toledo: Arzobispado de Toledo, 1991).

Missale Hispano-Mozarabicum, 2 vols. (Toledo: Arzobispado de Toledo, 1991).

Pinell, Jordi. *Liturgia hispánica*, Biblioteca litúrgica 9 (Barcelona: Centre de Pastoral Litúrgica, 1998).

Vives, José, Tomás Marín Martínez, and Gonzalo Martínez Díez, eds., *Concilios Visigóticos e Hispano-Romanos*, España Cristiana 1 (Barcelona-Madrid: Consejo Superior de Investigaciones Científicas Instituto Enrique Flórez, 1963).

MUJERISTA

Mujerista Theology engages in theological praxis that have as its goal the liberation of U.S. Latinas, hence from the Spanish word *mujer*, which translates as woman. Its main proponent, Ada María Isasi-Díaz, has documented and analyzed the accounts of daily life and faith of U.S. Latinas, principally by means of ethnographic and meta-ethnographic studies, and has coined the name "Mujerista Theology." Other methods of study, such as sociological and psychological interpretation and analysis, are also employed as methodological resources in Mujerista Theology. Yolanda Tarango has been engaged with the tasks of Mujerista Theology since the beginnings of its articulation in the 1990s in the United States.

The majority of Latinas in the United States live in poor conditions and are marginalized through political and economic institutions by the dominant social group. Mujerista Theology, as a specific liberation theology contextualized in the life and faith of U.S. Latinas, sees Latinas as moral agents in the communal "historical project" of achieving and maintaining their own liberation from the complex and oppressive forces that surround them. Salvation and human history go hand in hand with Liberation Theology, as well as in the theology of mujeristas. The historical project of liberation of U.S. Latinas, according to Mujerista Theology, is one of securing the fullness of life that God destined for them concretely within the realities and experience of day-to-day living. The fullness of life that is sought by mujerista Latinas starts with survival, the satisfaction of both the basic needs to sustain physical life and the wants that make for a full and pleasant daily existence.

Armed with a hermeneutics of liberation, mujerista Latinas in the United States engage themselves in the communal struggle (La Lucha) against the dynamics of oppressive powers and arrive at their self-determination. By analyzing their stories of oppression and their faith stories of empowerment, they can come to denounce, for example, the benefits that the privileged part of the world collects from a global economy that exploits the other part of the world. In most cases, the countries of origin of U.S. Latinas, or that of their parents or grandparents, happen to be precisely in that exploited part of the world. In the praxis of Mujerista Theology, the

conscientization of U.S. Latinas about their oppressive social and even ecclesial locations intermingles with their theological and ethical reflection by actually surviving the oppressive reality and constructing a different one for themselves as individuals and as a community. In this way, the theological praxis of Mujerista Theology can emerge only from the grassroots foundation of both the pain and the hope of the community. Theology and ethics are inseparable, then, in the praxis of liberation of U.S. Latinas. Their new reality is constructed precisely through the combination of both the social analysis and the empowerment that their faith provides them.

The Latina voices that are lifted up ask about how God is present in their daily lives, and who is God for them, in the first place. They ask themselves how their own beliefs and popular religiosity interact with their daily lived existences. Even though there are significant differences between the various groups of Latinas, such as generational, socioeconomic, national heritage, degree of adaptation to the cultural environment of the United States and particular mestizaje mix, Latinas find a unity in the forces that oppress them all: sexism, ethnic/racial prejudice, and socioeconomic discrimination. The forms of discrimination are more subtle after the 1960s in the United States, and so they have become much more insidious and much more difficult to point out to those who do not experience their sting. Latinas know that discrimination is alive and well, and they see it every day in institutions that keep subtly supporting the status quo. In this context, U.S. Latinas point out the social sin that hurts them individually and communally. Through the faithful analysis of their context, Latinas see the social dimension of sin, and confront it. The structures of power that deny Latinas the abundance of life that was meant for them and all by God are thus unmasked and challenged. Latinas claim the justice that they deserve and their right to belong fully to social institutions that organize communal life, be it the economic market or the church.

Mujerista Latinas' theological reflections nourish their firm belief that they belong to God's family on this earth (the "kin-dom" of God), and in the particular country of which they are now part, the United States of America. Latinas give priority to their own conscience in their social interactions and in their analysis of the reality that surrounds them. The Hispanic culture in general holds the ethical role of conscience highly. Many are the everyday expressions in Spanish that point to that fact, as in the following: "No tiene conciencia," "He does not have a conscience," referring to an individual who has broken an ethical rule of the community; or "No le duele la consciencia," "His conscience doesn't hurt," even though the person has done something unacceptable. Essential then to Mujerista Theology is a process of conscientization about the contextual realities that trap the Latinas viz-à-viz the hope and strength that their faith instills in them. The conscientization method utilizes the action-reflection-action model with the dual goal of survival and liberation. Latinas become subjects of their own history, and not mere victims of the oppressive forces, by recognizing in community their socio-political rights and claiming them in the name of the dignity conferred on them by God. In that way, mujerista Latinas in the United States walk toward their preferred future, steadily surviving and enjoying their lives in the fullness that God intended for them.

Alicia Vargas

References and Further Reading

Isasi-Díaz, Ada María. *Mujerista Theology: A Theology for the Twenty-First Century* (Maryknoll, NY: Orbis Books, 1996).

———. *En la Lucha in the Struggle: Elaborating a Mujerista Theology* (Minneapolis: Fortress Press, 2004).

Isasi-Díaz, Ada María, and Yolanda Tarango. *Hispanic Women: Prophetic Voice in the Church* (Minneapolis: Fortress Press, 1992).

Perez, Arturo, Consuelo Covarrubias, and Edward Foley, eds. *Asi Es: Historias de espiritualidad hispana* (Collegeville, MN: The Liturgical Press, 1994).

MULATEZ

The term "mulatez" refers to people of African and European mix racial heritage. As a racial and cultural symbol, it points to the ways in which mulatto/as act and position themselves in relation to others and how they are seen and positioned in society. These ways of positioning the self in relation to society open and close possibilities of actions for mulatto/as in societies where race plays a central role in determining social, political, religious, and economic arrangements. Under the legacy of Spanish colonialism, and later U.S. imperial interests, social arrangements were developed that placed whiteness at the top of the social hierarchy, Blacks at the bottom, with the middle arranged by various degrees of separation or closeness to whiteness vis-à-vis blackness. In the resulting racialized social structure, mulatto/a bodies lived in the existing tension among whiteness, blackness, and other racial conceptions that developed in the Americas and the Caribbean.

Mulatez importance is in its symbolic meanings as a social construct. Competing ideologies, political projects, and science are among the factors that contribute to the conceptualization of mulatez. On a cautionary note, "mestizaje" and "mulatez" are not synonymous. Although some scholars use both terms interchangeably, often in an attempt to gather together experiences thought of as shared by people of mixed descent, for mulattos the mixing of the two terms functions as a way to conceal their blackness. For this reason, in the remainder of this entry, mestizaje will not be part of the discussion.

Measuring blackness in the Americas and the Spanish-speaking Caribbean is quite common. The gradation of blackness either grants certain privileges or denies them, depending on closeness to blackness. The closer an individual is to being Black the more parallel the degradation of societal conditions where racism is prevalent. The ways of defining blackness range from characteristics of skin tones, hair textures, facial features, ways of speaking, and/or cultural productions. From its usage as a pejorative term that originally referred to mules, "mulatez," as some scholars argue, is gaining increasing usage as a self-identification of marginalized people of mixed African descent within the Latino/a population. These scholars insist that it is possible to speak of a mulatto culture without being racially (as it regards physical appearance) Black. This can occur in places where African ancestry has played an important role in the development of symbolic practices. For example, some scholars seem to be in agreement that Puerto Rico is "whitening" faster than any other nation in the Spanish-speaking Caribbean. Whatever truth exists in this claim, the African influence is undeniable. Musical production (particularly bomba, plena, salsa, and Latin Jazz), cuisine, the arts *máscaras* and *vegigantes*, popular festivities like *La Fiesta de Santiago Apóstol* at Loíza Aldea, and literature underscore the African influences on the Island. African culture, rhythm, and instrumentation strongly influence music, graphic arts, cuisine, and linguistic patterns of the Caribbean and the Americas.

The sociological and anthropological literature is ambiguous on how to theorize "mulatez." As per literature, what it means to be a mulatto/a is understood in relation and attitudes toward blackness. Any negative attitude that is attached to blackness in a particular society by extension also applies to mulatto/as as long as they appear to be of African descent; on the other hand, privileges and advances could be possible if the mulatto/a is of light complexion. This explains the historical lack of theorizing about differences between mulattos and African slaves or free Blacks that extended beyond the privileges of social and economic advantages available to light-skinned mulatto/as, often serving in houses of Whites.

From Central, South American, and the Caribbean, attitudes toward mulatto/as are diverse. For example, in Perú and Colombia it is common to make a distinction between what the elites consider high culture, referred to as *la cultura*, and those practices often considered "popular" (of lesser importance) and Black simply as *cultura*. The article *la* creates a demarcation between these two cultures, reflecting ingrained social attitudes toward anything African. Also, the word *negrear* (to "negroize") is used to denote insult or a way to ask for better treatment. "No me negrees" (do not "negroize" me) is a common way to complain against poor treatment, thus underscoring the reality that there exists a way in which *negro/as* (Blacks) can be treated that is not acceptable to Whites. In countries of the Spanish-speaking Caribbean, like Puerto Rico and the Dominican Republic, mulatez is often considered on a scale of degree to blackness, from the most African looking to those who could almost pass as White—which, not surprising, is considered the best. Dominicans often refer to their racial heritage as *indios* while labeling their Haitian neighbors as Blacks. In Puerto Rico, the term *jabao* refers to a light skin mulatto/a attempting to pass as White. In Haiti and Trinidad, *negritude* is embraced as a source of national identity and resistance. As it can be intuited from this discussion, mulatez is positioned in the intersection of whiteness and blackness, often forcing a choice between the privileges of whiteness or the stigma of blackness.

During the late seventeenth to the nineteenth centuries, an ideology of racial improvement gained strength among the Creole elite. Because the prevailing view about those from African descent was that they were primitive, White masters justified their use of the female slave body as a sexual object as an attempt to improve and purify the race through the infusion of "white" blood, a process known as *la limpieza de sangre* (the washing of the blood). This ideology of *blanqueamiento* (whitening) has survived until this day. It is often said that by marrying White, or at least a person of lighter skin, the race is improved.

With the growing influence of the United States in the Caribbean during the late nineteenth and early twentieth centuries, conceptions of race became more radicalized. The racial project that dominated the United States introduced a different form of racism to Spanish-speaking countries. The "one drop rule" prevalent in the American South was enough to consider most Hispanics Black. When U.S. troops arrived in the Caribbean, they considered the inhabitants of the Great Antilles Blacks. Prior to and after the Spanish-American War period, political cartoons routinely depicted Cubans, Puerto Ricans, and Filipinos as Blacks using the same images previously used to portray African Americans. The evolutionary uplifting of these "new peoples" was construed as the "White men's burden." They were perceived as lacking the ability to self-govern and needing civilization, with arguments similar to those used in the United States to condone segregation and disenfranchisement of Blacks. Census data show that the racial understanding of the United States had a great impact on the self-conceptions of these countries. The number of those who classified themselves as mulatto/as crossed racial lines over to White, Indian, or other, particularly in the Spanish-speaking Caribbean. Whitening became a better strategy for advancement.

Usually, discussions of racism focus on the struggles between peoples in the margin and those sectors in society that subjugate them to subaltern places. Often neglected are analyses of internal racism among marginalized communities. The Latino/a community in the United States is no different. Whatever the reasons for this neglect, the experiences of Afro-Latino/as and mulatto/as have been submerged in Pan-Hispanic identities that promote "brownness" as a self-understanding of the Latino/a community in the United States. Whether intentional or not, it is hard to deny that mestizaje, as a category of self-understanding, privileges indigenous elements of Latino/a culture over African ones, a problematic matter for Afro-Latino/as and mulatto/as.

How Black must one be to be mulatto? Often heard in the African American communities are discussions surrounding the question of being "black enough." This will, without a doubt, become an issue when blackness is discussed among mulatto/as. Brownness may signify a strong indigenous descent, but more commonly in the Caribbean it points to greater racial mixing—Spanish, Indian, and African. It could also point to blackness as a "fair skin African-descent," who may or may not be Latino/a. Such formulations already imply a deprecation of blackness. The cultural question to then ask in the context of U.S. society is why is a "fair skin" African American seen as Black, but a "fair-skin" mulatto of Latino/a descent seen as brown?

Religion and Mulatez

Recently, the concept of mulatez has entered the Latino/a religious discourse as a way to reclaim practices, traditions, and cultural artifacts of African descent. In the Latino/a discourse, mulatez functions in three interrelated ways: first, as a marker of racial and cultural identity; second, as an epistemological principle by which to understand the world; and third, as a religious identity.

As the discussion of mulatez in theology, as well as biblical and theological studies, gains force, Ada María Isasi-Díaz, Michelle González, Samuel Cruz, and Miguel De La Torre are at the forefront on the theorizing of mulatez. For these authors, "mulatez" offers a space from which to speak with a particular Black Latino/a voice as an aid to theorize Latino/as' cultural, religious, and political lives in U.S. society. One of the developments of using "mulatez" in religious discourse is that it provides mutually enriching conversations with the African American theological tradition. This requires extensive engagements with African American religious scholars and revisioning Latino/a history in the United States.

For Isasi-Díaz, the use of "mulatez" becomes an ethical option. "Mulatez" enables Latino/as to engage in ways of coping, struggling, and flourishing as a community against oppressive powers of racism and sexism. As a cultural category, for Isasi-Díaz, using "mulatez" acknowledges the mingling of elements from diverse cultures, Hispanic as well as those learned from the dominant culture. These elements come together to form how Latina/os see the world and fuel their struggle for a just society.

Michelle González criticizes the Mexican American domination of Latino/a religious discourse and its privileging of a particular kind of popular religiosity, which cannot claim to represent the multiple Latino/a communities. She engages African American religious construction of blackness because of its exclusion of the Afro-Latino experience. Although she claims that Afro-Latino/as do not have the history of racism in the United States like their African American counterpart, they and their ancestors have been victims of the large slave traffic. In addition, the historical contribution of Latino/as to U.S. society, and their growing numbers, a significant portion of whom are of African descent, warrants that they be included in the conversation of race. Gonzalez also addresses the African elements of popular religion, particularly within the Cuban and Cuban American community. Devotions to saints, in particular to La Caridad, are surrounded by racial understanding that needs careful analysis.

Samuel Cruz notes that the major efforts outlining popular religiosity have been made by Catholic scholars on Catholic popular devotions. Little attention has been paid to the "Africanization" of Protestantism, the ways in which local traditions of Latino/as communities, migrants, and those rooted in the mainland, are incorporated into the Protestant traditions. In his studies, Cruz connects Pentecostalism and Afro-Caribbean religions, particularly Santería. He demonstrates that strong African influences are present in how Caribbean Pentecostalism relates religion to the world. He compares Pentecostal understandings of prayer, blessings, the spiritual world, exorcism, and prophecy to the beliefs and rituals of Santería. He concludes by showing how many elements of the African worldview found their way into Pentecostalism.

The use of "mulatez" by White Latina/o scholars within the religious discourse has been criticized by some Hispanics. Miguel De La Torre questions the usefulness of "mulatez" in religious and theological discourse due to its racist connotations. His primary concern is that the term "mulatez" is neither used nor accepted as a form of self-description by predominately White Latino/a communities (i.e., Miami, Florida) due to inter-Hispanic racism, but, rather, an imposition made mostly by White Latino/as scholars onto the community. Furthermore, some Black and biracial communities find the term "mulatto" racially offensive. De La Torre insists that any White scholar who attempts to use the category "mulatez" is reifying a racist ideology that undermines *negritude* and silences mulatto/as who are excluded not only from U.S. society, but by the Hispanic community.

Conclusion

All who consider themselves mulatto/as do not experience mulatez in the same way. In societies where the racial hierarchy is prevalent, it is possible for light-skinned mulatto/as to experience certain privileges and perhaps be granted certain social standing that will be denied to darker skinned mulatto/as. Skin coloration and perception of race as "Whites" may help many Latino/as on the road to social advancement in the United States.

Through personal, social, and cultural preconceptions, the viewer may attribute certain characteristics and abilities to the mulatto/a. However, an individual may self-identity as a person of mulatto descent as an exercise of affirming a particular subjectivity and way of acting in the world. What exactly being a mulatto/a means, then, depends on lived experiences, geographical location, and particular views of race, culture, and ethnicity from which one speaks. Although mulatez initially had a clear racialized understanding, it has been used in other ways to describe general cultural traits not limited to general physiognomy.

At the same time, in the various engagements with mulatez, it is becoming increasingly difficult to see how these authors deal with the "hard facts" of African elements in the Latino/as communities. On the positive side, interest in the discussion of mulatez opens space to uncover how Africanized worldviews and forms of expressions can be included in U.S. Latino/a religious discourse from which they are often missing. Literary movements that deal with blackness such as Afro Cuban poetry, the Nuyorican Poets, Latino/a music, and graffiti, among other forms of cultural and artistic expression, are increasingly relevant as fountains of inspirations and resistance. On the negative side, including mulatez in the U.S. Latino/a religious discourse presents the problem of deciding what aspects of African culture will be included in theological reflection. What elements of Afro-Caribbean and Afro-Latino/a religiosity can be included in Christian theological reflection? How are we to analyze elements of ritual practices in Christian churches that reflect African influences or that are derived from them? Pertinent to the Latino/a academy is the question of who speaks in the voice of Afro-Latino/as: are they White Latino/a scholars, or Afro-Latino/as? The shortage of religious history of slavery in the Caribbean and the Americas from a Latino/a religious perspective in the United States needs to be addressed as well.

Elias Ortega-Aponte

References and Further Reading

Andrews, G. R. *Afro-Latin America 1800–2000* (New York: Oxford University Press, 2004).

Cruz, Samuel. *Masked Africanisms: Puerto Rican Pentecostalism* (Dubuque, IA: Kendall Hunt Publishing Company, 2005).

De La Torre, Miguel A. "Rethinking Mulatez." *Rethinking Latino(a) Religion and Identity*, ed. Miguel A. De La Torre and Gastón Espinosa (Cleveland: The Pilgrim Press, 2006).

Gonzalez, M. A. *Afro-Cuban Theology: Religion, Race, Culture, and Identity* (Gainesville, FL: University Press of Florida, 2006).

Isasi-Díaz, A. M. *La Lucha Continues: Mujerista Theology* (Maryknoll, NY: Orbis Books, 2004).

Torres, A., and N. E. Whitten, Jr. *Blackness in Latin America and the Caribbean Vols. I-II* (Bloomington: Indiana University Press, 1998).

MYSTICISM

Derived from a Greek word meaning "initiation," *mysticism* signifies mystery, divine inspiration, esoteric spirituality, or awe stemming from an experience of ultimate reality. From a Christian theological perspective, "mysticism" refers to the experience of direct knowledge of God, or to the religious practices of mystics and saints aimed at attaining communion with God. Among the various Latino/a religious cultures of North America, the general understanding of mysticism is grounded in the story of the famous Roman Catholic male and female mystics of early modern Spain and the Spanish colonies of the Americas.

There is a threefold pattern common to almost all mystical states reported among different religious traditions around the world. Broadly speaking, the three stages are the following: Initiation, Purification, and Fulfillment. The

Engraving depicts Saint Teresa of Avila interceding for souls in Purgatory, an engraving by Schelte Adams Bolswert after a painting from the workshop of Peter Paul Rubens, circa 1600. Teresa of Avila (1515–1582) was a Spanish mystic, Carmelite nun, and author during the Counter Reformation. (Getty Images)

initiatory stage usually involves a spontaneous mystical experience, or a calling to know God more intimately, followed by a sense of longing either to understand the initial outpouring of spiritual feelings and phenomena or to duplicate the feelings of the original experience. The mystic, or seeker, often reports an inability to reproduce the experience and its altered state of mind at will. The various mystical writers and contemplative visionaries spanning the history of Christianity have also referred to this purification stage as "purgation" or cleansing, which in traditional Christian mystical theology is reported as lasting from a few months to several decades. During this middle stage of spiritual unfolding, the mystic engages in different practices, or exercises, aimed at furthering one's ability to perceive and discern the nonmaterial realities of the soul and the world of Spirit as well as deepening one's intimacy with God. Among these practices are various forms of prayer and meditation aimed at stilling the mind and quickening the faculties of the soul, such as reciting verses from the Holy Scriptures, chanting or singing, walking, rhythmic breathing, fasting, even staring at a bowl of water, a mirror, or a lighted candle. There is a connection between certain forms of physical, mental, or emotional exhaustion and the onset of mystical states of consciousness. In the classic Christian understanding of such exercises, however, it is only by the Grace of God through Jesus Christ and the abiding power and gifts of the Holy Spirit that the mystic enters the third stage of mystical knowledge referred to as the "fulfillment" of his or her quest for knowledge of God. This final stage of mystical unfolding and consciousness is signified by terms such as "union" or "enlightenment."

Hispanics, whether self-identifying as Roman Catholic, Protestant, or Pentecostal, are familiar with the famous Spanish mystics Teresa of Avila (1515–1582) and John of the Cross (1542–1591), each of whom was also a leader in the Catholic Counter-Reformation. Although in her youth she suffered from both physical and emotional illnesses, and later struggled with acute anxiety over the writing and dissemination of her visionary works, Teresa of Avila eventually took up the pen and became one of most influential and revered mystics of the sixteenth-century Catholic Reformation. After her mother's death, Teresa's father took her to an Augustinian convent to be raised and educated by nuns. Saint

Teresa's theology was influenced by the Augustinian tradition and accounts for some of the existential dynamics evident in her understanding of human suffering and Grace. Her autobiography, *La Vida de la Santa Madre Teresa de Jesus* (ca. 1565), along with *The Interior Castle* (1577) and *The Way of Perfection* (ca. 1567), provided a metaphorical and pedagogical model of Christian spirituality for the men and women entering the Carmelite Order. Despite the prevailing ascetic stereotype of the Christian mystic, and despite opposition from conservatives in the older Carmelite ranks, Teresa undertook the reform and expansion of Carmelite convents throughout Spain, a task that exemplified the notion of "faith in action" that was so central to the Catholic Reformation. She advocated for "deep prayer" among the laity while believing that it pleased God when both clergy and laity followed this contemplative practice.

Teresa's colleague, John of the Cross, joined her in reforming their beloved Carmelite Order, and he also wrote some of the most dynamic and beloved Christian mystical poetry of all time. His poems, *Living Flame of Love*, and the *Spiritual Canticle*, together with his treatise on mystical union with God, the *Ascent of Mount Carmel*, are today ranked among the spiritual classics of Christianity. John's *Dark Night of the Soul* traces the soul's longing for union with God through a series of sensorial trials and spiritual awakenings spanning the trajectory of the mystical path. His mastery of Castilian prose and verse has drawn comparisons with Miguel de Cervantes as both of these writers made major contributions to the foundations of the Spanish language.

The inspiration for the founding of the Jesuit Order was revealed to the Spanish soldier, Ignatius of Loyola (1491–1556), while recovering from a canon blast that severely wounded his leg during Pentecost week in May 1521. Later that month while convalescing back in Loyola, he began pondering how he might serve God and the Church rather than his former military career. Ignatius's diaries and personal reflections witness that he was blessed with mystical gifts and visions such as experiencing the love of the Trinity, seeing lights floating through the air, having the gift of tears, being aware of angelic presences, and hearing music emanating from heavenly sources. Ignatius possessed a profound familiarity with the mystical power of the Holy Spirit in transforming persons and communities. His major work, known as the *Spiritual Exercises*, focused on silent prayer and close scriptural readings that followed the major stages of Christ's earthly life in relation to the Holy Trinity. The Society of Jesus, or the Jesuit Order, has been promoting contemplative retreats based on Saint Ignatius's book for nearly 500 years and has been on the vanguard of social justice and liberation movements since its founding.

There were many more men and women throughout the Americas over the next several centuries who felt called to a life of deep prayer and mystical piety, perhaps even influenced by the publication of the works of Saint Teresa and Saint John during the early 1600s. The commitment of the Jesuits to justice and education inspired many to take up Saint Ignatius's *Spiritual Exercises*. Even though they are not well known outside of Roman Catholic circles, these men and women were significant contributors to the story of Hispanic mysticism. Among their ranks were notable women mystics such as the Peruvian Creole nun, Rosa de Santa Maria (1586–1617), who following her canonization in 1671 became the Virgin Patroness of the Americas as Saint Rose of Lima. We find also a Mexican nun who became the first female theologian of the Americas, Sor Juana Inés de la Cruz (ca. 1648–1695). The Chilean nun, Ursula Suarez (1666–1749), critiqued the colonial division of labor and the subservient roles assigned by society to both secular and religious women. Although her story was not published in Chile until 1984, she has emerged in recent years as a Chilean role model of saintly piety and social activism at the intersections of race, class struggle, and gender oppression. These and other women saints and mystics pushed the frontiers of the gender divide in Spanish America while emerging as strong voices for feminist and liberation concerns, long before these issues appeared on the horizons of even the most progressive colonial theologians.

Another important mystical figure and writer of the Hispanic religious tradition was the Spanish priest, Miguel de Molinos (1640–1696), who founded Quietism in the seventeenth century, a movement which later influenced the rise of Methodism. Father Molinos and his followers believed that humanity's most solemn perfection could be attained by denying the egotistical concerns and worldly desires of the self in favor of the soul's complete fusion with the essence of God. Hence by rendering the mind inactive (or quiet), the faculties of the soul and the divine presence take hold of the individual and will begin leading the believer to spiritual perfection. A few years after publishing *The Spiritual Guide* (1675), Molinos was accused of heresy by Pope Innocent XI, arrested by the Spanish Inquisition, and sentenced to life in prison in 1687. Although the basic ideas of Quietism were present in earlier Christian heresies, Father Molinos's late seventeenth-century version of this school of mystical thought and practice perhaps resembled Protestant notions of personal piety and justification far too much for the Papacy and the Spanish Inquisition to leave him without censure. Molinos died in a papal prison at Rome, which was then under the control of the Spanish Empire.

The lives and works of Spanish and Latin American mystics still inspire Roman Catholic Hispanics across South, Central, and North America to ponder the pathways of mystical piety aligned with "faith in action" while serving the needs of the marginalized and oppressed. On the other hand, the widespread and popular appeal of these exemplary Christian mystics and saints' lives has also touched the hearts and minds of numerous non-Catholic Latino/as. Hence, although there is not a clearly defined Protestant Hispanic tradition of mysticism, certain forms of Protestant and Pentecostal piety, devotion, pneumatological feeling, and spiritual practices can be described as fostering mystical states of mind or knowledge of God.

Albert Hernández

References and Further Reading

Teresa of Avila. *The Collected Works of St. Teresa of Avila*, 3 vols., trans. Kieran Kavanaugh and Otilio Rodriguez (Washington, DC: Institute of Carmelite Studies Publications, 1976–1985).

John of the Cross. *The Collected Works of St. John of the Cross*, trans. Kieran Kavanaugh and Otilio Rodriguez (Washington, DC: Institute of Carmelite Studies Publications, 1991).

Ellwood, Robert S. *Mysticism and Religion*, 2nd ed. (New York: Seven Bridges Press, 1998).

Gonzalez, Michelle A. *Sor Juana: Beauty and Justice in the Americas* (Maryknoll, NY: Orbis, 2003).

McGinn, Bernard. *The Presence of God: A History of Western Christian Mysticism*, 4 vols. (New York: Crossroad Publishing, 1991–2005).

Myers, Kathleen Ann. *Neither Saints, nor Sinners: Writing the Lives of Women in Spanish America* (New York: Oxford University Press, 2003).

Peers, E. Allison. *Spanish Mysticism: A Preliminary Survey* (Whitefish, MT: Kessinger Publishing, 2003).

Index

Ecclesiotypical dimensions, 568
as ideal symbol of virgin and mother, 247, 341, 347–348
Immaculate Conception of, 569
incorporated within Santería, 37
Native Americans on, 534
as the New Eve, 568, 569
as Our Lady of Providence, 472
Perpetual Virginity, 569
as Queen of May, 457
respect for feminine deities symbolized by, 87
search for inn, 644
song of the anawim, 642–643
Virgin-Whore dichotomy, 516–517
as warrior figure for the Spanish, 534
See also Marian devotions
Virgin of Guadalupe. *See* Our Lady of Guadalupe
Virgin of Montserrat, 533
Virgin of the Rosary, 522
Visigothic era, 381, 382, 482–483, 532
Vivar, Rodrigo Díaz de, 484
Voodoo, 207, **577–582**, 580 (photo)
Voter registration drives, 361, 561
Voting Rights Act (1965), 253
Voudoun, 502

Wahlberg, John, 313
Walker, Theron, 296
Walkout (film), 442
Walsh, Monsignor Bryan O., 410–412
The War Brides Act, 43, 46
War on Poverty, 135
Watchtower (Russell), 312
Water spirits, 717
The Way of Perfection (Teresa of Avila), 392
Way of the Cross, 686
Weber, Max, 176, 450
Wesley, John, 415, 618
West, Cornel, 16
Whipple, Bishop Benjamin, 233
White Legend, 80
White supremacy, 16–17, 20
Whitson, R. E., 145

Who Are We? Challenges to America's National Identity (Huntington), 55–56, 515
Wilkerson, David, 24, 426
Wilson, Woodrow, 50
Witchcraft (*brujería*), 179, 193, 274–275, 417–419, 503, 537
Women:
Abuelita (little grandmother) theology, 347
abuse vs., 125, 398, 529, 570–571
altars, 33
within Catholic Charismatic movement, 95–96, 97
Chicano Movement, 137–138
education and occupational status, 125, 250, 257–258, 321
Espiritualistas, 224, 226
extended families, 126
female slaves as sexual objects, 387
gender roles, 246–247, 249, 250
grassroots Christianity usually led by, 716, 724
as healers, 278
Las Hermanas (The Sisters), 107, 213, 363, 413–414, 764
Hispanic Women: Prophetic Voice in the Church, 661–662
Latina evangélica theology, 327–329
Latino/a literature, 331
legal system of Roman law, 339
machista attitudes, 247
Marianismo, 341, 346–348
marimacha, 339
Mujerista theology, 158–159, 259–260, 335–337, 383–385, 552, 673, 736
Mujerista theology, Isasi-Díaz on, 242, 252, 258, 648, 744–745
Muslims, 307–308
parteras (midwives), 31
Pentecostal movement, 429, 433
rezadora (female prayer leaders), 31
sexual behavior of, 348
as single parents, 249, 250
El Teatro Campesino, 137